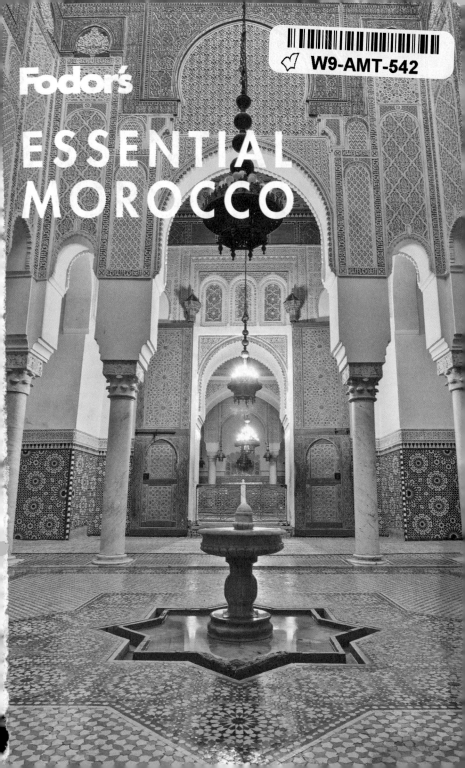

Fodor's
ESSENTIAL
MOROCCO

Welcome to Morocco

For centuries, Morocco has inspired travelers with its colorful energy, fascinating history, and dazzling combination of Arab, European, and African influence. From vibrant and bustling medinas to the sparse but breathtaking Sahara, the country packs a remarkable variety of adventures into its corner of North Africa. Surfers catch waves at windswept Atlantic coast beaches and hikers trek the scenic Atlas Mountains. Kasbahs and mosques offer a glimpse of a more mystical time, while hip cafés and high-design riads reflect Moroccans' modern, cosmopolitan side.

TOP REASONS TO GO

★ **Exotic Cities:** Sultry Marrakesh, market-filled Fez, historic Rabat.

★ **History:** Ancient ruins, mosques, and Amazigh villages invite discovery.

★ **Beaches:** From Agadir to Essaouira, surfing and sunbathing abound.

★ **Souks:** Traditional crafts, leather, rugs, and more are for sale in bright markets.

★ **Food and Drink:** Stewed tagines, saffron couscous, smoked zaalouk, mint tea.

★ **Trekking:** The rugged High Atlas and vast Sahara await exploration by camel or on foot.

Contents

Fodor's Features

MAPS

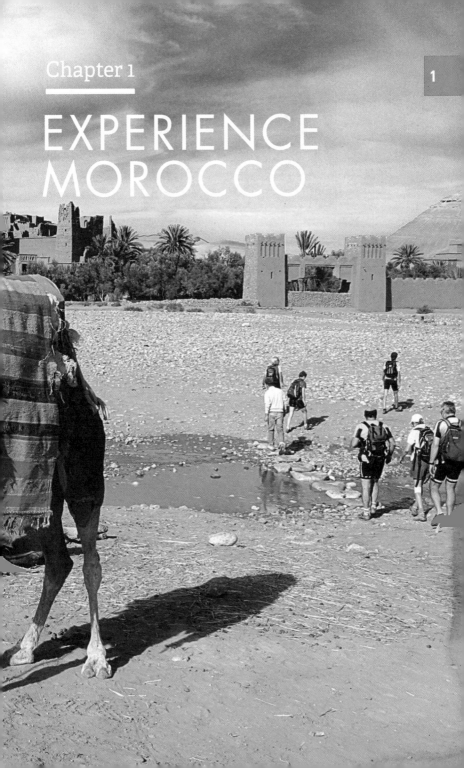

Chapter 1

EXPERIENCE MOROCCO

18 ULTIMATE EXPERIENCES

Morocco offers terrific experiences that should be on every traveler's list. Here are Fodor's top picks for a memorable trip.

1 Camel Trekking

Camel treks are a unique way to explore the rolling sand dunes and abandoned kasbahs of the Moroccan desert, one of the most gorgeous regions on earth. (Ch. 8)

2 Mint Tea

Enter any shop, café, or home and you'll be greeted with a cup of refreshing mint tea, the quintessential sign of hospitality in Morocco.

3 Ben Youssef Medersa, Marrakesh

One of the best-preserved historic sites in Marrakesh, this 16th-century Koranic school and its expansive courtyard is a breathtaking work of architecture. (Ch. 3)

4 Kasbah des Oudayas, Rabat

Originally built by Muslim refugees from Spain, Rabat's imposing 12th-century fortress and its quaint walled garden offer a glimpse into the city's long history. (Ch. 4)

5 Amazigh Villages

The semi-nomadic Amazigh tribes still live in mountain and desert villages, where they continue ancient traditions and you can experience their famed hospitality. (Ch. 7)

6 Sahara Desert Camping

The windswept Saharan sand dunes make for the ultimate camping experience. Settle into a simple Bedouin tent for unforgettable stargazing and spectacular sunsets. (Ch. 8)

7 Marrakesh Souks

Wind your way through the narrow and colorful labyrinths of the city's medina to haggle for handcrafted rugs, clothing, jewelry, pottery, and more. (Ch. 3)

8 Hiking the High Atlas

From North Africa's tallest peak to the epic Cascades d'Ouzoud waterfalls, a trek through the High Atlas Mountains is the perfect respite from urban Morocco. (Ch. 7)

9 The Old City of Fez

Fondouks, medersas, mosques, and palaces dating back a thousand years fill the 9,500 alleyways of Fez's medina, making it the world's most active medieval city. (Ch. 6)

10 Surfing the Atlantic Coast

The magnificent coastline between Agadir and Essaouira draws surfers and other watersport fanatics, thanks to its huge waves and extreme winds. (Ch. 9)

11 The Goat Trees

Argan oil, a luxury beauty product, comes from trees that grow only in Morocco. Goats also climb these trees to feast on the nuts, making for a strange photo-op. (Ch. 9)

12 Moroccan Music Festivals

Morocco's rich musical heritage is best experienced through its festivals, from the Gnaoua World Music Festival in Essaouria to the World Sacred Music Festival in Fez.

13 Hammams

An important part of Moroccan culture, hammams are a cross between a sauna and a Turkish bath. You can choose from inexpensive public ones to luxurious private ones.

14 Cooking Classes

Shop for ingredients at a souk, then learn to make aromatic tagines. Café Clock offers great classes in Marrakesh and Fez. (Ch. 3 and Ch. 6)

15 Chefchaouen

Founded in the 15th century in the foothills of the Rif Mountains, the blue village of Chefchaouen is considered one of Morocco's most picturesque places. (Ch. 5)

16 Renting a Riad

While found throughout the country, Marrakesh in particular has a superb collection of restored 16th-century palaces that have been turned into charming guesthouses. (Ch. 3)

17 Roman Ruins at Volubilis

The well-preserved Volubilis was once the capital of the Roman province of Mauritania and still contains intricate mosaics and majestic columns from the time. (Ch. 6)

18 Hassan II Mosque, Casablanca

Casablanca's huge Hassan II Mosque is known as the country's most exceptional representation of Moroccan artistry. (Ch. 4)

WHAT'S WHERE

1 Marrakesh.
Marrakesh is the
meeting point between
Morocco's north and
south, Arab and
Amazigh, big city and
small town. If you visit
only one city in
Morocco, make it
Marrakesh.

**2 Rabat and
Casablanca.**
Casablanca, Morocco's
economic capital, and
Rabat, the political
capital, are the country's
most Europeanized
cities. Meanwhile, the
Atlantic beaches offer
miles of wild surf, sand,
and sea.

**3 Tangier and the
Mediterranean.** Many
of Morocco's most
dramatic social and
economic contrasts are
painfully evident in
and around Tangier.
The mountain strong-
hold at the blue city of
Chefchaouen and the
coastal city of Tetouan
are also worth visiting.

**4 Fez and the Middle
Atlas.** The Arab-Islamic
and Imazighen
chapters in Morocco's
history are most
evident in the cities of
Fez and Meknès. Side
trips to the Roman
ruins at Volubilis and
the holy town of
Moulay Idriss are
musts. The Middle Atlas
mountain range has
great natural beauty.

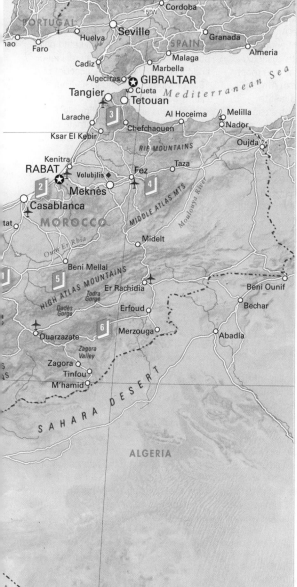

5 The High Atlas. You can trek the High Atlas on foot or by mule and taste rural Morocco at its most colorful and hospitable. Decent roads offer pleasant rides to Setti Fatma and the ski resort Oukaïmeden.

6 The Great Oasis Valleys. No trip to Morocco is complete without a taste of the desert, and some of Morocco's best scenery is on the way out to Merzouga or M'hamid, where crumbling kasbahs, arid hills, and date palm oases cling to the few rivers that sustain this region. The Dadès and Todra gorges seem impossibly sculpted in the late afternoon light.

7 Agadir and the Southern Atlantic Coast. Busy Agadir contrasts with Essaouira's bohemian vibe. Agadir, Tafraoute, and Tiznit are connected by curvy mountain roads studded with deserted hilltop kasbahs and villages. People-watching is wonderful here, as women's wraps vary within the region, from austere black or navy full-body coverings in Taroudant to brightly flowered garments along the coast.

Morocco Today

POLITICS

Morocco is a democratic constitutional monarchy, with the king having ultimate authority. After the fall of several Middle Eastern regimes during the Arab Spring of 2011 and unrest in neighboring Algeria, the world's gaze shifted nervously to Morocco. Widely regarded as the most moderate and stable of North African nations, the kingdom acted fast to appease dissenters. Although a cautious modernizer in the past, King Mohammed VI, who had already introduced some economic and social liberalization, revised the constitution and brought forward elections in response to protests. His ability to calm the populace, many of whom remember the far fierier reign of his father, Hassan II, ensured the stability of his kingdom and won him the trust of Western nations. Encouraged by Mohammed VI's popularity with his people, Washington granted Morocco the status of non-NATO ally and the relationship with the United States remains strong and firm. However, after the gruesome death of a fishmonger in late 2016, ongoing protests in the northern province of Rif have shown there is still a desire for better governance and equality throughout Morocco, especially for the Amazigh people, Morocco's dominant ethnic group. In 2019 the Amazigh language of Amazigh finally became an official language.

Elections in 2021 overwhelmingly ousted the Islamist PJD party who had maintained the parliamentary majority for a decade. Billionaire businessman Aziz Akhannouch, of the liberal RNI party, was named prime minister and seven women took up ministerial positions.

ECONOMY

Morocco enjoys a vibrant tourist trade and exports of handicrafts, produce, nuts, and oils. The country is also investing in global value chains such as textiles, automobiles, renewable energy, and aeronautics. As with other African countries, the kingdom's principal wealth comes from natural resources, with Morocco's key raw material being phosphate (used in pesticides, animal feed, and fertilizers). Agriculture accounts for 13% of Morocco's annual GDP, but significantly accounts for nearly 75% of jobs in rural areas and 38% nationally. Poor harvests due to drought, climate change, or disease have a severe socioeconomic impact.

WOMEN'S RIGHTS

In recent years, King Mohammed VI has had to balance the demands of feminist organizations calling for an expansion of women's rights with resistance from the country's Islamic political parties, who fiercely oppose change. In the beginning of the century, Morocco made sweeping reforms to its family-law code, the Moudawana, creating one of the most progressive family codes in the Arab world. The new Moudawana gave women significantly more rights and protections. They now have the right to request a divorce, the legal age of marriage has leapt from 15 to 18, and polygamy is now severely restricted. Women also now have the right to child support and shared custody. In 2011, the country passed a new constitution guaranteeing gender equality, but incongruities remain; generations of customary practices are hard to reverse and the application of the new laws is patchy, especially in more rural areas. To help with this transition, Morocco has introduced female Islamic preachers and guidance counselors called Morchidat, whose role is to help women and girls distinguish between customs, Islam, and the law in asserting their rights. There is also a huge gulf between urban and rural outlooks and opportunities: while 90% of girls between ages 15–17 will attend school in urban areas, only 40% of girls in rural areas will attain that level of education. The Democratic Association of Moroccan Women continues to fight for urgent reforms to Morocco's Family Code and for the reform of the inheritance laws in which a female heir is entitled to only half that of her male siblings.

RELIGION

An estimated 99% of Moroccans are Muslim, with the king being able to trace his lineage to the prophet Mohammed. The second most practiced religion is Christianity, which predates Islam; only a few Jewish Moroccans remain today, although they were a significant part of the population pre–World War II. Moroccans are, on the whole, tolerant of other people's beliefs. As in most Islamic countries, a faith of any sort is easier to understand than no faith at all. Muslim prayers are said five times a day, with men tending to gather in mosques upon hearing the call to prayer. It is common to see men praying elsewhere, such as by the side of the road, in fields, or even corners of the office. Women tend to pray in the home and seldom stop work to pray in public throughout the day. It is considered highly impolite to interrupt a person who is praying and it's also advisable not to cross in front of them. Fasting takes place during the holy month of Ramadan, which falls in the ninth month of the lunar cycle.

Despite a close regard for Islam, Moroccans tend to interpret its laws in a less conservative way than many Muslim countries. Travelers familiar with other Islamic nations, such as Pakistan or Saudi Arabia, may be surprised by the fact that modesty in women's dress emphasizes covering the skin rather than disguising the female form. It is not uncommon to see young girls wearing skin-tight

jeans with long-sleeve T-shirts and headscarves, rather than the voluminous coverings commonly seen in other Muslim regions. Female visitors find it useful to carry a long scarf or sarong to cover their shoulders or hair upon occasion. There are times when bare arms and low necklines attract unwelcome attention. Similarly, beachwear, shorts, and skirts above the knee are best restricted to the beach. Men are not expected to wear shorts in formal or mixed company.

MUSIC

Music is integral to daily and ritual life in Morocco, both for enjoyment and ceremony, and as social commentary. It emanates from cell phones, car radios, homes, and stores and markets everywhere. While Western popular music and Arabic artists are well-liked, the traditional and folk music of Morocco provide a sense of cultural identity and pride. In the Rif, it's considered a virtue for young Amazigh women to compose and sing poetry, or *aita,* recalling deed of Riffian heroes; in Casablanca, *rai* (opinion) music, born of social protest is popular among young men; cobblers in the Meknès medina may work to the sound of violin-based Andalusian classical music or the more folksy Arabic *melhoum,* or "sung poetry." You know you've reached the south when you hear the banjo strum of Marrakesh's roving storytellers. *Gnaoua* music is best known for its use in trance rituals but has become a popular form of street entertainment; the performers' brass *qraqeb* hand cymbals and cowrie-shell-adorned hats betray the music's sub-Saharan origins. This rich culture of sound has been modernized in recent years with fusions of Western-influenced pop music and traditional Moroccan beats. Morocco's music festivals are growing every year in size, quality, and recognition.

What to Eat and Drink in Morocco

COUSCOUS

Couscous is made from semolina flour that's blended, by hand, with water until it forms tiny grainlike balls. It's then steamed and usually served with a meat or chicken stew and vegetables. The instant couscous found in the United States has been precooked and dried.

TAJINE

The name of this quintessential, slow-cooked Moroccan stew that's served almost every day in Moroccan homes refers not only to its conical terracotta cooking pot, but to the dish itself: tasty, aromatic stew. Classic versions are chicken tajine with preserved lemon and green olives or lamb with dried prunes and almonds.

PASTILLA

This Moroccan delicacy consists of a crust of buttery filo pastry around a filling of shredded chicken with crushed almonds, spices, eggs, and sugar. Once upon a time, pigeon was the bird of choice, but that's rare these days. The baked pies are sprinkled with sugar and cinnamon.

DATES

The Drâa and Tafilalet oases in Southern Morocco are the date capitals of Morocco, with over 45 varieties grown there, including the prized *mejdool* date, a type once reserved for kings and sultans. November is harvest season and the town of Erfoud, in eastern Morocco, celebrates with an annual Date Festival.

AMLOU

Morocco's answer to peanut butter is a blend of almonds, argan oil, and honey. It's often homemade, and can be found in local stores or country markets, especially near Essaouira where the argan trees grow. Amlou is ideal for breakfast with fresh, warm flatbread.

ZAALOUK AND TAKTOUKA

These are two of cooked salads that are usually served as an appetizer. *Zaalouk* is made with eggplant, tomato, garlic, olive oil, and spices, while *Taktouka* is based on tomatoes and roasted green peppers.

Tagine

HARIRA

Harira is a hearty, tomato-based soup traditionally served for the break of fast (*l'ftour*) during Ramadan. Recipes vary, but most are based on a meat broth, with tomatoes, lentils, chickpeas, onion, celery, and spices. During Ramadan harira is served with dates on the side as well as honey-soaked pastries called *chebakia*.

MECHOUI

This is a traditional way of preparing lamb, in which the whole animal is slow-roasted for several hours on a spit over charcoals, typically in a closed pit or in a mud-built kiln. A whole lamb is usually reserved for special occasions but mechoui can be found at street stalls, where hunks of the tender roasted meat are served, simply seasoned with salt and cumin.

BRIOUAT

These bite-size, triangular, deep-fried filo pastry parcels can be either sweet or savory. As a premeal appetizer, fillings might include mildly spiced ground meat, melted cheese, shrimp, or vegetables. Honey-drenched almond briouats are a popular treat during Ramadan.

MINT TEA

More than just a drink, mint tea is a ritual that represents hospitality, and merchants in the bazaar may offer you a some of this "Berber whiskey." It's usually served in colorful glasses alongside pastries. The leaves are Chinese gunpowder tea, washed to extract the bitterness, then boiled with fresh mint and a heap of sugar.

Morocco's Top Outdoor Adventures

CAMEL-TREKKING IN THE SAHARA

Head south of Zagora or to Merzouga to meet the blue-robed descendants of nomads offering camel treks in the desert. From one-hour rides to multiday wilderness expeditions, there are local operators who can set you up for an incredible, if not necessarily comfortable, adventure on a single-humped dromedary.

DESERT CAMPING

Whether you're "wild-camping" with open fire and a sleeping mat or "glamping" with carpets and king-size beds, a night under the stars is magical. Godd options are the dunes of Erg Chigaga or Erg Chebbi, or the luxury camps of Agafay, near Marrakesh.

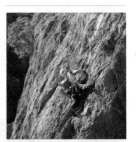

ROCK CLIMBING

Morocco offers single-pitch and multipitch routes suitable for beginners to experienced climbers. Popular locations are the Todra Gorge, Tafraoute, Aïn Belmusk near Marrakesh, and Akchour in the Rif Mountains. It's best to book your climb through a specialist agency or bring your own equipment.

SUMMIT DJEBEL TOUBKAL

At 4,167 meters, Djebel Toubkal, in the High Atlas, is North Africa's highest peak. To reach the summit requires a good level of physical fitness as well as surefootedness for the stony trails, but does not require technical climbing skills. The expedition typically takes two to three days from the trekking base of Imlil, where you can hire a qualified mountain guide.

HOT-AIR BALLOONING

A typical experience at one of Marrakesh's balloon flight outfits will launch you just after dawn, then slowly ascending to a height of 1,000 meters as the sun rises. Stunning vistas of villages, countryside, and the High Atlas Mountains open up in the distance. The flight lasts about an hour and is typically followed by breakfast.

WATER SPORTS

The Atlantic coast from Essaouira to Agadir is dotted with surfing, windsurfing, and kite-surfing schools. Hard-core surfers are attracted to the waves of Taghazout, near Agadir. Sidi Kaouki, near Essaouira, has challenging waves for keen windsurfers.

CYCLING AND MOUNTAIN-BIKING

With a good map and a bike, the possibilities are endless, whether you're interested in biking on paved roads or off-road on dirt tracks. Local outfitters in Marrakesh offer guides, bike rental, and tours that range from easy city cycles to challenging multiday explorations.

Hiking and trekking

MULE-TREKKING

If you want to travel like a local, with zero carbon footprint, think about going on a mule trek. Imlil is the ideal base for mule-trekking in the High Atlas, but day-rides and multiday treks with local guides can also be arranged through local accommodations and tour operators in the less-explored Dadès Gorge, Skoura Oasis and Drâa Valley.

HIKING AND TREKKING

Morocco's spectacular landscapes of mountains, oases, deserts, and coastline make for fabulous hiking. Imlil and the Ourika Valley are hot spots, easily accessible for day treks from Marrakesh. Aït Bougmez (aka "happy valley") is relatively undiscovered and harder to reach, but with pretty hamlets and a way of life unchanged for centuries. It's worth taking a few days to explore with a local guide.

Morocco's Best Historic Sites

MEDERSA BOU INANIA, FEZ

With its hard-to-miss green-tile minaret and its marble floors, cedar ceilings, carved stucco walls, and intricate hand-cut *zellij* tiling, this medersa is widely considered the most beautiful of the Koranic schools of the 14th century. It's one of Morocco's finest examples of Merinid architecture.

AÏT BEN HADDOU, NEAR OUARZAZATE

The best-known fortified village, or *ksar*, in Morocco has appeared in films and TV (including Lawrence of Arabia and Game of Thrones) but for centuries was a key link in a chain of fortresses that guarded the caravan trade route from the Sahara. It's a splendid example of 17th- and 18th-century southern Morocco architecture built from earth, with crenelated towers decorated with Imazighen motifs.

CHELLAH RUINS AND GARDENS, RABAT

The landscaped gardens, necropolis, and ruins here are fascinating. The story is that a citadel was built by the Romans in 40 AD and Muslim dynasties over the centuries added a mosque, the ramparts, the gates, and the gardens.

VOLUBILIS ROMAN RUINS

Morocco's most impressive archaeological site was a flourishing community during the 1st and 2nd centuries AD, as the farthest flung outpost of the Roman Empire. Today the UNESCO World Heritage site has vestiges of Roman villas, marketplaces, temples, and mosaics.

PLACE DJEMÂA EL FNA, MARRAKESH

Way back when, this was the meeting place for Imazighen tribes from the Atlas mountains, country farmers, and trans-Saharan caravans. Snake charmers, acrobats, and orange juice sellers can be found during the day; at night it's a cornucopia of musicians, sizzling food grills, and sideshows.

HASSAN II MOSQUE, CASABLANCA

Inspired by the Koranic verse "the throne of God was upon the water," the Hassan II mosque sits partly on land and partly on sea, on a promontory on the Atlantic Coast. It features breathtaking Islamic architecture with a high-tech laser atop the minaret, beaming toward Mecca.

Aït Ben Haddou

FEZ EL-BALI
The oldest part of the oldest Imperial city of Morocco, Fez's medieval medina is a labyrinth of narrow streets concealing fondouks, fountains, souks, craftworkers, riads, and mosques.

PREHISTORIC ROCK CARVINGS
There are more than 300 sites of prehistoric rock engravings in Morocco. Many, with carvings around 5,000 years old, are in the Drâa Valley and pre-Sahara regions.

BAYT DAKIRA, ESSAOUIRA
An old family house in the once-thriving Jewish quarter, or "Mellah," the museum and cultural center also houses the beautifully renovated Simon Attias synagogue. The site celebrates the Judeo-Islamic heritage of Essaouira, which was once the only Muslim city in the world to have a majority Jewish population.

HERI ES SOUANI, MEKNÈS
These royal granaries were built in the 18th century to store grain for the sultan's thousands of horses, potentially over a long period of time. An ingenious system of under-floor water ducts kept the thick-walled chambers cool, sort of like an ancient refrigerator. The ruins of the adjacent royal stables are testament to a ruler who, some say, treated his horses better than people.

Recommended Tour Operators

Morocco's infrastructure has improved in recent years, making travel around the country by train or car quite easy. There are still two areas, though, where it's helpful to have a local guide. Despite some development in rural Morocco's infrastructure, the High Atlas remains relatively undiscovered and full of unspoiled charm. To fully enjoy and understand the area, though, suitable transport (organized in advance or upon arrival in the region) and an experienced driver are key. The same is true for the desert, where arranging camels, four-wheel-drive transportation, and tented camps is best done through a well-connected local guide.

Even the smallest one-man-band tour operators in Morocco now have an Internet presence, and it is possible to book tours and excursions online through internationally renowned or local outfits. For both the High Atlas and Sahara regions, local guides are easily found in Marrakesh or, for the High Atlas, in the small hill stations, most notably Imlil. A homegrown guide personalizes your traveling experience, often suggesting unknown restaurants and small riads, or organizing (with your permission) a visit to their home. The plus side here is the authentic cultural experience; the downside may be a lack of reliability, possibly poor vehicle maintenance, and limited English. All the good hotels in Marrakesh can make these arrangements, even with little prior notice. Prices vary greatly, but you should expect to pay around $150 a day for a vehicle and driver-guide (and you should tip around $10 per day). If recruiting locally, expect to pay in dirhams—in cash, rather than credit card. If making these arrangements in advance, check how experienced a tour operator or guide is.

You tend to get what you pay for in Morocco, and almost anything is possible, with operators capable of arranging all manner of tours. High-end travel, for example, might include air-conditioned luxury transport, five-star accommodations, spa treatments, and lavish meals. Another option might be experience-based: with quad biking, ballooning, cooking classes, a trip to a local *moussem* (festival), or skiing in Oukaïmeden. Very popular these days are ecotours, which typically arrange stays in unspoiled Imazighen hamlets or eco-lodges; visit local cooperatives, such as argan oil or carpet-weaver co-ops; and shower under breathtaking waterfalls.

LUXURY TOURS

Many large international tour companies offer ultraluxurious tours. On the plus side, you have the backing of an established and respected operator and are able to pay by credit card prior to travel. On the minus, the choice of luxury in rural parts of Morocco is limited, and you may miss out on some of the simple charms of the country.

Abercrombie and Kent. Pioneers for years in the luxury travel market, this hugely respected outfitter offers a number of small group tours and tailor-made packages to Morocco. ☎ 800/611–4711, ⊕ www.abercrombiekent.com, ✉ from $4295 per person.

Travel Exploration. This upmarket, female-owned company guarantees in-depth, authentic travel experiences that are curated to deliver an insider's view of the country. Private tours include a combination of architecture, culture, arts and crafts, gastronomy, rural adventure, special workshops, food tours, and Jewish heritage, all led by expert local guides. ☎ 800/787–8806, ⊕ www.travel-exploration.com, ✉ from $300 per person per day touring.

EXPERIENTIAL TOURS

Plan-it Morocco. Plan-It Morocco promises a new world of sensory experiences in the old world of Fez and throughout the country. The experienced company founders—Australian Michele Reeves and Briton Gail Leonard—are passionate about sharing their discoveries in and around this ancient city and across Morocco. They create experiences that let you taste, smell, feel, and hear Morocco rather than merely seeing it. Their culinary adventures, which incorporate tastings, cooking classes, and supplier tours are immensely popular. ☎ 0535/63–87–08, ⊕ www.plan-it-morocco.com, ✉ from $80 per person for day trips.

ADVENTURE TOURS

Amazing Toubkal Treks. Hassan Fadil and his team of qualified Imazighen mountain guides are specialists in trekking in the High and Central High Atlas as well as the M'Goun regions. They offer a wide range of itineraries including ascents of Mt. Toubkal, treks into Aït Bougemez Valley, or a complete 22-day traverse of the entire Atlas region. ☎ 0652/61–89–04 in Morocco, ⊕ www.amazing-toubkal-trek. com, ✉ from €150 per person.

Epic Morocco. For tailor-made trekking tours around Morocco, Epic Morocco is great, taking you off-the-beaten track. Whether you're looking for luxury guesthouses or the great outdoors, they do their best to tailor everything to your needs, and they come armed with impressive knowledge of the hiking and biking trails of the country. They also do high-octane adventures like paragliding off Toubkal and rallies across the desert. ☎ 2081/50–61–31 in Morocco, ⊕ www.epicmorocco.co.uk.

Moroccan Mountain Guides. This team of young, passionate Amazigh and Spanish guides specializes in the High Atlas. They offer home-stays and hotels with a family atmosphere as well as cultural tours in more remote areas. There's a strong slant to ecotours, including mountain biking, horse-riding, Toubkal ascents, and bivouacs. English, Spanish, French, Arabic, and Imazighen speakers are available. Half-day and full-day treks typically start in the High Atlas or excursions can be organized from Marrakesh. ☎ 0672/84–51–71 in Morocco, ⊕ www.moroccomountain-guides.co.uk, ✉ from $70 per day.

SAHARA TOURS

Desert Majesty. Based in Ouarzazate, this company offers budget 4x4 tours using local drivers who know the region inside and out. One of their tours combines the desert with the Anti-Atlas region around Taroudant. ☎ 0671/66–04–94 in Morocco, ⊕ www.desertmajesty.com, ✉ from $200 per day.

SheherazadVentures. This English–Moroccan boutique tour company offers tailored private travel throughout Morocco, specializing in the Sahara Desert and the Great South. It's good for families and couples who want hands-on cultural activities, an authentic desert experience, and top-notch service. ☎ 0615/64–79–18 in Morocco, ⊕ www.sheherazadventures. com, ✉ from $400 a day for two people.

What to Watch and Read

ANOTHER SKY, DIRECTED BY GAVIN LAMBERT

In this 1954 film, a young Englishwoman falls in love with an Amazigh street musician. When he mysteriously disappears, she sets off across the Atlas Mountains to find him. It's beautifully shot, with authentic scenes of life during the French protectorate.

HIDEOUS KINKY

The 1998 film adaption of this autobiographical novel by Esther Freud stars Kate Winslet. It's 1970s Marrakesh and a young Englishwoman with two small children tries to live the bohemian dream.

BABEL (2006), DIRECTED BY ALEJANDRO GONZÁLEZ IÑÁRRITU

While holidaying in Morocco with her husband (Brad Pitt), a woman (Cate Blanchett) is accidentally shot by two young goat-herders. Film locations include the Atlas Mountains and a rural village where local Imazighen try to save her life.

HORSES OF GOD (2012), DIRECTED BY NABIL AYOUCH

In this fictional tale set in Casablanca, religious fundamentalists groom a group of boys from the slums to perpetrate the 2003 Casablanca terror bombings. The stark realism and social commentary are gripping. English subtitles.

ROCK THE CASBAH, DIRECTED BY LAILA MARRAKSHI

In this 2013 comedy/melodrama set in Tangiers, three Moroccan sisters come together for the funeral of their father (Omar Sharif). Secrets, lies, and family feuds are revealed. English subtitles.

THE CALIPH'S HOUSE: A YEAR IN CASABLANCA BY TAHIR SHAH

In this 2006 memoir, Anglo-Afghan writer Tahir Shah moves his family to Morocco to restore a ruined house in the shantytown of Casablanca. Mischievous djinns, gangster neighbors, and adventures in the Sahara provide a taste of Moroccan culture at its most unpredictable.

DREAMS OF TRESPASS: TALES OF A HAREM GIRLHOOD BY FATEMA MERNISSI

In this memoir, Fatema Mernissi, a leading Moroccan feminist, recounts her childhood in a traditional family harem in 1940s Fez. Several generations of women and girls share living space and duties that sometimes united them and at other times cause friction.

THE SAND CHILD BY TAHAR BEN JELLOUN

In this 1985 novel, a father with seven daughters desperately wants a son, but the eighth child is another girl. The infant is named Ahmed and is raised as a boy so she can enjoy all the privileges that are granted to men in Islamic society.

THE DJINN IN THE SKULL: STORIES FROM HIDDEN MOROCCO BY SAMANTHA HERRON

Writer Samantha Herron spent time in the Drâa Valley with a family of nomads and immersed herself in folklore and the art of storytelling. In this 2015 collection she weaves elements of traditional tales with her own vivid imaginings, creating new fables of modern Morocco.

ADVENTURES IN MOROCCO (2020) BY ALICE MORRISON

An honest and often hilarious account of Scottish author Alice Morrison going to Morocco to run the six-day Marathon des Sables; 1,001 nights later she's still there, having fallen in love with the country. Bartering in the souks, herding goats, and thrashing around in pigeon excrement are just some of her adventures.

Renting a Riad

For an authentic Moroccan lodging experience, venture into the medinas of Rabat, Fez, Meknès, Marrakesh, or Essaouira and stay at a traditional riad.

WHAT IS A RIAD?

These beautiful dwellings are usually tucked away behind heavy wooden doors set into featureless walls on blind alleys called *derbs*. Traditional riad-style houses were the domain of wealthier families, usually passed down from one generation to the next. They usually have traditional decorative and structural elements, including colorful hand-cut tiles (*zellij*), silky *tadelakt* walls of finely pressed and waxed plaster, painted cedar-wood ceilings, and arched colonnades. The living rooms are on the ground floor, with sleeping quarters on the upper floors. At the center of a riad is an ornamental garden with a fountain or water feature, and rooms look inward through windows of wrought iron or wooden latticework.

In more recent times, with changing fashions and the development of modern *nouvelle villes* by colonial rulers, many Moroccans relinquished their old houses for dwellings with 20th-century sanitation and modern amenities but the faded charms and beauty of traditional riads have captured the imagination of foreign investors, who often buy them as holiday retreats; many have been restored lovingly to their former glory with sumptuous attention to detail and the addition of state-of-the art facilities. Restored riads offer boutique accommodations in Morocco's walled cities, usually with three to six bedrooms over two levels, often with a plunge-pool and a sun terrace.

WHAT'S INCLUDED?

Riads that operate as guesthouses and rent individual rooms function like small hotels, with an on-site manager and staff who attend to housekeeping, catering, security, and concierge services. The room price usually includes breakfast. If you want complete privacy but top-notch service, then you'd book exclusive use of an authorized guesthouse riad and customize the on-site services as desired. A less expensive option is to rent a privately owned riad where you can self-cater and treat the place as home. For private riads you must check if electricity, water, heating, or firewood is included. Additional meals, private transport, guides, special activities, and excursions can normally be arranged for an additional cost. In some areas of some medinas, alcohol is strictly frowned upon and even prohibited. Check in advance if you can order wine or beer with your meals or bring liquor onto the property.

HOW MUCH DOES IT COST?

Riads come in all sizes and levels of luxury, so prices range anywhere from 300 DH to 3,000 DH per room per night for those run as a guesthouse. To rent an entire midprice riad with four bedrooms, expect to pay around 4,000 DH to 6,000 DH per night, usually with a minimum of two nights required. A luxury four-room riad, with staff, will cost around 8,000 DH–12,000 DH per night.

FINDING A RIAD

A simple Internet search will turn up hundreds of riads at different price categories. Most individual riads are privately owned and locally managed, so inquire directly via the official website, rather than through third-party booking sites, after you've checked out their customer reviews. **Owners Abroad** (⊕ *www.owners-abroad.org*) has a selection of midpriced private riad homes to rent direct from owners. For the high end of the market, agencies such as **VillaNovo** (⊕ *www.villanovo.com*) organize exclusive rentals of premier properties with full concierge service.

THE DYNASTIES OF MOROCCO

For centuries, Morocco, whose essence lies in a culturally rich mosaic of Arabic, European, and African influences, has lured and intrigued foreigners. With a complex and tumultuous history dating back more than 5,000 years, Morocco today is as unique and exotic as the diverse ethnic civilizations that have shaped everything here from language, music, art, and architecture to politics, education, and the economy.

 At the crossroads between East and West, Africa and Europe, Morocco has attracted invading conquerors seeking a strategic foothold in fertile valleys, desert oases, and coveted coastal outposts on the Atlantic and Mediterranean. Excavations from the 12th century BC show the remains of Phoenician settlements in ancient times. It was not until the 7th century, when Arabian invaders introduced Islam, that the Moroccan political landscape became more spectacular, often extreme, with radical religious reformers founding Muslim kingdoms in the midst of Christian encroachments and nomadic Berber tribal rule. Rural Berber tribes engaged in lawless conflict, battling it out with bloody family feuds in the harsh Sahara and unforgiving cliffs of the Atlas mountains. Successive invasions by Arab, French, and Spanish civilizations ensued, but the indigenous Berbers survived, remaining an integral component of today's Morocco. European colonization ultimately gave way to Morocco's independent state and a centralized constitutional government, still ruled today by monarchs, descended from the Alaouite Dynasty.

(left) Casablanca's Hassan II Mosque (top) Tomb of Moulay Ismail, Méknes

(left) A mosaic in the Roman ruins at Volubilis (above) an aerial view of the city of Moulay Idriss (right) a Roman coin excavated near Essaouira, on Morocco's Atlantic coast

Predynastic Morocco

1200 BC – AD 700

As Phoenician trading settlements expanded along the Mediterranean, the Romans also began to spread west through North Africa, declaring Volubilis its capital, whose ruins stand outside of Meknès. In the 2nd century BC, the Romans annexed Volubilis, Lixus, Chellah, and Mogador. Volubilis, orginally a Berber settlement, expanded dramatically under the Romans. The first Arab invasions occurred circa AD 682, collapsing the Roman Empire.

Idrissid Dynasty

682 – 1000

Under the regime of Oqba Ibn Nafi, Arabs spread the religion of Islam and its holy language, Arabic, both of which took hold (to varying degrees) throughout Morocco. In 788, exiled from Baghdad, Moulay Idriss I established the first Islamic and Arab dynasty that lasted almost 200 years. He set out to transform the village of Fez into the principal city of western Morocco. In 807, Idriss II, his son, founded Fez el-Bali (literally, Fez the Old) as the new intellectual capital in the Fez River's fertile basin—the Oued Fez, also known as Oued el-Yawahir,

the River of Pearls. Attracted by its importance, Andalusian and Tunisian Muslims arrived and established one of the most significant places of learning during its time—the Kairaouine University. The Fez medina is divided into two quarters on either side of the Fez River. The Andalusian Quarter originally housed refugees from Moorish Spain, who had begun to flee the Reconquista (the Christian re-conquest of Spain); the Kairaouine Quarter originally housed refugees from the Kairaouine. By the 10th and 11th centuries, the Bedouin tribe known as the Benu Hilal descended upon rural regions, destroying farmlands and villages.

Rome annexes Morocco	Moulay Idriss I establishes first Arab-Islamic dynasty in Morocco	Berber Merinid Dynasty established
400	800	1200	1600

(top left) Aït Ben Hadou, a ksar near Ouarzazate (near right) the entrance gates to Chellah, Rabat (far right) the towering minaret for the Koutoubia Mosque in Marrakesh

Almoravid Dynasty
1060–1150

From the south, one of the major Berber tribes emerged to create the Almoravid Dynasty, which led conquests to control desert trade routes to the north. By 1062, the Almoravids controlled what is now Morocco, Western Sahara, and Mauritania. Youssef Tashfin established Marrakesh as his capital, building fortressed walls and underground irrigation channels, and conquered Tlemcen—what is today Algeria. He eventually extended his kingdom north into Spain by 1090.

Almohad Dynasty
1150–1248

The Almohad Dynasty, started by radical reformer Ibn Toumert (the Torch) in the High Atlas village of Tinmal, gave rise to an empire stretching across Spain, Tunisia, and Algeria. The Almohads built the current capital of Rabat and its famous landmarks, Marrakesh's iconic Koutoubia mosque, and the Giralda Tower in Seville. After 100 years of rule, the Almohad empire collapsed because of civil warfare, causing Berbers to return to local tribes.

The Merinid Dynasty
1248–1472

The nomadic Banu Merin Berber tribe from the Sahara established the Merinid Dynasty, pushing westward into northeastern Morocco and ousting the Almohads, who were once their masters. As Merinid tribesmen waged holy wars, they seized control of the Fez el-Jdid, constructing numerous Islamic mosques and madrassas (colleges). Tribal in-fighting served to weaken the dynastic rule while invaders from Portugal captured coastal cities.

(far left) Asilah, a city in
northern Morocco (near left)
the Saadian Tombs in the
Marrakesh medina (above) the
fortified walls of Taroudant

The Wattisid Dynasty

1472 – 1554

Facing mounting territorial occupation by the Portuguese in what are now Tangier, Essaouira, and Agadir, the Merinids lost control to the Wattisids, due to the rising perception that a ruler was only legitimate if they descended from the Prophet Mohammed. The Wattisids reigned between 1472 and 1554 from Fez, relinquishing rule because of Moorish conquests on the Moroccan side of the Straits of Gibraltar. By 1492, Muslims had lost control of Spain and sought refuge back in the Maghreb.

The Saadian Dynasty

1554 – 1669

As the first Arab kingdom since the Idrissids, the Saadian Dynasty drove out the Christians. Lacking any loyalty to Berber tribes, they also proclaimed their superiority as direct descendants of the prophet Mohammed. The Saadi family originally settled in the Drâa Valley near Zagora in the 12th century and later in the Sous near Taroudant, which became the Saadian capital until they declared Marrakesh their sultanate in 1524. The greatest of the eleven Saadian sultans, Ahmed el Mansour, reigned for more than 25 years, building ties with England's monarchy against Spain. He commanded an army to conquer the West African Songhai empire and led a gold rush on the Niger River. His impact on Morocco as "The Victorious" ended when he died in 1603, leaving his vast kingdom to his sons, who continued to reign for the next 60 years in both Marrakesh and Souss but failed to keep order and peace. General anarchy swept the country as Jewish and Muslim refugees from Catholic Spain arrived on chaotic shores while bands of pirates (the notorious Barbary pirates) sailed from Rabat and Salé.

Moulay Rashid captures Marrakesh from Saadiens	Morocco signs a treaty with Spain	Morocco becomes a French protectorate	Moroccan independence
1700	1800	1900	2000

In Focus | THE DYNASTIES OF MOROCCO

(far left) Moulay Ismail, who united and liberated Morocco from European powers in 1672 (near left) the gardens of the Museum of Moroccan Arts, Fez (bottom right) Tangier's waterfront promenade

The Alaouite Dynasty

1669 – 1894

The Alaouite Dynasty, led by Moulay Rashid, captured Marrakesh in 1669. By 1672, the ruler Moulay Ismail seized Meknès, launching years of brutal holy wars while effectively liberating the country from European powers and laying the foundation for European trade relations. In 1767, Morocco signed a peace treaty with Spain and a trading agreement with France. In 1787, a U.S. peace treaty was signed. But the 19th century saw losses of territory to France.

European Conquest

1906 – 1956

By 1906, the majority of Africa was under European rule. Morocco, though still independent, was on the verge of bankruptcy after years of borrowing from European powers, in particular France. The Treaty of Fez in 1912 distributed Morocco's regions between Spain and (mostly) France, declaring the country as a French protectorate with Rabat as its capital. It was during this time that the Glaoui, who controlled one

of the High Atlas passes from their kasbah at Telouet, became allies with the French. Uprisings took place in the 1920s, and by the 1930s and 1940s, violent protests across the country heightened as the independence movement of the Istiqulal Party gained strength in Fez. Writers including Paul Bowles settled in Tangier, an international zone since 1923, and began an artistic counter-culture there. By 1955, the situation had reached a boiling point; France granted Morocco independence in 1956.

(above) The Mohammed V
Mausoleum, Rabat (right)
Agadir's popular beachfront

Return of the Alaouite Dynasty

1956 – 1961

In 1956, Mohammed V returned from exile to regain the Moroccan throne. The Glaoui-French alliance was broken, and the Glaoui Dynasty went into an immediate decline. When Mohammed V died unexpectedly in 1961, his son, Hassan II, inherited the responsibility to continue social and political reforms, building up the country and maintaining his position as the country's spiritual leader. Hassan II was instrumental during the 1970s and 1980s in developing foreign relations between North Africa and the world.

A New Morocco

1961 – 1987

The ascension of King Hassan II reflected the dynamic yet insecure spirit of a country in transition. Radical left-wing supporters emerged as serious threats to the monarchy. The Socialist Union of Popular Forces campaigned for radical reforms, a view shared by newly-independent Algeria, which briefly engaged in a territorial war with Morocco over disputed frontiers. Militants tried but failed to assassinate King Hassan II five times between 1963 and 1977. Rioting leftists took to the streets in violent protest against what they considered autocratic, absolute rule. At the same time, beach resorts were being built in Agadir in the 1970s and early 1980s, creating an influx of European beach-goers.

The desolate Western Sahara region in the deep south became one of Africa's most controversial and longest-running territorial conflicts beginning with the Green March of 1975, when Morocco exerted its control over the territory. The area remained a powder keg for explosive behavior throughout the 1980s, as stakes remain high to own the area's valuable natural resources, including phosphate deposits, fish reserves, and oil.

On Nov. 6 1975, Hassan II orders "Green March" into Western Sahara	Mohammed VI becomes King	New family code gives women more power	Political reforms after "Arab Spring" uprisings
1980	**2000**	**2010**	**2020**

In Focus | THE DYNASTIES OF MOROCCO

(above) Moroccan women can be both modern and traditional (right) Quartier des Habous, Casablanca

The Progressive Years

1987 – 1999

Morocco granted more local control and even elected a house of representatives. Infrastructure began to improve. The Casablanca Stock Exchange installed an electronic trading system in the early 1990s. A busy film economy, which had begun in the early 1960s, began to develop in Ouarzazate. With the death of King Hassan II in 1999, his son, Mohammed Bin al Hassan, was immediately enthroned as Mohammed VI at the age of 36 in a peaceful transition.

Modern Morocco

1999 – 2011

When King Mohammed VI married engineer Salma Bennani in 2002, she became the first wife of a Moroccan ruler to be publicly acknowledged and given a royal title. Following many years of hard work by activists, women's rights have since improved. The minimum age for matrimony has risen to 18, and women have more freedom of choice in marriage and divorce. Women have also won seats in parliamentary elections. Terrorist bombings in 2003 and 2011 raised fears of Islamic extremists, but King Mohammed VI has tried to expand constitutional reforms to create more freedom and limit the powers of the monarchy. Morocco has sought member-

ship in the EU, but the stalemate in Western Sahara has hindered the region's stability and prosperity. Significant investments have been made in tourism, infrastructure, and renewable energy, including the world's largest solar power plant near Ouarzazate. The king continues to implement reforms and retain the affection of his people despite the 2011 Arab Spring, which toppled the regimes of many of Morocco's neighbors. In 2019, the Berber Amazigh language became an official language to be used alongside Arabic and French in government offices and public buildings. The Berber tifinagh alphabet can be seen on road signs, buildings, and official documents.

Kids and Families

Morocco is a treasure trove of adventures for families with children. The Imperial cities of Fez and Marrakesh in particular, are rich with fascinating sights, smells, and sounds. Kids can marvel at the snake charmers and acrobats of the Djemâa el Fna or enjoy the twisting alleys of Fez's medieval medina. The Volubilis ruins near Fez may captivate teenage imaginations and the dinosaur fossils and rock carvings of the Sahara are often a hit with younger kids. In the south, Kasbah Aït Benhaddou is a must, especially for those who recognize it from movies like *Gladiator* and the TV series *Game of Thrones*.

GETTING AROUND

Travel is best by rental car or a private vehicle with a driver. There is stunning scenery to admire, but journeys between destinations can take several hours, so stock on snacks, drinks, diapers, and toilet tissue—and make sure to include travel-free days in your itinerary and check that a child-seat can be provided if required. Streets are often badly paved (if at all), so a stroller may prove impractical.

WHAT TO BRING

Disposable diapers are available in city supermarkets and in small shops but the quality is often not the same as in Western countries, so you may want to bring your own. In rural areas you may struggle to find diapers, so stock up if touring. The same goes for baby formula. Pack plenty of sun hats and sunscreen, which are expensive in Morocco and not always available. Always carry bottled water.

WHAT TO EAT

Most hotels and restaurants in larger towns have Westernized children's menus, but eating like the locals will allow your family to discover many tasty Moroccan dishes. Grilled meat skewers (*brochettes*) of lamb, beef, or chicken can be stuffed into local bread to make on-the go sandwiches. *Kefta* are basically meatballs with mild spices and sometimes served as a main course in a *tajine* with a tomato sauce and eggs. For snacks, nuts, dates, and seasonal fruit are abundant and inexpensive.

WHERE TO STAY

Larger cities and seaside resorts offer modern hotels, guesthouses, and private apartments. Traditional Moroccan *riads* are found in the walled medinas of the Imperial Cities, though they're not advisable for small children since there are often steep stairs and unguarded balustrades. Rented apartments are a good way to keep costs down, but check the security of the neighborhood and confirm that there's a local contact in case of problems. In rural areas, family-friendly guesthouses offer local charm and can range from simple to luxurious. Desert camps in the Sahara offer standard or luxury tents suitable for children of all ages.

OUTDOOR ACTIVITIES

Morocco has outdoor adventures for the timid and the brave. Mule-trekking in the High Atlas, with visits to Imazighen villages is good for all ages, as is a camel ride along the beach. Quad-biking for older kids is popular in the palm groves of Marrakesh and the desert. In the Cascades of Ouzoud you can see native Barbary apes or splash under the waterfalls. For a unique wilderness adventure, head to the Sahara for camel-trekking and camping.

Bike rides and hiking can be tailored to suit all ages and abilities almost anywhere in Morocco. Near Marrakesh, **Terres d'Amanar** (⊕ *www.terresdamanar. com*) activity center offers archery, climbing, zip lines, and crafts workshops while **Oasiria** (⊕ *www.oasiria.com*) is a waterpark with slides and pools. The southern Atlantic Coast is peppered with beaches and surf schools; Essaouira is an ideal base for learning to surf.

Chapter 2

TRAVEL SMART

Updated by
Sarah Gilbert

★ **CAPITAL:**
Rabat

♦ **POPULATION:**
36,910,000

$ **CURRENCY:**
Moroccan dirham (MAD)

$ **MONEY:**
ATMs common; credit cards
accepted, but cash is needed
for markets, tipping, etc.

💬 **LANGUAGE:**
Modern Standard Arabic and
Tamazight (Amazigh) are the
official languages; French is
widely spoken

☎ **COUNTRY CODE:** 212

⚠ **EMERGENCIES:**
19 (police) or 15
(ambulance/fire)

🚗 **DRIVING:**
On the right

⚡ **ELECTRICITY:**
220v/50 Hz; plugs have two
round prongs

🕐 **TIME:**
Six hours ahead of New York

⊖ **DOCUMENTS:**
Stay for up to 90 days with
valid passport

📱 **MAJOR MOBILE
COMPANIES:** Maroc
Telecom, Inwi, Méditel

Tangier ○

RABAT ✪   ○ Fez
Casablanca ○

MOROCCO

○
Marrakesh

Agadir ○

Atlantic Ocean

**WESTERN
SAHARA**

Getting Here and Around

Air

Morocco is served by major airlines from North America, Europe, and the Middle East. The national carrier, Royal Air Maroc, flies to more than 80 destinations worldwide; look for special promotions on the airline's website.

Casablanca Mohammed V Airport (CMN) serves as the main entry point for nonstop flights from the United States. Morocco can also easily be reached through European hubs such as London, Paris, Amsterdam, Madrid, and Berlin, on major carriers and budget airlines, including easyJet, Ryanair, and Air Arabia.

AIRPORTS AND FLIGHTS

From Casablanca, there are frequent connections to popular destinations throughout the country, such as Marrakesh (RAK), Fez (FEZ), Essaouira (ESU), Agadir (AGA), Ouarzazate (OZZ), Rabat (RBA), and Tangier (TNG). Consider taking domestic flights if traveling long distances within Morocco, or if time is short.

GROUND TRANSPORTATION

Casablanca Mohammed V Airport has a train station under the Terminal 1 arrivals hall, with trains running hourly between 3 am and 10 pm, making travel to and from the airport easy and hassle-free. The ride to the city takes around 45 minutes. Taxis are also always available outside the arrivals hall; official fares to the city (around 300 DH) and other destinations are posted on a board at the taxi stand. Most hotels offer a transfer service to/from the airport on request.

Boat

If traveling from Spain, it's easy to take a ferry across the Strait of Gibraltar. There are numerous daily ferries from Tarifa and Algeciras, with the shortest crossing

from Tarifa to Tangier at around 45 minutes. Algeciras to Tangier or Ceuta (an autonomous Spanish territory in mainland Morocco, Sebta in Morocco) are other options.

Unfortunately, disembarking in Tangier can be a less than relaxing way to enter Morocco as you're likely to be greeted by hawkers offering everything from sunglasses to watches and city tours. Do your best not to engage with them, or try a firm "no thanks/non merci/la shukran."

Bus

Buses are the most popular means of public transport, and the two major national bus companies offer reliable, comfortable service with the option of superior buses, online booking, and guaranteed seats.

CTM (Compagnie de Transports Marocains) runs services to most areas of the country, with designated CTM stops, which are not necessarily in the central bus station. Another major bus company, Supratours, is owned by ONCF (Morocco's national rail service) and offers through-ticketing on buses whose departure times are coordinated with the arrival of trains.

If you're really going off the beaten track, there are a number of smaller bus companies known as "souk buses" that cover rural areas not served by CTM or Supratour. They are not always comfortable, clean, or safe, but they can be hailed in every village they pass through.

The bus station—known as the *gare routière*—is generally on the outskirts of town, although some cities have separate CTM or Supratours stations; check before you set off. It's best to arrive at least half an hour before your bus is scheduled to leave, giving you time to check your large pieces of luggage in the hold.

FARES

Fares are inexpensive; it's about 95 DH for the three-hour journey from Marrakesh to Essaouira. Expect to pay no more than 10 DH to store luggage. Additionally, most CTM, and some Supratours, stations have inexpensive luggage storage facilities.

It's advisable to book tickets a few days in advance as popular routes can fill up quickly. The bus stations can be chaotic, but it's easy to book online. Note that the CTM website and app is only in French or Arabic; ask at your hotel for help if necessary.

 # Car

Renting a car isn't necessary if you're only planning to visit major cities, but sometimes it's the best or only way to explore Morocco's coastal towns, mountainous rural areas such as the Middle or High Atlas, and the southern oases.

Roads are generally in good shape, and mile markers and road signs (in both Arabic and French) are easy to read. Note that many rural destinations are still only reached by *pistes* (dirt paths), and these rough roads can damage a smaller car.

Also bear in mind that traffic becomes more erratic during Ramadan and, no matter what time of year, when you're driving on open roads, grand taxi drivers tend to drive down the middle, so slow down and honk the horn as you approach a bend.

Hiring a car and an official, licensed driver (check credentials if you book directly with the driver) is an excellent but more expensive way to get to know the country and to tap into local knowledge and connections. Drivers also serve as protectors from potential faux guides and tourist scams.

BOOKING YOUR TRIP

You can hire anything from a compact Fiat to a four-wheel-drive SUV, a boon for touring the Atlas Mountains and southern oases. Expect to pay from around 350 DH to 9,000 DH for a premium car per day, including unlimited mileage. Child seats and GPS are extra and payable at pick-up, so availability can't be guaranteed.

The best place to rent a car is at Casablanca's airport, as the rental market is very competitive—most cars are new, and discounts are often negotiable. Most recommended agencies have offices here and branches in the city, as well in other major cities. To get the best deal, book through a comparison website such as www.rentalcars.com.

You can also negotiate the rental of a grand taxi with a driver for a given itinerary just about anywhere in Morocco. The advantage is that you don't have to navigate; the disadvantage is that the driver may have his own ideas about where you should go and will probably not speak English. For ease—and higher prices—local tour operators can provide high-quality vehicles with multilingual drivers.

■TIP→ **Rental cars are nearly always stick shift but automatics are available.**

GASOLINE

Gas is readily available and generally cheaper than in Europe. Unleaded fuel (*sans plomb*) is around 12 DH a liter, and diesel (*gasoil*) is around 10 DH. Most gas stations provide full service; leave around 3 DH–5 DH tip. Increasingly, gas stations take credit cards and have restrooms; some have cafés.

Getting Here and Around

PARKING

When parking in the city, make sure you're in an authorized parking zone— avoid curbs painted with red-and-white stripes. Most zones will have a *gardien de voitures* (car parking attendant) who will look after your car for a small tip, around 2 DH–5 DH. In cities, there are parking garages or you can purchase a ticket from a curbside machine, valid for a set duration.

ROAD CONDITIONS

Road conditions are generally very good and the network of *autoroutes* (toll roads) and toll-free expressways has expanded considerably in recent years. Autoroutes run from Tangier in the north, to Agadir in the south, taking in Casablanca, Rabat, and Marrakesh. There are periodic tollbooths charging from 5 DH to 20 DH; make sure to carry loose change in coins as booths generally don't accept credit cards.

Expect the unexpected: many drivers think nothing of driving on the opposite side of the road or reversing at high speed along busy roads, while taxis often pull up to the side of the road without notice.

On rural roads expect the occasional flock of sheep or herd of goats to cross the road at inopportune times; in the south you'll even see road signs warning of camel crossings. In the mountains, side-pointing arrows designate curves in the road but be aware that some dangerous curves can come unannounced. In the countryside you're more likely to encounter potholes, narrow roads, and speeding taxi drivers.

Night driving should be avoided; it requires extreme caution, especially outside of cities where many roads are unlit. Beware of inadequate or unfamiliar lighting on vehicles at night, particularly on trucks—it's not uncommon for them to have red lights at the front and white lights at the rear. Ubiquitous ancient mopeds rarely have working lights or reflectors—the same goes for donkey and mule carts, bicycles, and pedestrians.

ROADSIDE EMERGENCIES

In case of a road accident, dial 15 for emergency ambulance and fire services, and for police dial 19 in cities, and 177 outside cities.

As emergency numbers in Morocco may not be answered quickly, it's wise to hail help from passersby and/or street police if possible. Even in the most rural areas, someone will appear to assist a stranded traveler. When available, it can be more effective to summon a taxi to reach medical help instead of relying on ambulance service.

RULES OF THE ROAD

Traffic moves on the right side of the road, as in the United States and most of Europe. There are two main rules in Morocco: the first is, "priority to the right," meaning that on traffic circles you must yield to traffic entering from the right; the second is, "every man for himself," as any car that is ahead of you— even by an inch—considers itself to have priority.

It's mandatory to wear seat belts for both drivers and passengers and failure to do so can result in a hefty fine. Talking on cell phones while driving is also illegal, though most Moroccans do it.

You must carry your car registration and insurance certificate at all times (these documents are supplied with rental cars). Morocco's speed limits, enforced by radar, are 120 kph (75 mph) on autoroutes, from 60 kph to 100 kph (37 mph–62 mph) on national routes, and 40 kph (25 mph) in built-up areas.

Commonly enforced penalties include speeding, not stopping at a stop sign, and running a red light. On-the-spot fines are payable to the issuing officer, or your driver's license may be confiscated. Always ask for the fine "ticket" as this reduces the risk of corruption.

Taxi

Moroccan taxis take two forms: *petits taxis* (small taxis that travel within city limits) and *grands taxis* (larger taxis that travel between cities). Grands taxis usually have designated stops and the driver will wait until the taxi is full before departing.

Taxis are color-coded according to city—in Casablanca and Fez they're red, in Rabat and Chefchaouen they're blue, etc. Petits taxis can be hailed anywhere and take a maximum of three passengers. The fare is metered and inexpensive: usually 5 DH to 30 DH for a short trip. Taxis often pick up additional passengers en route, so if you can't find an empty cab, try hailing a taxi with one or two passengers already; the driver should run a separate meter for each passenger. Passengers traveling together pay one fare.

Grands taxis travel fixed routes. Two passengers can squeeze in front with the driver, and four can sit, very cramped, in the back. Don't expect air-conditioning, a luxurious interior, or even fully functioning windows or seatbelts, though some of the ancient Mercedes sedans are being replaced by modern minivans. Fares for these shared rides are inexpensive and you can also buy several seats to make it a more comfortable ride; if you charter a grand taxi for a specific journey, negotiate a price in advance.

Train

Morocco's punctual rail system is run by the ONCF (Office National des Chemins de Fer) and is great for getting between the four imperial cities (Fez, Meknès, Rabat, and Marrakesh); the network is less extensive in the south and along the Mediterranean coast.

Fares are relatively inexpensive compared to the United States and Europe; for example, a first-class (*première classe*) ticket from Casablanca to Marrakesh costs 171 DH ($18.50). A first-class ticket guarantees a reserved seat and is worth the extra money, especially during busy periods. Long-distance trains seat six people to a compartment in first class, and eight to a compartment in second class (*deuxième classe*), which is still a comfortable option.

Launched in late 2018, Al Boraq (named after a mythical winged creature from Islamic folklore) is Africa's first high-speed, LGV train. It's cut the journey time between Tangier and Casablanca in half, to just over two hours, running at top speeds of 320 kph; there are plans to expand the line to Marrakesh.

You can buy train tickets online or at any station up to six days in advance. Purchasing your ticket on the train is pricier and can only be done in cash.

🔘 Tram

Casablanca and Rabat have shiny new tram services, which have taken the burden off the urban buses and taxis and lessened some of the traffic. Tickets are easy to purchase on platforms, and announcements are in French and English.

Essentials

 ## Accommodations

Accommodations in Morocco range from opulent to extremely basic, with everything in between. Hotels can be on a par with those of the United States and Europe, but five-star comforts begin to disappear the farther off the beaten path you venture. Hotels can lack amenities, particularly in smaller towns and villages, but they often make up for a lack of luxury with genuine charm, hospitality, character, and location.

HOTELS

Hotels are classified by the Moroccan government with one to five stars, plus an added category for five-star luxury hotels, but this rating is not the equivalent to North American and European ratings, and standards can vary. As a rule of thumb, in hotels with three or more stars, all rooms have private bathrooms, and there is usually air-conditioning.

High season in Morocco depends on the region. If you're visiting the imperial cities and the High Atlas, it's generally from mid-March to mid-May and September through October. On the Mediterranean and Atlantic coasts, July and August is peak season for domestic tourism, and in the desert, September through November are the most popular months.

RIADS

Many traditional *dars* and *riads* (medina houses with an interior courtyard, or interior garden in the case of a riad) have been sensitively restored, beautifully furnished, and turned into unique boutique hotels and B&Bs, where you can get a real taste of Moroccan heritage.

As well as booking a room, it's often possible to rent the entire property, especially in the most popular cities, such as Marrakesh and Fez; perfect for families or small groups. It's also possible

to rent rural retreats and coastal villas. Most properties are available on popular booking engines such as booking.com, Tripadvisor, and Airbnb, or book direct and you may get preferential rates.

Communications

INTERNET

Free Wi-Fi is widely available in hotels, restaurants, and cafés—although speeds can vary—so it's easy to keep in touch with a laptop, tablet, or smartphone.

PHONES

The country code for Morocco is 212. Moroccan landline numbers start with 05, and all mobile phone numbers start with 06; many Moroccan businesses have both numbers.

CALLING WITHIN MOROCCO

Within Morocco, always dial the four-digit area code, even if you're calling locally.

You must purchase a *télécarte*, or phone card, to use public phones on the street. Or head to a Téléboutique; these little shops have individual coin-operated phones, which you need to feed with dirhams to make a call.

CALLING OUTSIDE MOROCCO

To call the United States from Morocco, dial 00, then 1 (the country code), then the area code and phone number.

You can make international calls by calling directly or via directory enquiries accessed by dialing 160. Many operators speak English, and all speak French. Calls from Morocco are expensive but it's possible to make free or cheap Internet calls if Wi-Fi is available. Otherwise, the cheapest option for direct international dialing is from a public phone, using a télécarte.

MOBILE PHONES

4G is widespread and GSM mobile phones with international roaming capability work well in cities, less so in the mountains and desert. Roaming fees can be steep, especially for data, so use Wi-Fi whenever possible. It's almost always cheaper to send a text message than to make a call; check rates with your provider.

Alternatively, if you just want to make local calls and you have an unlocked mobile phone, you can buy a prepaid SIM card in Morocco. The three major mobile-phone companies, Inwi, Maroc Telecom, and Méditel, all offer packages from around 100 DH.

■ TIP→ **You will need your passport to buy a SIM card.**

⊕ Customs and Duties

The following may be imported without duty: 150 ml of perfume, 250 ml of eau de toilette, 1 liter of spirits, 1 liter of wine, 200 cigarettes or 50 cigars or 400 grams of tobacco. Prohibited items include arms and ammunition, drugs, and any books, video, or audio material containing "immoral, sexual or offensive" material.

⊕ Dining

Moroccan cuisine is varied and delicious. Dining establishments range from outdoor food stalls and family-run restaurants to elegant and expensive eateries with prices approaching those of Europe. Moroccan restaurants commonly offer delicious tagines, couscous, and grilled kebabs served with bread and salad; on the coast, charcoal-grilled fish is a good choice, and you can often choose your

meal from the daily catch. Marrakesh and Fez are the places for wonderful feasts in Arabian Nights surroundings, and Casablanca has a diverse dining scene. The listed restaurants in this guide represent the best in each price range and cuisine type.

MEALS AND MEALTIMES

Hotels normally serve a generous continental breakfast (*petit déjeuner continental* in French) with an array of Moroccan breads and pastries, often included in the room rate. If it's not included, you can buy an equivalent meal at numerous cafés at a much lower price. The more expensive hotels offer expansive buffets. Breakfast is usually served from 8 to 10 or 10:30 but caffeine lovers should be able to get a coffee before that.

Lunch (*déjeuner*) in Morocco is typically the most leisurely meal of the day and large, and is served between noon and 2:30. A typical lunch menu consists of salad, a main course with meat and vegetables, and fruit. In restaurants this is generally available à la carte. On Friday, the traditional lunch is a bowl piled high with fluffy couscous topped with vegetables and meat.

At home, lunch and dinner are often served communal-style, on one big platter. Moroccans only eat with their right hands and use bread as an all-purpose utensil to pick up meat and sop up the juices. In restaurants, bread will always be served in a basket and utensils will be offered to foreigners. All restaurants, no matter how basic, have sinks for washing hands before and after your meal.

Hotels and restaurants usually begin dinner service at 7:30, although in a Moroccan home you probably won't sit down to eat until 9 or 10 pm. Dinner (*diner*) in international restaurants is generally à la carte, although many of

Essentials

the fancier restaurants serve prix-fixe menus, with at least three courses, often more. If you're a vegetarian or have other dietary requirements, mention this when you make a reservation; most restaurants will prepare special dishes with advance notice.

Unless otherwise noted, the restaurants listed in this guide are open daily for lunch and dinner, although during Ramadan, everything changes and many cafés and restaurants are closed during the day; the *iftar* meal breaks the fast and is served precisely at sunset. Many people wake up for an additional meal, the *suhur*, before sunrise. Hotels and tourist-oriented restaurants continue to serve meals to non-Muslim guests as usual, but don't be surprised if there's a slight break in service at sunset when the staff have their meal.

PAYING
For price charts deciphering the price categories of restaurants and hotels, see "Planning" at the beginning of each chapter.

Larger and pricier restaurants generally take credit cards; MasterCard and Visa are the most widely accepted. Outside cities and larger towns, most restaurants are cash-only.

RESERVATIONS AND DRESS
Reservations are generally a good idea at more popular spots, but might not be possible at places on the cheaper end of the scale: we mention them only when they're essential or not accepted. Book as far ahead as possible, and reconfirm as soon as you arrive. Jacket and tie are rarely required.

WINES, BEER, AND SPIRITS
Although alcohol is forbidden by Islam, it isn't illegal in Morocco and there are hotels, restaurants, and bars that are licensed to serve it. In fact, the country has an increasing number of vineyards producing red, white, rosé, and *vin gris* (very light rosé) wines, particularly in the Meknès region. There are breweries too; Heineken is produced under license in Casablanca, and local favorites include Casa, a pale lager, and Flag Spéciale. The French supermarket, Carrefour sells alcohol, except during Ramadan, when liquor sections are usually closed.

Electricity
The electrical supply in Morocco is 220 volts, 50Hz; wall outlets take the two-pin plug, found in Europe. To use electrical appliances from the United States, bring a converter and adapter; they may need a transformer, so check if they're dual-voltage. A flashlight is a useful thing to carry, especially in rural areas.

Emergencies
In case of emergency, dial 15 for ambulance and fire services, and for police dial 19 in cities and 177 outside cities. Pharmacies are plentiful and can deal with minor ailments. There's always a late-night pharmacy available; details are usually posted on pharmacy doors or ask at your hotel.

Health
Medical care is available throughout the country but varies in quality. Larger cities have excellent private clinics while the rest of the country depends on government-run clinics and dispensaries; in rural areas, English-speaking medical support may not be available. Ensure that you have adequate insurance to cover

medical care; in an emergency, contact your embassy or consulate.

Although Moroccan water is generally safe (in cities at least), it's advisable to stick to bottled water and try to resist the temptation to add ice to beverages unless you know it's been made from bottled water. Use reasonable precautions and eat only well-cooked foods, but mild cases of diarrhea should respond well to Imodium. Be sure to drink plenty of fluids; if you can't keep fluids down, seek medical help immediately.

Note that scorpions and snakes live in the desert. They rarely pose a serious problem; however, it's advisable not to walk barefoot. Dog bites pose the risk of rabies; always get a rabies vaccination at the earliest possible opportunity if you are bitten. Many medinas have a huge street cat population; they look cute but avoid petting them as they can carry diseases.

In summer and in the desert, there's a risk of sunburn, heatstroke, and dehydration so be sure to drink plenty of water and seek shade where possible. If you do get dehydrated, pharmacies sell rehydration treatments.

■ TIP→ **Pack your own high-SPF sunscreen; it's widely available but very expensive.**

COVID-19
Although COVID-19 brought travel to a virtual standstill for most of 2020 and into 2021, vaccinations have made some travel possible again. Remaining requirements and restrictions—including those for nonvaccinated travelers—can, however, vary from one place (or even business) to the next. Check out the websites of the CDC and the U.S. Department of State, both of which have destination-specific, COVID-19 guidance. Also, in case travel is curtailed abruptly again, consider buying trip insurance.

Just be sure to read the fine print: not all travel-insurance policies cover pandemic-related cancellations.

OVER-THE-COUNTER REMEDIES
Pharmacists are a good source of advice on everyday ailments and many medicines, including antibiotics and painkillers, are available over the counter, including aspirin (Aspro) and ibuprofen (Analgyl).

Avoid temporary tattoos with black, rather than natural brown henna; they can cause a severe allergic reaction in some people.

Hours of Operation
Banks are open Monday to Friday 8:15 to 3:45. Post offices are open Monday to Friday 8:30 to 4:30, and government offices have similar schedules.

Museums are generally open all day but may close for lunch. Standard pharmacy hours are 9 to 12:30 and 3:30 to 8:30; your hotel can help you find which pharmacies are open around the clock. Medina shops are typically open every day from about 9 to 6, but may be closed Friday afternoon and Sunday.

On Friday, the day of prayer, many businesses close down for the day or at least around the noon prayer. During Ramadan schedules change, usually with later opening times and earlier closing.

HOLIDAYS
The two most important religious holidays in Morocco are the four-day Eid al-Fitr (Feast of the Breaking of the Fast), which marks the end of the monthlong Ramadan fast, and three-day Eid al-Adha (Feast of the Sacrifice), when sheep are sacrificed to commemorate the prophet Ibrahim's willingness to sacrifice his son. Another holiday is the one-day Eid

Essentials

al-Mouloud, commemorating the birth of the prophet Mohammed. All banks, offices, and some shops are closed during these festivals.

Ramadan, which lasts around 30 days, is not a holiday per se but it does change the pace of life. Because the Islamic calendar is lunar, the dates for Ramadan and other religious holidays are around 11 days earlier each year.

Morocco's other holidays are as follows: January 1, New Year's Day; January 11, Anniversary of the Independence Manifesto; May 1, Labor Day; July 30, The Feast of the Throne (commemorating the coronation of King Mohammed VI); August 14, Oued ed-Dahab, or Allegiance Day; August 20, Revolution Day; August 21, Youth Day; November 6, Green March Day; November 18, Independence Day.

❂ Mail

Post offices are available everywhere and visible by their yellow-and-blue signs. Outgoing airmail is reliable. Note that if you mail letters at the main sorting office of any city, they will often arrive several days sooner than if you mail them from elsewhere. Airmail letters to the United States take about 14 days, and a 20-gram airmail letter or postcard costs about 25 DH to send.

SHIPPING PACKAGES

The best way to ship a package home is with an international courier service such as DHL, UPS, or FedEx. However, be warned that certain goods may be confiscated by customs, such as artisanal daggers and undocumented artworks. If you buy a carpet or large handicraft item, the shop will be able to organize shipping, but it might double the price of your purchase.

ⓢ Money

Prices in Morocco are low compared to both North America and Europe; fresh produce, public transportation, and labor are very cheap. Sample costs below are in U.S. dollars.

Meal in cheap restaurant, $5–$15; meal in expensive restaurant, $30–$100; 1.5 liters of bottled water, $0.60; cup of coffee, $1.30; museum admission, $2–$7; liter of gasoline, $1.30; short taxi ride, $1–$2.

Because the dirham's value can fluctuate, some upscale hotels, tour operators, and activity specialists geared toward tourists publish their prices in euros, but also accept dirhams and usually credit cards.

ATMS AND BANKS

You'll usually get a better rate of exchange at an ATM than you will at a *bureau de change*, hotel, or even international bank, even accounting for the fees your bank may charge. Reliable ATMs are attached to banks in major cities, and there's one in the arrivals hall at Casablanca's airport. Banque Populaire, BMCI, Société Générale, and Attijariwafa Bank all accept major credit cards.

CREDIT CARDS

MasterCard and Visa are widely accepted at all but the most basic hotels, restaurants, and shops—Amex less so—but there's often a 5% surcharge to cover bank fees. It's wise to inform your credit-card company before you travel, and keep a record all your credit card numbers in a safe place.

Although it's usually cheaper (and safer) to use a credit card for large purchases (so you can cancel payments or be reimbursed if there's a problem), note that some credit card companies and the banks that issue them add substantial percentages to foreign transactions, whether in foreign currency or not; check with your provider.

CURRENCY AND EXCHANGE

The national currency is the dirham (DH), which is divided into 100 centimes. There are bills for 20, 50, 100, and 200 DH, and coins for 1, 5, and 10 DH. There is usually more than one style of banknote in circulation at any time.

The dirham is a closed currency and can only be bought on arrival in Morocco; the exchange rate for the U.S. dollar is the same at all banks, including those at the airport. It's advisable to only exchange or withdraw the amount you think you'll need as dirhams can't be taken out of the country, although they can be exchanged upon departure, as long as you've kept the exchange receipts.

🌐 Passports

U.S. citizens with a valid passport can enter Morocco and stay up to 90 days without a visa.

📍 Restrooms

Be warned that some public toilets are squat-style. It's customary to tip the attendant in a public toilet around 3 DH.

■ TIP → **Always carry hand sanitizer and your own toilet paper or tissues.**

➕ Safety

Morocco is a relatively safe destination. Violent crime is rare. People who pester you to hire them as guides in places like Marrakesh and Fez are a nuisance but not a threat to your safety. Pickpocketing, however, can be a problem. In souks, open markets, and other crowded areas,

carry your backpack or purse in front of you. Cell phones, cameras, and other portable electronics are big sellers on the black market and should be kept out of sight whenever possible. Bags and valuables can also be snatched by thieves on mopeds. Keep an eye on your belongings at crowded beaches, as it is not unheard of for roving gangs to make off with your stuff while you're swimming.

Morocco, along with its neighbors, has experienced social unrest and international terrorism over the past few years, just like its North African and European neighbors. The country has, however, been widely praised for its handling of these issues, and foreign governments frequently accord Morocco a lower security (i.e., a higher safety) rating than its neighbors.

Female travelers—and especially single female travelers—sometimes worry about treatment on the streets of Morocco. There really isn't anything to worry about; you'll most likely be leered at, spoken to, and sometimes followed for a block. Women walking alone are targeted by vendors hoping to make a sale. This attention, while irritating, isn't threatening. Don't take it personally; Moroccan women endure it as well. The best way to handle it is to walk purposefully, avoid eye contact, and completely ignore men pestering you. If they don't let up, a firm reprimand with the Arabic "*hashuma*" ("shame"), or the French "*Laissez-moi tranquille*" ("Leave me alone") should do the trick. If this still doesn't work, look for a local police officer or head into a restaurant or museum.

Essentials

🧳 Packing

The average temperature in Morocco is 63.5°F (17.5°C), with minimums around 50°F (9.4°C) in winter (colder in the mountains) to above 80°F (27°C) in summer, and significantly hotter in the desert. But unless you visit in the sweltering heat of July and August or a biting cold snap in January, you'll most likely need to pack for a range of temperatures.

Casual clothes are fine in Morocco but it's wise to dress modestly. Apart from the beach, tank tops and shorts are not acceptable for either sex, especially in rural areas and medinas, where both women and men should cover their arms and legs. Crucial items to bring include comfortable walking shoes, sandals, and, for women, a large shawl or scarf which can be wrapped around your head or arms for respect or your shoulders for warmth.

It's also smart to pack your own toilet paper and tissues, hand sanitizer, travel-size baby wipes, sunscreen, Imodium, and tampons. A French phrasebook can also come in handy.

💲 Taxes

Tourists pay a lodging tax between 20 DH and 50 DH, per person per night, based on the city and the category of hotel. Travel agents always quote with all taxes included but if you book directly with the hotel, it's worth asking about the tax rate.

There are no airport taxes above those originally levied on the ticket price. VAT (Value Added Tax) is 20% and it's possible to get a refund on certain purchases if you've spent at least 2,000 DH.

🕑 Time

Morocco observes Greenwich Mean Time year-round (five hours ahead of Eastern Standard Time), so for most of the year it's on the same clock as the United Kingdom: five hours ahead of New York and one hour behind Continental Europe. Morocco observes Daylight Saving Time during the same period as Continental Europe, except when Ramadan is in summer, when the country temporarily goes back into Winter Time, which is two hours behind Continental Europe or four hours ahead of New York.

💲 Tipping

Tipping is standard practice in Morocco and always appreciated, but there are no hard-and-fast rules and it's always at your discretion. If you're hiring a guide, a minimum tip of 100 DH for a half a day, or 200 DH for a full day is standard; private drivers get a minimum of 200 DH per day; in restaurants, people generally tip 10% of the bill; hotel porters and restroom attendants get around 3 DH, and in taxis, you can round up to the nearest 5 DH.

📍 Visitor Information

The Moroccan National Tourist Office maintains Visit Morocco (🌐 *www.visitmorocco.com/en*), a website in eight languages, including English. The tourist office also has Much Morocco (🌐 *www.muchmorocco.com*), a website aimed specifically at English-speaking markets.

Contacts

Air

AIRLINES Air Arabia.
⊕ www.airarabia.com. **Air France.** ☎ 800/237–2747 ⊕ www.airfrance.com. **Brussels Airlines.** ✉ Brussels Airlines General Aviation zone, b. house, Bldg. 26☎ 0800/401–1801 reservations (from within U.S.) ⊕ www.brusselsairlines.com. **Easyjet.** ⊕ www.easyjet.com. **Iberia.** ☎ 800/722–4642 in U.S. ⊕ www.iberia.com. **KLM.** ☎ 0800/618–0104 in U.S. ⊕ www.klm.com. **Royal Air Maroc.** ☎ 0522/48–97–97 in Morocco, 800/344–6726 in U.S. ⊕ www.royalairmaroc.com.

AIRPORTS Moroccan Airports Authority (ONDA). ☎ 080/1000–224⊕ www.onda.ma.

GROUND TRANSPORTATION ONCF. ☎ 2255 ⊕ www.oncf.ma/en.

Boat

Baleària. ⊕ www.balearia.com/en. **FRS.** ☎ 956/68–18–30 in Spain⊕ www.frs.es/en. **Southern Ferries Ltd.** ☎ 0844/815–7785 in U.K. ⊕ www.southernferries.co.uk. **Trasmediterránia.** ☎ 902/45–46–45 in Spain ⊕ www.trasmediterranea.es.

Bus

CTM. (Compagnie de Transports Marocains). ✉ Km 13.5 Rte. de Casa-Rabat Sidi Bernoussi, Casablanca☎ 0800/09–00–30⊕ www.ctm.ma. **Supratours.** ✉ Av. Hassan II, next to train station, Guéliz☎ 0890/20–30–40 ⊕ www.oncf.ma.

Car

Europcar. ☎ 0522/53–91–61 Casablanca Mohammed V International Airport⊕ www.europcar.com. **Sixt.** ☎ 0600/07–78–00⊕ www.sixt.com. **Thrifty.** ☎ 08022/00–77–78 ⊕ www.thrifty.ma.

Train

ONCF. ☎ 2255 24-hr information line⊕ www.oncf.ma/en.

Customs and Duties

Government of Morocco Customs Administration. ☎ 080/100–7000⊕ www.douane.gov.ma.

Embassies

U.S. Embassy. ✉ Km 5.7, Av. Mohamed VI, Souissi ☎ 0537/63–72–00 Rabat ⊕ ma.usembassy.gov.

Visitor Information

ONMT. ☎ 0537/67–40–13 in Rabat, 212/221–1583 in New York⊕ www.visitmorocco.com, www.muchmorocco.com.

Great Itineraries

The Imperial Cities: The Classic Tour of Morocco

For longer stays in Morocco, tailor your tour around more exhaustive exploring of regions and adventurous diversions. If time is limited, focus on the major experiences and sights. This weeklong holiday gives you enough time to sample the best of Morocco. Remember to add a day on each end for travel time (a direct flight from New York to Casablanca takes approximately eight hours), and pace yourself to see the most important places.

DAY 1: ARRIVAL IN CASABLANCA

Flights generally arrive in Casablanca in the early morning. The city doesn't have that many sights and only requires a few hours to see them all. As your starting point, visit the **Hassan II Mosque** and the Mohammed V Square designed in French colonial, Art Deco style. You're going to be exhausted anyway after a transatlantic flight, so spend your first night in Casablanca; however, if you want to make an early start in the morning, travel one hour along the coast to Rabat.

DAY 2: RABAT

Explore the capital city of Rabat. The best sights in the city are the **Hassan Tower** and **Mohammed V Mausoleum, Chellah Gardens and Necropolis,** and **Oudayas Kasbah** overlooking the Atlantic Ocean. In the late afternoon, drive to Meknès to spend the night.

DAY 3: MEKNÈS AND VOLUBILIS

Begin your tour by passing the **Bab Mansour** and visiting the holy **Mausoleum of Moulay Ismail,** which is open to non-Muslims. Walk toward the lively Place el-Hedime, which leads to the medina. Tour the open bazaars of the medina streets; enjoy an inexpensive classic Moroccan

lunch; and visit the food souk near the row of pottery stands. The **Museum of Moroccan Art** in the 19th-century Dar Jamai palace and **Heri el Souani** (Royal Granaries) are recommended stops. In the afternoon, drive 30 minutes to the ancient Roman archaeological ruins of **Volubilis.** When you approach, the Triumphal Arch rises in the open field. Count on 90 minutes for a thorough visit. The Tangier Gate, House of Orpheus, House of Columns, and House of Ephebus are must-sees. You can spend the night near Volubilis at Moulay Idriss, or head back to Meknès.

DAYS 4 AND 5: FEZ

Try to arrive in Fez as early as possible so you can spend two full days exploring everything the **Fez el-Bali, Fez el-Djedid,** and **Ville Nouvelle** have to offer: medieval monuments, artisan workshops, public squares, ancient tombs, cultural museums, chaotic souks, atmospheric cafés, and palatial gardens. The blue-tiled gate of **Bab Boujeloud** is the gateway to the main alley of Talaa Kebira. The most important sites include the **Bou Inania medersa, Attarine madrassa, Mausoleum of Zaouia Moulay Idriss II** (peek in from the doorway—it's not open to non-Muslims), and **Karaouine Mosque and University** (the latter generally considered the oldest academic institution in the world, with a recently renovated library). Visit the restored **Nejjarine fondouk** for the best examples of woodworking craftsmanship. Watch the full fabrication process of the leather tanneries from a rooftop terrace. Shop for the famous blue-and-white Fassi pottery. Discover the area of the **Royal Palace** (Dar el-Makhzen) that leads to the active Mellah quarter beyond the Fez el-Djedid. Watch the sunset over the medina from the **Merenid tombs** or **Musée des Armes** atop the hills of the Borj Nord, or from the **Borj Sud,** south of the walled city. Indulge in an authentic Fassi

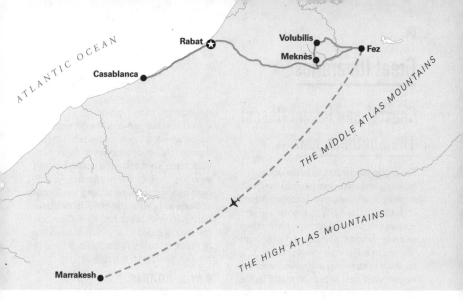

dinner in a riad courtyard. Spend two nights here.

DAYS 6 AND 7: MARRAKESH

The quickest way to travel the 398-km (242-mile) distance between Fez and Marrakesh is by plane (direct with Air Arabia). After dropping your bags at your hotel in Marrakesh, hit the ground running. The best place to start is the famed **Djemâa el Fna,** the perfect gateway into the labyrinth of souks, including the **Souk des Teinturiers** for leather, **Souk Addadine** for metalwork, and **Souk Zarbia,** the main carpet market. The **Ali ben Youssef Medersa, Dar Si Saïd** museum, **Palais Bahia,** and **Koutoubia Mosque** are important sites (though non-Muslims cannot enter the mosque). Walk south of the Palais Bahia to explore the bustling streets of the Mellah, the former Jewish quarter and largest in Morocco. In the evening, splurge on a feast, or head to the open grills on the busy main square. On your second day, take a petit taxi for a relaxing promenade through the **Ville Nouvelle** and lush **Majorelle Gardens and Museum,** where you can do some bird-watching and see an extraordinary collection of Imazighen ceramics, textiles, jewelry, and art. After, head back toward the medina and visit the 16th-century **Saadian Tombs** for one of the country's finest

Tips

■ One of only two mosques in Morocco non-Muslims can enter is the Hassan II Mosque in Casablanca (the other is the Tinmel Mosque in the High Atlas mountains). Visits are allowed only between prayer times (with official on-site guides) at 10 am, 11 am, and 3 pm. The 3 pm tour tends to be quieter, as bus groups visit in the morning.

■ During Ramadan, check for special hours; while many sites are open on holy days, some local restaurants and cafés close for the day or entire month.

■ Make your visit more special by attending an annual outdoor event, such as the World Sacred Music Festival held in Fez or the Mawazine Music Festival in Rabat featuring leading names in Arabic, African, and Western music.

representations of Islamic *zellij* (tile) work. Plan a relaxing hammam treatment to rejuvenate after a week of touring.

Great Itineraries

Coastal and Inland Oases: The Southern Tour

For those who want to escape the bustling medinas and touristy feel of the imperial cities, the Southern Atlantic coastline is the perfect alternative, with miles of deserted beaches, enchanting seaside villages, and colorful exotic landscapes to enrich the mind and spirit. The scenery is stunning and varied with rocky wilderness, vast seascapes, and fertile plains. Much of the area (except for Agadir) remains pristine and gets relatively few visitors. Swim, surf, sunbathe, birdwatch, and breathe in fresh ocean air. Laid-back towns, surfer havens, coastal resorts, and unexpected oases offer a holistic way to learn about local culture, food, language, and history.

DAY 1: MARRAKESH

Fly directly to Marrakesh Menara International Airport. Rent a car in the airport terminal, and check in to a hotel in Guéliz. Take a taxi to enjoy a delectable Moroccan dinner and experience the exotic activity of the **Djemâa el Fna,** the city's main square. Don't miss the city's excellent nightlife, with live street entertainment, local clubs, bars, and theater performances showcasing the fusion of Amazigh, Arab, African, and Andalusian influences in music and dance.

DAY 2: ESSAOUIRA

Rise early to drive west to the relaxing, picturesque port city of Essaouira. After you check into your hotel, take a walking tour of the harbor and town of whitewashed houses, and then stop to have lunch near the port. Don't miss the fresh charcoal-grilled sardines and shrimp in seaside food stalls. The town is a hub for contemporary Moroccan artists—check out art galleries showcasing self-taught naive artists of the region. Shop the colorful pedestrian-only medina streets for ceramics, thuya wood, *babouches* (leather slippers), and woven fabrics. Watch the sunset on the ocean horizon atop the ramparts of the **kasbah.** For the best panoramic view, access the fortress at **Skala de la Ville,** the cliffside sea bastion lined with brass cannons. Dine on fresh local seafood at a casual open grill or in one of many restaurants around the medina and along the beachfront.

DAY 3: AGADIR

Head south to Agadir, stopping off for magnificent sea views on the undisturbed sand dunes of Morocco's most beautiful beaches. **Sidi Kaouki, Tafedna,** and **Taghazout** are the most well-known beaches to sunbathe and dip your toes into the Atlantic waters. **Taghazout** attracts surfers and offers brisk ocean breezes. When you finally arrive in Agadir, visit the hilltop **kasbah** and **fish stalls** by the harbor. Enjoy dinner and one night here.

DAY 4: TIZNIT

Continue your journey to Tiznit, famous for its silver and wool blankets. Stay one night in Tiznit to experience local Amazigh living and hit its wonderful market, especially if you are looking for jewelry.

DAY 5: TAFRAOUTE

On Day 5, discover the natural beauty of the Anti-Atlas region, passing palm groves, almond orchards, rocky landscapes, fertile valleys, and fortified towns. Pass through the small villages **Igherm** and **Oumnast** before enjoying the beauty of Tafraoute. Explore the **Ameln Valley** region, then return to town in the late afternoon. Spend the night at the Auberge Kasbah Chez Amaliya, under hillsides scattered with pisé villages.

DAY 6: TAROUDANT

Take a relaxing drive toward Taroudant, where the atmosphere is very low-key and you can walk around the open markets and historic ramparts. The red-ocher-walled city is known for handcrafted leather items and aromatic spices. There are two main souks in the town. In the medina, don't miss the jewelry souk, fish market, kasbah, and pretty gardens. Listen for Tashelheit, the Amazigh dialect of the southern Souss region. On Sunday, locals from surrounding areas sell produce, livestock, and various wares near the main gate. A short loop drive east, about 10 km (6 miles) from Taroudant, takes you through the fertile Souss Valley plains and barren terrain leading toward the ruins of the Kasbah de Frieja. Spend the night in Taroudant.

DAY 7: RETURN TO MARRAKESH

Count on at least four hours to return to your starting point. If you plan to depart on the same day, head straight to the Menara airport. If you decide to stay one more evening, head back to the famed Djemâa el Fna, and shop for last-minute souvenirs in the **Souk des Teinturiers** for leather, **Souk Addadine** for metalwork, and **Souk Zarbia** for carpets. The **Ali ben Youssef Medersa, Dar Si Saïd** museum, **Palais Bahia**, and **Saadian Tombs**

Tips

■ Go off the beaten track—head to coastal destinations of Oualidia and Mirleft, a small village fast becoming a trendy spot for surfers and sun worshippers.

■ For an outdoor adventure, arrange a horse ride on the beach or rent ATVs through several stables or quad-trek companies.

■ To avoid serious problems, buy and carry a supply of bottled water to beat the heat on beaches and while walking through the villages and open terrain of the Anti-Atlas. Bring sunscreen. Both are difficult to find on the road.

■ Carry a Moroccan-Arabic phrase book. Neither English nor the standard Arabic of the Middle East are widely spoken in rural regions.

are important sites. If time and energy permit, walk south of the Palais Bahia to explore the bustling streets of the Mellah, the largest former Jewish quarter in Morocco.

Great Itineraries

Quintessential Morocco: The Grand Tour

In just over two weeks you can experience a lot of Morocco: coastal havens on the Atlantic coast, the High Atlas Mountains, pre-Saharan palmeries, Amazigh and Moorish architecture, rural hillside towns, and exquisite imperial cities. Allow three weeks for a more relaxed pace.

DAYS 1 AND 2: TANGIER, TETOUAN, AND CHEFCHAOUEN

The best way to enjoy Tangier is by taking a walking tour along the beachfront. Enter the medina and see the **Grand Mosque** and large market at the **Grand Socco.** Head to the north side of the mosque to enter the beautiful **Mendoubia Gardens** before meandering through the smaller alleyways to the **Petit Socco.** From here, reach the 15th-century **kasbah** and sultanate palace of **Dar el-Makhzen,** which houses the **Museum of Moroccan Arts** and **Museum of Antiquities.** Visit the historic **American Legation Cultural Center and Museum** commemorating the first diplomatic relations between the United States and Morocco. Enjoy a leisurely dinner by the water. On Day 2, pick up a rental car and drive southeast through the Rif Mountains to visit **Tetouan,** the historic town and UNESCO World Heritage site dating from the 8th century. Continue onto the stunning blue-washed hillside city of **Chefchaouen**; stay in Casa Hassan-Dar Baibou, which is nestled in the heart of the medina.

DAY 3: MEKNÈS AND VOLUBILIS

Start early on Day 3. Drive through **Ouazzane** en route to Fez, stopping off at the Roman ruins of **Volubilis.** Spend at least 90 minutes walking the grounds. The Tangier Gate, Diana and the Bathing Nymphs mosaic, House of Orpheus,

House of Columns, and House of Ephebus are must-sees. Then continue onto Meknès, arriving by midday. Pass the **Bab Mansour** and visit the holy **Mausoleum of Moulay Ismail,** which is open to non-Muslims. Walk toward the lively place el-Hedime, which leads into the medina. Tour the open bazaars of the medina streets and have some lunch. Near the row of pottery stands, visit the food souk. The **Museum of Moroccan Art** in the 19th-century Dar Jamai palace and **Heri el-Souani** (Royal Granaries) are recommended stops. Late in the afternoon, get back in the car and continue to Fez, arriving by nightfall, and splurge on a sumptuous Fassi meal in a riad or former palace.

DAYS 4 AND 5: FEZ

Spend Day 4 exploring the Fez **medina,** absorbing the view from one of many rooftop terraces overlooking this ancient labyrinth or atop the hill of the **Musée des Armes** for an incredible panorama of the whole city. Tour the Fez el-Bali and Fez el-Djedid. Don't miss the blue-tiled gate of **Bab Boujeloud, Bou Inania medersa, Attarine madrassa, Zaouia Moulay Idriss II, Nejjarine fondouk,** and **Karaouine Mosque and University.** For the morning of Day 5 you could sign up for a Moroccan cookery class at your riad or at Café Clock, shop for ingredients in the souk, and prepare your own lunch. Alternatively visit the **tanneries** to find leather bargains and then explore the **Quartier des Potiers** for famous blue-and-white Fassi pottery and to learn how it's made. Spend the night in Fez.

DAY 6: MIDDLE ATLAS MOUNTAINS TO ERFOUD

In the morning of Day 6 head start the seven-hour journey south through olive groves and small villages to reach the **Azrou Cedar Forest,** where you can see the indigenous macaque Barbary apes in their natural habitat. You'll then pass

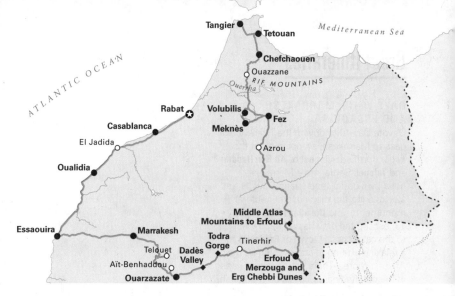

through the ski resort of **Ifrane** and head over the **Middle Atlas Mountains** before descending to the apple-growing regions of **Midelt**, where you can have lunch. Following this, the **Ziz Valley** and gorge lead you to the edge of the **Sahara** at **Erfoud**, where you can spend the night in a hotel. If you wish to reach the **Erg Chebbi** dunes this day, then an additional two hours takes you to Merzouga (the days are too short in winter to get there before sunset).

DAY 7: ERFOUD, MERZOUGA, AND ERG CHEBBI DUNES

Spend a relaxed morning visiting the many fossil workshops in **Erfoud** and the **Tahiri Paleontology Museum** in **Rissani**. A two-hour drive then takes you to the edge of the dunes at **Merzouga**, where you can arrange a camel trek and a hotel or a desert camp for the night.

DAYS 8 AND 9: TODRA GORGE, DADÈS VALLEY, OUARZAZATE

Rise very early on Day 8 to catch the sunrise over the **Erg Chebbi dunes,** and then get on the road to **Tinerhir**. Visit the spectacular **Todra Gorge** and stay overnight in this dramatic region. On Day 9 explore the rugged landscape on the **kasbah** route in the Dadès Valley, passing stunning cliffs and canyons and the

Tips

■ If you'd rather stick mainly to the four imperial cities, take the train instead of a rental car. It's inexpensive, reliable, and fast.

■ A car is the best and sometimes only way to reach Morocco's mountainous area, small coastal villages, and rural regions, where roads are often rough and dirt.

■ Avoid driving at night. Roads are not well lighted, if at all.

■ Consider an adventure tour like camel riding in the Sahara, white-water rafting on the Ahansal River, or hot-air ballooning over the Ourika Valley.

■ Avoid faux guides and unlicensed tour drivers.

palm-lined oasis of Skoura on the road to **Ouarzazate**. Treat yourself to a night at the wow-factor Hotel Sultana Royal Golf outside Ouarzazate, or stay in the 17th-century courthouse of the pacha at Dar Kamar next to the kasbah.

Great Itineraries

DAYS 10–13: MARRAKESH AND ESSAOUIRA

Devote Day 10 to driving the Tizi-n-Tichka pass to Marrakesh, stopping off at the *ksour* (fortified villages) of **Aït Ben Haddou** and **Telouet.** Settle into a Marrakesh hotel by nightfall, and spend Days 11 and 12 exploring the medina, architectural monuments, and **Djemâa el Fna.** On Day 13, escape the crowds and head west to the calm coastal town of **Essaouira** for a relaxing afternoon and evening by the Atlantic shores. There are charming riads in the old medina, or hotels on the beach.

DAYS 14–16: OUALIDIA, CASABLANCA, AND RABAT

Day 14 takes you north along the coast to **Oualidia,** where you should try some of the famous oysters, then on to the former Portuguese port town of **El Jadida.** Spend the night here at the charming Hotel L'Iglesia. On Day 15, check out the stunning ocean-side **Hassan II Mosque** in Casablanca before heading up to Rabat for your last day. Wander through Rabat's **Rue des Consuls** for last-minute purchases on your way to the 12th-century **Kasbah des Oudayas,** savoring your final taste of imperial Morocco. Casablanca is about an hour away by train for your departure Day 16.

On the Calendar

March

Marathon des Sables, Southern Morocco.
Dubbed the "Toughest Footrace on Earth," this six-day, 251-km (156-mile) ultramarathon across the Sahara desert is not for the faint of heart or weak of knee. ⊕ *www.marathondessables.com*

1-54 Contemporary African Art Fair, Marrakesh. The Moroccan edition of this global art fair sees leading galleries gather at the iconic La Mamounia hotel and other venues around the city. ⊕ *www.1-54.com/marrakech*

April

Printemps Musical des Alizés, Essaouira.
Drawing a roster of world-class musicians to play at intimate venues around the city, this three-day festival is a must for classical music buffs.

May

Festival of the Roses, Kelaa M'Gouna.
Expect folk music, dancing, and fragrant rose-related products of every kind at this three-day festival, ending with the crowning of the Queen of the Roses.

June

Fes Festival of World Sacred Music, Fez.
At this enchanting nine-day festival, everything from rock to African jazz and Sufi chanting rings out across the medina, and many concerts are free. ⊕ *www.fesfestival.com*

Festival Mawazine, Rabat. Attracting more than 2 million visitors, this nine-day music fest showcases international headliners—past rosters include the likes of Elton John and Stevie Wonder—alongside world music stars. ⊕ *www.festivalmawazine.ma*

Gnaoua World Music Festival, Essaouira.
For four days, the city sways to hypnotic Gnaoua rhythms, which has roots in sub-Saharan Africa, fusing Islamic Sufism with African traditions. ⊕ *www.festival-gnaoua.net*

July

Jazzablanca, Casablanca. This nine-day music festival features famous and up-and-coming jazz—along with pop, rock, blues, and funk—artists from Morocco and around the globe. ⊕ *www.jazzablanca.com*

National Festival of Popular Arts, Marrakesh. This five-day spectacular features Amazigh musicians, acrobats, storytellers, and snake charmers from all corners of Morocco, and beyond.

September

TANJAzz, Tangier. This entertaining and ever-growing jazz festival has been attracting a host of international and local musicians for more than 20 years. ⊕ *www.tanjazz.org*

Imilchil Marriage Festival, Midelt Province.
Dressed in their finery, thousands of young Imazighen converge on the High Atlas village of Imilchil for this ancient and lively spouse-picking festival.

Chapter 3

MARRAKESH

Updated by
Amanda Mouttaki

◉ Sights   **🍴 Restaurants**   **🛏 Hotels**   **🛍 Shopping**   **🍸 Nightlife**

★★★★★   ★★★★★   ★★★★★   ★★★★★   ★★★★☆

WELCOME TO MARRAKESH

TOP REASONS TO GO

★ **Djemâa el Fna:** One of the world's most exuberant marketplaces, the Djemâa is an unforgettable place to wander amid sizzle and smoke.

★ **Souk shopping:** Lose yourself (literally) in the alluring lanes of the bazaars and souks of the "red city" labyrinth.

★ **Authentic accommodations:** Stay in a riad and sip mint tea in an airy, bougainvillea-filled courtyard haven.

★ **Historic sights:** Step back in time to bygone dynasties as you explore elaborate tombs and palaces of sultans, and the tranquil beauty of the intricate medersa.

★ **Dance till dawn:** From intimate clubs with belly dancers and hookah pipes to full-on techno raves with international DJs, Marrakesh is the hedonistic capital of Morocco.

Negotiating the twisting and turning alleys deep in the medina is a voyage in itself. A small street is called a *rue* in French or a *zenqa* in Arabic; an even smaller alley is called a *derb*.

1 Medina. The old walled city contains the bulk of the attractions, the souks, and *riads*. It's a warren of narrow derbs, where it's easy to get lost.

2 Guéliz. Northwest of the medina, Guéliz is the modern administrative center, home to the tourist information office, fashionable boutiques, art galleries, cafés, restaurants, and banks; Avenue Mohammed V runs down its spine.

3 The Palmery. The Palmery is a 30,000-acre oasis, 7 km (4½ miles) north of the medina between the roads to Casablanca and Fez. Once a series of date plantations, it's now a hideaway for the rich and famous, with luxury hotels and secluded villas among the palms.

Marrakesh is Morocco's most intoxicating city. It's often referred to as the "Red City" or the "Rose City" due to the reddish color of all the buildings, which were originally constructed from local red clay (all new construction must be one of the approved red or pink hues). Once a trading and resting place on the ancient caravan routes from Timbuktu, Marrakesh has barely paused for breath and is still a magical, ever-changing destination.

Lying low and dominating the Haouz Plain at the foot of the snowcapped High Atlas Mountains (a marvelous sight on a sunny day), the city was stubbornly defended against marauding tribes by successive sultans. They maintained their powerful dynasties and surveyed their fertile lands from the Menara Garden's tranquil olive groves and lagoon, and the Agdal Gardens' vast orchards. Today, exploring the city has never been easier. A crackdown on hustlers who hassle and an undercover Tourist Police mean that you're freer than ever before to wander and wonder.

The medina is Marrakesh's miracle—a happy clash of old and new, in turn beguiling and confusing. Virtually unchanged since the Middle Ages, Marrakesh's solid, salmon-pink ramparts encircle and protect its mysterious labyrinthine medina, hiding palaces, mansions, and bazaars. Pedestrians struggle to find their balance on the tiny cobbled lanes among an endless run of mopeds, donkey carts, and wheelbarrows selling a mixture of sticky sweets and saucepans. Take your time, and take it all in.

Planning

When to Go

Marrakesh can get quite cold in the winter and after the sun goes down. Although the sun shines almost year-round, the best time to visit is in spring (February to April), when the surrounding hills and valleys are an explosion of colorful flowers, and fall (October and November), when the temperature is comfortable enough to warrant sunbathing. The only exception in that period is during Easter week, which brings crowds. July and August can be unbearably hot, with daytime temperatures regularly over

100°F. Christmas and New Year's is peak season and the city fills to bursting, with hotels and riads booked up months in advance.

Planning Your Time

To get a true feel for the charm and chaos of Marrakesh, a visit of at least five full days is recommended. Deciding what area to stay in depends largely on personal taste and budget. Inside the ancient walled **medina,** cozied up in a traditional riad, you'll never be far from the souks and historic sights. Most are reached on foot through a muddle of alleys with a taxi stand usually no more than a short walk from the front door. Small taxis can navigate to other points in the medina or elsewhere. Families may prefer to opt for modern hotels in **Hivernage** or **Guéliz**, where the vibe is more European. The streets here are safe (though the paving often broken and hazardous) and taxis are plentiful for the short hop to the medina. Farther afield is the **Palmery,** oozing exclusivity and offering boutique hotels for idyllic days of total relaxation to a soundtrack of birdsong. The drawback here is that transport into town gets costly, at around 150 DH for a taxi each way.

Getting Here and Around

AIR

Menara Airport in Marrakesh receives domestic flights from Casablanca and direct international flights from the United Kingdom, Europe, and Scandinavia. Flights from the United States, Canada, Brazil, and the Middle East pass through Casablanca.

The trip from the airport to town is only 15 minutes by car, taxi, or bus. On first arriving in Marrakesh, it's wise to ask your hotel or riad to arrange a private transfer direct from the airport. It may cost around 200 DH (for four people) but makes for a far less stressful arrival.

BIKE

A relatively new initiative in Marrakesh, inspired by hosting the prestigious COP22 UN Climate Change Conference in 2016, means that there are now banks of bicycles for hire at key touristic hubs like Theatre Royal, Palais de Congrès, Koutoubia mosque, and Jardin Majorelle. Payment is made through a mobile phone app in order to unlock the bike and you get charged by the hour or by the day. Look for the racks of orange and gray bicycles called **Medina Bike.**

BIKE CONTACTS Medina Bike. ✉ *Marrakesh* ☎ *0612/64–47–34* ⊕ *www. medinabike.ma.*

BUS

Intercity buses all leave from Marrakesh. Use the *gare routière* at Bab Doukkala for national public buses, or the Supratours or Compagnie du Transports au Maroc (CTM) bus stations in Guéliz. Buses arrive at the gare routière from Casablanca, Rabat, Fez, Agadir, Ouarzazate, and other cities. CTM and Supratours buses have their own terminals, but also stop at the gare routière. They are quicker, safer, and more comfortable than public buses to most key destinations. Supratours, which has its office next door to the train station on Avenue Hassan II, links up with Morocco's train network, with bus routes to destinations south and west of Marrakesh. Visit the ONCF (national rail network) website for information and timetables for Supratours. Ticket reservations must be done in person.

Public Bus No. 19 departs the airport every 30 minutes from 6:30 am to 9:30 pm daily. It stops at Place Djemâa el Fna and continues through to Guéliz, serving most of the main hotels along avenues Mohammed V and Mohammed VI (cost 30 DH).

Within Marrakesh, the public Alsa City Bus runs all over town; fares are a standard 4 DH.

BUS CONTACTS ALSA City Bus. ✉ *Marrakesh* ☎ *0524/33–52–70* ⊕ *www. alsa.ma.* **Compagnie de Transports au Maroc.** ✉ *Gare Routière, Bab Doukkala* ☎ *0800/09–00–30 call center* ⊕ *www. ctm.ma.* **Supratours.** ✉ *Av. Hassan II, next to train station, Guéliz* ☎ *0890/20–30–40* ⊕ *www.oncf.ma.*

CAR

Marrakesh is in the center of the country, so it connects well by road with all other major destinations. Most of these roads are good two-lane highways with hard, sandy shoulders for passing. There is a freeway connecting Marrakesh to Casablanca and Rabat in the north and Agadir to the southwest. Most of the major international car rental agencies have branches here as well as Moroccan companies like Label Voiture and Medloc Maroc.

Within the Marrakesh medina, driving is not recommended. Cars can pass through some of the medina's narrow alleys, but not all, and unless you know the lay of the land you risk getting stuck and being hard-pressed to perform a U-turn. Outside the medina, traffic is frenetic and locals freely admit that stoplights and lane markings are mostly decorative and rarely observed. It can be hazardous to drive here as well. Leave your car at a guarded parking lot and walk.

RENTAL CARS Avis. ✉ *Marrakech Menara Airport, Hivernage* ☎ *0524/43–31–69* ⊕ *www.avis.com.* **Europcar.** ✉ *63, bd. Zerktouni, in Afriqui gas station forecourt, Guéliz* ☎ *0524/43–12–28* ⊕ *www.europcar.com.* **Hertz.** ✉ *154, av. Mohammed V, Guéliz* ☎ *0524/43–99–84* ⊕ *www.hertz. ma.* **Label Voiture.** ✉ *Appt. 20, Immeuble 90, bd. Zerktouni, 1st fl., Guéliz* ☎ *0524/42–15–19* ⊕ *www.labelvoiture. com.* **Medloc Maroc.** ✉ *1st fl., no. 3, 75,*

rue Ibn Aicha, Guéliz ☎ *0524/43–57–57* ⊕ *www.medloc-maroc.com.*

TAXI

Petits taxis in Marrakesh are small, beige, metered cabs permitted to transport three passengers within the city limits only. A petit taxi ride from one end of Marrakesh to the other should cost around 20 DH (50% extra from 8 pm to 6 am). The journey is sometimes shared with other passengers if plans coincide. When getting into the taxi, make sure the driver sets the meter (*le compteur*) on the dashboard for your journey. Taxi Vert is a dial-a-cab service that allows you to preorder a petit taxi for a specific pickup for 15 DH on top of the metered charge, very useful for late at night.

Grands taxis are either old four-door Mercedes or newer minivans. Most often they simply take a load of up to six passengers on short hauls to suburbs and nearby towns, forming a reliable, inexpensive network throughout each region of Morocco. They can also be chartered for private hire for excursions and airport transfers.

■ TIP→ **Negotiate a price directly with the driver or through your hotel if chartering a special trip.**

The standard charge for a run from the airport into the medina in petits taxis starts at about 100 DH during the daytime and 150 DH after 8 pm, but you will have to negotiate. Grand taxis cost 100 DH to 150 DH during the day, 150 DH to 200 DH after 8 pm.

Uber does not operate in Morocco but Careem, Roby, and Taxi Vert are similar ride-hailing services; simply download the app, book a car, and pay online. Roby charges a small service fee for each ride but otherwise prices do not fluctuate with demand.

TAXI CONTACTS Taxi Vert. ✉ *Marrakesh* ☎ *0524/40–94–94.*

TRAIN

Marrakesh is connected by good train service to Tangier, Rabat, Casablanca, and Fez. The train station is located on Avenue Mohammed VI at the junction with Avenue Hassan II in Guéliz and is Morocco's main southern terminus. Advance reservations can be made for first class only. Per day there are six trains to Tangier, eight to Fez, and nine to Casablanca.

TRAIN CONTACT ONCF. ⊠ *Av. Mohammed VI, at av. Hassan II, Guéliz* ☎ *2255 call center (from local phones only)* ⊕ *www.oncf.ma.*

Guides and Tours

Guides can be helpful when navigating the medina's serpentine streets. They can point out little-known landmarks and help you understand the city's complicated history. You are best off booking a licensed guide through a tour company or your hotel's staff should be able to suggest one to suit your interests. Although guides can be very knowledgeable about the city, don't rely on them for shopping. Store owners will inflate prices in order to give the guides kickbacks. The going rate for a city guide is 300 DH for a half day, 600 DH for a full day.

A number of companies offer full-day excursions (or longer) departing from Marrakesh by bus, 4WD, or motorbike and sidecar.

TOUR COMPANIES AND GUIDES

Legendes Evasions

SPECIAL-INTEREST TOURS | This highly respected local agency runs chauffeured vehicle tours to some of the Imazighen villages around Marrakesh. Day trips start at around 2,200 DH for up to six people per car. ⊠ *Galerie Elite, 212, av. Mohammed V, 1st fl., Guéliz* ☎ *0524/33–24–83* ⊕ *www.legendesevasions.com.*

Marrakech Insiders

SPECIAL-INTEREST TOURS | Established in 2015, Marrakech Insiders has a small fleet of supercool vintage bikes and experienced local riders that offer a different perspective on the city—discover the medina, the nouvelle ville, the outlying Palmery, or the Agafay desert of Marrakesh. Tours start at 1,400 DH (per bike) and you can be picked up at your hotel. ⊠ *Guéliz* ☎ *0669/69–93–74* ⊕ *www.marrakechinsiders.com.*

Mohammed Lahcen

WALKING TOURS | If you want a top-notch private guide for Marrakesh, you can't beat English-speaking Mohammed Lahcen. His going rate for a guided tour is 300 DH for a half day, 600 DH for a full day (depending on number of people). ⊠ *Tangier* ☎ *0661/20–06–39* ✎ *bab_adrar@hotmail.com.*

Sahara Expedition

SPECIAL-INTEREST TOURS | This budget agency runs daily group excursions and tours throughout the region, including Ourika Valley and Essaouira. Three-day sprints via minibus to the Sahara desert at Merzouga start from 1,000 DH per person with very basic hotels. ⊠ *22, bd. Mohammed Zerktouni, Guéliz* ☎ *0524/42–97–47* ⊕ *www.saharaexpe.com/.*

Said el-Fagousse

WALKING TOURS | The amiable Said el-Fagousse has encyclopedic knowledge of Marrakesh's secret treasures and Moroccan history. Originating from the desert village of M'Haimd el Ghizalne, he is a qualified guide for both city and nationwide destinations. His rates are 400 DH for a half day, 700 DH for a full day. ⊠ *Tangier* ☎ *0661/78–32–98* ✎ *moroccotourguide@gmail.com.*

SheherazadVentures

CULTURAL TOURS | This Marrakesh-based English-Moroccan company organizes private tailored tours for families and small groups, with a cultural focus.

They're specialists in Southern Morocco and Sahara offering active day excursions from Marrakesh, as well as nationwide tours. Rates start around 1,500 DH per person per day for two people. ✉ *Appt. 55, Residence Ali (C), Av. Mohammed VI, near Café Cesar, Guéliz* ☎ *0615/64–79–18* ⊕ *www.sheherazadventures.com.*

Hotels

Marrakesh has exceptional hotels. The spas are superb, and the loving attention to detail is overwhelming. If, however, you'd prefer not to spend a fortune sleeping in the bed where a movie star once slumbered, solid budget riads and midrange boutique options abound. They're small, clean, and suitably Moroccan in style to satisfy adventurous penny-pinchers.

To take on the historic heart of Marrakesh and live like a pasha of old, head to one of the medina's riads. Riad restorations, many by ultrafashionable European expats, have taken over the city; you'd trip over them, if only you knew where they were. Anonymous doors in the narrow, twisting derbs of the medina, and especially the souks, transport you to hidden worlds of pleasure. There are cheap ones, expensive ones, chic ones, funky ones, plain ones. Riads normally have around four to six rooms arranged around a courtyard and each room can be rented individually on a nightly basis. For special events and larger gatherings, it's worth considering booking the whole property.

Marrakesh is something of a Shangri-la for designers who, intoxicated by the colors, shapes, and patterns of the city, feel free to indulge themselves in wildly opulent and ambitious designs. Although it isn't all tasteful, much of the decor and style in Marrakesh hotels and riads is fascinating.

Most of the larger hotels (classified with three, four, or five stars by the Moroccan government) are in Guéliz, Hivernage, and in the zone touristique located beyond the Agdal Gardens heading out of town on Route de Ourika. There are also many superb guesthouses just a few miles out of town in the surrounding countryside.

∎ TIP→ **Anybody with mobility issues or physical limitations should note that staying in a traditional riad usually involves a walk from the nearest parking area through narrow streets to reach the front door and climbing stairs to access the bedrooms and terrace. There are rarely elevators in all except very few of the larger luxury riads or boutique hotels.**

Hotels and riads vary their prices wildly between high and low season. This means that if you time your trip right you can find some great deals. High season runs from March to May and from October to December, with spikes at Christmas, New Year's, and Easter.

Hotel reviews have been shortened. For full information, visit Fodors.com.

WHAT IT COSTS in Dirhams

$	$$	$$$	$$$$
under 700 DH	700 DH–1,500 DH	1,501 DH–3,500 DH	over 3,500 DH

Restaurants

Marrakesh has arguably the largest selection of restaurants in Morocco, which serve equal parts Moroccan and international cuisine at varying price points. Restaurant dining, once reserved mainly for the wealthy or very special occasions, is now part of the norm for virtually all Marrakshis. Options vary from inexpensive snack bars, cafés, and fast-food restaurants to the more pricey French bistros, sushi bars, and sophisticated Moroccan fine-dining options. In restaurants where alcohol is served, meal prices tend to be high as licenses are expensive. Home entertaining, however, with lavish meals to impress visitors, is still very much part and parcel of the old Marrakshi way of life. To get an idea (albeit a rather expensive one) of traditional yet sumptuous Moroccan entertaining, treat yourself to an evening at one of Marrakesh's popular riad gastronomique restaurants in the medina.

■ TIP → **Morocco is a Muslim country, so don't assume that all restaurants will serve alcohol. Licenses are expensive and, inside the medina especially, are very hard to come by.**

You can also eat well at inexpensive sidewalk cafés in both the medina and Guéliz. Here, don't miss out on a famous local dish called *tanjia*, made popular by workers who slow-cook lamb or beef in an earthenware pot left in hot ashes for the whole day. Food is cooked and served from an outdoor street-kitchen with shared tables, but it's a hearty meal with locals for around 30 DH.

Most restaurants in Marrakesh tend to fall into two categories. They're either fashionable, flashy affairs, mostly in Guéliz and the outlying areas of Marrakesh, which serve à la carte European, Asian, and Moroccan cuisine, or they're more traditional places, often tucked inconspicuously into riads and old palaces in the medina. Both types can be fairly pricey, and, to avoid disappointment, are best booked in advance. They also tend to open quite late, usually not before 7:30 in Guéliz and 8 in the medina, although most people don't sit down to eat until 9 or 9:30. In recent years a third dining category, the dinner-cabaret, has become a popular format, attracting tourists, expats, and well-heeled Moroccans for their entertainment value, if not necessarily for their cuisine.

There's no set system for tipping. Your check will indicate that service has been included in the charge; if not, tip 10% or 15% for excellent service.

Dining reviews have been shortened. For full information, visit Fodors.com.

WHAT IT COSTS in Dirhams

$	$$	$$$	$$$$
under 80 DH	80 DH–150 DH	151 DH–300 DH	over 300 DH

Safety

Like other Moroccan cities, Marrakesh is quite safe. While women—particularly those traveling alone or in pairs—are likely to suffer from catcalls and whistles, there is generally little physical risk. The city does have its fair share of pickpockets, especially in markets and other crowded areas; handbags should be zippered and held closely, and wallets placed in inside pockets. The old city shuts down relatively early, so don't wander its dark alleys late at night. The Moroccan Tourist Police take their jobs very seriously, so don't hesitate to call on them. They operate undercover so are hard to identify, but in the medina they are never far away; ask any guide or shopkeeper to alert them if you're in trouble. Their office is on the northern side of the Place Djemâa el Fna. Additional armed foot patrols are visible and vigilant at key locations in the city and throughout the popular tourist areas.

CONTACTS Brigade Touristique (Tourist Police). ⊠ *Pl. Djemâa el Fna, Marrakesh* ☎ *0524/38–46–01.*

Shopping

Marrakesh is a shopper's bonanza, full of the very rugs, handicrafts, and clothing you see in the pages of magazines back home. Most bazaars are in the souk, just north of Djemâa el Fna and spread through a seemingly never-ending maze of alleys. Together, they sell almost everything imaginable and are highly competitive. Bargaining here is hard, and you can get up to 80% discounts. So on your first exploration, it's often a better idea to simply wander and take in the atmosphere than to buy. You can check guideline prices in some of the more well-to-do parts of town, which display fixed price tags for every object.

There are a number of crafts and souvenir shops on Avenue Mohammed V in Guéliz, as well as some very good Moroccan antiques stores and designer shops that offer a distinctly modern take on Moroccan clothing, footwear, and interior decoration. These allow buyers to browse at their leisure, free of the souk's intense pressures. Many have fixed prices, with only 10% discounts after haggling. Most of these stores are happy to ship your purchases overseas. Bazaars generally open between 8 and 9 am and close between 8 and 9 pm; stores in Guéliz open a bit later and close a bit earlier, some breaking for lunch. Some bazaars in the medina close on Friday, the Muslim holy day. In Guéliz, most shops are closed on Sunday.

BARGAINING

Bargaining is part of the fun of shopping in the medina's souks. Go back and forth with the vendor until you agree on an acceptable price. If you are not sure if the vendor's "lowest price" is really the lowest, slowly leave the store—if the vendor follows you, then you can negotiate further. If bargaining is just not your thing and you don't mind paying a little extra, consider the shops of Guéliz. Although these shops are not as colorful as the souks, a reasonable variety of high-quality goods are on offer.

SHOPPING GUIDES

Many guides have (undeclared) affiliations with certain shops, and taking on a guide may mean you'll be delivered to the boutique of their choice, rather than your own discovery. You should be fine on your own, as long as you keep your eyes peeled for mini-adventures and overly aggressive sellers. Small boutique shopkeepers who can't afford to tip guides will thank you for it.

There are also a few personal shopping guides working in Marrakesh (mostly expats), trying to strike the best deal for the customer and take the pain out of seeking, finding, and haggling for those "must-have" items.

FONDOUKS

If you tire of the haggling in the souk but still want to pick up a bargain, try visiting a *fondouk*. These were originally storehouses, workshops, and inns frequented by merchants and artisans on their journeys across the Sahara (known as *caravanserai* in the Middle East), and are still in use today, particularly by merchants bringing carpets and other goods from surrounding villages; others are staffed by artisans at work on goods destined for the market. They're easily recognized by courtyards full of junk, usually with galleries on upper levels. Fondouks always keep their doors open, so feel free to look around. Because you deal with the artisans directly, there's less of a markup on prices. There are a couple of fondouks on Dar el Bacha as you head toward the souk, and on Rue Bab Taghzout by the fountain known as Shrob ou Shouf ("Drink and Look").

Visitor Information

The Delegation Regionale du Tourisme office in Guéliz is the only tourist information office; it has maps, brochures, and general tourist information for Marrakesh and the surrounding area. The office is closed on weekends.

Medina

If you can see the ramparts, you're either just inside or just outside the medina. In some respects not much has changed here since the Middle Ages. The medina is still a warren of narrow cobblestone streets lined with thick-walled, interlocked houses; designed to confuse invaders, the layout now serves much the same purpose for visitors. Donkeys and mules still deliver produce, wood, and wool to their destinations, and age-old crafts workshops still flourish as retail endeavors.

■ TIP→ **When walking the narrow streets of the medina, keep to the right-hand side (and keep your shoulder bag to the right also) as mopeds often zip through at great speed with little respect for window-shopping pedestrians.**

Sights

★ Ali ben Youssef Medersa
NOTABLE BUILDING | If you want a little breath taken out of you, don't pass up the chance to see this extraordinarily well-preserved 16th-century Koranic school, North Africa's largest such institution. The delicate intricacy of the *gibs* (stucco plasterwork), carved cedar, and *zellij* (mosaic) on display in the central courtyard makes the building seem to loom taller than it really does. As many as 900 students from Muslim countries all over the world once studied here, and arranged around the courtyard are their former sleeping quarters—a network of tiny upper-level rooms that resemble monks' cells. The building was erected in the 14th century by the Merenids in a somewhat different style from that of other medersas; later, in the 16th century, Sultan Abdullah el Ghallib rebuilt it

almost completely, adding the Andalusian details. The large main courtyard, framed by two columned arcades, opens into a prayer hall elaborately decorated with rare palm motifs as well as the more-customary Islamic calligraphy. The Koranic school closed in 1960, but the building was restored and opened to the public in 1982. In 2018 the building closed for further restoration and is expected to reopen in 2022. ⊠ *Off Rue Souk el Khemis, Medina* ☎ *0524/44–18–93* 🖾 *20 DH for medersa, 60 DH combination ticket with Musée de Marrakech.*

Ali ben Youssef Mosque
RELIGIOUS BUILDING | After the Koutoubia, this is the medina's largest mosque and Marrakesh's oldest. The building was first constructed in the second half of the 12th century by the Almoravid sultan Ali ben Youssef, around the time of the Qoubba Almoravid. In succeeding centuries it was destroyed and rebuilt several times by the Almohads and the Saadians, who changed its size and architecture accordingly; it was last overhauled in the 19th century, in the then-popular Merenid style. Non-Muslims may not enter. ⊠ *Just off Rue Souk el Khemis, Rue Assouel, next to Ali ben Youssef Medersa, Medina.*

★ La Bahia Palace
CASTLE/PALACE | This 19th-century palace, once home to a harem, is a marvelous display of painted wood, ceramics, and symmetrical gardens. Built by Sultan Moulay el Hassan I's notorious Grand Vizier Bou Ahmed, the palace was ransacked on Bou Ahmed's death, but you can still experience its layout and get a sense of its former beauty. Don't forget to look up at smooth arches, carved-cedar ceilings, *tadlak* (shiny marble) finishes, gibs cornices, and *zouak* painted ceilings. Fancy a room? Each one varies in size according to the importance of each wife or concubine. In 2020 the entire palace was repainted and some areas restored.

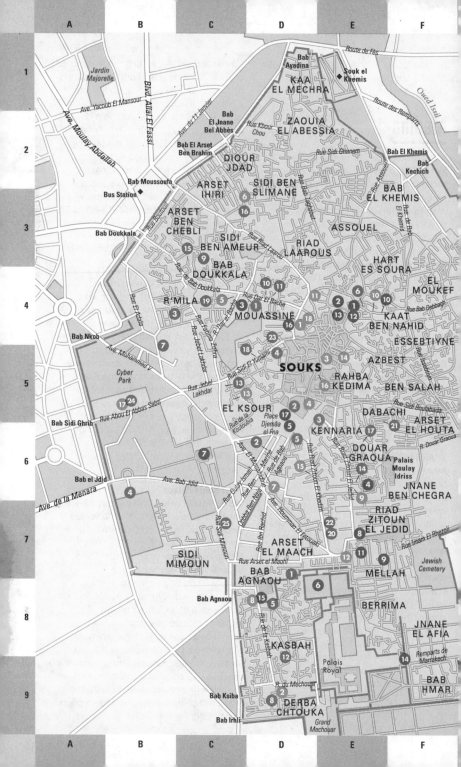

Medina

Route de Fès
TO →
FÈZ & MEKNES

Bab Debbagh

Bab Lalla
Aouda Saadia

Rue Rachidia

ARSET
SIDI
YOUSSEF

Bab Aylen

Oued Issil

Bab Ghemat

Route de Ouarzazate

Rue Belaid

Ave. Hodis

0 — 1/2 mi
0 — 1/2 km

Sights ▼

1 Ali ben Youssef
   Medersa **E4**
2 Ali ben Youssef
   Mosque **E4**
3 Dar el Bacha Musée **C4**
4 Dar Si Saïd **E6**
5 Djemâa el Fna **D6**
6 El Badi Palace **E8**
7 Koutoubia Mosque **C6**
8 La Bahia Palace **E7**
9 Lazama Synagogue **E7**
10 Maison de la
    Photographie **E4**
11 Mellah **E7**
12 Musée de
    Marrakech **E4**
13 Qoubba Almoravid **E4**
14 Ramparts **F9**
15 Saadian Tombs **D8**
16 The Secret Garden **D4**
17 Souks **D5**
18 Tanneries **G4**

Restaurants ▼

1 Café Arabe **D4**
2 Café Clock **D9**
3 Café des Épices **E5**
4 Chez Lamine Hadj
   Mustapha **D5**
5 Dar Moha **C4**
6 Dar Yacout **C3**
7 Hadj Brik **D6**
8 Kasbah Café **D8**
9 La Famille **E6**
10 Le Foundouk **E4**
11 Le Jardin **D4**
12 Le Tanjia **E7**
13 Le Tobsil **C5**
14 L'Mida **E5**
15 Marrakech Henna
    Art Cafe **D6**
16 Nomad **E5**
17 Royal Mansour **B5**
18 Terrasse des Épices **D4**

Quick Bites ▼

1 Bacha Coffee **C4**
2 Café Argana **D5**
3 Café de France **E5**
4 Dar Cherifa **D5**
5 Grand Balcon du
   Café Glacier **D6**

Hotels ▼

1 Dar Alfarah **D7**
2 Hotel Ali **D6**
3 La Maison Arabe **C4**
4 La Mamounia **B6**
5 La Sultana **D8**
6 Le Farnatchi **E4**
7 Le Naoura
   Marrakech **B5**
8 Les Jardins de la
   Medina **D9**
9 L'Hotel **C3**
10 Palais Khum **D4**
11 Riad Adore **D4**
12 Riad Baya **D9**
13 Riad el Fenn **C5**
14 Riad le Clos des Arts **E6**
15 Riad Le Limoun **C3**
16 Riad les Trois Mages **C3**
17 Riad Linda **E6**
18 Riad l'Orangeraie **D5**
19 Riad Malika **C4**
20 Riad Nesma **E7**
21 Riad 107 .... **E5**
22 Riad Samsli **E7**
23 Riad Snan13 .... **D4**
24 Royal Mansour **B5**
25 Villa des Orangers **C7**

KEY

1 *Exploring Sights*
1 *Restaurants*
1 *Quick Bites*
1 *Hotels*

Did You Know?

The Bahia Palace has some of the finest examples of Andalusian and Moorish architecture in the country, but the grand Cour d'Honneur courtyard, with its Italian Carrara marble floor is an unrivaled highlight.

■ **TIP →** **If you use an on-site guide, you should also tip 30 DH–50 DH.** ⊠ *Rue Riad Zitoun el Jdid, near Pl. des Ferblantiers, Medina* ⬛ *70 DH for adults, 30 DH for kids.*

Dar el Bacha Musée (*Museum of the Confluences*)

HISTORIC HOME | Built in 1910, Dar el Bacha was once the home of the infamous Thami el Glaoui who, during the French protectorate of Morocco, was considered one of the most powerful men in the south of the country. This palace was where he would host and entertain famous guests such as Josephine Baker, Winston Churchill, and Charlie Chaplin.

The building was renovated and opened to the public for the first time in 2018 and features exemplary Moroccan craftsmanship. Zellij-tiled walls in multiple different styles, a traditional courtyard resplendent with citrus trees and local fauna, and rooms housing exhibits that tell the story of coexistence between the faiths in Morocco are some of the highlights. ⊠ *Rue Lalla Fatima Zahra, Medina* ⬛ *60 DH* ☉ *Closed Mon.*

Dar Si Saïd

ART MUSEUM | **FAMILY** | This 19th-century palace is now a museum with an excellent collection of antique Moroccan crafts including pottery from Safi and Tamegroute, jewelry, daggers, caftans, carpets, and leatherwork. The palace's courtyard is filled with flowers and cypress trees, and furnished with a gazebo and fountain. The most extraordinary salon is upstairs; it's a somber room decorated with gibs cornices, zellij walls, and an amazing carved-cedar ceiling painted in the zouak style (bright colors in intricate patterns). Look for the prize exhibit, a marble basin with an inscription indicating its 10th-century Córdoban origin. The basin, which is sometimes on loan to other museums, was once given pride of place in the Ali ben Youssef Mosque in the north of the souk. It was

brought to Morocco by the Almoravid sultan in spite of its decorative eagles and griffins, which defy the Koran's prohibition of artistic representations of living things. ⊠ *Riad Zitoune El Jdid, Derb Si Saïd, Medina* ☎ *0524/38–95–64* ⊕ *www. fnm.ma/musee-dar-si-said-de-marrakech/* ⬛ *20 DH* ☉ *Closed Tues.*

★ Djemâa el Fna

MARKET | The open square market at the center of the medina is Marrakesh's heartbeat and a UNESCO World Heritage site. This centuries-old square was once a meeting point for regional farmers and tradesmen, storytellers and healers. Today it's surrounded by bazaars, mosques, and terraced cafés with balcony views over the action. While it's relatively quiet during the day, food stalls and performers begin to appear in the late afternoon.

Djemâa el Fna comes to life at night when it fills with a variety of performers enticing locals and visitors alike. Gnawa dancers sway clanking their *krakebs* (castanets) and strumming on traditional guitars while traditional storytellers regale locals with tales from the past. By sunset the square is full, and smoke rises from the makeshift stalls that are set up every evening and offer grilled meats on paper-lined tables.

All day (and night) long you can get fresh orange juice from the green carts that line up around the square, starting at 4 DH a glass. You can also pose for a photograph with one of the roving water sellers (you'll be expected to pay at least 10 DH for the privilege), whose eye-popping costumes carry leather water pouches and polished-brass drinking bowls—we don't recommend drinking from the offered cup of water. Or snack on sweet dates, apricots, bananas, almonds, sugar-coated peanuts, and walnuts from the dried fruit–and–nut stalls in the northwest corner. It's a festival atmosphere every night of the week!

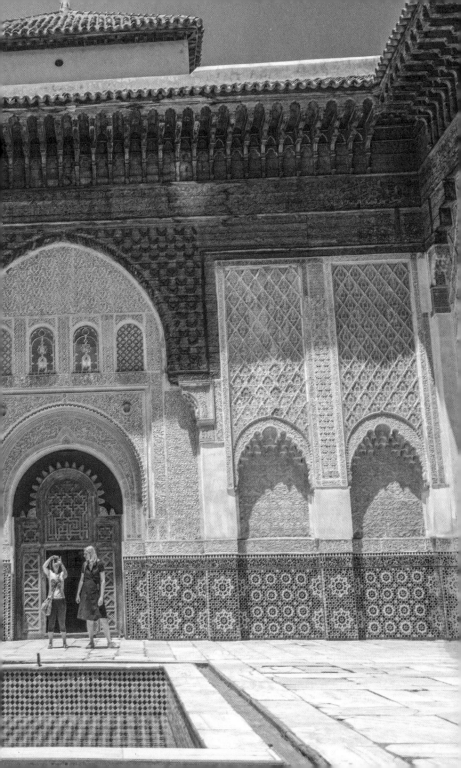

Day or night, there's always something entertaining to see at the Djemâa el Fna.

It's worth noting that while these days this is a wonderful bazaar, once upon a time the Djemâa's purpose was more gruesome: it accommodated public viewings of the severed heads of sinners and criminals. Djemâa actually means "meeting place" and el Fna means "the end" or "death," so as a whole it means something along the lines of "assembly of death" or "meeting place at the end of the world."

⚠ **Watch out for pickpockets and be wary of ladies here offering henna applications as they're not always aboveboard.** ✉ *Medina*.

El Badi Palace

CASTLE/PALACE | This 16th-century palace was once a playground for Saadian princes and visiting diplomats—a mammoth showpiece for opulent entertaining. Today it's a romantic set of sandstone ruins, policed by nesting storks. Sultan Ahmed el Mansour's lavish creation was ransacked by Moulay Ismail in the 17th century to help him complete his own palace at Meknès. But it's not hard to see why the palace, whose name translates as "The Marvel," was once among the world's most impressive monuments. A huge swimming pool in the center (still there today, but empty) is flanked by four others, along with four sunken orange orchards. The main hall was named the Koubba el Khamsiniyya, referring to its 50 grand marble columns. Along the southern wall is a series of belowground corridors and underground dungeons. It's a vast, calm, and mystical place. Also on display is a collection of goods from the minbar (pulpit from which the imam gives services) of the Koutoubia Mosque. If you use an on-site guide (otherwise unpaid), who can bring the place to life, you should also tip 30 DH to 50 DH. ✉ *Ksibat Nhass, Medina* ✛ *Enter ramparts and enormous gateway near Pl. des Ferblantiers* ☎ *0524/37–81–63* 💰 *70 DH for adults, 30 DH for kids.*

★ Koutoubia Mosque

NOTABLE BUILDING | Yacoub el Mansour built Marrakesh's towering Moorish mosque on the site of the original 11th-century Almoravid mosque. Dating from the early 12th century, it became a model for the Hassan Tower in Rabat and the Giralda in Seville. The mosque takes its name from the Arabic word for book, *koutoub*, because there was once a large booksellers' market nearby. The minaret is topped by three golden orbs, which, according to one local legend, were offered by the mother of the Saadian sultan Ahmed el Mansour Edhabi in penance for fasting days she missed during Ramadan. The mosque has a large plaza, walkways, and gardens, as well as floodlights to illuminate its curved windows, a band of ceramic inlay, pointed *merlons* (ornamental edgings), and various decorative arches. Although non-Muslims may not enter, anyone within earshot will be moved by the power of the evening muezzin call. ✉ *South end of Av. Mohammed V, Medina.*

Lazama Synagogue

SYNAGOGUE | One of the few remaining synagogues still in operation, the Lazama synagogue was established in 1492 and renovated several times since, with the latest being at the turn of the 20th century. Visitors are permitted inside to learn about Morocco's Jewish history and see the blending of traditions and cultures. ✉ *Derb Manchoura, Mellah* ⊕ *www.jmarrakech.org/* 💰 *10 DH* 🕙 *Closed Sat.*

Maison de la Photographie

ART MUSEUM | This restored riad, in the heart of the medina, houses a rare collection of original black-and-white photos and glass negatives that depict life in Moroccan communities between 1862 and 1960. The archive, which was established in 2009, is constantly growing and there are regular thematic exhibitions. There is also a very pleasant roof terrace café. ✉ *46, rue Souk Ahel Fes, near Medersa Ben Youssef, Medina* ☎ *0524/38–57–21* ✉ *maisondelaphotographiemaroc@gmail.com* ⊕ *www.maisondelaphotographie.ma* 💰 *50 DH.*

Mellah

NEIGHBORHOOD | As in other Moroccan cities, the Mellah is the old Jewish quarter, once a small city within the city. Although it used to be home to a thriving community, along with rabbinical schools and scholars, today there are only a few Jewish inhabitants. You can visit the remains of a couple of synagogues with the help of an official guide, or local kids will be happy to point the way in return for a few dirhams. The Lazama Synagogue is open daily and is still used for weddings and bar mitzvahs. It has a pretty, blue-tiled inner courtyard. The Mellah gets its name from the Arabic word for salt, and some say that the Jewish residents who lived here acquired their wealth through the salt trade.

■ **TIP**→ **The Mellah district has undergone many renovations in recent years, but visitors might want to avoid walking alone in the more residential areas, past the Lazama Synagogue.** ✉ *Mellah.*

Musée de Marrakesh

HISTORY MUSEUM | The main reason to come to this small, privately owned museum next door to the Ali ben Youssef Medersa is not the exhibitions of regional pottery, ceremonial daggers, and traditional costume, but rather the stunning central atrium, a tiled courtyard containing a huge lampshade that resembles a descending UFO. Set within the restored 19th-century Menebhi Palace, this is a perfect place to relax while enjoying Moroccan architecture and gentle music piped through speakers. There are occasional exhibitions in the courtyard of beautiful artifacts or paintings, but they're poorly displayed and lack English translations. ✉ *Pl. ben Youssef, Medina* ☎ *0524/44–18–93* ⊕ *www.museedemarrakech.ma* 💰 *50 DH.*

The 16th-century El Badi Palace was once decorated with gold, turquoise, and crystal; these were carried off in 18th century, when the palace was destroyed by Sultan Moulay Ismail.

Qoubba Almoravid

NOTABLE BUILDING | Newly renovated and open to the public for the first time in 2021, this is the city's oldest monument and the only intact example of Almoravid architecture in all of Morocco (the few other ruins include some walls here in Marrakesh and a minaret in El Jadida). Dating from the 12th century, this masterpiece of mechanical waterworks somehow escaped destruction by the Almohads. It was once used for ablutions before prayer in the next-door Ali ben Youssef Mosque (relying on the revolutionary hydraulics of *khatteras*, drainage systems dug down into the water table), and also had a system of toilets, showers, and faucets for drinking water. It was only excavated from the rubble of the original Ali ben Youssef Mosque and Medersa in 1948. ⊠ *Pl. Ben Youssef, Medina* 🖂 *50 DH adults, 20 DH kids.*

Ramparts

NOTABLE BUILDING | The medina's amazingly well-preserved walls measure about 33 feet high and 7 feet thick, and are 15 km (9 miles) in circumference. The walls are fashioned from local reddish ocher clay laid in huge blocks. The holes that are visible on the exterior surface are typical of this style of construction, marking where wooden scaffold supports have been inserted as each level is added. Until the early 20th century, before the French protectorate, the gates were closed at night to prevent anyone who didn't live in Marrakesh from entering. Eight of the 14 original *babs* (arched entry gates) leading in and out of the medina are still in use. Bab Agnaou, in the kasbah, is the loveliest and best preserved of the arches.

■ TIP→ **The best time to visit the walls is just before sunset, when the swallows that nest in the ramparts' holes come out to take their evening meal.** ⊠ *Medina.*

Saadian Tombs

CEMETERY | This small, beautiful, 16th-century burial ground is the permanent resting place of 166 Saadians, including its creator, Sultan Ahmed el Mansour, the Golden One. True to his name, he did it in style—even those not in the lavish mausoleum have their own colorful zellij graves, laid out for all to see, among the palm trees and flowers. Because the infamous Moulay Ismail chose not to destroy them (he was apparently superstitious about plundering the dead), these tombs are one of the few Saadian relics left. He simply sealed them up, leaving only a small section open for use. The complex was rediscovered only in 1917 by General Hubert Lyautey during the French protectorate. Passionate about every aspect of Morocco's history, the general undertook the restoration of the tombs.

The central mausoleum, the **Hall of Twelve Columns,** contains the tombs of Ahmed el Mansour and his family. It's dark, lavish, and ornate, with a huge vaulted roof, carved cedar doors and *moucharabia* (carved wooden screens traditionally used to separate the sexes), and gray Italian marble columns. In a smaller inner mausoleum, on the site of an earlier structure containing the decapitated body of the Saadian dynasty's founder, Mohammed esh Sheikh, is the tomb of El Mansour's mother.

■ TIP→ **Get here either early or late to avoid the crowds and to see the monuments swathed in soft golden sunlight.**

If you use one of the on-site guides (who are unpaid), you should tip 30 DH to 50 DH. ⊠ *Rue de la Kasbah, next to mosque, Kasbah* ⌑ *70 DH adults, 30 DH kids.*

★ The Secret Garden

GARDEN | The Secret Garden, or *Le Jardin Secret,* opened to the public in 2016 after several years of intensive excavation, restoration, and planting. Once one of the largest private riads in the medina, the 16th-century site is home to beautiful Islamic architecture, the lush Exotic and Islamic gardens, an ancient, but still operational, water management and irrigation system, and the original watchtower that has commanding views over the whole medina. The restored Pavilions, which were once formal reception rooms, now house a small café and an exhibit of photographs that show the property's excavation and reconstruction. There are areas to sit and relax, a bookshop, café, and exhibition rooms. Well-informed guides are on-site and provide free tours of the gardens. Entry to the Tower is an extra 40 DH. ⊠ *121, rue Mouassine, Medina* ☏ *0524/39–00–40* ⊕ *www.lejardinsecretmarrakech.com* ⌑ *80 DH.*

★ Souks

MARKET | The vast labyrinth of narrow streets and derbs at the center of the medina is the souk—Marrakesh's marketplace and a wonder of arts, crafts, and workshops. Every step brings you face-to-face with the colorful handicrafts and bazaars for which Marrakesh is famous. In the past, every craft had a special zone within the market—a souk within the souk. Today savvy vendors have pushed south to tap trading opportunities as early as possible, but the deeper in you venture, the more you will be rewarded by better prices and by seeing artisans at work—metalworkers, carpenters, tailors, and cobblers just to name a few. Look for incongruities born of the modern era. Beside handcrafted wooden pots for kohl eye makeup are modern perfume stores; where there is a world of hand-sewn djellabas at one turn, you'll find soccer jerseys after the next; fake Gucci caps sit beside handmade Imazighen carpets.

■ TIP→ **As you wander through the souk, take note of landmarks so that you can retrace your steps without too much trouble. Once the shops' shutters close, they're often unrecognizable.**

Did You Know?

The 77-meter-tall minaret of the Koutoubia Mosque is the tallest structure in Marrakesh and local laws prohibit any new building being taller than the mosque.

The farther north you go the more the lanes twist, turn, and entwine. Should you lose your way, retrace your steps to the busiest thoroughfare and then look for the brown painted signs (usually found at key intersections) indicating the direction of Place Djemâa el Fna. But mostly you'll rely on people in the souk to point the way. If you ask a shopkeeper rather than a loitering local, you'll be less likely to encounter a "faux guide."⊠⊠ *Medina* ✛ *North of Pl. Djemâa el Fna.*

Tanneries

HISTORIC SIGHT | For a whiff of Marrakesh life the old way, the tanneries are a real eye-waterer, not least because of the smell of acrid pigeon excrement, which provides the ammonia that is vital to the tanning process. Six hundred skins sit in a vat at any one time, resting there for up to two months amid constant soaping, scrubbing, and polishing to get the leather strong, supple, clean, and ready for use. Once the hides have been stripped of fur, washed, and made supple through this six-week process, the final stage involves soaking and rubbing in a mix of ground mimosa bark and water, which eventually turns the grayish-green hides into the natural reddish-brown or "tan" shade that we always expect in our natural leather goods. The tanned skins are dried in the sun and then sold direct to the artisans near Ben Youssef Mosque. Additional color dyeing takes place after the skins have been purchased by the artisans in another part of the souk.

Thirteen tanneries are still in operation in the Bab Debbagh area in the northeast of the medina. Simply turn up Rue de Bab Debbagh and look for the tannery signs above several open doorways to both the right and left of the street. To visit one of them, just pop in and the local manager will offer you mint leaves to cover the smell, explain the process, and guide you around the vats of dyes. In return he'll hope for a healthy tip to share with

his workers; this is a dying art in a poor dyeing area, so the more you can tip, the better.

■TIP→ **Finding the tanneries can be frustrating. It's best to arrive via taxi and ask for Bab Debbagh (the tanneries are straight ahead through the gate) or the Place el Mokf (Avenue Bab Debbagh is at the top on the left). Alternatively, task an official guide to include the visit as part of a city walking tour, but beware of false guides who are plentiful and forceful in this area.**

⊠ *Av. Bab Debbagh, Medina.*

Restaurants

The medina is full of wonderful food options that range from simple street fare to high-end dining.

Café Arabe

$$ | **ITALIAN** | This Italian-owned three-story restaurant in the heart of the medina serves both Moroccan and Italian food. The trendy terrace, complete with a trickling fountain and relaxing music, is a good place to stop for drinks, while the ground-floor, shaded patio is better suited to a lunchtime visit. **Known for:** homemade pastas; cocktails on the terrace; gardenlike courtyard for dining. Ⓢ *Average main: DH150* ⊠ *184, rue el Mouassine, Medina* ☎ *0524/42–97–28* ⊕ *www.cafearabe.com.*

Café Clock

$ | **MOROCCAN** | **FAMILY** | An outpost of the popular Café Clock in Fez, this so-called cultural café combines a fun vibe with tasty contemporary Moroccan cuisine. Signature dishes include camel burgers, a blue cheese and fig salad, veggie platters, and homemade ice cream. **Known for:** cultural activities and live music; camel burgers; vegetarian food options. Ⓢ *Average main: DH70* ⊠ *224, Derb Chtouka, Kasbah* ☎ *0524/37–83–67* ⊕ *www.cafeclock.com.*

Marrakesh Street Food

Marrakshis have perfected the art of cooked street food, traditionally the province of the working class. There are hundreds of sidewalk grills scattered throughout both the medina and Guéliz, serving tasty, inexpensive, and satisfying meals. From midday to midnight, choose from grilled minced beef, sausage, lamb chops, brochettes, Moroccan salads, and french fries, supplemented by bread, olives, and hot sauce. As you'll guess, no credit cards are taken.

Djemâa el Fna

For the ultimate grilling experience, there's only one place: the Djemâa el Fna. By dusk, more than a hundred stalls sizzle and smoke their way through mountains of fresh meat and vegetables. Step up to the stall of your choice and order from the wild array of perfectly done veggies, salads, *kefta* (beef patties), merguez sausages, beef brochettes, couscous, and even french fries. In cooler months or during Ramadan, try a bowl of hearty *harira* (chickpea, lentil, and meat soup). The meal starts with free bread (to weigh down your paper place setting) and the hot dipping sauce called harissa. The mint tea at the end should be free, too.

Vendors will do anything to attract your attention, from dragging you to a seat, chasing you down the lanes, and best of all, performing the occasional comic rundown of classic English phrases ("It's bloody marvelous!") with matching Cockney accent.

TIP→ Eat where the Moroccans eat: they know what to order, and how much to pay.

Street Food Tours

If you find the idea of dining at one of the stalls on the square, or eating alone in Marrakesh, a little bit daunting, there are organized evening food tours to show you the ropes, sample the flavors, and guide you through the street entertainment. To join a mixed group try **Marrakech Food Tours** (www.marrakechfoodtours.com) or for a more bespoke, private tour try **Tasting Marrakech** (www.tasting-marrakech.com).

Café des Épices

$ | CAFÉ | FAMILY | In keeping with the name, this café in the medina's "spice square" offers spiced teas and coffees along with a range of freshly squeezed fruit juices, smoothies, and light snacks, salads, and sandwiches. Ever popular, it expanded into the neighboring property and teeters over three levels with a great rooftop view over the veiled women selling basketware and woolly hats below. **Known for:** great location; highly photographable; well-priced tasty snacks and juices. $ *Average main: DH60* ⊠ *75, Rahba Lakdima, Medina* ☎ *0524/39–17–70* ⊕ *www.cafedesepices.ma.*

Chez Lamine Hadj Mustapha

$ | |Although the row of severed lambs' heads out front may not be everyone's idea of culinary heaven, Marrakshis love Chez Lamine Hadj Mustapha, and you'd be missing out not to try it. English TV chef Jamie Oliver chose this spit-and-sawdust street restaurant in a filming trip for a gutsy example of Moroccan roast lamb specialty, *mechoui*—it's served as a simple sandwich or as a laden plateful priced by weight. **Known for:** authentic Marrakesh cuisine; rustic atmosphere; there's a slightly more elegant outpost in Guéliz. $ *Average main: DH75* ⊠ *18–26, Souk Ablouh, Mellah* ▬ *No credit cards.*

Dar Moha

$$$$ | **MOROCCAN** | You can dine on delicious adaptations of traditional dishes—such as tiny melt-in-the-mouth *pastilla* (sweet pigeon pie) filled with a vegetable puree—at this lovely restaurant with a reputation for *nouvelle cuisine marocaine*. Andalusian lutes and Gnaoua music accompany dinner, which is a fixed five-course tasting menu at 530 DH; lunch is à la carte, with a limited menu for children. Alcohol is served. **Known for:** serves alcohol; modern Moroccan gastronomy; beautiful courtyard seating. [$] *Average main: DH520* ✉ *81, rue Dar el Bacha, Medina* ☎ *0524/38–64–00* 🌐 *www.darmoha.ma.*

★ **Dar Yacout**

$$$$ | **MOROCCAN** | Come hungry for the five-course traditional Moroccan feast served at this restaurant located deep in the medina. Aperitifs are taken on the rooftop, which has stunning panoramic views of the Koutoubia Mosque, and then you can choose to dine beside the pool on the lanterned terrace, in a vaulted upstairs room, or in the lush, cushion-filled main salon. **Known for:** plentiful amount of food served; sumptuous Moroccan dining; magical fairy-tale setting. [$] *Average main: DH700* ✉ *79, Sidi Ahmed Soussi, Bab Doukkala* ☎ *0524/38–29–29* 🌐 *www.daryacout.com* 🕒 *Closed Mon. No lunch.*

La Famille

$$ | **VEGETARIAN** | **FAMILY** | In a tiny garden, off one of the medina's main shopping streets, the French owner serves a constantly changing menu derived from fresh local ingredients; think enormous main-course salads or pizzettas topped with anything from carrots and apples to raspberries, mint, and beetroot. Homemade cakes, fresh-brewed coffee, and freshly squeezed juices are served through the afternoon. **Known for:** no alcohol; charming garden space; creative food. [$] *Average main: DH80* ✉ *42, Riad Zitoun Jdid, Medina* ✣ *Near Bahia Palace* ☎ *0524/38–52–95* 🕒 *Closed Mon. No dinner.*

Le Foundouk

$$ | **MOROCCAN** | This French-run restaurant hidden at the souk's northern tip is regularly booked with upscale tourists and expats, and the candlelit roof terrace is a popular spot for balmy summer nights or predinner cocktails. The menu features traditional Moroccan fare as well as lighter international dishes such as sea-bass fillet served in a clam sauce, or vegetarian risotto. **Known for:** serves alcohol; filled with character in a historic setting; intriguing international cuisine. [$] *Average main: DH150* ✉ *55, Souk Hal Fassi, Kat Bennahid, near Medersa Ben Youssef, Medina* ☎ *0524/37–81–90* 🌐 *www.foundouk.com* 🕒 *Closed Wed. No lunch.*

Hadj Brik

$ | **MOROCCAN** | If you want to eat with the locals, this is the perfect spot, though be forewarned that the menu is meat-only. Everything is ordered by weight and you'll get side dishes of olives as well as a tomato and onion salad. **Known for:** unpretentious, quick service; perfectly charcoal-grilled meats; a go-to spot for locals. [$] *Average main: DH50* ✉ *Rue Beni Marine, Marrakesh* 💳 *No credit cards.*

Le Jardin

$$ | **MOROCCAN** | Building on the success of his Café des Épices, Moroccan entrepreneur Kamal Laftimi opened this laid-back spot in the heart of the souks. The menu features classic Moroccan dishes, but there are plenty of options for vegetarians and pescaterians, as well as delicious desserts. **Known for:** excellent desserts; cool, tranquil setting; fun mocktails. [$] *Average main: DH120* ✉ *32, Souk el Jeld, Sidi Abdelaziz, Medina* ☎ *0524/37–82–95* 🌐 *www.lejardinmarrakech.com.*

Crowds throng Marrakesh's Jardin Majorelle but the recently renovated "Secret Garden," in the medina, is still a peaceful sanctuary.

Kasbah Café

$$ | MOROCCAN | Perfectly positioned just opposite the entrance to the Saadian tombs, this Spanish-owned café is a welcome retreat for those who find themselves "kasbahed-out" at the end of a trek through the monuments of Marrakesh. The menu features Moroccan standards, as well as pizza, salads, and a cool gazpacho. **Known for:** lovely rooftop terrace. $ *Average main: DH130* ✉ *Rue de la Kasbah, opposite Saadian tombs, Kasbah* ☎ *0524/38–26–25* ⊕ *www.kasbahcafemarrakech.com.*

Marrakech Henna Art Cafe

$ | FUSION | FAMILY | This lovely, small café caters to vegetarians, vegans, and gluten-free diners as well as meat-eaters, with options that range from Moroccan classics like harira soup and vegetarian couscous to fusion dishes such as a tabbouleh couscous or falafel sandwiches with a cooked salad of tomatoes, bell peppers, garlic, toasted paprika, and olive oil. **Known for:** lots of vegetarian options; easy to find; organic henna tattoos. $ *Average main: DH50* ✉ *35 Derb Sqaya, Riad Zeitoun Kdim, Marrakesh* ☎ *06/66779304* ⊕ *www.marrakechhennaartcafe.com* ☾ *Closed Wed.*

L'Mida

$$ | MOROCCAN | Just off the Rehba Kdima ("Spice Souk"), L'Mida is a pleasant spot serving a fresh, modern take on Moroccan flavors. There are plenty of meaty options, but vegetables get the royal treatment in dishes like a seven-vegetable vegan couscous and Amazigh gnocchi with chestnut butter and garlic confit. **Known for:** modern Moroccan flavors; amazing rooftop views; unique desserts. $ *Average main: DH100* ✉ *78 bis, Derb Nkhal, Rehba Kdima, Marrakesh* ☎ *0524/44–36–62* ⊕ *www.Imidamarrakech.com.*

Nomad

$$ | MOROCCAN | Tucked into a side street off the so-called Spice Square in the souks, Nomad has become a local favorite for modern Moroccan cuisine in a quirky outdoor setting, with cushioned benches and festoons of woven lanterns that light up in the evenings. The menu offers takes on traditional Moroccan dishes as well as lighter options such as vegetarian pastilla with goat cheese and caramelized onions. **Known for:** excellent desserts; no alcohol; modern Moroccan food. $ *Average main: DH120* ✉ *1, Derb Aarjan, off Rahba Lkdima, Medina* ✛ *Near Café des Epices* ☎ *0524/38–16–09* ⊕ *www.nomadmarrakech.com.*

Royal Mansour

$$$$ | **MOROCCAN** | The prestigious Royal Mansour hotel is home to four restaurants, each with a different vibe, but La Grande Table Marocaine, which serves classic Moroccan dishes with a modern twist, is the one worth a splurge. **Known for:** casual-chic evening dress code; the finest Moroccan cuisine; exclusive and elaborate setting. $ *Average main: DH500* ✉ *Rue Abou Abbas el Sebti, Medina* ☎ *0529/80–82–82* ⊕ *royalmansour.com.*

Le Tanjia

$$ | **MOROCCAN** | This stylish restaurant is a good bet for a special night out, with traditional Moroccan cuisine and live acoustic North African and Arabian music. The three-tiered restaurant is centered on a rose-filled fountain of the inner patio where the musicians play from early evening. **Known for:** lively atmosphere; Marrakshi specialty tanjia, a slow-cooked meat dish; easy to access via taxi. $ *Average main: DH150* ✉ *14, Derb J'did, next to Pl. des Ferblantiers, Medina* ☎ *0524/38–38–36* ⊕ *tanjiaoriental.com/.*

Terrasse des Épices

$$ | **INTERNATIONAL** | **FAMILY** | On a rooftop hidden deep within the northern quarter of the souks, this all-day (and evening) restaurant is a popular spot for expats, tourists, and trendy locals. The menu mixes Moroccan and international cuisine, with everything from fish tagine and tanjia (slow-cooked beef or lamb) to pasta dishes and steaks. **Known for:** one of few informal medina restaurants serving alcohol; upbeat ambience; rooftop views overlooking the souks. $ *Average main: DH120* ✉ *15, souk Cherifia, Sidi Abdelaziz, Medina* ☎ *0524/37–59–04* ⊕ *www.terrassedesepices.com.*

Le Tobsil

$$$$ | **MOROCCAN** | The tables are strewn with rose petals and lanterns line the walls of this intimate spot, the perfect setting for a romantic, fine-dining feast. The traditional Moroccan fixed menu (700 DH), featuring not one but two tagines (first poultry, then lamb), couscous, starter, and dessert, is wheeled out in serious style. **Known for:** very good Moroccan cuisine; elegant and romantic setting; generous portions. $ *Average main: DH700* ✉ *22, Derb Abdellah ben Hessaien, R'mila Bab L'Ksour, Medina* ☎ *0524/44–15–23* ⊗ *Closed Tues. and July and Aug.*

☕ Coffee and Quick Bites

Café culture, with top-notch people-watching, is nowhere busier than on the Djemâa el Fna, where several terraces compete for the best view of the square. Look elsewhere, though, if you want quality coffee and snacks.

Bacha Coffee

$$ | **CAFÉ** | The airy courtyard in the 1910 building that houses the Dar el Bacha Musée is all palm trees and colorful tiles: it's a perfect oases for a quick bite. There are over 100 types of coffee, from all over the world, and perfect pastries, as well as a selection of main dishes. **Known for:** top-class service; wide range of coffees; jaw-dropping interior decorations. $ *Average main: DH100* ✉ *Inside Dar el Bacha Musée, Rte. Sidi Abdelaziz, Medina* ⊗ *Closed Mon.*

Café Argana

$ | CAFÉ | FAMILY | The multilevel terraced seating area at this café on the square means there are several prime viewing opportunities. It's one of the fancier cafés on the square, having been completely rebuilt in 2017. **Known for:** great views. $ *Average main: DH70* ✉ *1–2, pl. Djemâa el Fna, Medina* ☎ *0524/44–27–57.*

Café de France

$ | CAFÉ | Though it's a bit past its prime, Café de France is a local institution and a great place for people-watching from morning till night. On the ground floor there's a tiny snack restaurant with bright plastic tables, serving sandwiches and quick bites until closing time. **Known for:** skip the food and just come for a drink and the atmosphere; good spot for after-dinner mint tea with a view; top floor views of the square. $ *Average main: DH40* ✉ *Pl. Djemâa el Fna, on northeast corner, Medina* ☎ *0524/44–23–19* ⊕ *www.cafe-france-marrakech.com.*

Dar Cherifa

$$ | MOROCCAN | An airy 16th-century riad turned café turned library turned art gallery, Dar Cherifa is wonderfully airy spot to take a break from shopping for a pot of mint tea. They also have the occasional cultural evening, including poetry readings, traditional music, and story-telling. $ *Average main: DH130* ✉ *8, Derb Cherfa Lakbir, Mouassine, Medina* ☎ *0524/42–65–50* ⊕ *www.dar-cherifa. com* ⊗ *Closed Wed. No dinner.*

Grand Balcon du Café Glacier

$ | CAFÉ | To the south of the square, this is a top choice for catching the sunset, but you'll have to compete for elbow room with all the amateur photographers who throng the best spot. Service is slow and soft drinks overpriced—but that's not unexpected for this bird's-eye view. **Known for:** closes relatively early (around 10 pm); great views; crowded at prime time. $ *Average main: DH70* ✉ *Pl. Djemâa el Fna, Medina* ☞ *Expect to purchase something to visit the top terrace.*

 # Hotels

Dar Alfarah

$$ | B&B/INN | FAMILY | This renovated riad near the Badi Palace in the Mellah quarter has rooms arranged over two floors, looking inward to the central patio pool and terrace, which is shaded by jasmine, bougainvillea, and banana palms. **Pros:** family-friendly; good location; plenty of atmosphere. **Cons:** service sometimes slow; bathrooms and showers need maintenance; small pool. $ *Rooms from: DH1000* ✉ *58, Derb Touareg, Ksibat N'Hass, Medina* ☎ *0524/38–42–69* ✉ *countuctdaralfarah@gmail.com* ⊕ *www.daralfarah.com* ⤴ *10 rooms* ☉ *Free Breakfast.*

Le Farnatchi

$$$ | B&B/INN | On the souk's northern tip is this lavish riad spread across five adjoining properties, known for its fabulous decor and elite clientele (Angelina Jolie and Russell Crowe have stayed here). **Pros:** vast suites; excellent service; great adjoining restaurant. **Cons:** steep stairs to access some rooms; edgy neighborhood; expensive. $ *Rooms from: DH3500* ✉ *2, Derb el Farnatchi, Qa'at Benahid, Medina* ☎ *0524/38–49–12* ⊕ *lefarnatchi.com/* ⊗ *Closed Aug.* ⤴ *10 suites* ☉ *Free Breakfast.*

L'Hotel

$$$$ | B&B/INN | The ambience at this hotel, opened by celebrated British designer Jasper Conran, is that of a stylish and elegant retreat within the medina, where peace and tranquillity reign supreme. **Pros:** free transfer to and from airport; excellent on-site restaurant; idyllic roof terrace. **Cons:** no twin rooms; restaurant menu is limited; no children allowed. $ *Rooms from: DH4800* ✉ *41, Derb Sidi Lahcen ou Ali, Bab Doukkala* ☎ *0524/38–78–80* ⊕ *www.l-hotelmarrakech.com* ⤴ *5 rooms* ☉ *Free Breakfast.*

Hotel Ali

$ | B&B/INN | A long-standing favorite among budget travelers and backpackers,

Hotel Ali is right at the edge of the main square and is constantly abuzz with activity, but don't expect many creature comforts. **Pros:** some rooms have private balconies; great place to meet fellow travelers; right on the main square. **Cons:** heating/air-conditioning not reliable; beds and room furnishings are worn; can be noisy. $ *Rooms from: DH400* ✉ *Rue Moulay Ismail, Medina* ✛ *55 yards from Dejmâa el Fna* ☎ *0524/44–49–79* ⊕ *www.hotel-ali.com* ▭ *No credit cards* ⮑ *39 rooms* ⎟⊙⎟ *Free Breakfast.*

Les Jardins de la Medina

$$$ | **HOTEL** | **FAMILY** | This 18th-century palace once belonging to the cousin of King Hassan II is now a luxurious boutique hotel with lush gardens hidden in the kasbah area of the medina. **Pros:** excellent restaurant; fabulous gardens; stylish decor. **Cons:** slow service; pool area rather cramped; 20-minute walk to reach main square. $ *Rooms from: DH2500* ✉ *21, Derb Chtouka, Kasbah* ☎ *0524/38–18–51* ⊕ *www.lesjardinsdelamedina.com* ⮑ *36 rooms* ⎟⊙⎟ *Free Breakfast.*

La Maison Arabe

$$$ | **HOTEL** | At the edge of the medina, with easy access to parking, taxis, and the main Djemâa el Fna square, La Maison Arabe is a stylish hotel offering old-fashioned charm and exceptional Moroccan hospitality. **Pros:** wonderful nooks; luxurious spa; renowned restaurant and cooking school. **Cons:** often fully booked; the outdoor restaurant overlooks the pool; some rooms are small. $ *Rooms from: DH2800* ✉ *1, Derb Assehbe, Bab Doukkala* ☎ *0524/38–70–10* ⊕ *www.cenizaro.com/lamaisonarabe/marrakech* ⮑ *37 rooms* ⎟⊙⎟ *Free Breakfast.*

★ La Mamounia

$$$$ | **HOTEL** | Since 1923, Morocco's most prestigious hotel has achieved legendary status for its opulence, grandeur, celebrity guest list, and hefty price tag. **Pros:** stunning architecture and interiors; one of the finest hotels in the world;

exquisite restaurants. **Cons:** exorbitant bar/restaurant prices; ground-floor rooms have no view of garden; some standard classic rooms. $ *Rooms from: DH6200* ✉ *Bab Jdid, Medina* ☎ *0524/38–86–00* ⊕ *www.mamounia.com* ⮑ *208 rooms* ⎟⊙⎟ *No Meals.*

Le Naoura Marrakech

$$$ | **RESORT** | **FAMILY** | This outpost of a well-respected French luxury hotel chain is ideally situated on the edge of the medina but an easy walk from the main sights. **Pros:** the private villas are exceptional; spacious standard rooms; central location. **Cons:** hotel rooms lack character; lack of outdoor garden spaces; noisy pool area. $ *Rooms from: DH2400* ✉ *Rue Djbel Alakhdar, Bab Doukkala* ☎ *0524/45–90–00* ⊕ *www.hotelsbarriere.com/en/marrakech/le-naoura.html* ⮑ *115 rooms* ⎟⊙⎟ *Free Breakfast.*

★ Palais Khum

$$ | **B&B/INN** | This exquisite, Italian-owned boutique riad is near the Dar el Bacha Royal residence, on a street filled with antiques dealers and quality boutiques. **Pros:** roof terrace; fabulous design; quiet location. **Cons:** pool is very close to restaurant; some rooms have no external window or view; no outdoor pool. $ *Rooms from: DH1500* ✉ *2, Derb el Henaria, off Rue Dar el Bacha, Medina* ✛ *Enter through gardens of its very own patisserie, Kremm Café, and there's an elevator to access all levels and terrace* ☎ *0524/39–03–89* ⊕ *www.palaiskhum.com* ⮑ *11 rooms* ⎟⊙⎟ *Free Breakfast.*

Riad Adore

$$$ | **B&B/INN** | The jewel in the crown of the English-owned Pure Riads collection, Riad Adore is decorated in cool, pale shades of white, beige, and gray, with *tadlak* walls and subtle lighting—it's an elegant and sophisticated guesthouse close to the main medina action. **Pros:** beautiful roof terrace; elegant design; great location. **Cons:** children under 12 not accepted; three-night minimum stay; small splash pool. $ *Rooms from:*

DH1800 ✉ *97, Derb Tizouagrine, off Rue Dar el Bacha, Medina* ☎ *0524/37–77–37* 🌐 *www.riadadore.com* 🛏 *10 rooms* 🍴 *Free Breakfast.*

Riad Baya

$ | **B&B/INN** | **FAMILY** | Nestled into a residential area of the kasbah, the intimate Riad Baya has a lovely central courtyard and rooftop terrace. **Pros:** can rent the whole riad; cozy, homey atmosphere; attentive staff. **Cons:** no nearby parking; 20 minutes from main square; not suitable for those who have trouble walking. [$] *Rooms from: DH650* ✉ *13 Derb Akerkour, Kasbah* ☎ *5/24 42 79 14* 🌐 *www.riadbaya.com* 🛏 *5 rooms* 🍴 *Free Breakfast.*

Riad el Fenn

$$$$ | **HOTEL** | English entrepreneur Vanessa Branson created this riad "adventure" in 2002, and since then it has been reworked and extended into a palace of individually conceived rooms designed with a stylish modern aesthetic. **Pros:** three pools and a spa; dripping with good taste; loads of communal spaces for relaxation. **Cons:** bar and restaurant get busy; cheapest small rooms are very dark; 7.5% compulsory service charge added. [$] *Rooms from: DH4500* ✉ *2, Derb Moulay Abdellah ben Hessaien, Bab Ksour, Medina* ☎ *0524/44–12–10* 🌐 *www.el-fenn.com* 🛏 *20 rooms* 🍴 *Free Breakfast.*

Riad le Clos des Arts

$$$ | **B&B/INN** | The Italian owners Georgina and Massimo have blended Moroccan flavors and craftsmanship with European style to create a riad that oozes sophistication. **Pros:** spacious rooms; on-site hammam; relaxed, family feel. **Cons:** can be difficult to find in the medina; no pool; no TV. [$] *Rooms from: DH1800* ✉ *50, Derb Tbib, Riad Zitoun Jdid, Medina* ☎ *5/24 37 51 59* 🌐 *www.leclosdesarts.com* 🛏 *9 rooms* 🍴 *Free Breakfast.*

Riad Le Limoun

$$ | **B&B/INN** | The decor is modern Moroccan meets cool hideaway at this chic riad, with a bright and airy interior. **Pros:** great rooftop terrace; all king-size beds; vegetarian food options. **Cons:** 20-minute walk to Djemâa el Fna; no ability to split beds; adults only. [$] *Rooms from: DH700* ✉ *66, Derb Lahcen O Ali, Bab Doukkala* 🌐 *riadlelimoun.com/* 🛏 *5 rooms* 🍴 *Free Breakfast.*

Riad les Trois Mages

$$ | **B&B/INN** | **FAMILY** | Tucked away in the Riad Laarouss neighborhood, Les Trois Mages is a delightful small riad with English-speaking staff and spacious, tastefully furnished rooms. **Pros:** cozy lounges; rooftop pool; great service. **Cons:** prices are set in GB sterling so can fluctuate; rooms get noisy when riad is full; far from the main square. [$] *Rooms from: DH1100* ✉ *11, Derb Jemaa, off Rue el Gza, Riad Laarouss, Medina* ☎ *0524/38–92–97* 🌐 *www.lestroismages.com* 🛏 *6 rooms* 🍴 *Free Breakfast.*

Riad Linda

$ | **B&B/INN** | A Scottish-owned riad with English-speaking staff, Riad Linda is an unpretentious and welcoming guesthouse that is an excellent value; it's decorated in contemporary Moroccan style, with individual touches such as vintage caftans displayed in bedrooms and enormous abstract modernist paintings by the owner. **Pros:** English-speaking staff; roof terrace; in the heart of the medina. **Cons:** rooms are small; far from nearest taxi drop-off point; no pool. [$] *Rooms from: DH650* ✉ *93, Derb Jemaa, Derb Dabbachi, Medina* ☎ *0524/39–09–27* 🌐 *www.riadlinda.com* 🛏 *6 rooms* 🍴 *Free Breakfast.*

Riad Malika

$$ | **B&B/INN** | Full of eccentric charm, the rambling Riad Malika occupies three old houses and was one of the first riads to become a guesthouse in the 1990s. **Pros:** cozy winter lounge; parking nearby; large

bedrooms. **Cons:** far from main square; heavily flowered interior courtyard may be allergen trigger; lots of stairs. [$] *Rooms from: DH1100* ✉ *29, Arsat Aouzal, Bab Doukkala* ☎ *0524/38–54–51* 🌐 *www.riadmalika.com* 🛏 *9 rooms* 🍴 *Free Breakfast.*

Riad Nesma

$ | **B&B/INN** | **FAMILY** | Proof that staying in a beautiful riad with elegant rooms does not have to break the bank, this Moroccan-run guesthouse is a real treasure, with a delightful roof terrace. **Pros:** roof terrace with pool and Jacuzzi; excellent value; great location. **Cons:** rooms opening onto patio are noisy; no ground-floor access; rooms are small. [$] *Rooms from: DH700* ✉ *128, Riad Zitouen Lakdim, Medina* ☎ *0524/44–44–42* 🌐 *www.riadnesma.com* 🛏 *24 rooms* 🍴 *Free Breakfast.*

Riad 107

$ | **B&B/INN** | This budget-friendly riad with great amenities (including air-conditioning) is in a quiet alley not far from Place Djemâa el Fna. Its simple decorations and traditional architecture give the property a peaceful vibe that's fresh and modern as well as cozy Moroccan—think colorful throws and cushions set against pale walls, a small tiled central courtyard, and a small plunge pool. **Pros:** stylish modern decor; safe and convenient location; splash pool. **Cons:** narrow stairs to terrace; street noise can affect ground-floor rooms; small rooms. [$] *Rooms from: DH600* ✉ *107, Derb Jdid, Douar Graoua, Medina* ☎ *0524/38–64–57* 🌐 *www.riad107.com* 🛏 *6 rooms* 🍴 *Free Breakfast.*

★ Riad l'Orangeraie

$$ | **B&B/INN** | **FAMILY** | With easy access from Bab Laksour and just a five-minute walk to Djemâa el Fna, this luxurious riad is a great base for exploring the medina. **Pros:** cozy fireplace in winter; English-speaking staff; great location. **Cons:** in-house meals expensive; 30% surcharge at Christmas and New Year; rooms next to the pool can be noisy. [$] *Rooms from: DH1500* ✉ *61, rue Sidi el Yemani, Mouassine, Medina* ☎ *666/61 23 87 89* 🌐 *www.riadorangeraie.com* 🛏 *7 rooms* 🍴 *Free Breakfast.*

Riad Samsli

$$ | **B&B/INN** | **FAMILY** | Made up of two adjoining houses around separate courtyards, Riad Samsli has 10 charming rooms at very good prices. **Pros:** English-speaking staff; allows children of all ages; lovely communal salons. **Cons:** no doors between bathroom and bedroom; some rooms are small; no ground-floor rooms. [$] *Rooms from: DH750* ✉ *24, Derb Jdid, Riad Zitoun Lkdim, Medina* ☎ *0524/42–77–49* 🛏 *10 rooms* 🍴 *Free Breakfast.*

Riad Snan13

$$ | **B&B/INN** | You'll get the best of both worlds at this unassuming riad that's close to all of the action of the medina but still secluded. **Pros:** excellent service and staff; lovely terrace; easy access to taxis. **Cons:** fills up quickly; first-floor room has no windows; hard to find. [$] *Rooms from: DH1300* ✉ *13, Derb Snan, Bab Lksour, Medina* 🌐 *riadsnan13.com/* 🛏 *6 rooms* 🍴 *Free Breakfast.*

★ Royal Mansour

$$$$ | **HOTEL** | Built and owned by King Mohammed VI of Morocco, the Royal Mansour opened in 2010 and is an ultraluxurious private medina within the medina, comprising 53 individual three-story riads complete with a private patio, sitting room, rooftop plunge pool, fireplace, and personal butler. **Pros:** finest Moroccan craftsmanship; complete privacy and luxury; fabulous spa treatments. **Cons:** no ground-floor bedrooms; can be difficult to book due to exclusive guest list; entire riads only can be booked (not individual rooms). [$] *Rooms from: DH13000* ✉ *Rue Abbou Abbas el Sebti, Medina* ☎ *0529/80–80–80* 🌐 *www.royalmansour.com* 🛏 *53 rooms* 🍴 *Free Breakfast.*

La Sultana

$$$$ | HOTEL | There's a certain over-the-top charm to this series of five inter-connected riads of palatial proportions, each with a different decorative theme inspired by previous ruling dynasties. **Pros:** stunning interiors; fireplaces in every room; impeccable service. **Cons:** least expensive rooms are small; small pool; in-house food is average. $ *Rooms from: DH4200* ✉ *403, rue de la Kasbah, Kasbah* ✛ *Head left just behind Saadian tombs* ☎ *0524/38–80–08* ⊕ *www.lasultanamarrakech.com* ⤴ *28 rooms* ⦿ *Free Breakfast.*

Villa des Orangers

$$$$ | HOTEL | Formerly the private residence of a Marrakesh judge, this exquisite 1930s property has all the understated glamour and class you'd expect from a Relais & Chateaux hotel, with unobtrusive service, libraries to hide away in, and guest rooms with enormous bathrooms. **Pros:** excellent restaurant; unsurpassed luxury; plenty of privacy. **Cons:** lots of stairs to climb; wood-paneled rooms rather gloomy; very expensive. $ *Rooms from: DH4900* ✉ *6, rue Sidi Mimoun, Medina* ☎ *0524/38–46–38* ⊕ *www.villadesorangers.com* ⤴ *27 rooms* ⦿ *Free Breakfast.*

Nightlife

BARS

For evening drinks in elegant surroundings, dress the part and head to one of Marrakesh's prestigious hotels such as **La Maison Arabe** or **La Mamounia** in the Medina.

Alcohol was once nearly unheard of in the medina, and while it's still unthinkable to swig liquor on the streets or even on outdoor plazas or terraces, there are a few good places to go for a drink within the city walls. Alcohol licenses are still hard to come by, though, and taxes are high; as a result, the drinks are expensive.

Café Arabe bar

BARS | The restaurant in this galleried, bougainvillea-strewn riad is known for the food but the sleek rooftop bar is also an excellent place to enjoy cocktails, Moroccan wine, or champagne. ✉ *184, rue el Mouassine, Medina* ☎ *0524/42–97–28* ⊕ *www.cafearabe.com.*

★ El Fenn

BARS | True to the name (El Fenn means "art" in the local dialect), this fashionable spot in the medina is a magnet for designers, artists, and photographers. Wine, beer, spirits, and a vast selection of cocktails are available and can be sipped fireside in winter, or under the rooftop tent with views across to the Koutoubia mosque. ✉ *Derb Moulay Abdellah ben Hessaien, Bab L'Ksour, Medina* ☎ *0524/44–12–10* ⊕ *www.el-fenn.com.*

Les Jardins de la Koutoubia bar

PIANO BARS | The attractive Art Deco styling and open-air courtyard at this piano bar in hotel Les Jardins de la Koutoubia create an elegant setting in which to enjoy a cocktail. ✉ *26, rue de la Koutoubia, Medina* ☎ *0524/38–88–00* ⊕ *www.lesjardinsdelakoutoubia.com.*

Kabana

BARS | Right near the Djemâa el Fna and with one of the best views of the Koutoubia minaret, Kabana is the latest hot spot on the Marrakesh night scene. Live DJs, an array of cocktails, and a full menu of snacks and main dishes are available. ✉ *1, Kissariat ben Khaled, R'mila, Medina* ☎ *0664/46–44–50* ⊕ *www.kabana-marrakech.com.*

Kosybar

LIVE MUSIC | The Kosybar and restaurant is a long-standing favorite for a late-night drink in the medina, accompanied by live jazz nightly, and a platter of sushi if you wish. There's a large roof terrace, with great views of the storks nesting in the nearby ramparts of the Badii Palace, and the interior restaurant and bar, with mosaic-tiled floors, wrought-iron balustrades, and fireplaces, are truly cozy. ⊠ *47, pl. des Ferblantiers, Kzadria, Medina* ☎ *0524/38–03–24* ⊕ *www.kosybar.com.*

La Maison Arabe bar

BARS | The intimate surroundings of the jazz bar at hotel La Maison Arabe provide a cozy fireside setting for cocktails and a tasty menu of light savory snacks. A resident pianist tickles the ivories every evening from 7 to 9. ⊠ *1, Derb Assehbe, Bab Doukkala, Medina* ☎ *0524/38–70–10* ⊕ *www.lamaisonarabe.com.*

Le Salama

BARS | A stone's throw from the Djemâa el Fna and up a narrow staircase, Le Salama is one of the few places in the medina where you can grab a cold beer or an aperitif without having to eat dinner. Drinks are served either at the bar area in the top terrace Sky Bar with views across to the Koutoubia. ⊠ *40, rue des Banques, Kennaria, Medina* ☎ *0524/39–13–00* ⊕ *www.le-salama.com.*

CASINOS

La Grand Casino de La Mamounia

CASINO | The casino at La Mamounia has a large room for roulette, poker, and blackjack; a slot-machine hall; and is open until 6 am, but you'll need to dress up to gain entrance to this exclusive establishment. ⊠ *Av. Bab Jdid, Medina* ☎ *0524/33–82–00* ⊕ *www.grandcasinomamounia.com.*

Shopping

Kasbah Chic

PRIVATE GUIDES | Personal shopper Patrizia Bell-Banner is an interior decorator living between London and Marrakesh. She knows her way through the best boutiques of the souks and out to the designer showrooms of the Sidi Ghanem industrial zone, and can point you in the direction of those special items you may be seeking. The price is around €300

Shopping Detour

Out beyond Guéliz, the industrial zone of **Sidi Ghanem** has become a hot shopping destination, where local designers and artisans have workshops and showrooms targeting the wholesale and export market. Riad owners, restaurateurs, hoteliers, expats, and tourists come here to buy superior-quality, contemporary-style housewares, ceramics, fashion, jewelry, and perfumes. About 5 km (3 miles) out of town on Route de Safi, it's recommended to hire a taxi to take you here, wait while you shop, then bring you back.

per day. ⊠ *Marrakesh* ☎ *0661/42–43–82* ⊕ *www.kasbahchic.com.*

THE SOUKS

You can find everything from dried fruit to handbags, carpets to candlesticks in the jumbled labyrinth of merchants and artisan workshops found in the souks of the Marrakesh medina. It's one of the wonders of the city, and stretches north from Place Djemâa el Fna to Ali ben Youssef Medersa. Each souk has a name that defines its specialty and that relates to the crafts guilds that used to control each area.

Heading north from Bab Fteuh square, near Place Djemâa el Fna, the souks are laid out roughly as follows: Souk Semmarine has textiles and souvenirs; Souk Rahba Kdima (aka "the Spice Souk") is spices, herbs, apothecaries, woolen hats, and baskets. Souk el-Kebir is full of carpets, leather goods, and wood wares; Souk Zarbia also has carpets. Souk des Bijoutiers/Souk Tagmoutyime is for jewelry; Souk el-Attarine has polished copper

Stalls filled with crafts and other goods fill the laneways around the Djemâa el Fna square in the center of the medina.

and brass as well as mirrors. Souk des Babouches/Souk Smata is the place for leather slippers, while Souk des Teinturiers/Souk Sebbaghine is all about fabric and wool. Several other souks—including Souk Chouari for wood carpenters; Souk Haddadine with blacksmiths; and Souk Cherratine with leatherworkers—are at the northern end.

Generally, credit cards are not accepted here, except at the more upmarket bazaars and shops, though this is changing. Most places are open daily from 9 to 9, though some close on Friday at midday. A small side market called Souk Cherifia is at the northern end of the souks beyond Souk Haddadine: the ground floor sells standard touristic items, but go up to the second floor near the entrance to La Terrasse des Épices restaurant and you'll find several fascinating little boutique outlets by up-and-coming young Marrakesh-based designers.

Carpet Souk

MARKET | The main carpet souk—called the Souk Zrabia or Le Criée Berbère—has a flat, shiny floor in the middle of the surrounding boutiques, to roll out the rugs to display to potential buyers. To get here head north on Rue Semarine, and just after the Souk el Attarine branches off left, take the next right turn off the street (which is now more properly named Rue Souk el-Kebir—the Big Souk Street). The carpet souk can also be reached from a passage in Rahba Qdima's northeast corner (to the right of Le Café des Épices). ✉ *Rahba Qdima, Medina.*

Leather Souks

MARKET | At the northeastern edges of the souk (just beyond the northern end of the main Rue Souk el Kebir) are the leatherworkers—busy cutting out templates for those leather slippers called babouches, hammering and polishing, and making up bags and satchels from several types of animal skins. Look for signs to the Souk des Sachochiers (bag makers),

Souk Chairia, and Souk Cherratine, all leather-working areas. The tanneries, where the raw hides have been prepared and dyed, are some 20 minutes' walk farther northeast from Souk Cherratine along Rue Bab Debbagh. Also in the northeast are a range of shops selling instruments, especially drums (Souk Moulay aii) and woven baskets (Souk Serrajine). ⊠ *Rue Souk Chairia, Medina.*

Rue Mouassine

MARKET | One of the easiest ways to head back to Djemâa el Fna from a day of souk shopping is to find Rue Mouassine, the souk's westernmost main north–south artery (the other main artery is Rue Souk Semarine, on the eastern side of the souks). Rue Mouassine is quite easy to find, and it's almost impossible to veer away from the correct path once you're on it; the simplest route is to take a counterclockwise loop from behind the Ben Medersa Mosque—when you hit the big mosque, you've hit Rue Mouassine. This is heavy souvenir territory, with the whole gamut of goods on display—lanterns, teapots, scarves, babouches, djellabas. The street spits you out into the northeast corner of Bab Fteuh square, and from there it's a short hop down to Djemâa el Fna.

■ **TIP →** **Look for Fnac Berbère, the Amazigh bookshop, on the southern section of Rue Mouassine (the southern section from the fountain to Bab Fteuh square is sometimes known as Rue Fehl Chidmi). It's a good landmark.**

⊠ *Medina.*

Souk des Babouches (slipper souk)

MARKET | Best approached by taking the main left fork onto Souk el-Attarine, where it branches off from Rue Souk el Kebir, and then continuing north for about 150 yards, the Souk Principal des Babouches—also called Souk Smata—is on the right-hand side and is filled with the namesake babouches, pointed

leather slippers so beloved of Moroccans. The small doorway opens up to an enormous emporium with examples in every color imaginable.

It can be hard to judge the proper value of these fairy-tale leather slippers, because price depends on so many things, such as the thickness of the sole, the number of layers, the presence or absence of a stepped heel, and of course the decoration. Use your nose, but be warned that a fair price can vary from 60 DH to 400 DH, depending on quality.

Look for the tiny wool boutique on the left as you come to the arch before the right turn for the babouches market. It's on the way to the Souk des Teinturiers (Dyers' Souk). You can see men rolling out wool to make into fetching striped handbags, and, best of all, into small balls, and looping them up into the most unusual necklaces going. ⊠ *Rue Souk Smata, Medina.*

Souk des Bijoutiers (jewelry souk)

CRAFTS | North of the carpet souk on Rue Souk El-Kebir you'll see an overhead sign for the Souk des Bijoutiers (also labeled Souk Tagmoutyime). Follow that just off to the right into a narrow mall, full of jewelry stores displaying their wares behind glass. It is by no means the only place in Marrakesh to buy jewelry, and buyers should proceed with caution if they're not well versed in stones or precious metals. ⊠ *Rue Souk Tagnaoutuyime, Medina.*

★ Souk des Teinturiers (fabric and wool souk)

MARKET | To get to the fabric and wool souk, use the Mouassine Mosque as a landmark, and keep the Mouassine fountain on your right while you continue until the street widens out with shops on either side. At the point where it branches into two alleys running either side of a shop selling handmade lamps and textiles, take an immediate sharp left

3

Marrakesh MEDINA

turn. Follow that derb and look for the helpful word "teinturies" in spray paint and then head right. Souk des Teinturiers is also called Souk Sebbaghine. The main square for fabric dyeing is hidden down a little shimmy to the right and then immediately left, but anyone can (and likely will) direct you. Here you'll see men dipping fabrics into vats full of hot dye. Look up to see scarves and skeins of wool hanging all over, in individual sets of the same bright colors.

For the best view, head into the dyers' square and ask to be led into the boutique. A dyer can show you the powders that the colors come from. A lovely bit of magic involves the fact that green powder dyes fabric red; red powder dyes things blue; and yellow powder dyes things purple. Head up the steep stairs and onto the roof if you're allowed—a spectacular view of industry unfolds, with headscarves and threads of every color hanging up to dry in separate color blocks all over the rooftops. ⊠ *Rue Souk Sebbaghine, Medina*.

Souk Haddadine (ironworkers souk)

MARKET | From Rue Souk el-Attarine, follow that main souk street as faithfully as possible and it will take you north, looping clockwise to the east, and through the ironmongers' souk, where you'll see blacksmiths at work, hammering out lanterns and wrought-iron chairs. ⊠ *Medina*.

Souk Lghzal (wool souk)

MARKET | North of Djemâa el Fna on Souk Semarine, you pass a fairly prominent derb (alley) that turns off to the left (Rue R'mila Bab Ksour, also called Rue el Ksour). Take the next right turn and wander down a few yards (toward the Spice Square or Rahba Qdima) and on the right you will find the small square of Souk Lghzal, the Wool Souk. Today women sell secondhand clothes in the square, and the odd djellaba. Head over to the apothecary stalls leading up to the

entrance to the square, and immediately to the right on entering it for spices and potions galore. ⊠ *Medina*.

★ Souk Rahba Qdima (Spice Square)

MARKET | Just a quick turn right and then left out of the Souk Lghzal (via Rue Souk Semarine) is the large square called Souk Rahba Qdima. This square is surrounded by small shops that sell everything from cure-alls to run-of-the-mill salt and pepper and just about everything in between. In the center of the square are lots of woven baskets and hats for sale. You'll also find ladies pounding henna leaves to create henna powder. If shopping isn't your for you, head to the rooftop of nearby **Nomad** for a glass of tea and a bird's-eye view. ⊠ *Souk Rahba Qdima, Medina*.

Souk Semarine

MARKET | Souk Semarine is the main street that runs from Djemâa el Fna into deeper parts of the souk. If you're beginning your exploration here, you'll at first see a mishmash of products but as you go farther specialty items begin to appear: rug shops, fine wood crafts, and stalls selling dazzling lamps and lighting fixtures are prominent.

From Djemâa el Fna take the street just to the left of Café Argana, which leads into the small Bab Fteuh square, then keep bearing right. To the left there is a *kissaria* (covered market), with dried fruits, herbs and spices, essential oils, and traditional colored eye kohls. Veer right into the covered market, past a couple of stands selling teapots and mint tea glasses, and take a left onto Rue Souk Semarine. It's signposted and lined with fabrics and inexpensive souvenirs. ⊠ *Rue Souk Semarine, Medina*.

SPECIALTY STORES
ANTIQUES
★ Khalid Art Gallery

ANTIQUES & COLLECTIBLES | Popular with the international jet set, the Khalid Art

Aromatic spices like ras el hanout (which literally means "head of shop" or "top shelf") make great gifts to take home.

Gallery is a gorgeous riad full of the most sought-after Moroccan antiques, Jewish-Moroccan treasures, and Amazigh pieces. Owner Khalid speaks excellent English and is an authority on most of the art coming out of Marrakesh. ✉ 14, rue Dar el Basha, Mouassine, Medina ☎ 0524/44–24–10.

★ Le Trésor des Nomades / Mustapha Blaoui

CRAFTS | The highly respected Le Trésor des Nomades—often referred to just by the name of its owner, Mustapha Blaoui—extends over several floors and two adjacent properties. Here you'll find antique doors, lanterns, vintage tribal carpets, mats from Mauritania, Amazigh jewelry, and all kinds of crafted furniture, housewares, and textiles. It's so well-known that there is no sign over the door.

■ TIP→ Shipping can be arranged for large purchases. ✉ 142, rue Bab Doukkala, Bab Doukkala ☎ 0524/38–52–40.

Twizra

CRAFTS | Prices are high at this general antiques and jewelry store in the kasbah—so bargain hard! They can (reliably) organize international shipping and also accept credit cards. ✉ 361, Bab Agnaou, Medina ☎ 0524/37–65–65.

ART
Galerie Dawiya

ART GALLERIES | At this small gallery, owners Dominique and Mohammed aim to create awareness of lesser-known Moroccan painters. There's a variety of styles, sizes, and prices from small watercolors to larger oil paintings and sculptural pieces. Credit cards are accepted. ✉ 129, rue Dar el Bacha, Medina ✛ Next to Bureau de Change ☎ 0524/39–05–52.

★ Riad Yima

ART GALLERIES | This riad turned art gallery and tearoom is filled with original artwork by owner Hassan Hajjaj who's known as Morocco's Andy Warhol. True to the artist's pop aesthetic, expect to find colorful portraits blending pop culture and the artist's own fashions. Smaller items include notebooks, posters, and upcycled lanterns made from sardine tins. ⌧ *52, Derb Aarjane, Rahba Lkdima, Medina* ☎ *0524/39–19–87* ⊕ *www.riadyima.com.*

CARPETS
Bazar de Sud

CRAFTS | Run by the Marrakshis Lamdagh-ri family since 1940, this shop works with more than 200 artisans and has a huge collection of old and new tribal carpets as well as antique Imazighen textiles.

■ TIP→ **Worldwide shipping can be arranged and credit cards are accepted.** ⌧ *117 and 14, souk des Tapis, Rahba Lak-dima, Medina* ☎ *0524/44–30–04* ⊕ *www. bazardusud.com.*

Palais Saâdiens

CRAFTS | This shop has an enormous selection of Imazighen, Bedouin, and trib-al carpets. ⌧ *16, rue Moulay Taib, L'Ksour, Medina* ☎ *0524/44–51–76.*

CLOTHING
Aya's

MIXED CLOTHING | This shop sells bespoke caftans and tunics made with the highest quality fabrics—cashmeres, linens, silks—all hand-embroidered. Celebrity clients include Julia Roberts, Tom Hanks, and Hugh Jackman. ⌧ *Derb Jdid, Bab Mellah, 11 bis, near Le Tanjia restaurant, Mellah* ☎ *0524/38–34–28* ⊕ *www.ayas-marrakech.com.*

Kitan

MIXED CLOTHING | The aesthetic is Japan-meets-Morocco at this boutique that stocks uniquely patterned clothing for men and women. Shop off the rack or, if you have a few days, have a one-of-a-kind piece made to fit. ⌧ *19, rte. Sidi Abdelaziz, Souk Jeld, Marrakesh.*

Max & Jan

MIXED CLOTHING | The flagship store for this contemporary fashion label has a selection of Moroccan designer accessories, fashion items for men and women, and a pricey collection of designs by the Swiss-Belgian duo Max & Jan. They also have a constantly changing showcase for other up-and-coming local designers. ⌧ *14, rue Amsefa, Sidi Abdelaziz, Medina* ☎ *0524/37–55–70* ⊕ *www.maxandjan.ma.*

Warda La Mouche

MIXED CLOTHING | This boutique stocks handmade clothing for women in great fabrics and colors, embellished with Moroccan traditional elements such as embroidery and tassels. The tunics are especially wearable and figure-flat-tering. Prices are reasonable for the quality of workmanship. Credit cards are accepted. ⌧ *127, rue Kennaria, Medina* ☎ *0524/38–90–63.*

CRAFTS
Al Nour

CRAFTS | This boutique displays lovely hand-embroidered items all created in a workshop that benefits and trains women with disabilities. Clothing, table linen, bed linen, and home accessories are some of the items available. ⌧ *57, rue el Ksour, Medina* ⊕ *www.alnour-tex-tiles.com/.*

Antiquités du Sahara

CRAFTS | Handcrafted jewelry from southern Morocco of Amazigh, Touareg, and Blue Men traditions is what this shop is known for. Camel-skin decorat-ed dromedary carry packs and ornately carved wooden Touareg tent pegs reminiscent of tribal caravans or bygone times also line the shelves. ⌧ *176, Rahba Lakdima, next to carpet market, Medina* ☎ *0524/44–23–73.*

Chabi Chic

CRAFTS | Some of the trendiest riads serve guests using the *beldi* (traditional) pottery with modern designs that are the hallmark of Chabi Chic. Product lines include serving ware, tea sets, and coasters as well as spices, carpets, and beauty products. They also have a store in the Sidi Ghanem Industrial zone in the Marrakesh outskirts. ⊠ *1, Derb Aarjane, Rahba L'Kdima, Medina* ✢ *Within Nomad restaurant* ☎ *0524/38–15–46* ⊕ *www. chabi-chic.com.*

Ensemble Artisanal

CRAFTS | It may be a bit touristy, but this is a great way to see all the wares of the souk in one hassle-free space. Many of the goods here display fixed prices (which are high) for handicrafts including babouches, embroidery, lanterns, bags, jewelry, carpets, and paintings. You can see baskets being woven, carpets on the loom, and other artisans at work. There's even a snack bar.

■ TIP➜ **If you enjoy bargaining, take a note of prices here and then aim to pay around 25% less in the souks.** ⊠ *Av. Mohammed V, Bab Doukkala* ☎ *0524/38–66–74.*

+Michi

CRAFTS | The stock here tends to tastefully redesigned takes on Moroccan classic items like babouche slippers and hand-sewn buttery soft leather bags. ⊠ *38 Souk Kimakhin, Medina.*

HEALTH AND BEAUTY
Naturom

SKINCARE | Handmade natural beauty products are the thing here, ranging from soap to shampoo bars to argan oil goods. It's a great place to stock up on bath supplies with a Moroccan touch. ⊠ *Riad Zitoun Jdid, Medina.*

Activities

COOKING SCHOOLS

With so many chic riads serving wonderful food, it's no surprise that cooking schools in Marrakesh are in demand. Tagines, couscous, and briouates (puff pastries) are all on the menu for the Maghrebian master chef in the making.

Café Clock Marrakech cooking school
COOKING CLASSES | The all-day course at Café Clock starts with a shopping trip to the local market before returning to the kitchen on the terrace of the riad in the Kasbah neighborhood. The group chooses from a menu of tagines or couscous, cooked salads, harira soup, Moroccan pastries, dessert, and flatbreads. Sometimes the day involves visiting a local community oven to bake bread. Classes are 600 DH per person (cash only) and must be reserved in advance. ⊠ *224, Derb Chtouka, Medina* ☎ *0524/37–83–67* ⊕ *www.cafeclock.com* ⌑ *600 DH.*

★ La Maison Arabe cooking school
COOKING CLASSES | Originally a fine Moroccan restaurant run by two revered French ladies in 1946 and frequented by the pasha and visiting royals, and a favorite of Sir Winston Churchill, La Maison Arabe is now a luxury boutique hotel that continues to enjoy a reputation for great Moroccan cuisine. It was one of the first establishments in Marrakesh to offer cooking courses, which are now open to guests and nonguests in groups of up to eight people at a time. Classes are run in the upstairs modern kitchen with a translator on hand (Arabic, English, French). Participants learn about the key spices and how to prepare signature Moroccan dishes such as tagines, couscous, pastilla, pastries, and Moroccan cooked salads. The standard class is about four hours long, and at the end you eat the meal you have prepared. There's also an express one-hour course to learn the basics of Moroccan cuisine. Prices start at 600 DH per person.

■ TIP➜ **La Maison Arabe has extended their cooking school to include their private garden property in the countryside just outside Marrakesh.** ⊠ *1, Derb Assehbe, Bab Doukkala* ☎ *0524/38–70–10* ⊕ *www. lamaisonarabe.com.*

Guide to Hammams

To escape the bustling souks and crowded cities—or simply to recover from hours of trekking and touring—a hammam is the perfect retreat to soothe both body and soul in a uniquely Moroccan way. Essential to Moroccan life, hammams are best described as something between a Turkish bath and a Finnish sauna. Like the tagines used to cook the national dish, hammams provide a mixture of baking and steaming. Water pipes run beneath marble-tiled floors, which are heated by wood fires belowground. At public hammams, these fires are the same ones used for the neighborhood's bread-baking ovens, which is why you'll usually find the hammam in the medina of any Moroccan town. Inside, water arrives through taps and creates a constant, light steam before being removed by drains at the center of the room.

Walking into a public hammam for the first time can be daunting if you're imagining a luxurious bathing chamber. These aren't full-service spas, like those now found in many upscale riads and hotels—but rather a basic, unadorned public bath, with no signs for the uninitiated. Most public hammams are a popular weekend stop for a family scrub-down since some private homes are without bathrooms. It's perfectly safe, but perhaps not the most hygienic environment. If you know what to expect, there is nothing like it to make you feel you are truly in Morocco.

Origins
Islamic public baths were originally cold, and only men were permitted to use them. When the prophet Mohammed came to believe that hot water could promote fertility, the heated hammam (the word means "spreader of warmth") was inaugurated, and its use was extended to women. It soon became central to Muslim life, with several in each city, town, and village to make hygiene available to everyone in accordance with the laws of Islam. The hammam's popularity also increased because the heat was thought to cure many types of diseases. The price of entry was—and still is—kept low so that even the poorest could afford it. Unlike the Roman baths, which were large, open, and designed for socializing, Moroccan hammams are mostly small, enclosed, and dimly lighted to inspire piety and reflection. In time the hammams drew people to socialize, especially women, whose weekly visits became an important chance for them to connect with friends and neighbors.

Choosing a Hammam
If you're looking for an authentic experience, head to a public hammam. If you're shy, have a higher budget, or seek a more luxurious experience, opt for a private one. It's worth noting that all hammams are gender-segregated. When looking for a public hammam, ask at your hotel for ones that are welcoming to foreigners. Entry to a public hammam is usually 20 DH; private hammams cost 200 to 500 DH depending on treatment package. Upscale spa treatments can add 600 to 1,000 DH.

What to Bring
In a public hammam, take basic toiletries: soap, shampoo, comb and/or hairbrush, razor, a towel, and an extra pair of underwear. Moroccan women never leave a hammam with wet hair

and there are no hair dryers so you might want to bring an extra towel to use as a turban when you leave. You may also want to bring a pair of flip-flops, as the hammam's tiled floors are slippery and hot. Other items like a small plastic water jug, a scrubbing glove called a *kessel* (or kees, or kis), some dark olive soap called *savon noir*, and mineral-laden clay for conditioning hair and skin called *rhassoul* can be purchased at a local grocer or pharmacy, or often at the hammam.

Don't bring any valuables; you'll leave your belongings in an open cubby (the attendants watch diligently over these, so bring 5 DH to 10 DH for a tip). If you hire a *tayeba*, an assistant, who will basically do everything from start to finish for you, tip 20 DH to 50 DH. Private hammams usually provide individual bags containing everything you need.

Etiquette

The atmosphere at a hammam is generally relaxed, with the echo of voices and splashing water resounding from each room. As a tourist, you may be stared at, but a big smile will ease anxiety. A warm "salaam" when you arrive will also help break the ice. Once you have stripped down to your underwear and stored your bagged belongings in a cubby, take two buckets from the entry room and enter the hammam. Most hammams consist of three interconnected rooms, usually dimly lit with tiny windows in a small, domed roof. The floors are often white marble tiles—both hot and slippery—so tread carefully. The first room is warm, the next hot, and the last is the hottest.

Choose a spot in the hot room first. Then go to the taps and fill your buckets, one with hot water, the other with cold for mixing. Go back and

rinse your sitting area, and sit on a mat (which is usually provided). You can either stay here to let your pores open or go to the hottest room for 15 minutes or so.

Apply the olive soap over your body. Sit for a while before rinsing it off, then begin scrubbing your skin with the kessel mitt. Particularly in women's hammams, one of the other bathers may offer to scrub your back; it's polite to allow her to scrub yours and offer to scrub hers in return. Now rinse off with jugs of water mixed from the hot and cold buckets. You may refill your buckets at any time. Apply the rhassoul over your hair, and comb or brush until it's silky smooth, then repeat.

Finally, lather your body with regular soap, followed by a final all-over rinse, including rinsing your sitting area before leaving. Wrapped in your towel, you can relax in the changing room before dressing and going outside. If you hired a tayeba, pay him or her now, and tip the attendant who looks after the belongings. (Moroccan women never leave a hammam with exposed wet hair, and you may want to wrap yours with a towel or scarf as well; this isn't such a big deal for men.)

Private hammams follow the same ritual. Towels are usually supplied or rented and specialized products are available for purchase. In hotels and upscale spas, you won't need to take anything with you, as attendants, towels, and all products are included in the fee. Tayebas in private hammams should be tipped 40 DH to 60 DH.

Souk Cuisine

COOKING CLASSES | The very popular day-long cooking classes run by Dutch cook Gemma van de Burgt will have you mastering the art of tagine preparation before you know it. Classes meet at Café de France to shop for spices and ingredients in the medina, then you'll prepare a meal together; small groups cook at Gemma's home, larger groups cook at Riad Safa in the north of the medina. The price includes recipes to take home, lunch, and a glass of wine. Children eight years and up are welcome, too. ✉ *5, Derb Tahtah, Zniquat Rahba, Medina* ☎ *0673/80–49–55* ⊕ *www.soukcuisine.com.*

CYCLING

Marrakech City Bike Tours

BIKING | You can take a two- or four-hour guided bike tour through the city's old quarters, via the ramparts or out to the Palmery. Prices start at 250 DH per person (based on two people minimum). ✉ *Marrakesh* ☎ *0661/24–01–45* ⊕ *www.marrakech-city-bike-tour.com.*

Pikala Bikes

BIKING | Dutch biking enthusiast Cantal Bakker founded the nonprofit Pikala Bikes (*pikala* is the word for bicycle in Moroccan Arabic) as a way to promote bicycle riding in Marrakesh while creating jobs for local youths. You can book guided tours with Pikala-trained bike guides around the city. Prices start at 250 DH. Bike rentals are also available. ✉ *Riad Laarouse, Marrakesh* ☎ *0612/86–07–39* ⊕ *pikalabikes.com/.*

HAMMAMS
PUBLIC HAMMAMS
Hammam el Basha

SPAS | As far as public hammams go, this is one of the largest and most accessible (it's 10 minutes north of Djemâa el Fna). Even in its current, rather run-down condition, you get a good sense of how impressive this hammam must have been in its heyday. Instead of the typical series of small, low rooms, here you bathe in large, white-tile chambers that give a pleasant sense of space. After your bath, you'll dry and dress in a huge domed hall inset with stone benches. There are segregated hours for men (morning) and women (afternoon). It's cash only and prices start at 20 DH. ✉ *20, rue Fatima Zohra, Medina* ☎ *No phone.*

Hammam Mouassine

SPAS | Believed to be the oldest operational hammam in Marrakesh, Hammam Mouassine first opened its doors in 1562. These days the clientele is primarily tourists and the experience quite basic. Prices start at 150 DH. ✉ *Sidi el Yamani, Medina* ☎ *0688/63–33–34* ⊕ *hammam-mouassine.business.site/.*

PRIVATE HAMMAMS
Les Bains de l'Alhambra

SPAS | This candlelit marble hammam has sunken baths filled with floating orange slices and bath oils and a colonnaded patio for relaxing. Hammam with scrub starts at 180 DH. Massages and other beauty treatments are on the menu, too. ✉ *9, Derb Rahala, Kasbah* ☎ *0524/38–63–46* ⊕ *www.lesbainsdelalhambra-marrakech.com.*

Les Bains de Marrakech

SPAS | A temple to exotic beauty treatments and therapies, Les Bains de Marrakech will bathe you in milk with orange water and rose petals, massage you with argan oil, and rub you down with mint-steamed towels. A basic hammam and scrub starts at 200 DH. Reservations are required. ✉ *2, Derb Sedra, Bab Agnaou, Kasbah* ☎ *0524/38–14–28* ⊕ *www.les-bainsdemarrakech.com* ⌁ *170 DH.*

Hammam de la Rose

SPAS | As you step into the cool blue relaxation room with subtle lighting and chic decor, you might mistake this city-center hammam for a nightclub; but the gentle music, perfume, and whispering staff are pure spa. The two hammams are steaming hot all day, and a traditional, or *beldi*, hammam with exfoliation and spice-infused cleanse costs 250 DH. Massages and other treatments are available, too, and a couple's hammam can be booked as well. ✉ *130, Dar el Bacha, Medina* ☎ *0524/44–47–69* ⊕ *www.hammamdelarose.com* ☜ *From 250 DH.*

Hammam Rosa Bonheur
SPAS | Close to the Bahia Palace this hammam is in a renovated riad and offers spa services including massages and facials to pair with your hammam. Rates start at 275 DH for a hammam. Don't worry about finding it: they'll pick you up from an easy-to-locate meeting spot for your appointment. ✉ *35, Derb al Arsaa, Riad Zitoun Jdid, Medina* ☎ *0661/38–78–71* ⊕ *hammamrosabonheur.com/.*

HOTEL HAMMAMS
La Maison Arabe hammam
SPAS | A morning or afternoon spent in this sumptuous hotel's hammam will make you feel like royalty. The staff may not scrub you quite as hard as you might want, but the hammam room is beautiful and the small pool filled with roses is just for you. It's popular, so reservations are essential. ✉ *La Maison Arabe, 1, Derb Assehbe, Bab Doukkala* ☎ *0524/38–70–10* ⊕ *www.lamaisonarabe.com* ☜ *650 DH for hammam and 30-min massage.*

La Mamounia hammam
SPAS | A visit to the Mamounia's hammam is an extravagance fit for special celebrations and allows you to spend some downtime at this famously exclusive establishment. The hammam and spa is open by reservation only, required for both hotel guests and nonguests. Prices start at about 1,200 DH. ✉ *Av. Bab el Djedid, Medina* ☎ *0524/44–44–09* ⊕ *www.mamounia.com.*

Spa Diane Barrière
SPAS | Underground at the Naoura Barrière hotel, this state-of-the-art spa offers not just hammams, scrubs, and scented beauty treatments, but a heated hydrotherapy pool with water jets, aquabikes, and other amenities. It's open to nonguests. A basic hammam with body scrub starts at 400 DH for 30 minutes and includes access to the hydro pool. ✉ *Le Naoura Marrakech Hotel, Rue Djbel Alakhdar, Bab Doukkala* ☎ *0524/45–90–00* ⊕ *www.hotelsbarriere.com* ☜ *400 DH.*

La Sultana Marrakech hammam
SPAS | In the Kasbah district, close to the Royal Palace, the hammam at the hotel La Sultana Marrakech offers a variety of treatments. Prices start at 500 DH for Royal hammam and 1,500 DH with 50-minute massage. ✉ *403, rue de la Kasbah, Kasbah* ☎ *0524/37–54–64* ⊕ *www.lasultanamarrakech.com.*

Guéliz

Guéliz is the "new city" of Marrakech, built by the French in 1912 for the Europeans to live in. It has a much more modern vibe than the medina, and the buildings that line the long, wide boulevards are Art Deco, Art Nouveau, and other contemporary architecture styles. There are many global brands like H&M, Zara, and Starbucks, but you'll also discover small, local designer boutiques tucked away as well. The smaller neighborhoods of Hivernage, Victor Hugo, and others fall under the general umbrella of Guéliz.

◉ Sights

★ Jardin Majorelle
GARDEN | Filled with green bamboo thickets, lily ponds, and an electric-blue gazebo, the Jardin Majorelle is a stunning escape. It was created by the French painter Jacques Majorelle, who lived in Marrakesh between 1922 and 1962, and then passed into the hands of another Marrakesh lover, the late fashion designer Yves Saint Laurent. There's a

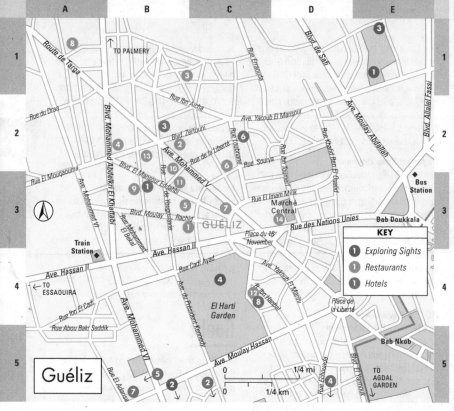

Guéliz

KEY

1 Exploring Sights

1 Restaurants

1 Hotels

French artist Jacques Majorelle made extensive use of bright blue paint when he built this garden; he later trademarked the name "Majorelle Blue."

fascinating Amazigh museum housed within the painter's former studio, with a permanent exhibit of tribal jewelry, costumes, weapons, ceramics, and rustic household tools and implements. There is also a shop and a delightful café. The Musée Yves Saint Laurent is next door.

■TIP→ **Try to visit the gardens in the early morning before the tour groups—you'll hear the chirping of sparrows rather than the chatter of humans.** ⊠ *Av. Yacoub el Mansour, main entrance on Rue Yves Saint Laurent, Guéliz* ☎ *0524/31–30–47* ⊕ *www.jardinmajorelle.com* ✉ *Garden 120 DH, museum 30 DH.*

Menara Garden

GARDEN | FAMILY | The Menara's vast water *bassin* and pavilion are ensconced in an immense olive grove, where pruners and pickers putter and local women fetch water from the nearby stream, said to give *baraka* (good luck). The elegant pavilion—or *minzah,* meaning "beautiful view"—was created in the early 19th century by Sultan Abd er Rahman, but it's believed to occupy the site of a 16th-century Saadian structure. In winter and spring snowcapped Atlas peaks in the background appear closer than they are; you might see green or black olives gathered from the trees from October through January. Moroccan families swarm here during the holidays and weekends to picnic. Come prepared as there's little shade in the main walking areas. ⊠ *Hivernage* ✛ *From Bab el Djedid, garden is about 2 km (1 mile) down Av. de la Menara.*

★ Musée Yves Saint Laurent

ART MUSEUM | Opened in late 2017, the stunning Yves Saint Laurent Museum is an ocher- and brick-color construction of cubic forms and curves, with patterns resembling threads of fabric. Inside, there is a vast collection of fashion and haute couture accessories as well as temporary exhibits and a reference library of botany, fashion, and Amazigh culture. It's next to the Jardin Majorelle, which contains the Villa Oasis, where the designer lived. A combination ticket for the garden and museum is available.

✉ *Rue Yves Saint Laurent, Guéliz* 🌐 *www.museeyslmarrakech.com* 🎫 *100 DH* 🕑 *Closed Wed.*

★ Parc el Harti

CITY PARK | FAMILY | This delightful, beautifully maintained public garden does not receive the attention it deserves. Paved pathways wind through cactus plantations, rose gardens, and exotic flowerbeds, past ornamental fountains, and through striking cascades of bougainvillea. It's the perfect escape from the city mayhem. ✉ *Rue El Qadi Ayad, Guéliz* ✥ *Entrance behind fountain on Pl. Novembre 16 (opposite main post office).*

🍴 Restaurants

Trendy Guéliz is known for its ever-changing restaurant scene but there are a number of long-standing classics as well.

Al Bahriya

$ | SEAFOOD | Cheap and cheerful, this restaurant is possibly the best catch in town. This no-frills Moroccan street restaurant in the heart of Guéliz (near La Grande Poste) is packed at night with locals getting their fish fix. **Known for:** yummy fried fish platter; popular with locals; quick service even when it's busy. [$] *Average main: DH60* ✉ *75 bis, av. Moulay Rachid, Guéliz* ☎ *0524/84–61–86* 💳 *No credit cards.*

★ Al Fassia Guéliz

$$ | MOROCCAN | Serving some of the best à la carte Moroccan food in the city, the affordable menu here includes tasty tagines, tender brochettes with saffron rice, couscous topped with caramelized onions, succulent tangia, and sweet-savory pigeon pastilla. There's an extensive choice of Moroccan wines, too. **Known for:** all-female family-run business; delicious and varied Moroccan dishes; traditional recipes from Fez. [$] *Average main: DH150* ✉ *55, bd. Zerktouni, Guéliz* ☎ *0524/43–40–60* 🌐 *www.alfassia.com* 🕑 *Closed Tues. and 3 wks in June and July.*

Amal Women's Association Restaurant

$ | MOROCCAN | FAMILY | A nonprofit center established the restaurant to help women from difficult backgrounds learn culinary skills and earn an independent living and the result is this friendly, brightly furnished restaurant and garden terrace, which attracts locals and expats for its excellent Moroccan and international dishes. The menu changes weekly but always has a mix of traditional Moroccan and international choices. **Known for:** reserve ahead for Friday couscous; great value; fresh, homemade items daily. [$] *Average main: DH60* ✉ *Rue Allal Ben Ahmed and Rue Ibn Sina, Guéliz* ☎ *0524/44–68–96* 🌐 *amalnonprofit.org/* 💳 *No credit cards* 🕑 *No dinner.*

Ayaso

$ | INTERNATIONAL | FAMILY | If you're looking for light, healthy meals or snacks Ayaso functions as both a restaurant and a specialty food store catering to vegan, vegetarian, and gluten-free diets. The fresh juices and smoothies are worth the stop alone. **Known for:** filling bowls and salads; vegan and gluten-free options; healthy breakfast menus. [$] *Average main: DH60* ✉ *6, bd. Zerktouni, Gueliz, Marrakesh* ☎ *0524/43–41–45* 🌐 *www.ayaso.bio.*

Azalai Urban Souk

$$ | MOROCCAN | The shaded entryway of this pretty little restaurant gives way to a small dining area lovingly decorated with comfy seating areas and lots of plants. It's a local favorite, especially for brunch. **Known for:** breakfast; hot or cold coconut lattes; unique approach to Moroccan flavors. [$] *Average main: DH120* ✉ *67, bd. Mansour Eddahbi, Gueliz, Marrakesh* ☎ *0669/29–31–62* 🌐 *azalai-urban-souk.business.site/.*

Catanzaro

$$ | ITALIAN | FAMILY | Perennially popular, this homey Italian spot has a good selection of salads, pasta, and pizzas at prices that make them a fabulous value. Alcohol is served, and at reasonable prices for this part of town. **Known for:** often fully booked on weekends; reasonably priced pasta and pizzas; consistent quality. $ *Average main: DH80* ✉ *Rue Tariq Ibn Ziad, Guéliz* ☎ *0524/43–37–31* ⏲ *Closed Sun.*

La Cuisine de Mona

$$ | **LEBANESE** | Just beyond the fringes of Guéliz, this tiny Lebanese restaurant is a winner on all counts, serving tasty Lebanese food, with a warm welcome in a quirky, colorful setting. The fresh meze platters include hummus, tabbouleh, baba ghanoush, marinated chicken wings, stuffed Lebanese bread, and shawarma. **Known for:** nice garden; cheerful ambience; good-value food but pricey drinks. $ *Average main: DH90* ✉ *Residence Mamoune 5, 115b, Quartier el Ghoul, off Rte. de Targa, Guéliz* ☎ *0618/13–79–59* 🌐 *lacuisinedemona.eresto.net* ⏲ *Closed Sun.*

★ **Grand Café de la Poste**

$$$ | **FRENCH** | This 1920s-style French café is a fabulous backdrop for salads, pastas, steaks, and seafood specials including oysters from Oualidia. It's long-standing favorite in the neighborhood, and a great place for a meal or a drink on the covered veranda. **Known for:** French cuisine; eclectic crowd; elegant service. $ *Average main: DH170* ✉ *Bd. el Mansour Eddahbi at Av. Imam Malik, just off Av. Mohammed V, Guéliz* ☎ *0524/43–30–38* 🌐 *www.grandcafedelaposte.restaurant.*

Le Loft

$$$ | **INTERNATIONAL** | Le Loft is popular for its chic setting and bistro menu of steaks, giant Caesar salads, pasta dishes, and various vegetarian options. Bentwood chairs, cushioned booths, bare brick walls, suspended industrial lighting, and huge pop-art prints give a funky, modern vibe. **Known for:** good cheeseburgers; lively ambience; good value two-course lunch menu. $ *Average main: DH160* ✉ *18, rue de la Liberté, Guéliz* ☎ *0524/43–42–16* 🌐 *www.restaurant-loft.com.*

MY Kechmara

$$ | **EUROPEAN** | **FAMILY** | This trendy spot has cool midcentury design, contemporary art on display, and some of the best salads in town. The menu pitches itself between French brasserie and Americana, with all-day dining including breakfast and after-work specials. **Known for:** family-friendly during the day; more happening in the evening; Sunday brunch offer; live music and DJs on the weekend. $ *Average main: DH120* ✉ *3, rue de la Liberté, Guéliz* ☎ *0524/42–25–32* 🌐 *www.mykechmara.com/food-menu.*

Patron de la Mer

$$$ | **SEAFOOD** | This fashionable restaurant that specializes in Mediterranean seafood is a great choice for a night out or long lunch. Delicious choices include seafood paella, grilled calamari, octopus tagine, lobster, and more. **Known for:** easy to find location; salt-crusted baked fish; wine available. $ *Average main: DH250* ✉ *Rue Oued el Makhazien, inside 2Ciels Hotel, Marrakesh* ✣ *Diagonal from the Royal Tennis Club* 🌐 *2ciels.com/en/rest/patron-de-la-mer-2/.*

+61

$$ | **AUSTRALIAN** | The seasonal menu at +61 reflects the laid-back Australian lifestyle, and all the produce is organic and grown within 30 minutes of Marrakesh. Cocktails and wine are served on-site. **Known for:** freshly made bread and pastas; contemporary, relaxed interior; seasonal mocktails and cocktails. $ *Average main: DH150* ✉ *96, rue Mohammed el Beqal, Gueliz, Marrakesh* ☎ *0524/20–70–20* 🌐 *plus61.com/* ⏲ *Closed Sun. and Mon.*

16Café

$$ | **INTERNATIONAL** | **FAMILY** | This modern terrace café at the edge of the Marrakesh Plaza, in the heart of Guéliz, is a popular lunch spot. The range of salads is imaginative, and even the half portion makes a satisfying meal; main dishes include chicken in mushroom sauce as well as several great pasta options. **Known for:**

big outdoor terrace on the Marrakesh Plaza; handmade pastries and cakes; lots of seating. $ *Average main: DH120* ⊠ *Marrakesh Plaza, Pl. du 16 Novembre, Guéliz* ☎ *0524/33–96–70* ⊕ *www.16cafe. com/.*

La Trattoria

$$$ | **ITALIAN** | The tables at this ever-popular Italian spot are tightly packed around the pool area and reservations are recommended if you want to eat the hallmark homemade ravioli and seafood pasta variations. Tapas and pre-dinner drinks can be enjoyed in the lush terrace bar, with jungle foliage in danger of dipping into your aperitif and background music courtesy of the resident pianist. **Known for:** beautiful inner garden; homemade pasta; relaxed atmosphere. $ *Average main: DH180* ⊠ *179, rue Mohammed el Béqal, Guéliz* ☎ *0524/43–26–41* ⊕ *www. latrattoriamarrakech.com.*

Hotels

The hotels in Guéliz tend to cater to package holiday groups, so unless you're with a family in need of a big hotel to drown out the noise you make, they may not appeal to you. They overflow with facilities but lack the character or personal service you find in an old riad. Still, we've found a few that buck the trend and are all in lively, city center locations.

Bab Hotel

$$ | **HOTEL** | This boutique hotel in the heart of Guéliz is chic and hypermodern in style, with trendy designer furniture, a space-age lounge bar, and minimalist bedrooms. **Pros:** spacious rooms; funky interior design; great location. **Cons:** patchy service; noisy neighborhood; small pool. $ *Rooms from: DH900* ⊠ *Rue Mohammed el Beqqal, at Bd. Mansour Eddahbi, Guéliz* ☎ *0524/43–52–50* ⊕ *www.babhotelmarrakech.ma* ⇆ *45 rooms* ⦿ *Free Breakfast.*

Le Caspien Hotel

$ | **HOTEL** | This modern hotel with a small pool, a restaurant serving international food, a bar area, and clean, spacious rooms and suites (many have twin beds), is a convenient local base in the heart of Guéliz. **Pros:** friendly and helpful staff; central location; good value. **Cons:** frequently booked by large groups; rooms at the front get street noise; unreliable Wi-Fi. $ *Rooms from: DH600* ⊠ *12, rue Loubnane, Guéliz* ☎ *0524/42–22–82* ⊕ *www.lecaspien-hotel.com* ⇆ *38 rooms* ⦿ *Free Breakfast.*

Dar Rhizlane

$$$ | **HOTEL** | Tucked into the residential neighborhood of Hivernage, Dar Rhizlane is a luxury boutique hotel that was designed to look like the capacious villas built during the French protectorate in the 1920s. **Pros:** excellent Moroccan restaurant; peaceful location yet near medina; wonderful service. **Cons:** least expensive rooms are cramped; breakfast not impressive; pool sunbathing area is small. $ *Rooms from: DH2100* ⊠ *Rue Jnane el Harti, Hivernage, Hivernage* ☎ *0524/42–13–03* ⊕ *www.dar-rhizlane. com* ⇆ *20 rooms* ⦿ *Free Breakfast.*

Diwane Hotel

$ | **HOTEL** | **FAMILY** | This city-center hotel has a huge, riad-style atrium, giving it some Moroccan charm along with standard hotel amenities such as a restaurant, bar, gym, spa, and pool. **Pros:** great value; excellent location; good-size pool. **Cons:** decor needs updating; buffet restaurant is inconsistent; smokey bars. $ *Rooms from: DH600* ⊠ *24, rue de Yougoslavie, corner of Av. Mohammed V, Guéliz* ☎ *0524/43–22–16* ⇆ *125 rooms* ⦿ *Free Breakfast.*

Es Saadi Marrakech Resort

$$$ | **HOTEL** | **FAMILY** | What started as Marrakesh's first casino has grown into a complex with two hotel properties as well as the Es Saadi casino and the

Festivals in Marrakesh

Since 2000, the high-profile **Marrakesh International Film Festival** has attracted the glitterati of the international movie world for screenings of Moroccan and international films throughout the city; previous special guests have included Susan Sarandon, Leonardo DiCaprio, and Martin Scorsese. Held in early December, it's the biggest, brightest, and glitziest event of the Marrakesh cultural calendar and attracts movie fans from near and far. Free public screenings are held at the Palais de Congrès, the Cinema Colisée, and Place Djemâa el Fna. For more information, visit the festival's website (www.festivalmarrakech.info).

Ramadan is the holy month of fasting, which lasts approximately 30 days, though the dates vary annually and each year start about 12 days earlier than the previous year; it's the ninth month of the Islamic lunar calendar. Muslims abstain from eating, drinking, and other worldly pleasures between sunrise and sunset. Each evening, the breaking of fast is marked by the *l'ftour* meal. Occasionally there are special musical concerts arranged in the late evenings to coincide with Ramadan. Visitors can experience l'ftour at several small street cafés in the medina and in Guéliz. **Aïd el-Seghrir** celebrates the end of Ramadan and is felt largely as a citywide sigh of relief. There are no big festivities, but families get together to share a meal. **Aïd el-Kebir,** the Day of Sacrifice, is the biggest of the religious celebrations, but has a somber tone; approximately 2½ months after the end of Ramadan, Muslims everywhere observe the last ritual of the pilgrimage to Mecca by slaughtering a sheep. Vegetarians and animal-lovers might want to avoid looking too closely.

Teatro nightclub. **Pros:** three swimming pools; family-friendly; spacious grounds. **Cons:** large pool/garden not open to all guests; big and impersonal; original hotel is a bit dated but Es Saadi Palace is magnificent. [$] *Rooms from: DH1800* ✉ *Rue Ibrahim el Mazini, Hivernage, Hivernage* ☎ *0524/44–88–11* 🌐 *www.essaadi.com* 🛏 *267 rooms* 🍴 *Free Breakfast.*

Four Seasons Resort Marrakech
$$$$ | RESORT | FAMILY | The Four Seasons is a luxurious mini-medina outside the walls of the old city: avenues of palm trees, arcades, and patios connect the low-rise pavilions, all surrounded by acres of exotic gardens, terraces, pools, and fountains. **Pros:** restaurants and bar on-site; pure luxury; family-friendly. **Cons:** patchy customer service; hefty price tag on extras arranged through the hotel; far from medina. [$] *Rooms from: DH6000* ✉ *1, bd. de la Menara, Hivernage, Hivernage* ☎ *0524/35–92–00* 🌐 *www.fourseasons.com* 🛏 *141 rooms* 🍴 *No Meals.*

Movenpick Mansour Eddhabi
$$$ | HOTEL | FAMILY | Although it's part of an international chain, the Movenpick Mansour has a distinctively Moroccan vibe, as well as a heated pool for winter swimming under the Marrakesh sun. **Pros:** multiple restaurants to choose from; great location; on-site yoga center. **Cons:** issues with air-conditioning; rooms lack character; connected to conference center so can have crossover traffic. [$] *Rooms from: DH2100* ✉ *Bd. Mohamed VI, Hivernage, Marrakesh*

☎ *0524/33–91–00* 🌐 *www.movenpick.com* 🛏 *503 rooms* 🍴 *Free Breakfast.*

2Ciels Hotel

$$ | **HOTEL** | This hotel is a great city-center base—downtown Guéliz is on the doorstep and it's close to modern restaurants, cafés, and nightlife—but it's also on a quiet corner close to the El Harti Gardens and Royal Tennis Club. **Pros:**; great location; underground spa; lovely rooftop bar. **Cons:** service can be slack; rooms are cramped; small pool. [$] *Rooms from: DH1500* ✉ *Av. Oued el Makhzine, Gueliz, Marrakesh* ☎ *0524/25–95–70* 🌐 *www.2ciels.com* 🛏 *85 rooms* 🍴 *Free Breakfast.*

🍸 Nightlife

BARS

In Guéliz, most of the modern tourist hotels have a bar with varying degrees of respectability that serves alcohol. A handful of hotels also feature a rooftop bar with views over the city; some are better than others. There are a few other late-night drinking dens scattered in the side streets south of Place du 16 Novembre along Avenue Mohammed V, but, it's worth noting that women are not always welcome. Night owls in search of something livelier should head to the trendy hangouts of Hivernage for upmarket nightclubs. Some restaurants around here have a small bar counter but usually patrons are obliged to order food.

Barometre

COCKTAIL LOUNGES | This classy spot attracts a hip crowd for excellent, though pricey, cocktails and food. ✉ *Rue Moulay Ali, Guéliz* 🌐 *lebarometre.net/.*

Café du Livre

BARS | A mash up of café, restaurant, and bar, the Café du Livre is a good place for a meal but it's also popular just as a place to meet for a drink. There's usually live music Friday and Saturday, but it can get very smoky. It's upstairs behind the Carré Eden shopping mall, just next to the Hotel Toulousaine. ✉ *44, rue Tarik ben Ziad, Guéliz* ☎ *0524/44–69–21.*

Comptoir Darna

BARS | A lively crowd gathers regularly at Comptoir Darna to take in the nightly cabaret show, enjoy the occasional live music, or to chill out with cocktails on the candlelit, plant-filled patio. The food is good, too, if expensive. There's a small dance floor for those who want to swirl to the tunes. ✉ *Av. Echouhada, Hivernage* ☎ *0524/43–77–02* 🌐 *www.comptoirmarrakech.com/fr.*

Lola Sky Lounge

BARS | The rooftop bar of the 2Ciels Hotel has sixth-floor views over the Royal Tennis Club, the old Marrakesh soccer stadium, and the Hivernage neighborhood. The bar serves tapas, beer, wine, cocktails, and coffee throughout the day and into the evening and has pleasant shaded seating areas with tables and reasonable prices. ✉ *2Ciels Hotel, Av. Oued el Makhazine, Guéliz* ☎ *0524/35–95–50* 🌐 *www.2ciels.com.*

Pearl Hotel Sky Lounge

BARS | This sky lounge, on the hotel's fourth-floor terrace, has the impressive views over the ramparts to La Mamounia and the Koutoubia mosque, as well as the Menara Gardens and beyond. It's the perfect spot for sunset drinks (or tea, coffee, or snacks). Added bonus: there's a doughnut-shape pool in the middle if you want to sunbathe and take a dip (for an extra 300 DH). ✉ *The Pearl Hotel, Angle Av. Echouhada and Rue des Temples, Hivernage* ☎ *0524/42–42–42* 🌐 *www.thepearlmarrakech.com.*

Le 68

WINE BARS | This tiny wine bar is a popular spot for early evening drinks and snacks. There's a good wine list available, and there's a small restaurant on the upstairs mezzanine that serves French cuisine at reasonable prices. ✉ *68, rue de la Liberté, Guéliz* ☎ *0524/44–97–42* ⊕ *www.le-68.com.*

CASINOS

Es Saadi casino

CASINO | Apart from La Mamounia, the only casino of note in Marrakesh is the one in the gardens of the Es Saadi hotel, set apart from the main building. Established in 1952, it was the city's first casino, though it's been renovated since then, and has a mixture of one-armed bandits and tables for roulette and blackjack. There are also poker games and tournaments, most nights from 6 pm to 8 am. ✉ *Hotel Es Saadi, Rue Ibrahim El Mazini, Hivernage* ☎ *0524/33–74–00* ⊕ *www.essaadi.com.*

DINNER SHOWS

★ Lotus Club

CABARET | The cabaret entertainment at Lotus Club is its raison d'être—and clearly built into the prices for drinks and food, which includes Mediterranean, Moroccan, and Japanese dishes. The show, entitled Oh La La!, features a burlesque-style revue of samba, Oriental, and Egyptian-inspired vignettes performed by corseted dancers flaunting feather boas, and live music from Moroccan guitar virtuoso Mahmoud "Mood" Chouki. Come around 9 pm to see the show. ✉ *Rue Ahmed Chawki, Hivernage* ☎ *0524/42–17–36* ⊕ *www.lotusclubmarrakech.com.*

NIGHTCLUBS

★ Buddha Bar

DANCE CLUBS | An impressive Buddha statue is stationed near the entrance of this hip nightspot, where an Asian vibe mixes with modern decor in the various salons. The music is an eclectic, ethnic world fusion with guest DJs, belly dancers, and even a Bollywood set. The restaurant offers a Pacific Rim fusion of Asian, Thai, Japanese, and Chinese cuisines. ✉ *Av. Prince Moulay Rachid,* *Hivernage* ✛ *Within Menara Mall complex* ☎ *0524/45–93–00* ⊕ *buddhabarmarrakech.com.*

L'envers

COCKTAIL LOUNGES | DJs, decently priced cocktails, and good food are all available at this trendy nightspot popular with a younger crowd. There are excellent cocktails and beer on tap. ✉ *29, rue Ibn Aicha, Gueliz, Marrakesh.*

Montecristo

DANCE CLUBS | In a beautiful Art Deco villa on the edge of Guéliz, Montecristo is a nonstop party destination every night of the week—on weekends it attracts crowds from Rabat and Casablanca—and it has a more intimate, eclectic vibe than the large cavernous clubs farther out of town. You can smoke *sheesha* on the roof terrace, dine downstairs, watch live bands in the lounge bar, or dance the night away to an ever-changing program of music in the first-floor club, but be aware of the omnipresent "working girls." ✉ *20, rue Ibn Aicha, Guéliz* ☎ *0524/43–90–31* ⊕ *www.montecristo-marrakech.com/en/.*

Palais Jad Mahal

DANCE CLUBS | There's an Indian maharaja vibe at the Palais Jad Mahal, once one of Hivernage's hippest nightspots and still a draw despite steep prices and iffy service. The atmosphere, excellent house band, belly dancers, and cabaret entertainment make it more than worthwhile. ✉ *10, rue Haroun Errachid, Hivernage* ☎ *0524/43–69–84* ⊕ *www.palaisjadmahal.net.*

Raspoutine

DANCE CLUBS | An outpost of the legendary Paris nightclub, Raspoutine attracts a beautiful crowd that dances the night away as DJs spin deep-house until the wee hours. There are plenty of red velour furnishings, drapes, and gilded mirrors hinting back to the original Champs-Elysée Russian-cabaret venue of the 1960s. There is no entry fee, but expect to pay top dollar for drinks at the elaborately decorated bar. Make sure to dress the part. ⊠ *10, rue Haroun Errachid, Hivernage* ✛ *Next to Palais Jad Mahal* ☎ *0616/60–94–70.*

SO Night Lounge

DANCE CLUBS | A stylish nightspot that attracts an upmarket crowd, SO has live music starting around 9 pm as well as resident DJs, a Moroccan restaurant, a licensed bar, and a garden terrace area to enjoy sheesha and alcohol-free cocktails. ⊠ *Sofitel, Rue Haroun Errachid, Hivernage* ☎ *0524/42–56–00.*

Le Théâtro

DANCE CLUBS | Hip, loud, and festive, Le Théâtro draws a late-night crowd for house music, live DJs, and circus cabaret acts. There's a cover charge most nights. ⊠ *Hotel Es Saadi, Rue Ibrahim El Mazini, Hivernage* ☎ *0664/86–03–39* ⊕ *www. theatromarrakech.com.*

Shopping

SPECIALTY STORES

ANTIQUES
Galerie Le Pacha

CRAFTS | This sprawling showroom is filled with inlaid furniture, antique doors, and an impressive carpet collection. ⊠ *79, bd. Moulay Rachid, Guéliz* ✛ *Next to Hotel Almas* ☎ *0524/43–04–76.*

La Porte d'Orient

ANTIQUES & COLLECTIBLES | This sibling of the medina's Porte d'Or sells Moroccan and Asian antiques. Shipping can be arranged. ⊠ *9, bd. Mansour Eddahbi, near Hotel Agdal, Guéliz* ☎ *0524/43–89–67.*

ART GALLERIES
BCK Gallery

ART GALLERIES | Exhibitions of contemporary art and sculpture from new and emerging Moroccan and international artists are on display here. In addition to their collections they host special events and art workshops. ⊠ *Résidence Al Hadika El Koubra, Rue Ibnou Aïcha Imm C, Guéliz* ☎ *0524/44–93–31.*

David Bloch Gallery

ART GALLERIES | This small modern gallery showcases up-and-coming contemporary Moroccan artists that lean toward graphic and urban styles. ⊠ *8 bis, rue des Vieux Marrakchi, Guéliz* ☎ *0524/45–75–95* ⊕ *www.davidblochgallery.com.*

Galerie Siniya28

ART GALLERIES | This gallery has a mission to support up-and-coming artists from Morocco and abroad while also democratizing art through access to young and amateur collectors. ⊠ *28, rue Tariq Ibn Ziad, 1st fl., Apartment 4, Marrakesh* ⊕ *galeriesiniya28.com/.*

Matisse Gallery

ART GALLERIES | This gallery has an interesting collection of works by young Moroccan artists, Moroccan masters, and the Orientalists. ⊠ *No. 43 Passage Ghandouri, 61, rue de Yougoslavie, Guéliz* ☎ *0524/44–83–26.*

★ Tindouf Gallery

ART GALLERIES | This gallery houses a permanent exhibit of Orientalist paintings, ornate inlaid furniture, and antique ceramics. There is a constantly changing program of exhibitions and works for sale by top-notch Moroccan artists and foreign painters living in the kingdom. ⊠ *22, bd. Mohammed VI, Guéliz* ☎ *0524/43–09–08* ⊕ *www.gallerytindouf.com.*

BEAUTY
L'Orientaliste

PERFUME | This charming shop specializes in exotic perfumes bottled in Marrakesh. There's also a selection of other items, including housewares including copper bowls, candlesticks, and Fez pottery. There are two locations on the same street. ⊠ *11 and 15, rue de la Liberté, Guéliz* ☎ *0524/43–40–74.*

CLOTHING

Atika Boutique

SHOES | This boutique is best known for its shoes, especially soft leather moccasins in every shade of the rainbow. ⊠ *34, rue de la Liberté, Guéliz* ☎ *0524/43–64–09.*

Hadaya

MIXED CLOTHING | This designer boutique sells T-shirts, sundresses, sandals, handmade shoes, funky bags, and accessories. ⊠ *31, rue Majorelle (also known as Rue Yves Saint Laurent), opposite Majorelle Garden, Guéliz* ☎ *0524/29–28–84.*

Intensité Nomade

MIXED CLOTHING | The chic caftan-inspired clothes here are for men and women, by designer Frédérique Birkemeyer. ⊠ *139, av. Mohammed V, Guéliz* ☎ *0524/43–13–33.*

Kaftan Queen

MIXED CLOTHING | Model-turned-fashion designer Sarah Buchan creates most of the modern bohemian styles on-site. The collection incorporates locally sourced materials and traditional Moroccan dressmaking techniques. ⊠ *61, rue Yugoslavie, Passage Ghandouri, Guéliz* ✛ *Opposite Cinema Coliée* ☎ *0524/42–07–97* ⊕ *www.kaftanqueen.store.*

Michele Baconnier

MIXED CLOTHING | This French designer boutique sells colorful high-end clothing, jewelry, babouches, and bags that offer a hip twist on contemporary design. ⊠ *12, rue des Vieux Marrakchis, Guéliz* ☎ *0524/44–91–78.*

Place Vendome

LEATHER GOODS | The gorgeous leather goods here are of excellent quality, typically much of better than what you'll find in the souks. ⊠ *141, av. Mohammed V, corner of Rue de la Liberté, Guéliz* ☎ *0524/43–52–63.*

CRAFTS

★ Ben Rahal Art

CRAFTS | This well-established shop has a magnificent array of Imazighen tribal rugs and antique carpets, and owner Mohamed Taieb Sarmi will painstakingly explain their origins and value. ⊠ *28, rue de la Liberté, Guéliz* ☎ *0524/43–32–73* ⊕ *www.benrahalart.com.*

Moor

CRAFTS | This sister shop to Akbar Delights in the medina sells a range of locally crafted items for the home as well as fashion items and accessories. You'll find handmade embroidered tunics and jackets, throw pillows, cushions, and painted lanterns. ⊠ *7, rue des Vieux Marrakchis, Guéliz, Guéliz* ✛ *Near Carré Eden Shopping Mall* ☎ *0671/66–13–07.*

★ 33 Rue Majorelle

CRAFTS | Just opposite the Majorelle Garden, this funky concept store stocks a range of fashions and quirky crafts, jewelry, and souvenirs from hip young Moroccan and European designers all working in and inspired by Marrakesh. ⊠ *33, rue Majorelle (also known as Rue Yves Saint Laurent), Guéliz* ☎ *0524/31–41–95.*

JEWELRY

Brins d'Orient

CRAFTS | The contemporary silver jewelry, all crafted on-site, incorporates traditional Moroccan motifs and semiprecious stones and an unusual modern slant. ⊠ *10, rue Majorelle, Guéliz* ☎ *0679/92–98–37 mobile.*

 Activities

HAMMAMS

Semlalia Hammam

SPAS | The oldest public hammam in Guéliz opened in 1965 and is still thriving. For the uninitiated, you can ask for somebody to help you through the process and they'll scrub you down with dark soap made from olives. For the basic use of the hammam you'll pay 20 DH; for the use of the hammam, black soap, exfoliation, and a *kaçal* (male or female attendant) to scrub you down, the cost is 100 DH. ✉ *48, bd. Mohammed El Khattabi Abdelkrim, Rte. de Casablanca, Guéliz.*

HOT-AIR BALLOONING
Ciel d'Afrique
BALLOONING | For a bird's-eye view of Marrakesh and the outlying plateaux, desert, and High Atlas Mountains, the French company Ciel d'Afrique is the most reliable and experienced. Balloon flights start at around 2,050 DH per person, including transfer to and from your hotel, and a Amazigh breakfast after you land. ✉ *Guéliz* ☏ *0524/43–28–43* ⊕ *www.cieldafrique.info* ☜ *2050 DH basic flight.*

QUAD BIKING
Dunes & Desert Exploration
FOUR-WHEELING | For those who like the more adrenaline-pumping entertainment of quad bikes, this outfitter is a one-stop shop that can also arrange hot-air-balloon rides, mountain biking, or even stand-up paddleboarding on Lake Takerkoust. One-hour quad rides in the Agafay Desert start at 300 DH. ✉ *Marrakesh* ☏ *0524/35–41–47* ⊕ *www.dunesdeserts.com* ☜ *300 DH.*

ROCK CLIMBING
Climb Morocco
ROCK CLIMBING | For beginners and experienced climbers, this professional outfit has AMGA trained instructors that run small groups for day climbs in the crags and crevices of the High Atlas Mountains, which are a two- to three-hour drive from Marrakesh. ✉ *Guéliz* ☏ *0669/88–71–55 same number for WhatsApp* ⊕ *www.climbmorocco.com.*

The Palmery

The expanse of palm groves to the north of the medina is sometimes called the Beverly Hills of Marrakesh, with its manicured golf courses, private villas hidden behind high walls, and luxurious gardens. There are also plenty of hidden hotel oases to spend the night. The Museum of the Palmery is also worth a visit for its exhibits of contemporary Moroccan art.

◉ Sights

★ Musée de la Palmeraie
GARDEN | Signposted on the Route de Fes as you head out to the Palmery, this enchanting walled garden with a contemporary art gallery is the creation of Marrakesh-born Abderrazzak Benchaabane—an ethnobotanist, perfume maker, garden designer, and local legend. The garden adjoins his home and exhibits his own collection of contemporary Moroccan art, paintings, and sculptures. Benchaabane was responsible for the restoration of the Jardin Majorelle at the request of Yves Saint Laurent in 1998, and the garden designs here clearly reflect his passion for creating beautiful natural spaces. The indoor gallery and arcades open out to a water garden with pergolas and pavilions, rose beds, and cactus gardens. ✉ *Dar Tounssi, Rte. de Fes, Palmery* ☏ *0661/09–53–52* ⊕ *www.museepalmeraie.com/* ☜ *40 DH.*

🍴 Restaurants

★ Ling Ling
$$$$ | CANTONESE | A meal at this Cantonese restaurant in the Mandarin Oriental is one of the finest dining experiences in Marrakesh. On warmer evenings opt for a table on the terrace for views of the pool garden, which is magically lit by lanterns that silhouette the surrounding palm trees. **Known for:** beautiful setting;

delicious food; fabulous cocktails. $ *Average main: DH350 ⊠ Mandarin Oriental, Rte. de Royal Golf, Palmery ⊹ Near Royal Golf Club, Rte. de Ouarzazate ☎ 0524/29–88–88 ⊕ www.mandarinoriental.com/marrakech.*

Hotels

Staying in the Palmery is a good choice if you're looking for a relaxing vacation and won't feel guilty about exchanging the medina's action for an idyll in your own private country palace. It's also close to Marrakesh's famous golf courses. The drawback is the 7-km (4½-mile) distance from Marrakesh, which necessitates a car, a taxi, or the use of infrequent hotel shuttles.

★ Dar Ayniwen
$$$ | HOTEL | FAMILY | Originally built as a family home in 1982, Dar Ayniwen (House of Palms) is now a luxurious small hotel amid 5 acres of gardens, where guests are immediately made to feel at home by the warm and attentive staff. **Pros:** friendly and welcoming service; unpretentious yet luxurious rooms; gorgeous gardens and pool. **Cons:** Internet unreliable; minimum two-night stay; meal service can be slow. $ *Rooms from: DH2500 ⊠ Tafrata, Palmery ☎ 0524/32–96–84 ⊕ www.dar-ayniwen.com ⇥ 10 rooms ⦿⦿ Free Breakfast.*

Dar Zemora
$$$ | HOTEL | The unpretentious charms of this country villa with an English-style garden is a delight, complete with croquet lawn, rose gardens, terraces, and swimming pool. **Pros:** complete tranquility; beautiful gardens; friendly English-speaking staff. **Cons:** not all rooms have private terrace; minimum two-night stay; meals are expensive. $ *Rooms from: DH2400 ⊠ 72, rue el Aandalib, Ennakhil, just off road to Fez, Palmery ☎ 0524/32–82–00 ⊕ www.darzemora.com ⇥ 7 rooms ⦿⦿ Free Breakfast.*

Les Deux Tours
$$$ | HOTEL | FAMILY | The Two Towers has a magnificent garden setting with accommodation in neoclassical villas designed by architect-owner Charles Boccara who is usually on-site to chat with guests. **Pros:** loads of communal areas; individual design; pretty pool and enormous garden. **Cons:** noise carries from other rooms; decor and upholstery somewhat tired; costs extra to have the pool heated. $ *Rooms from: DH2500 ⊠ Douar Abiad, Circuit de la Palmeraie, Palmery ☎ 0524/32–95–27 ⊕ www.les-deux-tours.com ⇥ 37 rooms ⦿⦿ Free Breakfast.*

Hotel Amanjena
$$$$ | RESORT | Just south of the Palmery, this fabulous hotel blends Moorish design details with ancient Egyptian architecture to make a peaceful paradise. **Pros:** staff is attentive without being overbearing; stunning architecture; incredible attention to detail. **Cons:** decor needs a refresh; few on-site activities; very expensive. $ *Rooms from: DH8800 ⊠ Old Rte. de Ouarzazate, Km 12, Palmery ☎ 0524/39–90–00 ⊕ www.amanresorts.com ⇥ 39 rooms ⦿⦿ Free Breakfast.*

Jnane Tamsna
$$$ | HOTEL | The word *jnane* means "garden," and this luxury property makes the most of its surroundings, with hacienda-style accommodations all surrounded by palms, olive trees, cactus gardens, herbs, and rose beds. **Pros:** exceptional gardens; plenty of pampering; charitable projects supported. **Cons:** service can be sluggish; meals expensive; swimming pools not heated year-round. $ *Rooms from: DH2000 ⊠ Douar Abiad, Circuit de la Palmeraie, Palmery ☎ 0524/32–84–84 ⊕ www.jnanetamsna.com/ ⇥ 26 rooms ⦿⦿ Free Breakfast.*

Ksar Char-Bagh
$$$$ | HOTEL | Rising like a Byzantine, 14th-century kasbah from the Palmery and surrounded by 10 acres of manicured

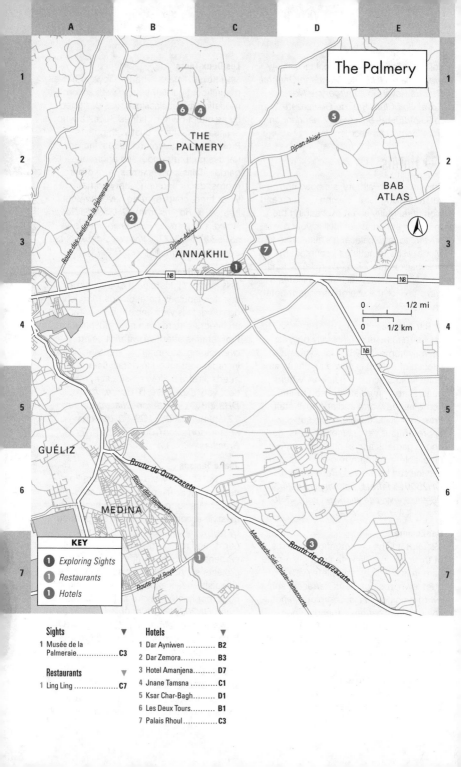

The Palmery

BAB ATLAS

THE PALMERY

ANNAKHIL

Djnan Abiad

Djnan Abiad

N8

N8

N9

GUÉLIZ

MEDINA

Route de Ouarzazate

Route des Remparts

Marrakech-Sidi Ghiate-Tamazourte

Route de Ouarzazate

Route Golf Royal

Route des Jardines de la Palmeraie

0   1/2 mi

0   1/2 km

KEY

1 *Exploring Sights*

1 *Restaurants*

1 *Hotels*

grounds, this Relais & Chateaux hotel is all about sumptuous, escape-it-all luxury. **Pros:** exclusive and private; beautiful decor; huge heated pool. **Cons:** extra services very expensive; restaurant more French than Moroccan; service sometimes falls short. $ *Rooms from: DH4500 ✉ Djnan Abiad, Circuit de la Palmeraie, Palmery* 📞 *0524/32–92–44* ⊕ *www.ksarcharbagh.fr* ⤴ *13 rooms* ⦿ *Free Breakfast.*

Palais Rhoul

$$$ | HOTEL | This sophisticated hotel set in 12 acres of gardens is the height of bohemian boutique chic, if a bit Beverley Hills. **Pros:** family-run, with owners on-site; the height of luxury; fabulous gardens. **Cons:** only main pool is heated; little English spoken; restaurant doesn't live up to the hype. $ *Rooms from: DH3300 ✉ Rte. de Fès, Circuit de la Palmeraie, Km 5 Dar Tounsi, Palmery* 📞 *0524/32–94–94* ⊕ *www.palais-rhoul.com* ⤴ *23 rooms* ⦿ *Free Breakfast.*

Nightlife

DINNER SHOWS

Le Blokk

CABARET | In the Palmery neighborhood, outside of town, Le Blokk is a dinner-cabaret venue with reasonably priced fixed-menu options (starting at 270 DH) for the Japanese and International cuisine (Moroccan dishes can be ordered by special request), though it's the live music and entertainment that are center stage. Talented singers perform songs from the last 50 years, followed by acrobatic performers who start to twirl from the ceilings around midnight. Top off the night with DJs spinning Oriental and Western dance music until around 1 am. Reservations are highly recommended. ✉ *Circuit de la Palmeraie, next to Mehdi Palace, Palmery* 📞 *0674/33–43–34* ⊕ *www.leblokk.com.*

🏃 Activities

With more than 300 days of sunshine a year, Marrakesh residents make the most of the outdoors. You can join them poolside at one of the upscale country retreats just outside of the city or find a shady spot in one of the city's gardens. Whatever you do, don't forget the sunscreen for outdoor activities. But also realize that in winter the weather can be unpredictable and sometimes rainy, which makes it the perfect time to plan a trip to a hammam or take a cooking class.

COOKING SCHOOLS

Jnane Tamsna cooking classes

COOKING CLASSES | All-day cooking classes are offered upon request in this delightful boutique guesthouse that has a thriving organic garden. An English-speaking chef gives instruction in the preparation of exquisite Moroccan recipes that are easy to replicate back home. You are invited to cook, eat lunch, and then relax by the swimming pool for the afternoon. Classes are 650 DH per person for a minimum of two people. ✉ *Douar Abiad, Circuit de la Palmeraie, Palmery, Palmery* 📞 *0524/32–84–84* ⊕ *www.jnane.com.*

GOLF

Marrakesh is a popular golfing destination and there are now more than 20 golf courses in and around town, with even more luxury resorts under construction.

Golf Amelkis Club

GOLF | The 27-hole (soon to be 36-hole) Golf Amelkis Club, designed by Cabell B. Robison, offers plenty of challenges with water features and bunkers. Unwind afterward with a drink at the bar in the kasbah-style clubhouse with the Atlas Mountains as a backdrop. ✉ *Km 12, Rte. de Quarzazate, Palmery* 📞 *0524/40–44–14* ⊕ *www.golfamelkis.com* 🔖 *From 400 DH for 9-hole course.*

Royal Golf Club

GOLF | The long-established Royal Golf Club is one of the oldest in Morocco, founded in 1933. It's a tree-filled haven, with the original 18-hole course and another more challenging 9-hole Menara course added in 2007. The casual Club House restaurant is open to nongolfers and has a delightful shaded terrace for a light and inexpensive lunch. ⌷ *Km 7, Rte. de Ouarzazate, Palmery ✢ 7 km (4½ miles) south of Marrakesh on old Ouarzazate road ☎ 0524/40–98–28 ⊕ www. royalgolfmarrakech.com ✆ From 600 DH for 9 holes.*

HORSEBACK RIDING
Les Cavaliers de l'Atlas

HORSEBACK RIDING | Half-day and full-day trekking excursions on horseback are offered from this ranch in the Palmery, starting at 500 DH for two people. Novices and experienced riders are catered to. Horseback riding out into the countryside at Lake Lalla Takerkoust and the Agafay Desert can also be arranged, with transportation. ⌷ *Palmery ✢ Near Ksar Char-Bagh luxury hotel ☎ 0672/84–55–79 ⊕ www.lescavaliersdelatlas.com.*

Chapter 4

RABAT AND CASABLANCA

4

Updated by
Helen Ranger

⊙ Sights
★★★★★

🍴 Restaurants
★★★★☆

🛏 Hotels
★★★★☆

🛍 Shopping
★★★☆☆

🍸 Nightlife
★★★☆☆

WELCOME TO RABAT AND CASABLANCA

TOP REASONS TO GO

★ **Modern-day Morocco:** However colorful the medieval cities of Marrakesh and Fez, and however enticing the Sahara and the mountain ranges, Rabat and Casablanca will show you the modern face of Morocco.

★ **Rabat's Kasbah des Oudayas:** Rabat's medieval kasbah has evocative architecture and a glorious garden overlooking the Bou Regreg River and the city of Salé.

★ **Casablanca's Hassan II Mosque:** One of the largest mosques in the world, this modern edifice makes elaborate use of traditional Moroccan craftsmanship.

★ **The old and the new in Casablanca:** Developed during the Protectorate, Casablanca's downtown architecture and the beachside promenade of La Corniche are a memorable mix of vintage French and modern Moroccan styles.

★ **Casablanca's southern beaches:** The splendid coastline between Casablanca and Oualidia features sublime beaches with famously surfable waves.

You can easily drive to Rabat from the northern cities of Tangier and Tetouan on the newer highway, although the older, slower coastal road is still open. From Rabat, you can go on to Casablanca, Azemmour, El Jadida, and Safi, where the highway ends. The coastal road will lead you farther south from this point—a good idea if you wish to explore the southern beaches, Essaouira, Marrakesh, or the Atlas Mountains. Either way you'll absorb plenty of coastal scenery. If you only have limited time to spend in the region, you may prefer to fly straight into Rabat as it's richer in traditional sights.

1 Rabat. Visitors are enticed by the cultured tranquillity of Rabat, where beautiful Moorish gardens are bordered by charming cafés. There are plenty of historic wonders, as well as nearby beaches.

2 Salé. The medina here is notable for its traditional way of life and impressive architecture.

3 Plage des Nations. Pleasant for a day at the beach, especially when combined with Jardins Exotiques.

4 Moulay Bousselham. A laid-back fishing village with a beach, on the edge of the bird-watching paradise of Merja Zerga National Park.

5 Skhirat Beach. Known for its lovely sandy beaches.

6 Oued Cherrat. A great beach, popular with surfers.

7 Casablanca. The buzzing economic heart of Morocco, with Hispano-Moorish and Art Deco architecture, a swathe of modern developments, and the splendid Hassan II Mosque on the sea.

8 Mohammedia. A charming coastal destination with beaches and fish restaurants.

9 Dar Bouazza. A fishing community and growing resort town with great beaches and oceanfront restaurants.

10 Azemmour. A wonderful place with an arty vibe and a whitewashed medina.

11 El Jadida. The fascinating old town here was built by the Portuguese.

12 Oualidia. A laid-back haven with a splendid lagoon.

Rabat and Casablanca, Morocco's most modern and elegant cities, straddle the North Atlantic coast, welcoming visitors with their varied histories and blossoming cultures.

As the political capital of Morocco, Rabat is a surprisingly sedate urban center, though it brims with historical interest and splendid architecture from both Arab and Art Deco periods. The royal city boasts many monuments from successive Arab dynasties as well as a simple unmarked cave on the coast that is thought to be one of the first sites ever inhabited by humans. Rabat and her more traditional twin city, Salé, watch one another over the River Bou Regreg, where they both offer traditional medinas full of market bustle as well as some of the most important historical sights in the country.

No more than 88 km (55 miles) southwest of Rabat is Casablanca, once an Amazigh town and now a thoroughly modern city, laid out by the French from 1912 until Moroccan independence in 1956, and now undergoing huge development. It's the undisputed commercial capital, with rich strata of history piled everywhere.

Despite the historical riches, Rabat, Casablanca, and their surrounding towns are somewhat removed from the tourism hubbub of places like Marrakesh, Fez, and Agadir, and you'll find yourself able to wander around relatively unhassled.

Breakers roll in all along Morocco's North Atlantic coast, contrasting markedly with the placid waters of Morocco's Mediterranean shore. From here, the ocean stretches due west to the United States. Much of this coast is lined with sandy beaches, and dotted with simple white *koubbas,* the buildings that house a Muslim saint's tomb.

What you can really sample when visiting this region is the urban side of North Africa, which overflows with modern structures in industrial, commercial, and leisure terms. Yet the old has been by no means ousted, so expect conspicuous contrasts: traditional dress alongside contemporary designs, and ancient Moorish edifices not far from trendy restaurants bubbling over with international tourists and young locals.

MAJOR REGIONS

Rabat and Around. Rabat is a rather laid-back urban center with stunning architecture and lots of historic attractions. Just outside the city, Salé is easy to get to and a wonderful window into Morocco's history and living traditions. The Jardins Exotiques is a nearby botanical paradise, while splendid beaches stretch both north and south along the Atlantic.

Casablanca and Around. The country's modern economic hub is an appealing blend of East and West. It's home to the massive Hassan II mosque as well as historic buildings, the long, waterside Corniche, excellent restaurants, and lots of international shopping. Nearby destinations like Mohammedia offer balmy beaches, relaxed restaurants, and calmer temperaments. A bit farther afield are artsy Azemmour, El Jadida with its fortified Cité Portugaise, and the popular beaches of Oualidia.

Planning

When to Go

During July, August, and the first part of September, temperatures are hot, beach towns are crowded, and hotels are typically more packed and expensive. April through June and October, the weather is delightful—easily warm enough to enjoy the beaches (although, depending on your tolerence level, it may be too cold to swim)—and most coastal resorts are pleasantly empty. If you don't want to swim or sunbathe, you can sightsee from November to March (and even then the weather can be quite warm). The relatively cool period lasts from around early December through the end of February, when temperatures on the coast can drop to 4°C–6°C (39°F–43°F).

Planning Your Time

Rabat has a relatively small airport, and more flights to this region land in Casablanca, so it may be best to start there. After a few days exploring the city that constitutes Morocco's economic heart, you'll probably be in search of some peace, so head north toward Rabat, stopping at Mohammedia for an afternoon. While in Rabat, spend a few days admiring the magnificent architecture, excellent museums, elegant restaurants, and lively medina. For an even more peaceful atmosphere, skip farther north to Moulay Bousselham, a bird-lover's paradise. To explore the southern parts of the area, stop by Azemmour and El Jadida on your way to Oualidia. You need a good two weeks to complete this tour fully, although some visitors prefer to focus on just the two cities and make brief day trips to some surrounding beach towns.

Getting Here and Around

AIR
The major airport in this region is Casablanca's Mohammed V International Airport, which is located about 30 km (19 miles) south of the city. While the airport in Rabat is increasingly well served, Casablanca's remains the most common international gateway for Americans traveling to Morocco, and many airlines fly there direct from North America, the Middle East, and Europe. Train, shuttle, or taxi services located outside the arrivals terminal can easily get you to the city proper, as well as to Rabat and other regional destinations.

BUS
You can reach some outlying destinations by bus if you don't wish to drive. CTM is the best bus company with air-conditioned vehicles (some with toilets and Wi-Fi) and assigned seats. The equally reliable Supratours is run by the railway company ONCF, and reaches towns not served by trains. With other bus companies, trips can be long and less than comfortable. Always make sure you use a reputable company—the roads here can be dangerous.

CTM. ✉ *2, av. Hassan II, Rabat* ☎ *0800/09–00–30* ⊕ *www.ctm.ma.*

CAR
If your stay in this region is limited to Casablanca and Rabat, you won't need a car at all. If, however, your aim is to relax in small coastal towns like Moulay Bousselham and Oualidia, a car is far more useful than the often slow and complicated public transportation to those places.

TRAIN
There is excellent nonstop train service between Casablanca (Casa Port station) and Rabat Ville (every 30 minutes at the beginning and end of the day; every hour otherwise). This is the best way to move between these two cities. You can also travel onward to Tangier, Fez, Meknès,

Marrakesh, and other destinations by train. This can be a comfortable and reasonably priced way to travel within the country. First-class carriages have air-conditioning or heating, assigned seats, and are less crowded than second class.

Travel between Casablanca (Casa Port station) and Tangier (3 hours) has been revolutionized by the El Boraq high-speed train. It stops at Rabat Ville, and at Kenitra, 30 minutes north of the capital, from where you can take an ordinary train to Meknès and Fez. The line is due to be extended from Casablanca to Marrakesh.

Festivals

There are some wonderful festivals in the region. Rabat's Mawazine music festival, usually staged between May and June, has achieved international recognition, bringing high-quality performers to Morocco. The capital also stages Jidar each September, a festival of street art: over nine days, local and international artists paint murals across the city. Casablanca hosts Jazzablanca each June, with four stages over nine days. L'Boulevard, which takes place in Casablanca in September, is an annual urban music festival that also incorporates street art.

Guides and Tours

This professional agency offers almost any kind of tour or break you could desire, from a Rif mountain escape to an urban exploration of one of the Kingdom's regal cities. It caters to all budgets and group sizes and is flexible in terms of trip type.

Hotels

It's always a good idea to book ahead in this part of the country, as Rabat and Casablanca fill up with business travelers, and the beach resorts are packed during the summer months. Casablanca has branches of the familiar brand-name hotels, and business hotels in both that city and Rabat may discount their published rates by applying corporate ones at the drop of a company's name. In the smaller coastal resorts you'll typically find midrange sea-view hotels with pools, but increasingly these towns also offer smaller, more personalized, bed-and-breakfast-type lodgings and traditional riads.

Hotel reviews have been shortened. For full information, visit Fodors.com.

WHAT IT COSTS in Dirhams			
$	$$	$$$	$$$$
RESTAURANTS			
under 90 DH	91 DH–130 DH	131 DH–180 DH	over 180 DH
HOTELS			
under 900 DH	900 DH–1,500 DH	1,501 DH–2,000 DH	over 2,000 DH

Restaurants

Morocco's northern Atlantic coast is the national center of seafood par excellence. Along the length of it the menus are remarkably similar: *crevettes* (prawns), *friture de poisson* (fried fish and octopus), *calamar* (squid), and various kinds of fish. *Fruits de mer* are always shellfish and prawns, not fish. In addition to seafood, Casablanca and Rabat offer many types of international cuisine— you'll find Italian and other Mediterranean restaurants, as well as Asian and even American eateries—and, of course, ones serving traditional Moroccan fare and French cuisine. Although it's tempting to think you can find good examples of the former anywhere, the best ones on this stretch of the coast are really limited to Casablanca and Rabat. (Locals eat Moroccan cuisine at home, so they tend to choose alternatives when dining out.)

Vegetarians should note that Moroccan salads—such as *zallouk* (eggplant puree) and *felfla matisha* (grilled pepper and fresh tomato)—are delicious.

Dining reviews have been shortened. For full information, visit Fodors.com.

Safety

Official guides in Morocco are identified by large, laminated badges worn on a lanyard around the neck. Be wary of the numerous unofficial guides who will offer to find you a hotel, take you on a tour, or, in some cases, supply hashish, or *kif,* for you. Some of them board the trains to lure unsuspecting visitors, and some will falsely claim to be students who merely wish to practice their English. To avoid these hustlers, you should appear confident and aware of where you are going. If you feel bullied or harassed, do not hesitate to summon police. As in any large city, pickpockets exist, and you should be alert and aware of your surroundings while walking around. Be careful to keep essential documents out of reach—an inside pocket is the most sensible, since bag-grabbing (often by motorcyclists) is quite common. If you have access to a reliable safe, it's smart to carry copies.

Rabat

55 km (34 miles) southwest of Keni-tra, 88 km (55 miles) northeast of Casablanca.

Rabat is a laid-back capital city with wide, clean streets, plenty of leafy parks, and a river estuary lined with restaurants and a sparkling marina. It's a city of contrasts: the voluptuously curvaceous, Zaha Had-id–designed theater rubs shoulders with the pirate kasbah (Kasbah des Oudayas); the small medina of whitewashed build-ings decorated with sandstone balances out the gracious consular mansions of

Souissi; and you can choose to cross the river via the modern Hassan II bridge or take a tiny rowboat.

A diplomatic center with a large com-munity of foreign residents, Rabat has a small medina and an array of histor-ical sites and museums, yet it exerts significantly less of the pressure that most travelers experience in a place like Marrakech. You'll generally find yourself free to wander and browse without being hassled to buy local wares or engage a guide, so it's an excellent place to get acquainted with Morocco. Attractive and well kept, with an array of good restau-rants and places to stay, it's arguably the country's most pleasant and easygoing city as far as tourists are concerned.

Rabat was founded in the 12th century by Abd al-Mu'min of the Almohad dynas-ty, as a fortified town—now the Kasbah Les Oudayas—on a rocky outcrop overlooking the River Bou Regreg. Abd al-Mu'min's grandson, Yacoub al-Man-sour, extended the city to encompass the present-day medina, surrounded it with ramparts (some of which still stand), and erected a mosque, from which the unfinished Hassan Tower protrudes as Rabat's principal landmark. Chellah, a neighboring Roman town now within Rabat, was developed as a necropolis in the 13th century.

In the early 1600s, Rabat itself was revived with the arrival of Muslims upon their expulsion from Spain, who populated the present-day medina. Over the course of the 17th century the Kasbah Les Oudayas grew notorious for its pirates, the Salé Rovers, and an inde-pendent republic of the Bou Regreg was established, based in the kasbah. The piracy continued when the republic was integrated into the Alaouite kingdom and lasted until the 19th century. Rabat was named the administrative capital of the country at the beginning of the French protectorate in 1912, and it remained the capital of the Alaouite kingdom when independence was restored in 1956. The Royal Palace continues to be the king's principal residence.

The city has grown considerably over the last 20 years, and today it has many important districts outside the kasbah, the medina, and the original French Ville Nouvelle. These include L'Océan, the seaside area that was once Spanish and Portuguese (during the French protectorate); Hassan, the environs of the Hassan tower; Agdal, a fashionable residential and business district; Ryad, an upscale residential district; and Souissi, an affluent enclave of wealthy folks and diplomats. Take a ride in a taxi, a tram, or your own car around the various neighborhoods to get a real understanding of the city as a whole.

GETTING HERE AND AROUND
AIR
Although most flyers still choose Casablanca as their arrival or departure point, Rabat does have its own, more modest, airport—Rabat-Salé, located 10 km (6 miles) northeast of the capital. It has domestic and international service. Getting into town costs about 200 DH by taxi.

AIRPORT CONTACTS Rabat-Salé Airport. ⊠ Rte. de Meknès, Rabat ☎ 0522/43–58–58 ⊕ www.onda.ma/en/Our-Airports/Rabat-Sale-Airport.

BUS
The bus station (gare routière) in Rabat is in the south of the city near the Prince Moulay Abdellah sports complex; from there you can take a taxi or a city bus into town. Service providers include CTM, Morocco's most reliable coach company.

CAR
You may prefer not to bother with a car if you're only visiting Rabat and Casablanca, but having one can be helpful if you want to explore farther afield. Major international agencies have rental outlets in Rabat itself or at the airport.

RENTAL CARS Avis. ⊠ 9, rue Abou Faris el Marini, Rabat ☎ 0522/66–72–72 ⊕ www.avis.ma. **Hertz.** ⊠ Rabat-Salé Airport, Rabat ☎ 080/02-00-77-78 ⊕ www.hertz.ma.

TAXI AND RIDESHARE
Rabat's petits taxis, which are blue, can get you from Point A to Point B, and you can flag them down just about everywhere in town. A typical metered fare will cost about 15 DH to 20 DH (after 8 pm there is a 50% surcharge). Be aware that drivers often claim to have no change, so that you'll have to pay more.

Ride-hailing services in Rabat and Casablanca are Blinc and Careem; simply download the app, book a car, and pay online.

TRAIN
Rabat has two train stations: one is Rabat-Agdal, the station that serves the high-speed train, Al Boraq; the other is Rabat-Ville, closer to most hotels and attractions. Rabat-Ville is just over two hours by train from Meknès, three hours from Fez, and four hours (via Casa Voyageurs in Casablanca) from Marrakesh. In addition, there are three trains daily (one of them overnight) from Rabat-Ville to Oujda. For Tangier, Al Boraq high-speed trains make the journey direct from Rabat-Agdal in 1½ hours (13 trains daily; five daily with a change at Kenitra to board Al Boraq), while there are also ordinary trains (eight daily, 4½ hours). Note that for onward travel from Tangier to Tetouan, Supratours has five buses daily (one hour).

TRAIN CONTACTS Office National des Chemins de Fer - Gare de Rabat Ville. (O.N.C.F.) ⊠ Av. Mohammed V, Rabat ⊕ www.oncf.ma.

TRAM
The Rabat-Salé tramway makes getting around Rabat and Salé easy and interesting. There are two lines: Line 1 runs from Salé Tabriquet, over the Bou Regreg

In 1195, Sultan Yacoub El Mansour began construction of what was intended to be a huge mosque; the minaret, seen here in the background (and now restored), known as the Hassan Tower, is all that was completed.

River, past the Hassan II Tower and the medina to Avenue Hassan II and the university.

Line 2 begins at Madinat Al Irfane and runs through Agdal, to Avenue Mohammed V and the Rabat Ville train station, through Bab Lamrissa and on to Salé and Hay Kamra.

Tickets are 6 DH and are available at station kiosks and machines. A ticket is valid for one hour if you are going in the same direction (i.e., you can get off and back on again using the same ticket, as long as you are going in the same direction within the hour). The trains run every 8 minutes during peak hours, otherwise every 15 minutes.

TRAM CONTACTS. ⊠ *8, rue Mohamed Errifai, Centre-Ville, Hassan* ⊕ *www.tram-way.ma/.* Tram Travel

GUIDES AND TOURS
Guided tours of several cities in this region are best reserved in your home country. Generally speaking, you can't

book a spot on a local guided tour upon arrival the way you can in many other countries. Atlas Voyages is recommended.

Atlas Voyages
This professional agency offers almost any kind of tour or break you could desire, from a Rif mountain escape to an urban exploration of one of the Kingdom's regal cities. It caters to all budgets and group sizes and is flexible in terms of trip type. ⊠ *22 Mahaj Ryad Centre, Hay Riad, Centre Ville* ☎ *0537/56–68–96, 0802/00–20–20* ⊕ *www.atlasvoyages. com.*

SAFETY
Rabat is considered one of the safest, least harried cities in Morocco. Travelers can generally expect minimal harassment from vendors and fake tour guides. Nonetheless, streets can be somewhat desolate after sundown, so visitors may prefer to use taxis then.

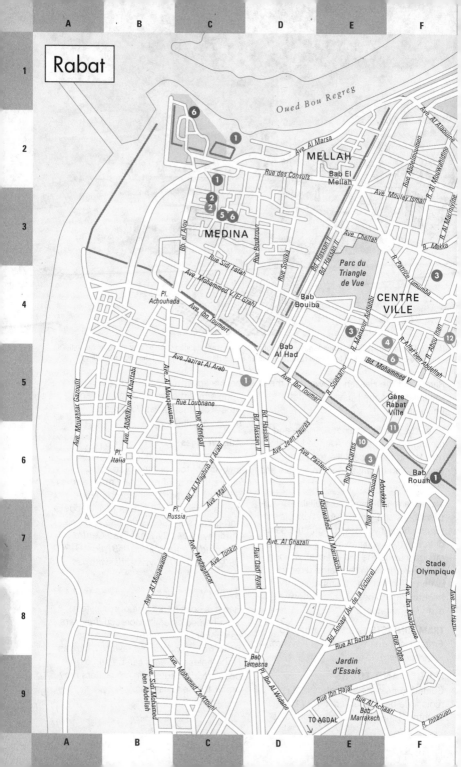

Rabat

Oued Bou Regreg

MELLAH

Ave. Al Marsa

Rue des Consuls

Bab El Mellah

Ave. Al Alaouine

Ave. Moulay Ismail

R. Abdelmoumen

R. Al Maghraoua

R. Al Maadouine

R. Mekka

MEDINA

Bd. Tarik

Rue Bannajine

Rue Soukka

Bd. Hassan II

Ave. Chellah

R. Patrice Lumumba

Rue Sidi Fatah

Ave. Mohammed V (El Gzah)

Pl. Achouhada

Ave. Ibn Toumert

Bab Bouiba

Parc du Triangle de Vue

CENTRE VILLE

R. Abou Inan

Ave. Jazirat Al Arab

Bab Al Had

Ave. Ibn Toumert

R. Mansou Addahbi

Bd. Mohammed V

R. Al Fatben Abdellah

Ave. Moukthar Gazouili

Ave. Abdelkrim Al Khattabi

Ave. Al Mouqawama

Rue Loubnane

Rue Senegal

R. Soekarno

Gare Rabat Ville

Pl. Italia

Bd. Al Maghrib al Arabi

Bd. Hassan II

Ave. Mali

Ave. Jean Jaures

Ave. Pasteur

Rue Decartes

Bab Rouah

Pl. Russia

Abdurkali

R. Abou Chouaib

R. Abdurwahb Al Marrakchi

Ave. Al Ghazali

Stade Olympique

Ave. Madagascar

Ave. Al Mouqawama

Ave. Tonkin

Ave. Dadi Ayad

Rue Dadi Ayad

Bd. Amass (Av. de la Victoire)

Rue Al Battani

Rue Opba

Ave. Ibn Khaldoune

Ave. Ibn Hazm

Bab Tamesna

Pl. Ibn Al Widane

Ave. Mohamed Zerkrouni

Ave. Sidi Mohamed ben Abdellah

Jardin d'Essais

Rue Ibn Hajat

Rue Al Achaari

Bab Marrakech

R. Innaouen

TO AGDAL

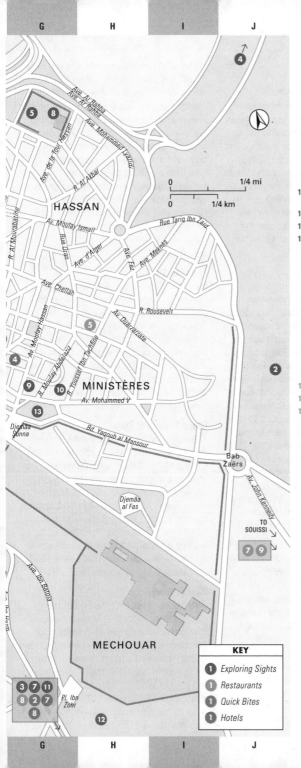

Sights ▼

1	Bab Rouah	**F6**
2	Chellah Ruins and Gardens	**J5**
3	Forêt Ibn Sina	**G9**
4	Grand Theatre of Rabat	**J1**
5	Hassan Tower	**G1**
6	Kasbah des Oudayas	**C2**
7	Lalla Soukaina Mosque	**G9**
8	Mohammed V Mausoleum	**G1**
9	Musée Mohammed VI d'Art Moderne et Contemporain	**G5**
10	Musée de l'Histoire et des Civilisations	**G5**
11	Rabat Zoological Gardens	**G9**
12	Royal Palace	**H9**
13	Sunna Mosque	**G5**

Restaurants ▼

1	Dar Naji	**D5**
2	Dinarjat	**C3**
3	La Casa Emma	**E6**
4	La Mamma	**F4**
5	Le Goéland	**H4**
6	Le Petit Beur	**F5**
7	Matsuri	**J7**
8	Paul	**G9**
9	Picolo's	**J7**
10	Restaurant Cosmopolitan	**E6**
11	Tajine wa Tanjia	**F6**
12	Ty Potes	**F4**

Quick Bites ▼

1	Café Maure	**C2**
2	Lily Gourmet	**G9**
3	Restaurant Café 7ème Art	**E4**

Hotels ▼

1	Dar El Kebira	**C2**
2	Dar Shâan	**C3**
3	La Tour Hassan	**F4**
4	Le Pietri Urban Hotel	**G5**
5	Riad Kalaa	**C3**
6	Riad Marhaba	**C3**
7	Sofitel Rabat Jardin des Roses	**G9**
8	Villa Mandarine	**G9**

Sights

Bab Rouah (*Gate of the Winds*)
HISTORIC SIGHT | Currently an art gallery, this city gate was built by Yaqoub al Mansour in 1197. To see it, go outside the city walls and look to the right of the modern arches. Originally a fortification, the gate has an elaborately decorated arch topped by two carved shells. The entrance leads into a room with no gate behind it; you have to turn left into another room and then right into a third room to see the door that once led into Rabat. ⊠ *Av. de la Victoire, Hassan, Centre Ville.*

★ **Chellah Ruins and Gardens**
RUINS | All that remains are ruins, but Chellah was an elaborate, independent city before Rabat ever existed. Presumably founded by Phoenicians, it dates from the 7th or 8th century BC. You'll see the remains of the subsequent Roman city, Sala Colonia, on your left as you walk down the path. Though these remnants are limited to broken stone foundations and column bases (with lots of resident storks), descriptive markers point to the likely location of the forum, baths, and market. Sultan Abu Saïd and his son Abu al Hassan, of the Merenid dynasty, were responsible for the ramparts, the entrance gate, and the majestic portals. The Merenids used Chellah as a spiritual retreat, and at quiet times the *baraka* (blessing) of the place is still tangible.

The entrance to the Merenid sanctuary is at the bottom of the path, just past some tombs. To the right is a pool with eels in it, which is said to produce miracles—women are known to toss eggs to the eels for fertility. The ruins of the mosque are just inside the sanctuary; you can still see the beautiful arches and the *mihrab* (prayer niche). Birds nest on the impressive minaret. On the far side of the mosque is a beautiful wall decorated with Kufi script, a type of Arabic calligraphy characterized by right angles. To the left of the mosque is the *zaouia*

(sanctuary), where you can see the ruins of individual cells surrounding a basin and some ancient mosaic work. Beyond the mosque and zaouia are some beautiful, well-maintained walled gardens. Spring water runs through them at one point, and they give Chellah a serenity that's quite extraordinary considering that it's less than a mile from the center of a nation's capital. From the walled gardens you can look out over the River Bou Regreg: you'll see cultivated fields below and cliffs across the river. On the right is a hill with a small white koubba. ⊠ *Chellah* 🚾 *70 DH.*

Forêt Ibn Sina
CITY PARK | This large, fenced park has several wide, well-packed dirt trails that pass through wooded areas. It's the perfect place for a run or a walk. There are always gardeners around to keep it tidy and plenty of other people taking the opportunity for a bit of exercise close to the city center. Access is next to the Sofitel Jardin des Roses. ⊠ *Foret Ibn Sina, Souissi.*

Grand Theatre of Rabat
THEATER | Perched on the banks of the Bou Regreg River, the gracious white curves of this Zaha Hadid–designed structure contrast with the nearby ancient Hassan Tower and the Mausoleum. Billed as the largest in Africa, the theater seats 1,800 people in its auditorium. There is a second, smaller theater as well as a restaurant, cafés, a bookstore, and outside auditorium that seats 7,000. ⊠ *Hassan* ⊕ *www.bouregreg.com/.*

Hassan Tower
NOTABLE BUILDING | At the end of the 12th century, Yacoub al Mansour—fourth monarch of the Almohad dynasty and grandson of Abd al Mu'min, who founded Rabat—planned a great mosque. Intended to be the largest in the Muslim world, the project was abandoned with the death of al Mansour in 1199. A further blow to the site occurred with the strong tremors of the 1755 Lisbon earthquake,

Rabat's medieval Kasbah des Oudayas was built high on a hill, overlooking the Bou Regreg River.

and this tower is the only significant remnant of al Mansour's dream. A few columns remain in the mosque's great rectangular courtyard, but the great tower was never even completed (which is why it looks too short for its base). Note the quality of the craftsmanship in the carved-stone and mosaic decorations at the top of the tower. From the base there is a fine view over the river. Locals come here at dawn to have their wedding photos taken. ⊠ *Hassan* 🖾 *Free*.

★ Kasbah des Oudayas

HISTORIC DISTRICT | Rabat's early history is based around this kasbah: built strategically on high ground over the mouth of the Bou Regreg River and the Atlantic, it was originally constructed for defensive purposes. Still inhabited, it once comprised the whole of the city, including the castle of Yaqoub al Mansour.

Walk up the steps to the huge, imposing ornamental gate, built, like Bab Rouah, by the Almohads. The gate's interior is now used for art exhibits. Enter the kasbah and turn right into Rue Jama (Mosque Street). The mosque, which dates from Almohad times (it was built in the mid-12th century), is on the left; it was supposedly reconstructed in the late 18th century by an English Muslim—Ahmed el Inglizi. Continue to the end of the road past a house called Dar Baraka, and you'll emerge onto a large platform overlooking the Bou Regreg estuary. Here there is the magnificent view across the river to the old quarter of Salé, and you can walk down to the water's edge. Go back along Rue Jama until you come to Rue Bazo on the left; this winds down the kasbah and past picturesque houses. Turn left, walk to the bottom of the street, and proceed down to the banks of the Bou Regreg to see the beautiful Jardin des Oudayas (Oudayas Garden), a walled retreat that you can explore at your leisure, and stop for tea at Café Maure. The garden (which is wheelchair accessible) was laid out in the early 20th century, but its enclosure dates from the beginning of the present Alaouite dynasty in the 17th century. At the top of the garden is the Musée des Oudayas (Oudayas Museum), featuring traditional costumes, and a 12th-century Koran.

✉ *Souissi* 🎫 *Museum 60 DH.*

Lalla Soukaina Mosque

NOTABLE BUILDING | Built in the 1980s by King Hassan II in honor of his grand-daughter, this mosque is proof that the tradition of Moorish architecture that produced the Court of Lions in Granada's Alhambra is alive and well. Notice the exquisite sandstone work on the walkways surrounding the mosque, and look up at the colorfully painted geometric designs on the ceilings. The mosque is surrounded by immaculately kept gardens. Non-Muslims may not enter, but there's plenty to admire from outside. ✉ *Edge of Souissi, beyond Ibn Sina Hospital, Souissi.*

Mohammed V Mausoleum

TOMB | The resting place of King Mohammed V, who died in 1961, this mausoleum is adjacent to the Hassan Tower and, thanks to a commanding position above the river, is similarly visible to anyone approaching Rabat from Salé. The tomb itself is subterranean; the terrace that overlooks it is approached by steps on each side. Looking down, you're likely to see someone ritually reading the Koran. Beyond the central sarcophagus of King Mohammed V are those of his sons Prince Moulay Abdallah and King Hassan II; the latter was interred here in July 1999 as world leaders stood by for his state funeral. Designed by a Vietnamese architect and built between 1962 and 1966, the tomb is cubical, with a pyramidal green-tile roof, a richly decorated ceiling, and onyx interior walls. A mosque, built at the same time, adjoins the tomb. ✉ *Hassan.*

Musée de l'Histoire et des Civilisations

(*Museum of History and Civilizations*)
HISTORY MUSEUM | Formerly known as the Musée Archéologique, this museum originally opened in 1931 and displays prehistoric, Roman, and Islamic-period artifacts discovered throughout the country. Roman pieces include many inscribed tablets; the Chellah and Volubilis sites are particularly well represented, and there's an ample collection of Roman bronze items. Also noteworthy is the plaster cast of the early human remains found at the Dar Es-Soltane caves, on the coast south of the city. ✉ *23, rue Brihi, Rabat* 🕿 *0537/20–03–98* ⊕ *www.fnm.ma/ musee-archeologique-de-rabat* 🎫 *20 DH includes entrance to the Mohammed VI Museum of Modern and Contemporary Art* 🕙 *Closed Tues.*

★ Musée Mohammed VI d'Art Moderne et Contemporain (*Museum of Modern and Contemporary Art*)

ART MUSEUM | Inaugurated in 2014, this striking must-see museum is an exquisite showcase of contemporary art pieces from across the nation. The permanent collection charts the evolution of Moroccan artwork from the 20th century onward, while the skillfully curated temporary exhibitions focus on fascinating themes. There's a nice café here, too. ✉ *2, av. Moulay Hassan, Centre Ville* 🕿 *0537/76–90–47* ⊕ *www.musee-mohammed6.ma* 🎫 *20 DH includes entrance to the nearby Museum of History and Civilisations* 🕙 *Closed Tues.*

Rabat Zoological Gardens

ZOO | **FAMILY** | Rabat's zoo is home to 1,800-odd animals representing 150 species, most of them residing in relatively wide enclosures. Covering more than 120 acres, it's divided into five themed ecosystems—Atlas Mountains, desert, savannah, rain forest, and wetlands—with the first of these being the highlight due to the presence of Atlas lions, which only exist in captivity. Elephants, giraffes, hippos, and hordes of magnificent oryx and gazelles also call this place home. After ogling them, you can learn more by visiting the educational farm or catching one of the scheduled daily events. ✉ *Km 13, Rte. de Kenitra, Rabat* 🕿 *0537/29–37–94* ⊕ *www.rabatzoo.ma* 🎫 *50 DH.*

Non-Muslims can't enter the modern Lalla Soukaina Mosque, but the architecture and the surrounding gardens are worth seeing.

Royal Palace (*Mechouar*)
CASTLE/PALACE | Built in the early 20th century, Morocco's Royal Palace is a large, cream-color building set back behind lawns. Its ornamental gate is accented by ceremonial guards dressed in white, blue, or red. The complex houses the offices of the cabinet, the prime minister, and other administrative officials. The palace is usually occupied by the royal family and closed to the public.

Sunna Mosque
MOSQUE | Rabat's largest and most important mosque was originally erected in the 18th century. Since then it's undergone various rebuildings but has nonetheless been sheltered from architectural anarchy, retaining its beauty and dignity to this day. The French had wanted to extend Avenue Mohammed V through the site; however, Moroccans resisted. Thanks to the martyrs of that confrontation, the mosque still stands on its sacred ground. Non-Muslims may not enter. ✉ *At top of Av. Mohammed V, Centre Ville.*

🍴 Restaurants

La Casa Emma
$$$ | **MEDITERRANEAN** | Light, airy, and full of greenery, La Casa Emma offers exquisite French cuisine featuring plenty of seafood, along with a wide range of tapas, pizzas, and pastas. There's an after-work vibe early evenings when locals congregate for cocktails and chill music. **Known for:** chic, people-watching spot; wide-ranging menu; great cocktails. [$] *Average main: DH175* ✉ *7, rue Tajmouati, Centre Ville* ☎ *0652/62–12–20.*

★ **Dar Naji**
$ | **MOROCCAN** | Loved by locals and visitors alike, Dar Naji is one of the city's most authentically Moroccan, medina-based restaurants and features interesting dishes more often found in Moroccan homes. Look for *trid* (soft layers of pastry layered with a meaty sauce) and *medfouna* (a rustic stuffed bread). **Known for:** excellent value; truly authentic menu; open nonstop midday to midnight. [$] *Average main: DH80* ✉ *Bab Al Had, Rue*

Jazirat Al Arab, Rabat ☎ *0537/26–25–28* 💳 *No credit cards.*

★ **Dinarjat**

$$$$ | **MOROCCAN** | In a palatial medina house, this atmospheric restaurant serves gourmet versions of traditional Moroccan cuisine, with live Andalusian music as a charming backdrop. Well-signposted from Avenue Laalou, it's in the medina close to Kasbah des Oudayas; in the evenings, a man with a lantern waits at the nearest medina entrance to guide you to the restaurant. **Known for:** romantic environment; gourmet Moroccan menu; impeccable service. [$] *Average main: DH200* ✉ *6, rue Belgnaoui, Medina* ☎ *0537/70–42–39.*

Le Goéland

$$$ | **FRENCH** | Located near the flower market on Place Pietri, Le Goéland is a convivial place that specializes in French-style cuisine, with lots of fresh fish and a good selection of tapas. On weekends, DJs spin into the early hours and a party atmosphere prevails. **Known for:** spirited atmosphere; genuine French cuisine; high-quality fish dishes. [$] *Average main: DH135* ✉ *9, rue Moulay Ali Cherif, Hassan* ☎ *0537/76–88–85* 🕒 *Closed Sun.*

La Mamma

$$ | **ITALIAN** | Rabat's original Italian restaurant serves pastas, pizzas, grilled meats, and other classic Italian fare. Expect an inexpensive and cheerful place with a central brick oven and a homey *cucina* vibe. **Known for:** extensive menu; well-priced Italian classics; speedy service. [$] *Average main: DH100* ✉ *6, Zankat Tanta, Centre Ville* ☎ *0537/70–73–29.*

Matsuri

$$$$ | **JAPANESE** | This Japanese franchise has restaurants in various Moroccan cities and is known throughout the country for its high-quality food. The Rabat branch is large and airy, with a relaxed vibe, a nonsmoking section, and a sushi conveyor belt. **Known for:** large menu; peaceful setting; nonstop service midday to midnight. [$] *Average main: DH220* ✉ *151, av. Mohamed VI, Rte. de Zaers, Souissi* ☎ *0537/75–75–72.*

Paul

$$$ | **FRENCH** | A café, bakery, and French restaurant all rolled into one, Paul is a popular spot in the Agdal district for coffee and pastries. The bakery, a standout in its own right, makes some of the best bread in town. **Known for:** refined, efficient service; unrivaled French pastries; beautiful terrace. [$] *Average main: DH150* ✉ *82, av. des Nations Unies, Agdal* ☎ *0537/67–20–00* 🌐 *paul-maroc.com/.*

Le Petit Beur

$$$ | **MOROCCAN** | If you're looking for genuine local food, Le Petit Beur (aka Dar Tagine) has it all: couscous, brochettes, tagines, and *harira* (a chickpea-based soup with vegetables and meat) served in a friendly, casual setting. The pretty tiled walls and painted ceilings add a further level of authenticity. **Known for:** affordable prices; high-caliber Moroccan menu; bustling atmosphere. [$] *Average main: DH140* ✉ *8, rue Damas, Centre Ville* ☎ *0537/73–13–22* 🌐 *www.lepetit-beur.ma* 🕒 *Closed Sun.*

Picolo's

$$$$ | **MEDITERRANEAN** | This friendly Mediterranean-style restaurant offers "cuisine du marché," or cooking from the market. It serves a broad selection of fish, meat, and pasta dishes in a charming setting: white linens top the tables in the cheery dining room, and the beautiful airy garden, where intimate tables snuggle amid the greenery, is a delight. **Known for:** great for outside dining; fresh produce from the market; lovely tapas. [$] *Average main: DH190* ✉ *149, rte. des Zaers, Souissi* ☎ *0537/63–69–69.*

Restaurant Cosmopolitan

$$$$ | **FRENCH** | Set in an exquisite Art Deco villa, this restaurant focuses on refined French classics. Alfresco diners can choose a seat on the swish yet

sunny garden patio; inside, the dining rooms stretch out with French poise. **Known for:** sophisticated atmosphere; fantastic 1930s-style dining areas; decadent dessert menu. $ *Average main: DH190* ✉ *Av. Ibn Toumart, Centre Ville* ☎ *0537/20–00–28.*

Tajine wa Tanjia

$ | MOROCCAN | This is the place to discover a delicacy from Marrakesh—the *tanjia* (a type of casserole slow-cooked in a large earthen jar in the coals at the hammam)—along with other authentic Moroccan dishes. It's cozy and friendly, with very reasonable prices. **Known for:** Moroccan music; bustling atmosphere; friendly, unpretentious service. $ *Average main: DH85* ✉ *9, rue Baghdad, Centre Ville* ☎ *0537/72–97–97* ▭ *No credit cards* ⊘ *Closed Sun.*

★ Ty Potes

$ | FRENCH | Set among verdant gardens, this enchanting eatery offers a menu that encapsulates the Brittany region of France: think luscious salads and buckwheat crepes oozing with all you can imagine, as long as it's (mostly) French. The experience is made even better by the fantastic service and the pleasant, knowledgeable staff. **Known for:** good wine list; Breton-style ingredients; great daily specials. $ *Average main: DH75* ✉ *11, rue Ghafsa, Hassan* ☎ *0537/70–79–65* ⊕ *www.typotes.com* ⊘ *Closed Sun. and Mon.*

☺ Coffee and Quick Bites

Café Maure

$ | MOROCCAN | FAMILY | The Café Maure is a charming place in the Oudayas gardens of the kasbah to pause for a glass of tea and local pastries. The shaded terrace is decorated with mosaic tilework and looks across the river to Salé. **Known for:** location in the Oudayas gardens; gazelle's horns pastries; lovely terrace. $ *Average main: DH50* ✉ *Oudayas Museum, 1, bd.*

Al Marsa, Medina ☎ *0537/73–15–37, 0658/31–71–81* ▭ *No credit cards.*

Lily Gourmet

$ | DESSERTS | This top-of-the-line patisserie has a spectacular array of cakes, tarts, macarons, cheesecakes, and cookies that you can take away in a box or enjoy on the spot. A pleasing array chairs and couches inside and out makes this a very pleasant spot for coffee and a treat. **Known for:** perfect for morning coffee or afternoon tea; laid-back atmosphere; beautiful cakes. $ *Average main: DH50* ✉ *6, rue Soumaya, Agdal* ☎ *0661/11–48–78* ⊕ *www.lily-gourmet.com.*

Restaurant Café 7ème Art

$ | MOROCCAN | FAMILY | This landmark café in downtown Rabat has been around since 1997 and serves the city's best milk shakes and ice cream in a large, leafy garden. Always busy with students and businesspeople, there's Wi-Fi to check your email while you drink your coffee. **Known for:** legendary desserts and coffee; efficient service; relaxed atmosphere under the trees. $ *Average main: DH65* ✉ *Av. Allal Ben Abdellah, Centre Ville* ☎ *0537/73–38–87.*

Hotels

Dar El Kebira

$$ | B&B/INN | This luxurious guesthouse in the heart of the Rabat medina impresses with its beautiful traditional architecture and decor. **Pros:** authentic Moroccan riad guesthouse; excellent service; traditional hammam. **Cons:** ground-floor rooms can be noisier than those upstairs; not easy to find in the medina (ask to be met on the periphery); no vehicular access, but staff will help with your luggage. $ *Rooms from: DH1265* ✉ *Rue des Consuls, 1 Impasse Belghazi, Medina* ☎ *0537/72–49–06* ⊕ *www.darelkebira. com* ⊐ *10 rooms* ⫿⃝⃝ *Free Breakfast.*

★ Dar Shâan

$$ | B&B/INN | This beautiful medina guesthouse has a lovely mosaic-tiled courtyard

The mausoleum of King Mohammed V is decorated with geometric patterns because Islamic traditions avoid figurative decorative images.

and comfortable rooms that faultlessly combine modernity with tradition. **Pros:** elegant rooms; stupendous views from the roof terrace; easy to find in the medina. **Cons:** top floor rooms can be noisy if children are using the rooftop pool; no bathtubs, only showers; no vehicular access. $ *Rooms from: DH1000* ⊠ *24, rue Jirari, Medina* ☎ *0537/72–20–20* ⊕ *www.dar-shaan.com* ⬅ *11 rooms* ⦿ *Free Breakfast.*

Le Pietri Urban Hotel

$ | HOTEL | In an excellent location in the center of town, between the Mohammed V art museum and the flower market, Le Pietri is a comfortable, modern hotel decorated with midcentury style and bold colors. **Pros:** easy walk to the railway station and the bus to the airport; helpful staff; an elevator. **Cons:** no walk-in showers: they're all over the bathtubs; no traditional Moroccan decor; no pool. $ *Rooms from: DH795* ⊠ *4, rue Tobrouk, Centre Ville* ☎ *0537/70–78–20* ⊕ *www.lepietri.com* ⬅ *35 rooms* ⦿ *Free Breakfast.*

★ Riad Kalaa

$$ | HOTEL | A gorgeous interior courtyard with a relaxing terrace and a small plunge pool, plus views of Rabat's rooftops help make this 17th-century medina house one of the most beautiful riads in town. **Pros:** there are several other riads in the same group; great service; very stylish. **Cons:** watch your head if your sleeping area is in a mezzanine; if there's a party on the terrace, it can be noisy; may be difficult to find (the riad will send someone to meet you on request). $ *Rooms from: DH1200* ⊠ *3–5, rue Zebdi, Medina* ☎ *0537/20–20–28, 0661/19–95–16* ⊕ *www.rabatriads.com* ⬅ *11 rooms* ⦿ *Free Breakfast.*

Riad Marhaba

$ | B&B/INN | This comfortable, well-restored spot has a welcoming atmosphere and attractive rooms that retain their medina-esque architectual features. **Pros:** rooftop terrace with great views; friendly atmosphere; comfortable rooms with a local look. **Cons:** medinas are pedestrianized, so arrange a porter if your bags are

The Museum of Modern and Contemporary Art opened in 2014 and was the first-large museum built in Morocco since the country's independence from France in 1956.

too heavy; as with all medina houses, rooms can be somewhat dark; a little tricky to find. [$] *Rooms from: DH570* ✉ *Rue Açam, Medina* ☎ *0537/70–65–54* 🌐 *www.riadmarhaba.com* 💳 *No credit cards* 🛏 *4 rooms* 🍴 *Free Breakfast.*

Sofitel Rabat Jardin des Roses

$$$$ | **HOTEL** | A somewhat imposing block of a hotel close to the Royal Palace, this luxury lodging allows guests to escape the city's bustle in 17 gorgeous acres of parkland, with the rose gardens for which the hotel is named. **Pros:** tranquil atmosphere; a true luxury hotel; beautiful grounds. **Cons:** relatively far from public transport; not for those looking for more intimate lodgings; expensive. [$] *Rooms from: DH2300* ✉ *Quartier Aviation, Av. Imam Malek, Impasse Souissi, Souissi* ☎ *0537/67–56–56* 🌐 *sofitelrabatjardin.guestreservations.com* 🛏 *229 rooms* 🍴 *No Meals.*

La Tour Hassan

$$$$ | **HOTEL** | If you want a luxury hotel that reflects classic Moroccan style, the Tour Hassan is ideal. **Pros:** lovely gardens and pool; near the city center; authentic decor. **Cons:** some rooms are a little small; rooms in north wing are near a bar and can be loud; rather expensive. [$] *Rooms from: DH3500* ✉ *26, rue Chellah, Hassan* ☎ *0537/23–90–00* 🌐 *www.latourhassanpalace.com* 🛏 *143 rooms* 🍴 *No Meals.*

★ Villa Mandarine

$$$$ | **HOTEL** | Located in a residential neighborhood, this spectacular villa offers all you need to be truly at ease: superb service, excellent decor with interesting art, and outstanding classic-meets-contemporary French and Moroccan cuisine. **Pros:** beautiful gardens; romantic setting; good on-site facilities, including a relaxing hammam. **Cons:** limited public transportation; away from the town center, so not ideal for those wanting proximity to nightlife or shopping; expensive. [$] *Rooms from: DH2300* ✉ *19, rue Ouled Bousbaa, Souissi* ☎ *0537/75–20–77* 🌐 *www.villamandarine.com* 🛏 *36 rooms* 🍴 *Free Breakfast.*

Nightlife

BARS AND CLUBS

Amnesia

DANCE CLUBS | Drawing a party-loving crowd, the city's original nightclub has been going strong for over 30 years and shows no sign of stopping. If you're after something lively, look no farther. The fun doesn't really start until after midnight. ⊠ *18, rue Monastir, Centre Ville* ☎ *0652/07–52–70.*

★ Le Bistrot du Pietri

LIVE MUSIC | Inside the Pietri Urban Hotel, Rabat's most popular jazz restaurant features superb musicians every Friday and Saturday night. Expect anything from bebop and Latin to jazz fusion. On weeknights, the bar fills up with the after-work crowd and gets lively. The food is excellent, too, with a menu embodying a good deal of Mediterranean tastes and some genuine inventiveness from the chef. ⊠ *4, rue Tobrouk, Centre Ville* ☎ *0537/70–78–20.*

Le Dhow

BARS | Permanently moored on the Bou Regreg River, this boat has several decks on which you can eat, drink, and people-watch while a DJ spins ambient music. Pull up a quirky armchair as the sun sets and watch the twinkly lights of the kasbah splash the historic walls of the medina, or gaze across the river to the marina in Salé. Tapas, burgers, salads, and pizzas are available on the lower deck bistro, and there's a more formal restaurant above. ⊠ *Quai de Bou Regreg, Av. Al Marsa, Rabat* ☎ *0537/70–23–02* ⊕ *www.ledhow.com.*

5ème Avenue Afro Club

DANCE CLUBS | Featuring DJs with music from Senegal, Mali, Ivory Coast, and more points south, the 5ème Avenue Afro Club is open from 6 pm to 4:30 am. ⊠ *4, av. Bin Al Ouidane, Agdal* ☎ *06389/97–51–31.*

O'Goethe 2.0

BARS | Part of the Goethe Institute, this combination bar-restaurant-cultural hub is packed every night. Drinks and food are reasonably priced, with pizzas being the favorite menu item, and the interior is charming. There's a large screen for televised sports, plus a garden out the back. There's often live music, too. ⊠ *26, rue Oqba Ibn Nafiq, Agdal* ☎ *0537/68–21–84.*

Shopping

Rabat's medina has shops offering Moroccan furniture, clothing, artwork, and locally made crafts, while the new city has various modern shopping centers. The **Agdal** neighborhood has a high concentration of furniture and antiques stores, while the lower part of **Avenue Mohammed V** is a good place to buy traditional Moroccan garments.

CRAFTS

Ensemble Artisanal

CRAFTS | Near the River Bou Regreg there is a series of small workshops where you can watch artisans create Morocco's various handicrafts. You'll find everything from traditional mosaic tile work, embroidery, leatherwork, and painted wood to brass, pottery, and carpets. Items can be purchased hassle-free at fixed prices, which are a little higher than the well-negotiated ones in nearby Rue des Consuls. ⊠ *6, av. al Marsa, Espace les Oudayas, Rabat* ☎ *0537/73–05–07.*

Rue des Consuls

CRAFTS | The medina's Rue des Consuls is the place to shop for handicrafts and souvenirs in Rabat: it's pedestrian-only, has a pleasant atmosphere, and imposes no real pressure to buy, aside from the typical encouragements. Among the treasures here are Imazighen jewelry, leather goods, wooden items, brass work, traditional clothing, and slippers. You can also peruse red and orange Zemmour carpets from Khémisset, near

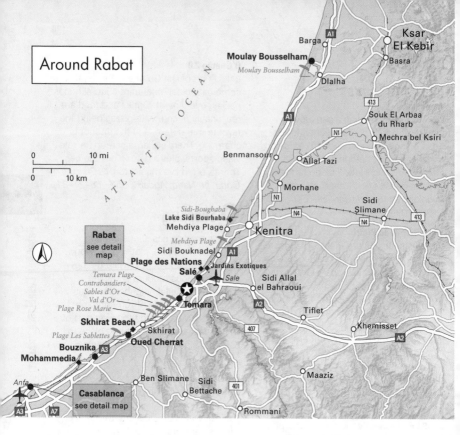

Around Rabat

ATLANTIC OCEAN

0   10 mi
0   10 km

Ksar El Kebir

Barga

Basra

Moulay Bousselham

Moulay Bousselham

Dlalha

Souk El Arbaa du Rharb

Mechra bel Ksiri

Benmansour

Allal Tazi

Morhane

Sidi Slimane

Sidi-Boughaba
Lake Sidi Bourhaba
Mehdiya Plage

Mehdiya Plage

Kenitra

Sidi Bouknadel

Plage des Nations

Jardins Exotiques

Salé

Sale

Sidi Allal el Bahraoui

Temara Plage
Contrabandiers
Sables d'Or
Val d'Or
Plage Rose Marie

Temara

Tiflet

Khemisset

Skhirat Beach

Plage Les Sablettes

Skhirat

Oued Cherrat

Bouznika

Mohammedia

Maaziz

Anfa

Ben Slimane

Sidi Bettache

Casablanca
see detail map

Rommani

Rabat
see detail map

Meknès; deep-pile Rabati carpets, in predominantly blue-and-white designs; and orange, black, and white Glaoui rugs. Some of the larger shops take credit cards.

■ TIP→ Try to visit on a Monday or Thursday morning when the entire street turns into a carpet market. ⊠ Rabat.

 Activities

GOLF

★ Royal Golf Dar es Salam

GOLF | Morocco's most famous golf club is on the road toward Romani, at the far edge of the Souissi area. Designed by Robert Trent Jones and ranked among the best in the world, it includes two 18-hole courses and one 9-hole course

in 162 verdant acres. ⊠ Km 9, Av. Mohamed VI – Rte. des Zaers, Souissi ☎ 0537/75–58–64 ⊕ www.royalgolfdares-salam.com ⅄. Greens fees 18 holes 1200 DH; 9 holes 650 DH.

HAMMAMS

Hammam & Spa Dar El Kebira

SPAS | In a lovely guesthouse in the medina, this spa offers an authentic hammam experience along with a host of other pampering treatments, including ones that utilize henna and traditional ghassoul clay. ⊠ 1, rue des Consuls, Impasse Belghazi, Medina ☎ 0537/72–49–06 ⊕ www.darelkebira.com/en/luxury-riad-rabat-services/hammam-spa.

Salé

37 km (23 miles) southwest of Kenitra, 13 km (8 miles) northeast of Rabat across the Bou Regreg River.

Salé, the country's second-most-populated city, is a great place to experience unspoiled, hassle-free Moroccan culture. It was probably founded around the 11th century, and in medieval times became the premier trading harbor on this part of the Atlantic coast. At the beginning of the 17th century, it joined Rabat in welcoming Muslims expelled from Spain. The two were rivals for more than 100 years following this, but Rabat eventually gained the upper hand. Today Salé appears poorer than its smart neighbor, but is an important cradle of Moroccan history. The medina alone is worth the journey both for its monuments and its authenticity. Expect to see more people in traditional dress or practicing traditional crafts than you would in most other Moroccan large-city medinas.

GETTING HERE AND AROUND
The Rabat–Salé tramway is the ideal option for traveling between the two cities, costing just 6 DH per ride. Note that only grands taxis can make the journey between Salé and Rabat, not petit taxis.

For extra romance, you can be rowed in a small blue boat over the river from Salé to the Kasbah Les Oudayas or to the Grand Théâtre. The 20- to 30-minute trip costs 50 DH.

TIMING AND PRECAUTIONS
Most travelers visit Salé just for the day. It's a relatively safe city, with very little harassment; however, if you do feel threatened, don't hesitate to summon police.

 Sights

Salé's most interesting sights are located in and around the medina—and there are plenty of them. A good place to

start your tour is at Bab Lamrissa, the southernmost entrance to the medina, next to the tram station. Walk northwest along the city wall, stopping off at the gold and spice markets in the center, then continue on to the Great Mosque and the Pirate's Prison. Don't worry if you lose track of where you are within the medina; many a shop will distract you but you're never far from an entry gate. If you stay at or eat at The Repose, you can ask for a copy of their excellent map of the medina.

If you feel like traveling a little farther afield, the Jardins Exotiques and the beautiful Plage des Nations to the north of the city are well worth a visit.

Abou el Hassan Merenid Medersa
NOTABLE BUILDING | Turn left around the corner of the Great Mosque, and you'll see on your right the Abou el Hassan Medersa. Built by the Merenid sultan of that name in the 14th century, it's a fine example of the traditional Koranic school. Like the Bou Inania in Fez or the Ben Youssef in Marrakesh, this madrassa has beautiful intricate plasterwork around its central courtyard, and a fine mihrab (prayer niche) with a ceiling carved in an interlocking geometrical pattern representing the cosmos. Upstairs, on the second and third floors, you can visit the little cells where the students used to sleep, and from the roof you can see the entire city. ✉ *Rue Ash al Shaiara, Salé* 🖬 *60 DH.*

Battlements and Fortresses of Salé
HISTORIC SIGHT | A heavily fortified town for centuries, Salé still has many traces of its eventful history preserved within the old medina walls. Many landmarks in the area have been named as national heritage sites or monuments. **Borj Bab Sebta** is an 11th-century, square-shape fortress situated at the Sebta gate into the old medina. **Borj Adoumoue**, also called the Old Sqala, is an 18th-century bastion, where cannons gaze over the waters to this day. Nearby is **Borj Roukni**,

also called Borj Kbira, or the large fortress, a semicircular, 19th-century edifice built to counter attacks by the French. There's also a fantastic kasbah (although in need of preservation) known as the **Gnawa Kasbah**, built by Moulay Ismail in the 1700s. This lies near the beach 3km north of the medina and is now home to the National Circus School Shems'y. ⊠ *Medina, Salé.*

★ Complexe des Potiers

STORE/MALL | Salé has long been known throughout the country, and beyond, for its local pottery. At this particular complex (just off the road toward Fez, to the right after the river from Rabat) visitors can browse through a whole series of pottery shops, each with its own style; you might also get the chance to chat with a potter or maybe even try your own hand at clay work. Other crafts have been added as well, notably bamboo and straw work and mosaic-tile furnishings. ⊠ *Oulja, Rte. Ain Houalla, Salé.*

Djemâa Kabir (*Great Mosque*)

MOSQUE | A few steps from the tomb of Sidi Abdellah ben Hassoun is the great mosque known as Djemâa Kabir. Built by the Almohad dynasty in the 12th century, this beautiful structure is the third-largest mosque in Morocco, after the Hassan II in Casablanca and the Kairaouine in Fez. Non-Muslims cannot enter. ⊠ *Zanqat Sidi Abdellah ben Hassoun, Salé.*

★ Jardins Exotiques (*Exotic Gardens*)

GARDEN | FAMILY | Just 10 km (6 miles) north of Salé, you'll find the extraordinary Jardins Exotiques, which were created in the mid-20th century by a Frenchman named Marcel Françòis, who used to play classical music to his plants. Planned to represent different regions (like Polynesia, Brazil, or Japan), the gardens are a haven for birds and frogs. There are two circuits of different lengths and the walkways and bridges make this a wonderful playground and educational experience for children, too. Since Françòis's death in 1999, the property has been maintained by the government and has recently been well restored. A touching autobiographical poem forms his epitaph at the entrance.

Many people combine a visit to the gardens with a day at the beach at Plage des Nations, another 10 km (6 miles) along the coast. A private taxi organized by your hotel costs 300 DH for the return trip, including the driver's wait while you explore the gardens. ⊠ *Km 13, Rte. de Kenitra, Bouknadel* ☎ *0537/82–27–56* ⊕ *www.jardinsexotiques.com* ⊠ *20 DH.*

Pirates' Prison (Borj Adoumoue)

HISTORIC SIGHT | The Borj Adoumoue, which means "fortress of tears," was a Pirates' Prison in the city walls of Salé and is now a museum. It was built by the Salé Rover pirates as their headquarters. Cannons pierce the walls and there are underground dungeons. ⊠ *Av. Sidi Ben Achir, Salé, Salé* ⊠ *20 DH.*

Sidi Abdellah ben Hassoun Tomb

TOMB | One of the streets in Salé's medina is Zanqat Sidi Abdellah ben Hassoun—named after the town's patron saint. His magnificent tomb is situated here, next to the Great Mosque. He died in Salé in 1604. ⊠ *Zanqat Sidi Abdellah ben Hassoun, Salé.*

Zaouia Tijania

NOTABLE BUILDING | Close to the Great Mosque (Djemâa Kabir) and the Abou el Hassan Merenid Medersa is the *zaouia*—a shrine to a Muslim saint of the Tijani order, a mystical Sufi sect founded by Shaykh Ahmad al-Tijani (1739–1815). ⊠ *Zaouia Tijania, Salé.*

🍴 Restaurants

Al Marsa

$$$$ | SPANISH | One of the swanky restaurants in Salé's marina, Al Marsa—meaning "port" in Arabic—serves Spanish food in a glass-enclosed dining room overlooking the Bou Regreg River. The menu revolves around fish and seafood, the produce is fresh, and the dishes imaginative (if Spanish cuisine isn't your thing, Al Marsa has a sister restaurant right next door, also called Al Marsa, serving Italian fare). **Known for:** great paella; stunning views; buzzy, European-style atmosphere. $ *Average main: DH220* ⊠ *Port de Plaisance, Marina Bouregreg, Salé* ☎ *0537/84–58–18* ⊕ *www.almarsa. ma.*

The Repose restaurant

$$ | **VEGETARIAN** | The sophisticated restaurant in The Repose riad is a destination in its own right, where the chef uses local ingredients to prepare an entirely vegetarian menu (unique in Morocco). Reservations are essential if you're not staying at the hotel. **Known for:** upscale setting; vegetarian; inventive, delicious food. $ *Average main: DH100* ⊠ *The Repose, 17, Zankat Talaâ, Ras Chejra, Medina, Salé* ⊕ *www.therepose.com/ copy-of-about.*

 ## Hotels

★ The Repose

$ | **HOTEL** | **FAMILY** | This outstanding riad is a veritable sanctuary set over three floors and run by a lovely Anglo-Moroccan couple. **Pros:** excellent service including a helpful, hand-drawn map; exceptional food; beautiful, restful environment. **Cons:** in a pedestrianized area, so no transport right to the door; interior is a little dark; can be hard to find. $ *Rooms from: DH495* ⊠ *17, Zankat Talaâ, Ras Chejra, Medina, Salé* ☎ *0537/88–29–58* ⊕ *www. therepose.com* ⇄ *7 rooms* ⵏ⃝ *Free Breakfast.*

 ## Shopping

Souk Laghzal

MARKET | A couple of times a week, usually Tuesday and Thursday, an auction is held in the wool market square. At this quirky event, a crowd sits in a circle around the auctioneer, who sells off an unpredictable array of items that might include an old caftan, a plastic chandelier, or a beautiful pottery piece—you never know. A jumble sale with heaps of low-priced clothing takes place nearby. As the square's name would suggest, this is also a wool area; you can buy dyed wool on one side of the square and wool products (carpets and the like) on the other. ⊠ *Medina, Salé.*

Plage des Nations

28 km (17 miles) northeast of Rabat, 4 km (2½ miles) north of Bouknadel.

On the coast just north of the small town of Bouknadel, the sandy expanse of Plage des Nations stretches north for several miles. A small development of holiday homes has sprung up here, along with a golf course to the north.

GETTING HERE AND AROUND

Shared grands taxis run regularly from Salé to Plage des Nations in summer. Private taxis can be chartered from Rabat, Salé, and Kenitra throughout the year. From Rabat, a round-trip including the driver's wait while you visit Jardins Exotiques en route to the beach, costs 300 DH.

TIMING AND PRECAUTIONS

Most travelers visit Plage des Nations for the day en route to Rabat, on their way north or as a day trip from Rabat. Combining the beach with a visit to the Jardins Exotiques is a great idea. Plage des Nations is generally safe, with minimal hassling of visitors. The beach, however, is rather secluded after sundown, so caution is advised for those desiring an evening walk on the shore.

 ## Sights

Plage des Nations

BEACH | This magnificent beach, also known simply as "Nations," is so long that even during the busiest times you'll probably find some space along the stretch. The water is swimmable, but there may be strong currents, so caution should be observed. The sands are cleaned daily in summer, although some litter is possible in colder months. It's a hot spot for surfers and paragliders; sunbathers can rent parasol and loungers for reasonable prices. The beach is accessed by driving along the N1 from Salé and turning left just north of the small town of Sidi Bouknadel, or ask your hotel to organize a round-trip by taxi. **Amenities**: lifeguards (in season); parking; food and drink. **Best for**: swimming; surfing; walking. ⊠ *Plage des Nations*.

Activities

Des Nations Sunrise Surf Club
SURFING | FAMILY | Recognized by the Fédération Royale Marocaine de Surf et Bodyboard (Royal Moroccan Federation of Surfing and Bodyboarding), this outfit offers classes for all ages and runs competitions. Equipment can be hired. ⊠ *Corniche, Plage des Nations* ☎ *0662/70–55–38*.

Moulay Bousselham

82 km (51 miles) northeast of Kenitra, 150 km (93 miles) northeast of Rabat, 125 km (78 miles) southwest of Tangier.

Equidistant from Rabat and Tangier, the laid-back fishing village of Moulay Bousselham has a breathtaking lagoon and beach. Situated in the Merja Zerga National Park, it's one of northern Morocco's prime bird-watching locations, with boat trips organized to see thousands of herons, pink flamingos, sheldrakes, gannets, and more. The whole area is considered a wetland protected by the Ramsar Convention (an international treaty working for the conservation of wetlands) as well as by the village's patron saint. The place has little more than a couple of streets with a smattering of cafés and souvenir shops. It's virtually empty in

the cooler months but very popular with Moroccans in summer.

GETTING HERE AND AROUND
To get to Moulay Bousselham from Rabat, Casablanca, Tangier, Meknès, or Fez, take the train to Souk el-Arbaa du Rharb, from where you can take the bus or a taxi to the bus station at Moulay Bousselham.

TIMING AND PRECAUTIONS
Most travelers stay in Moulay Bousselham for a couple of nights. It's generally considered safe, with most annoyances stemming from vendors hawking their wares. The village does become somewhat desolate after sundown, so take the usual precautions.

TOURS
Hassan Dalil
BOAT TOURS | Bird expert Hassan Dalil offers excursions on the lagoon in his own boat. He's very pleasant and knowledgeable, and speaks English. He can also take you to see the rare marsh owls at dusk. Give him a call or ask for him at the café in town. ⊠ *Moulay Bousselham* ☎ *0668/43–41–10* ☞ *100 DH per person for a 2-hr boat excursion.*

Sights

Merja Zerga National Park (*Blue Lagoon*)
NATIONAL PARK | FAMILY | Moulay Bousselham is at the head of the Merja Zerga National Park, a vast lagoon stretching over 17,000 acres. This region is one of the most important wetland reserves in North Africa and is a major stopover for countless birds migrating from Norway, Sweden, and the United Kingdom to Africa: the birds fly south at the end of summer and winter at Merja Zerga before continuing on to West Africa and even South Africa. They stop off again on their way back to Europe in spring, so spring and fall are the times for bird-watching. The Ramsar Convention site holds between 50,000 and 100,000 waders at any one time, including

The Legend of the Blue Lagoon

The legend of the Blue Lagoon and Moulay Bousselham dates from the 10th century, when the saint Saïd ben Saïd immigrated to the Maghreb from Egypt, following a revelation instructing him to pray where the sun sets over the ocean. He had a disciple called Sidi Abdel Jalil who, according to the story, saw Saïd ben Saïd fishing with a hook and asked him why a man with such great powers needed one. To show that he required no aids himself, Sidi Abdel Jalil put his hands into the water and pulled out fish as numerous as the hairs on his hand. Provoked by this act, Saïd ben Saïd took off his *selham* (cloak), swept it along the ground, called out, "Sea, follow me," and proceeded to walk inland. He did not stop until he had walked 10 km (6 miles). The sea followed him, and so the lagoon was formed. After this, Saïd ben Saïd was called Moulay Bousselham—"Lord, Owner of the Cloak." Both Moulay Bousselham and Sidi Abdel Jalil are buried in the town.

shelduck, marbled teal, coot, pied avocet, and slender-billed curlew. The pink greater flamingos on their way to and from Mauritania are particularly spectacular. ✉ *Moulay Bousselham.*

Moulay Bousselham's Tomb
RELIGIOUS BUILDING | At the foot of the village, near the sea, you'll find the tomb of Moulay Bousselham, which attracts hundreds of pilgrims every summer. Like Sidi Abdel Jalil's somewhat smaller one, it is a white building capped with a dome. ✉ *Moulay Bousselham zaouia, Moulay Bousselham.*

Hotels

La Maison des Oiseaux
$ | **B&B/INN** | **FAMILY** | Notable for having a beautiful garden right opposite the lagoon, the cute but somewhat faded "Bird House" is a low-key B&B with a few basic rooms, a library, and an artist's studio upstairs. **Pros:** very genuine welcome; friendly atmosphere; unpretentious accommodations. **Cons:** little to do in the area after nightfall; basic but presentable rooms; can be difficult to find. [$] *Rooms from: DH500* ✉ *Douar Riahi, Moulay Bousselham* ☎ *0661/30–10–67* 🌐 *moulay.bousselham.free.fr/la_maison_des_oiseaux.html* 💳 *No credit cards* 🛏 *11 rooms* 🍴 *Free Breakfast.*

★ **Vila Bea**
$$$ | **HOTEL** | With staggering lagoon views and a bright retro-esque style, this bewitching hotel has all the requisite elements of a relaxing retreat. **Pros:** incomparable views; stylish decor; excellent service. **Cons:** few dining options outside the hotel; little to do in the way of social life; expensive for the area. [$] *Rooms from: DH1540* ✉ *41, front de mer, Moulay Bousselham* ☎ *0537/43–20–87* 🌐 *www.vilabea.com* 🛏 *8 rooms* 🍴 *Free Breakfast.*

Temara

11 km (7 miles) southwest of Rabat.

The closest beach town to Rabat, Temara has a pleasant beach and a small port. It can be reached by car from the R322 from Rabat, or from the highway. Otherwise, take the train from Rabat and get off at Temara station; the beach is a short walk away.

Sights

Dar Es-Soltane Caves (*Les Grôttes de Harhoura*)

CAVE | On the coast at Temara, just south of Rabat, is a series of caves that are some of the earliest identified sites of human habitation. The easiest one to visit is on the landward side of the coastal road, across from Contrabandiers Beach, though you can't go inside. It's easy to spot, with a grassed area and iron railings in front, and is known as El Harhoura. Casts of the prehistoric human skeletons discovered here in the 1930s by Armand Ruhlmann are on display in the Museum of History and Civilizations, in Rabat. ✉ *Temara.*

Temara Plage

BEACH | FAMILY | This small beach with wonderful sand can be empty during colder months, but it's very much the opposite in summer. It's a short walk from the train station. **Amenities:** food and drink; lifeguards (in summer); parking. **Best for:** sunset; swimming; walking. ✉ *Temara.*

Restaurants

Restaurant Miramar

$$ | MOROCCAN | This popular restaurant and café sits right next to the rocky beach at Temara, overlooking the sea. It's the perfect place for fresh fish, though meat-eaters are not forgotten. **Known for:** friendly staff; fabulous sunsets; shellfish and pastas. $ *Average main: DH120* ✉ *Plage Harhoura* ☎ *0537/74–76–56.*

Skhirat Beach

20 km (12 miles) southwest of Rabat.

Southwest of Rabat, toward Casablanca, is lovely Skhirat Beach. It's close to the capital and perfect for a day by the sea.

GETTING HERE AND AROUND
While it's easiest to reach Skhirat by car, you can take the train from Rabat Ville station to Bouznika station. From there, grab a cab to the Plage Bouznika (8 DH). Grands taxis also run from Rabat to Skhirat (12 DH).

Sights

Contrabandiers Beach

BEACH | Connected to Temara Plage by a walkway across the rocks, pretty Contrabandiers Beach draws throngs of sunbathers, swimmers, and surfers in summer. As is always the case on this coastline, currents can be extremely dangerous, so don't plan to take a dip unless you're a strong swimmer. Locals will rent you a beach umbrella, and there are usually several vendors who walk up and down the sand selling ice cream and other snacks. **Amenities:** food and drink; lifeguards (in summer); parking. **Best for:** swimming; surfing; walking. ✉ *Skhirat.*

Skhirat Plage

BEACH | To say that Skhirat Plage is loved by Moroccans during the summer months—and by some faithful souls year-round—is an understatement. The long stretch of fine, golden sand lying just beyond the Royal Palace of Skhiratis is perfect for strolls but also a known surfing spot, as the plethora of boards reveals. Swimmers love it, too, but beware of dangerous currents—lifeguards are not always present. **Amenities:** food and drink; lifeguards (in summer); parking. **Best for:** swimming; surfing; walking. ✉ *Skhirat.*

 Restaurants

⭐ **Les Trois Palmiers**

$$$$ | MEDITERRANEAN | Sliding glass windows run the length of this restaurant, and open onto the beach between Temara and Skhirat. The inventive menu features Oualidia oysters, fish or prawn carpaccio, and plenty of fresh fish, as well as some Spanish dishes such as paella and fish *fiduea* (sort of a paella made with noodles instead of rice). **Known for:** superb sea views; excellent fish-oriented menu; upbeat tapas bar. $ *Average main: DH200* ⊠ *Plage Val d'Or, Temara* ☎ *0550/00–96–79* ⊕ *www. troispalmiersrestaurant.com.*

Oued Cherrat

36 km (22 miles) from Rabat.

Oued Cherrat is a small beach destination with superb ocean views and excellent surf conditions. Once a wild and relatively unfrequented stretch of sand, it's now a lot more popular, with development underway, although it's still less crowded than other North Atlantic beaches during the summer months.

GETTING HERE AND AROUND
Coming by car, take the highway from Rabat toward Casablanca, taking the Bouznika exit and then the coastal road toward Oued Cherrat. You can also take a train from Rabat Ville station to Bouznika station. From there, taxis to the Plage Oued Cherrat are around 10 DH. Grands taxis also go from Rabat to Bouznika (20 DH).

🍴 Restaurants

Eden Island Beach Club
$$$ | SEAFOOD | FAMILY | Between Skhirat and Bouznika, this excellent place to eat, drink, and disconnect serves an excellent menu of mostly fish-based options, with salads and proper desserts thrown in. The location is fabulous—right on the beach, with two pools, and areas for eating and relaxing separated by rustic bamboo canes. **Known for:** wonderful sea views; wide range of seafood; often live music at sunset. $ *Average main: DH180* ⊠ *Plage Oued Cherrat, Eden Island* ☎ *0661/29–69–38* ⊕ *www.edenisland-beachclub.com* ⊗ *Closed Dec.–Mar.*

Bouznika

40 km (25 miles) southwest of Rabat.

Bouznika Bay is one of the prettiest areas in the region and much loved by both Rabat and Casablanca locals. A grands taxis from Rabat to Bouznika should cost about 20 DH.

◉ Sights

Bouznika Bay
BEACH | This bay is one of the prettiest in the region and much loved by both Rabat and Casablanca locals. For this reason, it gets exceptionally crowded when the weather is hot: crowds hit the golden sands and surfers stream into the waves. It's a lovely place out of season, too—perfect for picnicking and exploring the tide pools. During summer, there is a good selection of restaurants and cafés. **Amenities:** food and drink; lifeguards; parking. **Best for:** surfing; swimming; walking. ⊠ *Plage de Bouznika, Rabat.*

🍴 Restaurants

Restaurant Kasbah Village
$ | PIZZA | FAMILY | This laid-back lounge and restaurant is a great place for coffee and a crepe, or pizza and a beer. It's right next to the beach on a peninsula that overlooks the sandy sweep of Bouznika bay. **Known for:** the views; laid-back vibe; reasonable prices. $ *Average main: DH80* ⊠ *Bouznika* ☎ *0661/30–24–82* ▭ *No credit cards.*

Mohammedia

25 km (16 miles) north of Casablanca.

A short drive from Casablanca, Mohammedia and the surrounding area have a long stretch of pretty bays, which draw droves of sunseekers during the summer. It was originally a port town and currently has a delightful harbor and yacht club plus a good choice of fish restaurants, as well as a food market. Charming wooden beach houses line the waterfront. North of town, the coast is good for swimmers, surfers, and sunbathers, although currents here can be dangerous.

On Saturday, there is a souk at Al Alia (a southeastern district of Mohammedia) that sells everything from *khlii* (preserved meat) to dentist chairs. It's a grand event for locals, and you can see donkeys, horses, and people heading that way for miles.

GETTING HERE AND AROUND

Trains from the Casablanca Port station leave at least once an hour for Mohammedia (20 minutes, 28 DH). A seat in a grand taxi from Casablanca costs approximately 12 DH.

In Mohammedia, you can take a relatively inexpensive petit taxi, with a minimum fare of 6 DH.

Sights

Plage Les Sablettes

BEACH | FAMILY | This long sandy bay attracts swarms of surfers, sunbathers, and families in summer when temperatures can get very high. **Amenities:** food and drink; lifeguards (in summer); parking. **Best for:** sunbathing; surfing; swimming; walking. ✉ *Plage les Sablettes, Mohammedia.*

Restaurants

Restaurant du Parc

$$$ | SEAFOOD | FAMILY | Befitting its name, this elegant restaurant is right on a park, in a 1950s building with a dining terrace. As is often the case in Mohammedia, the menu bears a distinct fish and seafood theme, so your choices will largely depend on what's been caught that day, though there is also a good selection of salads and meat dishes, plus some Moroccan fare and French-influenced desserts. **Known for:** book ahead on weekends; platters of fish friture: fried fish and shellfish; family favorite since 1950. [$] *Average main: DH150* ✉ *Bd. Zerktouni, Mohammedia* ☎ *0523/32–22–11.*

★ **Restaurant du Port**

$$$ | SEAFOOD | This boat-shape fish restaurant next to the port is the most famous place to eat in town. The splendid food isn't cheap, but it's worth every last dirham because the chef insists on using top-quality ingredients and each dish is crafted with imagination and sophistication. **Known for:** interesting, wide-ranging wine list; creative cuisine; excellent desserts. [$] *Average main: DH180* ✉ *1, rue du Port, Mohammedia* ☎ *0523/32–24–66* 🌐 *www.restoport.ma.*

Hotels

Sphinx Boutique Hotel

$$ | HOTEL | This enticing boutique hotel, set in a clean-lined 1950s villa, flawlessly balances modern comfort and vintage elegance. **Pros:** chic but friendly atmosphere; stylish and comfortable; wonderful garden. **Cons:** nearby nightclub can be noisy; parking can be limited; some rooms are small and looking a bit tired. [$] *Rooms from: DH950* ✉ *Bd. Moulay Youssef* ☎ *0523/31–00–73* 🛏 *18 rooms* 🍴 *Free Breakfast.*

Nightlife

Le Roof Sky Lounge

DANCE CLUBS | The classy bar above the Restaurant du Port draws a fun-loving crowd. DJs make this the chic place to party as the sun sets over the ocean; there's also food available for those in need of a bite. ✉ *1, rue du Port* ☎ *0523/32–24–66* 🌐 *www.roof.ma.*

🏃 Activities

★ Bautilus

SAILING | FAMILY | Since Mohammedia is essentially a port town, the thing to do here is try your hand at boating. It's an ideal way to explore the coast. Whether you're a beginner or more experienced, you can choose from a variety of small vessels, including canoes, catamarans, and motorboats. Bautilus is run by Mehdi and Hicham, two passionate sailors who can also arrange sailing excursions, fishing trips, and other on-the-water activities. Sailing lessons start at 250 DH and motorboat trips costs 2,000 DH for a half day or 3,000 DH for a full day. Canoe trips are priced at 250 DH per person for groups of eight or more. ⊠ *Base Nautique de Mohammedia* ☎ *0665/19–69–87, 0645/46–02–28* ⊕ *www.bautilus.com.*

Casablanca

91 km (57 miles) southwest of Rabat.

Casablanca is Morocco's economic hub and its largest, most modern metropolis. The city's vibrant economy has resulted in plenty of good restaurants and hotels, a burgeoning arts and culture scene, and large shopping centers featuring world-renowned brands. Here you'll find a busy sea port, the country's major airport, an enormous amount of business and housing development, a lovely seaside corniche with prestigious neighborhoods, an efficient tramway, and a big traffic problem. The city has its own stock exchange, and working hours tend to transcend the relaxed pace kept by the rest of Morocco. People from all over the country have migrated to the city to find work, and there's a large community of expats, mostly French.

True to its name—*casa blanca* in Spanish (white house), which, in turn, is Dar El Beida in Arabic—the city is a conglomeration of white buildings. Present-day Casablanca, known colloquially as "Casa" or "El Beida," was only founded in 1912, so it lacks the abundance of ancient monuments that abound in Morocco's other major urban centers; however, there are still some landmarks, including the famous Hassan II Mosque, while Mauresque and Art Deco architecture from the Protectorate years graces the downtown area.

GETTING HERE AND AROUND
AIR

From overseas, Casablanca's Mohammed V Airport is the busiest gateway to Morocco itself: you'll find a modern arrivals hall, fairly efficient and usually courteous staffers, and a not-so-complicated continuation of your journey by train or car. Passport control can sometimes be slow, however. Trains connect the airport to the national network from 6:50 am to 10:50 pm (although you should always check online for changes); taxis are available to the city of Casablanca at comparatively expensive but fixed rates (280 DH–350 DH).

AIRPORT CONTACTS Mohammed V International Airport. ⊠ *Rte. de Nouasseur, N11, Casablanca* ☎ *0522/53–90–40* ⊕ *www.onda.ma/en/Our-Airports/Casablanca-Mohammed-V-Airport.*

BUS

Buses are fine for short trips, like Casablanca to El Jadida or Safi, but trips longer than a couple of hours can be interminable, hot, and dusty. Inquire at the station for schedule and fare information. In Casablanca the Compagnie de Transports au Maroc (CTM) bus station is by far the most convenient, because the other stations are on the outskirts of town.

BUS CONTACTS CTM Casablanca. ⊠ *Gare Routiere CTM, 23, rue Léon l'Africain, Centre Ville* ☎ *0800/09–00–30* ⊕ *www.ctm.ma.*

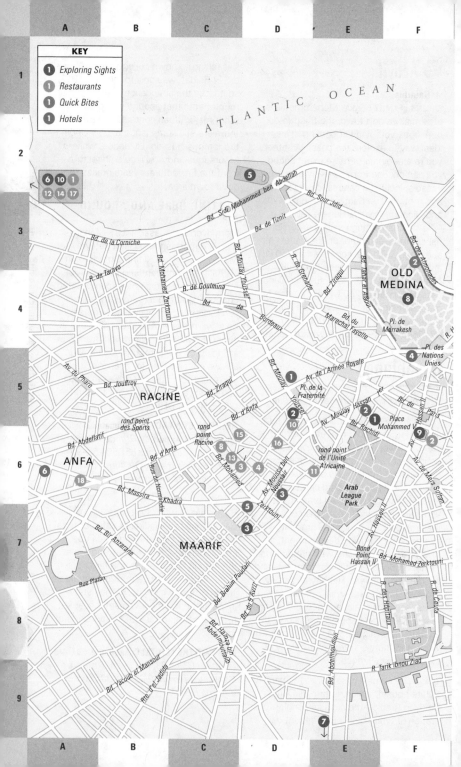

Casablanca

Sights ▼

1	Abderrahman Slaoui Museum....	E5
2	American Center for the Arts	D5
3	Downtown Casablanca...........	D7
4	Habous............................	H8
5	Hassan II Mosque	D2
6	La Corniche......................	A2
7	Museum of Moroccan Judaism	E9
8	Old Medina	F4
9	Place Mohammed V...............	F6
10	Sidi Abderrahman	A2

Restaurants ▼

1	À Ma Bretagne.....................	A2
2	Al-Mounia	F6
3	Bacco e Venere....................	C6
4	Bondi Coffee Kitchen	D6
5	Brasserie la Bavaroise...........	G5
6	Casa José Puerto.................	G4
7	Golden China.......................	G4
8	Iloli...............................	H5
9	La Bodega	H5
10	La Cantine de Gauthier..........	D5
11	Le Bistrot Chic	E6
12	Le Cabestan	A2
13	Le Kimmy'z.........................	C6
14	Le Petit Rocher...................	A2
15	Le QuatorZe	C6
16	Le Rossignol.......................	D6
17	Lily's	A2
18	Paul...............................	A6
19	Restaurant du Port de Peche	G4
20	Taverne du Dauphin..............	G4

Quick Bites ▼

1	Frédéric Cassel Patisserie.........	J9
2	La Sqala............................	F3
3	Venezia Ice	G8

Hotels ▼

1	Barceló Anfa	D5
2	Hôtel & Spa Le Doge	E5
3	Hôtel Gauthier.....................	D6
4	Hyatt Regency Casablanca........	F5
5	Kenzi Tower	D7
6	Le Casablanca Hotel	A6

CAR

You may not want a car if you are staying in Casablanca, as driving here is almost a hazardous sport. However, it is possible to rent one if you are planning to explore the country. Others may prefer moving onto their next destination, such as Fez or Marrakesh, before picking up a vehicle.

RENTAL CARS Avis. ✉ *Bd. Zayid Ou Hmad, Centre Ville* ☎ *0522/31–24–24* ⊕ *www.avis.com.*

TRAIN

Casablanca has three train stations: Casa Port, Casa Voyageurs, and Casa l'Oasis (the former two both downtown, the latter in the Oasis neighborhood). By train you can travel quickly and pleasantly to Marrakesh, Fez, Rabat, Tangier, and smaller towns like El Jadida and Azemmour. Direct trains from the airport go to both Casa Voyageurs and l'Oasis.

Trains to Rabat depart every half hour (the train is by far the best way to move between Casablanca and the capital). From Casa Voyageurs it is less than three hours by train to Marrakesh (12 trains daily), 3½ hours from Meknès (18 trains daily), and four hours to Fez (18 trains daily). There are three trains daily from Casa Voyageurs to Oujda (one overnight, 10 hours). There are 13 trains daily from Casa Port to Tangier, changing at Kenitra where you pick up Al Boraq high-speed train (total journey time three hours). However, you should always check online for changes to timetables.

CONTACTS Office National des Chemins de Fer, Casa-Oasis. *(O.N.C.F.)* ✉ *Gare de Casa Oasis, Rte. de L'Oasis, Casablanca* ☎ *22–55* ⊕ *www.oncf.ma.* **Office National des Chemins de Fer, Casa-Port.** *(O.N.C.F.)* ✉ *Gare de Casa Port, Tangier* ☎ *22–55* ⊕ *www.oncf.ma.* **Office National des Chemins de Fer, Casa-Voyageurs.** *(O.N.C.F.)* ✉ *Gare de Casa Voyageurs, Bd. Bahmad, Centre Ville* ☎ *22–55* ⊕ *www.oncf.ma.*

TRAM

The tramway has given this city something to be very proud of: it's safe, clean, affordable, and runs on time, which is no mean feat. With the tram, you can easily navigate from some of Casablanca's major locations, such as the Ain Diab beach area, the old pedestrianized town center around boulevard Mohammed V, and the old medina. It also makes a link between some of the city's more affluent areas and the less salubrious suburbs. For now, the tram comprises 71 stations that run along two lines covering 47 km (29 miles). The website includes a route finder and downloadable plan.

Tickets cost 6 DH. The tram runs from 5:30 am to 10:30 pm on weekdays and until 11:30 pm on weekends.

GUIDES AND TOURS

CONTACTS Visit Morocco. ✉ *3, rue Ahmed Ben Bouchta, Anfa, Casablanca* ☎ *0522/36–16–32* ⊕ *www.visitmorocco.ma.* **Taste of Casablanca Food Tour.** ✉ *Casablanca* ☎ *0630/84–70–14* ⊕ *www.tasteofcasablanca.com.*

TIMING AND PRECAUTIONS

Many visitors spend at least a couple of nights in Casablanca, often using it as a base to visit other places in the area. As in any large city, travelers should be cautious after dark when walking in the center and around the old medina. It is best to use a taxi late at night when returning from restaurants, bars, or nightclubs.

Sights

★ Abderrahman Slaoui Museum

ART MUSEUM | One of the city's few museums, the Abderrahman Slaoui is hidden away in a splendid Art Deco villa. Permanent exhibits feature a collection of the nation's treasures, including delicate crystal perfume bottles, Jacques Majorelle paintings, vintage prints, and 300-year-old jewelry from Fez. The museum has a café spilling out onto the rooftop, and a

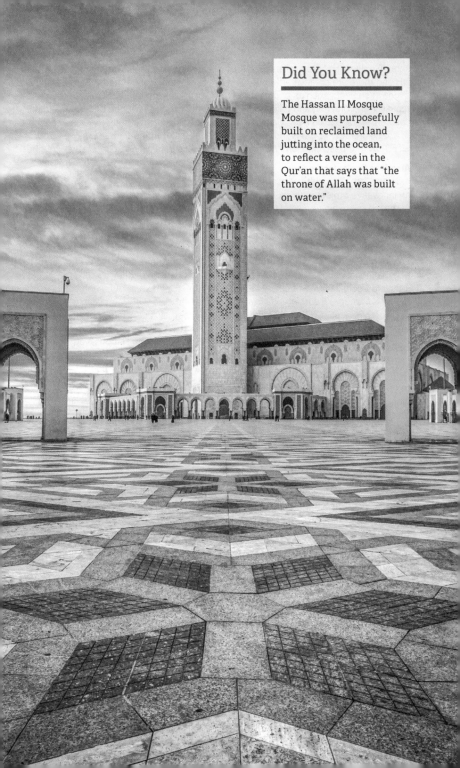

shop. Guided visits are available for 100 DH and there are creative art workshops in subjects such as photography, tapestry, and drawing and painting for children. ✉ *12, rue du Parc, Casablanca* ☎ *0522/20–62–17* ⊕ *www.musee-as.ma* 🎫 *60 DH* ⊗ *Closed Sun. and Mon.*

American Center for the Arts

ARTS CENTERS | This cultural center is an innovative project with six floors of purpose-built exhibition space, meeting and event rooms, a state-of-the-art 160-seat theater, roof terraces, residences, and a café. Part of the nearby American Language Center, it has a full program of exhibitions, dance, theater, and other artistic pursuits, all free of charge. ✉ *2, rue Khlil Matrane, Gauthier, Casablanca* ☎ *0522/27–77–65, 0522/27–52–70* ⊕ *aca.org.ma.*

La Corniche

PROMENADE | Get a feel for Casa's Atlantic setting by stopping at a Corniche café to relish the sun and breeze. The lovely landscaped walkway along the sea is a favorite with families. On weekends, this area is bursting with people settling in the seafront line of cafés and restaurants, basking in the beach resorts, and walking up and down the wide pavement. In the evenings, nightclubs and bars open their doors for all kinds of partygoers. You can also walk along the extended Corniche from the lighthouse at El Hank to the Hassan II Mosque. ✉ *Le Corniche, Casablanca.*

Downtown Casablanca

NEIGHBORHOOD | The area of the city bordered by Avenue des FAR, Place des Nations Unies, Place Mohammed V, and Avenue Abdullah Al Mediouini contains the remaining examples of Mauresque and Art Deco architecture built by the French in the early years of the Protectorate (1912–56), when Casablanca was the jewel in the French Empire's crown. While much has been lost, the city is restoring large swathes of these buildings including the Central Market

and the enormous Hotel Lincoln, both on Boulevard Mohammed V. Some excellent examples are Le Petit Poucet bar also on this boulevard, the Cinema Rialto on Rue Bouchaib, and the Bank al Maghrib on Boulevard de Paris. Many apartment blocks in this area sport pretty wrought-iron balconies and swags of cement flowers and fruit on the buildings. ✉ *Casablanca.*

Habous

NEIGHBORHOOD | Also known as the New Medina, the Quartier des Habous was built by the French in a 1930s tourism drive, to offer a sanitized version of a "real" medina. Today it's a curiously attractive mixture of French colonial architecture with Moroccan details. Capped by arches, its shops surround a pretty square with trees and flowers. As you enter the Habous, you'll pass a building resembling a castle; this is the Pasha's Mahkama, or court, completed in 1952. The Mahkama formerly housed the reception halls of the Pasha of Casablanca, as well as a Muslim courthouse; it's currently used for district government administration. On the opposite side of the square is the Mohammed V Mosque—although not ancient, this and the 1938 Moulay Youssef Mosque, in the adjacent square, are among the finest examples of traditional Maghrebi (western North African) architecture in Casablanca. Look up at the minarets and you might recognize a style used in Marrakesh's Koutoubia Mosque and Seville's Giralda. Note also the fine wood carving over the door of the Mohammed V. The Habous is well-known as a center for Arabic books; most of the other shops here are devoted to rich displays of traditional handicrafts aimed at locals and tourists.

■ **TIP →** **This is the best place in Casablanca to buy Moroccan handicrafts.**

You can also purchase traditional Moroccan clothes such as kaftans and djellabas (long, hooded outer garments). Immediately north of the Habous is

Casablanca's Royal Palace. You can't go inside, but the outer walls are pleasing; their sandstone blocks fit neatly together and blend well with the little streets at the edge of the Habous. ⌧ *Quartier Habous, Casablanca.*

★ Hassan II Mosque

MOSQUE | Casablanca's skyline is dominated by this massive edifice, decorated with magnificent *zellij* (mosaic tiles). The building's foundations lie partly on land and partly in the sea, and at one point inside you can see the water through a glass floor. The main hall holds an astonishing 25,000 people and has a retractable roof so that it can be turned into a courtyard. The minaret is more than 650 feet high, and the mezzanine floor (which holds the women's section, about 6 feet above the main floor) seems dwarfed by the nearly 200-foot-high ceiling. Still, the ceiling's enormous painted decorations appear small and delicate from below.

Funded through public subscription, designed by a French architect, and built by a team of 35,000, the mosque was erected between 1987 and 1993 and is one of the largest in the world, its minaret being the tallest. It was built in Casablanca primarily so that the largest city in the kingdom would have a monument worthy of its size. Except for the ruined Tinmel mosque in the High Atlas Mountains, this is the only mosque in Morocco that non-Muslims are allowed to enter. One-hour guided tours of the mosque are offered daily (six per day, Saturday to Thursday; four on Friday). There are reduced hours during Ramadan. Be sure to dress conservatively, and note that you will be required to remove your shoes at the entrance.

■ TIP→ **If you fly out of Casablanca, try to get a window seat on the left for a good view of the mosque in relation to the city as a whole.**

⌧ *Hassan II Mosque, Bd. de la Corniche, Casablanca* ☎ *0522/48–28–86* ⊕ *www. fmh2.ma/* ⌧ *140 DH.*

Museum of Moroccan Judaism

HISTORY MUSEUM | Set in a lovely villa in the suburb of Oasis, this museum has a permanent exhibition of traditional ceremonial objects, clothing, lamps, and furniture from various synagogues around Morocco. There's also a temporary exhibition space that often shows photographs and art. Phone ahead to make sure it's open. ⌧ *81, rue du Chasseur Jules Cros, Oasis, Casablanca* ☎ *0522/99–49–40* ⊕ *www.jewishmuseumcasa.com* ⌧ *50 DH* ⊙ *Closed Sat.*

Old Medina

HISTORIC DISTRICT | The simple whitewashed houses of the medina, particularly those closest to the harbor, form an extraordinary contrast to Morocco's economic and commercial nerve center just a few hundred yards away. European consuls lived here in the 19th century during the early trading days, and there is still a youth hostel and a few cheap hotels within. Today it boils over with busy Moroccan shoppers, vendors, and beggers. The medina has its own personality and charm, due in part to the fact that many Casa residents living in more affluent areas never set foot here. Near Place des Nations Unies a large conglomeration of shops sells watches, leather goods, crafted wood, and clothes. It's best avoided at night unless you're accompanied by a local you know well. ⌧ *Casablanca.*

Place Mohammed V

PLAZA/SQUARE | Casablanca's version of London's Trafalgar Square has illuminated fountains, plenty of pigeons, and a series of grand buildings. This is the center of downtown and has some imposing Mauresque and Art Deco buildings. Coming from the port, you'll pass the main post office on your right, and on your left as you enter the square is its most impressive building, the courthouse, built in the

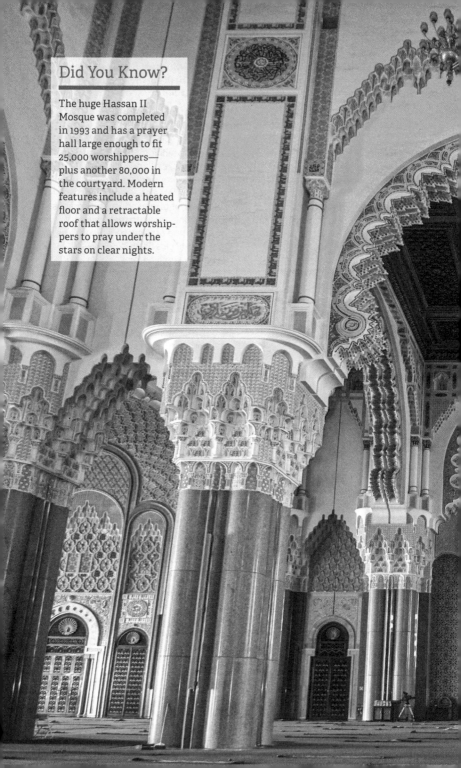

Did You Know?

The huge Hassan II Mosque was completed in 1993 and has a prayer hall large enough to fit 25,000 worshippers—plus another 80,000 in the courtyard. Modern features include a heated floor and a retractable roof that allows worshippers to pray under the stars on clear nights.

1920s. On the other side of Avenue Hassan II from the post office is the ornate Bank Al Maghrib; the structure opposite, with the clock tower, is the Wilaya, the governor's office. The more modest buildings on the right side of the square house the notorious customs directorate (where importers appeal punitive taxes). Now that the tram serves this area, it's easy to get here from nearly anywhere else in the city. ⊠ *Pl. Mohammed V, Casablanca.*

Sidi Abderrahman

RELIGIOUS BUILDING | If you follow the Corniche to its southwestern edge, you will see the tomb of Sidi Abderrahman, a Sufi saint, just off the coast on a tiny island. Moroccans come to this shrine if they are sick or if they feel they need to rid themselves of evil spirits. Before the bridge was built in 2013, it was accessible only at low tide, at which point you would simply walk to the small collection of white houses, built practically one on top of the other. Non-Muslims are allowed to visit and have their futures told by a resident fortune-teller, although access to the shrine itself is prohibited. The other side of the island is one of the most exciting places in Casablanca to sit and watch the wild Atlantic swell. Be sensitive to the people who live here, as they will not appreciate being taken for museum exhibits and may object to having their pictures taken.

■ **TIP** → **On the sands, just in front of the tomb, you can enjoy some snails, or pancakes if you prefer, and Moroccan mint tea along with the locals.** ⊠ *Casablanca.*

 Restaurants

À Ma Bretagne

$$$$ | FRENCH | Located on the Corniche close to Morocco Mall, with wall-to-wall sea-view windows, this is an elegant, modern spot for French provincial cuisine. The kitchen excels in its fish and shellfish dishes; for a sweet finish,

the warm chocolate tart is spectacular. **Known for:** waterside setting; refined French ambience; stylish dining room. $ *Average main: DH220* ⊠ *Bd. de la Corniche, Sidi Abderrahman, Casablanca* ☎ *0522/39–79–79.*

Al-Mounia

$$$ | MOROCCAN | FAMILY | Casablanca's first and most cherished Moroccan restaurant has dining rooms with a quintessential Moroccan atmosphere and a lovely patio with a centuries-old tree. The excellent cooking has a refined touch: the salads are delectable, and the tagines bubble with the most sensational of aromas. **Known for:** a rare Moroccan restaurant in contemporary Casa; warm, convivial service; traditional decor. $ *Average main: DH150* ⊠ *95, rue Prince Moulay Abdallah, Casablanca* ☎ *0522/22-26–69* ⊙ *Closed Sun.*

Bacco e Venere

$$ | ITALIAN | FAMILY | Priding itself on the use of authentic ingredients, this excellent Italian restaurant focuses on classic fare, like perfect pizzas, fresh pasta, and, for bigger appetites, mouthwatering meat and fish dishes. There's a cute terrace if you want to eat alfresco. **Known for:** pizza cooked in a wood-burning oven; lively atmosphere; excellent antipasto. $ *Average main: DH95* ⊠ *50, av. Hassan Souktani, Gauthier, Casablanca* ☎ *0662/74–32–81* ⊕ *www.baccoevenere.com.*

Le Bistrot Chic

$$$$ | BISTRO | This place prides itself on fine wines, treating customers to a fantastic range of options from France and beyond. There's a proper bistro ambience in the dining area, which offers reasonable prix-fixe menus for both lunch and dinner, while the mezzanine bar serves French-style tapas, including a very respectable cheese board. **Known for:** elegant crowd; informative staff; intimate atmosphere. $ *Average main: DH200* ⊠ *8, rue Taha Hussein, Gauthier,*

Casablanca ☎ *0522/29–78–78* ⏲ *Closed Sun.*

La Bodega

$$$ | **SPANISH** | Every night is fiesta night at La Bodega, opposite the Central Market: come for tapas and a drink or stay for a full meal from the typically Spanish menu—think *jambon serrano* (thinly sliced, dry-cured Spanish ham) and paella. The restaurant has a fun atmosphere, with themed live music each evening and popular dance floor: Tuesday, for instance, is salsa time, and a pro will give tips if you feel like improving your moves. **Known for:** lively atmosphere; high-quality Latin fare; tempting fixed-price menu at lunch. [$] *Average main: DH150* ✉ *129, bd. Allal Ben Abdellah, Casablanca* ☎ *0522/54–18–42* 🌐 *www.bodega.ma* ⏲ *No lunch Sun.*

Bondi Coffee Kitchen

$ | **AUSTRALIAN** | **FAMILY** | Imported 100% Arabica specialty coffee beans and top-notch baristas make this Australian/Moroccan-owned spot a good place to settle in for a coffee alongside breakfast served all day or any of the inventive salads, sandwiches, and pastas. The service is efficient and the vibe is laid-back. **Known for:** good Wi-Fi; vegetarian and vegan options; great coffee beverages. [$] *Average main: DH85* ✉ *31, rue Sebou, Gauthier, Casablanca* ☎ *0651/68–77–07.*

Brasserie la Bavaroise

$$$$ | **FRENCH** | For a supreme culinary experience, head to Brasserie la Bavaroise where the menu is awash with delectable French favorites, sumptuous steaks, sophisticated fish dishes, and beguiling desserts. The restaurant has a contemporary look that's elegant without being stuffy, and an atmosphere to match. **Known for:** efficient yet unobtrusive service; exceptional French menu; handsome dining room. [$] *Average main: DH220* ✉ *133, bd. Allal Ben Abdellah, Casablanca* ☎ *0522/31–17–60* 🌐 *restopro.ma/bavaroise* ⏲ *No dinner Sun.*

★ **Le Cabestan**

$$$$ | **MEDITERRANEAN** | Located right near the Corniche lighthouse, you approach this restaurant through a pretty, candlelit garden and inside you'll have spectacular ocean views: you can look down from a window seat onto blue rock pools as you savor delicious fish dishes. The menu focuses on fine Mediterranean cuisine, with a lively tapas bar that draws a cocktail- and champagne-loving crowd until the early hours. **Known for:** late-night music and dancing; stellar ocean views; glittering clientele. [$] *Average main: DH250* ✉ *90, bd. de la Corniche, Phare d'el Hank, Casablanca* ☎ *0522/39–11–90* 🌐 *www.le-cabestan.com.*

La Cantine de Gauthier

$$$$ | **FRENCH** | A top choice in the well-heeled Gauthier district, little Cantine de Gauthier oozes as much French chic as a Parisian bistro. It's a casual spot that serves delicious French meat and fish dishes, though the well-priced sharing plates of charcuterie and cheese attract the after-work crowd for an apéro. **Known for:** draft beer available as well as excellent French wines; chic, laid-back ambience; intimate setting. [$] *Average main: DH190* ✉ *3, rue Abou Adil El Allaf, Gauthier, Casablanca* ☎ *0520/13–91–31* ⏲ *Closed Sun.*

Casa José Puerto

$$ | **SPANISH** | This upscale Spanish tapas restaurant is a favorite among residents and always abuzz with diners and drinkers—which makes it a great place to meet true Casablancans. Products are local and fish is supplied daily, with typical options including calamari and *patatas bravas*; for those missing pork, there's even real chorizo and *jamón,* all accompanied by a selection of wines and beers from here and abroad. **Known for:** opens early for an after-work crowd; lively atmosphere; extensive menu. [$] *Average main: DH130* ✉ *26, bd. Felix Houphouet Boigny, Casablanca* ☎ *0522/29–70–12.*

Golden China

$$ | **CHINESE** | If you need a break from
tagines, Golden China is just the place.
The red-and-gold decor, dark wood furniture, and softly played Asian music sets
the tone, while the authentic menu offers
a wide variety of poultry, seafood, meat,
vegetarian, and noodle dishes. **Known for:**
Centre Ville setting; city's oldest authentic Chinese restaurant; exceptionally
varied menu. $ *Average main: DH120*
⊠ *12, rue el Oraibi Jilali, Casablanca*
☎ *0522/27–35–26* ⊙ *Closed Sun.*

Iloli

$$$$ | **JAPANESE** | If you're yearning
for Japanese food in Morocco, Iloli is
widely regarded as the best place to go,
and you can choose to sit on the airy
terrace; inside at tables or at the counter
to watch the sushi chefs in action; or
upstairs on sofas and armchairs. The
menu has plenty of sushi and sashimi, as
well as cooked options. **Known for:** popular set menus; alcohol is available; lovely
desserts. $ *Average main: DH260* ⊠ *Rue
Najib Mahfoud, Gauthier, Casablanca*
☎ *0608/86–66–33* ⊕ *www.iloli-restaurant.
com/.*

Le Kimmy'z

$$$$ | **FRENCH** | There's a bit of everything
at this multilevel space, starting with a
buzzy bar area on the ground floor that
serves wine and tapas and is popular
with the after-work crowd. Head upstairs
for dinner at the restaurant, which has a
French-inspired menu that's known for
its market-fresh produce and excellent
steaks. **Known for:** vibey atmosphere;
excellent wine list and cocktails; music
and DJs in the evening. $ *Average main:
DH210* ⊠ *7, rue Najib Mahfoud, Gauthier,
Casablanca* ☎ *0662/14–91–83* ⊕ *www.
lekimmyz.com.*

★ Lily's

$$$$ | **ASIAN** | The setting at Lily's is quite
magnificent, with carved wood screens,
butterflies on the ceiling, bamboo
growing through the wooden floors, and
spectacular sea views through every
window. The food is pretty spectacular,
too, featuring Japanese, Thai, Korean,
and Vietnamese dishes. **Known for:** Asian
decor makes for a Zen-like atmosphere;
superb fish dishes; indulgent desserts.
$ *Average main: DH200* ⊠ *92, bd.
de la Corniche, El Hank, Casablanca*
☎ *0522/36–12–71* ⊕ *www.lilys.ma.*

★ Paul

$$ | **FRENCH** | A branch of the popular
French café, bakery, and restaurant
group, this Paul location is in the beautiful Art Deco Villa Zevaco, with a fabulous
garden. The milk shakes and desserts
are decadent, and the rustic breads
are beloved throughout the city; for
something more substantial, the pastas,
burgers, steaks, and fish are all good,
too. **Known for:** well-heeled clientele;
extravagant breakfasts; good value prix-
fixe lunch. $ *Average main: DH130* ⊠ *Vil-
la Zevaco, corner of Bd. d'Anfa and Av.
Moulay Rachid, Casablanca* ☎ *0522/36–
60–00* ⊕ *www.paul-maroc.com.*

★ Le Petit Rocher

$$$$ | **MEDITERRANEAN** | For fine dining or
drinks with a fantastic view, the super-el-
egant Petit Rocher is just the ticket: its
unrivaled position lets you gaze over the
sublime Atlantic waves and the Hassan II
Mosque. Enjoy delicious Mediterranean
cuisine and good wine in the restaurant
area, or settle down at the bar where
fabulous cocktails are poured and a
DJ often spins. **Known for:** after-dinner
party atmosphere in the bar; exceptional ocean-side setting; seafood dishes.
$ *Average main: DH250* ⊠ *Complexe au
Petit Rocher, El Hank, Bd. de la Corniche,
Casablanca* ☎ *0522/36–26–26* ⊕ *www.
lepetitrochercasa.com.*

Le QuatorZe

$$$$ | **FRENCH** | With decor featuring a
long leather banquette, retro-style chairs,
and a wall of family-style photos and
old plates, this homey spot run by two
sisters, Zineb and Malika, is a wonderful
find, though easy to miss: it's up a few
steps in a lovely old house. The French

menu is limited but exquisite, featuring lots of fish. **Known for:** intimate atmosphere; artistically presented French food; good wine list. $ *Average main: DH200* ✉ *14, rue Najib Mahfoud, Gauthier, Casablanca* ☎ *0522/20–96–52* ◷ *Closed Sun. and Mon.*

Restaurant du Port de Peche

$$$ | SEAFOOD | FAMILY | Tucked away inside the port (to find the restaurant, enter the port by the gate and turn left toward the fishing port), this family-friendly spot is one of Casablanca's oldest fish restaurants and always draws a crowd at lunchtime. What to choose depends on what's been caught that day, so be sure to ask the waiters for advice. **Known for:** reasonable prices; oysters are a specialty; no-nonsense service. $ *Average main: DH180* ✉ *Port de Pêche, Casablanca* ☎ *0522/31–85–61* ◷ *Closed Sun.*

★ Le Rossignol

$$$ | MEDITERRANEAN | Another offering in the buzzing district of Gauthier, Le Rossignol is billed as a French restaurant but has all sorts of interesting dishes thanks to a chef who has worked all over the world. You'll find Lebanese meze and mac 'n' cheese with truffles, excellent salads, fish dishes, and a very upmarket burger, not to mention great breakfast options. **Known for:** open breakfast to late night; vibey atmosphere; good options for vegetarians. $ *Average main: DH150* ✉ *Angle Rue Taha Hussein et Rue Kacem Amine, Gauthier, Casablanca* ☎ *0522/27–58–45.*

Taverne du Dauphin

$$ | SEAFOOD | One of the city's most established fish-and-seafood restaurants, the Dauphin is a convivial alternative to more expensive eateries offering a similar menu. The prices—coupled with its placement in the town center, near the port and on the edge of the old medina—make it a bustling spot, with some tables spilling out onto the pavement. **Known for:** unpretentious service; throwback atmosphere and decor; superb fish

dishes. $ *Average main: DH125* ✉ *45, bd. Félix Houphouet Boigny, Casablanca* ☎ *0522/22–12–00* ◷ *Closed Sun.*

☕ Coffee and Quick Bites

Frédéric Cassel Patisserie

$ | CAFÉ | They serve a full café menu of breakfast, brunch, lunch, and dinner but the real draw is the glorious array of cakes, French macarons, cookies, and chocolates that grace the display cabinets at this beautiful French patisserie in upmarket Anfa. The interior is modern and airy but there's also a terrace where you can have coffee and watch all the beautiful people. **Known for:** good coffee and indulgent cakes; great terrace; chic but laid-back atmosphere. $ *Average main: DH80* ✉ *8, bd. Moulay Rachid, Anfa, Casablanca* ☎ *0522/94–93–82.*

La Sqala

$$$ | MOROCCAN | FAMILY | A Casablanca institution, this pretty, blue-and-yellow-theme open-air restaurant is set into the city ramparts overlooking the marina. It may serve the best Moroccan breakfast in town; a pastry and mint tea make for a perfect break from sightseeing; and they also serve splendid Moroccan salads and tagines for lunch and dinner. **Known for:** no alcohol; excellent Moroccan food in a city that doesn't have many Moroccan restaurants; beautiful gardens. $ *Average main: DH135* ✉ *Bd. des Almohades, Casablanca* ☎ *522260960* ⊕ *www.sqala. ma.*

Venezia Ice

$ | ICE CREAM | FAMILY | This is a great place to stop off if you're taking a walk along the seaside promenade, La Corniche. In a prime position overlooking the sea, this branch of the ever-popular Venezia Ice serves breakfast, salads, burgers, and sandwiches, and, of course, their excellent ice cream. **Known for:** efficient service; multiple flavors of ice cream; beach and sea views. $ *Average main: DH25* ✉ *Above Tahiti Beach Club, La*

Corniche, Casablanca ☎ 0674/30–29–63 🌐 www.venezia-ice.com.

Hotels

Barceló Anfa

$$$ | **HOTEL** | **FAMILY** | This smart addition from the Barceló hotel group has spacious and tastefully decorated public areas and generous-size rooms. **Pros:** upper floors have great city views; helpful staff; walk-in showers. **Cons:** can feel a little generic; off-site restaurants generally have more character; bathrooms open to the rooms (though toilet is separate). [$] *Rooms from: DH1600 ✉ 44, bd. d'Anfa, Casablanca ☎ 0520/00–90–00 🌐 www.barcelo.com/en-ww/barcelo-anfa-casablanca/ 🛏 206 rooms 🍴 Free Breakfast.*

★ Le Casablanca Hotel

$$$$ | **HOTEL** | Drawing on the Art Deco flavor of Casablanca's history, this exquisite hotel combines fabulous interior design aspects of the 1920s with modern facilities, such as in a built-in TV in the mirror above the bathtub, super-comfortable beds, and top-rate Wi-Fi. **Pros:** impeccable service; superb bathrooms; several wonderful bars and restaurants on-site. **Cons:** no kids under 12; expensive; some might find bedroom decor less than restful. [$] *Rooms from: DH4500 ✉ 19, bd. Moulay Rachid, Casablanca ☎ 0522/64–97–97 🌐 www.lecasablanca-hotel.com 🛏 68 rooms 🍴 No Meals.*

★ Hotel & Spa Le Doge

$$$ | **HOTEL** | A refuge amid the cacophony of Casablanca, this Relais & Châteaux boutique hotel is an Art Deco delight that offers high-quality accommodations and personalized services consistent with brand standards. **Pros:** sublime decor; faultless service; high-quality restaurant and rooftop bar. **Cons:** 1930s-inspired style won't suit all tastes; expensive; parking can be a challenge. [$] *Rooms from: DH1610 ✉ 9, rue du Docteur Veyre, Casablanca ☎ 0522/46–78–00 🌐 www.hotelledoge.com 🛏 16 rooms 🍴 Free Breakfast.*

Hotel Gauthier

$$ | **HOTEL** | Named for the chic district it's located in, the Gauthier is a boutique hotel with a modern, quirky vibe. **Pros:** lovely terrace; contemporary decor; comfortable yet stylish rooms. **Cons:** some rooms are dark; service can be slow at busy times; beginning to look a little worn around the edges. [$] *Rooms from: DH1400 ✉ 2 bis, rue Ilya Abou Madi, Gauthier, Casablanca ☎ 0522/22–32–24 🌐 www.hotelgauthier.com 🛏 35 rooms 🍴 Free Breakfast.*

Hyatt Regency Casablanca

$$$$ | **HOTEL** | Casablanca's most conspicuous hotel occupies a large site next to Place des Nations Unies and overlooks the old medina. **Pros:** excellent service and facilities; popular Black House disco; upper-floor rooms have fantastic views. **Cons:** expensive; lacks the intimacy of smaller lodgings; rather blocklike exterior. [$] *Rooms from: DH2100 ✉ Pl. des Nations Unies, Casablanca ☎ 0522/43–12–34 🌐 www.hyatt.com 🛏 255 rooms 🍴 No Meals.*

Kenzi Tower

$$ | **HOTEL** | In the heart of the Maarif shopping district, this sophisticated spot has excellent facilities—including a fitness center, indoor pool, and full-service spa—as well as panoramic views of the Hassan II Mosque and the ocean beyond. **Pros:** rooftop bar; fantastic views; central location. **Cons:** on a busy road; off-site restaurants are generally a better option; not every room has a city view. [$] *Rooms from: DH1475 ✉ Twin Center, Bd. Mohammed Zerktouni, Casablanca ☎ 0522/97–80–00 🌐 www.kenzi-hotels.com/kenzi-tower 🛏 237 rooms 🍴 No Meals.*

🍸 Nightlife

Most Casablanca nightlife for the younger set happens out along Boulevard de la Corniche, around a 50 DH taxi fare from the center of town. Exceptions are the major hotel discos, such as the Black House in the Hyatt Regency.

BARS

⭐ Le Cabestan Bar

COCKTAIL LOUNGES | The bar area inside Le Cabestan Ocean View restaurant heats up after dark, drawing the glitterati of the city who drink, dance, and gossip the night away as the DJ spins. Spectacular coastal views and briny air add to the unforgettable experience. ⊠ *Cabestan, 90, bd. de la Corniche, Casablanca* ☎ *0522/39–11–90* ⊕ *www.le-cabestan. com.*

Rick's Café

BARS | Within the walls of a restored medina riad, Rick's Café evokes, of course, the romantic Casablanca from the classic 1942 Humphrey Bogart film—which wasn't actually shot here. The pianist, Issam, plays jazz nightly and also organizes jazz jams next to the bar. Service is efficient and the restaurant menu blends American, French, and local cuisines. You can dine while sitting atop a high stool at the bar or settle in at one of the intimate tables. The cocktails are perfectly crafted and there's a comprehensive wine list. ⊠ *248, bd. Sour Jdid, Pl. du Jardin Public, Tangier* ☎ *0522/27–42–07* ⊕ *www.rickscafe.ma.*

⭐ Le Wynn

WINE BARS | Take a stool at the bar or squeeze around a table and enjoy fantastic wine along with excellent cheese and charcuterie at this chic French brasserie. This is a great place to meet local Casablancans. ⊠ *7, rue Omar Ben Abi Radia, Casablanca* ☎ *0522/26–37–12.*

DANCE CLUBS AND LIVE MUSIC

Brooklyn Bar

DANCE CLUBS | If you're looking for a place to drink and dance, head to Brooklyn Bar, which blends the scenes of New York City and Casablanca nightlife. There's a rooftop area, too. ⊠ *56, bd. de la Corniche, Ain Diab, Casablanca* ☎ *0661/25–96–98.*

Vertigo

LIVE MUSIC | In downtown Casablanca, Vertigo offers a great mix of entertainment, from DJs to live music to quirky theater. It's a small place but pulls in a cultured crowd of all origins and ages. Drinks are reasonably priced as is the simple but appetizing menu. Entrance fees vary according to what's on. ⊠ *110, rue Chaouia, opposite Hotel Transatlantique, Casablanca* ☎ *0664/09–45–25.*

🛍 Shopping

Casablanca's main shopping area is in **Maarif**, just south of Boulevard Zerktouni. The Maarif market is famous among Casablancans, stocking fruits, vegetables, fish, spices, and olives, as well as flowers and argan products. The Twin Center shopping mall is also here, as well as a number of European retailers and all manner of specialty shops devoted to everything from chocolate to porcelain. Built on a grid, you'll find that the lower part, nearer Boulevard Bir Anzarane, is more traditional, with lots of hole-in-the-wall places selling local products.

Several other shopping centers have been built in recent years: Marina Mall on the sea near the Hassan II Mosque, Anfa Place Mall on the Corniche, and Morocco Mall, the largest mall in Africa, on the western edge of the city.

The top place to shop for traditional souvenirs and handicrafts is the **Quartier des Habous.** It offers the best variety and prices, but you should still try to get an idea of market prices before starting to bargain. In close proximity to some of

Casa's luxury hotels, the shops lining **Boulevard Houphouet Boigny** offer few deals, and their business is mostly geared to tourists. They do present a broad sampling of all things Moroccan, however, and are convenient for last minute, one-stop shopping.

CRAFTS
Coco Corner

HOUSEWARES | This chic spot stocks all sorts of desirable home decor objects, furnishings, and accessories. The keyword here is design, and nothing is conceived without elegance. ✉ *89, av. Stendhal, Val Fleuri, Cité Plateau, Casablanca* ☎ *0522/99–00–10* ⊕ *www. coco-corner.com.*

Exposition Nationale d'Artisanat

CRAFTS | If bargaining isn't your thing but you want to bring home some wonderful handicrafts, this multilevel government-run emporium is the perfect alternative. It's stocked with authentic crafts from all over Morocco. ✉ *3, av. Hassan II, Casablanca* ☎ *0522/26–70–64.*

SHOPPING CENTERS AND MALLS
Anfa Place Mall

MALL | FAMILY | This mall overlooks the sea opposite the Abdul-Aziz Saud Mosque, right before the Megarama cinema. There's a pretty good selection of shops—most containing clothing and accessories—as well as a supermarket and stores selling books and cosmetics. Right outside, you'll find a number of restaurants and cafés overlooking an accessible stretch of beach. ✉ *Bd. de la Corniche, Casablanca* ☎ *0522/95–46–46* ⊕ *www.anfashopping.com.*

Morocco Mall

MALL | FAMILY | At the end of the Corniche, just after the Sidi Abderrahman islet, sits one of Africa's largest malls. It features all kinds of stores and a sizeable food court. There's also an IMAX theater, a large supermarket, and an adventure playground for kids that includes an ice rink. ✉ *Corner of Bd. de la Corniche and Bd. de L'Ocean Atlantique, Casablanca* ☎ *0801/00–12–30* ⊕ *www.moroccomall. net.*

Activities

BEACH CLUBS
The Tahiti Beach Club

SWIMMING | FAMILY | This is the most polished of the semiprivate clubs found along the Corniche in Ain Diab. Public entry here is 200 DH per person during the week and 250 DH on the weekend, including a parasol and lounge chair. Along with sun and sand, it offers many recreational activities for both adults and children—including several pools, a trio of top-notch restaurants with ocean views, a spa, a gym, a kids' club, and a surf school. ✉ *Bd. de la Corniche, Casablanca* ☎ *0522/79–80–25* 💰 *From 200 DH.*

HAMMAMS
It's best not to take valuables to the hammam, so leave your jewelry, credit cards, and most of your cash in the hotel safe. Most people like to keep undergarments on, too, so bring a spare pair to change into.

PUBLIC HAMMAMS
Hammam Le Pacha

SPAS | Popular with locals, these private baths stick to tradition without forgetting the pampering principle. Use of the hammam with combo exfoliation/soaping costs 80 DH and towels are 50 DH. You can also reserve a massage—prices vary according to duration and type. ✉ *484, bd. Gandhi, Casablanca* ☎ *0522/77–42–41.*

Hammam Ziani

SPAS | This is a friendly and authentic hammam offering a range of typical services, such as exfoliation and soaping at 80 DH. They also offer packages that include massages and algae wraps that come highly recommended. ✉ *59, rue Abou Raqraq, Casablanca* ☎ *0661/16–66–27 0661166627* 💰 *60 DH.*

Azemmour

75 km (46 miles) southwest of Casablanca.

Azemmour, situated on both the banks of the Oum Errabi River and the Atlantic Ocean, makes a fantastic weekend or day-trip destination from Casablanca. The charming small town has a medina with a Portuguese flavor, warm locals, and a quality of light that has inspired artists for centuries. The town's history stretches far back, but the Portuguese built the current Azemmour in 1513, and it proudly claims Estavanico, or "Stephan the Moor," as a former resident. Estavanico, born Mustafa Azemmouri in 1500, was captured and sold as a slave in 1522. He later joined the Spanish Narváez expedition with Álvar Núñez Cabeza de Vaca, and became the first African to explore North America.

GETTING HERE AND AROUND

The train from Casablanca to Azemmour Halte (1½ hours) leaves from Casa Port station, with trains running about every two hours during the day. By car, the drive from Casablanca to Azemmour takes about an hour. Bus service to Azemmour is unreliable as the route is seasonal.

If you're staying in a riad here, take a petit taxi from the train or bus station (about 10 DH) to one of the gates of the Azemmour medina; once there, it's best to call your riad to have an escort lead you from the entrance to the premises. The small medina streets and alleys are a gentle maze, and not easy to navigate alone—but once you've spent some time walking them, you'll get your bearings. What's more, most locals are friendly and will try to help if you become lost.

BUS CONTACTS CTM. ⊠ *Gare Routiere, Bd. Moulay Al Hassan, Azemmour* ☎ *0800/09–00–30* ⊕ *www.ctm.ma.*

TRAIN CONTACTS Office National des Chemins de Fer. *(O.N.C.F.)* ⊠ *Azemmour Halte* ☎ *0890/20–30–40* ⊕ *www.oncf.ma.*

Sights

Azemmour's medina is divided into three parts—the Mellah (or Jewish Quarter), the kasbah, and the old medina—and, to appreciate the attractions within it fully, you should arrange for a guide (it's easiest to do so through your riad). While the area retains much of its traditional charm, the influence of local and foreign artists is also visible. Lured by Azemmour's unique lighting, many artists have chosen to set up shop here; and as you wander the medina streets, their murals are a delightful surprise. It's worth stopping into one of the studios or galleries to see the artists and their work.

Although the new town offers quite a contrast, it warrants a visit as well. Located on the opposite side of the road to the medina, it contains the tomb of Sidi Bouchaib, a saint recognized for his abilities to heal dementia. Only Muslims can enter, but everyone can peep into the initial porch or just admire the architecture outside. From there, wander down through the busy thoroughfare, Boulevard Ahmed Choufani, which is unfrequented by tourists but full of locals. It's flanked by a multitude of hole-in-the-wall shops selling old-school wares, many of which are related to healing and spells. Expect to find anything from leeches and fox tails to animal bones, all used in traditional medicine.

Ahmed el-Amine

ART GALLERY | Perhaps Azemmour's most renowned resident artist, Ahmed el-Amine has been painting in and around the medina for nearly two decades. He still lives here, working out of this studio. ⊠ *6, Derb el-Hantati* ☎ *0523/35–89–02.*

Galerie Akwas

ART GALLERY | The medina's original gallery exhibits the work of artists from

On the banks of the Oum Errabi River, the town of Azemmour, with its whitewashed medina, is an easy day trip or weekend getaway from Casablanca.

across the nation. It was founded by Abderrahmane Rahoul, former director of the Ecole Supérieure des Beaux Arts in Casablanca, who is a well-known and highly respected visual artist himself. ✉ *4, Bab El Makhzen, Azemmour* ☎ *0661/41–08–31.*

★ Maison d'Artisanat

CRAFTS | FAMILY | This regional handicrafts center is well worth a visit. There's a large courtyard where exhibitions are often held, a shop selling crafts at fixed prices, and an auditorium. Around the courtyard and upstairs are the workshops of local craftspeople as well as classrooms to teach young people these skills. Look out for the beautiful Azemmouri embroidery.

✉ *Av. Allal Ben Abdellah, Azemmour* ⊕ *www.maison-artisanat.com.*

Plage el Haouzia

BEACH | FAMILY | Before the Mazagan Beach Resort was built between Azemmour and El Jadida, you could walk along the sand from one community to the other. While that's no longer possible, this is still a stunning beach and one of the cleanest on the coast. There's also a shipwreck that's fun to explore. **Amenities:** food and drink; lifeguards (in summer). **Best for:** sunsets; surfing; swimming; walking. ✉ *Plage al Haouzia, Azemmour.*

Shrine of Rabbi Abraham Moul Niss

TOMB | Rabbi Moul Niss is the most revered of the Jewish saints in Azemmour and his shrine draws many local and international pilgrims. Little is known of him but it's said that miracles have happened here for hundreds of years. His shrine contains a cave with a plaque and some ceremonial objects, and there's a courtyard outside with benches, which makes this a pleasant place for reflection. It's not always possible to get inside, but ask locally for the guardian and give him a small tip. ✉ *Azemmour.*

🛏 Hotels

★ L'Oum Errabia

$ | **HOTEL** | This delightful guesthouse at the river's edge effortlessly mixes charm and chic. **Pros:** wonderful river views; fabulous design and atmosphere; excellent location. **Cons:** some rooms are rather dark; difficult to find alone; can be a little noisy when busy. $ *Rooms from: DH800* ✉ *25, Impasse Chtouka* ☎ *0523/34–70–71* 🛏 *9 rooms* ◎ *Free Breakfast.*

Riad 7

$ | **B&B/INN** | Containing just five pretty but compact rooms, this riad gives tradition a twist by focusing on contemporary decor while still highlighting the carefully preserved features of the ancient building it inhabits. **Pros:** cozy, intimate atmosphere; centrally located in the old medina; well-restored traditional building. **Cons:** lots of stairs; some rooms are small; as is often the case with medina houses, rooms can be a bit dark. $ *Rooms from: DH550* ✉ *2, Impasse Chtouka, Azemmour* ☎ *0523/34–73–63, 0661/38–34–47* ⊕ *www.riad7.com* 🛏 *5 rooms* ◎ *Free Breakfast.*

🏃 Activities

In addition to water sports like surfing and kayaking, boat trips and fishing excursions along the river can be arranged at most riads. You can hire a rowboat next to the marina; prices are displayed on a board. Beaches just south of the town are also beautiful for a stroll or swim.

El Jadida

103 km (64 miles) southwest of Casablanca.

El Jadida it best known for its fabulous fortified old town, built by the Portuguese in the 16th century and now a designated UNESCO World Heritage site. (The name El Jadida actually means "the New" and has alternated more than once with the town's original Portuguese name, Mazagan.) Yet this place has other enticements for tourists, too—including a large sand-rimmed bay and a pretty promenade lined with palm trees and cafés.

GETTING HERE AND AROUND

The train to El Jadida is every two hours during the day from Casa Port station in Casablanca, and the train station is located in the Ville Nouvelle, 4 km (2½ miles) south of the old town. Buses are fine for trips from Casablanca (CTM one- to two hours, DH 55); frequent ones also come from Safi and Oualidia in the south. In El Jadida, one bus station, the Gare Routière, serves all bus companies and grand taxis.

El Jadida has inexpensive metered petit taxis. For local runs, however, it is always advisable to establish an agreed-upon fare before getting in. The going rate for such trips is around 10 DH. The petit taxi station is next to the bus station. Grand taxis are available for intercity journeys, like El Jadida to Oualidia (60 DH), as well as for longer trips to Marrakesh (80 DH) or Essaouira (75 DH).

BUS INFORMATION CTM. ✉ *Gare Routiere, Av. Mohammed V, El Jadida* ☎ *0800/09–00–30* ⊕ *www.ctm.ma.*

TRAIN INFORMATION Office National des Chemins de Fer. *(O.N.C.F.)* ✉ *Av. Ben Badis, El Jadida, 4 km (2½ miles) south of El Jadida's Cite Portugaise* ⊕ *www. oncf.ma.*

TIMING AND PRECAUTIONS

Most travelers stay in El Jadida for one or two nights. It's generally considered safe; however, the Cité Portugaise area is poorly lighted at night and the new town has a few seedy bars and clubs. You should exercise caution if visiting after sundown.

The Gothic arches and pools of water of El Jadida's ancient underground cistern are illuminated by a round window overhead.

Sights

Church of the Assumption
CHURCH | Walking down Rua da Carreira, you'll see on the left the old Portuguese Church of the Assumption. Erected in 1628, it's a fine example of late-Gothic Manueline-style architecture. ⊠ *Eglise de l'Assomption, Rua da Carreira, Cite Portugaise, El Jadida.*

★ Cité Portugaise
HISTORIC DISTRICT | El Jadida's main attraction is the atmospheric Cité Portugaise, which was built for military purposes in the early 1500s, overtaken by the Moroccans in 1769, and registered as a UNESCO World Heritage Site in 2004. Impressive (and still imposing) stone walls make it difficult to miss. The Portuguese city was originally a rectangular island with a bastion on each corner, connected to the mainland by a single causeway. Take the entrance on the right where you'll see that the Portuguese street names have been retained. ⊠ *Cité Portugaise, El Jadida.*

Fortress
MILITARY SIGHT | At the end of Rua da Carreira (Rue Mohammed Al Achemi), you can walk up ramps to the walls of the fortress. Looking down from the heights, you'll see a gate that leads directly onto the sea and, to the right, El Jadida's fishing harbor. ⊠ *Rua da Carreira, Cite Portugaise, El Jadida.*

Grand Mosque
MOSQUE | Beyond the Portuguese Cistern on Rua da Carreira is a fine old mosque, and its original construction makes it one of the focal points of the city. The beautiful white minaret is unique in that it has five sides, all with rounded edges. ⊠ *Rua da Carreira, Cite Portugaise, El Jadida.*

Jewish cemetery
CEMETERY | El Jadida was once home to a very large Jewish population—traces of which are still visible in the city's Mellah, the Jewish quarter of the old medina. If you walk around the walls to the other side of the fortress, you get clear views over the Jewish cemetery. ⊠ *Cimitiere Juif, El Jadida.*

Portuguese Cistern
NOTABLE BUILDING | The photogenic Portuguese cistern is where water was stored when El Jadida was still the fortress of Mazagan (some say it originally stored arms). A small amount of water remains, illuminated by a single shaft of light, reflecting the cistern's gorgeous Gothic arches, a stunning effect. According to local legend, this massive spot wasn't rediscovered until 1916, when a Moroccan Jew stumbled on it in the process of enlarging his shop—whereupon water started gushing in. ✉ *Rua da Carreira, Cite Portugaise, El Jadida* 🎟 *60 DH.*

Sidi Bouzid Beach
BEACH | **FAMILY** | This beautiful stretch of sand extends southwest away from El Jadida; you can access it by taking the coastal road about 5 km (3 miles) out of town. It's an ideal place to stroll or watch the sunset. Swimming is great here too, although currents can be strong. **Amenities:** food and drink; lifeguards (in summer); parking. **Best for:** sunsets; swimming; walking. ✉ *Plage de Sidi Bouzid.*

🍴 Restaurants

★ La Capitainerie
$$ | **MOROCCAN** | In the stylish Hotel L'Iglesia, La Capitainerie has tables that spill out onto the esplanade as well as a lovely dining room that highlights local tradition by displaying numerous period objects. The menu revolves around seafood with a Moroccan edge; you can order à la carte or choose a fixed-price menu; both change daily. **Known for:** intimate atmosphere; unique setting; small but appealing menu. [$] *Average main: DH110* ✉ *Eglise Espagnole, Cite Portuguaise, El Jadida* ☎ *0523/37–34–00* 🌐 *www.liglesia.com/en/diner-iglesia.php.*

Restaurant du Port
$$ | **SEAFOOD** | This old-school fish restaurant, located between the port and ramparts, serves the catch of the day straight out of the water. You can also sit at the bar and dine tapas-style while enjoying the reasonably priced alcohol beverages. **Known for:** great location; simple menu; unpretentious decor. [$] *Average main: DH100* ✉ *Port d'El Jadida* ☎ *0523/34–25–79* 💳 *No credit cards* 🕒 *No dinner Sun.*

Tchiquito
$ | **SEAFOOD** | For fresh fish, an easygoing atmosphere, and low prices, Tchiquito, just outside the medina walls, is the way to go. Be prepared to meet lots of people from the surrounding neighborhoods, as this seems to be everyone's favorite fish place. **Known for:** homey service; local ambience; inexpensive prices. [$] *Average main: DH50* ✉ *Rue Ben Tachfine, El Jadida* ☎ *0667/94–90–39* 💳 *No credit cards.*

🛏 Hotels

Dar Al Manar
$$ | **B&B/INN** | This delightful guesthouse just outside of town is an ideal place to unwind. **Pros:** relaxing environment; beautiful gardens; intimate atmosphere. **Cons:** no alternate dining options nearby; only five rooms and can book up fast; a little out of town. [$] *Rooms from: DH1000* ✉ *Phare Sidi Mesbah, El Jadida* ✥ *Near Sidi Mesbah lighthouse* ☎ *0523/35–16–45, 0661/49–54–11* 🌐 *www.dar-al-manar.com* 🛏 *5 rooms* 🍽 *Free Breakfast.*

★ L'iglesia
$$$ | **HOTEL** | One of Morocco's most chic hotels is partly built within the walls of the old Spanish church, St. Anthony of Padua, in the heart of the centuries-old Cité Portugaise. **Pros:** historical setting; unique interiors; gorgeous building. **Cons:** few other restaurant options in the area; expensive for the area; if you stay in the converted church, breakfast is in a different building. [$] *Rooms from: DH1700* ✉ *Eglise Espagnole, Cite Portuguaise, El Jadida* ☎ *0523/37–34–00* 🌐 *www.liglesia.com* 🛏 *14 rooms* 🍽 *Free Breakfast.*

El Jadida, with its beaches and walled old town, is a pretty spt on the Atlantic Coast, between Casablanca and Essaouira.

Mazagan Beach Resort

$$$$ | **HOTEL** | **FAMILY** | Mazagan is a spectacular seaside resort between Azemmour and El Jadida. **Pros:** lots of leisure activities; luxury accommodations; sprawling property. **Cons:** very large, so lacks intimacy; expensive; not accessible by public transportation. [$] *Rooms from: DH3500* ✉ *16 km (10 miles) northeast of El Jadida, Plage de Mazagan, El Jadida* ☎ *0523/38–80–60* 🌐 *www.mazaganbeachresort.com* 🛏 *500 rooms* 🍴 *No Meals.*

Pullman Mazagan Royal Golf & Spa

$$ | **RESORT** | **FAMILY** | This luxury hotel has large, well-equipped rooms that are decorated in a classy contemporary style. **Pros:** on the beach; quiet area; good for golf. **Cons:** no off-site eateries nearby; somewhat impersonal; no public transportation. [$] *Rooms from: DH1450* ✉ *Km 7, P4302, El Jadida* ☎ *0523/37–91–00* 🌐 *www.all.accor.com/hotel/2960/index.en.shtml* 🛏 *121 rooms* 🍴 *Free Breakfast.*

Activities

GOLF

Mazagan Golf Club

GOLF | Designed by South African golfer Gary Player, this is a links course—meaning that it literally links the land with the sea. The 72 par, 18-hole course follows the natural contours of the dunes and delivers panoramic water views. ✉ *Mazagan Beach Resort, 16 km (10 miles) northeast of El Jadida* ☎ *0523/38–80–76* 🌐 *www.mazaganbeachresort.com* ⛳ *Greens fees are 750 DH for 18 holes.*

Royal Golf El Jadida

GOLF | This 18-hole course next to the Atlantic is a good course, even though it's less sophisticated than the nearby one at the Mazagan Beach Resort. ✉ *Km 7, Rte. de Casablanca, El Jadida* ☎ *0523/37–91–00* ⛳ *Greens fees are 600 DH on weekends.*

Oualidia

175 km (109 miles) southwest of Casablanca, 89 km (55 miles) southwest of El Jadida. From El Jadida, follow sign to Jorf Lasfar.

This small beach town is famous nationwide for its oysters (if you visit the oyster parks, you can learn how they're cultivated). But what really attracts the large influx of travelers each summer is its bay, which is arguably one of the most picturesque places on Morocco's entire Atlantic coast. The fine sand is gently lapped by a sapphire lagoon, and in the distance white breakers collide beyond the cliffs. The main beach is surrounded by a promontory to the south, a gap where the sea enters the lagoon, an island, and another promontory to the north. Around the corner, a second beach seems wholly untouched, and dunes bearing tufts of grass alternate with little rocky hills.

The town is split into two sections: most hotels and restaurants are in the lower town, around the lagoon and beach. The business end of town with the market and bus station is up on a cliff. If you arrive by bus, arrange for your hotel to collect you or walk the 3 km (2 miles) down the hill. Taxi drivers can be persuaded to take you for an extra tip to cover the cost of their return journey.

Sand and sea aside, there aren't many "sights" here. If you have a car, however, the drive south along the coastal road from El Oualidia to Essaouira is a rewarding one with magnificent views—especially in spring, when the wildflowers are out. The town also has a Saturday souk, which is definitely worth a visit.

GETTING HERE AND AROUND
Grands taxis and local buses offer services to Essaouira and El Jadida from Oualidia. Both depart from a stop near the post office on the main road. There is also regular bus service north and south.

If you are traveling here by car from Marrakesh, follow the road to Safi and take the scenic coast road to Oualidia. If you are driving from El Jadida, follow the coast road down to Oualidia and allow extra time for possible congestion.

TIMING AND PRECAUTIONS
El Oualidia is a great choice for a stopover on the way north or south, or as a relaxing beach weekend destination.

Sights

Koubba (*Saint's Tomb*)
NOTABLE BUILDING | Just off the beach about 28 km (17 miles) south of Oualidia, the koubba of an unnamed saint is built on a rock in such a way that it's only accessible at low tide. Some of the cliffs here are truly magnificent, reminiscent of the Atlantic coast of Ireland. ✛ *On coast near Zaouiet Sidi Radi.*

Restaurants

Ostrea II
$$$ | SEAFOOD | The menu at Ostrea II features various types of seafood, but most people come for the oysters—which can be accompanied with wine chosen from a respectable list and followed by a classic French dessert. Just after entering town, a sign for the restaurant points toward the lagoon. Head down the twisty road, then grab a table inside overlooking the oyster park or out on the lagoon-side terrace. **Known for:** all-day service; fresh oysters cultivated right in front of the restaurant; great views. $ *Average main: DH150* ⊠ *Parc a Huites No. 007, Oualidia* ☎ *0523/36–63–24, 0664/49–12–76.*

Restaurant à l'Araignée Gourmande
$$$ | SEAFOOD | FAMILY | This unpretentious, family-friendly spot looks out over the beach and lagoon. Not surprisingly, the menu is seafood-oriented—lobster, of course, is the priciest item listed, but it's superb—and there are other options like omelets and salads, plus a

small selection of desserts. **Known for:** lovely views plus beach access; friendly, no-frills service; moderately priced menu. $ *Average main: DH140 ⊠ Plage Oualidia ☎ 0523/36–64–47.*

 Hotels

Dar Beldi

$ | **B&B/INN** | **FAMILY** | Located in the upper town, a short car ride from the lagoon, this pretty guesthouse rambles over various levels interspersed with lovely patios and plants. **Pros:** lovely for families; pretty and peaceful; individually decorated rooms. **Cons:** there's no restaurant (but breakfast is included); some rooms are dark; a little far from the beach. $ *Rooms from: DH550 ⊠ Douar Moulay Adessalam, Oualidia ☎ 0523/36–62–88 ➪ 5 rooms ⍟ Free Breakfast.*

L'Hippocampe

$$ | **HOTEL** | **FAMILY** | Overlooking the lagoon, this family-run hotel offers clean, functional rooms arranged around a truly beautiful, flower-filled garden. **Pros:** cozy in winter, too; easy beach access; friendly staff. **Cons:** indoor dining area lacks intimacy; gets very busy in summer; rooms aren't particularly inspiring. $ *Rooms from: DH1450 ⊠ Plage Oualidia ☎ 0523/36–61–08 ⊕ www.hippocampe-oualidia.com ➪ 23 rooms ⍟ Free Breakfast.*

★ La Sultana Oulidia

$$$$ | **HOTEL** | Breathtakingly beautiful and discrete, this luxurious little boutique hotel on a secluded corner of Oualidia's lagoon is worth the price if you're in the mood to be truly pampered. **Pros:** flawless service; beautiful location; luxury facilities and furnishings. **Cons:** the atmosphere may be too tranquil for some; a little awkward to reach without a car; high prices. $ *Rooms from: DH7200 ⊠ Parc a huitres 3, Oualidia ☎ 0523/36–65–95 ⊕ www.lasultanahotels.com/oualidia ➪ 12 rooms ⍟ No Meals.*

 Activities

SURFING

Gentle waves make Oualidia's lagoon a great place to learn how to surf, while experienced surfers will find fairly consistent waves on the Atlantic beaches south of town. Offshore winds are southeasterly, and there are left- and right-hand waves and reef breaks. Winter is the best season for surfing, particularly in January.

Surfland

SURFING | **FAMILY** | This school runs surfing holidays for both adults and children, with English-speaking instructors. Camping accommodations are available but surfers staying elsewhere can join up without a reservation if there's space. Lessons cost 350 DH (equipment included). ⊠ *Oualidia ☎ 0523/36–61–10, 0661/14–64–61.*

TANGIER AND THE MEDITERRANEAN

Updated by
Sarah Gilbert

 Sights   Restaurants   Hotels   Shopping   Nightlife

★★★★★   ★★★★☆   ★★★☆☆   ★★☆☆☆   ★★☆☆☆

WELCOME TO TANGIER AND THE MEDITERRANEAN

TOP REASONS TO GO

★ **Tangier:** Morocco's cultural melting pot, this vibrant port city is rapidly modernizing, but retains the bohemian charm that has attracted visitors for centuries.

★ **The mountain stronghold of Chefchaouen:** This captivating city is one of Morocco's fairy-tale towns, with a blue-painted medina and beautiful views.

★ **The Rif Mountains:** Morocco's most northerly mountains offer everything from easy rambles to more strenuous multiday hikes amid spectacular scenery.

★ **Laid-back Asilah:** Check out the eye-catching street art that graces the walls of this coastal town's whitewashed medina, then sit down to a seafood feast.

★ **Beaches of Tamuda Bay:** This stretch of coast dubbed the Moroccan Riviera is known for upscale resorts, fine dining, and water sports.

Set across from mainland Europe, Tangier has a long history that has produced a unique and diverse city filled with traces of the past. Founded by the Carthaginians in the 5th century BC and colonized by the Romans, Arabs, Portuguese, Spanish, and French over the following centuries, it has combined the architecture, cultures, and culinary traditions from each civilization that sought to capture it. Side trips down the Atlantic coast reveal the laid-back seaside town of Asilah and Larache's ancient ruins of Lixus. Along Morocco's Mediterranean coast, Tamuda Bay offers sweeping beaches and gentle breezes. The trip south from Spanish-influenced Tetouan to the Riffian mountain town of Chefchaouen takes you through fertile valleys where the pace of life slows remarkably.

1 Tangier. A fusion of cultures, Tangier offers lively souks, laid-back cafés, and access to both the Atlantic and the Mediterranean coastlines.

2 Cap Spartel. A landmark lighthouse marks the meeting point of the Mediterranean and Atlantic, as well as the start of a string of beaches.

3 Asilah. Every summer, this pretty seaside town hosts an international arts festival, when the medina turns into an open-air art gallery.

4 Larache. This Atlantic port city at the mouth of the Loukkos River is home to the fascinating archaeological site of Lixus.

5 Ceuta. Get a taste of España in northern Morocco— along with vino, jamón, and tapas—at this historic Spanish port city.

6 Tamuda Bay. The expanding luxury development along Morocco's Mediterranean coast combines five-star resorts, golf courses, water sports, and endless beaches.

7 Tetouan. Between the Mediterranean Sea and the Rif Mountains, and famed for its fine crafts, the city retains its Spanish influence.

8 Chefchaouen. This town is a favorite of locals and tourists for its photogenic blue-hued medina, pure mountain air, and leisurely pace.

Sitting between the Atlantic Ocean, the Mediterranean Sea, and the backbone of the Rif Mountains, Tangier and the north hold all the allure of varied, dramatic landscapes and intriguing towns that many people associate with the country, as well as an energy unparalleled in the rest of Morocco.

The port city of Tangier offers a glimpse of evolving urban Morocco, with its increasing sophistication, polyglot inhabitants, palm-lined boulevards, and extensive infrastructure for travelers. South of Tangier, on the Atlantic, are the magnificent views from Cap Spartel and coastal towns. By the turquoise Mediterranean, Tamuda Bay is known for luxurious modern resorts and water sports, while a bit inland, untouristy Tetouan, known for fine crafts, retains its Spanish heritage. To the south, in the captivating town of Chefchaouen in the Rif Mountains, regional dress and a traditional, agricultural way of life persist.

As for beaches, there's no shortage of outstanding strands around Tangier and northern Morocco. From crowded city beaches to empty sand, Atlantic rollers to the calm shores of the Mediterranean, there's something for everyone.

MAJOR REGIONS

The Atlantic and Mediterranean Coasts. The Atlantic and Mediterranean coasts of northwestern Morocco present splendid views and gentle breezes that make a refreshing change from urban Tangier. Cap Spartel, an easy trip from Tangier, has spectacular views of the meeting of the Atlantic and Mediterranean. South on the Atlantic are coastal towns such as Asilah, a fishing village known for a lively art festival and good seafood, and Larache, a sleepy spot with a seaside promenade. On the Mediterranean, Ceuta, with its fine buildings, is an autonomous bit of Spain in Africa. South of Ceuta are the developing towns of Tamuda Bay, with resorts and water sports for visitors.

Chefchaouen and the Rif. Inland, in a valley near the Rif Mountains, Tetouan has a long history tied in part to Spain, as well as a historic medina and a reputation for fine woodwork and leather making. South of Tetouan, past quiet, fertile valleys, the hillside Rif Mountain town of Chefchaouen has a dramatic setting, a beautiful, blue-painted medina, and access to waterfalls and hikes.

Planning

When to Go

The region has a temperate, coastal climate throughout the year. In Tangier and along the Mediterranean Coast, winter brings rain and surprisingly cool temperatures, whereas the summer months of June through September see hot and sunny days. Spring and autumn are the best times for hiking the Rif Mountains. On the coast, the traditional high season lasts from July to the end of August, when an influx of domestic as well as foreign tourists means that airports and seaports get busier, rooms are hard to find, and the medinas, cafés, and beaches overflow.

Planning Your Time

First-time visitors to the region would make best use of their time by basing themselves in Tangier. The city's tangible history, bohemian air, and abundance of good hotels ensure a good starting point for exploring all that the surrounding area has to offer. Traveling to Tetouan and Larache (for the ruins of Lixus) is possible in separate day trips by taking CTM buses; however, joining an organized tour or taking a grand taxi (fares should be decided before departing) directly from Tangier is much easier. Another option is to take a break from city-hopping on the beaches of Tamuda Bay. You can get an overview of the region in a week, but it's worth spending at least four days in Tangier. Although those short on time can visit Chefchaouen in a day, staying two days in this relaxed Riffian town will offer a better sense of this unique corner of Morocco.

Getting Here and Around

AIR
Tangier Ibn Battouta Airport is becoming more popular for full-service and low-cost airlines, offering domestic and international connections. Tetouan's smaller regional Sania Ramel Airport connects to a small number of domestic destinations and European cities in the summer.

BOAT AND FERRY
Ferries are a popular way to get to Tangier, especially from Europe. Tanger Ville is a passenger port with regular ferries to and from Tarifa in Spain; it's also a stop for several major cruise lines. The Tanger Med cargo port is a passenger terminal with connections to and from Algeciras and Barcelona in Spain, Marseille and Sete in France, and Genoa in Italy.

BUS
CTM and Supratours run buses around the region, including daily between Tangier, Larache, Tetouan, Chefchaouen. CTM even has an overnight 10-hour bus to Marrakesh, as well as a 5½-hour bus to Casablanca.

CAR
Renting a car in Tangier to explore the region is possible and manageable (though cars with automatic transmissions are still scarce and roads tend to get very busy in summer), as is hiring local drivers (and their cars) for varying lengths of time through local travel agencies. You can also haggle with taxi drivers who may allow you to hire their services for the day to travel to areas directly surrounding Tangier.

TAXI
Grands taxis (taxis that travel fixed routes indicated by their parking stations and leave only when full, meaning with six people) are a good way to get from point to point. They travel between cities as well as along fixed routes within Tangier. To avoid a squeeze or unpredictable delay, offer to pay for more than one

spot. There are also *petits taxis* that travel within the city limits.

TRAIN

There are frequent intercity train connections between the Tanger Ville train station and Marrakesh, Rabat, Fez, and Casablanca; prices are very cheap, even for first-class tickets. Morocco's first high-speed rail line, Al Boraq, cuts the journey from Tangier to Casablanca to just over two hours, with stops at Kenitra and Rabat. Trains also depart from Tangier to the popular seaside town of Asilah.

Guides and Tours

In the port area of Tangier there are still plenty of unlicensed guides wanting to show you around; give them a firm "no thanks/ *non merci* / *la shukran*." Most licensed guides sport a badge and work for tour companies; you can also find them in any tourist office or book one online in advance.

Plan-it Morocco is a well-established outfit offering excellent cultural tours, such as a tasting trail of Tangier's medina, a tour of the gems of Tangier's Andalusian architecture, and an exploration of the city's rich literary and artistic heritage that includes talking to local artists. The company also has a street art tour of Asilah's seaside medina.

CONTACTS Plan-it Morocco. ☎ *0535/63–87–08* ⊕ *www.plan-it-morocco.com.*

Restaurants

As much of a mosaic as the region itself, northern Moroccan cuisine combines influences from several other cultures. Most notably, Spanish tapas, without ham (though there is a cured turkey variety that is mischievously called *jambon de dinde,* or "turkey ham"). The abundance of fresh seafood makes it a natural choice in coastal areas. Fresh grilled sardines, shrimp, and calamari are standard

fare here, as are larger Mediterranean catches such as sea bream, swordfish, sole, and St. Pierre (John Dory); they also appear in tagines. Tangier and the major regional towns have no shortage of restaurants and cafés, but they tend to get quite busy in the summer months, and the most popular restaurants require reservations.

Dining reviews have been shortened. For full information, visit Fodors.com.

Hotels

Accommodations in the north range from opulent to downright spare, with everything from luxury resorts to boutique hotels to family-run guesthouses. You'll have a range of options in most areas, though rooms do book up during July and August. Hotels in Tamuda Bay and many in Tangier are on a par with those of Europe, but the farther you venture off the beaten path, the farther you might feel from a five-star welcome. Still, what these lodgings might lack in luxury, they often make up in charm, character, and, most of all, location.

During high season, prices can rise quite drastically, but booking ahead can secure some superb rooms; all but the most basic B&Bs take debit or credit cards.

Hotel reviews have been shortened. For full information, visit Fodors.com.

WHAT IT COSTS in Dirhams			
$	$$	$$$	$$$$
RESTAURANTS			
under 100 DH	100 DH–150 DH	151 DH–200 DH	over 200 DH
HOTELS			
under 500 DH	500 DH–1,000 DH	1,001 DH–1,500 DH	over 1,500 DH

Tangier

32 km (20 miles) across the Strait of Gibraltar from Tarifa, Spain; 250 km (155 miles) north of Rabat; 340 km (211 miles) north of Casablanca.

At the crossroads of Europe and Africa, Christianity and Islam, the legendary port city of Tangier is like nowhere else in Morocco. It's certainly a melting pot—a place where it's not uncommon to see modern Tanjawa (as residents of Tangier are called) sharing the sidewalk with rural Riffians in traditional dress and eccentric expats. Many people have fallen for its louche charms, from Winston Churchill to the Rolling Stones, and from Woolworth heiress Barbara Hutton to the Beat poets. It's easy to see why: the whitewashed kasbah walls shimmer in the sunlight and there are plentiful intimate corners in the serpentine medina, towering palms, French balconies, Spanish cafés, and other remnants of times gone by.

Newer additions to the cityscape include a state-of-the-art marina—the largest port in Africa—and a high-speed train that will whisk you to Casablanca in just over two hours. At a slower pace, literature lovers can follow in the footsteps Paul Bowles, author of *The Sheltering Sky,* who made Tangier his home for more than 50 years, and William S. Burroughs, who wrote *Naked Lunch* at the hotel El Muniria (you don't want to stay here these days but the bar is cool). Today there's a creative renaissance underway, with contemporary galleries springing up around the city.

At the highest point of the medina, the whitewashed kasbah is all sunlit squares, sea views, and fresh breezes, and it's home to some of the city's finest lodgings and eateries. From there, the medina's warren of alleyways winds down—steeply, in parts—to the bustling Petit Socco. Below that, the larger Grand Socco (also known as Place du 9 Avril)

joins the medina to the wide boulevards of the Ville Nouvelle, which are lined with cafés, shops, and galleries. The revamped port area includes the contemporary architecture of Tanja Marina Bay, at the western end of the sweeping Corniche.

GETTING HERE AND AROUND
AIR
Tangier Ibn Battouta International Airport is just 15 km (9 miles) from Tangier's city center; taxis wait outside the terminal. Several airlines fly to Tangier through European gateways, including Air Arabia (from London Gatwick and Amsterdam), Iberia (from Madrid), Vueling (from Barcelona), and Royal Air Maroc and Ryanair from several European cities. Many of the airlines have local offices.

BOAT AND FERRY
Ferries are a popular option for locals and tourists alike, with frequent connections from Tarifa and Algeciras in Spain from a number of ferry companies.

The Spanish company FRS and French company Inter Shipping operate a regular 45-minute catamaran service between Tarifa and the city's port, Tanger Ville (400 DH per passenger one-way); the ticket includes a land transfer to Algeciras.

FRS, Trasmediterranea, and Balearia also operate services from Tanger Med—the largest port in North Africa, 40 km (25 miles) east of Tangier—to Algeciras; these take around 60 minutes. Grandi Navi Veloci offers 30-hour sailings to and from Barcelona.

CONTACTS Balearia. ☎ 0539/93–44–63 *in Tanger Med* ⊕ *www.balearia.com.* **FRS.** ☎ 0539/94–26–12 *in Port Tanger Ville* ⊕ *www.frs.es.* **Grandi Navi Veloci.** ☎ 010/209–4591 *in Italy* ⊕ *www.gnv. it.* **Tanger Ville Port.** ☎ 0539/33–23–32 ⊕ *www.tangerport.com/en.* **Tanger Med Port.** ☎ 0539/33–70–00 ⊕ *www.tmpa. ma.* **Trasmediterranea.** ☎ 801/00–35–36 *in Morocco* ⊕ *www.trasmediterranea.es.* **Inter Shipping.** ⊠ *Tangier*

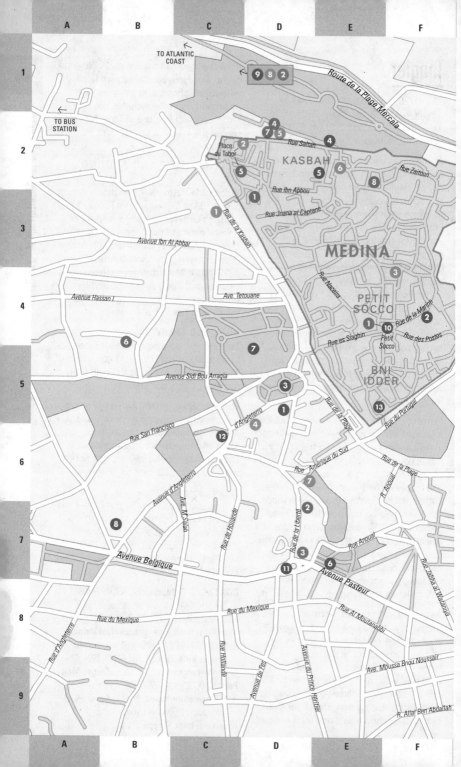

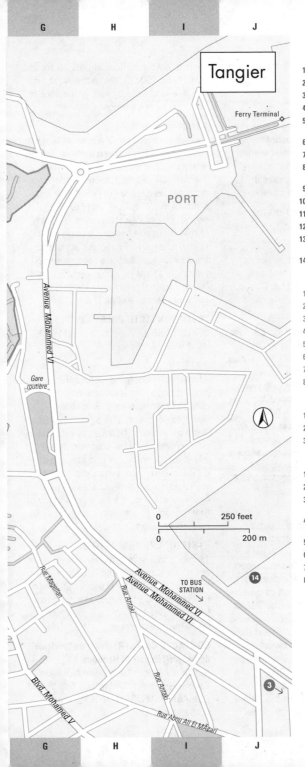

Sights ▼

1	Cinémathèque de Tanger	**D5**
2	Grand Mosque	**F4**
3	Grand Socco	**D5**
4	Kasbah	**E2**
5	Kasbah Museum of Mediterranean Cultures	**E2**
6	La Terrasse des Paresseux	**E7**
7	Mendoubia Gardens	**D5**
8	Mohamed Drissi Gallery of Contemporary Art	**B7**
9	Parc Perdicaris	**D1**
10	Petit Socco	**F4**
11	Place de France	**D7**
12	St. Andrew's Church	**C6**
13	Tangier American Legation Museum	**E5**
14	Tanja Marina Bay	**J7**

Restaurants ▼

1	Café à l'Anglaise	**C3**
2	El Morocco Club	**C2**
3	Hammadi	**F4**
4	Restaurant Darna	**D5**
5	Restaurant Nord-Pinus	**D2**
6	Salon Bleu	**E2**
7	Saveurs de Poisson	**D6**
8	Villa Josephine	**D1**

Quick Bites ▼

1	Café Centrale	**E4**
2	Café Hafa	**D1**
3	Gran Café de Paris	**D7**

Hotels ▼

1	Dar Nour	**D3**
2	El Minzah Hotel	**D7**
3	Hilton Tanger City Center Hotel & Residences	**J9**
4	Hotel & Restaurant Nord-Pinus	**D2**
5	La Maison Blanche	**C2**
6	La Maison de Tanger	**B4**
7	La Tangerina	**D2**
8	Saba's House	**E2**

☎ *0539//34–38–34* ⊕ *www.intershipping. es/en.*

BUS

Tangier-Tetouan-Al Hoceima's regional bus operator is CTM. Several buses run daily between Tangier, Tetouan, Chefchaouen, and many other cities within the region. The company even has an overnight 10-hour bus to Marrakesh, as well as a 5½-hour bus to Casablanca.

CONTACTS CTM. ☎ *0800/09–00–30* ⊕ *www.ctm.ma.*

CAR

Several major car-rental companies operate in Tangier if you want to rent a car to explore this region of Morocco. Cars can be rented out of the airport, city center, and at ferry ports.

CONTACTS AirCar. ✉ *Tangier Ibn Batouta International Airport, Terminal 1, Tangier* ☎ *0539/39–36–10* ⊕ *www.aircar.ma.* **Avis.** ✉ *Tangier Ibn Battouta International Airport, Tangier* ☎ *0539/39–30–33* ⊕ *www. avis.com.* **Budget.** ✉ *7, av. Prince Moulay Abdellah, Tangier* ☎ *0531/06–09–50* ⊕ *www.budget.com.* **Europcar.** ✉ *87, Av. Mohammed V, Ville Nouvelle, Tangier* ☎ *0539/94–19–38* ⊕ *www.europcar.com.* **Hertz.** ✉ *Tangier Ibn Battouta International Airport, Tangier* ☎ *0802/00–77–78* ⊕ *www.hertz.co.uk.*

TAXI

In the Ville Nouvelle, abundant petits taxis are the safest and most efficient way to get around. Petits taxis have a meter, so insist that the driver turn it on. You can wave one down by indicating the general direction you wish to travel; if the driver is going your way, he'll stop. For longer distances, or if you are among a group of four or more, you'll need the larger grand taxi, which can be called from most major hotels. A 10-minute petit taxi ride should cost about 10 DH; in a grand taxi (by yourself), the same journey would be about 30 DH. From the Tanger Ville port and airport to the city center or kasbah, daytime prices should be around 30 DH and 100 DH, respectively; at night, taxi fares increase by half. Make sure to confirm the price before departing.

TRAIN

Tangier is served by ONCF, and thanks to Al Boraq, the high-speed rail line, journey times to other major cities have been dramatically reduced; there are connections to Casablanca (just over 2 hours), Marrakesh (5½ hours), and Fez (3½ hours). Tanger Ville train station is 3 km (2 miles) outside the city, a short taxi ride from the medina. First-class accommodations or sleeper cars are recommended for longer journeys, especially overnight ones. Regional trains also link to the seaside town of Asilah.

TRAIN CONTACTS ONCF. (*ONCF*) ✉ *Tanger Ville Railway Station* ☎ *0890/20–30–40* ⊕ *www.oncf.ma.*

SAFETY

Tangier has become a much safer place since it became the favorite city of the current Moroccan king, who recognized its potential to be a great tourist destination and subsequently increased police presence. Use common sense when exploring by day and stay out of dark alleys at night. When in doubt about walking through dimly lit areas, take a taxi. Tourists should keep a photocopy of their passports with them at all times in case the police ask to see it.

VISITOR INFORMATION

Tangier's tourist information center is open weekdays and can usually supply information about local events as well as brochures and some rudimentary maps, but if you need or want a good city map, you'll have to buy one.

CONTACTS Conseil Régional du Tourisme de Tanger-Tétouan-Al Hoceima. ✉ *2, Résidence la Marina, 1st fl., Ville Nouvelle, Tangier* ✣ *Corner Av. Mohammed VI and Rue Ahfir* ☎ *0539/34–11–33* ⊕ *www. visittanger.com.*

Medina

Tangier's medina is relatively compact and reasonably easy to navigate, although there are some steep hills. Start by exploring the kasbah, the highest and oldest section; step through the Bab Al Bahr for views over the Straits of Gibraltar and discover the Kasbah Museum in a former sultan's palace. Then walk downhill, past cupboard-size stores and the hole-in-the-wall Cafe Baba—frequented by the Rolling Stones—to the hubbub of the medina's main square, the Petit Socco, where a café terrace is perfect for people-watching. Take time to dip into the food market near the Grand Socco, with its marvelous pyramids of spices and mounds of multihue olives.

 ## Sights

Grand Mosque

MOSQUE | The towering white-and-green-tiled minaret of the largest mosque in the city makes it one of the most recognizable sights in the medina. Built on the ruins of a European-built church in 1685 by Sultan Moulay Ismail, it was a tribute to and celebration of Morocco's return to Arab control. ■TIP→ **While only Muslims are allowed to enter the mosque, it makes a great photo stop as you explore.** ⊠ *76, rue de la Marine, Medina.*

★ Kasbah

HISTORIC DISTRICT | Sprawling across the medina's highest point, Tangier's kasbah is a fusion of sun-drenched squares, where the Mediterranean sun bounces off pristine white walls—a relic of the Portuguese in the 16th century—and shade-filled alleyways, making it the ideal place for relaxed wandering. Don't miss Place de la Kasbah, with the Dar el Makhzen (a sultan's palace turned fascinating museum) at one end, and the iconic Bab al Bhar gate at the other. Step through the gate for stunning views over

the port and across the ocean to Spain. The Bab el-Assa has a fountain covered in beautiful *zellij* tiles, ornate stucco, and carved wood. The kasbah is also home to some of the city's most atmospheric restaurants and lodgings. You can reach it from the Grand Socco by walking up Rue d'Italie, which turns into the steep Rue de la Kasbah, and entering through the Bab el Kasbah at the top. Or dive into the medina and get there—with a few twists and turns en route—walking upward along Rue Amrah. A petit taxi can take you there as well. ⊠ *Kasbah.*

★ Kasbah Museum of Mediterranean Cultures

HISTORY MUSEUM | This former sultan's palace now houses a beautiful museum, with arts and crafts—including carpets, jewelry, ceramics, illuminated manuscripts, and textiles—alongside an overview of the region's rich history from the Paleolithic period to colonial times. There are finely crafted examples of carved and painted cedar ceilings and the marble columns in the courtyard were taken from the ancient Roman city of Volubilis; other notable objects are the mosaic Voyage of Venus and the life-size Carthaginian tomb. There's also a lovely Moroccan-Andalusian garden to stroll through and a rooftop café with stunning views. Exit the palace via the former treasury of Moulay Ismail, the Bit el Mal; look for the giant, knobby wooden boxes that once held gold and precious gems. A palace has been here since the 12th century, but the current building was reconstructed in the 18th century by Ahmed Ben Ali. ⊠ *Pl. de la Kasbah, Kasbah* ☎ *0539/93–44–81* ⊕ *www.fnm. ma* ⊠ *20 DH* ⊗ *Closed Tues.*

Petit Socco

PLAZA/SQUARE | Stopping off in this permanently busy square is a quintessential Tangier experience, with a cast of characters passing through who are bound to give you a taste of Moroccan

Tangier History

Tangier's strategic position at the crossroads of the Mediterranean and Atlantic, as well as Europe and Africa, has long attracted attention. Following Carthaginian, Roman, and then Arab conquerors, Portugal seized Tangier in the 15th century, only to hand it over to Great Britain in the 17th century as part of Catherine of Braganza's dowry on her marriage to King Charles II. British control of Tangier was short-lived, though; in 1684 it fell into the hands of the Sultan Moulay Ismail.

In the 19th century, France, Spain, and Great Britain all battled for control, and the country became a French protectorate in 1912. However, it was agreed that Tangier was too important to be controlled by any one power, and the city was declared an international zone, initially administered by France, Spain, and Great Britain, and then, by 1924, eight European powers. The city's unique status, complete with special tax laws and loose governance, drew a cosmopolitan crowd of artists, writers, and free spirits. Tangier became fabled for its hedonistic excesses. It was a safe haven for international spies, and rumor has it that secret agents used Tangier as a meeting point during World War II.

After Morocco gained independence in 1956, the international population—and investors—dwindled, and the city's magnificence began to retreat into the realm of myth. Now, with the support of the king, this gritty port city is sweeping away decades of neglect with major civic and cultural renewal, including a new marina, ferry terminal, and fishing port, and a high-speed train service to Casablanca.

Modern-day Tangier may be more subdued than the sybaritic haven of its past, yet it still has a distinctly bohemian appeal. Like Morocco's zellij tiles, the city is an amalgam of centuries and nationalities that appears to change shape depending on the angle from which it's viewed.

daily life. Pick from three old-school cafés: what is now the Hotel Fuentes used to be the German post office during the International Zone era. The square is a great place to take a break before plunging back into the souks that surround it, or you can let gravity take you down past the Grand Mosque to the viewing platform looking out onto the port. ⊠ *Medina*.

★ **Tangier American Legation Museum**
HISTORY MUSEUM | As the first public real estate and the only U.S. National Historic Landmark outside the country, the Tangier American Legation Museum pays testament to the long-standing relationship between Morocco and the United States.

Since the stately building was donated to the U.S. government by Sultan Moulay Suleiman in 1821, the museum has amassed a large collection of paintings, books, maps, and portraits. Exhibits to look out for include the original correspondence between George Washington and the sultan, and an amusing letter home from a panicked ambassador who was given an unusual goodwill gift by the Moroccan people: a now-extinct Barbary lion. Don't miss the Paul Bowles wing, dedicated to the American author's life in Tangier. ⊠ *8, rue d'Amérique, Tangier* ☎ *0539/93–53–17* ⊕ *www.legation.org* ⊠ *20 DH; guided tours 50 DH per person* ⊙ *Closed Sun.*

With all the fishing boats in Tangier's harbor, you know you can find fresh seafood for dinner.

🍴 Restaurants

Café à l'Anglaise

$$ | **MOROCCAN** | The decor of this cute café-restaurant reflects Tangier's mix of cultures. The chef only makes a handful of main dishes a day depending on market finds—perhaps *briouates* (small pastries stuffed with meat or cheese) or kebabs—and when they're gone, they're gone. **Known for:** lovely roof terrace; unique artichoke tagine; vegetarian and vegan-friendly options. $ *Average main: DH120* ✉ *37, rue de la Kasbah, Medina* ☎ *0635/18–67–66.*

★ El Morocco Club

$$$ | **MOROCCAN** | In 1931, an American architect renovated a kasbah mansion and turned it into El Morocco Club. Today it's three venues in one: a sophisticated restaurant serving a fusion of Mediter-ranean and Moroccan cuisine, a pretty café terrace, and a seductively lit piano bar. **Known for:** laid-back lunches at the café terrace; elegant setting; restaurant

reservations essential. $ *Average main: DH200* ✉ *Pl. du Tabor, Kasbah, Tangier* ☎ *0539/94–81–39* ⊕ *www.elmorocco-club.ma* ⊗ *Closed Mon.*

Hammadi

$ | **MOROCCAN** | Decorated in over-the-top Moroccan style, with banquettes covered with rich brocade and plump cushions, Hammadi (named after the affable owner) is never dull. Try traditional dishes such as the house *pastilla* (a meat pie), chicken tagine, or *kefta* (beef patties), along with a cup of freshly brewed mint tea. **Known for:** alcohol menu available; live Andalusian music daily; go at dinner to avoid tour groups. $ *Average main: DH90* ✉ *2, rue de la Kasbah, Medina* ☎ *0539/93–45–14.*

Restaurant Nord-Pinus

$$$$ | **MOROCCAN** | Boasting an undeni-ably romantic ambience with intimate nooks, antique furniture, and sparkling stained-glass lights, this hotel restaurant serves traditional Moroccan dishes with a creative twist. The catch of the day is popular, along with dishes like chicken and olive tagine cooked over a wood fire. **Known for:** tempting desserts; views over the sea and the Corniche; reservations are essential. $ *Average main: DH400* ✉ *11, rue Riad Sultan, Kasbah, Kasbah* ☎ *0539/22–81–40* ⊕ *www.nord-pi-nus-tanger.com.*

Salon Bleu

$ | MOROCCAN | Decked out in dazzling blues and whites, this seaside house behind Place de la Kasbah has been turned into a tea salon and restaurant by the owners of the guesthouse Dar Nour. Tuck into delicious Moroccan dishes in the intimate salons or on the terrace with stunning sea views across to Spain. **Known for:** delicious desserts; good-value set menus; special mint tea. $ *Average main: DH60* ✉ *Pl. de la Kasbah, Kasbah, Tangier* ☎ *0529/27–16–18.*

☕ Coffee and Quick Bites

Café Centrale

$ | MOROCCAN | Front-row seating can be had at the pavement tables of this café smack bang in the middle of the Petit Socco. It's a good place to catch your breath with a coffee or freshly squeezed orange juice and a crepe as you watch an intriguing cast of characters wander past. **Known for:** good mint tea; Tangier institution; credit cards not accepted. $ *Average main: DH20* ✉ *Petit Socco, Tangier* ▭ *No credit cards.*

🛏 Hotels

Dar Nour

$$ | B&B/INN | In the heart of the medina and boasting 360-degree views, this charming inn (the name means "House of Light") is partly built right on the kasbah's western ramparts. **Pros:** cool rooftop bar; personal service; cozy atmosphere and stylish decor. **Cons:** no access for cars; can be difficult to find;

steep stairs. $ *Rooms from: DH785* ✉ *20, rue Gourna, Kasbah, Tangier* ☎ *0662/11–27–24* ⊕ *www.darnour.com* ⤵ *10 rooms* ⦿ *Free Breakfast.*

Hotel & Restaurant Nord-Pinus

$$$$ | HOTEL | The spacious suites at this 18th-century former palace have been artfully decorated in a mix of antique and contemporary furniture and sumptuous fabrics; shaggy rugs, carved cedarwood, and handcrafted wall tiles help give the place a truly Moroccan feel. **Pros:** spectacular panoramic views; sophisticated style; at the highest point of the medina. **Cons:** service can be leisurely; might be too intimate for some; steep stairs to upper floors. $ *Rooms from: DH2195* ✉ *11, rue Riad Sultan, Kasbah, Tangier* ☎ *0593/22–81–40* ⊕ *www.nordpinustan-ger.com* ⤵ *5 rooms* ⦿ *Free Breakfast.*

★ La Maison Blanche

$$$ | B&B/INN | This elegant town house has been sensitively transformed into a tranquil haven amid the mayhem of the medina, with light-filled rooms (named after notable kasbah visitors) that have been individually decorated in exquisite French fabrics and antiques. **Pros:** delicious breakfasts with a view; classic Moroccan riad architecture; extremely helpful staff and owner. **Cons:** small property; pedestrian-only access (but very close to parking); steep stairs to upper floors (there is one ground-floor room). $ *Rooms from: DH1200* ✉ *2, rue Ahmed Ben Ajiba, Kasbah, Tangier* ☎ *0661/63–93–32* ⊕ *www.lamaisonblanchetanger. com* ⤵ *9 rooms* ⦿ *Free Breakfast.*

La Maison de Tanger

$$$ | B&B/INN | Every guest room in this traditional hotel is completely unique, each individually decorated and with balconies looking out to the hotel gardens and the sea in the distance. **Pros:** beautiful garden with swimming pool; intimate and relaxed atmosphere; great staff. **Cons:** pedestrian-only access; steep stairs to upper floors; can be difficult to

The Tangier American Legation Museum chronicles the long friendship between Morocco and the United States, including correspondence that dates back to George Washington.

find. $ Rooms from: DH1200 ⊠ 9, rue Al Mabara, Marshan ☎ 0539/93–66–37, 0660/68–88–52 ⊕ www.lamaisondetanger.com ⤳ 9 rooms ⦿ Free Breakfast.

★ Saba's House

$$$$ | B&B/INN | A luxe makeover has given this traditional riad six striking suites—named after some of the city's celebrity fans, including Elizabeth Taylor—in which contemporary pieces have been artfully blended with traditional Moroccan design. **Pros:** superb staff; stunning terrace views; marble hamman. **Cons:** no children allowed; small property; steep stairs. $ Rooms from: DH2800 ⊠ 61, rue Cheikh Mohammed Ben Seddik, Kasbah, Tangier ☎ 0539/33–13–87 ⊕ www.sabashouse.com ⤳ 6 suites ⦿ Free Breakfast.

★ La Tangerina

$$ | B&B/INN | At the highest point of the kasbah, this light, bright riad is stylishly decorated in Belle Époque–meets–Moroccan style, with vintage finds, large parlor palms, black-and-white checkered floors, atmospheric lanterns, and colorful carpets. **Pros:** hamman in the cellar; stunning ocean views from terrace; friendly, helpful staff. **Cons:** no restaurant (you can order dinner ahead, though); rooms facing street can be noisy in summer; steep stairs to upper floors. $ Rooms from: DH660 ⊠ 19, rue Riad Sultan, Kasbah, Tangier ☎ 0539/94–77–31 ⊕ www.latangerina.com ⤳ 10 rooms ⦿ Free Breakfast.

Nightlife

Les Fils du Detroit

LIVE MUSIC | Older musicians hold Arab-Andalous music jam sessions here every evening around 6 pm in the closet-size but wonderfully atmospheric Les Fils du Detroit (the Sons of the Strait). Sometimes your presence is enough to get the band going, strumming their ouds and guitars. You'll pay just the price of a mint tea, but it's nice to leave a tip for the musicians. ⊠ Rue Ben Abbou, off Pl. de la Kasbah, Kasbah, Tangier.

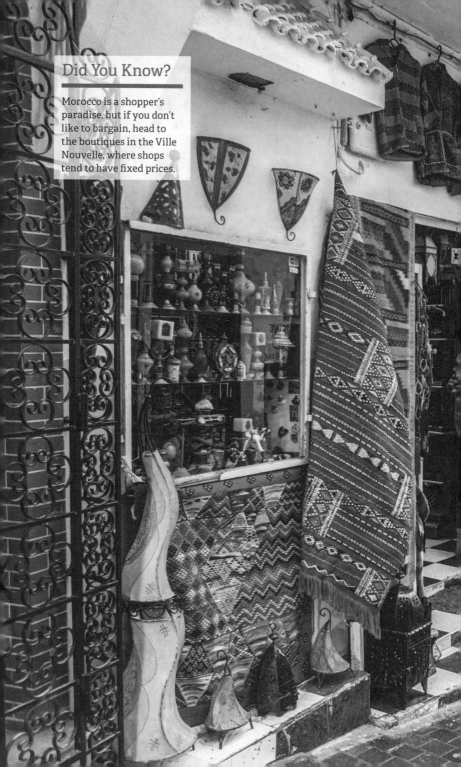

★ Hotel & Restaurant Nord-Pinus Bar

BARS | The laid-back terrace bar at this chic hotel is the perfect spot for sundowners as you gaze across the sea to Spain. Pair your negroni or chilled Moroccan rosé with some nibbles—plump olives, salted almonds—and drink in the views until stars dot the sky and the city lights sparkle. ⊠ *11, rue Riad Sultan, Kasbah, Tangier* ☎ *0661/22–81–40* ⊕ *www. nordpinustanger.com.*

Piano Bar

PIANO BARS | The Piano Bar at El Morocco Club harks back to the era of the International Zone, with its red leather seating, dark-wood paneling, and seductive lighting. Indulge in cocktails and tapas—perhaps a half-dozen oysters—sit back under the black-and-white photos of the city's celebrity visitors, and listen to the tinkling piano or perhaps a top DJ. ⊠ *El Morocco Club, Pl. du Tabor, Kasbah, Tangier* ☎ *0539/94–81–39* ⊕ *elmoroccoclub.ma/en.*

 ## Shopping

Shopping in Tangier can be just as mystifying and thrilling as it is in Marrakesh. Be ready to haggle for better prices; learning a few numbers in Arabic helps to earn the respect of vendors and makes it more likely you'll get a good deal. Ville Nouvelle boutiques offer standard Moroccan items, such as carpets, brass, leather, ceramics, and clothing, at higher—but fixed—prices. The more unusual and creative high-quality items, however, are mostly in the specialty shops throughout the medina. Don't be afraid to stop at small, unnamed stores, as these often stock real off-the-beaten-path treasures.

ANTIQUES

★ Boutique Majid

CRAFTS | One of the finest antiques shops in Morocco has an array of antique textiles, silks, rich embroideries, vintage rugs, and Amazigh jewelry (often silver with coral and amber), as well as wooden boxes, household items, copper, and brass, collected from all over Africa on the owner's regular scouting trips. Prices are high, but the quality is indisputable, and it's worth a visit just to hear tales from Majid himself. International shipping is also available. ⊠ *66, rue les Almohades, Tangier* ☎ *0539/93–88–92* ⊕ *www. boutiquemajid.com.*

ART GALLERIES

Galerie Conil

ART GALLERIES | This interesting gallery specializes in contemporary and art brut (art created outside academic traditions), with exhibitions of painting, sculpture, photography, and mixed media from up-and-coming and established Moroccan artists. The gallery has three locations around Tangier, and this one is tucked behind the Petit Socco. ⊠ *7, rue du Palmier, Tangier* ☎ *0534/37–20–54* ⊕ *www.facebook.com/galerieconil.*

CRAFTS

Bleu de Fes

CRAFTS | If you don't know a Beni Ouarain rug from a Boucherouite, this store is the place to come. Sip a mint tea as vintage and contemporary rugs from around the country are unfurled in a kaleidoscope of colors; don't forget to haggle. ⊠ *65, rue les Almohades, Tangier* ☎ *0539/33–60–67* ⊕ *www.facebook.com/bleudefesrugs.*

Volubilis Boutique

CRAFTS | Opposite the Café Centrale, the colorful Volubilis Boutique has been in business since 1972, stocking handmade leather boots, shoes, and bags for both men and women, as well as traditional clothes with a Western twist. Ask the friendly owner, artist Mohamed Raiss el Fenni, to show you his delicate watercolor and highly original ice-cream stick paintings. ■ TIP→ **The shop closes for lunch.** ⊠ *15, Petit Socco, Tangier* ☎ *0539/93–13–62.*

LOCAL DESIGN

★ Las Chicas

OTHER SPECIALTY STORE | Just outside the Bab el Kasbah, Tangier's first concept store is a delight. Putting a contemporary spin on traditional Moroccan style, the eclectic stock includes clothing, accessories, original art, housewares, and cosmetics. They promote Moroccan design, from Hassan Hajaj lampshades to couture clothing from Noureddine Amir and Fadila El Gadi, as well as Las Chicas' own designs. A pretty upstairs café serves delicious cakes, quiche, and other light bites, and there's a ground-floor gallery space. ✉ 52, rue Kacem Guennoune, Tangier ☎ 0539/37–45–10 ⊕ www.facebook.com/laschicasdetanger.

★ Laure Welfling

CRAFTS | The vibrant boutique of this eponymous French designer and stylist is filled with richly embroidered evening dresses and multihued silk caftans, all hand-sewn by Tangier's finest tailors. Other chic accessories include hats, shoes, jewelry, and housewares. The high prices reflect the quality. ✉ 3, pl. de la Kasbah, Kasbah, Tangier ☎ 0539/94–97–89 ⊕ www.facebook.com/laurwelfling.

Ville Nouvelle

In Tangier's Ville Nouvelle, built in the late 19th and early 20th century, striking Art Deco buildings rub shoulders with lavish Spanish-style villas, reflecting the city's cosmopolitan past. One place to start exploring is the Grand Socco, the former marketplace seen in many a sepia-tinted photograph, where the 1930s Cinéma Rif has been brought back to life. Then take in the café culture of Place de France and stroll Boulevard Pasteur for some old-school shopping, and be sure to take in the views over the city to the sea from the Terrasse des Paresseux. Plenty of petits taxis are available if you want to explore farther afield.

◉ Sights

Cinémathèque de Tanger (Cinema Rif)
ARTS CENTER | This popular cinema and cultural center, formerly the Cinéma Rif, is in a renovated, whitewashed Art Deco theater dating from 1938; it offers retrospective screenings and cutting-edge films across two screens. Old Spanish film flyers dazzle from under their glass frames at the café, where there is a full menu of intriguing, ciné-inspired cocktails and some light bites. The colorful, comfy chairs spill out onto the legendary Grand Socco marketplace, perfect for people-watching. ✉ Pl. du 9 Avril (aka Grand Socco), Ville Nouvelle ☎ 0539/93–46–83 ⊕ www.cinemathequedetanger.com ☎ Films 25 DH ☉ Closed Mon.

★ Grand Socco (Place du 9 Avril 1947)

PLAZA/SQUARE | This large, palm-lined plaza sits at the junction of old and new, linking the medina to the Ville Nouvelle. Tangier's main marketplace in times past is now known as the Place du 9 Avril, the date of King Mohammed V's famous speech requesting independence. The keyhole-shape Bab el Fahs, the main entrance to the medina, stands at the bottom. As late as the 1940s, when the new city was just beginning, the door was locked at night to seal off outsiders—hence the name, meaning "Inspection Gate." ✉ Pl. du 9 Avril 1947, Ville Nouvelle.

Mendoubia Gardens

CITY PARK | Next to the Grand Socco and flanked by a row of colonial-era buildings, this large, grassy park draws families and young couples, especially on weekends. On a peak of the central hill, surrounded by historic cannons, an engraved stone monument displays the speech King Mohammed V gave to the French asking for Moroccan independence in 1947. ✉ Pl. du 9 Avril, Ville Nouvelle.

Tangier's palm-ringed Grand Socco plaza marks the entrance to the medina.

Mohamed Drissi Gallery of Contemporary Art

ART GALLERY | Located in the stately former British Consulate building built in 1890, this gallery, run by Morocco's ministry of culture, shows mostly traveling exhibitions of contemporary art. A lovely garden surrounds the building. ⊠ *52, rue d'Angleterre, Ville Nouvelle* ☎ *0539/94–99–72* 🖃 *Free* 🕙 *Closed Sun.*

Parc Perdicaris

CITY PARK | FAMILY | A 15-minute taxi ride from the center of Tangier and around halfway to Cap Spartel, this sprawling coastal park (also known as Park Rmilat) makes a great break from the city. Its shady pine, mimosa, and eucalyptus groves, ocean views, signposted trails, and picnic spots make it popular with local families, especially on weekends. You can also see the restored house of Ion Perdicarus (the son of an American ambassador to Greece, born in 1840) and imagine his kidnapping by the Rifi bandit El Raissouni, with whom he later

became friends. ⊠ *Ville Nouvelle* ✛ *Off P4601* 🖃 *Free*.

Place de France

PLAZA/SQUARE | Famous for its café scene in the first half of the 20th century, Place de France is one of the Ville Nouvelle's main squares, named for the French consulate in one corner of the square. During World War II, legend has it that it was a popular haunt for European secret agents and shady deals; more recently it was the star of a thrilling chase scene in the 2007 film *The Bourne Ultimatum*. ⊠ *Pl. de France, Ville Nouvelle*.

★ St. Andrew's Church

CHURCH | Consecrated in 1905, this towering Anglican church—famously painted by Matisse in 1912–13 from his room at the Grand Hotel Villa de France—gives a sense of the flourishing interfaith relations that Tangier was once famous for. The Lord's Prayer is engraved in Arabic behind the altar, and quotes from the Koran appear across the Moorish-style walls. The church is built on land donated by Sultan Hassan. A cemetery surrounds St. Andrew's and holds the grave of British journalist Walter Harris (1866–1933; he lived in and wrote about Morocco), as well as British and Commonwealth soldiers who died fighting in North Africa during World War II. The caretaker is almost always on-site, and for a small donation to the church, he will share his knowledge about the church and those buried here. ✉ *50, rue d'Angleterre, Ville Nouvelle* ⏲ *Closed Fri.*

Tanja Marina Bay

MARINA/PIER | Morocco's first urban marina sits at the western end of the golden sweep of city beach, with space for superyachts, restaurants such as La Table du Marché and Chiringuito, and the trendy nightclub 555 Famous Club. It's perfect for a leisurely promenade, and on a clear day, you can see Tarifa in Spain. ✉ *Av. Mohammed VI, Ville Nouvelle* 🌐 *www.tanjamarinabay.ma.*

La Terrasse des Paresseux

PLAZA/SQUARE | A row of cannons pointed in the direction of Spain lines the so-called Idler's Terrace, known for its sweeping views; some say this is meant to stop Spanish invaders, or perhaps the French, the British, or the Portuguese. The terrace is a popular stop for locals, and on a clear day it's possible to see the outline of Spain on the horizon. ✉ *Bd. Pasteur, Ville Nouvelle.*

🍴 Restaurants

Restaurant Darna

$ | MOROCCAN | Stop for lunch at this community center, whose name means "Our House," and you won't just enjoy a scrumptious home-style meal; you'll also be supporting local women and children in need. The traditional couscous served on Friday shouldn't be missed, especially when eaten in the sun-drenched, tiled patio. **Known for:** shop with handcrafted products; daily chalkboard specials; delicious desserts. [$] *Average main: DH60* ✉ *Rue Jules Cot, off Pl. du 9 Avril, Ville Nouvelle* ☎ *0539/94–70–65* ⏲ *No dinner.*

★ **Saveurs de Poisson**

$$$ | SEAFOOD | At this iconic, cash-only restaurant, the menu and the price are fixed, so just sit down and prepare to enjoy four courses, designed to be shared by the table. The main event is always the catch of the day—perhaps St. Pierre, dorado, or sole. **Known for:** fruit juice from a secret recipe; reservations are essential; no-frills setting but full of atmosphere. [$] *Average main: DH200* ✉ *2, Escalier Waller, off Rue de la Liberté, Ville Nouvelle* ☎ *0539/33–63–26* 💳 *No credit cards* ⏲ *Closed Fri.*

Villa Josephine

$$$$ | FRENCH | A visit to Villa Josephine—perched on a hilltop estate, a 15-minute drive west of the city—is like stepping back to the glamorous 1920s, when it was a summer retreat for the rich and famous. Dress to impress for cocktails in the wood-paneled library and bar before dining on a classic French menu—perhaps steak with béarnaise sauce—on the terrace or in the dining room lit by crystal candelabra. **Known for:** reservations are recommended; beautiful property, furnished with antiques; romantic ambience. [$] *Average main: DH525* ✉ *231, rte. Sidi Masmoudi, Ville Nouvelle, Ville Nouvelle* ☎ *0539/33–45–35* 🌐 *villajosephine-tanger.com/.*

☕ Coffee and Quick Bites

Café Hafa

$ | MOROCCAN | West of the Kasbah, overlooking the Strait of Gibraltar and set up on seven levels plunging toward the sea, this laid-back cliff café opened in 1921 and soon became the favorite sunset-watching haunt of locals and bohemian visitors. Waiters impressively deliver 16 steaming cups of sweet tea at a time, along with bowls of *bissara* (traditional pea soup). **Known for:** legendary café; local flavor; credit cards not accepted. $ *Average main: DH10* ✉ *Rue Hafa, Ville Nouvelle* ⊟ *No credit cards.*

Gran Café de Paris

$ | MOROCCAN | This fabled café has been gracing a corner of the buzzy Place de France since 1927, and its brown leather seats, wood paneling, and mirrors galore will make you feel like you're back in the 1950s with William Burroughs (he wrote here) or in *The Bourne Ultimatum* (a scene was filmed here). The terrace is the perfect place to watch the world go by over an orange juice or café au lait. **Known for:** credit cards not accepted; delicious croissants; good coffee. $ *Average main: DH20* ✉ *Pl. de France, Ville Nouvelle* ☎ *No phone* ⊟ *No credit cards.*

Hotels

El Minzah Hotel

$$ | HOTEL | Built in the 1930s, one of Tangier's most iconic hotels has faded somewhat (despite a recent renovation) but still offers beautiful gardens, a large swimming pool, several restaurants, and a stunning courtyard lined with photos of celebrity visitors. **Pros:** can be reached by vehicle; retains an old-world charm; pool bar. **Cons:** Wi-Fi can be patchy; service is not always five star; rates can be expensive. $ *Rooms from: DH909* ✉ *85, rue de la Liberté, Ville Nouvelle* ☎ *0539/33–34–44* ⊕ *www.leroyal.com* ⬎ *140 rooms* ⦿ *Free Breakfast.*

★ Hilton Tanger City Center Hotel & Residences

$$$ | HOTEL | FAMILY | Morocco's only five-star Hilton, this hotel just a few blocks from the Mediterranean shows a whole other side to Tangier, from its showstopping lobby to the stylish rooms. **Pros:** rooftop pool and bar; excellent service; great views from the restaurant. **Cons:** not directly on the beach; no spa; a 40-minute walk to the mediina. $ *Rooms from: DH1400* ✉ *Pl. du Maghreb Arabe, Ville Nouvelle* ☎ *0539/30–97–00* ⊕ *www3.hilton.com* ⬎ *180 rooms* ⦿ *Free Breakfast.*

Nightlife

BARS

Tangerinn Pub

BARS | A late-night libation at the Tangerinn Pub in El Muniria hotel, a vestige of the former International Zone, is the opportunity for literary nostalgia. After all, your bar stool may have supported the likes of William Burroughs (who wrote *Naked Lunch* in what was formerly Room 9), Allen Ginsberg, and Jack Kerouac. They probably wouldn't recognize it today, though; on weekends it teems with beer-drinking expats and young Moroccans, and techno blasts from the speakers. The hotel itself has seen better days and is not the best option for a good night's sleep. ✉ *Hotel El Muniria, 1, rue Magellan, Ville Nouvelle* ☎ *0610/04–72–27.*

Tangerino

BARS | Facing the beach, this contemporary restaurant-bar-lounge channels a marine theme, complete with a wooden fishing boat and nets hanging from the ceilings. Enjoy delicious tapas at the bar or a huge dish of paella in the dining room—you'll be getting some of the freshest seafood around. There's a well-stocked bar, too. ✉ *Corniche de Tanger, 186, av. Mohammed VI, Ville Nouvelle* ☎ *0539/94–39–73.*

DANCE CLUBS

555 Famous Club Tanger

DANCE CLUBS | Sitting at the far point of Tanja Marina Bay, this nightclub (an import from Marrakesh) can hold up to 1,500 revelers. The light show is high-tech, the music—dance, R&B,

Latin—from the resident DJs is loud, drinks are expensive, and the party doesn't really get going until after midnight. They also have a neighboring tapas restaurant, Sky 5, with great views over the water. ⊠ *Tanja Marina Bay, Av. Mohammed VI, Ville Nouvelle* ☎ *0654/08–53–21* ⊕ *www.facebook.com/555FamousClubTanger.*

Shopping

ANTIQUES
Galerie Tindouf
ANTIQUES & COLLECTIBLES | Across from the Hotel Minzah, this pricey antiques shop specializes in home furnishings and period pieces from old Morocco, with an especially large inventory of antique rugs. The owners also run the Bazaar Tindouf right down the street, where Moroccan ceramics, wood, iron, brass, and silver, plus embroidery and rugs, are piled floor to ceiling. ⊠ *72, rue de la Liberté, Ville Nouvelle* ☎ *0539/93–86–00.*

ART GALLERIES
Galerie Dar D'Art
ART GALLERIES | This contemporary "house of art" showcases local and international artists year-round in a plethora of media and styles. Staff are knowledgeable about the small but strong art scene in Tangier and Morocco. ⊠ *6, rue Khalil Metrane, Ville Nouvelle* ☎ *0539/37–57–07* ⊕ *www.facebook.com/galeriedardart.*

BOOKS AND STATIONERY
Librarie des Colonnes
BOOKS | Opened in 1949, this historic and charming independent bookstore was frequented by Tangier's literati, including Paul Bowles, Tennessee Williams, and Truman Capote. More recently it was saved from closure by Yves Saint Laurent's partner, Pierre Bergé; covetable books still cram the shelves. The store closes on Sunday. ⊠ *54, bd. Pasteur, Ville Nouvelle* ☎ *0539/93–69–55.*

CRAFTS
Fondouk Chejra (*Weaver's Market*)
CRAFTS | Housed on the second floor of an old inn, this weaving cooperative overlooks what used to be the large courtyard where visitors parked their animals. Weavers and their looms are tightly packed into cupboard-size stores, where walls are lined with naturally dyed blankets, throws, curtains, linens, thick wool djellebas, and cactus silk (also known as vegan or Sabra silk) scarves. It can be tricky to find; ask a local to show you the portal that leads into the complex, below the Waller steps. ⊠ *To left of Escalier Waller, off Rue de la Liberté, Ville Nouvelle.*

PERFUMES
Parfumerie Madini
PERFUME | Founded in 1919, this famous Moroccan perfume house produces some of the world's most highly regarded oud (a resinous oil) fragrances, as well as copies of some of the most recognizable scents by the likes of Chanel and Dior. The perfumery is owned by Sidi Madini and has been passed down through his family for more than 500 years. ⊠ *5, bd. Pasteur, Ville Nouvelle* ☎ *0539/93–43–88.*

Activities

GOLF
Royal Country Club de Tanger
GOLF | This scenic 18-hole course weaves between cypress, pine, and fir trees. Founded in 1914, it's the oldest in Morocco and one of the oldest in Africa, just 3 km (2 miles) outside of the city center. Lessons are available. ⊠ *Rte. de Boubana, Ville Nouvelle* ☎ *0539/93–89–25* ⊕ *royalgolfdetanger.com/en/* ⋈ *300 DH (9 holes); 500 DH (18 holes)* 🏌 *18 holes, 6627 yards, par 70.*

The Cap Spartel lighthouse looks over both the Atlantic Ocean (to the left) and the Mediterranean (to the right).

Cap Spartel

12 km (7 miles) west of Tangier.

A short drive from Tangier, the jutting promontory of Cap Spartel sits high above the rocky coastline, offering splendid views from the most northwesterly point of mainland Africa and the meeting point of the Atlantic and the Mediterranean. A shady, tree-lined road leads up to a large 19th-century lighthouse and panoramic vistas over the water.

If you drive approximately 8 km (5 miles) south of Cap Spartel, you can look down toward the beach and see the small ruins of Cotta, a Roman town dating from the 3rd century BC. It was known for its production of garum, a pungent anchovy paste that was exported throughout the Roman Empire.

Several uninterrupted miles of golden beaches run south from Cap Spartel, including Sol and Achakkar, and Sidi

Kacem below the Caves of Hercules. This is the Atlantic and there's generally a lot of wind, which makes the beaches good for windsurfing and sometimes surfing. The currents can be tricky, though, so staying close to shore is recommended for safety.

GETTING HERE AND AROUND
Cap Spartel is most easily reached by grand taxi from Tangier, around 200 DH for a round-trip. If driving, take Route Rahrah and Avenue Ahmed Balafrej.

 Sights

Cap Spartel Lighthouse
LIGHTHOUSE | At 985 feet above sea level, the land around the lighthouse offers amazing views over the water: on a clear day, it's possible to see the meeting point of the dark blue of the Atlantic and the turquoise of the Mediterranean. Built by Sultan Mohammed III in 1864, this lighthouse was maintained by Britain, France, Spain, and Italy until Morocco's

independence from France in 1956. ✉ *Cap Spartel* ✥ *Turn right off Av. Ahmed Balafrej.*

Caves of Hercules

CAVE | **FAMILY** | Six kilometers (4 miles) south of Cap Spartel are the Caves of Hercules, a popular tourist attraction tied to the mythical Hercules, who's said to have rested here after his labors. One cave has been decorated with amateurish paintings; the other has been left in its natural state and is famed for its windowlike opening in the shape of the African continent, through which the surf crashes. Legend has it that the cave leads to a subterranean tunnel that crosses the Mediterranean. At one of the many cafés by the entrance to the caves, you can sit under a parasol and take in the sea views over a cold drink. You can tour the caves on your own if you're not with a guide or a group. ✉ *Cap Spartel* 🎟 *5 DH.*

🍴 Restaurants

Café Restaurant Cap Spartel

$ | **MOROCCAN** | **FAMILY** | In a prime spot next to the Cap Spartel Lighthouse, this popular restaurant has a sweeping terrace to take in the views. Its wide-ranging menu includes paninis and sweet and savory crepes, as well as salads and fresh fish. **Known for:** stunning sunset panoramas; alfresco dining; family-friendly food and vibe. [$] *Average main: DH50* ✉ *Cap Spartel* ☎ *0539/93–37–22* 🌐 *www.caferesto-capspartel.com.*

Asilah

40 km (25 miles) southwest of Tangier, 52 km (32 miles) south of Cap Spartel.

Straddling the cliffs of the north Atlantic coast, this sleepy fishing village is famed for its annual arts festival (usually in July or August), which lasts more than a month. It also has several relaxing beaches, as well as restaurants that offer some of the region's freshest fish and seafood dishes. In summer, the bite-size medina heaves with day-trippers from Tangier and Spain, so it's worth spending the night if you can.

Asilah was founded by the Phoenicians around 1500 BC. A prosperous trading town, it was invaded by the Carthaginians, Romans, Normans, and Portuguese, among others. It was officially Spanish territory before being returned to Morocco in 1956.

GETTING HERE AND AROUND

Asilah can be reached from Tangier by grand taxi or car via the N1 and A5. Another option is the train, a 40-minute ride from Tanger Ville station.

👁 Sights

★ **Asilah Arts Festival** (*Cultural Moussem*)

ARTS FESTIVALS | At one of North Africa's largest cultural festivals, Moroccan and international artists are invited to literally paint the town, leaving vibrant murals on the picturesque medina's whitewashed walls. Everyone from Japanese artists to Sufi chanters, along with thousands of spectators, descends on the town for more than a month of exhibitions and concerts. The festival is usually in July or August, though the date can change and dates may be released on short notice. Some events require tickets. ✉ *Asilah* 🌐 *www.assilah.net* 🎟 *Free.*

🍴 Restaurants

★ **Casa Garcia**

$ | **SEAFOOD** | Locals and visitors alike flock to this marine-theme, Spanish-style seafood restaurant for no-nonsense fresh fish, paella, and seafood. The terrace is a nice place to linger over a bottle of Moroccan wine. **Known for:** buzzing on weekends, so make reservations;

fantastic seafood tagines; extensive drinks menu. $ *Average main: DH85* ✉ *51, rue Moulay Hassan Ben El Mehdi, Asilah* ☎ *0539/41–74–65.*

★ Dar Al Maghrebia

$ | MOROCCAN | For authentic Moroccan cuisine at great-value prices, look no further than this small, family-run restaurant. Dine in the cozy salon or at one of the pavement tables, and choose from an array of brochettes, tagines, pastillas, and *briouates* (stuffed pastries). **Known for:** virgin cocktails; good for vegetarians; friendly staff. $ *Average main: DH80* ✉ *7, rue Al Banafsaj, Asilah* ☎ *0671/04–30–87.*

Oceano Casa Pépé

$ | MOROCCAN | This small, well-located restaurant sits just outside Bab al-Kasaba, the medina's main gate. The current menu is overly expansive, but the fried fish is always a good choice. **Known for:** serves alcohol; fish and seafood; popular with groups. $ *Average main: DH90* ✉ *8, pl. Zellaka, Asilah* ☎ *0539/41–73–95.*

★ La Perle d'Asilah

$$$ | FRENCH FUSION | At Asilah's finest restaurant, the sophisticated menu is largely French, with a dash of Asian and Moroccan. A chalkboard highlights the daily specials—perhaps John Dory, crab, or roasted *poussin* (young chicken); there are great-value two- and three-course prix-fixe menus, too. **Known for:** terrace dining; excellent service; indulgent desserts, such as chocolate fondue. $ *Average main: DH185* ✉ *Rue Allal Ben Abdallah and Av. Melilla, Asilah* ☎ *0618/41–87–58.*

Hotels

★ Dar Azaouia

$$ | B&B/INN | Sitting just outside the medina walls, this beautiful traditional dar artfully blends modern European style with traditional Moroccan design in a sensitive restoration by its multilingual Belgian owner. **Pros:** friendly and helpful staff; excellent breakfast served at the time of your choice; road access. **Cons:** no children under 12; small property; steep stairs. $ *Rooms from: DH850* ✉ *18, rue 6, Asilah* ☎ *0672/11–05–35* ⊕ *www.darazaouia-asilah.com* ➥ *8 rooms* ⬚ *Free Breakfast.*

Dar Manara

$$ | B&B/INN | This Spanish-owned riad has been nicely restored and converted into an intimate B&B with small but attractive rooms and plenty of laid-back lounging spaces. **Pros:** short walk to transport; rooftop terrace; helpful staff. **Cons:** steep stairs to the rooms; pedestrian-only access; small property, so need to book ahead. $ *Rooms from: DH700* ✉ *23, rue M'Jimaa, Asilah* ☎ *0539/41–69–64* ⊕ *www.asilah-darmanara.com* ➥ *5 rooms* ⬚ *Free Breakfast.*

★ Hotel Al Alba

$$ | HOTEL | With bright, traditional-style rooms, this hotel reflects the medina and sky with its fresh blue-and-white color scheme, stained-glass skylights, and plant-filled patios. **Pros:** one block from the sea; friendly, multilingual staff; on-site hammam and spa. **Cons:** some rooms are small; steep stairs to upper floor; outside the medina. $ *Rooms from: DH800* ✉ *35, Lot Nakhil, Asilah* ☎ *0539/41–69–23* ⊕ *www.hotelalalba.com* ➥ *12 rooms* ⬚ *Free Breakfast.*

⬤ Shopping

Bazar Atlas

CRAFTS | There are stacks of handwoven carpets from all corners of the country for sale here, along with singular green-glazed ceramics unique to Tamegroute in southern Morocco. International shipping is available. ✉ *25, rue Tajira, Asilah* ☎ *0661/10–33–45.*

Factory

CRAFTS | Tucked away down a medina street (close to Dar Manara guesthouse), this bijou jewelry store stocks one-of-a-kind and limited-edition pieces in both classic and contemporary designs. Items are handcrafted in sterling silver and adorned with semiprecious stones from Morocco, the Middle East, and as far afield as Asia. ✉ *34, rue M'jimma, Asilah* ☎ *0655/10–99–20.*

Larache

48 km (30 miles) south of Asilah, 80 km (50 miles) southwest of Tangier.

If you're visiting the ancient ruins of Lixus, the sleepy—outside of July and August—town of Larache is worth a look for its Spanish-built Place de la Libération. This grand, oval-shape plaza with a fountain at its center is studded with palm trees and encircled by handsome Hispano-Moorish buildings. On the plaza's eastern side, the imposing, tiled Bab Al Khemis is the centerpiece of an arched walkway that leads into the blue-and-white medina and the colonnaded marketplace, the Zoco de la Alcaiceria. Fresh produce and housewares are sold here from open-fronted stores, wooden carts, or straight off the cobblestones. The popular Balcón Atlántico, a seaside promenade that runs along the rocky shore, is one block west of the Place de la Libération.

GETTING HERE AND AROUND

Larache can be reached from Tangier by either a grand taxi or a CTM bus, which leaves from Tangier's central bus station. By car, drive south along the A5.

Sights

★ Lixus

RUINS | Perched on a hilltop with stunning views over the Loukos Estuary, Lixus is a fascinating archaeological site, just 10 minutes from Larache and one hour from Tangier. Although the site may not as famous or imposing as the Roman ruins of Volubilis near Meknès, you'll be able to explore without the crowds. Only a small portion of Lixus has been excavated, but the main attractions are an amphitheater, a column-lined road, and a mosaic of a sea god (half man, half crab). Also notable is the religious center of the town, at the summit, which retains the foundations for the places of worship of each civilization to have settled there—from Phoenicians in the 7th century to the Carthaginians to the Romans. The Romans believed it was here that Hercules picked the golden apples of the Garden of the Hesperides. A visitor center has an interesting display charting what's known of the site's history, and the guardians (Mohammed speaks excellent English) at the entrance are informative and happy to show you around; a tip of around 100 DH is appreciated. You can reach the site by petit taxi from Larache; arrange for your driver to pick you up after your visit. ✉ *Larache* ✥ *Off National Rte. 1* 🎫 *60 DH.*

Restaurants

Grand Café Lixus

$ | INTERNATIONAL | Since 1920 this Larache landmark has occupied a prime spot on the main square. Inside, it's all Art Deco splendor with towering columns, gilded chandeliers, and a grand piano; or you can grab a terrace table, perfect for people-watching over a breakfast of French or Moroccan pastries and perhaps a pizza in the evening. **Known for:** popular with locals; excellent coffee all day; Moroccan and international menu. [$] *Average main: DH30* ✉ *Pl. de la Libération, Larache.*

Hotels

Hotel Espana

$ | HOTEL | Set in a striking Hispano-Moorish building, this 1920s grande dame has retained a certain period charm despite somewhat dated decor. **Pros:** Andalusian decor in public areas; central location on main square; friendly staff. **Cons:** no elevator; charge for parking; Wi-Fi can be patchy. [$] *Rooms from: DH380* ✉ *6, Av. Hassan II, Larache* ☎ *0539/91–31–95* 🛏 *42 rooms* 🍴 *Free Breakfast.*

Ceuta

78 km (49 miles) northeast of Tangier.

The autonomous Spanish city of Ceuta, with its relaxed air, sweeping beaches, imposing buildings, pretty plazas, and buzzy tapas bars, makes for a pleasant stopover if you're heading to or from Algeciras in Spain. Set on a rocky peninsula jutting into the Mediterranean, Ceuta—known as Sebta in Morocco—was once one of the finest cities in the north. Originally thriving under its Arab conquerors, the city was extolled in 14th-century documents for its busy harbors, fine educational institutions, ornate mosques, and sprawling villas. Smelling prosperity, the Portuguese seized Ceuta in 1415; the city passed to Spain when Portugal itself became part of Spain in 1580, and it remained under Spanish rule after Moroccan independence.

Since 1995, Ceuta has been an autonomous city and a military base, with an economy boosted by its duty-free status. However, its strategic position on the frontier between Europe and Africa means that it's become a hot spot for the trafficking of drugs and migrants from sub-Saharan Africa. This is demonstrated by the high security around its small border.

GETTING HERE AND AROUND

Ceuta can be reached from Tangier by either a grand taxi or a CTM bus. You'll be greeted at the border with a lengthy, often chaotic, customs and immigration process, sometimes taking up to several hours.

Balearia, Trasmediterranea, and FRS operate numerous ferries a day to/from Algeciras in Spain to Ceuta, a trip that takes approximately one hour (around €35).

ESSENTIALS

VISITOR INFORMATION Ceuta Tourism Services. ✉ *Calle Edrissis, Ceuta* ☎ *0856/20–05–60* 🌐 *www.ceuta.es.*

👁 Sights

Castillo del Desnarigado

HISTORY MUSEUM | Just under Ceuta's lighthouse, and named for a flat-nosed Amazigh pirate who made the cove his home in 1417, this fort built in the 19th century now houses a museum of military history showcasing the evolution of weapons from the 16th to 19th centuries. You can look out across Ceuta's port and, on clear days, take in a stunning view of Gibraltar from the ramparts. ✉ *Carr. Castillo del Desnarigado, Ceuta* ☎ *0956/51–40–66 in Spain* 🎟 *Free.*

El Chorrillo Beach

BEACH | At Ceuta's longest and most popular city beach, the sand is nothing special but the clear water is relatively calm year-round. It gets crowded in summer. **Amenities:** food and drink; showers; toilets; water sports. **Best for:** swimming. ✉ *Ceuta.*

★ Murallas Reales

MILITARY SIGHT | Ceuta's monumental Royal Walls date back a millennium and have been added to over the years by the Arabs, Portuguese, and Spanish to strengthen the town's fortifications. The strikingly modern Museo de los Muralles Reales, set in the walls, displays interesting art exhibitions. Crossing the San Felipe moat gives you a fine view over the walls. ✉ *Av. San Francisco Javier, Ceuta.*

It's believed that Ceuta's massive stone walls date back to the 5th century, though subsequent Arab, Portuguese, and Spanish rulers added to them.

★ Plaza de África

PLAZA/SQUARE | The lovely Andalusian-style square is at the heart of the old city and worth exploring. Check out the memorial that honors soldiers who took part in the Hispano-Moroccan war of 1859. Flanking the main plaza is a pair of impressive churches, both built on the sites of former mosques: to the north is the baroque Nuestra Señora de África (Our Lady of Africa), and at the southern end is the larger and even more ornate cathedral. ✉ *Plaza Nuestra Señora de África, Ceuta.*

Restaurants

The city's cuisine is a hybrid of Spanish and Moroccan influences, and with the Mediterranean at Ceuta's doorstep, seafood is on the menu—from shrimp sautéed in a spicy pepper sauce to creamy baked whitefish to enormous grilled sardines. Moroccan influences are present in the form of couscous, as well as sweet-salty combinations such as prunes with roast lamb. A favorite pastime here is tapas, including *jamón serrano* (air-cured ham), paired with a cold cerveza or a glass of vino.

Parador de Ceuta Restaurant

$$$ | **SPANISH** | This retro-look dining room serves classic Spanish dishes such as *jamón ibérico* (cured leg of pork), seafood paella, and grilled octopus. Dramatic lighting is provided by attractive Andalusian lanterns hanging from the high ceiling like a constellation. **Known for:** high prices for the city; creative daily specials; romantic vibe. $ *Average main: €16* ✉ *Parador de Ceuta, 15, Plaza Nuestra Señora de de África, Ceuta* ☎ *956/51–49–40 in Ceuta* ⊕ *www.parador.es.*

🛏 Hotels

Parador de Ceuta

$$ | **HOTEL** | A reliable option in Ceuta, this aging grande dame is conveniently located on the main square. **Pros:**

pleasant garden; good-size rooms; good restaurant. **Cons:** food and drink can be expensive; service is slow; dated decor. [$] *Rooms from: €75* ✉ *15, Plaza Nuestra Señora de África, Ceuta* ☎ *956/51–49–40 in Spain* 🌐 *www.parador.es* 🛏 *106 rooms* 🍴 *No Meals.*

Tamuda Bay

12 km (7½ miles) south of Ceuta, 22 km (14 miles) north of Tetouan, 80 km (50 miles) east of Tangier.

Going back to its Roman roots for the first part of its name, Tamuda Bay is a new luxury development that stretches from Fnideq to M'diq on the Mediterranean coast. It's being dubbed the "Moroccan Riviera" for its upscale international resorts—a Ritz-Carlton is in the works—with fine-dining restaurants and luxury spas, long stretches of golden sand, gin-clear water, and almost year-round sunshine. It's the perfect break from city-hopping, and if you get bored with lounging by the pool, the Rif Mountains are on your doorstep for exploring.

GETTING HERE AND AROUND

The hotels in Tamuda Bay are about a 90-minute drive from Tangier by the N2 or by the A4 and N16. It's possible to arrange a driver from Tangier.

Hotels

★ **Banyan Tree Tamouda Bay**

$$$$ | RESORT | FAMILY | Morocco's first Banyan Tree is an all-villa resort, each with a private pool and just a pebble's throw from a sweep of shell-strewn beach, that pays homage to the region's history with its sparkling white Andalusian-Moroccan–style architecture. **Pros:** good variety of dining options; gorgeous villas; excellent facilities. **Cons:** not all restaurants and activities are available in low season; spa is pricey; main pool and villa pools aren't heated. [$] *Rooms from: DH3000* ✉ *Oued Negro, Rte. Nationale 13, Fnideq, Tamuda Bay* ☎ *0539/66–99–99* 🌐 *www.banyantree.com* 🛏 *92 villas* 🍴 *Free Breakfast.*

Sofitel Tamuda Bay Beach and Spa

$$$$ | RESORT | With its striking architecture, modern design, and vibrant colors, the Sofitel pays homage to the Riviera lifestyle, fusing the atmosphere of the Mediterranean and the Rif to create a unique resort. **Pros:** cool vibe; location right on the beach; nightclub with DJ. **Cons:** some areas looking tired; service can be less than five stars; breakfast isn't always included. [$] *Rooms from: DH4100* ✉ *Rte. de Sebta, M'diq, Tamuda Bay* ☎ *0539/71–62–00* 🌐 *www.sofitel-tamudabay.com* 🛏 *104 rooms* 🍴 *Free Breakfast.*

Tetouan

40 km (25 miles) south of Ceuta, 63 km (39 miles) southeast of Tangier.

Sheltered in a valley between the Mediterranean Sea and the backbone of the Rif Mountains, Tetouan is a fascinating fusion of Andalusian flavor and Riffian tradition. The whitewashed medina, a UNESCO World Heritage site, remains largely untouched by time and tourism and retains its quotidian life and authenticity. Tetouan is also famed for its fine crafts, particularly wood and leatherwork.

The city has a long and storied history, beginning with its founding in the 3rd century BC by the Imazighen, who named it Tamuda. The Romans destroyed it in the 1st century AD and built their own city in its place, the ruins of which you can still see on the city's edge. The medina and kasbah were built in the 15th and 16th centuries and improved upon thereafter. Tetouan was governed by Andalusians until the Alaouite sultan Moulay Ismail took it back in the 17th century.

Tetouan, perched on a hill with its whitewashed buildings, is nicknamed "White Dove."

Tetouan's proximity to Spain made it the main contact point between Andalusia and Morocco throughout the 20th century; it was the capital of the Spanish protectorate from 1913 until independence in 1956. The city's imposing Hispano-Moorish buildings stand in testament to the opulence of a bygone era.

GETTING HERE AND AROUND

Tetouan's small Sania Ramel Airport (TTU) is just 5 km (3 miles) outside town and has direct flights to Casablanca with Royal Air Maroc.

CTM is the region's main bus company and runs several buses daily to Tangier, Chefchaouen, and Larache.

ESSENTIALS

VISITOR INFORMATION Tetouan Tourism Office. ⊠ *Av. Mohammed V, Tetouan* ☎ *0539/96–19–15.*

Sights

Archaeological Museum

HISTORY MUSEUM | Close to Place Al Jala, this three-room museum holds a small collection of Roman mosaics and statuettes, coins, bronzes, and pottery found at various sites in northern Morocco such as Lixus and Cotta. It also has pictures of the archaeological site of Tamuda (which resembles Stonehenge), where Anteus is fabled to have been buried after his battle with Hercules. There are further exhibits in the garden. ⊠ *2, av. Mohammed Ben Larbi Torres, Tetouan* 🖼 *10 DH* ⊘ *Closed Tues.*

Dar El Oddi

NOTABLE BUILDING | A hidden gem in the medina, this beautiful 1920s mansion has been painstakingly restored by the El Oddi family and opened to the public as a small but fascinating cultural space. Among the ornate zellij tiles, carved stucco, and stained glass, there are collections of photographs, postcards, and stamps (miniature works of art) honoring the city's history. There's also a souvenir shop and a small peaceful café to sip a mint tea. ✉ *5, Derb Oddi, Medina, Tetouan* ☎ *0539/72–16–71* ⊕ *dareloddi. com/* 🎫 *25 DH* ☾ *Closed Mon.*

Medina

MARKET | Tetouan's UNESCO-protected medina—established in the 8th century—is one of Morocco's most compact and interesting. Surrounded by a wall and accessed by seven gates, it includes a Jewish quarter, the Mellah, as well as exceptional 19th-century Spanish architecture from the period of the protectorate. Crafts, secondhand clothing, food, and housewares markets are scattered through the medina in charming little squares, such as the Souk el Hout Al Kadim (the old fish market); there's even a small tannery near the Bab Mkabar. Tetouan's medina is relatively straightforward, so don't hesitate to deviate from the main path and explore; it's hard to get lost. ✉ *Bab er-Rouah, Tetouan.*

Place Hassan II

PLAZA/SQUARE | If you follow the pedestrian Avenue Mohammed east, past Spanish houses with wrought-iron balconies and tilework, you'll soon arrive at Place Hassan II, an open square with the Royal Palace to the north. On the east side is the Bab er-Rouah, the entrance to the historic covered market, and the Mellah is to the south. On the west side, look up to see Dar Tair (House of the Bird), an old Spanish apartment building crowned with a majestic bronze statue of a man sitting atop an eagle; it's close to Rue Zawiya, where you'll find some good dining options. ✉ *Tetouan* ✛ *Eastern end of Av. Mohammed.*

Place Moulay El Mehdi

PLAZA/SQUARE | A leisurely stroll through Tetouan begins most naturally at the Place Moulay El Mehdi, a large circular plaza ringed with cafés, a post office, and the Spanish church of Nuestra Señora de las Victorias; the church glows with strings of lights in the evening. The plaza is a favorite spot for the evening promenade and often the site of outdoor concerts. ✉ *Av. Mohammed V, Tetouan.*

★ Royal Artisan School (*Escuela de Artes y Oficios / Dar San'aa*)

COLLEGE | Just across from Bab el Okla, this prestigious school was founded in 1919 to preserve Morocco's rich craft heritage. Here you can watch the masters passing on their skills, including wood painting, pottery making, and embroidery, and also buy directly from the artisans. The Moorish-Andalusian building is a work of art in itself, with a colonnade inscribed with Kufic inscriptions, stained-glass details, and a vibrant zellij tiles. ✉ *Av. Mohammed Ameziane, Tetouan* ✛ *Opposite Bab el Okla* ☎ *0539/97–27–21* 🎫 *50 DH* ☾ *Closed Fri. afternoon and weekends.*

Tetouan Museum of Modern Art (*Centro de Arte Moderno de Tetouan*)

ART MUSEUM | The north's most prominent showcase of contemporary Moroccan art, this museum is set inside a beautiful, castlelike former train station. The dazzlingly white minimalist interiors display paintings by the likes of Mohammed Drissi, Mohammed Hamri (of the Jajouka musicians and Rolling Stones fame), and Hassan Echair, as well as sculpture, photography, and temporary exhibitions. ✉ *Av. Al Massira, Tetouan* ☎ *0539/71–89–46* ☾ *Closed Mon.*

🍽 Restaurants

In recent years the town has seen an expanding number of good restaurants. Although a fair percentage of them are in foreign-owned riads, the restaurants still retain local charm.

★ Restaurant Blanco Riad

$$ | **MOROCCAN** | Set within a jasmine-scented courtyard, this is one of the prettiest dining spots in the city. The

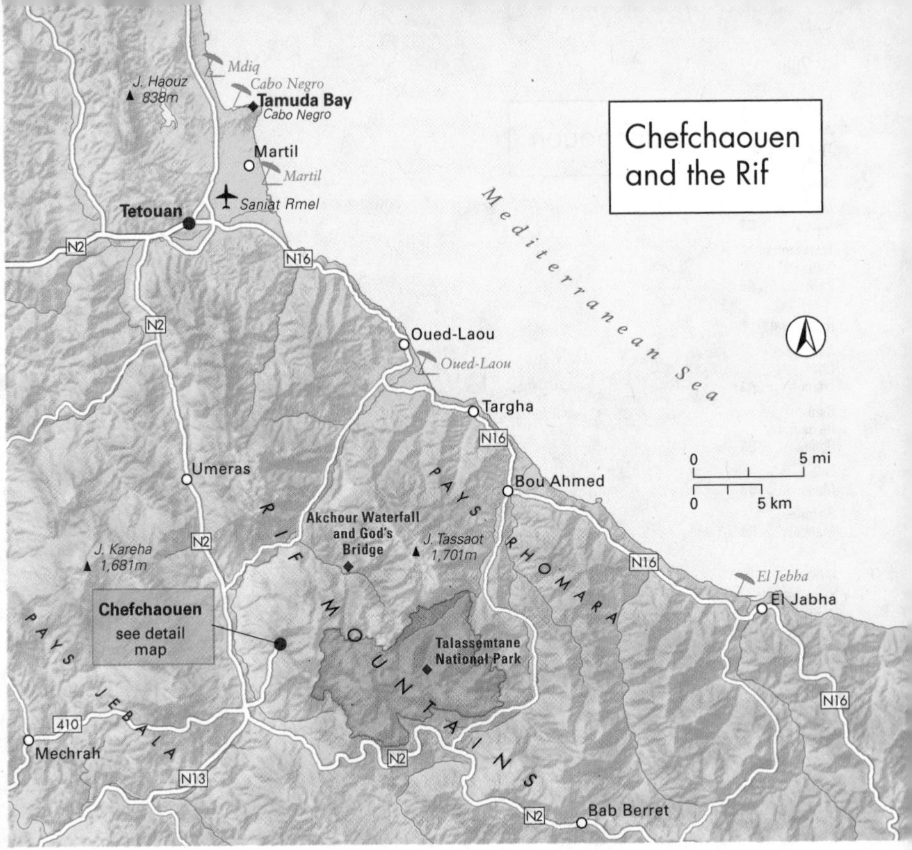
Chefchaouen and the Rif
Mediterranean Sea
Mdiq
Cabo Negro
Tamuda Bay
Cabo Negro
J. Haouz 838m
Martil
Martil
Saniat Rmel
Tetouan
N2
N16
N2
Oued-Laou
Oued-Laou
Targha
N16
Umeras
RIF MOUNTAINS
PAYS RHOMARA
Bou Ahmed
0 5 mi
0 5 km
Akchour Waterfall and God's Bridge
J. Tassaot 1,701m
J. Kareha 1,681m
N2
N16
El Jebha
El Jebha
Chefchaouen see detail map
PAYS JEBALA
Talassemtane National Park
N16
410
Mechrah
N2
N13
N2
Bab Berret

food is equally as good as the setting, thanks to a menu of modern Moroccan cuisine featuring dishes such as orange, carrot, and saffron salad, and seafood cannelloni. **Known for:** popular with locals, so reserve ahead; no alcohol but lots of fresh juices and smoothies; homemade nougat ice cream. [$] *Average main: DH100* ✉ *25, rue Zawiya Kadiria, Tetouan* ☎ *0539/70–42–02* 🌐 *www.blancoriad.com/en.*

Restaurant Restinga
$ | MOROCCAN | A narrow alleyway leads off Avenue Mohammed V to a small courtyard with a large fig tree as its centerpiece; you can dine inside or out at the restaurant here. Try the platter of fried fish, which might include calamari, sole, rouget, and shrimp. **Known for:** credit cards not accepted; alcohol served with complimentary tapas; popular with locals. [$] *Average main: DH50* ✉ *21, av. Mohammed V, Tetouan* 💳 *No credit cards.*

Restaurant Riad El Reducto
$ | MOROCCAN | The restaurant in this Spanish-run hotel is one of best options for a great homemade meal short of being invited into a Tetouani home. Fine Moroccan dishes include chicken pastilla, fish skewers, and delicious nut-based pastries, as well as Spanish *croquetas* (fritters). **Known for:** includes straightforward options for unadventurous diners; beautiful Moorish-style decor; alcohol available. [$] *Average main: DH90* ✉ *38, Zanqat Zawiya, Tetouan* ☎ *0539/96–81–20* 🌐 *www.elreducto.com.*

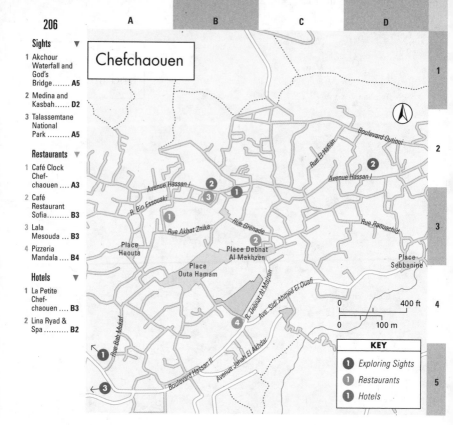

Chefchaouen

🛏 Hotels

★ Blanco Riad Hotel & Restaurant

$$ | HOTEL | The inner courtyard of this beautifully designed, Spanish-run riad in the medina dates back to the 17th century, and during the Spanish protectorate, the palace housed the pasha (governor). **Pros:** excellent restaurant; tranquil atmosphere; traditional hammam. **Cons:** steep stairs to the upper floors; small property; pedestrian-only access. $ *Rooms from: DH525* ⊠ *25, rue Zawiya Kadiria, Tetouan* ☎ *0539/70–42–02* ⊕ *www.blancoriad. com/en* ⤳ *8 rooms* ⏐◎⏐ *Free Breakfast.*

Riad El Reducto

$$ | HOTEL | This traditional riad—built for the Moroccan prime minister during the Spanish protectorate in 1810—has five spacious rooms above the courtyard restaurant and five in the quieter neighboring building, all individually decorated with Andalusian tiles and Moroccan details. **Pros:** wonderful restaurant; friendly staff; great views from the roof terrace. **Cons:** pedestrian-only access; steep stairs to the terrace; busy courtyard restaurant means the surrounding rooms can be noisy. $ *Rooms from: DH550* ⊠ *38, Zanqat Zawiya, Tetouan* ☎ *0539/96–81–20* ⤳ *10 rooms* ⏐◎⏐ *Free Breakfast.*

🛍 Shopping

Look out for wood and leather goods made by Tetouan's master craftsmen. And *mendils,* the striped, multicolor cloth used by Riffian farmers for all-purpose protection from the elements, are made and sold in a little square northeast of Bab er-Rouah.

Chefchaouen's History

Founded in 1471 by Moulay Ali ben Rachid as a mountain base camp for launching attacks against the Portuguese at Ceuta, Chefchaouen was historically off-limits to Christians until the arrival of Spanish troops in 1920. Before then it was allegedly only visited by three Europeans. Vicomte Charles de Foucauld—French military officer, explorer, and missionary—managed to make it inside the walls disguised as a rabbi in 1883. In 1889, British journalist Walter Harris, intrigued by the thought of a city closed to Westerners that was so near Tangier, used a similar strategy to gain access to Chefchaouen while researching his book *Land of an African Sultan*.

A third visitor, American William Summers, was less lucky and was caught and poisoned in 1892.

Remote Chefchaouen's isolationism increased with the arrival of Muslims expelled from Spain at the end of the 15th century and again at the start of the 17th. Jews expelled from Spain with the Muslims chose various shades of blue for the facades of their houses, while the Muslim houses remained green or mauve. When the Spanish arrived, they were stunned to find Chefchaouen's Sephardic Jews speaking and writing a medieval Spanish dialect that had been extinct in Spain for four centuries.

Ensemble de l'Artisanat

CRAFTS | At this government-sponsored crafts center, rug weavers, leatherworkers, woodworkers, and jewelry designers create and sell their wares. Prices are fixed but the quality is excellent, and there can be a certain value in not having to haggle. It's closed Sunday. ☒ *Av. Hassan I, Tetouan* ☎ *0539/99–20–85*.

Chefchaouen

65 km (40 miles) south of Tetouan, 112 km (70 miles) southeast of Tangier.

Built on a hillside high in the Rif Mountains, Chefchaouen, known as the Blue City, is a world apart from its Spanish-style neighbors, with a slower pace of life that seems somehow in tune with the fertile valleys, abundant natural springs, wildflowers, and low-lying clouds hovering above the surrounding mountains. From Rifi Imazighen dressed in earth-tone wool djellabas (long, hooded robes) and sweaters (ideal for cold, wet Rif winters) to the signature blue-washed houses lining its narrow streets, Chefchaouen has maintained its unique identity throughout the years. The medina has been walled since its earliest days, and is still off-limits to cars.

Somehow, even the burgeoning souvenir shops don't make much of a dent in the town's mystique. Chaouen, as it's often called, is an ideal place to wander through the picturesque medina, walk up into the looming mountains above the valley, and sip mint tea in an open square. No other place in Morocco has its otherworldly, bohemian appeal—making the town a place that ranks as a consistent favorite among travelers to the region.

GETTING HERE AND AROUND

CTM has several buses daily, including service to and from Tangier, Tetouan, Casablanca, and Rabat. Grands taxis can be taken from Tangier (around 650 DH per person, one-way) or from Tetouan (around 35 DH per person, one-way) directly to Chefchaouen.

BUS CONTACTS CTM – Gare Routière.
☎ *0539/98–76–69* ⊕ *www.ctm.ma.*

Sights

Akchour Waterfall and God's Bridge
WATERFALL | The village of Akchour in Talassemtane National Park—a 50-minute grand taxi ride northeast of Chefchaouen—is the starting point for two beautiful and relatively easy hikes. Take the left-hand path at the hydroelectric dam, and the Akchour waterfall is around a 45-minute walk away. From there you have the option of continuing on a four- to five-hour round-trip hike to another, much larger waterfall. You can also choose to go right at the dam; on the other side of the river, you can head up on a steep path to God's Bridge, a natural stone bridge. Several small cafés offering mint tea and tagines sprinkle the paths, as do wildflowers. Be aware that some locals might try to sell you things, some of them illegal. ⊠ *Akchour.*

★ Medina and Kasbah
NEIGHBORHOOD | Chefchaouen boasts one of the most picturesque medinas in Morocco, a compact and crowd-free area that's a delight to explore, with almost every building along its tangle of alleyways painted in a dazzling blue hue. Photo opportunities abound at every turn. At its heart is the cobbled main square, Place Outa el Hammam. Looming over the medina are the dusky red walls of the 13th-century kasbah, now home to a lovely Andalusian garden and a small ethnographic museum. ■TIP→ **Climb the tower for incredible views of the medina and the mountains beyond.** ⊠ *Pl. Outa el Hammam, Chefchaouen* 🛒 *Medina free; kasbah 60 DH.*

Talassemtane National Park
NATIONAL PARK | Established in 1989, the 145,000-acre Talassemtane National Park is a beautiful 45-minute drive from Chefchaouen. Its Mediterranean ecosystem hosts a unique variety of Moroccan pine as well as more than 239 plant species, many of which are endangered, such as the black pine and the Atlas cedar. The numerous hiking options include the popular hike to the Akchour Waterfall and God's Bridge. ■TIP→ **It's recommended to use a guide on longer hikes.** ⊠ *Chefchaouen* ☎ *039/98–72–67* 🛒 *Free.*

 Restaurants

★ Café Clock Chefchaouen
$ | MOROCCAN | The hugely popular Café Clock company has arrived in a cool blue riad in Chefchaouen. It comes with the same relaxed vibe as its counterparts in Fez and Marrakesh, as well as menu favorites like camel burger and a wide variety of fish dishes. **Known for:** range of cultural programs; cooking classes; vegetarian and vegan-friendly. Ⓢ *Average main: DH95* ⊠ *Derb Tijani, Chefchaouen* ☎ *0539/98–87–88* ⊕ *www.cafeclock. com.*

Café Restaurant Sofia
$ | MOROCCAN | Popular with both locals and visitors, the town's first female-owned restaurant has a menu that showcases traditional dishes made with the freshest ingredients. Dine alfresco under an awning; don't miss the shrimp tagine or the fluffy seven-vegetable couscous. **Known for:** credit cards not accepted; family owned and run; outdoor seating. Ⓢ *Average main: DH50* ⊠ *Pl. Outa el Hammam, Escalier Roumani, Chefchaouen* ☎ *0671/28–66–49* ▤ *No credit cards* ⊘ *Closed Mon.*

Lala Mesouda
$ | MOROCCAN | This great-value restaurant, with its carved-wood chairs, colorful banquettes, and bare stone walls, is one of the top choices in town for Moroccan dishes full of home-cooked flavor. House specialties include regional favorites such as bissara and hearty tagines, as well as plenty of options for vegetarians. **Known for:** vegetarian options; great service; atmospheric decor. Ⓢ *Average main:*

There are many theories about why the walls of Chefchaouen were painted blue, though it's believed the practice began, at least in part, in the 15th century, soon after the city was founded.

DH50 ✉ *Av. Hassan II, Chefchaouen* ☎ *0539/98–91–33.*

Pizzeria Mandala

$ | **ITALIAN** | **FAMILY** | Take a break from tagines and head to this popular restaurant just outside the medina. Pizza and pasta are the mainstays of the menu, but they also serve meat dishes and good-size salads. **Known for:** delicious desserts; family-friendly option; delivery to area hotels. Ⓢ *Average main: DH60* ✉ *Av. Hassan II, Chefchaouen* ☎ *0539/88–28–08.*

 Hotels

★ Lina Ryad & Spa

$$$$ | **HOTEL** | The large, bright suites at this upscale hotel come with traditional Moroccan touches, such as brass lanterns and dark-wood doors. **Pros:** excellent guests-only restaurant; great location in heart of the medina; heated pool. **Cons:** courtyard-facing suites can be noisy; steep stairs and no elevator; pedestrian-only access. Ⓢ *Rooms from: DH1550* ✉ *Av. Hassan I, Chefchaouen*

☎ *0645/06–99–03* ⊕ *www.linaryad.com* ⤳ *17 suites* ⦿❙ *Free Breakfast.*

★ La Petite Chefchaouen

$$ | **B&B/INN** | Restoring this riad was a labor of love for the well-traveled Moroccan owner, and he's met his own high standards with the clean, contemporary look here. **Pros:** delicious dinners on request; extremely helpful staff; stunning views from the terrace. **Cons:** lacks traditional Moroccan decor; steep stairs; pedestrian-only access (but they'll help with luggage). Ⓢ *Rooms from: DH1000* ✉ *169, av. Hassan Ier, Chefchaouen* ☎ *0661/57–22–72* ⊕ *www. lapetitechefchaouen.ma* ⤳ *5 rooms* ⦿❙ *Free Breakfast.*

 Shopping

Chefchaouen is one of the north's best places to shop for quality traditional crafts. Wool items and leather goods are the main local export; look in small medina stores for thick blankets, rugs, bags, and shoes.

L'Art de L'Artisanat Berbère
CRAFTS | Handcrafted carpets, blankets, and throws are piled floor to ceiling at this friendly cooperative, from colorful kilims to abstract Azilal rugs; you can even watch the families making them. Bargaining is expected, and all purchases can be shipped internationally. Tucked down a narrow derb near the Bab el-Ain, the co-op can be tricky to find, so ask a local. ⊠ *23, derb Bab el Moukaf, Bab el-Ain, Chefchaouen* ☎ *0539/98–60–71.*

★ La Botica de la Abuela de Aladdin
OTHER HEALTH & BEAUTY | This small, sweet-smelling store—the name means Aladdin's Grandma's Apothecary—is a riot of color and awash with the fragrances of rose, amber, sandalwood, vanilla, Damascus jasmine, and more. The owner creates around 20 different types of handmade soaps, body oils, lotions, and solid perfumes made from all-natural, organic ingredients. Beautifully packaged, they make perfect gifts to take home. ⊠ *17, rue Targi, Chefchaouen* ☎ *0631/86–43–86* ⊕ *abuelaaladin.business.site.*

Ensemble Artisanat
CRAFTS | The small cooperative workshop produces high-quality goods that are beautiful and inexpensive, including hand-painted wood boxes, weavings, original art, and leatherwork. ⊠ *Pl. el Majzen, just outside medina walls, Chefchaouen.*

 ## Activities

Less visited than the High Atlas mountains, the Rif Mountains around Chefchaouen still offer all manner of walking opportunities, from easy rambles along the banks of the Ras el-Maa River to more ambitious full-day hikes, such as scaling Jebel el-Kalaa, which looms over the town, and multiday hikes in Talessemtane National Park.

Chapter 6

FEZ AND THE MIDDLE ATLAS

Updated by
Sarah Gilbert

 Sights
★★★★★

 Restaurants
★★★★☆

 Hotels
★★★★☆

 Shopping
★★★☆☆

 Nightlife
★★☆☆☆

WELCOME TO
FEZ AND THE MIDDLE ATLAS

TOP REASONS TO GO

★ **Fez el-Bali:** The world's largest active medieval city promises a sensorial vacation from modern life with its bustling passageways, craftspeople, and covered markets.

★ **The food souk in Meknès:** On Place el-Hedim, sample famous olives, aromatic spices, and dried fruit, available in a dizzying array of colors and flavors.

★ **Volubilis:** A short trip from Meknès, these well-preserved Roman ruins are considered the most impressive in the country.

★ **Skiing at the Moroccan Aspen:** Attracting both royalty and the Moroccan elite, the highest peak of the Michlifen ski resort rises to 6,500 feet.

★ **Overland adventures:** Hike through the forested slopes and fertile valleys of the Middle Atlas to get a glimpse of life in less-visited Amazigh villages.

Situated between the mountainous Middle Atlas and the valleys of the Rif, Fez and Meknès are rewarding visits with historic monuments, sumptuous palaces, imposing ramparts, and vibrant markets. Fez is by far the more significant destination. Meknès is a calmer city where you can experience authentic local life, with fewer visitors and hustlers. Side trips to the Roman ruins of Volubilis and the sacred village of Moulay Idriss are highly recommended if time permits. The Middle Atlas, the northernmost part of the three Atlas Mountain chains, is a cool, green oasis on the way to or from the Sahara. Explore places like Ifrane, known as "Morocco's Switzerland," the Amazigh towns of Azrou and Sefrou, beautiful forests, and picturesque mountain ranges.

1 Fez. The labyrinthine heart of Morocco's oldest imperial city, Fez el-Bali is the world's largest still-active medieval medina; it's an entrancing jumble of markets, museums, and mosques.

2 Meknès. Founded in the 11th century, this former capital has a more manageable ancient medina than Fez, as well as the monuments of Moulay Ismail's Imperial City.

3 Moulay Idriss. Morocco's holiest town is a hidden jewel, with white-washed buildings clustered across two hills;

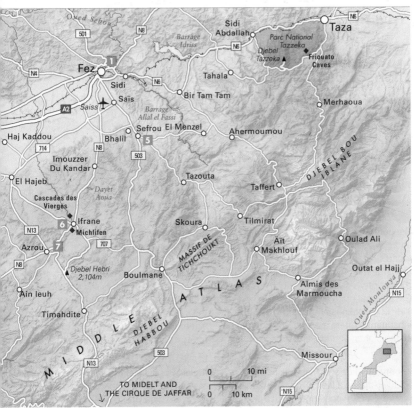

climb to the top for views over the fertile countryside.

4 Volubilis. This outpost of the Roman Empire, now a UNESCO World Heritage site, boasts impressive ruins scattered across a plain near the foothills of Mt. Zerhoun.

5 Sefrou. Once a hub of North African trade, the picturesque Amazigh market town was a center of Morocco's multiculturalism. It's famed for the annual Cherry Festival.

6 Ifrane. This French-built mountain resort has a European vibe, plus fresh air, verdant forests, and tranquil lakes. Avid skiers can even hit the slopes.

7 Azrou. Surrounded by forests of towering cedars, this peaceful Amazigh mountain stronghold changes tempo on Tuesday, when the souk and hundreds of people come to town.

Designated as UNESCO World Heritage sites, the imperial cities of Fez and Meknès, both former capitals, are ancient centers of learning, culture, and craftsmanship. They remain two of Morocco's most authentic and fascinating cities, outstanding for their history and culture, and Fez rivals Marrakesh as a top visitor destination and host of international festivals.

Recognized as Morocco's intellectual and spiritual center, Fez has one of the world's oldest universities as well as the largest intact medieval quarters. It is the country's second-largest city (after Casablanca), with a population exceeding 1 million. Meknès, with nearly 650,000 inhabitants, offers a chance to experience all the sights, sounds, and smells of Fez on a smaller, more manageable scale.

In between Fez and Marrakesh, the Middle Atlas is a North African arcadia, where rivers, woodlands, and valley grasslands show off Morocco's inland beauty. Snowy cedar forests, ski slopes, and trout streams are not images normally associated with the country, yet the Middle Atlas unfolds like an ersatz alpine fantasy less than an hour from medieval Fez. To remind you that this is still North Africa, Barbary apes scurry around the roadsides, and the traditional djellaba (hooded gown) and hijab (head covering) appear in ski areas.

Most travelers to Morocco will get a glimpse of the Middle Atlas as they whiz between Fez and Marrakesh, or between Meknès and points south. The central highland's Amazigh villages, secret valleys, scenic woods, dramatically barren landscapes, and high plains blanketed with olive groves lie in stark contrast to the exotic imperial cities. For this reason alone, the region is rewarding to discover for its integrity and authenticity.

MAJOR REGIONS

Around Fez and Meknès. The Roman ruins of Volubilis and the holy city of Moulay Idriss are highly recommended side trips. Volubilis was the Roman Empire's farthest-flung capital, and it's home to some of the country's best archaeological treasures. Moulay Idriss has Morocco's most sacred shrine, the tomb of founding father Moulay Idriss I. Both sites are key to understanding Moroccan history, and it's possible to see both places in one day. Most tours from Meknès or Fez will cover both if you don't have your own transport, although you may not spend as much time in Moulay Idriss as it deserves.

The Middle Atlas. Spreading south and east of Fez and heading north towards the Rif Mountains, the Middle Atlas is the northernmost of the three Atlas mountain ranges. The snow-tipped peaks near Ifrane, the lofty cedars of Azrou, and authentic Amazigh towns such as Sefrou and Bhalil are the main attractions in this heavily forested zone.

Planning

When to Go

Busloads of tourists and intense heat tend to suppress the romance of just about anything. Try to visit Fez and Meknès between September and April, before the high season or extreme heat makes it uncomfortable to sightsee. Spring and autumn are really the best time to visit any part of Morocco.

The Middle Atlas is relatively cool year-round, and often snowbound midwinter with temperatures dropping below 0°C (32°F). For skiing or driving through the snow-filled peaks around Ifrane or Azrou's cedar forest (occasionally snowed in from January to March, but normally well plowed), come between December and April. April through June is the best time to hike. The high tourist season in the mountains runs mid-March through summer. The most popular festival is the annual Fes Festival of World Sacred Music, currently held in June.

Planning Your Time

If you're short of time, Fez should be your priority. The ancient monuments of the medina and the leather tanneries can be explored in one or two days, although you should devote longer to losing yourself in the medieval city's labyrinthine alleyways. A third day could be spent visiting the

smaller and more manageable imperial city of Meknès and the impressive Roman ruins of Volubilis. With more time and transport—a rental car or tour—Fez makes the ideal base for day trips to alpine-style Ifrane and the Middle Atlas towns of Sefrou and Azrou. If you really want to experience Amazigh culture, spend the night in the troglodyte village of Bhalil; or visit the Holy City of Moulay Idriss, just a stone's throw from Volubilis.

Getting Here and Around

Most visitors to the Middle Atlas set down in Fez, the region's largest city. Traveling within Fez is best done on foot, but taking a petit taxi to points of interest such as the Ville Nouvelle is an inexpensive option. To visit Meknès or Volubilis, take a train, bus, grand taxi (negotiate a price before the journey), or tour. To visit the Middle Atlas, you'll need a car or a tour.

AIR

International and domestic flights operate regularly from the state-of-the-art Fès-Saïss Airport terminal, including direct flights to Marrakesh. The airport serves the Middle Atlas as well as Fez and Meknès. You can't fly directly into Fez from the United States; you must connect in Europe or Casablanca. Upon arrival, petits taxis wait outside the airport terminal and train station and carry two to four people. Grands taxis carry six people. Avoid unofficial drivers who hang around the terminals and charge false rates. Taxis should have their meters running. Most drivers request cash payment.

BUS

The CTM is Morocco's best bus company and has services from most major cities to Fez and Meknès. In the Middle Atlas, Azrou and Ifrane are all served by daily CTM buses, if somewhat sporadically;

or grab a grands taxi. If you're flying into Casablanca, the bus to Ifrane and to Azrou takes around six hours.

CAR

The easiest way to tour the well-paved regions in and around Fez and the Middle Atlas is by car. GPS or a good map is a necessity if you plan to venture far from the beaten path. The best map to use is the Michelin Map of Morocco 742; if you can't find this map at home, ask your car-rental company to provide one. Road signs at major intersections in larger cities are well marked to point you in the right direction. Little white pillars alongside routes indicate the distance in kilometers to towns.

If you're traveling farther afield into the Middle Atlas, a car is essential. Depending on where you're coming from, it's best to rent a vehicle in Fez. Be aware that many secondary roads are unpaved and require a four-wheel-drive vehicle. Ensure your car is equipped with a spare tire and emergency fuel. Weaving through mountain passes, roads can be dangerously narrow, steep, and winding.

TRAIN

Fez and Meknès are served by the ONCF train station that goes east to Oujda, south to Marrakesh, and west to Tangier, Rabat, and Casablanca. Fez and Meknès are also connected by regular local trains, a 45-minute trip.

Restaurants

Every Moroccan city has its own way of preparing the national dishes. *Harira,* the spicy bean-based soup filled with vegetables and meat, may be designated as Fassi (from Fez) or Meknessi (from Meknès), and the versions vary slightly in texture and ingredients. Few of the basic medina restaurants in Fez and Meknès are licensed to serve alcohol. Some

proprietors allow oenophiles to bring their own wine, as long as they enjoy it discreetly. Larger hotels and luxury *riads* (renovated guesthouses and villas) have well-stocked bars that serve wine, beer, and cocktails, as do more upscale restaurants.

Most of the Middle Atlas hotels we recommend have fair to excellent restaurants, but venture to stop at small-town crossroads or souks for a homemade bowl of harira for around 10 DH. Note: some locals may frown upon alcohol of any kind. Be discreet if you carry your own wine or beer.

Dining reviews have been shortened. For full information, visit Fodors.com.

Hotels

Hotels in Fez range from the luxurious and the contemporary to more personal, atmospheric riads that offer everything from an Arabian Nights fantasy to authentic traditional living, and more upscale but still boutique versions, such as Palais Amani. Hotels in or near Fez el-Bali are best, as the medina is probably what you came to see. In Meknès, choices are more limited, with a few gems competing at the top end, but Ifrane's Michlifen Resort & Golf draws local elites for its Anglo-European styling. The Middle Atlas offers a selection of good hotels, although some of the inns and auberges off the beaten path should be thought of as shelter rather than full-service hotels, as lodging tends to be unmemorable.

Hotel reviews have been shortened. For full information, visit Fodors.com.

WHAT IT COSTS In Dirhams

	$	$$	$$$	$$$$
RESTAURANTS				
	under 200 DH	200 DH–300 DH	301 DH–400 DH	over 400 DH
HOTELS				
	under 1,200 DH	1,200 DH–1,600 DH	1,601 DH–2,000 DH	over 2,000 DH

Safety

In general, Fez and Meknès are safe cities. In Fez—less in Meknès—pickpocketing and unwanted hassle from hustlers and faux guides will be the biggest concern. Harassment from those offering to be tour guides or drivers is best avoided by smiling and firmly saying "no thank you," preferably in French ("non merci") or Arabic ("la shukran"). Try not to become visibly agitated, as it could exacerbate the situation.

You can safely explore Fez medina during the day, but ask at your hotel if there are any areas you should avoid after dark. If you get off track, turn around and head back to a more populated area. If you are followed, enter a store, hotel, restaurant, or café and ask for help. At night, poorly lit medina alleyways can be intimidating but are not necessarily unsafe. Often hotels and restaurants will dispatch someone to escort you to your destination.

From December through January, heavy snowfall may cover Middle Atlas roads; however, the snow-removal systems in places such as Azrou's cedar forest are relatively good, with cleared driving routes. More remote roads (marked in white on the Michelin map of Morocco) will be difficult to access or completely closed in snowy conditions.

Tours

FISHING

Morocco, surprisingly, offers trout fishing in the foothills of the High Atlas and in the Azrou Cedar Forest. European brown trout and rainbows, nearly all stocked fish or descendants of repopulated fisheries, thrive in select highland environments. March through May are the prime angling months. Permits and further orientation are available through the Administration des Eaux et Forêts offices in Rabat.

Administration des Eaux et Forêts
✉ 605, Rabat-Chellah, Rabat ☎ 0535/76–30–15 ⊕ www.eauxetforets.gov.ma.

HORSEBACK RIDING

For the equestrian, several stables offer mountain or rural outings on horseback. Try Le Centre Equestre et de Randonnée Aïn Amyer.

Le Centre Equestre et de Randonnée Aïn Amyer
HORSEBACK RIDING | The company, based on the outskirts of Fez, houses the famous Moroccan Barb species of horse, a desert breed with stamina, in its stables. They have a range of riding circuits that cover the country; depending on your time and expertise, it's possible to go on a ride of several hours—perhaps to the ruins of Volubilis—or on 10-day expeditions around the desert or High Atlas. ✉ Aïn Amyer, Km 2.5, Rte. d'Immouzzer, Fez ☎ 0661/17–44–04 ✉ azzmsefer@yahoo.fr ✉ From 200 DH per hr for a short ride with guide.

RAFTING

One of the best ways to see Morocco is through the natural beauty of its flowing rivers and dramatic canyons. Morocco Rafting specializes in river-rafting tours. Adventure holidays are available with a range of activities that combine rafting, kayaking, canyoning, and tubing.

Morocco Rafting

WHITE-WATER RAFTING | This company—open since the late 1990s—specializes in white-water rafting tours in the Middle and High Atlas; the season starts in March. They also run hot-air ballooning, quad biking, and kitesurfing adventures. ⊠ *Marrakesh* ☎ *01709/802203 in U.K.* ⊕ *www.rafting.ma* ✉ *From $695 per person for a 3-day rafting trip.*

Fez

Fez is one of the world's most spectacular city-museums and an exotic medieval labyrinth—mysterious, mesmerizing, and sometimes overwhelming. Passing through one of the *babs* (gates) into Fez el-Bali is like entering a time warp, with only the numerous satellite dishes installed on nearly every roof as a reminder you're in the 21st century, not the 8th. As you maneuver through crowded passages illuminated by shafts of sunlight streaming through thatched roofs of the *kissaria* (covered markets), the cries of *"Balek!"* ("Watch out!") from donkey drivers pushing overloaded mules—overlapped with the cacophony of locals bartering, coppersmiths hammering, and the muezzin, the citywide call to prayer—blend with the odors of aromatic spices, curing leather, and smoking grills for an incredible sensorial experience you will never forget.

PLANNING YOUR TIME
FESTIVALS
★ **Fes Festival of World Sacred Music**

MUSIC FESTIVALS | Sponsored by the Spirit of Fez Foundation, a nonprofit association working to maintain the city's cultural heritage, the annual Fes Festival of World Sacred Music focuses on a different theme each year and has become an international favorite, attracting some of the world's finest musicians and intellectual scholars for the Fes Forum roundtable debates. Concerts are held in diverse venues across the city, including the imposing Bab Al Makina. There are also free concerts, including Sufi Nights, held daily in a palatial dar. It's currently held in June (the date varies with Ramadan), but check the website for specifics. ⊠ *Fez* ☎ *0535/74–05–35* ⊕ *www.fesfestival.com.*

GETTING HERE AND AROUND

Fez is an enigmatic, intriguing city best explored on foot. Walking beneath one of the imposing arched babs and into the medina's maze of cobbled streets stimulates all the senses. Summer months can be unbearably hot with little air circulation, especially along canopied and crowded alleyways. The best time to tour is the morning; crowds and temperatures won't be too intense. Nights are cool throughout the year with a refreshing desert breeze. Remember that Friday is a traditional day of prayer, and many establishments in the medina are closed.

GUIDES AND TOURS

There's much to be said in favor of employing a good guide in Fez: you'll be left alone by faux guides and hustlers, and if your guide is good you'll learn much and be able to see more of your surroundings than when you're reading and navigating as you move around. On the other hand, getting lost in Fez el-Bali is one of those great travel experiences. Maps of the medina really do work, and numerous signs on medina walls point you to important sites, restaurants, and hotels.

The tourist office and your hotel are the best sources for official guides vetted by the ONMT. They cost around 300 DH per day, plus tips, more if you include touring regions or special destinations by car.

VISITOR INFORMATION

CONTACTS Fez Tourist Office. ⊠ *Av. Mohammed Es Slaoui, Ville Nouvelle* ☎ *0535/94–24–92.*

Fez's Bou Inania Medersa has impressive carved stucco walls and ceramic tiles, but don't confuse it with the Bou Inania Medersa in Mèknes, which is also a work of art.

DINING

In the country's culinary capital, foodie pleasures are everywhere: from simple food stalls and cafés to gourmet Moroccan fare in ancient palaces. Traditional Moroccan recipes are sometimes given a contemporary twist by innovative chefs, and there are French- and Mediterranean-influenced dishes to sample. For something quick and filling, you can always grab a 10 DH bowl of cumin-laced pea or bean soup at one of the many stands and stalls near the medina's main food markets just inside Bab Boujeloud, or take a sightseeing break with a honey-laden pastry and some fresh mint tea. For a heartier meal, try slow-cooked tagines, grilled meat, and vegetable-topped couscous. Taste Fassi specialties on a fascinating street-food tour, and don't leave without sampling pigeon pastilla, a heavenly combination of sweet and sour flavors. It's often made with chicken nowadays, but the Ruined Garden, in the medina, will cook the authentic dish to order with a day's notice.

LODGING

Staying in Fez's medina offers such a unique experience that you're best off choosing a hotel either in or very near medieval Fez el-Bali. Choose an atmospheric riad, boutique hotel, or resort-style hotel. There are also some good new hotels in the Ville Nouvelle. There are no hotels in Fez el-Djedid.

Fez el-Bali

Fez el-Bali is a living medieval city, crafts workshop, and market that has changed little in the past millennium. With no cars allowed and a tangle of more than 9,000 narrow alleyways, it invites the walker on an endless and absorbing odyssey. Exploring this honeycomb of ancient streets, filled with often chaotic crowds and the occasional donkey to dodge, is a challenging adventure. Fez isn't really yours, however, until you've tackled it on your own, become hopelessly lost a few times, and survived to tell the tale.

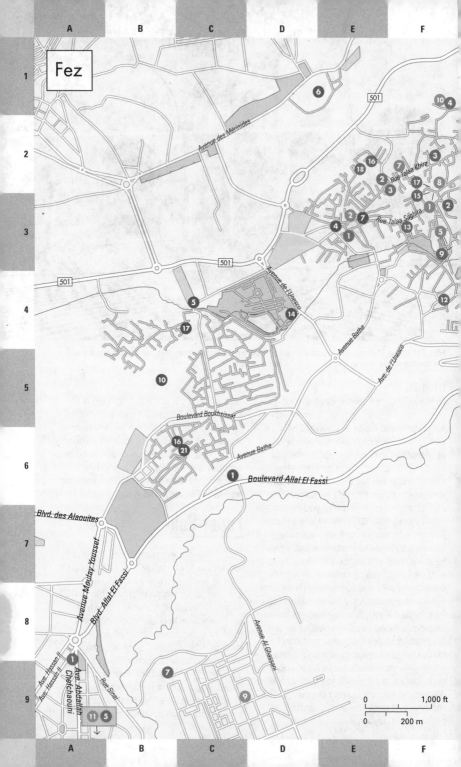

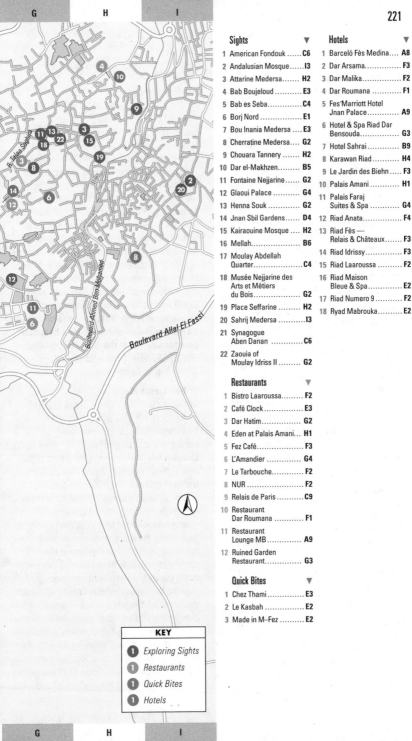

Sights ▼

1 American Fondouk **C6**
2 Andalusian Mosque......**I3**
3 Attarine Medersa.......**H2**
4 Bab Boujeloud **E3**
5 Bab es Seba.............**C4**
6 Borj Nord **E1**
7 Bou Inania Medersa **E3**
8 Cherratine Medersa....**G2**
9 Chouara Tannery **H2**
10 Dar el-Makhzen.........**B5**
11 Fontaine Nejjarine......**G2**
12 Glaoui Palace **G4**
13 Henna Souk **G2**
14 Jnan Sbil Gardens......**D4**
15 Kairaouine Mosque **H2**
16 Mellah...................**B6**
17 Moulay Abdellah
   Quarter..................**C4**
18 Musée Nejjarine des
   Arts et Métiers
   du Bois.................**G2**
19 Place Seffarine **H2**
20 Sahrij Medersa **I3**
21 Synagogue
   Aben Danan **C6**
22 Zaouia of
   Moulay Idriss II **G2**

Restaurants ▼

1 Bistro Laaroussa.........**F2**
2 Café Clock...............**E3**
3 Dar Hatim...............**G2**
4 Eden at Palais Amani...**H1**
5 Fez Café.................**F3**
6 L'Amandier **G4**
7 Le Tarbouche............**F2**
8 NUR **F2**
9 Relais de Paris **C9**
10 Restaurant
   Dar Roumana **F1**
11 Restaurant
   Lounge MB **A9**
12 Ruined Garden
   Restaurant..............**G3**

Quick Bites ▼

1 Chez Thami...............**E3**
2 Le Kasbah **E2**
3 Made in M–Fez **E2**

Hotels ▼

1 Barceló Fès Medina....**A8**
2 Dar Arsama..............**F3**
3 Dar Malika...............**F2**
4 Dar Roumana **F1**
5 Fes Marriott Hotel
   Jnan Palace............**A9**
6 Hotel & Spa Riad Dar
   Bensouda...............**G3**
7 Hotel Sahrai **B9**
8 Karawan Riad **H4**
9 Le Jardin des Biehn **F3**
10 Palais Amani **H1**
11 Palais Faraj
   Suites & Spa **G4**
12 Riad Anata...............**F4**
13 Riad Fès —
   Relais & Châteaux.......**F3**
14 Riad Idrissy..............**F3**
15 Riad Laaroussa **F2**
16 Riad Maison
   Bleue & Spa.............**E2**
17 Riad Numero 9 ....**F2**
18 Ryad Mabrouka.........**E2**

KEY

① Exploring Sights
① Restaurants
① Quick Bites
① Hotels

Sights

Andalusian Mosque

MOSQUE | The grand carved doors on the mosque's north entrance, domed Zenet minaret, and detailed cedarwood carvings in the eaves, which bear a striking resemblance to those in the Musée Nejjarine, are the main things to see here, as the mosque itself is set back on a small elevation, making it hard to examine from outside. It was built in AD 859 by Mariam, sister of Fatima al-Fihri, who had erected the Kairaouine Mosque on the river's other side two years earlier with inherited family wealth. The gate was built by the Almohads in the 12th century. ⊠ *Rue Nekhaline, Fez el-Bali, Fez* ☞ *Entrance restricted to Muslims.*

Attarine Medersa

HISTORIC SIGHT | Graceful proportions, elegant, geometric carved-cedar ornamentation, and its excellent state of preservation make this 14th-century building one of the best representations of Moorish architecture in Fez. Named for local spice merchants, the former Koranic school was founded by Merenid sultan Abou Saïd Othman as a students' dormitory attached to the Kairaouine Mosque next door. ⊠ *Boutouil Kairaouine, Fez el-Bali, Fez* 🖼 *20 DH.*

★ Bab Boujeloud

NOTABLE BUILDING | This Moorish-style gate dating to 1913 is considered the principal and most beautiful point of entry into Fez el-Bali, even though it's 1,000 years younger than the rest of the medina. It was built by General Hubert Lyautey, Moroccan commander under the French protectorate. The side facing toward Fez el-Djedid is covered with blue ceramic tiles painted with flowers and calligraphy; the inside is green, the official color of Islam—or of peace, depending on interpretation. ⊠ *Pl. Pacha el-Baghdadi, Fez el-Bali, Fez.*

Borj Nord

MILITARY SIGHT | Sitting high above the city, this former fortress, now the national Museum of Arms, was built in 1582 under the command of Saadian sultan Ahmed el Mansour to guard and control Fez el-Bali. In 1963, a huge collection of weapons originally housed in the Batha Museum was brought to the historic site, creating an interesting display. Sabers, swords, shields, and armor from the 19th century showcase the history of how arms played a social role in tribal hierarchy. Especially important is the arsenal of sultans Moulay Ismail and Moulay Mohammed Beh Abdellah—the elaborate Amazigh guns encrusted in enamel, ivory, silver, and precious gems date back to the 17th century. It's a 20-minute walk uphill from the medina or a short petit taxi ride. ■TIP→ **Walk up to the crenellated rooftop in late afternoon for a beautiful panoramic view of the city.** ⊠ *Borj Nord, Fez* 🕿 *0535/64–52–41* 🖼 *10 DH* ⊗ *Closed Mon. and at lunchtime.*

★ Bou Inania Medersa

NOTABLE BUILDING | From outside Bab Boujeloud you will see the green-tile tower of this *medersa* (school), generally considered the most beautiful of the Kairaouine University's 14th-century residential colleges. It was built by order of Abou Inan, the first ruler of the Merenid dynasty, which would become the most decisive ruling clan in Fez's development. The main components of the stunningly intricate decorative artwork in this now-nonoperating school are the green-tile roofing; the cedar eaves and upper patio walls carved in floral and geometrical motifs; the carved-stucco midlevel walls; the ceramic-tile lower walls covered with calligraphy (Kufi script, essentially cursive Arabic) and geometric designs; and, finally, the marble floor. Showing its age, the carved cedar is still dazzling, with each square inch a masterpiece of handcrafted sculpture involving long hours of the kind

A visit to the Chouara Tannery is fascinating but rather smelly; it's a good idea to hold a sprig of fresh mint to your nose while you're there.

of concentration required to memorize the Koran. The black belt of ceramic tile around the courtyard bears Arabic script reading "this is a place of learning" and other such exhortatory academic messages. ⊠ *Talâa Kebira, Fez el-Bali, Fez* 🚏 *20 DH*.

Cherratine Medersa

NOTABLE BUILDING | Constructed in 1670 by Moulay Rachid, this is one of Fez's two Alaouite medersas and an important historical site. More austere than the 14th-century medersas of the Merenids, the Cherratine is also more functional, designed to hold over 200 students. It's interesting primarily as a contrast to the intricate craftsmanship and decorative intent of the Merenid structures. The entry doors beautifully engraved in bronze lead to the *douiras*, narrow residential blocks consisting of a honeycomb of small rooms. ⊠ *Ras Cherratine, Fez el-Bali, Fez* 🚏 *20 DH*.

★ Chouara Tannery

HISTORIC SIGHT | The city's famous medieval tanneries are at once beautiful, for their ancient dyeing vats of reds, yellows, and blues, and unforgettable, for the malodorous smell of the sheep, goat, cow, and camel skins. The terrace overlooking the dyeing vats is high enough to escape the place's full fetid power and get a spectacular view over the multicolor vats. Absorb both the process and the finished product on Rue Chouara, just past Rue Mechatine (named for the combs made from animals' horns): numerous stores are filled with loads of leather goods, including coats, bags, and babouches (traditional slippers). One of the shopkeepers will hand you a few sprigs of fresh mint to smother the smell, before explaining what's going on in the tanneries below—how the skins are placed successively in saline solution, quicklime, pigeon droppings, and then any of several natural dyes: poppies for red, turmeric for yellow, saffron for orange, indigo for blue, and mint for green. Barefoot workers in shorts pick up skins from the bottoms of the dyeing vats with their feet, then work them manually. Though this may look like an undesirable job, the work is relatively well paid and still in demand for a strong export market. ⊠ *Rue Chouara, Fez el-Bali, Fez.*

Fontaine Nejjarine

FOUNTAIN | This ceramic-tile, cedar-ceiling public fountain is one of the more beautiful and historic of its kind in Fez el-Bali. The first fountain down from Bab Boujeloud, Fontaine Nejjarine seems a miniature version of the nearby Nejjarine fondouk, with its geometrically decorated tiles and intricately carved cedar eaves overhead. ⊠ *Pl. Nejjarine, Fez el-Bali, Fez.*

Glaoui Palace

CASTLE/PALACE | Among the medina's many hidden palaces, the extraordinary Dar al Glaoui is one of its most atmospheric. The Pasha of Marrakesh's second home—he ruled over most of southern Morocco in his day—has fallen into disrepair since Morocco's independence from France in 1956, when his power waned. But amid the crumbling ruins of the late-19th-century structure, evidence of former grandeur is visible in the exquisite cedarwood doors, intricate stucco, tiled salons, and the carved wooden balconies that line its patios. The large estate comprised 17 buildings and two gardens, with ornate salons, an enormous kitchen, Koranic school, garages, stables, a harem, and a hammam. Abdou—an artist and one of the remaining family members—or his sister will show you some of its treasures. ⊠ *1, rue Hamia Douh, Fez el-Bali, Fez* 🖾 *50 DH.*

Henna Souk

MARKET | This little henna market is one of the medina's most picturesque squares, with a massive, gnarled fig tree in the center and rows of spices, hennas, kohls, and aphrodisiacs for sale in the tiny stalls around the edges. The ceramic shops on the way into the henna souk sell a wide variety of typically blue-and-white Fassi pottery. At the square's end is a plaque dedicated to the Maristan Sidi Frej, a medical center and psychiatric and teaching hospital built by the Merenid ruler Youssef Ibn Yakoub in 1286. Used as a model for the world's first mental hospital—founded in Valencia, Spain, in 1410—the Maristan operated until 1944. ⊠ *Fez el-Bali, Fez.*

Kairaouine Mosque

MOSQUE | Built in AD 857 by Fatima, the daughter of a wealthy Kairaouine refugee, this is considered one of the most important mosques in the Western Muslim world, and one look through the main doorway will give you an idea of its immensity. With about 10,760 square feet, the Kairaouine was Morocco's largest mosque until Casablanca's Hassan II Mosque came along in the early 1990s. It became the home of the West's first university and the world's foremost center of learning at the beginning of the second millennium. Stand at the entrance door's left side for a peek through the dozen horseshoe arches into the mihrab (marked by a hanging light). An east-facing alcove or niche used for leading prayer, the mihrab is rounded and covered with an arch designed to project sound back through the building. Lean in and look up to the brightly painted and intricately carved wood ceiling. If you get there just before prayer times, the two huge wooden doors by the entrance will be open, providing a privileged view of the vast interior. For a good view of the courtyard, head to the rooftop of the Attarine Medersa. ■ **TIP→ Note that entry is restricted to Muslims.** ⊠ *Bou Touil, Fez el-Bali, Fez.*

Did You Know?

The Musée Nejjarine des Arts et Métiers du Bois is a marvel of geometric tiles and intricately carved cedar eaves---and also an excellent example of a medieval fondouk, or travelers inn. These were built around a courtyard so that the traveling merchants could store their goods and their animals in the courtyard, and sleep in the rooms upstairs.

The Kairaouine Mosque is not open to non-Muslims but you can usually get a peek through the door to see the mosque's majestic interior.

Musée Nejjarine des Arts et Métiers du Bois

OTHER MUSEUM | A 14th-century, three-story Nejjarine fondouk, the Inn of the Carpenters is now home to a fascinating museum that displays Morocco's various native woods, 18th- and 19th-century woodworking tools, and a series of antique wooden doors and pieces of furniture. Enjoy a mint tea on the rooftop terrace with panoramic views over the medina. Don't miss the former jail cell on the ground floor or the large set of weighing scales, a reminder of the building's original functions—commerce on the ground floor and lodging on the levels above. ■ TIP→ **Check out the palatial, cedar-ceiling public bathrooms, certainly the finest of their kind in Fez.** ⊠ Pl. Nejjarine, Fez el-Bali, Fez ☎ 0535/74–05–80 ⛫ 20 DH.

Place Seffarine

PLAZA/SQUARE | In this open, triangular space that is home to metalworkers, copper and brass bowls, plates, and buckets are wrought and hammered over fires around the square's edge, and the smells of soldering irons permeate the air. Look toward the Kairaouine Mosque at the top of the square to see the Kairaouine University library. It holds a collection of precious manuscripts, including a 9th-century Koran, but is currently open only to Muslim scholars. ⊠ Pl. Seffarine, Fez el-Bali, Fez.

Sahrij Medersa

COLLEGE | One of the medina's finest medersas was built by the Merenids in the 14th century and named for the *sahrij* (pool) on which its patio is centered, with rich chocolate-color cedar wall carvings and some of the oldest *zellij* mosaic tiling in the country. It's still a working school, so head up the narrow steps leading to empty rooms over the central patio and you may hear the chanting of Koranic verses. ⊠ Andalusian Quarter, Fez el-Bali, Fez ⛫ 20 DH.

Zaouia of Moulay Idriss II

RELIGIOUS BUILDING | Originally built by the Idriss dynasty in the 9th century in honor of the city's founder—who was just 33 at the time of his death—this *zaouia* (sanctuary) was restored by the Merenid dynasty in the 13th century and has became one of the medina's holiest shrines. Particularly known for his *baraka* (divine protection), Moulay Idriss II had an especially strong cult among women seeking fertility and pilgrims hoping for good luck. The wooden beam at the entrance, about 6 feet from the ground, was originally placed there to keep Jews, Christians, and donkeys out of the *horm*, the sacred area surrounding the shrine itself. Inside the horm, Moroccans have historically enjoyed official sanctuary—they cannot be arrested if sought by the law. You may be able to catch a glimpse of the saint's tomb at the far right corner through the doorway; look for the fervently faithful burning candles and incense, and the tomb's silk-brocade covering. Note the rough wooden doors themselves, worn smooth with hundreds of years of kissing and caressing the wood for *baraka* (blessing). Entrance is restricted to Muslims only. ✉ *Bou Touil, Fez el-Bali, Fez* ✥ *On north side of mosque.*

🍴 Restaurants

L'Amandier

$$ | MOROCCAN | This fine-dining Moroccan restaurant sits on the top floor of Palais Faraj, with stunning views over the medina, making it especially romantic at night. The decor is sleek and sophisticated, the service is attentive, and the chef has re-created age-old Fassi recipes that reflect a variety of Mediterranean influences. **Known for:** reservations are essential; excellent wine list; outdoor dining in summer. [$] *Average main: DH220* ✉ *Palais Faraj, Bab Zhiat, Fez el-Bali, Fez* ☎ *0535/63–53–56* 🌐 *www.palaisfaraj.com.*

★ **Bistro Laaroussa**

$ | MOROCCAN | On Riad Laaroussa's lovely roof terrace, you can indulge in your choice of two distinct dining experiences while enjoying stellar views over the medina. Opt for the bistro menu (lunch and dinner) and feast on Mediterranean-influenced dishes, perhaps seafood risotto and crème brûlée. **Known for:** menu of Moroccan wines; reservations required for Moroccan prix-fixe dinner option; market-fresh Mediterranean and Moroccan dishes. [$] *Average main: DH130* ✉ *Riad Laaroussa, 3, Derb Bechara, Fez el-Bali* ☎ *0674/18–76–39* 🌐 *riad-laaroussa.com* 🕒 *Closed Wed.*

★ **Café Clock**

$ | ECLECTIC | Set in the heart of the medina, this crosscultural café is a Fez institution. It's the perfect place to take a sightseeing break with a tea or mocktail, or a bite from the eclectic menu of Moroccan and international fare, like the justly famous camel burger; there are vegetarian-friendly options as well. **Known for:** relaxed vibe; cultural events; cooking workshops. [$] *Average main: DH85* ✉ *7, Derb el Magana, Fez el-Bali, Fez* ☎ *0535/63–78–55* 🌐 *www.cafeclock.com.*

Dar Hatim

$ | MOROCCAN | They say the best Moroccan food is served at home, and Dar Hatim is the next-best thing. In the convivial, exquisitely tiled dining room of this cash-only, family home-turned-restaurant, you can choose from several three-course set menus of traditional Moroccan dishes. **Known for:** options for vegetarians; reservations are essential; authentic cooking classes. [$] *Average main: DH190* ✉ *19, Derb Ezaouia Fondouk Lihoudi, Fez el-Bali, Fez* ☎ *0535/52–53–23* ✎ *darhatim@gmail.com* 💳 *No credit cards.*

Eden at Palais Amani

$$$$ | **MOROCCAN** | Dining under the stars in this Andalusian-style, gardenlike oasis is a delight, surrounded by citrus trees and next to a twinkling fountain, or eat inside the Art Deco–influenced dining room. The chefs take traditional recipes and give them a contemporary presentation, creating a three-course dinner using seasonal produce from the market, a five-course wine-tasting menu for groups, and a lighter tapas menu that can be eaten on the rooftop terrace. **Known for:** à la carte lunch options; Moroccan-meets-Mediterranean cuisine; pre- and postdinner cocktails in the rooftop bar. $ *Average main: DH450 ⊠ Palais Amani, 12, Derb el Miter, Oued Zhoun, Fez el-Bali, Fez* ☎ *0535/63–32–09* ⊕ *www.palaisamani.com.*

★ Fez Café

$ | **MEDITERRANEAN** | **FAMILY** | This popular bistro-style café-cum-restaurant is set in the delightful oasis of Jardin des Biehn. The daily changing chalkboard menu reflects the Moroccan chef's love of Gallic gastronomy, as he happily mixes Moroccan and French culinary influences, using fresh ingredients from the market and the owners' organic garden. **Known for:** reservations essential; dining in gorgeous garden or inside; good vegetarian and family-friendly choices. $ *Average main: DH160 ⊠ 13, Akbat Sbaa, Douh, Fez el-Bali, Fez* ☎ *0535/63–50–31* ⊕ *www.jardindesbiehn.com* ⊗ *Closed Thurs.*

NUR

$$$$ | **MOROCCAN** | Chef Najat Kaanache returned to her Moroccan roots to create this chic riad-turned-restaurant. The seasonally inspired tasting menu—around eight courses, though you can ask for a five-course option for a shorter meal—changes often, reflecting the market finds of the day with a focus on artful presentation and inspired flavor combinations. **Known for:** stylish setting;

contemporary Moroccan cuisine with global influences; Moroccan wines. $ *Average main: DH700 ⊠ 7, Zkak Rouah, Fez el-Bali, Fez* ☎ *0694/27–78–49* ⊕ *www.nurfez.com* ⊗ *No lunch. Closed Mon.*

★ Restaurant Dar Roumana

$$ | **MEDITERRANEAN** | One of the city's best fine-dining eateries is in the strikingly beautiful courtyard of hotel Dar Roumana, where Moroccan chef Youness Toumi creates two- and three-course fixed-price Mediterranean menus with a Moroccan twist. The menu makes the most of seasonal produce from top local producers in creative salads, such as figs with crispy pancetta, goat cheese, and date dressing, and a meat or fish dish like a perfectly cooked veal T-bone or panfried John Dory. **Known for:** top-notch wine list; intimate, romantic riad setting; reservations essential. $ *Average main: DH275 ⊠ Dar Roumana, 30, Derb El Amer, Zkak Roumane, Fez el-Bali, Fez* ☎ *0535/74–16–37* ⊕ *www.darroumana.com* ⊗ *No lunch. Closed Mon.*

★ Ruined Garden Restaurant

$ | **MOROCCAN** | **FAMILY** | Set in the romantic remains of a ruined riad associated with Riad Idrissy, this casual alfresco restaurant comes complete with crumbling mosaic floors, fountains, and lush foliage. The à la carte menu and daily specials focus on street food–style dishes prepared using fresh produce from the souk. **Known for:** authentic Fassi dishes; sophisticated take on Moroccan street food; cooking classes. $ *Average main: DH100 ⊠ Sidi Ahmed Chaoui, Siaj, Fez el-Bali, Fez* ☎ *0649/19–14–10* ⊕ *www.ruined-garden.com* ⊗ *Closed 2nd half July.*

Le Tarbouche

$ | **ECLECTIC** | Compact and colorful, this convivial café-restaurant occupies a superb spot on one of the medina's main streets. Try their take on Moroccan tabbouleh made with couscous or get a *merguez* (spicy sausage) pizza to go—or grab one of the outdoor tables, perfect for people-watching over an avocado milkshake, caramel iced coffee, or homemade rosemary lemonade. **Known for:** good options for vegetarians; fresh and creative menu; cash required for payment. [$] *Average main: DH55 DH* ✉ *43, Talaa Kbira, Fez el-Bali, Fez* ☎ *0654/85–80–94* 🌐 *www.facebook.com/letarbouchefes* 💳 *No credit cards.*

Coffee and Quick Bites

Chez Thami

$ | **MOROCCAN** | This is a good, convivial place to enjoy a drink or a snack, with the added bonus of first-rate people-watching at the top of one of the medina's busiest thoroughfares. Thami's has expanded over the years from a single table and four chairs under the shade of a mulberry tree to a full-fledged restaurant. **Known for:** no credit cards; good-value traditional dishes; kefta-and-egg tagine. [$] *Average main: DH65* ✉ *Rue Tala'a Sghira, Fez el-Bali, Fez* ✥ *Near Bab Boujeloud, at top of Tala'a Sghira* ☎ *0660/43–35–05* 💳 *No credit cards.*

Le Kasbah

$ | **MOROCCAN** | Spread over several levels, this good-value restaurant just below Bab Boujeloud offers an entertaining view of the street life below. The menu is average tourist fare, so you're probably better off sticking to a mint tea. **Known for:** popular with tourists; terrace overlooking the medina; good people-watching. [$] *Average main: DH70* ✉ *Talaa Kbira, Fez el-Bali, Fez* ☎ *0535/74–15–33.*

Made in M–Fez

$ | **MOROCCAN** | After a morning pounding the medina alleyways, this cute and contemporary café on the Talaa Kbira is the perfect place to take a break with a fresh juice or mint tea, *malawi* (Moroccan pancakes), or a more substantial tagine. The chocolate mousse comes highly recommended. **Known for:** friendly staff; modern Moroccan menu; no credit cards. [$] *Average main: DH50* ✉ *246, Talaa Kbira, Fez el-Bali, Fez* ☎ *0535/63–41–16* 💳 *No credit cards* ⏲ *No dinner.*

Hotels

Dar Arsama

$ | **B&B/INN** | This tranquil and intimate property has been sensitively restored by its creative, multilingual owners, Violeta from Spain and her Fassi husband, Adil, who have blended traditional and modern decor in the five spacious rooms and filled the house is filled with family heirlooms, vintage finds, and Violeta's original artwork. **Pros:** delicious food; friendly hosts; cultural activities offered. **Cons:** pedestrian-only access; steep stairs; small property. [$] *Rooms from: DH580* ✉ *Derb Sidi Safi, 14, Talaa Seghira, Fez el-Bali, Fez* ☎ *0673/22–75–42* 🌐 *www.dar-arsama.com* 🛏 *5 rooms* 🍴 *Free Breakfast.*

★ **Dar Malika**

$ | **B&B/INN** | Tucked down a quiet street in the heart of Fez medina, this 300-year-old traditional house has been lovingly restored with the addition of some contemporary comforts, such as satellite TV and a Bluetooth speaker. **Pros:** good for families or small groups; traditional decor; friendly and helpful staff. **Cons:** one room has a separate bathroom; steep stairs (but there's a ground-floor room); pedestrian-only access (but a five-minute walk from parking). [$] *Rooms from: DH600* ✉ *22, Ferrane Couicha, Fez el-Bali, Fez* ☎ *0677/31–39–04* 🌐 *darmalikafez.com* 🛏 *4 rooms* 🍴 *Free Breakfast.*

★ **Dar Roumana**

$ | **B&B/INN** | The House of the Pomegranate is a sumptuously restored residence, with four stunning suites (another is planned for 2022 opening) that showcase the work of Fez's famous artisans in their carved cedarwood doors and lofty ceilings, mosaic tile floors, and intricate plasterwork. **Pros:** excellent restaurant;

rooftop terrace; great service. **Cons:** pedestrian-only access; steep stairs to upper-floor rooms; hard to find (but they have a porter). [$] *Rooms from: DH856* ✉ *30, Derb el Amer, Fez el-Bali, Fez* ☎ *0535/74–16–37* 🌐 *www.darroumana.com* 🛏 *4 suites* 🍴 *Free Breakfast.*

Hotel & Spa Riad Dar Bensouda

$$ | **HOTEL** | Soaring ceilings, carved cedarwood, ornate stucco, and intricate zellij tiling reflect the sensitive restoration of this 17th-century mansion. **Pros:** friendly, efficient staff; central but tranquil location; public spaces include a lounge and rooftop terrace. **Cons:** good but limited restaurant menu; pedestrian-only access; relatively minimalist furnishings may not appeal to all. [$] *Rooms from: DH1200* ✉ *14, Zkak El Bghel, Fez el-Bali, Fez* ☎ *0524/42–64–63* 🌐 *riaddarbensouda.com* 🛏 *18 rooms* 🍴 *Free Breakfast.*

★ **Le Jardin des Biehn**

$$ | **B&B/INN** | Attracting a global clientele, this *maison d'hôtes* with a French flavor is a serene experience from the moment you step through the ocher-color passageway into the luxuriant garden filled with sweet-scented jasmine and roses, as well as olive and citrus trees. **Pros:** eclectic decor with antiques and crafts; spa and hammam, plus small pool; lovely café restaurant. **Cons:** can be too intimate for some; may get chilly in winter; pedestrian-only access. [$] *Rooms from: DH1570* ✉ *13, Akbat Sbaa, Fez el-Bali, Fez* ☎ *0535/74–10–36, 0664/64–76–79* 🌐 *www.jardindesbiehn.com* 🛏 *14 rooms* 🍴 *Free Breakfast.*

★ **Karawan Riad**

$$$$ | **B&B/INN** | The nomadic French owners of this contemporary caravansary spent a decade reinventing this palatial 17th-century riad, where seven sumptuous suites now sit around a vast courtyard of soaring columns. **Pros:** good restaurant; spacious, beautifully decorated rooms; roof terrace. **Cons:** can be hard to find; steep stairs to upper floors; pedestrian-only access. [$] *Rooms from: DH3480* ✉ *21, Derb Ourbia, Fez el-Bali, Fez* ☎ *0535/63–78–78* 🌐 *www.karawanriad.com* 🛏 *7 suites* 🍴 *Free Breakfast.*

★ **Palais Amani**

$$$$ | **HOTEL** | With only 18 tastefully decorated rooms and suites (some with two bathrooms), the upscale Andalusian-style property creates an intimate setting centered on an inner courtyard garden meticulously landscaped with a canopy of lush lemon and orange trees by a marble fountain. **Pros:** elevator helpful for accessibility; personalized service in tranquil setting; spacious, chic rooms. **Cons:** can be expensive; pedestrian-only access (but close to parking); no pool. [$] *Rooms from: DH2160* ✉ *12, Derb el Miter, Oued Zhoun, Fez el-Bali, Fez* ☎ *0535/63–32–09* 🌐 *www.palaisamani.com* 🛏 *18 rooms* 🍴 *Free Breakfast.*

Palais Faraj Suites & Spa

$$$$ | **HOTEL** | In a lavish 19th-century former palace just outside the medina walls, the 31 suites blend contemporary furnishings with acres of marble, intricately carved cedarwood, ornate zellij tiling, and sparkling chandeliers—the work of a four-year renovation led by experts in Moorish architecture. **Pros:**; road access; first-rate facilities including spa and restaurant; large swimming pool. **Cons:** Wi-Fi can be patchy; less intimate than a riad; not in the heart of the medina. [$] *Rooms from: DH2230* ✉ *Bab Ziat, Quartier Ziat, Fez el-Bali, Fez* ☎ *0535/63–53–56* 🌐 *www.palaisfaraj.com* 🛏 *31 suites* 🍴 *Free Breakfast.*

Riad Anata

$$ | **B&B/INN** | The Belgian owner has given this traditional house a lighter, more contemporary feel while staying true to its Moroccan roots, decorating the five rooms—named after colors—in pale tones, with smooth *tadlak* (waterproof plaster) walls and splashes of

vibrant color from throws, rugs, and local artwork. **Pros:** rooftop terrace with wading pool; personal service; close to taxis and parking. **Cons:** steep stairs; small property; lacks ornate Moroccan decor. [$] *Rooms from: DH1200* ✉ *Derb El-Hamia, Fez el-Bali, Fez* ☎ *0535/74–15–37* 🌐 *www.riad-anata.com* 🛏 *5 rooms* 🍴 *Free Breakfast.*

Riad Fès – Relais & Châteaux

$$$$ | **HOTEL** | For an architecturally refined interpretation of riad living, head to this luxurious hotel: it's a perfect blend of character, modern convenience, creature comforts, and outstanding service. **Pros:** sumptuous spa; quiet location; elegant appointments and finishes throughout. **Cons:** pricey restaurant; pedestrian-only access; not for those who want a completely nonsmoking hotel. [$] *Rooms from: DH2500* ✉ *5, Derb Zerbtana, Fez el-Bali, Fez* ☎ *0535/74–12–06* 🌐 *www.riadfes.com* 🛏 *30 rooms* 🍴 *Free Breakfast.*

★ **Riad Idrissy**

$ | **B&B/INN** | Meticulously restored, this delightful riad's triple-height courtyard and five rooms are resplendent with dazzling zellij tiles and ornate stuccowork. **Pros:** beautiful decor including Moroccan antiques; charming and attentive staff; access to the Ruined Garden restaurant in the mornings. **Cons:** pedestrian-only access; steep stairs to upper-floor rooms; may feel too small and personal for some. [$] *Rooms from: DH800* ✉ *Derb Idrissy, Fez el-Bali, Fez* 🌐 *www.riadidrissy.com* 🛏 *5 rooms* 🍴 *Free Breakfast.*

★ **Riad Laaroussa**

$$ | **B&B/INN** | Built around a lush courtyard garden—a tranquil oasis from the medina's mayhem right on the doorstep—this 17th-century palace was in disrepair before being rescued and rebuilt by its French-American owners, utilizing the skills of the city's finest craftspeople. **Pros:** personalized service; heated swimming pool and courtyard garden; large rooftop terrace. **Cons:** pedestrian-only access; steep stairs to upper floors; intimate property, so may not appeal to all. [$] *Rooms from: DH1200* ✉ *3, Derb Bechara, Fez el-Bali, Fez* ☎ *0674/18–76–39* 🌐 *www.riad-laaroussa.com* 🛏 *12 rooms* 🍴 *Free Breakfast.*

Riad Maison Bleue & Spa

$$$ | **HOTEL** | Originally the private residence of Moulay Bel Arbi El Alaoui, a famous 20th-century judge and theologian, this property has been renovated and expanded several times over the years, and high ceilings and intricately carved stucco and cedar walls surround central patios and fountains. **Pros:** historic building; central location; swimming pool and spa. **Cons:** some rooms can be dark; restaurant can be overpriced; steep steps to upper floors. [$] *Rooms from: DH1700* ✉ *33, Derb El Mitter, Ain Zliten, Fez el-Bali, Fez* ☎ *0535/74–18–73* 🌐 *www.maisonbleue.com* 🛏 *18 rooms* 🍴 *Free Breakfast.*

Riad Numero 9

$ | **B&B/INN** | It's just like staying at a friend's house (a friend with impeccable taste, that is), and what it lacks in size—there are just three bedrooms around the courtyard, each on a different level—it more than makes up for in style. **Pros:** beautifully decorated with crafts and antiques; perfect for small groups; central location. **Cons:** credit cards aren't accepted; windows open onto the courtyard; the smallest room is not en suite. [$] *Rooms from: DH1000* ✉ *9, Derb Lamsside, Fez el-Bali, Fez* ✉ *stephen@riad9.com* 🌐 *www.riad9.com* 💳 *No credit cards* 🛏 *3 rooms* 🍴 *Free Breakfast.*

Ryad Mabrouka

$ | **B&B/INN** | Carefully restored, this Andalusian-style town house in the heart of the medina is consistently a pleasure: every detail is polished, from magnificent doors and crafted furnishings to a pretty garden. **Pros:** rooftop terrace; small but well-maintained outdoor pool; good service. **Cons:** pedestrian-only access; steep steps; not for families with young children. ⓢ *Rooms from: DH1100* ✉ *25, Derb el Miter, Fez el-Bali, Fez* ☎ *0535/63–63–45* ⊕ *www.ryadmabrouka.com* ⇆ *8 rooms* ⍣ *Free Breakfast.*

Nightlife

BARS

★ Le Golden Bar

BARS | This Art Deco–influenced bar attracts sophisticated locals and visitors as much for the medina views as the creative cocktails. While you're perched atop the hotel Palais Faraj Suites & Spa, with sweeping vistas on three sides, you can sample a well-crafted cocktail, a glass of fine local wine, or beer from a comfortable couch. The intimate spot also hosts live music, and a large alfresco terrace overlooks the jumble of medina rooftops. ■**TIP**➔ **Get there for sunset to watch the old city turn to gold.** ✉ *Palais Faraj Suites & Spa, Bab Ziat, Quartier Ziat, Fez el-Bali, Fez* ☎ *0535/63–53–56* ⊕ *www.palaisfaraj. com.*

Shopping

Fez el-Bali is a gigantic souk. Embroidery, pottery, leather goods, rugs and carpets, copper plates, brass pots, silver jewelry, textiles, babouches, and spices are all of exceptional handmade quality and sold at comparatively low prices, considering the craftsmanship that has remained authentic for nearly a thousand years.

CRAFTS

★ The Anou Cooperative

CRAFTS | The first store from the award-winning Anou Cooperative showcases fair-trade shopping at its finest. Owned and managed by a group of more than 600 artisans from around Morocco, the cooperative was set up to cut out the middleman and give 100% of the price tag back to the makers. You can meet the artisans, try a workshop, or just shop till you drop for handcrafted rugs, jewelry, leather bags, ceramics, and more; then enjoy a mint tea on the rooftop terrace. ✉ *Derb el Magana, Fez el-Bali, Fez* ✢ *Off Rue Talaa Kebira, next to Café Clock* ☎ *0662/73–48–53* ⊕ *www.theanou.com/ fezstore.*

L'Art du Bronze

CRAFTS | Hundreds of handcrafted bronze, copper, and silver objects, antique and new, are sold at affordable prices. ✉ *35, rue Talaa Sghira, Fez el-Bali, Fez* ☎ *0661/19–50–81.*

Coin Berbère

CRAFTS | A family affair, this long-established carpet and antiques shop has been in the Bouzidi-Idrissi family for decades. Besides stocking tribal carpets in all hues and textures, from shaggy Beni Ourain to tightly woven kilims, the store carries ornate silver jewelry, Fassi pottery, silk caftans, and antique wooden doors. They can ship everything to your door, too. ✉ *67, Talaa Kbira, Fez el-Bali, Fez* ☎ *0535/63–69–46* ⊕ *www.coinberber. com.*

Fondouk Chemmaine–Sbitriyine

CRAFTS | These two adjoining 13th-century fondouks are dedicated to disappearing crafts, such as ornate Fassi embroidery, wooden hammam buckets, and fire bellows, making it easy to buy direct from the artisans. Then use the elevator and head to the roof terrace for stunning medina views. It's part of an ambitious project involving the Millennium Challenge Corporation, in which several long-abandoned fondouks—medieval inns built around a courtyard, where traveling merchants parked their animals on the ground floor, stored their goods, and slept upstairs—have been restored to their former glory, with soaring stone

After the sun sets, the lights of Fez's car-free medina illuminate the city.

columns and fragrant cedarwood balconies. ⊠ *Sbitriyine, Fez el-Bali, Fez.*

Maison de Broderie et de Brocard de Fès
CRAFTS | Discover the intricate work of local embroiderers, including beautiful tablecloths and napkins. ⊠ *2, Derb Blida, Fez el-Bali, Fez* ☎ *0535/63–65–46.*

Aux Merveilles du Tapis
CRAFTS | Hamid Hakim, proprietor of this carpet shop, gives an impeccably seasoned and erudite presentation of Moroccan rugs and carpets as well as the architecture and traditional life in a privileged Moroccan residence. This 14th-century palace has exquisite ceilings of carved cedar restored and enriched with olive oil. Mr. Hakim's assistants roll and unroll a large selection of rugs with great flair and precision while serving an excellent mint tea. Prices are steep and tough negotiating is required—don't feel pressured to buy unless you are comfortable with the price. The store is large enough to accept credit cards and ships rugs overseas—and they really do arrive. ⊠ *22, Derb Sebaâ Louyet, near Pl. Seffarine, Fez el-Bali, Fez* ☎ *0535/63–87–35.*

Place Seffarine
CRAFTS | The picturesque Place Seffarine is the place for all things metal: bowls, boxes, candleholders, and ornate lamps. You can watch the artisans as they rhythmically hammer the copper and brass into shape outside their workshops. For a ringside seat, stop for a mint tea break at the Crémerie La Place. ⊠ *Pl. Seffarine, Fez el-Bali, Fez.*

Terrasse de Tannerie
LEATHER GOODS | Shop for butter-soft leather bags, jackets, slippers, and poufs at this labyrinthine shop overlooking the tanneries. With enough time, you can get something made to order. Be sure to bargain hard. ⊠ *10, rue Chouara, Fez el-Bali, Fez* ☎ *0535/63–66–25.*

FOOD

Herboriste Seddik

OTHER FOOD & DRINK | In this quaint shop, the shelves are stacked with herbs, spices, and all kinds of traditional beauty products such as argan oil, as well as flower extracts and medicinal plants. Ask for the *ras el hanout* spice mix to re-create Moroccan flavors at home. Cash is required for payment. ⊠ *15, rue Chouara, near Chouara Tannery, Fez el-Bali, Fez.*

LOCAL DESIGN

★ Le Boutique du Jardin

OTHER SPECIALTY STORE | At Le Jardin des Biehn's bijoux boutique, contemporary Fassi designs—including handcrafted leather bags from Italian designer Alfred Berlin that use leather from the 11th-century tanneries, and handwoven blankets from Artisan Project, founded by Palestinian American Nina Mohammad-Galbert, who works with local weavers—sit side by side with vintage *boucherouite* rag rugs and classic caftans. ⊠ *13, Akbat Sbaa, Douh, Fez el-Bali, Fez* ⊕ *www.jardindesbiehn.com.*

★ Medin'Art

OTHER SPECIALTY STORE | The city's first concept store, in the heart of the medina, stocks the work of predominantly Moroccan or Moroccan-based designers who are breathing fresh life into ancient crafts. Expect to find stylish bags and accessories from Les Maures Collection, shoes from CEO, T-shirts from Rock da Kasbah, housewares from Ytto, and Km 13's purses and jewelry made from recycled tires. ■**TIP→ Fixed prices take the hassle out of haggling, too.** ⊠ *19 bis, Zkak Ihjarm Talaa Sghira, Fez el-Bali, Fez* ☎ *617/57–50–79.*

Activities

COOKING CLASSES

Café Clock Cooking Workshop

COOKING CLASSES | At this one-day cooking workshop you'll uncover the secrets of Moroccan cooking from souk to plate. Fassi cuisine originated in the fondouks (traditional inns) where people from numerous cultures—Andalusian, Indian, and Persian among them—crossed paths, and you'll start by choosing a menu of salad, main course, and dessert. Then shop for ingredients in the souk with one of the café's Moroccan chefs before rustling up everything from tagines to couscous in the kitchen—or on the roof terrace for larger groups—and sitting down to enjoy the fruits of your labor. ⊠ *7, Derb el Magana, Fez el-Bali, Fez* ☎ *0535/63–78–55* ⊕ *www.cafeclock.com* 🖃 *600 DH.*

The Courtyard Kitchen at Dar Namir

COOKING CLASSES | If you want to discover more about modern Moroccan cooking, sign up for a half- or full-day private class (maximum group is six people) with the knowledgeable Tara Stevens, author of the cookbook *Clock Book.* It's as hands-on as you want it to be; after discussing the menu you'll learn about herbs and spices, age-old cooking techniques, Moroccan wine, and more as you rustle up five sophisticated dishes. These might include traditional bread *khobs* flavored with wild marjoram, a deconstructed chicken, lemon, and olive tagine, and chocolate olive-oil cake. Enjoy the fruits of your labor on the roof terrace, washed down with some of that aforementioned wine. ⊠ *24, Derb Cheikh el Fouki, Fez el-Bali* ⊕ *www.darnamir.com* 🖃 *4-hr classes from €95 (euros preferred) per person.*

HAMMAMS AND SPAS

Les Bains Amani

SPAS | Indulge in a luxurious hammam experience at this cross between a traditional hammam and a European-style spa. Les Bain Amani's mosaic-tiled hammam offers a private, romantic, candlelit treatment that, unlike those in a local hammam, couples can enjoy together. Follow up with a relaxing massage using organic products in one of the treatment rooms. Yoga classes are also available. ✉ *Palais Amani, 12, Derb el Miter, Oued Zhoun, Fez el-Bali, Fez* ☎ *0535/63–32–09* ⊕ *www.palaisamani.com* ✉ *Hammam from 390 DH; massage from 490 DH.*

★ Spa Laaroussa

SPAS | After a hard day's sightseeing, there's no better place to relax and unwind than Riad Laaroussa's beautifully restored 17th-century bathhouse, a private space with dark-gray tadlak walls and white Carrara marble slabs. As you steam, you'll be treated to an aromatic body scrub and face mask of rhassoul clay, mined in the Atlas mountains. Afterward, indulge in one of the city's best massages with essential oils infused with fragrant orange blossom and jasmine. The spa treats up to two people (women and/or men) at the same time, and it gets busy, so book in advance. ✉ *Riad Laaroussa, 3, Derb Bechara, Fez el-Bali, Fez* ☎ *0674/18–76–39* ⊕ *www.riadlaaroussa.com* ✉ *Hammam from 350 DH* ☞ *Reservations essential.*

Fez el-Djedid

Fez el-Djedid, or New Fez—built in the 13th century—has three distinct attractions: the green oasis of the Jnan Sbil Gardens, the Royal Palace to the west, and the Mellah, or Jewish Quarter, to the south. It lies southwest of Bab Boujeloud between Fez el-Bali and the Ville Nouvelle, and was built by the Merenid dynasty as a government seat and stronghold.

It remained the administrative center of Morocco until 1912, when Rabat took over the role and diminished this area's influence. If you need a bite to eat when you're exploring Fez el-Djedid, the medina is just a 10-minute walk away.

Sights

Bab es Seba

NOTABLE BUILDING | Named after the seven brothers of Moulay Abdellah, who reigned during the 18th century, the Bab es Seba (also known as Bab Dekkakin) connects two open spaces originally designed for military parades and royal ceremonies, the Petit Méchouar and Vieux Méchouar. It was from this gate that the corpse of Prince Ferdinand, brother of Prince Henry the Navigator of Portugal, was hanged head-down for four days in 1443 after being captured during a failed invasion of Tangier. ✉ *Av. Moulay Hassan, Fez el-Djedid, Fez.*

Dar el-Makhzen

CASTLE/PALACE | Fez's Royal Palace and gardens are closed to the public, but even from the outside they're an impressive sight; inside are various palaces, 200 acres of gardens, and parade grounds, as well as a medersa founded in 1320. From Place des Alaouites, take a close look at the door's giant brass knockers, made by artisans from Fez el-Bali, as well as the imposing brass doors themselves. The street running along the palace's southeast side is Rue Bou Ksissat, one side of which is lined with typically ornate residential facades from the Mellah's edge. ⚠ **Security in this area is high and should be respected. Guards watch visitors carefully.** ✉ *Fez el-Djedid, Fez.*

★ Jnan Sbil Garden

GARDEN | Gardens play an important role in Moroccan culture, and this gorgeous green space just outside the medina walls is one of the oldest in Fez. Once part of the Royal Palace, it was donated

The manicured Jnan Sbil Gardens, with fountains and lush foliage, is a peaceful respite from Fez's busy medina.

to the city in the 19th century by Sultan Moulay Hassan. A stroll around the shady pathways of this well-restored garden, with time to admire its many towering palms, rose bushes, lakes, and fountains, is the perfect escape from the medina's hubbub. ⊠ *Av. Moulay Hassan, Fez el-Djedid, Fez* 🎫 *Free* ⏲ *Closed Mon.*

Mellah

HISTORIC DISTRICT | Known for its characteristically ornate balconies and forged-iron windows, the Mellah was created in the 15th century when the Jews, forced out of the medina in one of Morocco's recurrent pogroms, were removed from their previous ghetto near Bab Guissa and set up as royal financial consultants and buffers between the Merenid rulers and the people. Fez's Jewish community suffered repressive measures until the beginning of the French protectorate in 1912. Faced with an uncertain future after Morocco gained independence in 1956, nearly all of Fez's Jews migrated to Casablanca, Israel, and the United States.

⊠ *Fez el-Djedid, Fez* ✛ *Accessible via Pl. des Alaouites or Bab el-Mellah.*

Moulay Abdellah Quarter

HISTORIC DISTRICT | Some highlights of this historic district include the vertically green-striped **Moulay Abdellah Mosque** and the **Great Mosque Abu Haq**, built in 1276. The neighborhood was designed by the Merenids as a government seat and a stronghold against their subjects, but the area lost its purpose when Rabat became the Moroccan capital under the French protectorate in 1912. Subsequently filled with brothels and dance halls, the quarter was closed to foreigners for years. ⊠ *Fez el-Djedid, Fez.*

Synagogue Aben Danan

SYNAGOGUE | Built in the 17th century, this is the one of the oldest synagogues in the region and one of the few that remain in the Mellah. It is rarely used as a synagogue today, but its rich cedarwood benches and beams, tiled floors, and brass chandeliers have been restored to their former splendor.

The guardian can show you its most important features, including the original gazelle-skin Torah scrolls and the subterranean mikvah (ritual bath). ✉ *Derb Djaj, Fez el-Djedid, Fez* 🎟 *20 DH.*

Ville Nouvelle

The 20th-century Ville Nouvelle is a modern neighborhood built by the French, with tree-lined avenues, fashionable boutiques, and upscale residences. There are no outstanding historical sites, but visit this area for contemporary modern cafés, restaurants, and hotels. Considerable commercial development is taking place to attract younger, affluent Fassis.

Sights

American Fondouk

OTHER ATTRACTION | You may have dodged a few donkeys laden with skins from the tannery as you explore the medina, and this long-established nonprofit organization is dedicated to improving the lives of these working animals—donkeys, mules and horses—by offering support to them and their owners. Visitors are welcome; just contact the fondouk to arrange a tour of the clinic and meet the animals. Ask about the organization's new project, Mules of the Medina, a stable just a 10-minute drive from the clinic. ✉ *1, rte. de Taza, Ville Nouvelle* ☎ *0535/93–19–53* 🌐 *www.fondouk.org* 🎟 *Free (donations welcome)* 🕒 *Closed weekends but can open for visits on request.*

Restaurants

Relais de Paris

$$ | **FRENCH** | If you seek a change from tagines, head to the sophisticated surrounds of the Hotel Sahrai and this classic French bistro, decked out in soothing neutral tones with floor-to-ceiling windows overlooking the terrace. Steak frites and chocolate fondant are the go-to dishes, washed down with a fine French red, but the catch of the day and Lebanese meze are also on the menu. **Known for:** perfect spot for a leisurely lunch; international menu suits many tastes; extensive wine and cocktail list. [$] *Average main: DH220* ✉ *Hotel Sahrai, Dhar el Mehraz, Ville Nouvelle, Fez* ☎ *0535/94–03–32* 🌐 *www.hotelsahrai.com.*

Restaurant Lounge MB

$$ | **MEDITERRANEAN** | The menu of this lounge bar and restaurant features French-influenced fare such as *magret de canard* (duck breast) and sole meunière, and international favorites such as Caesar salad and hamburgers, backed up with an impressive wine list. One of the city's most stylish eateries, the minimalist design channels industrial chic with rough-hewn stone walls, slate floors, and floor-to-ceiling windows, complemented by sleek contemporary furniture. **Known for:** Mediterranean menu also includes Moroccan specialties; two-level space with lounge bar on mezzanine; creative cocktails. [$] *Average main: DH200* ✉ *12, rue Ahmed Chaouki, Ville Nouvelle, Fez* ☎ *0535/62–27–27* 🌐 *www.mbrestaurant-lounge.com.*

Hotels

Barceló Fès Medina

$ | **HOTEL** | Despite its name, this contemporary hotel from a Spanish chain actually sits in a prime spot at the edge of the Ville Nouvelle, with stellar views over the medina. **Pros:** spacious rooms; located between old and new Fez; spa and swimming pool. **Cons:** lacks an authentic Moroccan feel; not as intimate as a riad; not in the medina. [$] *Rooms from: DH660* ✉ *53, av. Hassan II, Ville Nouvelle, Fez* ☎ *0535/94–88–00* 🌐 *www.barcelo.com* 🛏 *134 rooms* 🍴 *No Meals.*

Continued on page 248

TRADITIONAL MOROCCAN CRAFTS

Shopping in Morocco is an experience you'll never forget. In Marrakesh and Fez, the warren of souks are both magical and chaotic, their narrow alleyways overflowing with products handcrafted using centuries-old techniques.

Medieval markets display the bright colors, bold patterns, and natural materials found throughout Morocco's rich arts and crafts tradition. Items are produced in artisan workshops dating back to ancient times, while stylish boutiques showcase the work of local designers giving these time-honored crafts a contemporary twist.

Handmade Moroccan arts and crafts demonstrate the influence of Berber, Arab, Andalusian, and European traditions.

Using natural resources like wool, copper, silver, wood, and clay, master craftsmen and their apprentices incorporate symbolic motifs, patterns, and color into wood carvings, textiles, ceramics, jewelry, and other decorative arts. Traditional processes, handed down through the generations, can be observed from start to finish. Be prepared to negotiate a good price for anything you'd like to buy: bartering is expected and considered an art form in itself.

(top left) Ceramic tagines (top right) leather slippers (bottom right) perfume bottles

242

THE BEST OF MOROCCAN CRAFTS

In Morocco's souks you can watch a weaver at the loom, a potter at the wheel, brass being beaten, wood being carved, and more. While prices may not be as cheap as they once were, hand-crafted goods can be found at any price point. Even the highest quality pieces are a fraction of what you'd pay back home.

LEATHER

Fine Moroccan leather is sought after worldwide. Fez and Marrakesh have working medieval tanneries, producing large quantities of items for export. Sold inexpensively in local markets are bags, belts, luggage, and beautifully embroidered footstools. Leather and suede jackets can be made to order. *Babouches* are the ultimate house slippers; myriad colors and styles are available, and they make an inexpensive gift.

SILVER

The most popular silver jewelry in Morocco is crafted by Berbers in the southern High Atlas and Anti-Atlas Mountains. Taroudant and Tiznit are well-known jewelry-producing cities, while desert nomads—Touaregs and Saharaouia—craft silver items for tribal celebrations. Look out for fibulas (ornamental clasps to fasten clothing), Touareg "crosses," chunky Berber necklaces studded with gemstones, delicate filigree, and hands of Fatima (or *khamsa*, meaning five, for the five fingers) that are said to offer protection from the evil eye. There's also a good variety of Moroccan Judaica that includes silver *yads* (Torah pointers), Torah crowns, and menorahs. Silver teapots, serving trays, and decorative pieces capture the essence of Moroccan metalwork with geometric designs and ornate detail.

SPICES

Markets overflow with pyramids of aromatic spices used extensively in local cuisine and natural cosemetics. To create tajines and couscous back home, look out for turmeric, cloves, ginger, paprika, and saffron. Ask shopkeepers for their *ras el hanout* ("top shelf") blend, a mix of eight spices including cumin, cinnamon, coriander, and allspice, used for stews and grilling.

TEXTILES

For centuries, weaving has been an important artisanal tradition in all regions of Morocco, to create beauty and spiritual protection, as well as functional items. The best buys are silk and wool scarves and shawls and traditional caftans and djellabas, as well as hand-embroidered napkins, runners, and tablecloths. With enough time and a master weaver, you can get fabric handwoven and create something unique to take home.

WOOD

From the forests of the Rif and Middle Atlas, cedar wood is used to create beautiful mashrabiyya latticework found on decorative household chests, doors, and tables. Essaouira is the source of all fragrant thuya-wood products. Here, only the gnarled burls that grow out of the rare coniferous tree's trunk are used to carve a vast variety of objects, from tiny boxes and picture frames to trays, games, and even furniture, often decorated with marquetry in ebony and walnut.

ARGAN OIL

Highly valued by the Berbers, argan oil has been used for centuries as an all-purpose salve for skin and nails, a hair conditioner, and a treatment for scars and acne. And with its strong nutty flavor, it's delicious for dipping bread or drizzling on salads. Traditionally, women hand-crack the nut between two stones, and pure argan oil is among the most expensive in the world. Low-priced varieties are often mixed with cheaper oils, so choose your products carefully and try to buy from a genuine women's cooperative.

The Origins of Argan: The oil from the Argania spinosa, a thorny tree that has been growing wild in Morocco for millions of years, is a prized commodity. Today, the tree grows in a triangular belt in southwest Morocco from Essaouira on the Atlantic coast down to Tafraoute in the Anti-Atlas Mountains and east as far as Taroudant. It takes about 20 kg (44 pounds) of sun-dried nuts to produce one liter of oil.

(top) Pressing argan oil in a traditional press
(bottom) argan oil and its source

MOROCCAN POTTERY

 Morocco has a deserved reputation as one of the world's best producers of artisanal ceramics, where myriad decorative styles, shapes, and colors vary from region to region.

From simple tagine pots to ornate platters, giant lidded urns to small jars decorated with silver filigree, this authentic craft makes for an inexpensive, high-quality, and practical souvenir.

FEZ

Morocco's most stunning ceramics are the distinctive blue-and-white Fassi pieces. On locally produced pieces you'll find the word *Fas* handwritten on the bottom. Fassi ceramics also come in a beautiful polychrome of teal, yellow, royal blue, and burgundy. Another design unique to Fez is the simple *mataisha* (tomato flower), which you'll recognize by the repetition of a small, four-petal flower. Fez is also at the forefront of experimental glazes—keep a look out for solid-color urns of iridescent chartreuse or airy lemon yellow that wouldn't look out of place next to a modernist piece by Philippe Starck or Charles Eames. Head to Ain Nokbi, the city's industrial quarter, to see potters in action.

(top) Blue-and-white Fassi ceramics (left) Moroccan teapot

ASSESSING POTTERY

Look for kiln markings left after the ceramics have been fired. Pottery fired en masse is put in the kiln on its side, so the edges of bowls are often painted after they have been fired. The paint tends to flake off after a while, giving the bowls a more rustic, or antiqued, look.

Another technique for firing en masse is to stack the bowls one on top the other. This allows for the glazing of the entire piece but results in three small marks on both the inside and outside of bowls from the stands on which they were placed. Small touch-ups tend to disrupt the fluidity of the designs, but such blemishes can be used as a bargaining angle to bring down the price.

You can spot an individually fired piece by its lack of any interior faults. Only three small marks can be seen on the underside of the serving dish or bowl, and the designed face should be immaculate. These pieces, often large, intricately glazed serving pieces, are the most expensive that you'll find.

THE ART OF NEGOTIATION

Everywhere in Morocco you will be engaged by experienced vendors who will pounce on you as soon as you blink in their direction. Your best defense is the proper mindset. For your first souk visit, browse rather than buy. Wander the alleyways and see what's for sale but avoid being pulled in to an intense negotiation. You can also visit one of the state-sponsored artisan shops found in most large cities, where prices are higher than the souk but fixed.

Once you've decided what you want to buy, decide how much you want to pay. Without appearing too enthusiastic, ask the price (in dirhams). But don't accept the first price you're given—if you definitely want something, offer a lower figure. If the vendor won't decrease the price enough, walk away. Chances are he will run after you, either accepting your best offer or making a reduction.

SAFI

Safi's flourishing pottery industry dates back to the 12th century. Produced near the commercial port of Jorf Lasfar—"yellow cliffs" in Arabic—because of the local yellow clay, the pottery is a distinctive mustard color. The potters' elaborate designs and colors rival those of Fez but are in black with curving lines of leaves and flowers, with less emphasis on geometric patterns. The pottery is predominantly overglazed with a greenish blue, although cobalt, brown, green, yellow, and red are also used.

TAMEGROUTE

In this sleepy desert town, distinctive green-glazed ceramics have been produced since the 17th-century, thanks to clay rich in copper. The remaining family-run potteries still use age-old techniques to create one-off pieces.

(top) Safi ceramic teapots

MOROCCAN RUGS

 Rugs have been woven in Morocco for millennia and there are almost as many designs as there are weavers, with endless varieties of patterns, shapes, and sizes. They can vary tremendously in quality, and you can find them everywhere from city souks to rural cooperatives and upscale boutiques.

BERBER RUGS

There are more than 40 different tribal groups in Morocco, each with its own weaving styles and designs. Woven by women traditionally for utilitarian as well as decorative purposes, with skills passed down through families, the rugs suit the region's climate. Usually made of sheep's wool, they're often decorated with intricate geometric symbols that tell a story of daily life. A single rug can take weeks or months to complete and no two rugs are ever alike.

URBAN RUGS

It's thought urban rugs have been woven in Morocco since the 18th century, inspired by imports from the Ottoman Empire, and most large cities have their own distinctive style or specific design. These pile rugs have higher knot counts (they're more "finely" woven) than Berber rugs. Antique Rabati rugs, which often have an ornate border around a central motif, in a color palette of rich jewel tones, are particularly sought after.

BUYING TIPS

■ **Check the color.** If artificially aged, the back of the rug will be darker than the front. Natural dyes are bright but usually uneven and artificial dyes can bleed if the rug gets wet.

■ **Check the knot count.** The higher the knot count per square inch, the higher the price. Examine the back of the rug to look for gaps.

■ **The age of rugs.** Rugs don't have labels with identification, provenance, or origin date. Genuine antiques are rare, and rugs are rarely more than 50 years old.

■ **Prices.** There's no set price but flat-weave rugs are generally cheaper than pile rugs and cotton is less expensive than wool. It's worth checking the fixed prices at an Ensemble Artisanal as a guide.

RUG STYLES TO LOOK OUT FOR

BENI OUARAIN
In the Middle Atlas mountains, women weave rugs with patterns of black and brown lines and geometric shapes on a shaggy, natural cream wool background; now often seen splashed across the pages of design magazines.

KILIM
These flat-weave rugs incorporate bands of geometric designs—often fortuitous Berber symbols—and are dyed with natural colors: blue from indigo, yellow from saffron, and red from the indigenous madder plant.

AZILAL
Woven in the High Atlas from wool or a mix of wool and cotton, these striking rugs combine thick pile, vibrant colors, and bold geometric markings in an abstract design.

BOUCHAROUITE
A lesson in recycling, these brightly colored rag rugs are hand-knotted from leftover fabric. In Moroccan homes, they're put rag-side down to keep in the heat on cold days.

TAZNAKHT
This region's wool rugs are a fusion of flatweave, embroidered, and knotted sections, with intricate motifs, such as diamonds and zigzags, in warm tones of mustard-yellow and tomato-red.

HANDIRA
From the Middle and High Atlas, these cream, blanket-like rugs are made from wool and cotton and studded with glittering sequins. They're traditionally used as bridal shawls, but make beautiful throws or wall hangings.

(top left) A modern rug showroom (top right) a rug souk (bottom right) flat-weave kilim

Fes Marriott Hotel Jnan Palace

$$ | HOTEL | FAMILY | Set in expansive grounds in the Ville Nouvelle, this was Marriott's first hotel in Morocco, catering to both leisure and business travelers with ultramodern, air-conditioned rooms that channel Moroccan decorative motifs and have marble bathrooms and terraces overlooking the gardens or the city. **Pros:** luxurious pool area; spacious guest rooms; numerous dining options. **Cons:** rooms can be tired; some rates don't include breakfast, which can be an expensive extra; lacks an authentic Moroccan feel. $ *Rooms from: DH1400* ⊠ *8, av. Ahmed Chaouki, Ville Nouvelle, Fez* ☎ *0535/94–72–50* ⊕ *www.marriott.com* ➭ *244 rooms* ⦿ *Free Breakfast.*

Hotel Sahrai

$$$$ | HOTEL | Perched on a hill looking down on the medina, this boldly designed and ultrastylish boutique hotel has brought a new level of contemporary luxury to Fez. Using Taza limestone, marble, wood, metal, and glass, French design guru Christophe Pillet has imitated the layout of the old city. **Pros:** luxurious Givenchy Spa; modern room design using marble, limestone, and wood; choice of restaurants and bars. **Cons:** outside the medina; can be expensive, but check for offers; not for those looking for traditional Moroccan style. $ *Rooms from: DH2500* ⊠ *Dhar el Mehraz, Ville Nouvelle, Fez* ☎ *0535/94–03–32* ⊕ *www.hotelsahrai.com* ➭ *50 rooms* ⦿ *Free Breakfast.*

 Nightlife

BARS

Jungle Bar

BARS | At the top of stylish Hotel Sahrai, the equally chic Jungle Bar draws a sophisticated crowd to an indoor-outdoor space decked out in tones of green and gold, with rich fabrics, tropical prints, and ambient lighting. It regularly hosts DJs, but the real star of the show is the view over the old city. There are plenty of luxurious alfresco daybeds to lounge on, so grab a creative cocktail and a front-row seat and watch the sun set as the medina fills with twinkling lights. ⊠ *Hotel Sahrai, Bab Lghoul, Dhar el Mehraz, Ville Nouvelle, Fez* ☎ *0535/94–03–32* ⊕ *www.hotelsahrai.com.*

 Shopping

ALC-ALIF English Bookstore

BOOKS | If you find yourself in the Ville Nouvelle, it's worth dropping by Fez's finest English-language bookstore, on the campus of the American Language Center. It's a treasure trove of books about Morocco, from literature and language to culture and cooking. The store closes for lunch. ⊠ *2, rue Ahmed Hiba, Ville Nouvelle, Fez* ☎ *0535/94–02–50.*

Poterie de Fès

The famous blue-and-white Fassi pottery is made here. You can see how craftsmen mold, glaze, and paint plates, dishes, bowls, and all things ceramic, as well as piece together mosaics with classic zellij tiling. From Bab Ftouh, it's a 20-minute walk west or a petit taxi ride to the potters' quarter. ⊠ *Quartier des Potiers, Aïn Nokbi, Fez* ✛ *Take Rte. N6 Sidi Hrazem* ☎ *0678/28–79–06.*

Meknès

60 km (37 miles) west of Fez, 138 km (85 miles) east of Rabat.

In the imperial city of Meknès, you'll spend most of your time in the medina, admiring the stunning Bab Mansour from the lively Place el-Hedim. Also worth exploring are the sights of the well-preserved imperial city, with its imposing walls and ornate palaces.

Occupying a plateau overlooking the Bouefekrane River, which divides the old from the new, Meknès was the base of one of the country's most famous rulers, Sultan Moulay Ismail. He came to power at the age of 27 and ruled from 1672 to 1727, during which time Meknès became Morocco's capital. Because the city is less inundated with tourists and more provincial than Fez, the pace is slower and less frenetic. Whether it was post–Moulay Ismail exhaustion or the 1755 earthquake that quieted Meknès down, the result is a pleasant middle ground between the brouhaha of Fez and businesslike Rabat.

GETTING HERE AND AROUND
AIR
Fès-Saïss Airport serves both Fez and Meknès. The taxi from the airport to Meknès takes about an hour and costs around 400 DH.

BUS
Regular CTM buses cover the Fez–Meknès route hourly. There are buses to Casablanca (around four hours, 90 DH), Tangier (around five hours, 100 DH), and Marrakesh (around eight hours, 180 DH).

BUS CONTACTS CTM Meknès. ✉ *Av. des Forces Armées Royales, Ville Nouvelle* ✛ *East of Ville Nouvelle between Av. des Forces Royales and Av. de la Gare* ☏ *0522/43–82–82* ⊕ *www.ctm.ma.*

CAR
You don't need (and probably don't want) a car if you're just visiting Fez and Meknès. If you're planning to explore the immediate region of the Middle Atlas, it's better to rent a car at Fez airport rather than in Meknès.

TAXIS
Grands taxis carry up to six passengers and make long-distance runs between Fez and Meknès. This can be faster, more comfortable, and better value than bus travel.

Metered petits taxis take up to four passengers, but cannot leave the city limits. If the driver refuses to turn on the meter or agree to a reasonable price, do not hesitate to get out. There is usually a 50% surcharge after 8 pm.

TRAIN
The most convenient train station in Meknès is the Rue el-Amir Abdelkader stop, close to the administrative center of the city. If you're coming from Fez, it will be the second stop.

PLANNING YOUR TIME
Meknès is a beautifully intact medieval city, easily explored in a short excursion from Fez. From the central Place el-Hedim, you can discover the medina's network of small open and covered streets flanked by shops and food stalls. To explore the Imperial City quarter, take a petit taxi or a more atmospheric *calèche* (horse-drawn carriage).

FESTIVALS
Meknès International Animated Film Festival
FILM FESTIVALS | Meknès's annual international animated film festival (FICAM) at the French Institute takes place each spring, though the month may vary. ✉ *Rue Ferhat Hachad, Ville Nouvelle* ☏ *0535/51–65–00* ⊕ *www.ficam.ma.*

RESTAURANTS
There are few culinary gems in Meknès, but chances are you'll want to sample local delicacies, snack on unusual dried fruits, and savor the ritual sweet pastries and mint tea, purported to be the best in the country. Good cafés and restaurants are scattered in the medina (many near Place el-Hedim).

NIGHTLIFE
Bars in the Ville Nouvelle tend to be quite seedy, and it's almost impossible to get an alcoholic drink in Meknès medina—although Collier de la Colombe has a decent wine list—so local nightlife tends to revolve around the Place el-Hedim, a low-key version of the Djemâa el Fna in Marrakesh. Check the schedule of the Institut Français in the Ville Nouvelle for

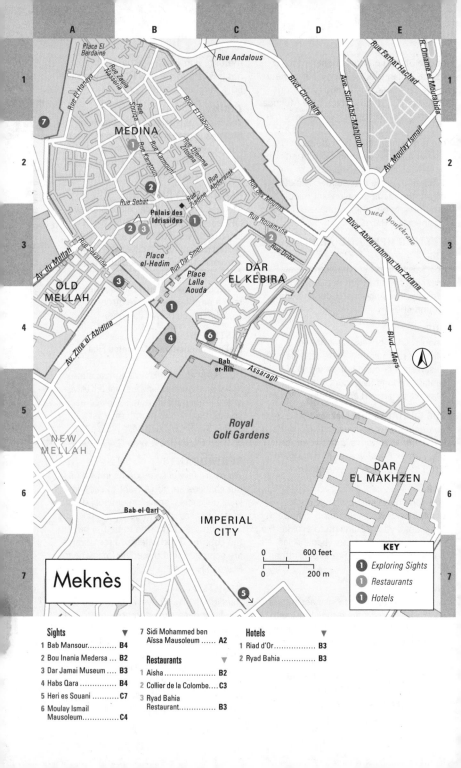

Meknès

KEY
- **1** Exploring Sights
- **1** Restaurants
- **1** Hotels

0 ――― 600 feet
0 ――― 200 m

concerts, films, and exhibitions. Summer concerts in the Heri es Souani are favorites of Meknès music lovers. Check with the tourist office for dates and dress warmly—the 12-foot walls built to cool oats and barley chill people as well.

VISITOR INFORMATION
CONTACTS Meknès Tourist Office.
✉ 27, pl. Administrative, Ville Nouvelle ☎ 0535/52–55–38.

The Imperial City

Moulay Ismail (1645–1727), of the Alaouite dynasty, enlarged Meknès over the decades and built a large imperial palace complex and substantial fortifications that are worth exploring. The imperial city covers a large area; the granaries are a 30-minute walk from the prison.

Habs Qara (*Prison of Christian Slaves*)
HISTORIC SIGHT | Closed at the time of writing, the green-tiled pavilion of Koubbat as-Sufara is where Moulay Ismail received ambassadors from abroad; the stairs to the right of the entrance lead down to the Habs Qara, immense subterranean slave quarters, built by an imprisoned Portuguese architect to earn his freedom. Here up to 60,000 enslaved people (of whom 40,000 were reportedly Christian prisoners of war) were shackled to the wall and forced to labor on the sultan's building projects. ✉ Imperial City, Meknès 🖭 60 DH.

★ **Heri es Souani** (*Royal Granaries*)
RUINS | The Royal Granaries were one of Moulay Ismail's greatest achievements during his reign, designed to store grain to feed his 10,000 horses for up to 20 years. To keep the grain from rotting, the granaries were kept cool by thick walls, hanging gardens, and an underground cistern with water ducts powered by donkeys. Behind the granaries are the ruins of the royal stables, where around 1,200 purebreds were kept. To the left of the door out to the stables, notice the symmetry of the stables' pillars from three different perspectives. Acoustically perfect, the site is now often used for concerts. The adjacent Agdal Basin served as a both a vast reservoir for the gardens and a lake. It's 2 km (1 mile) south of Moulay Ismail's mausoleum, so take a petit taxi in hot weather. ✉ Heri es Souani, Imperial City, Meknès 🖭 70 DH.

Moulay Ismail Mausoleum
TOMB | The mausoleum of Sultan Moulay Ismail, who died in 1727, is a beautiful structure with deep ocher-hue walls inside that lead to a private sanctuary, on the left, heavily decorated with colorful geometric zellij tiling. At the end of the larger inner courtyard is the sacred chamber with his tomb, surrounded by hand-carved cedar-and-stucco walls, intricate mosaics, and a central fountain. The mausoleum was closed at the time of writing, but check for reopening. ■ TIP→ **Non-Muslim visitors are allowed in to the first courtyards but not the tomb.** ✉ Imperial City, Meknès 🖭 Free.

The Medina

The focal point of the medina is the Place el-Hedim, and a walk around this sprawling square takes in several of the city's major sights, including the striking Bab Mansour and the Dar Jamai Museum.

★ **Bab Mansour**
NOTABLE BUILDING | Looming over the Place el-Hedim, this huge, horseshoe-shape triumphal arch is widely considered to be North Africa's most beautiful gate, completed in 1732 by a Christian convert to Islam named Mansour Laalej (whose name means "victorious renegade"). The marble Ionic columns supporting the two bastions on either side of the main entry are thought

The colorful zellij tiles on the exterior walls of the Sultan Moulay Ismail's burial place are examples of traditional geometric designs.

to have been taken from the Roman ruins at Volubilis. The taller Corinthian columns came from Marrakesh's El Badi Palace, part of Moulay Ismail's campaign to erase any vestige of the Saadian dynasty that preceded the Alaouites. Ismail's last important construction project, the gate was conceived as an elaborate homage to himself and the dynasty's strong Muslim orthodoxy, rather than a defensive stronghold—hence its intense decoration of green and white tiles and engraved Koranic panels, now faded with age. The Arabic inscription along the top of the gate reads: "I am the most beautiful gate in Morocco. I'm like the moon in the sky. Property and wealth are written on my front." ⊠ *Rue Dar Smen, Medina, Meknès* ✛ *South of Pl. el-Hedim.*

Bou Inania Medersa
HISTORIC SIGHT | Arguably just as beautiful and more well-preserved than its better-known Fassi namesake, the Meknès version is a showcase for Merenid

design; this Islamic educational institution, now a historic site, was finished in 1358. From the cupola to the enormous bronze doors on the street, virtually every inch of this building is covered with decorative carving or calligraphy. The central fountain was for ablutions before prayer. Head upstairs to visit the small rooms that overlook the courtyard. These housed the 60 communal *tolba*, or student reciters. ■**TIP**→ **The rooftop terrace has one of best panoramic views of Meknès's medina.** ⊠ *Rue Nejjarine, Medina, Meknès* ⧉ *60 DH.*

Dar Jamai Museum
OTHER MUSEUM | Closed for renovation at the time of writing, this 19th-century palace sits on the north side of the Place el-Hedim and houses a museum of Moroccan arts, with an outstanding collection of carpets, jewelry, ceramics, needlework, and woodwork. Built by a powerful family of viziers (high government officials), the palace itself

is stunning, especially the carved-cedar ceilings, interior Andalusian garden, and *menzah* (pavilion). ✉ *Pl. el-Hedim, Medina, Meknès* ✣ *North side of the square* ☎ *0555/53–08–63* 🎟 *10 DH.*

Sidi Mohammed ben Aïssa Mausoleum

TOMB | Just outside the medina walls, within the confines of an extensive cemetery, is the mosque and mausoleum of one of Morocco's most famous saints, Sidi Mohammed ben Aïssa (aka Cheikh El Kamel, 1467–1526). He founded the legendary Aïssaoua Sufi brotherhood, and each year his followers come from all over North Africa to gather at the shrine at the annual *moussem* (festival) on the eve of the birth of the prophet Mohammed. The festival date varies with the lunar calendar, but expect processions through Meknès, the brotherhood's singular music, and ecstatic dances, often imitating animals. Ben Aïssa was said to have made a pact with the animal world and to possess magical powers, such as the ability to transform leaves into gold and silver coins. The brotherhood was once known for such voluntary rituals as swallowing scorpions, broken glass, and poison; members also mutilated themselves with knives in prayer-induced trances. **■ TIP→ Entry to the mausoleum is restricted to Muslims.** ✉ *Medina, Meknès.*

🍴 Restaurants

Aisha

$ | MOROCCAN | Head to this cupboard-size restaurant for outstanding Moroccan cheap eats, perhaps freshly made bread and thick harira soup, a plate of grilled brochettes, or fluffy couscous. Portions are generous, and a full meal will cost less than a cup of coffee back home. **Known for:** vegan and vegetarian options; accepts cash only; local atmosphere. [$] *Average main: DH70* ✉ *14, rue Kababine, Medina, Meknès* ☎ *0620/57–47–30* 💳 *No credit cards.*

Collier de la Colombe

$ | MOROCCAN | A five-minute walk to the left inside Bab Mansour, this graceful medina space with intricate carvings, giant picture windows, and terraces overlooking the Boufekrane River and Ville Nouvelle is a good place to enjoy authentic Moroccan specialties. The menu is classic Moroccan, with highly recommended pastilla (a house specialty), tender grilled lamb, spicy beef brochettes, and mouthwatering fish tagines. **Known for:** good selection of wine and beer; excellent value for the price; polished but friendly service. [$] *Average main: DH100* ✉ *67, rue Driba, Medina, Meknès* ☎ *0535/55–50–41* 🌐 *lecollierdelacolombe.com.*

Ryad Bahia Restaurant

$ | MOROCCAN | Traditional Moroccan fare—choose from an à la carte or set menu—is prepared with fresh produce from the souk and served at candlelit tables in this riad's pretty courtyard. Typical dishes include hearty harira, an array of salads, and tasty tagines. **Known for:** intimate riad setting; friendly owners and staff; nonguests must reserve dinner ahead. [$] *Average main: DH90* ✉ *13, Tiberbarine, Medina, Meknès* ✣ *Behind Dar Jamai Museum* ☎ *0535/55–45–41* 🌐 *www.ryadbahia.com.*

🛏 Hotels

Meknès has not yet attracted the same level of development and active restoration of riads as Fez, although there are an increasing number of places to stay in the medina, which is the biggest draw.

Riad d'Or

$ | B&B/INN | This traditional guesthouse rambles across three 18th-century buildings; it's the kind of place where you might climb a staircase and chance on a plant-filled patio. **Pros:** panoramic terrace with a small pool; central location near Place el-Hedim; large, well-appointed rooms. **Cons:** decor can be tired; unreliable heat and air-conditioning; can be noisy. $ *Rooms from: DH400 ⊠ 17, Derb Ain El Anboub, Medina, Meknès* ☎ *0535/53–38–71* ⊕ *riadormeknes.com* ⟿ *21 rooms* ⦿ *Free Breakfast.*

★ Ryad Bahia

$ | B&B/INN | Tucked behind the Dar Jamai Museum, this 14th-century family house has been lovingly restored and furnished, and it's an impressive anthology of ceramics, rug weaving, and woodworking crafts. **Pros:** knowledgeable owners; outstanding service; family-friendly atmosphere. **Cons:** no alcohol allowed on premises; small property; long walk from parking lot. $ *Rooms from: DH670 ⊠ 13, Tiberbarine, Medina, Meknès* ⊹ *Behind Dar Jamai Museum* ☎ *0535/55–45–41* ⊕ *www.ryadbahia.com* ⟿ *13 rooms* ⦿ *Free Breakfast.*

Shopping

The diminutive Meknès souk is easier to manage than Fez. Getting lost here is difficult; it just isn't that big. Meknessi merchants and craftspeople can be as exceptional as those in Fez, and what's more, they're easier to negotiate with. Just be prepared, if you try to tell a rug seller that you're pressed for time, to hear, "Ah, but a person without time is a dead person."

CRAFTS

L'Art de la Damasquinerie

CRAFTS | At this family-run workshop, Ezzouak Abdelhak specializes in the fast-disappearing art of damascening (meticulously inlaying a thread of gold, silver, or copper onto a metal surface), creating exquisite decorative objects and jewelry. ⊠ *86, Souk Srairia, Medina* ☎ *0621/76–44–97* ⊕ *www.facebook.com/damasquinerie.*

Ensemble Artisanal

CRAFTS | The government-run Ensemble Artisanal is, as always in Moroccan cities, a good place to watch craftspeople at work and check for fixed-price, quality handcrafted products and prices before haggling in the souks. ⊠ *Av. Mohammed VI, Medina, Meknès.*

FOOD

Souk Atriya

FOOD | A tour through this gastronomic oasis stuffed with all manner of products heaped in elaborately arranged cones and pyramids—prunes, olives, spices, nuts, dates, and sugary pastries in every conceivable shape and color—is a veritable feast for the senses. Meknès is famed for its olives, and the variety on display and the painstaking care with which each pyramid of produce has been set out is nearly as geometrically enthralling as the decorative designs on the Bab Mansour. The food souks and kissaria (covered market) run along one side of the medina square. ■ TIP→ **The kissaria is a good place to stock up on Moroccan spices and aromatic herbs.** ⊠ *Pl. el-Hedim, Medina, Meknès.*

THE SOUKS

Beginning from Place el-Hedim, just past the pottery stands brimming with colorful tagine vessels, a narrow alleyway leads into the souks and kissaria (covered markets). **Souk Atriya,** the food souk, has a wonderful display of everything from spices to dried fruit to multihued olives. The **Souk Nejjarine,** the woodworkers' souk, leads into the rug and carpet souk. Farther on in this direction is the **Souk Bezzarine,** a buzzing flea market along the medina walls. Farther up to the right are basket makers, ironsmiths, leather workers, saddle makers, and, near Bab el-Djedid, makers of odd items like tents and musical instruments. The **Souk es-Sebat** begins a more formal section, where each small section is devoted to fabric and clothing, beginning with babouches (leather slippers).

The town of Moulay Idriss, where the country's founder, Moulay Idriss is buried, draws pilgrims from all over the world.

Moulay Idriss

23 km (14 miles) north of Meknès, 3 km (2 miles) southeast of Volubilis, 83 km (50 miles) west of Fez.

Moulay Idriss is Morocco's most sacred town, the final resting place of the nation's religious and secular founder, Moulay Idriss I. Born in 745, he is said to be a descendant of the prophet Mohammed, and he ruled from 788 until his death in 791. It is said that five pilgrimages to Moulay Idriss are the spiritual equivalent of one to Mecca, earning it the nickname the "poor man's Mecca." Non-Muslims are not allowed inside the tomb, and until 2005 were not allowed to spend the night in town. A splash of white against Djebel (Mt.) Zerhoun, the picturesque town tumbles down two hillsides. The pace of life is leisurely, visits are normally hassle-free, and people-watching in the main square offers a view of Moroccan life that hasn't changed for centuries.

Moulay Idriss attracts thousands of pilgrims from all over Morocco to its colorful moussem (festival) in August. Non-Muslims are welcome to attend the secular events, which are a fascinating glimpse into Islamic life and celebrations, with traditional music and parades.

GETTING HERE AND AROUND
Buses (15 DH) leave Meknès for Moulay Idriss every 15 minutes from 6 am until 10 pm. Or take a grand taxi from the Institut Français de Meknès (Rue Ferhat Hachad, between the medina and the Ville Nouvelle) for 10 DH.

TIMING AND PRECAUTIONS
Moulay Idriss is a holy town and requires utmost respect for its sacred rituals and customs, so act and dress accordingly. Each Saturday there's a lively local market. During Ramadan, most shops and restaurants are closed during the day, but you can buy picnic food from the market or eat on the terrace at the hotel Dar Zerhoune. It's thoughtful not to eat and drink on the street during this time.

Moroccan Wines

During their occupation of the Maghreb, the Romans exercised their viticulture skills and exploited the climate and the soil, but upon their departure, and with the strengthening of Islam, the grapes literally withered on the vine. Under the French protectorate the vineyards were revived, but fell into state hands once the French left in 1956, marking a second decline in production. The French once again took the helm in the 1990s, replacing all the vines and planting them in sand, which maintains the heat and kills phylloxera (the organism that once decimated French vineyards in the 19th century). The harvest is at the end of August and bottling takes place in France.

Moroccan reds are quite low in tannin; the whites are reasonably sharp and benefit from chilling. Wines of note are Médallion and Volubilis (reds and whites), both at the high end of the price range, but don't exclude bargains like the tasty Guerrouane Gris (a slightly orange-color rosé) or the Président Sémillon Blanc. Look out for Gérard Depardieu Lumière, a Syrah blend produced from vineyards owned by the French actor.

◉ Sights

Moulay Idriss Medersa

HISTORIC SIGHT | An outstanding historic site from the Merenids, the Moulay Idriss Medersa was built in the 14th century by sultan Abou el Hassan. The medersa, hidden in the town's steep and twisting streets, has a striking cylindrical minaret constructed in 1939 that is the only one of its kind in Morocco, standing as testimony to Turkish and Arab influences. Originally built with materials from Volubilis, the minaret is decorated with green ceramic tiles bearing inscriptions of the 114 *suras* (chapters) of the Koran. Only Muslims can enter the medersa. ✉ *Moulay Idriss Zerhoun.*

Sidi Abdellah el Hajjam Terrace

VIEWPOINT | From the Sidi Abdellah el Hajjam Terrace, in the Khiber quarter, you will have the best vantage point to see the holy village of Moulay Idriss and its sacred sanctuaries. The adjoining quarter across the gorge is called Tasga. ✉ *Moulay Idriss Zerhoun.*

Zaouia of Moulay Idriss I

TOMB | This important shrine and mausoleum of the Idrissid dynasty's patriarch, Moulay Idriss I, who died in 791, is marked by a wooden bar so that people bow their head on entering. Entry is restricted to Muslims, but for a good view over the green-tiled minaret and rooftop of this landmark building, climb to a vantage point overlooking the religious sanctuary. The hike through the town's surrounding alleys up one of the many hills is invigorating and a symbolic bow to Morocco's secular and spiritual history. ✉ *Moulay Idriss Zerhoun.*

🍽 Restaurants

The main street through Moulay Idriss (up to the parking area just in front of the mausoleum) has a line of small restaurants serving everything from brochettes of spicy meat to harira. In front, you'll see stands where tagines cook over hot coals for hours until the meat is tender; the kefta tagine is the one to try.

Restaurant at Dar Zerhoune
$ | **MOROCCAN** | This cozy riad serves home-cooked traditional Moroccan cuisine to guests and nonguests on the roof terrace, with sweeping views over Moulay Idriss, the ruins of Volubilis, and the mountains beyond; there's also an air-conditioned salon. Dishes make the most of fresh, local ingredients; opt for the three-course set lunch or dinner—perhaps the famed Moulay Idriss kefta or a tasty tagine, or choose something lighter such as Greek salad (made with local cheese) or vegetable soup. **TIP→ Book in advance if you'd like afternoon tea.** **Known for:** Moulay Idriss kefta; a lighter take on traditional dishes; convivial atmosphere. [$] *Average main: DH100* ✉ *42, Derb Zaouk, Moulay Idriss Zerhoun* ☎ *0642/24–77–93* 🌐 *www.darzerhoune.com.*

★ **Restaurant at Scorpion House**
$$$$ | **MOROCCAN** | Indulging in a long, leisurely lunch looking down on the sacred city of Moulay Idriss and the plains of Meknès is certainly something to savor, especially when it's served on the terrace at Scorpion House. Private groups—from 2 to 40 people at a time—can enjoy a menu personalized in advance (all dietary requirements are catered for) and including grilled meats, fish, and seasonal Moroccan salads, rounded off with fruit and sweet treats. **Known for:** advance reservations required; authentic Moroccan cruise with a contemporary touch; incredible views on beautiful property. [$] *Average main: DH600* ✉ *54, Drouj El Hafa, Moulay Idriss Zerhoun* ☎ *0655/21–01–72* 🌐 *www.scorpionhouse.com* ⏲ *No dinner.*

Hotels

★ **Dar Zerhoune**
$ | **B&B/INN** | With a prime perch atop a hill, overlooking the tranquil Holy City of Moulay Idriss, this welcoming, Western-owned guesthouse is the perfect place to unwind after the hurly-burly of Fez. The air-conditioned rooms and lounging spaces have been lovingly decorated in a modern Moroccan style. **Pros:** authentic local tours; friendly staff; panoramic roof terrace. **Cons:** small property; no TV (but books and board games are available); quiet town. [$] *Rooms from: DH600* ✉ *42, Derb Zaouk, Moulay Idriss Zerhoun* ☎ *0642/24–77–93* 🌐 *www.darzerhoune.com* 🛏 *6 rooms* 🍴 *Free Breakfast.*

Volubilis

28 km (17 miles) northwest of Meknès, 88 km (53 miles) west of Fez, 3 km (2 miles) west of Moulay Idriss.

Volubilis, a UNESCO World Heritage site and one of Morocco's best-preserved Roman ruins, was the capital of the Roman province of Mauritania (Land of the Moors), Rome's southwesternmost incursion into North Africa. Favored by the confluence of the rivers Khoumane and Fertasse and surrounded by some of Morocco's most fertile plains, this site has probably been inhabited since the Neolithic era.

Volubilis's municipal street plan and distribution of public buildings are remarkably comprehensible examples of Roman urban planning. The floor plans of the individual houses, and especially their incredibly well-preserved mosaic floors depicting mythological scenes, provide a rare connection to the sensibilities of the Roman colonists who lived here 2,000 years ago.

Multilingual official guides at the entrance to the site provide one-hour tours for 250 DH. If you prefer to see Volubilis on your own (less informative but more contemplative), make a clockwise sweep, starting at the modern visitor center. After crossing the little bridge over the Fertasse River, climb up to the plateau's

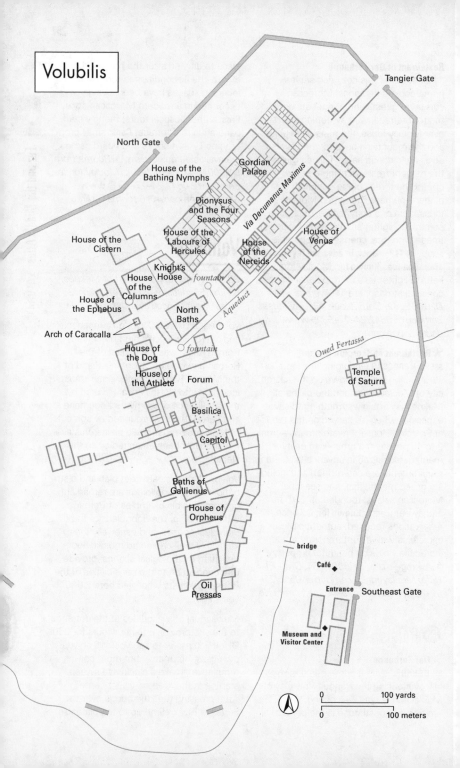

Volubilis

Tangier Gate

North Gate

House of the Bathing Nymphs

Gordian Palace

Dionysus and the Four Seasons

Via Decumanus Maximus

House of the Labours of Hercules

House of the Cistern

House of the Nereids

House of Venus

Knight's House

fountain

House of the Columns

Aqueduct

House of the Ephebus

North Baths

Arch of Caracalla

House of the Dog

fountain

Oued Fertassa

House of the Athlete

Forum

Temple of Saturn

Basilica

Capitol

Baths of Gallienus

House of Orpheus

bridge

Café ◆

Oil Presses

Entrance   Southeast Gate

Museum and Visitor Center ◆

0   100 yards

0   100 meters

Volubilis, with its extensive Roman ruins, is one of Morocco's most impressive archaeological sites.

left edge, and you'll soon come across an Amazigh skeleton lying beside a sculpture; the head points east, a deliberate placement suggesting early Islamization of the Amazigh populace here.

GETTING HERE AND AROUND

Volubilis is a 30-minute drive north from Meknès and an hour's drive west from Fez. Sometimes marked on road signs as "Oualili," Volubilis is beyond Moulay Idriss on Route N13, which leaves R413 to head northeast 15 km (9 miles) northwest of Meknès. Grands taxis to Volubilis are available from Meknès and Fez for around 350 DH and 1,000 DH round-trip, respectively. A one-way grand taxi from Moulay Idriss is 30 DH. From Fez, the only regularly scheduled bus connection to Volubilis is via Meknès.

TIMING AND PRECAUTIONS

Volubilis is an expansive site that requires intense walking and sun exposure. Tour earlier in the day or late in the afternoon, wear a hat, and carry plenty of water. The site is open daily, from 8:30 am until sunset; admission is 70 DH. A small, shady café (built around a tree near the site's car park) sells drinks and snacks, but for a more substantial meal, head to Moulay Idriss.

VISITOR INFORMATION

CONTACTS Volubilis Visitor Center. ⊠ *Main Gate, Volubilis.*

Sights

As you start a clockwise exploration of the site, the remains of Roman olive presses can be seen to the left, evidence of the importance of the olive-oil industry that supported 20,000 inhabitants of this 28-acre city. The first important mosaics are to the right in the House of Orpheus, consisting of a dolphin mosaic and one depicting the Orpheus myth in the Tablinum, a back room used as a library and receiving room. Past the public Baths of Gallienus, in a room to the right, are a dozen sets of footprints raised slightly above floor level in what was a communal bathroom. The wide-paved street leading up to the Capitol, the Basilica, and the Forum is the Cardus Maximus, the main east–west thoroughfare of any Roman town. Across the forum were the market stalls. The triumphal Arch of Caracalla, built in AD 217, destroyed by the 1755 Lisbon earthquake, and restored in 1932, is down to the left at the end of Decumanus Maximus, the main north–south street. As you look south through the arch, the first building to the left is the House of the Dog, named because of an unearthed bronze dog sculpture. The House of the Knight has an incomplete but beautifully designed mosaic of Dionysus. Beyond the northernmost gate—the Tangier Gate—stands the Palace of the Gordians, the residence of the administrators. The best mosaics are found in the House of Venus. Look for Diana Bathing with Nymphs and the Abduction of Hylas.

■ TIP→ Volubilis can get very hot, as the ruins offer no shade. Wearing a hat and bringing plenty of water are essential. The ground is uneven and sometimes rocky, so wear your best pair of walking shoes or sneakers.

Arch of Caracalla

RUINS | Rising out of fertile plains and olive groves, the impressive triumphal arch of Volubilis is the center point of the ancient Roman site. Decorated only on the east side, it is supported by marble columns, built by Marcus Aurelius Sebastenus to celebrate the power of Emperor Caracalla. ⊠ Volubilis.

Dionysus and the Four Seasons

RUINS | The house of Dionysus and the Four Seasons is about halfway down the Decumanus Maximus; its scene depicting Dionysus discovering Ariadne asleep is one of the site's most spectacular mosaics. Elsewhere along the Decumanus Maximus, the small spaces near the street's edge held shop stalls,

while mansions—10 on the left and 8 on the right—lined either side. ⊠ Volubilis.

House of the Bathing Nymphs

RUINS | Named for its superb floor mosaics portraying a bevy of frolicking nymphs in a surprisingly contemporary, all but animated, artistic fashion, the House of the Bathing Nymphs is on the main street's right side. The penultimate house has a marble bas-relief medallion of Bacchus. As you move back south along the next street below and parallel to the Decumanus Maximus, a smaller, shorter row of six houses is worth exploring. ⊠ Volubilis.

House of the Ephebus

RUINS | The ancient town's greatest mansions and mosaics, including the famous House of the Ephebus, line the Decumanus Maximus from the town brothel north to the Tangier Gate, which leads out of the enclosure on the uphill end. The house, just west of the Arch of Caracalla, is named for the nude, ivy-crowned bronze sculpture discovered here (now on display in Rabat). The cenacula, or banquet hall, has colorful mosaics with Bacchic themes. Opposite the House of the Ephebus is the House of the Dog, where a bronze canine statue was discovered in 1916 in one of the rooms off the triclinium, a large dining room. ⊠ Volubilis.

House of Orpheus

RUINS | One of the most important houses in the Roman ruins is the House of Orpheus, the largest house in the residential quarter. Three remarkable mosaics depict Orpheus charming animals with his lyre, nine dolphins symbolizing good luck, and Amphitrite in her sea horse–drawn chariot. Head north from here to explore the public Baths of Gallienus and freestanding Corinthian pillars of the Capitol. ⊠ Volubilis.

★ House of Venus

RUINS | Volubilis's best set of mosaics, not to be missed, is in the House of Venus. Intact excavations portray a chariot race, a bathing Diana surprised by the hunter Actaeon, and the abduction of Hylas by nymphs—all still easily identifiable. The path back down to the entrance passes the site of the Temple of Saturn, across the riverbed on the left. ⊠ *Volubilis.*

Sefrou

33 km (20 miles) southeast of Fez.

With cooler temperatures than nearby Fez, the Amazigh market town of Sefrou makes a pleasant summer day trip to explore the tranquil, well-preserved medina and the covered market, where the stalls are set behind bright-green shutters. In the fondouks, traditional artisans ply their trades. Try to time a visit with the Thursday souk or the famed Cherry Festival in June.

Sefrou lies in the River Agay's fertile valley at an altitude of 2,900 feet. It actually predates Fez and was the first stop on the caravan routes between the Sahara and the Mediterranean. Originally populated by Amazigh converts to Judaism, who came north from the Tafilalt oases and from Algeria in the 13th century, the town has a Mellah that is one of the oldest in Morocco. It remained a nucleus of Jewish life until independence in 1956, when virtually all of the Jewish community left the country.

◉ Sights

Bhalil

TOWN | The small Amazigh village of Bhalil, an off-the-beaten-track gem around 5 km (3 miles) from Sefrou, is built across a hillside, with picturesque pastel-color houses that line the narrow, winding streets. The houses may appear conventional from the outside, but step inside and you'll discover that many of them are built into the rock face. This design keeps out the scorching summer heat as well as the icy winter chill, and Bhalil's modern-day troglodytes normally use the cave as a living and dining space. This tranquil village is set at the foot of Djebel Kandar, and it makes a good base for walking, from leisurely rambles to more strenuous all-day hikes.

■ **TIP**→ **You'll often find the women of Bhalil sitting outside their houses sewing intricate djellaba buttons.** ⊠ *Bhalil.*

Culture Vultures Sefrou

CULTURAL TOURS | In addition to tours in Fez, Culture Vultures runs tours to three ancient fondouks around Sefrou's main square, visiting everyone from slipper makers to embroiderers. The tour includes lunch, as well as insight into the town's rich heritage at the Sefrou Museum of Multiculturalism (closed Friday); the founder describes it as "a micro museum with a macro message." The company also runs a small gallery of contemporary art, H'biza, which strives to present inspiring work. Pop into their office to see what artists-in-residence and presentations are coming up. ■ **TIP**→ **Book tours up to three days in advance via email.** ⊠ *33, al Kasba, Sefrou* ⊕ *culturevultures.ma* ≣ *€135 for 1 or 2 people, including tips for the artisans.*

Sefrou Cherry Festival

CULTURAL FESTIVALS | The town is most famous for its annual four-day Festival des Cerises, or Cherry Festival, which celebrates the yearly harvest in June with food, music, elaborate costumes, parades and cultural activities, including fantasias (a musket-firing cavalry charge) and the crowning of the Cherry Queen. It has been celebrated since 1920 and is now on UNESCO's intangible cultural heritage list. During the festival, a procession ventures across the Aggai River to the Kef el-Moumen caves, home to ancient tombs, including one for the prophet Daniel, a pilgrimage venerated by Jews and Muslims alike. According to legend, seven followers of Daniel slept here for centuries before miraculously resuscitating. ✉ *Sefrou.*

🍴 Restaurants

Al Farah Restaurant

$ | **MOROCCAN** | A mulberry tree shades the best of the small restaurants in Huddadine (Ironmonger) Square in the center of Sefrou's picturesque medina. Try the delicious rotisserie chicken, brochettes, fries, and salad. **Known for:** credit cards not accepted; simple home cooking; good place to observe daily life. [$] *Average main: DH30* ✉ *Pl. Huddadine, Sefrou* 💳 *No credit cards* 🕒 *No dinner.*

🛏 Hotels

★ **Dar Kamal Chaoui**

$ | **B&B/INN** | Kamal and Bea Chaoui have turned their family home in the tranquil troglodyte village of Bhalil into a delightful B&B with five rooms thoughtfully decorated with local touches—perhaps a donkey pannier or an intricately painted wooden door as a headboard—all with handwoven blankets across the beds. **Pros:** good walking; charming English- and French-speaking owners; dinners can be ordered. **Cons:** small property; off the beaten track; quiet area may not appeal to all. [$] *Rooms from: DH770* ✉ *60, Kaf Rhouni, Bhalil* ☎ *0678/83–83–10* 🌐 *www.kamalchaoui.com* 🛏 *5 rooms* 🍽 *Free Breakfast.*

Ifrane

58 km (36 miles) southwest of Sefrou, 63 km (39 miles) south of Fez.

Built in 1929 during the French protectorate to create a *poche de France* (pocket of France) for French expats, Ifrane has alpine chalets, contemporary villas, and modern boulevards that have become the place to see and be seen for the local elite, whose wealth is visibly flaunted with Western designer clothing in European-style cafés and a luxury resort and spa overlooking Azrou's cedar forest. Nicknamed "Morocco's Switzerland," Ifrane sits at an altitude of 5,460 feet and is visibly well maintained, with manicured gardens, tree-lined streets, and Swiss-style architecture. As a royal mandate, the Al Akhawayn University, an English-language public university with an American curriculum, opened in the mid-1990s and has become one of the country's finest. Grands taxis congregate at the bus station, 2 km (1.3 miles) southwest of town.

ESSENTIALS

TAXIS Ifrane Taxi Stand. ✉ *Gare Routière, Ifrane.*

VISITOR INFORMATION Délégation du Tourisme d'Ifrane. ✉ *Av. Mohammed V, Ifrane* ☎ *0535/56–68–21.*

👁 Sights

Known primarily as an upscale ski-resort town, Ifrane is also famous for its cold-water trout fishing and hiking trails around the **Cascades des Vierges** (Waterfall of the Virgins). Zaoula de Ifrane, a small village just north of the city, is home to local artisans. Near the well-photographed stone Atlas lion statue in the center of town, the royal palace of the ruling Alaouite dynasty is still in use by the ruling kingdom and off-limits to the general public, with high security in the area.

🍴 Restaurants

Cafe Restaurant La Paix

$ | **INTERNATIONAL** | **FAMILY** | This modern, family-friendly eatery is popular with both locals and visitors for its great location. The menu offers a range of international

The bucolic countryside and mountains around Ifrane are often covered in snow in winter, making this Morocco's most popular ski area.

dishes, including steak frites and pizza, as well as authentic Moroccan tagines; it also serves fresh juices and good coffee, as well as French pastries. **Known for:** terrace seating; buzzy atmosphere; credit cards not accepted. $ *Average main: DH70* ⊠ *Av. de la Marche Verte, Ifrane* ☎ *0535/56–66–75* ▭ *No credit cards.*

🛏 Hotels

★ Michlifen Resort & Golf
$$$$ | RESORT | Near the Michlifen ski slopes, this luxurious chalet-style retreat is less than an hour and a world away from the world's largest medieval city. **Pros:** many options for spa goers and sports lovers; beautiful mountain views; sumptuous suites. **Cons:** service can be leisurely; the region's priciest hotel (but check website for offers); limited public transportation. $ *Rooms from: DH4500* ⊠ *Av. Hassan II, Ifrane* ☎ *0535/86–40–00* ⊕ *www.michlifen.com/en* ↪ *70 rooms* ❏ *Free Breakfast.*

🏃 Activities

SKIING
Just a few miles apart, Michlifen and Djebel Hebri are the two ski resorts nearest Ifrane and within day-trip range of Fez. A day on the slopes is a pleasant option, but keep your expectations modest: the four trails are relatively simple. Skis and sleds can be rented at the resorts.

Azrou

17 km (10 miles) southwest of Ifrane, 67 km (40 miles) southeast of Meknès, 78 km (47 miles) southwest of Fez.

Life moves at a mellow pace in this small Amazigh market town, except on Tuesday when people descend from nearby villages for one of the region's largest souks. Held in an open area 1½ km (1 mile) northeast of the town, it draws locals for its vast selection of produce, livestock, clothes, and more, but you might pick up a rug at a bargain price. Follow the market's mayhem with a mint tea break in Place Mohammed V, the tranquil main square, where you'll find several cafés and shops.

Occupying an important junction of routes between the desert and Meknès and between Fez and Marrakesh, Azrou—from the Amazigh word for "rock"—is named for the city's quarry of black volcanic rocks. It was one of Sultan Moulay Ismail's strongholds after he built an imposing fortress (now in ruins) here in 1684. For centuries Azrou remained unknown, a secret mountain town that invading forces never fully located, thanks in part to a cave system designed for concealment and protection.

Sights

Cèdre Gouraud Forest

FOREST | Southeast of town, Azrou's cedar forest is a source of great pride throughout the country, with Moroccan cedars, some more than 400 years old, that grow to heights of close to 200 feet and cover some 320,000 acres on the slopes of the Middle Atlas, the High Atlas, and the Rif at altitudes between 3,940 and 9,200 feet. Cedar is much coveted by woodworkers, particularly makers of stringed musical instruments. Living among the enormous cedars to the south of Azrou are troops of bold Barbary macaques and birdlife ranging from the redheaded Moroccan woodpecker to owls and eagles. Flora include the large-leaf peony, the scarlet dianthus, and the blue germander, all of which attract butterflies, including the cardinal and the colorful sulfur Cleopatra. You can pick up information and maps of the forest showing trails and hikes at the Ifrane Tourist Office, a 25-minute drive away. ✉ *Azrou.*

Ensemble Artisanal

CRAFTS | Azrou's artisan center, just off the P24 to Khénifra (and a mere five-minute walk from Place Mohammed V), is a collection of small crafts shops selling carpets, kilims, leatherwork, and cedarwood and stone carvings. ✉ *Bd. Mohammed V, Azrou.*

Hotels

Le Palais des Cerisiers

$$ | **HOTEL** | Outside of town en route to Azrou's cedar forest, this pretty, Alpine-style hotel is set in a stone mansion on verdant grounds and well equipped with classic wood furnishings, air-conditioned and centrally heated rooms, serene mountain views, and indoor and outdoor swimming pools. **Pros:** bar with billiards table; spa and wellness center; mountain bikes for exploring. **Cons:** high rates for the area; uninspiring decor; need a car to get there. [$] *Rooms from: DH1200* ✉ *Rte. du Cèdre Gouraud, Azrou* ☎ *0535/56–38–30* 🌐 *www.lepalaisdescerisiers.com* 🛏 *20 rooms* 🍴 *Free Breakfast.*

Chapter 7

THE HIGH ATLAS

7

Updated by
Amanda Mouttaki

⊙ Sights   🍴 Restaurants   🛏 Hotels   🛍 Shopping   🍸 Nightlife

★★★★★   ★★★☆☆   ★★★☆☆   ★★☆☆☆   ★☆☆☆☆

WELCOME TO THE HIGH ATLAS

TOP REASONS TO GO

★ **Hike North Africa's tallest peak:** Djebel Toubkal, which soars to 13,671 feet, is only a two-day climb. Trekkers can find everything they need at the base of the mountain.

★ **Adrenaline junkies getting their fix:** From mountain biking to skiing to skydiving and hot-air ballooning, outdoor activities in magical surroundings abound. Even just driving through the jaw-dropping mountains can be an adventure, with panoramas you have to see to believe.

★ **Magnificent views in high style:** Some truly first-class hotels have opened their doors to travelers in the High Atlas; the best contribute to the local community.

★ **Amazigh tradition and culture:** Life in the Atlas has barely altered over hundreds of years. While the arrival of electricity, the Internet, and new roads has brought changes, you'll still find Amazigh culinary, agricultural, linguistic, and artisanal heritage alive and well.

The two routes over the Tizi-n-Test (Test Pass) and Tizi-n-Tichka (Tichka Pass) are spectacular. For serious trekking, the area around Imlil is the best place to base yourself. There are also less-strenuous walks along many of the dirt roads in the region, for instance along the Agoundis River. Alternatively, visitors can make the hotels around Ouirgane their base, exploring the area on muleback or simply lounging by the pool. From Ouirgane, the Tinmel Mosque and the Goundafi Kasbah can easily be reached on a day trip. The Aït Bougmez Valley is a paradise for gentle exploration, with easy treks through the apple and cherry trees or a medium-grade scramble through the gorges and caves.

1 Cascades d'Ouzoud. Impressive waterfall that can be enjoyed as a day trip from Marrakesh.

2 Aït Bougmez Valley. Known as the "happy valley," this remote mountain region is breathtakingly lovely.

3 Imlil and the Ourika Valley. Imlil is base camp for trekking the High Atlas.

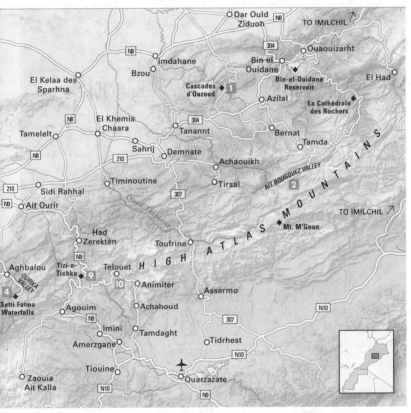

4 Setti Fatma. A popular day trip from Marrakesh, where you can hike to cascading waterfalls.

5 Oukaïmeden. Morocco's best-known ski resort villa is high in the Atlas mountains.

6 Lalla Takerkoust Lake. A large, man-made lake popular for water sports.

7 Ouirgane. A small village in the High Atlas, just south of Marrakesh, with gorgeous natural scenery.

8 Tizi-n-Test pass. A stretch of mountain road that connects Marrakesh and Taroudant with switchbacks through the High Atlas.

9 Tizi-n-Tichka pass. A mountain pass connecting Marrakesh and Ouarzazate over the High Atlas, along an old caravan path.

10 Telouet. A 19th-century kasbah village once home to the ruling Glaoui family.

TREKKING IN THE ATLAS

There are few better antidotes to the marvelous mayhem that is Marrakesh than the clear air and amazing vistas offered by the High Atlas Mountains. From gentle strolls through unspoiled Imazighen villages to full-blown, weeklong mountain treks, outfitters can cater to all levels of experience and budget.

Most travelers to the High Atlas associate it with one thing: Djebel Toubkal, North Africa's highest peak, scraping the clouds at 13,671 feet. It is indeed a magnificent sight, and for most of the year it's a relatively easy climb; from late April to early October a strong pair of legs (and boots) will suffice. As the focal point of the range, Djebel Toubkal is very popular in high season, but over its 600-plus-mile length, the High Atlas has over 400 peaks that exceed 10,000 feet, so there are plenty of alternatives. In typical Moroccan style, flexibility is the name of the game. Pretty much any type or length of trek can be organized, from a half-day excursion to lengthy expeditions involving mules and guides. Your level of fitness will determine which you choose.

SAFETY ADVICE

In most cases, you will need to hire a licensed mountain guide to accompany you. Conditions change quickly and it's easy to get lost in the mountains, so never walk alone; always tell someone where you are going, and when you hope to return. Take suitable quantities of food; warm, lightweight clothing; a hat and sunscreen; and a first-aid kit and water-purifying tablets (not bottled water). Most important, wear comfortable boots. Please leave no traces of your visit.

It is generally agreed that the launch point for any foray into the High Atlas is the largest Amazigh village in the region, Imlil (although it's still quite small). Here, accommodations are both plentiful and cheap, though they can feel a little faded.

In the shadow of Djebel Toubkal, Imlil is quiet but has a purposeful bustle, offering all that is necessary for a trek. Everything is for hire: boots (though bring your own if possible), jackets, sleeping bags, crampons, and even a mule, which can carry the loads of four people over most terrain.

GUIDES

Detailed maps of the region are scarce (and those that exist don't list many of the small villages and passes), but with a guide you shouldn't need one. Imlil is bursting with people willing to lead an expedition. Official guides can be found at the Bureau des Guides et des Accompagnateurs à Imlil, in the main square, or you can ask for a recommendation from your hotel or guesthouse. Official mountain guides undergo rigorous training and take exams within the French mountaineering system. In terms of cost, expect to pay 400 DH to 600 DH per day for a guide, plus more for food and accommodations. If a guide is arranging a trek for you, they will also arrange the food and

accommodations; just be sure to agree on the price beforehand. Mules come in at a very reasonable 150 DH along with their mule driver. It's also expected for you to tip your guide; a standard tip is 100 DH per day for the guide and cook, and 50 DH per person per day for the mule and regular driver.

TREKKING ROUTES

The choice of route will depend on your level of experience, the season, the length of time, and your budget. The obvious option is to attack Djebel Toubkal—you can be up and down in two days. Head south from Imlil past Sidi Chamarouch and make the easy ascent. Overnight on the mountain in one of two refuges (basic lodgings that offer beds, showers, food, and hot drinks) at the base of the mountain.

Those with more time and stamina may opt for a circular route, east from Imlil. Over five days, you might visit Tacchedirt, Tizi Likemt (at an impressive 11,663 feet), spend the second night at Azib Lkemt, and the third in Amsouzerte. To the west, Lac d'Ifni (a serene mineral-rich lake) awaits, then back to the one of the refuges before descending to Imlil. Another popular circular route goes up through Tizi Mizk, via Azeeb Tamsoult.

The High Atlas region is made for outdoor adventures—the perfect antidote to the animation of Marrakesh. You can hang glide, hot-air balloon, quad bike, and ride mules, but perhaps best of all, you can walk (in the winter, you can even ski).

This is also the heart of Amazigh mountain culture, so it's the perfect place to experience their hospitality and explore their customs. If trekking isn't your thing, you can relax and wander through the fruit orchards, gorge on in-season fresh peaches and walnuts, and learn about the carpets woven by the women of the region, over a cup of hot wild-thyme tea.

The High Atlas Mountains rise as a natural fortress between the fertile Haouz Plain around Marrakesh and the deserts of the south. Trapping moisture that blows in from the Atlantic, the mountains pass this bounty along to the land and to the thin rivers that vanish into the southern desert. To reach the mountains, even today's travelers must go through one of the routes guarded by age-old passes: Tizi-n-Test in the west or Tizi-n-Tichka in the east. They benefit from some glorious spots to stay, and the chance to take a quiet look at some intriguing relics of Moroccan history.

MAJOR REGIONS

The Central High Atlas and the Aït Bougmez Valley. The Central High Atlas is relatively unscathed by modernity. A large road-building initiative by the Moroccan government means that most areas are accessible, but they retain their wildness and their local traditions. The contrast in scenery is quite extraordinary in this area. One minute you will be looking up at a forbidding peak of bare rock, then the next at a patchwork of apple orchards. Aït Bougmez is the prettiest valley in Morocco with its lush greenery punctuated by hilltop shrines and ancient granaries. The region's crowning glory is Mt. M'Goun, which stretches up over 13,000 feet, making it the second-highest peak in North Africa.

Imlil and Ourika Valley. The village of Imlil is the preeminent jumping-off point for the high country, a vibrant mountain retreat whose existence has been given over to preparing walkers for various climbs around the peaks. The Ourika Valley, only 20 minutes outside of Marrakesh, is another gateway to the High Atlas peaks. It's a haven of green gorges and sparkling yellow wheat fields at the foot of snowcapped mountains. At the very end of the valley is Setti Fatma, a great base for trekkers. It's also where city families come for the weekend to escape the summer heat, so expect a playful party atmosphere filled with kids. There are countless cafés and restaurants along the road to Ourika.

Through the Tizi-n-Test Pass. To the west of Djebel Toubkal, the southern road from Marrakesh through Ouirgane carves its way through the High Atlas Mountains and offers spectacular views all the way to the Tizi-n-Test pass and beyond. Ouirgane is a great base for trekking and exploring, and has some fantastic lodging options. South of Ouirgane is best done as a road trip, with stops for occasional sights and breath-taking views.

Through the Tizi-n-Tichka Pass. Completed in 1936, the Tizi-n-Tichka has been widened and improved, but has lost none of its excitement or the hairpin bends beloved (or feared) by drivers. Though the road is safer and wider than the one over the Tizi-n-Test, it can be a dangerous drive, especially in winter weather. The scenery is relatively low-key; if you're just passing through en route to the southern oases, the vista from the Tichka road itself is amazing—especially in spring—and the Glaoui Kasbah at Telouet is worth a look.

Planning

When to Go

The mountains are at their most stunningly beautiful in March and April when the irises are blooming and the cherry trees are flowering. Hiking can be done all year round, but high season is the spring and fall. Attempting the summits in winter means that you need proper equipment and might encounter weather that will impede your plans, but you will be rewarded with empty mountains and peaceful, snow-filled scenery. Summer here is cooler than in the desert and in Marrakesh, but the sun is still strong and you will need lots of water if you decide to trek.

FESTIVALS
The most famous of festivals in this region is the **Imilchil Marriage Festival**, held each year in September. Legend has it that a "Romeo and Juliet" story

happened here ages ago; since then, an annual festival is held for young people to choose their own partner. Though lately the festival has been attracting more and more tourists, it is still very much a local tradition and visitors may feel out of place. The **Setti Fatma Moussem**, held in August, still contains the religious elements of a *moussem* (pilgrimage festival). Foreigners are welcome and will be pulled into the games and entertainment.

Planning Your Time

There is much to see in this region but since the roads are narrow and serpentine, the slopes are steep, and the terrain is bumpy, allow plenty of time for getting around. Seven to 10 days is recommended to really see the mountains and to get a good trek in. Any real mountain hike will begin in Imlil. The village of Tacchedirt is worth the five-hour trek, as is the more demanding two-day ascent to the great Toubkal. Afterward, explore the route to the pretty village of Ouirgane, and, to complete a circle back in the Marrakesh direction, stop at the barrage of Lalla Takerkoust, a pretty settlement with some pleasant eateries and accommodations.

Alternatively, you can take Route 210 out of Marrakesh, heading toward the Ouzoud Falls before continuing on to the reservoir Bin el-Ouidane. From here, head back down through Azilal and farther south to the magnificent valley of Aït Bougmez, which can serve as a base for trekking. Whatever you do, definitely don't miss out on getting up to the mountains themselves; even a short, half-day hike on a day trip from Marrakesh is well worth it. Imlil is just a 1½-hour drive from Marrakesh, making a day trip quite doable.

Getting Here and Around

AIR

There's no air travel directly into the High Atlas, but getting to the region isn't as difficult as it might seem. The closest airport is Marrakesh Menara, both to the Central High Atlas regions east of the city and to the areas south of Marrakesh, including the Ourika Valley. Many of the better hotels can arrange direct airport transfers from Marrakesh on your behalf, though this may come at an additional charge.

BUS

You can take a bus from an airport or another major city, but this can be time-consuming. If going to areas north and east of Marrakesh, try to avoid the marathon bus that goes from Marrakesh to Fez (via Beni-Mellal); buses run from Beni-Mellal up to Azilal, a common departure point for hiking excursions, departing approximately every three hours between 7 am and 4 pm. Buses also reach destinations in the High Atlas south of Marrakesh.

CAR

Unless you are taking a guided excursion, a car is the best way to explore off-the-beaten path towns at your own pace. If you have any intention of wandering into the hinterland independently, be sure you're driving a four-wheel-drive vehicle, and consider carrying more than one spare tire as well as emergency fuel. It's best to rent a car in Marrakesh and travel on from there.

See Travel Smart for more information on rental cars.

TAXI

You can also take a *grand taxi*. These used to be large, old, yellow Mercedes, but are now being traded in for modern cars (although they are usually still yellow). Prices are per seat, which means you have to wait until the car is filled with passengers to take off, but if you don't want to wait, you can buy up the empty seats or hire the entire car. Be sure to agree on and settle the fare prior to setting off.

Safety

The High Atlas is generally very safe and Imazighen have a treasured code of hospitality, but travelers should still take precautions. Rural sentiments are quite different from urban ones, so women should dress more conservatively than in larger cities. The biggest safety concern is, of course, for trekkers. While there are some instances where you can hike on your own, you will be safer and learn much more about the local environment if you take a guide. You can not summit Toubkal or any of the other major summits on your own; always take a trained, licensed guide and consider going with a group.

Restaurants

There are a few excellent restaurants in some of the major hotels, but beyond these, fare is limited mostly to what's available in small hotel restaurants and cafés—mostly tagines. Avoid alcohol except in hotels. In general, drinking won't raise any eyebrows as long as you're among other tourists, but the practice of carrying wine and spirits into the backcountry is not appreciated by villagers. Alcohol is *haram* (forbidden by the Koran), but on a more earthly level, it's simply not very socially acceptable.

Restaurant reviews have been shortened. For full information, visit Fodors.com.

Hotels

Some more sophisticated hotels in the High Atlas are located in or around Ouirgane, Lalla Takerkoust, and Ourika, which are quickly becoming sought-after refuges from the sometimes excessive stimulation of Morocco's cities. There are a couple of stunning kasbahs around Imlil. Most other lodging in the region consists of inexpensive *gîtes* (backpackers' refuges). Heterosexual couples staying in private homes while trekking will be assumed to be married. It's best not to disabuse your hosts of their assumptions. Note that it's illegal for a Moroccan and non-Moroccan of opposite sexes to spend the night together if they are not married; if one member of the heterosexual couple is Moroccan, a marriage certificate is likely to be required.

Hotel reviews have been shortened. For full information, visit Fodors.com.

WHAT IT COSTS In Dirhams			
$	$$	$$$	$$$$
RESTAURANTS			
under 90 DH	90 DH–120 DH	121 DH–150 DH	over 150 DH
HOTELS			
under 400 DH	400 DH–650 DH	651 DH–1,000 DH	over 1,000 DH

What to Wear

As weather in this region can be unpredictable, it's best to bring layers. It gets very hot in the summer and very cold in the winter, and you always need something warm for nighttime, regardless of the season. A hat and scarf are vital to protect against the sun. A down jacket, or something equally warm, is necessary for most of the year (note that heating is not a given in guesthouses). Solid footwear, such as boots or sneakers, is important, especially if you're planning on doing a trek. Sandals are socially acceptable and a sturdy, sensible pair can be useful for strolls, although not for demanding hikes. Both women and men should dress conservatively. Women will be better received by locals if they wear longish sleeves, avoiding short skirts and shorts. Both genders should be aware that pants are more practical when mule riding.

Tours

A good local tour guide will be able to plan with you, and accompany you, on a thorough visit of the region. As well as organizing accommodation and transport (which can be a headache), they'll be able to point you in the right direction of safe and appropriate treks and worthwhile points of interests while supplying all the cultural information you may require. There is also the language advantage; remember that in the mountains, Arabic or a Amazigh dialect is mostly spoken and a language-savvy guide is an invaluable asset. Be sure to research tour guides and companies in advance as there are some less reputable organizations around. If you are using a guide, ask if they are licensed.

★ **Argan Xtreme Sports**
BICYCLE TOURS | Argan Xtreme has a great fleet of bikes for on- and off-road bike tours. They offer a variety of tours from Marrakesh into the Atlas, with options for all abilities from family-friendly to professional bikers. Day and multiday excursions are available, and they also do tours in and around Marrakesh. ⊠ *AXS Bicycle Shop, Rue Fatima El Fihria, Marrakesh* ☎ *524/40–02–07 in Morocco, 314/374–2008 in U.S.* ⊕ *www.argansports.com.*

The Imazighen

The Imazighen are the indigenous people of North Africa, whose regions of occupation stretch from Egypt right across to Morocco and then down into Mauritania and Mali. They make up roughly 40% of the Moroccan population and the Amazigh language has been adopted as one of the three official state languages.

Amazigh (singular) and Imazighen (plural) is the preferred term, rather than "Berber," which is thought to derive from the Latin word "barbarus" used by the Romans to describe foreigners, especially those from the untamed hinterlands of their empire. These mountain communities were Jewish and Animist until the conquest of Morocco by Islam in the 7th century, and there was a large, residual Jewish population in Morocco until the mid-20th century, when many moved to Israel.

Amazigh Languages

There are three main divisions of the Amazigh languages: Taririft in the Rif area; Tamazight in the Mid-Atlas; and Tashlahit in the High Atlas, Anti-Atlas, and Souss. There is no linguistic connection to Arabic, although Moroccan Arabic and the Amazigh languages have infiltrated each other. They used to be primarily oral languages, but in 2003, the Neo-Tifinagh alphabet was adopted.

The Amazigh Way

Attention to local sensitivities is much appreciated and often rewarded with the celebrated Amazigh hospitality. Smiling goes further than anything in creating good will. Dressing modestly is always appreciated. Smoking is an urban phenomenon, so everyone (particularly women) should smoke discreetly.

If children ask for pens or sweets, the polite way to refuse is to say, "*Allah esahel*," which means "God make it easy on you." If you would like to contribute something to these regions, ask your hotel or guide how you can do so through one of the local associations that provide much of the local health care and education in the region. Always be sure to ask permission before you photograph Moroccans.

Pathfinders Treks

WALKING TOURS | This local Amazigh company offers tours with a focus on showing visitors the real Morocco. All the guides speak excellent English and are specialists in mountain and trekking tours (they also offer tours to the desert). The company is particularly passionate about sustainable tourism and supporting local communities. ✉ *Douar Tagadirt Ait Ali, Imlil* ☎ *0639/60–74–75* ⊕ *www.pathfinderstreks.com.*

Cascades d'Ouzoud

153 km (95 miles) northeast of Marrakesh.

No trip to the Atlas would be complete without a stop at these impressive falls, which are approachable from the S508 via the 1811. You will most likely hear the roaring water before you get your first glimpse, especially in late spring when the melting snow swells the rivers. The cascades, which are a popular destination for holidaying Moroccan families as well as foreigners, are rarely seen without a rainbow halo. You might see wild Barbary apes playing in the trees—avoid feeding them as they can get aggressive. Locals say the apes fall into three categories: those liking olives, those liking tourists, and those disliking both and preferring to hide.

There are a number of pop-up snack places at the falls. They are cheap, but may not always be the most reliable in terms of hygiene. There are public toilets in the car park. The colorful boats that sashay toward the gushing torrent are really fun to take a ride on, but do be careful. Remember that swimming in the basin carved out of the rock at the base of the falls is strictly forbidden, although you can jump in off the small bridge farther down and swim down to the rock pool.

Downstream, past the Ouzoud falls on the 1811 road, is the Amazigh hillside village of **Tanaghmelt.** Nicknamed "the Mexican village," the small community is connected by a web of narrow alleyways and semi-underground passages. You may also wish to continue up the 1811 (toward the P24) to see the **river gorges** of the Oued-el-Abid.

GETTING HERE AND AROUND

Around 170 km (105 miles) of good road separate Marrakesh from the Cascades d'Ouzoud, a journey that takes some two to three hours of driving. Leaving Marrakesh, take the Fez road (N8). Continue for around 60 km (37 miles). Turn right toward Azilal (the S508). Approximately 20 km (12 miles) before Azilal, turn left, following signs to Ouzoud.

Hotels

La Kasbah d'Ouzoud

$$ | **HOTEL** | **FAMILY** | Within this traditional kasbah, you can choose from spacious rooms or bungalows dotted around a pool and beautiful gardens. **Pros:** lush garden setting; beautiful building; excellent food. **Cons:** rather basic rooms; patchy Wi-Fi; if the phone signal is weak, the credit card machine doesn't work. $ *Rooms from: DH650* ✉ *C/R Ait Taguelle, Tanaghmelt* ☎ *0523/42–92–10* 🌐 *www.kasbahouzoud.com* 🛏 *13 rooms* 🍴 *Free Breakfast.*

Riad Cascades d'Ouzoud

$$ | **HOTEL** | At this haven of beautifully designed spaces, materials, and colors designed by a former architect, one of the highlights is the panoramic roof terrace. **Pros:** amazing location; perfect blend of elegance and comfort; welcoming and authentic. **Cons:** the walkway in front can get busy with tourists; basic amenities; some rooms on the small side. $ *Rooms from: DH650* ✉ *Tanaghmelt* ☎ *0523/42–91–73* 🌐 *www.ouzoud.com* 🛏 *9 rooms* 🍴 *Free Breakfast.*

The Aït Bougmez Valley

100 km (62 miles) southeast of Cascades d'Ouzoud; 182 km (113 miles) east of Marrakesh.

Also known as the valley of happiness, this Atlas valley was basically cut off from the rest of the world until 2001; before then, only a narrow, overgrown track led into the heavenly series of hamlets perched above a river and the richest of flora. Here, slopes dotted with beehives lead down into a grove of walnut and apple trees. The valleys are filled with vegetables and fruit grown using traditional farm techniques; there's not a tractor in sight, only donkeys, simple ploughs, and one seriously hardworking community.

Today, there is an excellent tarmac road that leads to Aït Bougmez. As a result, more visitors come to the area, but it still remains relatively secluded and retains its charm and authenticity. There is a huge variety of terrain in this relatively small area, so there are many options for

Did You Know?

The Cascades d'Ouzoud are particularly impressive in winter and spring, when the water is at its strongest. The crowds are heaviest in summer, though, when the water is warm enough for swimming.

hikers and bikers. There's of course the challenge of M'Goun mountain for those who want to test themselves, but for the less ambitious, just hiking through the rich fields at the base of the valley and enjoying the pure, refreshing air is a delightful experience.

Almost all houses here continue to be made from the traditional pisé bricks and baked earth, and you'll notice that most have living roofs, since sheaves of grasses are incorporated into the structure. One of the prettiest sights is the poppies peeping from them in spring. Life here is very simple, so don't expect any luxury spa hotels. There are also no restaurants in Aït Bougmez, but you can have a meal in practically any guesthouse with a little advance notice. Of course, you will also be invited in for tea by friendly villagers—be sure to say yes to experience that acclaimed hospitality.

Remember that you are deep in the mountains, and safety is vital. It is easy to get lost. Always travel with a guide, and be aware that much of this terrain is totally deserted for miles and miles on end. In winter, it gets incredibly cold and it's not uncommon to have minor snowstorms.

GETTING HERE AND AROUND
From Marrakesh, expect to spend 3½ hours getting to the Aït Bougmez valley. Leaving Marrakesh on the Route de Fez, take the right turn after 60 km (37 miles) toward Azilal. From Azilal, follow signs to the Aït Bougmez valley. It's a long but bewitchingly beautiful road that calls for careful, unhurried driving through mountain roads that are almost exclusively U-shape. It's also possible to reach Aït Bougmez by grand taxi from Marrakesh with a change at Azilal. Be aware that the last taxi leaves Azilal around 2 pm in order to make it to Aït Bougmez before nightfall.

Sights

Prehistoric dinosaur footprints
RUINS | FAMILY | Kids and adults alike love treading in these giant tracks of both carnivorous and herbivorous dinosaurs that are estimated to be about 185 million years old. There are several dinosaur-footprint sites in the region, but the easiest to find are those in the village of Ibaklliwne. As the road leads into the Aït Bougmez hamlets, it splits in two—this is actually a double valley. Follow the right-hand branch, leading into Tabant, the main village complete with a couple of cement structures, a school, and an administrative building. Follow this track for about 1½ km (1 mile) past the schoolhouses into the village of Ibaklliwne, where you'll find the dinosaur footprints on the hillside. ⊠ *Ibaklliwne, Ait Bougmez* 🖼 *Free.*

Sidi Moussa Marabout
RUINS | A 2½-hour walk from the base of the valley will take you to the steep slope of Sidi Moussa Hill. Here stands a circular earthen building, a shrine to the saint Sidi Moussa (*Moussa* means "Moses" in Arabic), which dates to at least 200 years ago. Sidi Moussa, revered for his skills in curing infertility, was buried here, and his tomb once attracted many visitors, although few still make the pilgrimage. Women thought to have fertility issues would leave a garment at the door and then spend the night inside. For a time the building was used as a collective granary before being restored by the Titmit Village Association. A guardian will serve you a glass of tea and give you a tour (pay him 20 DH minimum or 10 DH per person—all proceeds go to the Association). ⊠ *Ait Bougmez* 🖼 *Free; tour, 20 DH.*

Hotels

Dar Itrane

$$$ | **HOTEL** | Tucked into the village of Imghlaus, Dar Itrane is an inconspicuous gem of a lodge, with little that isn't utterly charming. **Pros:** wonderful views; delightful and helpful staff; delicious homemade food. **Cons:** can get cold at night; rooms are basic; smaller beds can be a bit slopey. [$] *Rooms from: DH700* ✉ *Imghlaus Village, Ait Bougmez* ☎ *0661/20–63–30* 🌐 *daritrane.com/* 💳 *No credit cards* 🛏 *17 rooms* 🍴 *Free Breakfast* ☞ *30% deposit required for reservation.*

La Montagne Au Pluriel

$ | **B&B/INN** | **FAMILY** | With a fabulous garden, friendly hosts, hot showers, and comfortable beds, this family-owned hotel is one of the most charming choices in the area. **Pros:** can arrange area hikes; gorgeous garden; lots of hot water. **Cons:** simple accommodations; can get cold at night; need to go to the roof terrace to get phone signal. [$] *Rooms from: DH150* ✉ *Agouti, Ait Bougmez* ☎ *0661/88–24–34* 🌐 *www.lamontagneaupluriel.fr* 💳 *No credit cards* 🛏 *30 rooms* 🍴 *Free Breakfast.*

Touda Ecolodge

$$ | **HOTEL** | **FAMILY** | This fantastic lodge occupies a prize position in the valley's deepest village, atop a hill with an unbeatable vantage point. **Pros:** tours and classes can be arranged; magnificent views; well-equipped accommodation. **Cons:** phone signal sometimes weak; gets cold at night; the road to get here may be difficult for some vehicles. [$] *Rooms from: DH600* ✉ *Village Zawiyat Oulmzi, Ait Bougmez* ☎ *0033/683–617–991 in France, 0662/14–42–85 in Morocco* 🌐 *www.touda.fr* 🛏 *9 rooms* 🍴 *Free Breakfast.*

Widiane Suites and Spa

$$$$ | **HOTEL** | Built in the middle of expansive parkland, on the edge of a huge lake and at an altitude certain to keep summers cool-ish and winters moderate, this glitzy hotel sets out to impress. **Pros:** hotel can arrange variety of activities in the area; the place to treat yourself; spacious, comfortable rooms. **Cons:** quite pricey; busy during Moroccan school breaks; opulence on this scale is jarring in contrast to rural surroundings. [$] *Rooms from: DH2800* ✉ *Chemin du Lac de Ben El Ouidane, Ait Bougmez* ☎ *0523/44–27–76* 🌐 *www.widiane.net* 🛏 *31 rooms* 🍴 *Free Breakfast.*

Shopping

Women's Cooperative of Imghlaus

CRAFTS | Up a dusty slope from the village of Imghlaus, in the Aït Bougamez valley, is a small, unassuming hut where you'd never know that inside was a veritable furor of singing voices and busy fingers. Inside, about 15 women create exquisite carpets in an organized production line. This cooperative is part of a fair-trade program that ensures the creators get the profits, with no middlemen involved. You can witness the fabrication process from beginning to end: the wool being cleaned, brushed, spun, and then fed through the loom. They'll also show you the natural tints they use: walnut for brown, petals for yellow, and a scarlet root for red. The women work in two shifts and it can take upward of a month to create a large rug. Design is important here; in Aït Bougmez, expect to find a certain motif repeated, and the older women may have this same motif tattooed on their chins or foreheads, an ancient tradition that revealed identity and was seen as beautiful. Prices vary, but expect a minimum of approximately 1,000 DH for a medium-size rug. You can buy directly here, or order online and have it mailed. There are also smaller items for sale. ✉ *Ait Bougmez* 🌐 *www.theanou.com.*

Activities

TREKKING

Hiking in this area is a true joy, thanks to the endless options and a huge variety of terrain in a relatively small area. Treks here are even suitable for families with children older than 11. A trek will give you insight into the valley, mountains, and underground gorges, with stops at villages, secret gorges, and orchards.

★ Epic Morocco

ADVENTURE TOURS | For bespoke, tailor-made tours around Morocco, Epic Morocco is great for trekking through the Aït Bougmez Valley. The company is committed to providing the best possible experiences within the country, taking you off the beaten track and into the real Morocco. Whether you're looking for luxury guesthouses or the great outdoors, they do their best to tailor everything to your needs, and they come armed with impressive knowledge of the hiking and biking trails of the country. They also do high-octane adventures like paragliding off Toubkal and rallies across the desert. ✉ *Appartement 8 Immeuble A, Residence le Gueliz, Guéliz* ☎ *2081/50–61–31* ⊕ *www.epicmorocco.co.uk.*

Imlil

64 km (40 miles) southeast of Marrakesh.

The ultimate home base for trekking the High Atlas, you'll find everything you need for your hike here: guides, rooms of varying price and quality, and equipment-rental shops. Imlil is a long strip of a village, built up around the main road.

⚠ **Storms may occasionally make the road into town impassable or treks to neighboring settlements impossible. Consider this if you're heading up in rough weather.**

GETTING HERE AND AROUND

Rental cars are available from numerous international and local agencies in Marrakesh but chances are you'll feel more comfortable with someone else doing the driving on these mountain roads.

You can get to Imlil from Marrakesh by grand taxi for 50 DH per seat or you can rent the whole car for 300 DH. You can also hire a private car and driver, but this will be more expensive at around 900 DH.

TIMING AND PRECAUTIONS

You can enjoy hiking for a day or spend an entire week trekking the region. The best time to visit is early or late summer or early fall, but winter is best avoided except for the most avid of outdoors enthusiasts. No matter what the season it's always recommended, and in many cases required, to hike with a guide.

The guides from the Bureau des Guides are fully qualified and mountain trained, and know the area thoroughly. Prices are 400 DH per day for hikes to a lower altitude and 500 DH per day if you are going up Mt. Toubkal.

VISITOR AND TOUR INFORMATION

Bureau des Guides. ✉ *Village Center, Imlil* ☎ *0524/48–56–26.*

 Sights

Djebel Toubkal

MOUNTAIN | You can unlock the adventurer inside by scaling this peak, the highest in North Africa. There are several ways to make the ascent, from hikes lasting several days to shorter options. The classic hike is a two- or three-day round-trip from Imlil. On Day 1, you hike to the foot of the mountain, which is an eight-hour walk, ascending at a moderate incline. There are two well-equipped refuges to spend the night that offer food and hot showers, as well as a campsite. On Day 2, you usually get up very early and leave

To get to the luxurious Kasbah de Toubkal from the village of Imlil, it's a short but steep hike or mule ride.

in the dark to get to the first big pass for sunrise, and then push to the top. You can then can either return to the refuge for another night and trek back the next day, or walk straight out back down to Imlil. While anyone can hike Toubkal it is best if you have some training and are in physically good shape to make the journey. It is required by the government to have a licensed guide, and there are police checkpoints along the way.

The road to Imlil is a left turn off the S501 (the Tizi-n-Test road that leads south from Marrakesh), just after Asni. The 17-km (11-mile) stretch is a spectacular expanse of scrub and cacti, which reaches out to the very foot of Ouanoukrim Massif. ✉ *Imlil.*

🍴 Restaurants

Food can be pretty basic in Imlil (primarily consisting of cafés that provide skewers and tagines), so if you're looking for something more gourmet, you may wish to seek out Kasbah du Toubkal, a 10-minute hike through the town. (There is a reception center on the main street.) The kasbah provides excellent Moroccan dishes to nonguests, in magnificent surroundings. Otherwise, most guesthouses will offer a full, home-cooked meal to nonguests.

Atlas Toubkal Imlil

$ | MOROCCAN | This restaurant located within a riad has stunning panoramic views from the rooftop terrace, along with delicious food. You'll find all the standard Moroccan dishes here, with a nice selection of well-portioned tagines. **Known for:** stunning views; good, inexpensive food; kofta (lamb) tagines. [$] *Average main: DH80* ✉ *Imlil* ✣ *Center of Imlil, just past bridge* ☎ *662/05–82–51* 🌐 *www.riadatlastoubkal.com* 💳 *No credit cards.*

Hotels

Some of Imlil's hotels are right on the main square as you enter the village, but there are plenty more tucked away. Given the rise in popularity for treks in the region, there is now a good choice of hotels catering to a variety of tastes and budgets. They can range from mattresses on the floor of someone's home to opulent suites in luxurious accommodations. A great way to meet locals and see everyday Moroccan life is to stay in a private home for about 100 DH a night per person.

Auberge Zaratoustra

$ | **B&B/INN** | This very pretty auberge is run by a friendly couple who offer convivial service and excellent home-cooked cuisine with a refined touch. **Pros:** warm welcome; run with care and attention; great food. **Cons:** no frills; gets quite cold at night; can be tricky to find. $ *Rooms from: DH350* ⊠ *Imlil* ☎ *0661/74–09–68* ⊕ *www.zaratoustra.com* ▤ *No credit cards* ⇥ *10 rooms* ⊺⃘ *Free Breakfast.*

★ Douar Samra

$$ | **HOTEL** | **FAMILY** | This charming, whimsical guesthouse was built from scratch using traditional methods and materials in the tiny hamlet of Tamatert, just past Imlil. **Pros:** can help organize guides and treks; eclectic design; best food in the Atlas Mountains. **Cons:** need to order a donkey to transfer your luggage up; a bit isolated if you want more action; can be hard to find. $ *Rooms from: DH450* ⊠ *Tamatert, Imlil* ⊹ *2 km (1 mile) from parking lot in Imlil. As you climb up, cross river, immediately on right is tiny, rocky track coming down stream's course. Follow this straight up and you come to Douar Samra in about ¼ mile* ☎ *0524/48–40–34, 0636/04–85–59* ⊕ *www.douar-samra.net* ⇥ *9 rooms* ⊺⃘ *Free Breakfast.*

Hotel and Café Soleil

$ | **HOTEL** | This simple, authentic hotel and café is on the main square of Imlil, and is a big hit with backpackers and trekkers.

Pros: hotel can organize treks and tours and will hold luggage for trekkers; great local color; very affordable. **Cons:** not soundproof so hard for light sleepers; can fill up in high season; basic accommodations. $ *Rooms from: DH400* ⊠ *Village Square, Imlil* ☎ *0524/48–56–22, 668/73–11–78* ⊕ *www.hotelsoleilimlil. com* ▤ *No credit cards* ⇥ *18 rooms* ⊺⃘ *Free Breakfast.*

★ Kasbah du Toubkal

$$$$ | **HOTEL** | Thank your stars that the short trek to this stunning yet simple kasbah keeps some guests away, so you can gaze over the snowcapped Atlas peaks in peace. **Pros:** hotel can organize tours, including a packed lunch; very intimate; excellent on-site hammam. **Cons:** seclusion might not be to everyone's liking; two-night minimum stay; luxury comes at a price. $ *Rooms from: DH1800* ⊠ *Imlil* ⊹ *Follow main road through Imlil and go right at fork, follow signs up hill, and keep going until you reach top* ☎ *0524/48–56– 11, 0661/91–85–98* ⊕ *www.kasbahdut-oubkal.com* ⇥ *14 rooms, 3 Amazigh salons (no en suite facilities), 1 house, 1 dorm* ⊺⃘ *Free Breakfast.*

★ Kasbah Tamadot

$$$$ | **HOTEL** | Should Hollywood set-makers get to work on a superdeluxe Moroccan mountain retreat, they might come up with something like this; this former villa of a prominent Italian art collector was even restored by Richard Branson himself. **Pros:** fantastic pool and spa; complete and absolute luxury; 20% of your breathtaking bill goes to the local community. **Cons:** expensive; hotel is a bit isolated; far removed from real Morocco. $ *Rooms from: DH5600* ⊠ *Rte. d'Imlil, Asni* ⊹ *The kasbah is just after Asni on road to Imlil, on left* ☎ *877/577–8777 U.S. toll-free, 0524/36–82–00* ⊕ *www.virgin-limitededition.com/en/kasbah-tamadot* ⇥ *24 rooms* ⊺⃘ *Free Breakfast.*

Setti Fatma

65 km (40 miles) southeast of Marrakesh.

Once you arrive at Setti Fatma, you'll notice the increase in crowds and, of course, more eating, lodging, and shopping options. But Setti Fatma is typically not the place to relax. It can be a nonstop party atmosphere for local Moroccans, which can be a lot of fun, just as long as you leave your longings for a quiet mountain retreat behind you.

One of the main reasons people make their way to Setti Fatma is to visit the seven waterfalls—a two-hour climb from the village center. If you don't want a hike this long, you can reach the first waterfall in about 20 minutes from the village. Setti Fatima is also a great setting-off point for walks into the mountains, where you can explore villages inaccessible by road.

GETTING HERE AND AROUND

A few kilometers along the 2017 from Tnine de l'Ourika, the road forks. Bear left toward Setti Fatma and the full beauty of the Ourika valley awaits you. Walnut trees line the river, which rushes to serve a number of pretty villages leading to Setti Fatma. The tiny village of Aghbalou is especially pretty, and a lovely place to spend a night.

You can take a grand taxi from Marrakesh to Setti Fatma; the price should be about 20 DH.

🍴 Restaurants

Restaurant-Hotel Azilal

$ | **MOROCCAN** | **FAMILY** | For only 50 DH, you can get a great meal here consisting of three courses made entirely by the family's mother. Go for a classic Moroccan salad (tomatoes and peppers) and a tagine of your choice and eat on the quaint platform overlooking the river. **Known for:** authentic cuisine; great home cooking; hearty portions. [$] *Average main: DH50* ✉ *Setti Fatma* ✣ *Near entrance of village on right, with an eating area on opposite side* ☎ *0668/88–37–70* 💳 *No credit cards.*

Timichi

$ | **MOROCCAN** | You need to cross a rickety bridge to get to this restaurant, which buzzes with the hum of local chatter, the sound of the trickling river, and the occasional Amazigh musician. The menu is predictable, with Moroccan salads, tagines, and a variety of sodas, but it's very tasty and the location is a great vantage point for people-watching. **Known for:** large portions; interesting people-watching; tasty tagines. [$] *Average main: DH60* ✉ *Setti Fatma* ✣ *At end of village, on left, over last makeshift footbridge* ☎ *0668/94–48–67* 💳 *No credit cards.*

🛏 Hotels

Auberge Le Maquis

$$ | **HOTEL** | **FAMILY** | One of the valley's first lodges, this friendly option guarantees excellent service, good food, and a snug bed for prices that won't break the bank. **Pros:** central heating (a rare find in these parts); fantastic welcome; free Wi-Fi throughout. **Cons:** not as secluded as some options; gets pretty cold at night; occasional noise from the road. [$] *Rooms from: DH580* ✉ *Km 45* ☎ *0524/48–45–31* 🌐 *aubergelemaquis.com/* 🛏 *11 rooms* 🍴 *Free Breakfast.*

La Perle de l'Ourika

$$ | **B&B/INN** | Perched on the edge of a ravine overlooking the river, this guesthouse offers you all the tranquillity you can't find in the center of Setti Fatma. **Pros:** very welcoming owner; stunning views; peaceful atmosphere. **Cons:** cold at night; not all rooms have en suite bathrooms; pretty basic accommodations. [$] *Rooms from: DH400* ✉ *Setti Fatma* ✣ *On left just before you enter main drag of village* ☎ *0682/62–82–50* 🌐 *www.laperledelourika.com* 🛏 *5 rooms* 🍴 *Free Breakfast.*

🛍 Shopping

Small stands line the road from before Ourika to Setti Fatma, selling crafts, pottery, and the carpets for which the Imazighen are so famous. Many of these small stands supply the great boutiques and bazaars of Marrakesh, so if you're in the mood for bargain hunting, you're likely to find a better deal here.

Oukaïmeden

20 km (13 miles) from Imlil.

Although you probably didn't go to Morocco for the snow, if you have a day or two to kill and you enjoy skiing, then a bit of powder isn't out of the question. The ski station at Oukaïmeden is a fun and increasingly popular place to visit, and a good place for novices to get in some practice without the stress of jam-packed slopes. On weekends, the mountains can get a bit crowded with enthusiastic Moroccans, but it is much quieter during the week. If you are a serious skier, then hire a guide and go off-piste; average skiers can just enjoy the novelty of skiing in northern African. The ski season lasts from late December until late March (and sometimes into April).

Hiking and climbing are two other great outdoor pursuits to experience in Oukaïmeden. There are numerous outfitters you can use to organize single-day or multiday tours for all levels of ability. There are also lots of fantastic hiking trails in the region; you can explore various routes with a guide or company, or find out information on how to hike on your own at your hotel. There are some lovely short walking trails, but don't go too far without a guide as the mountains can be quite harsh.

GETTING HERE AND AROUND

Transport can be a problem here, as a grand taxi from Marrakesh will drop you off, but might prove unreliable for pick ups when you want to move on. There is no scheduled bus service. In the busy ski season, you should be able to find shared taxis or even minibuses shuttling between the resort and Marrakesh. Otherwise ask your hotel in Marrakesh to book you a private car and driver or head here on a guided tour.

TIMING AND PRECAUTIONS

For skiers, Oukaïmeden is often a day trip from Marrakesh. There are a few hotels for those wishing to spend the night. Oukaïmeden, being a resort, is extremely safe. Just be sure to bring warm clothes.

GUIDES AND TOURS

Climb Morocco

ROCK CLIMBING | **FAMILY** | Based in Marrakesh, this American-owned outfit can organize tours of different lengths and for differing abilities. All of their climbing guides have been thoroughly trained and specialize in guiding single and multipitch rock climbing excursions as well as bouldering trips. 🌐 *www.climbmorocco.com.*

🍴 Restaurants

Chez Juju

$$ | **FRENCH** | **FAMILY** | For sophisticated dining in Oukaïmeden, you'll instantly appreciate Juju's yesteryear feel, modeled after alpine-style accommodations. The restaurant has been operating for more than 60 years and serves distinctly French dishes such as cassoulet and *tartiflette,* alongside some Moroccan choices like tagines. **Known for:** also has relatively upscale hotel rooms attached; nice wine menu; cozy, retro atmosphere. [$] *Average main: DH110* ✉ *Village center, Oukaimeden* ☎ *0524/31–90–05* 🌐 *www.hotelchezjuju.com.*

Hotels

Club Alpin Français

$ | **B&B/INN** | Offering a safe place to sleep for trekkers, skiers, and summer ramblers alike, this very simple and basic dormitory-style accommodation is clean and well run. **Pros:** can organize treks; relaxing and clean; easy to access. **Cons:** not much privacy; not many amenities; very basic accommodations. [$] *Rooms from: DH130* ✉ *Oukaimeden* ✥ *On right as you first enter Oukaïmeden* ☎ *0524/31–90–36* 🌐 *www.ffcam.fr* 💳 *No credit cards* 🛏 *158 beds (82 dormitory style, total of 76 beds in rooms for 4 or 8 people)* 🍴 *Free Breakfast.*

Lalla Takerkoust Lake

86 km (53 miles) northwest of Oukaïmeden, 40 km (25 miles) south of Marrakesh.

Thanks to the abundance of water, the Lalla Takerkoust dam is a good cooling-off point in the region. Fed by the river Oued Nfis, the lake has a shoreline stretching 7 km (4 miles) and offers fabulous views of the High Atlas peaks. It was originally made by the French to ensure the surrounding Houz Plains were watered. There are various activities available such as trekking, horseback riding, and quad biking, as well as water sports (although the ethics of such activities on a reservoir are somewhat questionable). There is also an increasing number of hotels and guesthouses in the area.

GETTING HERE AND AROUND

If you have your own car, take the R203 out of Marrakesh, in the direction of Tahannout and Asni. After around 5 km (3 miles), take the R209, better known as the Route du Barrage, off to the right. Continue until you reach the village of Lalla Takerkoust.

Otherwise, the village can be reached from Marrakesh by bus or grand taxi. The problem with both of these options is that you'll be dropped in the village of Lalla Takerkoust and will need to continue to the lake either on foot or with a local taxi, who will charge at least 100 DH. The easiest option is to ask your hotel for help. Most will organize a taxi transfer for you.

Sights

Lalla Takerkoust Lake

NATURE SIGHT | **FAMILY** | This reservoir is around 80 years old and a very established feature of the region, built by the French during the protectorate period. The water level fluctuates depending on rainfall and snowmelt, as it is fed from the mountains above. There are a few Jet Skis and paddleboards available to rent and take on the lake, which is not illegal but still questionable, given that this is a working reservoir. Swimming is forbidden since there is no lifeguard, but it's not uncommon to see people taking a dip, especially in the hotter months when temperatures rise. The most popular activity here is simply walking around the lake, which affords lovely views of the region as well as the local birdlife. ✉ *Lalla Takerkoust.*

Hotels

Jnane Tihihit

$$$ | **HOTEL** | **FAMILY** | Not far from the lake, this paradisiacal farm and guesthouse hides out behind the dusty, unassuming village of Makhfamane. **Pros:** delicious food; exemplary gardens; total immersion in nature. **Cons:** natural pool might not be to everyone's tastes; this is a working farm; the road to get here is very bumpy. [$] *Rooms from: DH890* ✉ *Douar Makhfamane, Lalla Takerkoust* ☎ *0670/96–59–70* 🌐 *www.jnane-tihihit.com/fr/* 🛏 *15 rooms* 🍴 *Free Breakfast.*

Le Petit Hotel du Flouka

$$$ | **HOTEL** | Set over a series of terraces leading down to the lake, this elegantly refurbished hotel is both relaxing and friendly. **Pros:** great views; congenial ambience; tasteful decor. **Cons:** restaurant can be busy; doesn't have a local feel; can get crowded on Sunday. [$] *Rooms from: DH800* ✉ *Rte. 203, Lalla Takerkoust* ☎ *664/49–26–60* 🌐 *www.leflouka.com* 🛏 *15 rooms* 🍴 *Free Breakfast.*

Activities

HORSEBACK RIDING

Les Cavaliers de L'Atlas

HORSEBACK RIDING | **FAMILY** | This is a reputable equestrian company that organizes all kinds of horseback excursions in the region. You can take a horse or pony out for anything from two hours to the whole day. It's a great way to discover the area and experience the lake or the nearby Agafay Desert from a different vantage point. Prices range from 400 DH for two hours, 780 DH for a half day, and 980 DH for a whole day, including meal and transfer if needed. ✉ *Lalla Takerkoust Lake, Lalla Takerkoust* ☎ *0672/84–55–79* 🌐 *cavaliersdelatlas.com/.*

PARAGLIDING

Fly Marrakech

HANG GLIDING & PARAGLIDING | One of the newest sports activities in the region is paragliding. With four qualified pilots and an on-site flight supervisor Fly Marrakech offers a safe way to try this unique and exhilarating sport. Meet at the flight location, or arrange for transportation from Marrakesh. Keep in mind there are weight and age limits and the activity is subject to weather conditions. ✉ *Near Lake Lalla Takerkoust* ☎ *0638/86–74–53* 🌐 *flymarrakech.ma/* 🎟 *750 DH.*

Ouirgane

60 km (37 miles) south of Marrakesh.

Ouirgane is one of Morocco's more luxurious bases for mountain adventures. It doesn't have the highest peaks, but it has a glorious choice of charming hotels and day trips that take in captivating scenery toward the mountainous Tizi-n-Test to the south. It's also a place to relax after climbing Djebel Toubkal or doing other High Atlas hikes.

"Sights" aside, by far the best thing to look at here is the surrounding countryside with its poppies in spring, yellow wheat in early summer, snowcapped mountains in winter, and rushing rivers and glorious, looming hills year-round. You can get out there in so many different ways, and your hotel (or a better-equipped one nearby) is the best way to rent equipment for outdoor activities.

Even if you keep close to town, you can explore the surrounding hills on foot or by bicycle, mule, horse, or quad bike. In town there's a lively Thursday morning souk. For many, Ouirgane is just a pleasant stop before tackling Tizi-n-Test but the charming village has a few auberges that make it a good starting point for treks.

GETTING HERE AND AROUND

If you have your own car, Ouirgane is a fairly short drive from Marrakesh. Failing that, a grand taxi costs 25 DH per person from Marrakesh; taxis from Tnine de l'Ourika are available for about 20 DH. The cheapest way is by bus (15 DH), which leaves Marrakesh's Gare Routière five times daily. However, it's easier to make the journey in a hired car with a driver.

Sights

Salt Mines

OTHER ATTRACTION | It is worth negotiating the potholed road to the salt mines just off the Amizmiz road (stop at the turning for the Amizmiz road and walk the last part). For centuries, local people have produced salt here from the saltwater river that cuts through the area, but today's relatively low value of the once highly prized natural commodity has greatly endangered the livelihoods of the salt-mining families. ✉ *Ouirgane* ✥ *From Ouirgane, take Amizmiz Rd.* ⏲ *Closed Sat. Usually only operational in warmer months.*

Shrine of Haïm ben Diourne
Site of one of the few Jewish festivals still held in Morocco, this complex contains the tombs of Rabbi Mordekai ben Hamon, Rabbi Abraham ben Hamon, and others. The shrine, known locally both as the "tigimi n Yehudeen" and "marabout Juif" (House of the Jews in Arabic and French, respectively), is a large white structure. The moussem (pilgrimage festival) generally happens in May. Tip the gatekeeper after a tour—anything between 5 DH and 15 DH is fine. ✉ *Ouirgane* ✥ *About 4 km (2½ miles) outside Ouirgane, the shrine is accessible on foot or by mule in less than an hour, or you can drive right up to gate on dirt piste. Turn left after about 1 km (½ mile) at Ouirgane's souk; follow road as it winds through village until you reach pink cubic water tank. Turn right and go to end of road, about 3 km (2 miles).*

🍴 Restaurants

La Bergerie
$$$$ | **FRENCH** | This delightful restaurant and guesthouse combines shaker style with *Little House on the Prairie,* and serves excellent French and Moroccan dishes. Specialties include wild boar, frogs' legs, and the wonderful *souris d'agneau* (a rich dish of slow-cooked lamb shank). **Known for:** attached inn is comfy and convenient; slow-cooked lamb shank; serves alcohol. [$] *Average main: DH180* ✉ *Marigha, Rte. de Taroudant, Km 59, Asni* ☎ *0524/48–57–17, 0661/15–99–06.*

★ Chez Momo
$$$ | **MOROCCAN** | **FAMILY** | Nestled in the foothills of the mountains near Ouirgane, Chez Momo is a delightful spot to sip a cocktail by the small pool or have a barbecue dinner seated on one of the chairs fashioned from tree trunks. After a feast you may find yourself inquiring about one of the seven cozy rooms and six suites, where a breakfast of morning coffee and *beghrir* (pancakes) is brought to your door each morning. **Known for:** stunning surroundings; delicious local cuisine; poolside dining available. [$] *Average main: DH130* ✉ *Rte. d'Asni, Km 61 from Marrakesh, Ouirgane* ✥ *Dirt road to Chez Momo is roughly 1 km (½ mile) south of bridge over Ouirgane River. Turn right at sign and continue about 164 feet downhill. Turn right again and park among olive trees* ☎ *0524/48–57–04, 0661/58–22–95* 🌐 *www.aubergemomo.com.*

🛏 Hotels

Domaine de la Roseraie
$$$$ | **HOTEL** | Spread over 60 acres of glorious gardens, with centuries-old olive trees, orchards, and magnificent roses, La Roseraie is the creation of one of the earliest pioneers of Morocco's hospitality industry. **Pros:** nice views; rooms hidden in private natural parkland; great amenities. **Cons:** decor is a bit faded; pool is not heated; quite costly. [$] *Rooms from: DH1900* ✉ *Rte. de Taroudant, Km 60, Ouirgane* ☎ *0524/43–91–28 reservations, 0524/48–56–94 hotel direct* 🌐 *www.laroseraie.ma* 🛏 *42 rooms* 🍴 *Free Breakfast.*

★ Domaine Malika
$$$$ | **HOTEL** | This small boutique hotel would not be out of place in one of the world's hippest capitals: how wonderful, then, that it is here in the High Atlas. **Pros:** beautiful hammam, pool, and olive grove; tasteful and unique decor; hotel

will organize tours, airport transfers, and cooking lessons. **Cons:** expensive for the area; two-night minimum stay; very small, so book ahead. $ *Rooms from: DH1500 ⊠ KM58 Rte. d'Amizmiz, Douar Marigha, Ouirgane ⊕ From Marrakesh, take Taroudant road in direction "Tahnanaoute." Before Ouirgane, in Douar of Maghira, turn right toward Amizmiz. The hotel is 500 meters ahead on left ☎ 0524/48–59–21 ⊕ domainemalika.com/ ⊘ Closed 2 wks in early Dec. ☞ 7 rooms, 1 large lodge for up to 19 people ⚏ Free Breakfast.*

★ Kasbah Bab Ourika

$$$$ | **HOTEL** | This luxurious retreat is a delightful example of how to build a near-perfect romantic getaway that's also eco-friendly. **Pros:** eco-friendly and gives back to the community; gorgeous ambience that's hard to top; staff can arrange activities and treks in the area. **Cons:** doesn't give a sense of true local culture; expensive; road to the kasbah is bumpy. $ *Rooms from: DH1500 ⊠ Ourika Valley ☎ 0668/74–95–47, 0661/63–42–34 ⊕ www.kasbahbabourika.com ☞ 30 rooms ⚏ Free Breakfast.*

Mohatirste

$ | **HOTEL** | For travelers looking for a simple, family-run hotel without a big price tag, this is a location to consider. **Pros:** can help arrange local activities; affordable; easy to access. **Cons:** vehicle needed to access other areas; limited amenities; basic accommodation. $ *Rooms from: DH350 ⊠ R203 just before Ouirgane ☎ 0524/48–50–68 ☞ 4 rooms ⚏ Free Breakfast ☞ Be prepared with cash as card use can be iffy.*

Activities

BIKING

You can rent bikes in town from hotels and inns like La Roseraie or La Bergerie (see above), or you can book a tour with outfitters like Argan Xtreme Sports or Marrakech Bike Action (see chapter Planner for details).

HORSEBACK RIDING

For horseback riding, La Roseraie is *the* place for the entire region (see above for info). You can rent horses for local rides or for full-blown tours in the mountains, complete with food and lodging in Atlas villages. Prices start at 200 DH for an hour.

WALKING

Every hotel around here will be able to fix you up with a walking guide to wander the local hills and rivers, and visit the salt mines, the remains of the Jewish settlement, and an Amazigh house, as you like. It's also only three days on foot (with the help of a mule or two) to the summit of Djebel Toubkal. The route bypasses Imlil, which is a plus for anyone wanting to avoid that well-known trekker base camp, though for some it has a genuine appeal.

Tizi-n-Test Pass

72 km (45 miles) southwest of Ouirgane.

The road to the Tizi-n-Test pass is one of Morocco's most glorious—and hair-raising—mountain drives. Heading south from Ouirgane to the pass takes you through the upper Nfis Valley, which was the spiritual heart of the Almohad Empire in the 12th century and later the administrative center of the Goundafi caids (local or tribal leaders) in the first half of the 20th century.

It's best enjoyed as a day trip by car from Ouirgane, especially as lodging options are few and seriously basic. There are plenty of cafés on the way, though, and you can also stop off at the Tinmel Mosque for a step back in history.

GETTING HERE AND AROUND

To experience the stunning mountain road that winds south toward Tizi-n-Test, you'll need transport. You can pick up a bus (a scary option) or a grand taxi (only

The 12-century Tinmel Mosque is one of only two mosques in Morocco that non-Muslims may enter.

slightly better) from Ouirgane. If you opt to drive yourself then you can take your time and drive within the speed limit. An alternative is to hire a car and driver through your hotel in Marrakesh (or a good hotel around Ouirgane).

Sights

Goundafi Kasbahs

RUINS | Most of the massive Goundafi Kasbahs, strongholds of the Aït Lahcen family that governed the region until independence in 1956, have long since crumbled away. But just past the small village of Talat-n-Yacoub, look up. A great hulking red kasbah sits at the top of the hill, amid a scene that is today eerily peaceful, with hawks nesting among the scraps of ornately carved plaster and woodwork still clinging to the massive walls. Built as a counterpart to the original Goundafi redoubt in Tagoundaft, the kasbah is a compelling testament to the concentration of power in an era said to be governed "tribally." Locals say the hands of slack workers were sealed into

the kasbah's walls during construction. There's usually not a tourist in sight.

It's a rocky, although fairly easy, walk up to it. From the kasbah you can see the Tinmel Mosque to the south, across the juncture of the Nfis and Tasaft Rivers. Just southeast are the mines of Tasaft. The Ouanoukrim Massif (the group of big mountains at the center of the High Atlas Mountains) dominates the view to the north. ⊠ *Above Talat-n-Yacoub, about 40 km (25 miles) south of Ouirgane, Talat-n-Yacoub.*

Tinmel Mosque

RUINS | One of only two mosques in the country that non-Muslims may enter (the other is Casablanca's enormous Hassan II mosque), Tinmel sits proudly in the hills and is well worth a visit. Built by Ibn Tumart, the first Almohad, its austere walls in the obscure valley of the Nfis formed the cradle of a formidable super-state and was the birthplace and spiritual capital of the 12th-century Almohad empire. Today the original walls stand firm, enclosing a serene area with row after row of pale brick arches, on a huge scale built to impress.

■ TIP → Admission to the mosque is free, but tip the guardian anything between 5 DH and 20 DH and he'll show you around and explain a little of the history. ⊠ Tinmel ✛ The signposted turnoff for mosque is about 4 km (2½ miles) south of Talat-n-Yacoub. Turn right, cross bridge, and follow path up other side of valley.

Tizi-n-Test

VIEWPOINT | The Tizi-n-Test pass climbs up to a staggering 6,889 feet and provides extraordinary views to the north toward the mountain peaks and south toward the Souss valleys. It's a hair-raising road trip calling for low gears and snail-like speeds, but the views are worth every second. ⊠ 76 km (47 miles) southwest of Ouirgane.

🍴 Restaurants

La Haute Vue

$ | CAFÉ | This small café right at the summit of Tizi-n-Test is the perfect place to take in the astounding view with some Moroccan cookies and mint tea on beautiful wrought-iron chairs made by the owner's son. It's also a good spot to stop along the road and wander up the hills. **Known for:** ironwork furniture; homemade cookies; sublime views. $ Average main: DH60 ⊠ Tizi-n-Test summit, 6,889 feet ☎ 0661/40–01–91 ▭ No credit cards.

🏨 Hotels

Berber Homestay

$ | HOUSE | FAMILY | If you want to really experience rural Moroccan mountain life, spend a night at the home of Said, who grew up in this small village in the Ijoukak Valley and has opened up his family home for visitors. **Pros:** comfortable rooms; amazing home-cooked food; complete immersion experience. **Cons:** can be cold in winter; remote location; not all rooms have a private bathroom.

$ Rooms from: DH250 ⊠ Ijoukak Valley ✉ berberhomstay@gmail.com ⊕ berber-homestay.com/ ▭ No credit cards ⇌ 3 rooms ❍ Free Breakfast ☞ Must be booked and paid in advance.

Dar El Mouahidines

$$ | B&B/INN | A very nice garden and a decent restaurant make this plain but functional hotel a nice place to stay near Tizi-n-Test. **Pros:** great start-off point for Adrar n'Iger; basic clean rooms; only hotel between Tinmel and the Tizi-n-Test pass. **Cons:** cold at night; remote; very simple accommodations. $ Rooms from: DH400 ⊠ Douar Tassouakt, Tinmel ✛ 8 km (5 miles) past Ijoukak on main road to Taroudant ☎ 0676/25–34–52 ⇌ 8 rooms ❍ Free Breakfast.

Tizi-n-Tichka Pass

110 km (68 miles) southeast of Marrakesh.

Winding its way southeast toward the desert, the Tichka Pass is another exercise in road-trip drama. Although the road is generally well maintained and wide enough for traffic to pass—and lacks the vertiginous twists of the Tizi-n-Test—it still deserves respect. Especially in winter, take warm clothes with you, as the temperature at the pass itself can seem another latitude entirely from the balmy sun of Marrakesh.

■ TIP → Sometimes gas can be difficult to find, particularly unleaded, so fill up before you hit the mountains. There's a station at the town of Aït Ourir, on the main road to Ouarzazate.

The road out of Marrakesh leads abruptly into the countryside, to quiet olive groves and desultory villages consisting of little more than a *hanut* (convenience store) and a roadside mechanic. You'll pass the R'mat River, the Oued Zat, and the Hotel Hardi. From here the road begins to rise, winding through fields that are either green with barley and wheat or brown with their stalks. At Km 55 you'll encounter the Hotel Dar Oudar in Touama. In springtime magnificent red poppies dot the surrounding fields.

On the way up into the hills, look for men and boys, often standing in the middle of the road, waving shiny bits of rock. These are magnificent pieces of quartz taken from the mountains that they sell for as little as 20 DH. On your left at Km 124 from Marrakesh you'll see the **Palais-n-Tichka,** a sort of Walmart for these shiny minerals, as well as other souvenirs. It's also a good restroom stop.

The road begins to climb noticeably, winding through forests and some of the region's lusher hillsides. A broad valley opens up to your left, revealing red earth and luminously green gardens. At Km 67 stands Mohammad Noukrati's Auberge Toufliht. From Toufliht there is little between you and the Tichka Pass but dusty villages, shepherds, and rock. You might find a decent orange juice, trinket, or weather-beaten carpet in villages like Taddert, but you'll probably feel pulled toward the pass. The scenery is rather barren, and as the naked rock of the mountains begins to emerge from beneath the flora, the walls of the canyon grow steeper and more enclosing.

Around Km 105 you'll see several waterfalls across the canyon. The trail down is precipitous but easy enough to follow; just park at the forlorn-looking refuge and the Café Tichka at Km 108. The trail winds to the left of the big hill, then cuts to the right and drops down to the falls after a short walk of half an hour or so. The Tichka Pass is farther along, at 7,413 feet above sea level. Depending on the season and the weather, the trip over the pass can take you from African heat to European gloom and back.

■ TIP→ **Warning: Always check the weather before embarking: winter storms can**

blow up very quickly and cause the road to be snow covered and impassable.

 ## Restaurants

Dar Oudar

$ | MOROCCAN | This restaurant that also has a few simple guest rooms is a good stop-off point before the climb to the Tichka Pass. The kitchen is justifiably proud of its reputation and makes delicious french fries and outstanding *kefta* (spiced minced beef) brochettes. **Known for:** starting point for the climb up the Tichka Pass; best french fries in the Atlas; tasty kefta brochettes. $ *Average main: DH60 ✉ Rte. de Ouarzazate, Km 56, Touama ☎ 0524/48–47–72 ⊕ www. daroudar.moonfruit.fr ⊟ No credit cards.*

La Maison Berbère

$ | MOROCCAN | This rest stop has made more of an effort than most of the others on this route, with a high ceiling and traditionally decorated salon permeated by the unmistakable smell of real coffee. Take a late breakfast or a tagine on the terrace at the back, overlooking a small garden and poppy-dotted fields. **Known for:** lovely views; easy stop-off point; hot mint tea. $ *Average main: DH50 ✉ 5 km (3 miles) before Taddert, Rte. de Ouarzazate ☎ 0524/37–14–67 ⊟ No credit cards.*

 ## Hotels

★ I Rocha

$$$ | HOTEL | Hidden on a promontory above the small Amazigh town of Tisselday, this is one of the best lodges in the region. **Pros:** hotel can arrange cooking courses, trekking, or telescope stargazing; lovely terrace; sparkling rooms. **Cons:** not all rooms have true double beds; rather isolated; wine prices inflated. $ *Rooms from: DH690 ✉ Tisselday ✛ Take signposted left at Tizirine (also called Douar Tisselday), halfway down main road that runs from Tizi-n-Tichka to Ouarzazate. Follow steep dirt track for*

It's best to take your time driving the Tizi-n-Tichka mountain pass, for safety and to enjoy the views.

500 feet 🖼 *0667/73–70–02, 0666/38–72–11* ⊕ *www.irocha.com* ⊟ *No credit cards* 🛏 *7 rooms* ⦿ *Free Breakfast.*

Telouet

116 km (72 miles) southeast of Marrakesh, 20 km (12 miles) east of P31.

The main reason for visiting Telouet is to see the incredible kasbah of the Glaouis (which is sometimes referred to simply as "Kasbah Telouet"). Built in the 19th century, the kasbah is now in near ruin, but the interior still hints of the luxury that once was. The village itself is not that remarkable.

It was from Telouet that the powerful Glaoui family controlled the caravan route over the mountains into Marrakesh. Although the Goundafi and Mtougi caids also held important High Atlas passes, by 1901 the Glaoui were on the rise. The legend goes that the Glaoui brothers saved the life of Sultan Moulay el-Hassan during a snowstorm, and in gratitude he gave them a collection of first-rate artillery. They then used it to subdue all their rivals, and were positioned to bargain when the French arrived on the political scene. The French couldn't have been pleased with the prospect of subduing the vast, wild regions of southern Morocco tribe by tribe. Thus the French-Glaoui alliance benefited both parties, with Madani el-Glaoui ruling as Grand Vizier and his brother Thami serving as pasha of Marrakesh.

GETTING HERE AND AROUND
Getting to Telouet isn't always easy. The best way, aside from with a tour group or hired car, is to take a grand taxi from Marrakesh or drive yourself.

TIMING AND PRECAUTIONS
The kasbah itself takes no more than three hours to explore. Take care, as parts of it are beginning to crumble.

Sights

Kasbah Telouet

RUINS | A formerly luxurious testament to the wealth of the Glaoui family, Kasbah Telouet is now in ruins but is still a wonderful place to explore. About five minutes south of Tizi-n-Tichka is the turnoff for the Glaoui Kasbah at Telouet. The road is paved but narrow, and winds from juniper-studded slopes down through a landscape of low eroding hills and the Assif-n-Tissent (Salt River). In spring, barley fields soften the effect, but for much of the year the scene is rather bleak.

Inside, walking through dusty courtyards that rise to towering mud walls, you'll pass through a series of gates and big doors, many threatening to fall from their hinges. Different parts are open at different times, perhaps according to the whims of the guard. Most of the kasbah looks ravished, as most of the useful or interesting bits had been carried off when the Glaoui reign came to its abrupt end in 1956. This sense of decay is interrupted when you get upstairs: here, from painted wood shutters and delicately carved plaster arabesques to exquisitely set tile and broad marble floors, you get a taste of the sumptuousness the Glaoui once enjoyed. Because it was built in the 20th century, ancient motifs are combined with kitschy contemporary elements, such as traditionally carved plaster shades for the electric lights. The roof has expansive views. ✉ *Telouet* 🎟 *Entry is free, but you should tip parking attendant and guardian of gate* ☞ *Parking for kasbah is down a short dirt road across from nearby auberge Chez Ahmed.*

Restaurants

Chez Ahmed

$ | **MOROCCAN** | This small but clean café and guesthouse is next door to the Kasbah Telouet parking lot and Ahmed, the owner, is very knowledgeable of Glaoui history and can organize tours of the surrounding area. He is also happy to sit and chat as well as feed you well for around 70 DH. **Known for:** history tours offered; knowledgeable and welcoming host; good but basic food. [$] *Average main: DH70* ✉ *Telouet* ☎ *0524/89–07–17* 💳 *No credit cards.*

Hotels

Kasbah Tigmi N'Oufella

$$ | **HOUSE** | This family home in an old kasbah has been converted to a bed-and-breakfast and it has a rooftop terrace with fabulous views of the High Atlas Mountains. **Pros:** mash-up of modern and traditional styles; easy to access; great cultural immersion. **Cons:** hot water not always reliable; not all rooms have a view; no other nearby options for meals. [$] *Rooms from: DH500* ✉ *Anguelez, Telouet* ✣ *From Telouet take P1506 to village of Anguelez, about 12 km* 🌐 *kasbah-haut-atlas.blog4ever.com/* 💳 *No credit cards* 🛏 *3 rooms* 🍴 *Free Breakfast* ☞ *Lunch and dinner can be prepared in advance (highly suggested).*

Chapter 8

THE GREAT OASIS VALLEYS

Updated by
Amanda Mouttaki

◉ Sights	🍴 Restaurants	🛏 Hotels	🛍 Shopping	🍸 Nightlife
★★★★★	★★★☆☆	★★★☆☆	★★☆☆☆	★☆☆☆☆

WELCOME TO
THE GREAT OASIS VALLEYS

TOP REASONS TO GO

★ **Desert dreams:** Live out those Lawrence of Arabia fantasies by sleeping on dunes under the stars.

★ **Dadès Gorge:** Follow mountain trails through some of Morocco's most beautiful scenery.

★ **Kasbah trail:** Marvel at and stay in ancient strongholds that dot the landscape.

★ **Morocco's Hollywood:** Spot celebs in Ouarzazate, home to visiting film crews.

★ **Flower power:** Visit the Valley of Roses in spring to see endless specimens in the wild.

The Great Oasis Valleys cover a huge area with some of Morocco's most characteristic wide-open spaces and tundra-like desolation.

1 Ouarzazate. Ouarzazate (pronounced wear-zaz-zatt) is a natural crossroads for exploring southern Morocco.

2 Aït Ben Haddou. One of Morocco's best known landmarks thanks to its appearance in countless films, this kasbah is a must-visit just outside Ouarzazate.

3 Skoura. This city lies in an oasis and palmeraie and is dotted with crumbling kasbahs.

4 Dadès Gorge. A series of rugged gorges cut out by the Dadès River and home to Morocco's fields of Damascus roses.

5 Todra Gorge. A gorge of tall limestone walls ebbs between a dry river bed and a pulsing river depending on the time of year. It's a popular destination for hikers and rock climbers.

6 Erfoud. One of the last cities before the Sahara desert is not on the radar for many visitors but it's a popular filming location thanks to its oasis and desert scenery.

7 Merzouga. Near Erg Chebbi, one of Morocco's largest sand dunes rising over 150 meters, Merzouga is an entry point for desert camping and other Sahara experiences.

8 Djebel Sarhro and Nekob. To get off the beaten path a visit to the Djebel Sarhro mountains in the Anti-Atlas range

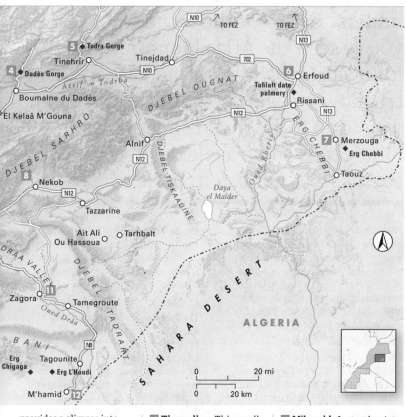

5 Todra Gorge
Tinehrir
Tinejdad
4 Dadès Gorge
Assif n Todrha
N10
702
TO FEZ
TO FEZ
N10
N13
Boumalne du Dadès
DJEBEL OUGNAT
6 Erfoud
Tafilalt date palmery
El Kelaâ M'Gouna
Rissani
N12
N13
DJEBEL SARHRO
Alnif
N12
7 Merzouga
Erg Chebbi
DJEBEL TISKAOUINE
ERG CHEBBI
Oued Rheris
8 Nekob
N12
Taouz
Tazzarine
Daya el Maider
Ait Ali Ou Hassoua
Tarhbalt
DRÂA VALLEY
DJEBEL TADRART
11 Zagora
Tamegroute
Oued Drâa
SAHARA DESERT
ALGERIA
B A N I
N9
Tagounite
Erg Chigaga
Erg L'Houdi
M'hamid
12

0   20 mi
0   20 km

provides a glimpse into rural Moroccan life. Nekob is the largest town in the area.

9 Agdz. One of the stops on the ancient caravan routes, the most prominent feature here is the Jebel Kissane along the Drâa River. A retreat to one of the hidden hotels in the palmeraie is a welcome oasis for travelers.

10 Tinzouline. This small city is one of Morocco's most important prehistoric sites. Near the city you can find cave drawings by early inhabitants.

11 Zagora. Few visitors spend more than mere hours in Zagora before embarking on a trip into the Sahara.

12 M'hamid. Just 45 km (28 miles) from Morocco's other towering sand dune Erg Chigaga, this desert outpost has less than 8,000 residents and is generally a last stop before entering the Sahara.

Morocco without the Sahara is like Switzerland without the Alps, and a desert sojourn is fundamental to an understanding of the country. After you've seen the Atlas Mountains, followed by palmeries and kasbahs, a trip down to the desert may seem a long way to go to reach nothing, and some Moroccans and travelers will warn you against it. Don't listen to them.

The void you encounter in the Sahara will remind you why prophets and sages sought the desert to purge and purify themselves. Unless you have oodles of time, though, you'll have to choose between the dunes of Erg Chebbi at Merzouga and Erg Chigaga beyond M'hamid, which are separated by 450 km (279 miles) of hard driving.

Of course, a vacation in the valleys isn't just about sublime Saharan sand. The asphalt might end and the desert begin at Merzouga and M'hamid, but in between are the oases flanked by the Todra and Dadès gorges—sister grand canyons separating the High Atlas from the Djebel Sarhro Massif. Both of these dramatic gorges appeal to hikers, and the Todra is a hot spot for climbers as well.

Permeating it all is a palpable sense of history. Once, the caravan routes from sub-Saharan Africa to Europe passed through Morocco's Great Oasis Valleys, with their cargoes of gold, salt, and slaves. From the Drâa Valley came the Saadian royal dynasty that ruled from the mid-12th to mid-17th century, and from

the Ziz Valley and the Tafilalt Oasis rose the Alaouite dynasty, which relieved the Saadians in 1669 and which still rules (in the person of King Mohammed VI) in 21st-century Morocco.

MAJOR REGIONS

The Dadès and Todra Gorges. These sister canyons, located within about two hours' drive from one another, northeast of Ouarzazate, have been carved into the rocks over millennia by the snowmelt waters of the High Atlas. Trekking and mountain biking are favorite activities for tourists.

Merzouga and the Dunes. If you opt to visit the south of Morocco, then it's almost criminal not to spend a night in the Sahara. The village of Merzouga is readily accessible by road, and the dunes of Erg Chebbi can be reached on foot or by camel.

The Drâa Valley. This fertile valley—extending along the shores of Morocco's longest river from Agdz, through Zagora as far as M'hamid—offers one of the most colorful and diverse landscapes in the kingdom. For those heading into the dunes at Erg Chigaga, Zagora is your last contact with modern services such as banks, pharmacies, and gas stations.

Planning

Getting Here and Around

The most convenient arrival and departure points for touring this vast region are the towns of Ouarzazate (if you're traveling from Marrakesh and the Atlantic coast) or Errachidia (if you're traveling from Fez, Meknès, or the Mediterranean coast). Given a choice, opt for Ouarzazate, as it is an interesting town in its own right. Ouarzazate is a key transport hub for forays into the Dadès and Todra gorges, the Drâa Valley, and the desert regions beyond Zagora. Errachidia is itself of little interest to travelers.

AIR

Royal Air Maroc serves Ouarzazate's Taourirt International Airport, offering direct flights daily from Casablanca and multiple ones per week from Paris. The airline also connects Casablanca with Errachidia and Zagora. *Petits taxis* (local taxis) provide ground transport from these airports; however, if you need to catch an early return flight, it's best to arrange transportation back to the airport through your hotel the night before.

BUS

Bus is the main mode of public transport south of Marrakesh. Compagnie du Transports au Maroc (locally known as CTM) and Supratours buses run to Ouarzazate, through the Drâa Valley, and down to Zagora and M'hamid.

CAR

The only practical way to tour the Great Oasis Valleys is by car. Being surrounded by gorgeous, largely unexplored hinterlands—like the Todra or Dadès gorges—without being able to explore safely and comfortably defeats the purpose

of coming down here. Driving the oasis roads requires full attention and certain safety precautions: make sure you have enough fuel, slow down when cresting hills, expect everything from camels to herds of sheep to appear in the road, expect oncoming traffic to come down the middle of the road, and be prepared to come to a full stop if forced to the right and faced with a pothole or other obstacle. Additionally, consider buying a local SIM and a data scratch card for your smart phone as Google Maps will be your friend. That said, there is a big road-building program in Morocco, so new roads may not be on your map. Also, many towns and villages have no signs, so you may have to stop and ask exactly where you are. Moroccans get around by asking directions; don't be afraid to do the same. If you haven't rented a car someplace else, you can rent one on arrival in Ouarzazate. Consider getting a 4x4: it's not essential but definitely makes life easier in some places.

Major agencies in Ouarzazate include Europcar and Hertz; Tafoukt is a local agency with a helpful owner, who offers the option of renting a car with a driver.

RENTAL CARS Tafoukt Cars. ✉ *88, rue Errachidia, Ouarzazate* ☎ *0667/35–87–99* ⊕ *tafoukt-cars.com.*

Planning Your Time

Doing the entire Great Oasis Valleys circuit is a serious undertaking, and you might miss the best parts for all the whirlwind traveling. So it's important to set priorities and carefully plan your itinerary. You could easily spend 14 days exploring. Allow at least five to seven if you want to include hiking time and a trip into the Sahara; then decide which dunes you want to discover—Erg Chebbi or Erg Chigaga.

From Ouarzazate, allot a minimum of two days to reach Erg Chebbi, traveling east through the Todra Gorge and Dadès Valley to Merzouga (this allows for an overnight stop in the Todra Gorge en route). On the return leg you can circle along the southern flanks of the Djebel Sarhro, passing via traditional villages like Nekob, into the Drâa Valley before arriving in Ouarzazate again.

Reaching Erg Chigaga from Ouarzazate requires a 4x4 vehicle and at least two days of driving (this again allows for an overnight stop). Head south through the Drâa Valley, admiring Agdz and Zagora en route to M'hamid; then continue off-road for about 50 km (31 miles) to the dunes. Returning to Ouarzazate, drive the route in reverse or loop back via Foum Zguid.

When to Go

You'll pay lower off-season rates and encounter fewer convoys of tourists if you travel the oasis routes in early December or mid-January through early March. High season begins in mid-March but doesn't fully kick in until April or Easter (whichever comes first). The Christmas and New Year period is also popular; if you want to visit a desert camp then, it's wise to book at least two months ahead. Summer is extremely hot in the desert and some hotels close during July and August, especially if this coincides with the holy month of Ramadan. If you plan to visit the Sahara in summer, traveling east via the Dadès and Todra gorges to Merzouga is slightly easier since the shaded depths of the canyons offer some respite from the sun. Likewise, a visit in the winter can mean freezing temperatures in the evening hours so be prepared with layers.

FESTIVALS
Each year villages here host a number of *moussems* (festivals) that are linked to the religious or agricultural calendar. These usually feature feasting, dancing, traditional music, and possibly a wonderful display of horsemanship called a fantasia. The downside is that they often don't have specific dates, so encountering one is largely a matter of luck. That said, there are a few festivals you can largely rely on: the **Rose Festival** of Kelaâ M'Gouna (Dadès Valley) in early May; the **International Nomads Festival** in M'hamid el Ghizlane (Drâa Valley) in mid-March; and the **Erfoud Date Festival** (Ziz Valley) in October. Check with the local tourist office or a nearby hotel for the exact dates about a month ahead of your visit.

Hotels

Hotels on the southern oasis routes generally range from mediocre to primitive, with several charming spots, simple but lovely gîtes (self-catering homes), and a few luxury establishments thrown in. This is not the place for major chains. Come with the idea that running water and a warm place to sleep are all you really need, and accept anything above that as icing on the cake. Bedding down outdoors on hotel terraces is common (and cheap) in summer, as are accommodations in *khaimas* (Amazigh nomad tents). The night sky is so stunning here that spending at least one night *à la belle étoile* (beneath the stars) seems almost mandatory. Any of the desert hotels and guesthouses in Merzouga or M'hamid will be able to arrange an unforgettable night under canvas, along with the necessary camel or 4x4 vehicle to get there. Basic bivouac camps, costing around 250 DH per person per night, typically have mattresses on the floor of large Amazigh tents and a shared bathroom block. Luxury tented camps—featuring private safari-style tents with Amazigh rugs, plush furnishings, and en suite chemical toilets—fulfill the Arabian Nights "glamping" fantasy; rates start at around 1,500 DH per person. Whatever you choose, bear in mind that many lodgings in remote areas still don't accept credit cards; double check the terms of payment and be sure to have sufficient cash on hand if required.

Hotel reviews have been shortened. For full information, visit Fodors.com.

WHAT IT COSTS in Dirhams			
$	$$	$$$	$$$$
RESTAURANTS			
under 70 DH	70 DH–100 DH	101 DH–150 DH	over 150 DH
HOTELS			
under 450 DH	450 DH–700 DH	701 DH–1,000 DH	over 1,000 DH

Restaurants

In the rural areas outside of Ouarzazate there are virtually no restaurants, just weathered street-side cafés with basic bathroom facilities (bring your own toilet paper!). These local spots can be great; just ask about the meal of the day, rather than look at the menu. Otherwise, lunch stops, complete with decent bathroom facilities, are best found in the hotels and auberges listed. For evening meals it is best to book your accommodation with half board. The fare you'll be served along the southern oases routes tends to be hearty and simple. *Harira* (a tomato and lentil soup) is more than welcome as night sets in and temperatures plunge. *Mechoui* (roast lamb) is a standard feast—if you can order it far enough in advance. Some of the best lamb and vegetable tagines in Morocco are simmered over tiny camp stoves in random corners and campsites down here. You may want to keep a bottle of wine in the car or in a day pack, as many restaurants (even in hotels) don't serve alcohol, but have no problem with customers bringing their own. Always ask first, though, as some places object.

Dining reviews have been shortened. For full information, visit Fodors.com.

Safety

You shouldn't have problems traveling this part of Morocco, but always exercise caution if going into remote areas.

Be prepared to be followed by local kids who may want to engage you in conversation. Rather than money (which just encourages begging), give them items such as pens or pencils. If they are selling homemade handicrafts, then, of course, give them a few dirhams for their efforts.

■ TIP→ **Where possible, make sure you engage a qualified guide through one of the official Bureaus de Guides or with a specialist company—this is especially important when trekking in the desert or mountains.**

Ouarzazate

204 km (127 miles) southeast of Marrakesh, 300 km (186 miles) southwest of Erfoud.

An isolated military outpost during the years of the French protectorate, Ouarzazate—which means "no noise" in the Tamazigh language—long lived up to its name. Today, however, the town is Morocco's Hollywood, and moviemakers can regularly be found setting up shop in this sprawling desert crossroads with wide, palm-fringed boulevards. Brad Pitt, Penélope Cruz, Angelina Jolie, Samuel L. Jackson, Cate Blanchett, and many more have graced Ouarzazate's suites and streets; and a film school here provides training in the cinema arts for Moroccan and international students. Yet despite the Tinseltown vibe and huge, publicly accessible film sets, Ouarzazate retains a laid-back atmosphere, making it a great place to sit at a sidewalk café, sip a café noir, and spot visiting celebs—or at least have a chat with the locals, who'll happily recount their experience working as an on-set extra (at its peak in the late 1990s, the movie industry provided casual work for almost half of the local population). Not surprisingly, though, the main attraction is still the cinematic surrounding terrain that made Ouarzazate a mainstay for filmmakers in the first place: namely, the red-glowing kasbah at Aït Ben Haddou; the snowcapped High Atlas; and the Sahara, with tremendous canyons, gorges, and lunarlike steppes in between.

GETTING HERE AND AROUND

The center of Ouarzazate is easily explored on foot. Avenue Mohammed V, the main street, runs from east to west with shops, cafés, banks, pharmacies, and tour agencies all along its length. Most hotels are near the Kasbah Taourirt; however, a cluster of boutique guesthouses dot the outlying palm groves, across the bridge in the direction of Zagora. If you're staying at the latter—or visiting the film studios—you'll need to rent a car or rely on cabs.

AIR

There are daily flights to Ouarzazate's Taourirt International Airport from Casablanca and twice-weekly ones from Paris. The airport is 3 km (2 miles) from the town center and can be reached by petits taxis.

BUS

Ouarzazate is well served by buses from Marrakesh (4 hours), Agadir (8½ hours), Casablanca (8½ hours), Taliouine (3½ hours), Taroudant (5 hours), Tinerhir (5 hours), Errachidia (6 hours), Erfoud (7 hours), Zagora (4½ hours), and M'hamid (7 hours). CTM buses run from the eastern end of Avenue Mohammed V. Supratours buses run from the western end of Avenue Mohammed V. Other public buses run from the *gare routière* (bus station) about 2 km (1 mile) from the town center, just off the N9 route

to Marrakesh. Shared *grands taxis* (long-distance taxis) will also bring you here from Marrakesh, Errachidia, Agadir, and Zagora; these can be hired for private day excursions, too.

CONTACTS CTM Ouarzazate. ✉ *Av. Mohammed V, next to main post office at east end, Ouarzazate* ☎ *0524/88–24–27* ⊕ *www.ctm.ma.* **Supratours.** ✉ *Av. Mohammed V, Ouarzazate* ☎ *0524/89–07–96* ⊕ *www.oncf.ma.*

GUIDES AND TOURS

Many travel agents and tour companies in Ouarzazate offer day excursions as well as longer outings that might include nights in the Dadès and Todra gorges or Saharan camping and camel trekking. You'll find them along Avenue Mohammed V, in Place el-Mouahidine, and frequently attached to hotels—just be sure to ask exactly what is being included in price (e.g., 4x4, driver, guide, meals, hotels, camel trip). Visitors who'd rather do a DIY driving tour will find car rental agencies along Avenue Mohammed V, too.

■ TIP→ **If you book a desert tour in advance, you'll avoid being hassled by touts when you reach Merzouga or M'hamid.**

Cherg Expeditions

GUIDED TOURS | Private day trips through the valleys and gorges or into the mountains to discover amethysts are led by Cherg Expeditions. You can sign on for multiday desert tours, too. Nearby destinations include the Fint Oasis and the kasbahs at Aït Ben Haddou. ✉ *2, pl. el Mouahidine, Ouarzazate* ☎ *0524/88–79–08, 0661/24–31–47* ⊕ *www.cherg.com.*

Zbar Travel

GUIDED TOURS | Well-priced tours and excursions throughout southern Morocco are offered by Zbar Travel, a respected English-speaking agency with a second office in M'hamid. ✉ *12, pl. Al Mouahidine, Ouarzazate* ☎ *0668/51–72–80* ⊕ *www.zbartravel.com.*

Atlas Studios pay tribute to the many movies filmed in Morocco, from classics like "Lawrence of Arabia" to modern blockbusters like "Gladiator."

TIMING AND PRECAUTIONS

For those traveling to the desert, this is an important town for stocking up on cash and purchasing essentials like maps, batteries, and other supplies. If you're heading south to M'hamid, it's also the last town where you will find a supermarket selling wine, beer, and liquor.

 Sights

Atlas Studios

FILM/TV STUDIO | FAMILY | If you're looking for things to do in Ouarzazate, visit Atlas Studios—Morocco's most famous studios—next to the Hotel Oscar. Guided tours start every 45 minutes, and the price is discounted if you're a guest of the hotel. It isn't Disney World, but you do get a sense of just how many productions have rolled through town—including Hollywood blockbusters like *The Mummy* and *Gladiator,* and classics like *Cleopatra* and *Lawrence of Arabia.*

■ TIP→ **Ask for Mohammed Brad Pitt as your tour guide.**

For another angle on the Ouarzazate film industry, check out the rather grand-looking kasbah off to the right just out of town on the way to Skoura. One enterprising local producer, frustrated by the increasingly expensive charges being levied on film crews wanting to film around real kasbahs, decided to build his own and undercut the competition. ⊠ *Tamassint, Rte. de Marrakesh, Km 5, next to Hotel Oscar, Ouarzazate* ☎ *0524/88–22–23* ⊕ *www.studiosatlas. com* ⊠ *80 DH.*

Fint Oasis

GARDEN | About 20 km (12 miles) outside of town, heading south via Tarmigte, the picturesque Fint Oasis is a popular destination for day-trippers. The track leading to it is rough but can be handled in a standard vehicle if you drive with extreme care. Head off-road toward the dark, rocky escarpment and the track eventually meets the river, where palm

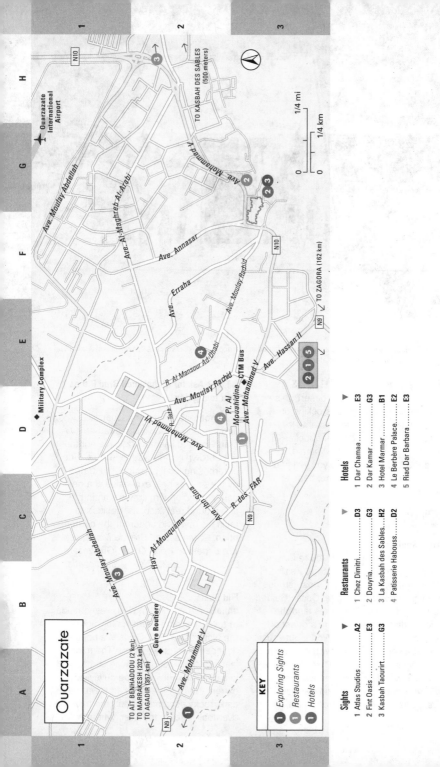

Ouarzazate

KEY

⓵	*Exploring Sights*
⓵	*Restaurants*
⓵	*Hotels*

Sights ▶

1 Atlas Studios	A2
2 Fint Oasis	E3
3 Kasbah Taourirt	G3

Restaurants ▶

1 Chez Dimitri	D3
2 Douyria	G3
3 La Kasbah des Sables	H2
4 Patisserie Habouss	D2

Hotels ▶

1 Dar Chamaa	E3
2 Dar Kamar	G3
3 Hotel Marmar	B1
4 Le Berbère Palace	E2
5 Riad Dar Barbara	E3

Ouarzazate International Airport

◆ Military Complex

Ave. Moulay Abdellah

Ave. Al-Maghreb Al-Arabi

Ave. Annasar

Ave. Errraha

Ave. Mohammed V

Ave. Moulay Rachid

R. Al Mansour Ad-Dhabi

Ave. Moulay Rachid

Pl. Al Mouahidine ◆ CTM Bus

Ave. Mohammed V

Ave. Hassan II

N10

N9 ↙ TO ZAGORA (162 km)

TO KASBAH DES SABLES (500 meters)

Ave. Mohammed V

Ave. Moulay Abdellah

Hay. Al Mouquama

Ave. Ibn Sina

R. des FAR

N9

◆ Gare Routière

Ave. Mohammed V

N9

TO AÏT BENHADDOU (2 km);
TO MARRAKESH (202 km);
TO AGADIR (357 km)

0   1/4 mi
0   1/4 km

trees spring into view. You can walk through Amazigh villages along the riverbed and stop for a simple lunch at one of the few local auberges.

■ **TIP→ Many agencies in Ouarzazate can arrange half- or full-day guided visits to the oasis.** ✉ *Tarmigte.*

Kasbah Taourirt

NOTABLE BUILDING | Once a Glaoui palace, the Kasbah Taourirt is the oldest and finest building in Ouarzazate. This rambling edifice was built of *pisé* (a sun-dried mixture of mud and clay) in the late 19th century by the so-called Lords of the Atlas.

■ **TIP→ It is worth hiring a guide at the entrance to take you around for about 100 DH.** ✉ *Av. Mohammed V, Ouarzazate* 🎫 *20 DH.*

🍴 Restaurants

★ Chez Dimitri

$$ | INTERNATIONAL | Founded in 1928 as the town's first store, gas station, post office, telephone booth, dance hall, and restaurant, Dimitri's is the fun and lively heart of Ouarzazate, and the food—whether Greek, Moroccan, or even Thai—is invariably excellent. The owners are friendly and helpful, and the signed photographs of legendary movie stars on the walls are sometimes enhanced by real stars at the next table. **Known for:** night-out ambience; great steaks; signed photos of stars. [$] *Average main: DH100* ✉ *22, av. Mohammed V, Ouarzazate* ☎ *0524/88–33–44, 0524/88–73–46.*

Douyria

$$ | MOROCCAN | Building up from the base of an old pisé (mud-built) home alongside the Kasbah Touarirt, this *douyria,* or "small house," marries tradition with contemporary flair. There are two Moroccan salon-style dining areas, with bold color schemes of lilac and lime, and the creative menu offers an interesting selection of starters and mains. **Known for:** terrace with views; camel tagine; original Moroccan dishes. [$] *Average main: DH100* ✉ *Av. Mohammed V, next to Kasbah Touarirt, Ouarzazate* ☎ *0524/88–52–88* 🌐 *www.restaurant-ouarzazate.net.*

La Kasbah des Sables

$$$ | INTERNATIONAL | Upon entering, you're greeted by a wall of lanterns reflected in a central pool, and meals are served in six intimate areas, each with a different decorative scheme (imagine an Amazigh salon or a patio with tables on terraces surrounded by water). The food is imaginative, mixing French-Moroccan influences in dishes such as confit of rabbit, with spices, honey, and peach sauce. **Known for:** Moroccan fusion food; beautiful decor; unique dining experience. [$] *Average main: DH120* ✉ *195 Hay Aït Ksif, Ouarzazate* ☎ *0524/88–54–28, 0673/52–07–20 mobile* ⏲ *Closed July.*

Patisserie Habouss

$ | CAFÉ | If you've got time to relax in Ouarzazate, there's no place better for people-watching than the terrace of Patisserie Habouss. Locals and visitors can be found indulging in its famous homemade gâteaux or honey-soaked Moroccan pastries accompanied by cinnamon coffee or freshly squeezed fruit juice. **Known for:** regional food at reasonable prices; excellent Moroccan pastries; nice views from the terrace. [$] *Average main: DH40* ✉ *Pl. Al Mouahidine, Ouarzazate* ☎ *0524/88–26–99.*

🛏 Hotels

★ Le Berbère Palace

$$$$ | HOTEL | Movie stars and magnates tend to stay at Ouarzazate's only five-star hotel when working on location. **Pros:** plenty of creature comforts; top-notch service; stunning gardens. **Cons:** pricey; can be difficult to get a room; breakfast not included and expensive. [$] *Rooms from: DH1700* ✉ *Av. Al Mansour Eddahbi, Ouarzazate* ☎ *0524/88–31–05*

⊕ www.hotel-berberepalace.com ⇆ 249 rooms ¶◎ No Meals.

Dar Chamaa

$$$ | B&B/INN | Poised on the outskirts of town, Dar Chamaa is a boutique riad that offers a contemporary take on traditional design. **Pros:** stylish accommodations with lots of mod-cons; good service; beautiful surroundings. **Cons:** not very helpful management; no access to anything else; out of the city. $ *Rooms from: DH880* ⊠ *Tajdar B-P 701, 8 km (5 miles) south of Ouarzazate center, Tajda* ✢ *From Ouarzazate center, follow road to Zagora across bridge and then turn left into palm groves (just after Hotel les Jardins de Ouarzazate)* ☎ *0524/85–49–54* ⊕ *www. darchamaa.com* ⇆ *18 rooms, 2 suites* ¶◎ *Free Breakfast.*

Dar Kamar

$$$ | B&B/INN | For anyone seduced by tales of Glaoui wealth and influence, this 17th-century pasha's courthouse has magisterial appeal. **Pros:** doting service; beautiful interiors; traditional hammam on-site. **Cons:** a little difficult to find; water pressure can be an issue; cheaper rooms (3rd category) get little daylight. $ *Rooms from: DH900* ⊠ *45, Kasbah Taourirt, Ouarzazate* ☎ *0524/88–87–33* ⊕ *www.darkamar.com* ⇆ *14 rooms* ¶◎ *Free Breakfast.*

Hotel Marmar

$ | HOTEL | What it lacks in amenities and decor this no-frills hotel more than makes up for in affordability and location near the bus stops in the center of town. **Pros:** some rooms have a/c and heat; central location; cheap, no-frills rooms. **Cons:** can be noisy; not all staff speak English; cash only. $ *Rooms from: DH270* ⊠ *19, av. Moulay Abdellah, Ouarzazate* ☎ *0524/88–88–87* ⊕ *www.hotel-marmar. com* ⊟ *No credit cards* ⇆ *200 rooms* ¶◎ *Free Breakfast.*

Riad Dar Barbara

$$ | B&B/INN | Run by an English-Moroccan couple, this guesthouse in a residential neighborhood on the outskirts of Ouarzazate has huge rooms with traditional decor, air-conditioning and heating, and en suite bathrooms that could use some updating. **Pros:** air-conditioning and heating; friendly English-speaking staff; spacious rooms. **Cons:** no pool; cash only; outside of town. $ *Rooms from: DH500* ⊠ *Tarmigt, 8 km (5 miles) south of Ouarzazate, Tajda* ☎ *0524/85–49–30* ⊕ *www. riaddarbarbara.com* ⊟ *No credit cards* ⇆ *8 rooms* ¶◎ *Free Breakfast.*

Shopping

Labyrinthe du Sud

CRAFTS | You'll discover a treasure trove of antiques, carpets, Touareg and Amazigh jewelry, and trinkets at Labyrinthe du Sud. Credit cards are accepted. ⊠ *Rte. de la Kasbah des Cigognes, Tajda* ☎ *0524/85–42–43.*

Activities

HAMMAMS AND SPAS

The following hammams and spas are open to all (even nonguests, if in a hotel).

Le Berbère Palace

SPAS | A common destination for movie stars filming in the nearby studios, this kasbah-style hotel has a deluxe hammam "Oasis," sauna, and Jacuzzi that are open to nonguests. Advance booking required. ⊠ *Av. El Mansour Addahbi, Ouarzazate* ☎ *0524/88–31–05* ⊕ *www.hotel-berbere-palace.com* ⊠ *Hammam from 150 DH.*

La Caravan des Épices

SPAS | This herbs and spice merchant sells every kind of medicinal root, leaf, mineral, spice, and ointment that you could imagine. On-site hammam services are also available by advance reservation. ⊠ *Rue El Mansour Eddahbi, Ouarzazate* ☎ *0661/34–81–14* ⊕ *www.caravane-epic-es.com* ⊠ *Hammam with exfoliation 250 DH, massage with essential oils 200 DH.*

The town of Aït Ben Haddou has been around since the 11th century, but has known recent fame as the backdrop of movies and TV shows, including "Game of Thrones."

Aït Ben Haddou

30 km (19 miles) northwest of Ouarzazate.

The *ksar* (fortified village) at Aït Ben Haddou is something of a celebrity itself. This group of earth-built kasbahs and homes hidden behind defensive high walls has come to fame (and fortune) as a backdrop for many films, including David Lean's *Lawrence of Arabia*, Ridley Scott's *Gladiator*, and as Astapor, the slave city in *Game of Thrones*. Of course, it hasn't always been a film set. It got going in the 11th century as a stop-off on the old caravan routes, with salt heading one way and ivory and gold heading back the other. Strewn across the hillside and surrounded by flowering almond trees in early spring, the red-pisé towers of the village fortress resemble a sprawling, dark-red sandcastle. Crenelated and topped with an ancient granary store, it's one of the most sumptuous sights in

the Atlas. The ksar is a UNESCO World Heritage site.

GETTING HERE AND AROUND

The village is easily reached by road. There are very few buses to Aït Ben Haddou, so if you don't have a car the best and cheapest option is to charter a grand taxi in Ouarzazate. On arrival, you'll find two main entrances to the kasbah. The first, by the hotel-restaurant La Kasbah, has ample safe parking and you can cross the riverbed via stepping-stones. Farther down the road is the second entry point opposite the Riad Maktoub. Here you can leave your car at the side of the road and then take a short stroll to a footbridge across the river to the kasbah.

🍽 Restaurants

There are a few café-restaurants on the roadside close to the parking areas of Aït Ben Haddou. However, you should avoid those with all the tour buses parked outside, as quality is invariably poor. Lodgings like Ksar Ighnda, and others listed below, offer reliable alternatives—they're open to the general public for lunch or dinner. Choose a smaller establishment, where you will find locals eating their lunch or sipping a coffee.

 ## Hotels

Kasbah Ellouze
$$$ | B&B/INN | Next to the old kasbah of Tamdaght, the rustic Kasbah Ellouze (Kasbah of Almonds) is brimming with character, though rooms are a bit dated overall. **Pros:** great food; kasbah setting; helpful staff. **Cons:** hot water not always reliable; cash only; rooms are dark and cold in winter. $ *Rooms from: DH900* ⊠ *Tamdakhte, 5 km (3 miles) north of Aït Ben Haddou on P1506, Aït Ben Haddou* ☎ *0524/89–04–59* ⊕ *www.kasbahellouze. com* ▭ *No credit cards* ☉ *Closed June and July* ⬉ *10 rooms* ⦿ *Free Breakfast.*

Ksar Ighnda
$$$$ | HOTEL | The most upmarket accommodation in the village, Ksar Ighnda stands on the grounds of an old mud-built ksar—though only the original olive trees remain in the garden near the pool. **Pros:** can accommodate larger groups; spacious gardens and common areas; one of the nicest hotels in the area. **Cons:** restaurant serves average-quality meals and meager breakfasts; not many options nearby; standard rooms are small. $ *Rooms from: DH1200* ⊠ *Douar Asfalou, 2 km (1 mile) east of Aït Ben Haddou, Aït Ben Haddou* ☎ *0524/88–76–44* ⊕ *www.ksar.ighnda.net* ⬉ *50 rooms* ⦿ *Free Breakfast.*

Riad Caravane
$$$ | B&B/INN | Influenced by the fashionable interiors of Marrakesh's hip riads, Riad Caravane has stylish rooms, a roof terrace looking out to the kasbah, and a small dipping pool. **Pros:** village atmosphere; chic design; easy walking access to Aït ben Haddou. **Cons:** hard to find; small dining area; some rooms are small.

$ *Rooms from: DH850* ⊠ *Ksar d'Aït Ben Haddou, Aït Ben Haddou* ☎ *0524/89–09–16* ⊕ *www.riad-caravane.com* ⬉ *8 rooms* ⦿ *Free Breakfast.*

Skoura

50 km (31 miles) southwest of El Kelaâ M'Gouna, 42 km (26 miles) northeast of Ouarzazate.

Surprisingly lush and abrupt as it springs from the tawny landscape, Skoura deserves a lingering look for its kasbahs and its rich concentration of date palm, olive, fig, and almond trees. Pathways tunnel through the vegetation from one kasbah to another within this fertile island—a true oasis, perhaps the most intensely verdant in Morocco. .

■TIP→ **Skoura is such a magical place, that if you're on a grand tour of the Great Oasis Valleys, think about basing yourself here (for at least two days) rather than Ouarzazate.**

With so many grand deep-orange-hue kasbahs in Skoura, a tour of the Palmery is compulsory. The main kasbah route through Skoura is approached from a point just over 2 km (1 mile) past the town center toward Ouarzazate. The 18th-century **Kasbah Aït Ben Moro** is the first fortress on the right (now restored and converted to a hotel); you can leave your car at the hotel, which will happily arrange for a local guide to walk you through the Palmery, past the Sidi Aïssa *marabout* (shrine to a learned holy man). Alternatively, continue along the main road for a few hundred meters till you find the Museum of Skoura. By the Amerhidil River is the tremendous **Kasbah Amerhidil,** the largest kasbah in Skoura and one of the largest in Morocco. The partially renovated edifice is open to the public.

Down the (usually bone-dry) river is another kasbah, **Dar Aït Sidi el-Mati,** while

The town of Skoura is known for its several vast stone fortresses; Kasbah Amerhidil is the largest.

back near the Ouarzazate road is the **Kasbah el-Kabbaba,** the last of the four fortresses on this loop. North of Skoura, on Route 6829 through Aït-Souss, are two other kasbahs: **Dar Lahsoune,** a former Glaoui residence, and, a few minutes farther north, the **Kasbah Aït Ben Abou,** the second largest in Skoura after the Amerhidil.

Sights

Museum of Memory

OTHER MUSEUM | Constructed and entirely funded by schoolteacher Abdelmoula el Moudahab, this small but fascinating private museum houses a collection of traditional Amazigh costumes, artifacts, manuscripts, and antiques belonging to several generations of local families. Abdelmoula, who speaks good English, can explain tribal differences and describe the various types of kasbahs and holy shrines found in the Skoura region. ☎ *0524/85–23–68* 🎫 *20 DH.*

Hotels

Chez Talout

$$$ | **B&B/INN** | A rustic farmhouse about 7 km (4½ miles) outside Skoura, Chez Talout is worth the trek for its warm welcome, wonderful food, and roof-terrace views across the palmery to Skoura's kasbahs. **Pros:** lush rural setting; excellent cuisine; lovely pool. **Cons:** cash only, and no alcohol available; Wi-Fi connectivity can be iffy in rooms; well off the beaten track. [$] *Rooms from: DH800* ✉ *Ouled Aarbiya, Talout, 7 km (4½ miles) southwest of Skoura, Skoura* ✢ *7 km (4½ miles) before Skoura if coming from Ouarzazate, turn left off main road just after Idelssane* ☎ *0662/49–82–83* 🌐 *www.cheztalout.com/en* 💳 *No credit cards* 🛏 *15 rooms* 🍴 *Free Breakfast.*

★ **Dar Ahlam**

$$$$ | **HOTEL** | A restored 19th-century kasbah, Dar Ahlam, "the House of Dreams," is one of Morocco's most exclusive and sumptuous hideaways and with its epic desert setting, impeccable service, and intimate more-house-than-hotel feel, you may never want to wake up. **Pros:** magical meals at your whim and location changes nightly; epitome of luxury; fairy-tale desert setting. **Cons:** reservations limited and must be made far in advance; remote location; pricey. [$] *Rooms from: DH13530* ✉ *Kasbah Madihi, Douar Oulad Cheik Ali, Koucheït, Skoura* ☎ *0524/85–22–39* 🌐 *www.darahlam.com* 🕒 *Closed Aug.* 🛏 *13 rooms, 1 villa* 🍴 *All-Inclusive.*

Les Jardins de Skoura
$$$ | **B&B/INN** | **FAMILY** | Styling itself as a *"maison de repos,"* this restored farmhouse casts such a spell over guests that many of them find it difficult to leave, staying on for days in its warm, lazy embrace. **Pros:** hospitable host; idyllic surroundings; excellent facilities. **Cons:** the road to get here is not navigable with anything larger than a taxi; pool is unheated; hard to cross the river if there is heavy rain. [$] *Rooms from: DH880* ✉ *Palmeraie de Skoura, Skoura* ✣ *2 km (1 mile) before Skoura (from direction of Ouarzazate), and after passing Kasbah Aït Ben Moro follow yellow arrow signs for left turn, additional 4 km (2½ miles) of track to get to house* ☎ *0524/85–23–24* 🌐 *www.lesjardinsdeskoura.com* 💳 *No credit cards* 🕒 *Closed July* 🛏 *5 rooms* 🍴 *Free Breakfast.*

★ **L'Ma Lodge**
$$$ | **HOTEL** | **FAMILY** | Set in the heart of the Palmery amid lush gardens (the owners planted 2,500 different plants), L'Ma Lodge is an exquisite escape from modern life. **Pros:** a haven of tranquillity; wonderful rooms; delicious food. **Cons:** water pressure can be hit or miss; can feel a bit isolated; there are only seven rooms so book early. [$] *Rooms from: DH1000* ✉ *Douar Oued Ali Khamsa, Skoura* ✣ *At end of village, turn left and then right opposite gendarmerie. After 3 km (2 miles), turn right at sign and follow white arrows* ☎ *0524/85–22–81, 0666/64–79–08 mobile* 🌐 *www.lmalodge.com* 🛏 *7 rooms* 🍴 *Free Breakfast.*

Activities

BICYCLE TOURS

Alfalfa Bicycle Tours
BIKING | Bicycling round the Palmery with a local guide is a delightful experience, allowing the ability to cover quite a bit of ground and to interact with locals who will be delighted to see you on a bike. Toufiq, the owner of Alfalfa, is knowledgeable and friendly. Bike tours are 80 DH for a half day or 120 DH if your legs feel up to a full day. ✉ *N10, Skoura* ✣ *Center of Skoura near Banque Populaire* ☎ *0611/72–30–05* ✉ *tmousaoui0@gmail.com.*

HORSEBACK RIDING

Skoura Equestrian Centre
HORSEBACK RIDING | This well-run spot just outside of town offers professional English-speaking riding instruction, as well as horseback excursions around the kasbahs of Skoura oasis; expect to pay 300 DH for two hours or 500 DH for a full day with picnic lunch. The center is managed by Sport-Travel Maroc in Marrakesh. You can also ask your hotel to book for you. Book in advance. ✉ *El Khamsa, 2 km (1 mile) north of Skoura on road to Toundout, Skoura* ☎ *0524/43–99–69* 🌐 *www.sporttravel-maroc.com.*

The Dadès Gorge

Boumalne du Dadès is 53 km (33 miles) southwest of Tinerhir, 116 km (72 miles) northeast of Ouarzazate.

Snaking its way up from Boumalne du Dadès, the narrow roadway that is gradually swallowed up by the gorge is captivating. Along the route you'll see sprawling, emerald-green valleys and classic kasbahs set against a backdrop of surreal wind-sculpted, geological formations. The immensity of the gorge itself is a humbling reminder of our own vulnerability to the forces of nature and time. The switchback road helter-skelters to the end of the tarmac at Msemrir, but (in good weather) you can loop across to Todra Gorge in a 4x4 vehicle or continue northward on a rocky piste to Imilchil. The scenery of the Dadès Gorge is astounding, and if you can break away on foot to explore further, you will encounter Amazigh nomad families living in caves and rocky crags carved into the mountainside.

GETTING HERE AND AROUND

The easiest access point for the Dadès Gorge is the town of Boumalne du Dadès, which is linked to Ouarzazate in the west and Errachidia in the east by the N10. CTM buses frequent this route, providing transportation to and from Boumalne du Dadès. Although there is no longer a CTM bus office in Boumalne du Dadès, tickets can be purchased from shops along the main street displaying the yellow sign reading "Espace Service." Tickets can also be purchased online (⊕ www.ctm.ma), though the system is sometimes not reliable.

The road through the gorge itself is mostly paved. Traveling beyond Msemrir requires a four-wheel-drive vehicle, and even then only if conditions are right. The piste routes can be treacherous, especially during the rainy season between December and February. If you do not have your own transport, grand taxis from Boumalne du Dadès will take you on the scenic drive.

TIMING AND PRECAUTIONS

The Dadès Gorge is beautiful all year. In summer the steep canyon walls and rushing rivers are refreshing after the heat of the desert. In winter, however, the region gets considerable rainfall that makes the pistes impassable. Always ensure you have a full tank of gas, a spare tire, and plenty of water if embarking on cross-country routes.

VISITOR INFORMATION

A small office at the bottom of the main street is manned by official mountain guides who can arrange and lead treks for you according to your abilities. If nobody is in the office, then ring the published telephone number (French-speaking only).

CONTACTS Bureau des Guides a Boumalne du Dadès. ⊠ *Av. Mohammed V, just after bridge on left (if coming from Dadès Gorge), next to WafaBank, Boumalne de Dadès* ☎ *0667/59–32–92.*

Sights

The town of Boumalne du Dadès marks the southern entrance to the Dadès Gorge, which is even more beautiful—longer, wider, and more varied—than its sister, the Todra Gorge. The 63 km (39 miles) of the Dadès Gorge, from Boumalne through Aït Ali and on to Msemrir, are paved and approachable in any kind of vehicle. Beyond that are some great rocky mountain roads for four-wheel-drive vehicles with good clearance. Boumalne itself is only of moderate interest, though the central market square is a good vantage point for a perusal of local life. The shops Artisanale de Boumalne and Maison Aït Atta merit a browse for their local products at local prices, particularly rosewood carvings and rosewater.

The lower Dadès Gorge and the Dadès River, which flows through it, are lined with thick vegetation. While the Todra has its lush date palmery, the Dadès has figs, almonds, Atlas pistachio, and carob trees. A series of kasbahs and *ksour* (plural of ksar, or fortified house) give way to Amazigh villages such as Aït Youl, Aït Arbi, Aït Ali, Aït Oudinar, and Aït Toukhsine—*aït* meaning "of the family" in the Tamazight Amazigh language.

Two kilometers (1 mile) up the road from Boumalne is the Glaoui Kasbah, once part of the empire of the infamous pasha of Marrakesh, T'hami el-Glaoui. The ksour

The diverse landscape and colorful rock formations make the Dadès Gorge one of Morocco's best hiking destinations.

at Aït Arbi are tucked neatly into the surrounding volcanic rock 3 km (2 miles) farther on from Glaoui Kasbah.

Ten kilometers (6 miles) from Aït Arbi is the village of Aït Sidi Boubker in the Tamlalt Valley, mostly known for the bizarre red rock formations called "Les Doigts de Singes" (or "Monkey's Fingers") after their curiously organic shapes carved by water and wind. A little farther beyond them are more sculpted rocks known as the "Valley of Human Bodies," where local legend says that lost travelers died of hunger and were transformed into rocks. After Aït Oudinar, where most of the lodging options are clustered, the road crosses a bridge and gets substantially more exciting and empty, and the valley narrows dramatically, opening up around the corner into some of the most stunning views in the Dadès. Six kilometers (4 miles) north of the bridge, the Hôtel la Kasbah de la Vallée has basic accommodations, a restaurant, and a licensed bar. A few kilometers from here, à staggering series of hairpin bends

descend into the belly of the camera-ready canyon.

Aït Hammou, the next village, is 5 km (3 miles) past the Kasbah de la Vallée. It makes a good base camp for walking north to vantage points over the Dadès River or, to the east, to a well-known cave with stalactites (ask the Hôtel la Kasbah de la Vallée for directions). At the top of the gorges is Msemrir, a village of red-clay pisé ksour that has a café with guest rooms. To go farther from Msemrir, you'll need four-wheel drive to follow the road (R704) that leads north over the High Atlas through Tilmi, the Tizi-n-Ouano, and Agoudal to Imilchil and eventually up to Route P24 (N8), the Marrakesh–Fez road. The road east from Msemrir climbs the difficult Route 3444, always bearing right, to another gorge-top town, Tamtattouchte. It makes for a great off-road drive.

🍴 Restaurants

Like other rural locales, the Dadès Gorge has few dining options, but lunch is served at most of the small auberges and hotels: as long as you turn up between midday and 3 pm, when the tagines are bubbling, you should be able to find a table. Chez Pierre and Dar Jnan Tiouira are particularly noted for their excellent food.

🛏 Hotels

Auberge Chez Pierre

$$ | **B&B/INN** | Clinging to the rocky face of the Dadès Gorge, this guesthouse is a wonderful place to both eat and stay in the area. **Pros:** fantastic food; beautiful situation; great service and decor. **Cons:** popular location with a few rooms; book ahead; no a/c; property and rooms accessed via steep stairways. [$] *Rooms from: DH700* ✉ *Douar Aït Arbi, 27 km (17 miles) north of Boumalne du Dadès, Rte. de Dadès Gorge, Boumalne de Dades* ☎ *0524/83–02–67* 🌐 *www.chezpierre.org* 🛏 *9 rooms* 🍴 *Free Breakfast.*

Auberge des Peupliers

$ | **B&B/INN** | An ideal base for anyone craving simple Amazigh hospitality, Auberge des Peupliers has cozy accommodations with distinctive clay sinks, electric heating, and en suite showers; newer rooms include traditional features (like carved motifs) and face out across the gorge, but there's not much else nearby. **Pros:** basic rooms at a value price; friendly, helpful service; offers good, local food. **Cons:** cash only; can be cold especially in winter; older rooms look shabby. [$] *Rooms from: DH250* ✉ *Aït Ouffi, 27 km (17 miles) north of Boumalne Dadès, Rte. de Dadès Gorge, Boumalne de Dades* ☎ *0524/83–17–48* 💳 *No credit cards* 🛏 *12 rooms* 🍴 *Free Breakfast.*

Chez Ichou

$$ | **B&B/INN** | A charming guesthouse in the Dadès Valley, Chez Ichou features modern, minimalist style with beautiful views of the gorge. **Pros:** clean, minimalist style; comfortable beds; great water pressure and bathroom amenities. **Cons:** can book up in high seasons; on the main road, can have noise; meals a bit more expensive than average. [$] *Rooms from: DH600* ✉ *23 Km de Boumalne Dadès, Aït Oudinar, Boumalne de Dades* ✣ *Follow N10 to Gorges du Dadès/R704 in Boumalne Dadès. At roundabout, exit onto Gorges du Dadès/R704. Drive 22.9 km, Chez Ichou is on your right* ☎ *0673/42–94–63* 🌐 *www.chezichou.com/* 🛏 *10 rooms* 🍴 *Free Breakfast.*

Dar Jnan Tiouira

$$$$ | **B&B/INN** | This kasbah and family-run guesthouse marries the traditional craftsmanship of the surrounding Amazigh tribes with the modern amenities discerning visitors expect. **Pros:** luxurious rooms; fabulous location; great food. **Cons:** staff not always on hand; some room layouts are a little awkward; steep ramps and stairs throughout. [$] *Rooms from: DH1200* ✉ *El Mastapha Hamdaoui, BP 28, Tinghir, Tamellalt, Boumalne de Dades* ✣ *22 km (13½ miles) north from Boumalne, Rte. de Dadès Gorge* ☎ *0667/35–18–60* 🌐 *darjnantiouira.com/en/* 💳 *No credit cards* 🛏 *11 rooms* 🍴 *Free Breakfast.*

★ **Ecobio Riad**

$ | **HOTEL** | Clinging to the cliff face, the views from this new eco-friendly riad are fabulously dizzying while rooms are are decorated in the pale colors of the bleached-out desert, using all natural, local materials, with homespun bedspreads and pristine en suites. **Pros:** environmentally aware; lovely views; pretty rooms. **Cons:** basic amenities; limited food options; on the road but isolated. [$] *Rooms from: DH300* ✉ *Douar Aït ibrirne, Boumalne de Dades* ☎ *0661/24–83–37* 🌐 *www.ecobioriad.com* 🛏 *6 rooms* 🍴 *Free Breakfast.*

The Sahara Desert

Life's truly picture-perfect moments come few and far between: a sea of sand dunes, shimmering gray, yellow, orange, and red throughout the day, is one of them. The Sahara is the most beautiful, enigmatic, and awe-inspiring natural wonder that you can experience in Morocco—but if at all possible, don't rush through the experience. Spend some time getting to know the people and their unique outlook on life as well.

Should you have time for it, an expedition into the deeper desert provides a glimpse into a forgotten world. You may enter the desert by camel or jeep, but you will be able to sleep in a traditional bedouin tent or something even more comfortable and luxurious. But it is not all about ancient worlds—you may even have the opportunity to sand board down the dunes.

Points of Entry

The two main desert destinations in Morocco are very different—Merzouga lies nine hours' drive due east of Ouarzazate via the Dadès and Ziz valleys; M'hamid is five hours' drive south of Ouarzazate via the Drâa Valley.

From Fez, Merzouga is the most convenient overnight desert stop. The onward route then takes you through the Todra and Dadès gorges before reaching Ouarzazate. The dunes near Merzouga, called Erg Chebbi, have sand piled high like a fancy hairdo, and you can dip your toe in as you like. The desert is easily accessible by road right to the edge of the golden sands. Here you can spend a night very happily in an oasis bivouac camp, sleeping under the stars, and another

back in Merzouga at an auberge or luxury hotel with majestic dune views.

M'hamid is the best entry point for the more adventurous and is the easiest place to reach if you are coming from Marrakesh. The paved road ends in the village, and beyond there's nothing but desert scrub, stony paths, and soft dunes. Erg Chigaga is the star attraction, some 50 km (31 miles) distant from the village. The sands go on for miles, and excursions by 4x4, camel, or a combination of both can be for as long or short as you like. Typically, a one-night trip by camel from M'hamid gets you to nearby Erg L'Houdi (The Dunes of the Jews); four days round-trip gets you to Erg Ezahaar (The Screaming Dunes), and five days gets you to the highest dunes in the region, Erg Chigaga.

Erg Chigaga can be reached by desert piste (unsealed dirt road) in a 4x4 in around three hours, so an overnight getaway is possible. Alternatively, a two-day camel trek from M'hamid will get you to Erg Chigaga, and you can book a 4x4 vehicle to bring you back the next day. Bivouacs in Erg Chigaga range from simple, nomad-style shared camps to superdeluxe private encampments.

What Should You Know?

Temperatures can reach 55°C (131°F) in June, July, and August. If you must go in summer, take sunset camel rides into the dunes, spend the night, and head back at dawn. The best (and busiest) time is between March and early May. October to February is nice, too, although it can be very cold at night from December through February.

The desert is unforgiving, and the inexperienced can easily become the expired. You must never attempt to visit the desert without an experienced guide. If you arrive in Merzouga or M'hamid without having prebooked a guided tour, make sure your guide is legitimate; the best thing is to book through one of the recommended local companies. The best way to avoid hassles is to make all arrangements in advance and arrange pick-up if you don't have your own transportation, or a roadside meeting if you do.

The impressive Erg Chebbi, near Merzouga, are more amenable to a quick in/out overnight, but they are a full 10-hour drive from Fez or two full days hard driving from Marrakesh. Erg Chebbi is very impressive, and solitary spots can be found on the fringes, with a good range of basic-to-deluxe accommodations. Southwest of M'hamid, however, you have eye-popping dunes that stretch for miles, including the Erg Chigaga. Ideally, allow at least two days (by camel) to get there from M'hamid, but a round-trip from Marrakesh is possible in three days with a 4x4.

Most tour operators, hotels, and auberges have their own permanent tented camps (bivouacs) hidden among the oases and dunes. Tents are usually good for between two and four people, but you can generally have a tent to yourself if traveling alone. If you want to keep the stars within eyeshot all night, you can also just sleep on a blanket on the sand. Most fixed camps have a restaurant tent (some serving alcohol), separate toilets, and washing facilities of some kind. In Merzouga and M'hamid, at the edge of the desert, there are also traditional auberges and plusher hotels of varying grades of luxury (some even have swimming pools).

What To Do in the Desert

You might think there's not much to do in the desert, but when there are no shops, no electricity, and no running water, just getting by becomes wonderfully time-consuming. You can cook bread in the sand; count stars and identify constellations until the sky caves in; climb to the crest of the dunes at sunset; and learn local drum beats by the campfire. Camel trips are de rigueur and in Erg Chebbi, near Merzouga, they rarely last more than three hours, with dinner generally waiting for you at your chosen bivouac camp. Beyond M'hamid, farther south, there's a much greater range of desert terrain to explore. Away from the fixed camps, the experience of camping *sauvage*, with just a nomad guide and camel for company, gives a fantastic insight into the real desert way of life. For thrill seekers there are quad bikes and buggies for desert safaris, or you can try your skills at boarding down the high dunes. Alternatively, just take it easy and watch the changing moods, colors, and textures of the dunes all day long.

Hotel Xaluca Dadès
$$$ | **HOTEL** | **FAMILY** | Part of the Group Xaluca chain, this vast hotel offers high-quality accommodation in a region that generally lacks luxury. **Pros:** plenty of family amenities; spacious, airy lounges; good for groups traveling together. **Cons:** popular with tour groups; ugly architecture; located at edge of Boumalne, far from the gorge. [$] *Rooms from: DH1000* ✉ *Rte. de Errachidia, Boumalne de Dades* ☎ *0524/83–00–60* 🌐 *www.xaluca.com* 🛏 *106 rooms* 🍴 *Free Breakfast.*

Activities

Mohamed Amgom
An experienced local guide, Mohamed Amgom offers treks in the Dadès Valley for 400 DH per day. He can also organize four-wheel-drive vehicles for excursions throughout the Dadès and Todra gorges. ☎ *0666/59–41–42.*

The Todra Gorge

194 km (121 miles) northwest of Rissani, 184 km (114 miles) northeast of Ouarzazate.

The towering limestone stacks of the Todra Gorge are breathtakingly beautiful, as is the winding route upward from Tinerhir, which leads you there through delightful groves of date palm, pomegranate, fig, and olive trees. The namesake river that carved the gorge also feeds vegetation, forming the Todra Oasis—Morocco's highest—cradled in the southern slopes of the High Atlas. This whole mountainous area is the heartland of the Aït Atta tribe of Imazighen, who have inhabited the region for centuries. Today it's also a top spot for trekking and rock climbing. Local hotels can organize guided hikes lasting several hours or several days. Mountaineers, ascending from the oasis to the steep cliffs of the gorge above, will also find plenty to keep them occupied, including several technical climbs for the experienced and some newer sections marked out for novices. Although hotels here may be able to offer you a guide and climbing equipment, the quality and condition of the latter cannot be vouched for, so bring your own or sign on for an organized tour run by a reputable outfitter.

GETTING HERE AND AROUND

The town of Tinerhir (also spelled "Tinghir"), on the main N10 route from Ouarzazate and Errachidia, is the most convenient access point for visiting the Todra Gorge. Long-distance buses travel here from Agadir, Casablanca, Marrakesh, Fez, Meknès, and Rabat. Buses also arrive from Ouarzazate (five hours), Errachidia (three hours), and Erfoud (four hours); most stop on Avenue Mohammed V, on the northern side of the main square.

To reach the gorge, take route R703 (3445) north toward Tamtattouchte, and follow the riverbed upward for about 15 km (9 miles). If you don't have your own vehicle, you can catch a grand taxi to take you up through the Todra palmery as far as the Todra Gorge; the 30-minute drive should cost about 30 DH per person. There are also minibuses that transport locals to the villages above the Todra Gorge; you can ask to be dropped off on the way through.

CONTACTS CTM Tinerhir. ✉ *Av. Hassan II, next to main square, Tinerhir* ☎ *0524/83–43–79* 🌐 *www.ctm.ma.*

TIMING

The steep sides of the gorge can often mean that the route through the gorge itself is in shade, but the effect of angled sunlight shifting across the rock face during the day creates a sublime canvas of red and orange. Mid- to late afternoon is the best time to visit.

Sights

The 15-km (9-mile) drive up from Tinerhir to the beginning of the Todra Gorge will take you through lush but slender palmeries, sometimes no wider than 100 feet from cliff to cliff. An inn and a café await near the spring, but you're better off not stopping, as the site itself isn't remarkable, and the concentration of hustlers and overhelpful children is dense.

The 66-foot-wide entrance to the Todra Gorge, with its roaring clear stream and its 1,000-foot-high rock walls stretching 325 feet back on either side, is the most stunning feature of the whole canyon, though the upper reaches aren't far behind. The farther off the beaten path you get, the more rewarding the scenery; a walk or drive up through the gorge on paved roads to Tamtattouchte is particularly recommended. There are some marked trails leading from Le Festival hotel.

From the thin palmery along the bottom, the walls of the Todra Gorge remain close and high for some 18 km (11 miles). Eagles nest in the Todra, along with choughs (red-beaked rooks), rock doves, and blue rock thrushes.

La Source des Poissons Sacrés (Springs of the Sacred Fish), about halfway to the beginning of the gorge, is so named for the miracle performed by a sage, said to have struck a rock once to produce a gushing spring, and twice to produce fish. Today the sacred source is frequented by young Amazigh women who are experiencing difficulties in conceiving children. (It is rumored that bathing in the water has about an 80% success rate.) You can also stop here to camp and have a refreshing drink.

Museum of the Oasis
MUSEUM VILLAGE | **FAMILY** | This small but ambitious community-oriented spot is well worth a stop if you're driving east from Tinerhir toward Merzouga. Housed in the 19th-century ksar of El Khorbat, it contains old maps, photos, antiques, and exhibits that document the traditional lifestyle of the southern oasis, with proceeds going to development and educational projects in the village. You can also buy locally made items at the craft workshop, and then enjoy a meal or spend a night in the atmospheric El Khorbat guesthouse ($$)—both are part of the same tourism initiative. ✉ *Aït Assem, Tinejdad* ✥ *48 km (31 miles) east of Tinerhir* ☎ *0535/88–03–55* 🌐 *www.elkhorbat.com* 🎟 *20 DH.*

Hotels

Auberge Baddou
$$ | **B&B/INN** | This small hotel is a worthy choice for budget accommodations at the far northern end of the Todra Gorge. **Pros:** friendly service; spotless rooms; nice pool area. **Cons:** central heating is an extra 150 DH per night in winter; cheaper rooms have shared bathrooms; rather isolated in unattractive village. [$] *Rooms from: DH450* ✉ *Aït Hani, Tamtetoucht* ✥ *29 km (18 miles) north of Tinerhir* ☎ *0672/52–13–89* 🌐 *auberge-baddou-todra.com* 💳 *No credit cards* 🛏 *18 rooms* 🍴 *Free Breakfast.*

Dar Ayour
$$ | **B&B/INN** | This pretty guesthouse sits at the edge of the river amid fig trees, olives, and date palms with the walls of the Todra Gorge towering above. **Pros:** small outdoor swimming pool; peaceful setting; good access to the gorge. **Cons:** bathrooms are basic; decor a bit dated; some rooms very small. [$] *Rooms from: DH600* ✉ *Km 17, Rte. des Gorges du Todra, Douar Tizgui, Tinerhir* ☎ *0524/89–52–71* 🌐 *www.darayour.com* 🛏 *18 rooms* 🍴 *Free Breakfast.*

★ **Le Festival**
$$ | **B&B/INN** | **FAMILY** | Made from the same mountain rock that surrounds

it, this quirky eco-hotel is owned and operated by the charming Addi Sror, who speaks excellent English. **Pros:** environmentally sensitive; dramatic isolation; great meals. **Cons:** three rooms in main house share a bathroom; few in-house amenities; castle and cave rooms are about 200 DH–300 DH extra per night. [$] *Rooms from: DH700* ✉ *Rte. des Gorges du Todra, 5 km (3 miles) north of Todra Gorge, 12 km (7 miles) south of Tamtattouchte, Tinerhir* ☎ *0661/26–72–51* ✎ *aubergelefestival@yahoo.fr* 🌐 *www.aubergelefestival-todragorge.com* 💳 *No credit cards* 🛏 *15 rooms* 🍴 *Free Breakfast.*

Erfoud

81 km (50 miles) south of Errachidia, 300 km (186 miles) northeast of Ouarzazate.

Any expedition to Erg Chebbi will entail passing through—or possibly spending a night in—Erfoud. Formerly a French administrative outpost and Foreign Legion stronghold, this frontier town on the Algerian border has a definite Wild West (in this case, Wild South) feel to it. Practical-minded travelers will be interested in the grid of low, dusty red buildings that house banks, shops, and other amenities.

The military fortress at Borj-Est, just across the Ziz to the east, provides the best possible view over the date palmery, the desert, and Erfoud from its altitude of 3,067 feet above sea level. Near the Borj-Est are quarries famous for their black marble, one of Erfoud's principal products; this luxurious solid is surprisingly rich in petrified marine fossils.

GETTING HERE AND AROUND

Erfoud sits at the southern end of the Ziz Oasis. From the north, the only way here is the N13 via Er-Rachidia. From Ouarzazate, take the N10 and turn onto the R702 just after the village of Tinejdad. This direct route avoids Errachidia. Buses to Erfoud depart from Errachidia (1½ hours), Fez (11 hours), Rissani (1½ hours), and Tinerhir (4 hours). From Errachidia you can take buses to Ouarzazate, Marrakesh, Midelt, and Meknès.

CONTACTS CTM Erfoud. ✉ *Complex Commerciale, Av. Mohammed V, Erfoud* ☎ *0535/57–68–86* 🌐 *www.ctm.ma.*

TIMING AND PRECAUTIONS

The biggest annual event is the Erfoud Date Festival, which coincides with the date harvest in October (the exact days vary from year to year). As with all the Moroccan Sahara regions, the best way to avoid excessive heat is to visit between February and May or September and November.

Sights

Tahiri Museum of Morocco

Midway between Erfoud and Rissani, this private museum is hard to miss—just look for the giant replica dinosaurs standing outside. Take a peek inside at the interesting, well-presented collection curated by Moroccan paleontologist Brahim Tahari; it includes fossils, bones, minerals, flints, crystals, and assorted oddities.

TIP→ There's a shop attached if you want to purchase your own bit of prehistory. ✉ *Km 17, Rte. de Rissani, Erfoud* ✎ *tahirifossils@gmail.com* 🎟 *Free, donations welcome.*

Restaurants

When hunger hits, your best option is to head to one of the hotels listed below. That said, there are a few simple eateries along the main street in the town center.

Pizzeria-Restaurant des Dunes

$$ | **MOROCCAN** | If you're craving pizza, try this tourist-friendly spot just opposite the gas station as you enter Erfoud from the direction of Errachidia. It serves standard pies plus a local variation on the theme

called *madfouna tafilalt* (aka Amazigh pizza), which is a baked flatbread stuffed with meat. **Known for:** welcoming terrace; pizza; cash only. [$] *Average main: DH80* ✉ *Av. Moulay Isamil, Erfoud* ☎ *0535/57-67-93* 🌐 *www.restaurantdesdunes.com* 💳 *No credit cards.*

Hotels

Kasbah Xaluca

$$$ | HOTEL | In a desert town that lacks any character-filled boutique accommodations, the rambling Kasbah Xaluca is the best choice available and offers a sense of authenticity combined with luxury facilities. **Pros:** all the modern conveniences; pretty pool area; attentive service. **Cons:** full of tour groups; not much character—large hotel feel; distance from dunes. [$] *Rooms from: DH1000* ✉ *Rte. Efoud à Errachidia KM 5, 5 km (3 miles) north of Erfoud, on road to Errachidia, Erfoud* ☎ *0535/57-84-50* 🌐 *www.xaluca.com* 🛏 *110 rooms, 24 suites, 8 bungalows* 🍴 *Free Breakfast.*

Shopping

No trip to Erfoud is complete without a visit to one of the many marble and fossil workshops. This section of desert was once a rich seabed filled with many types of marine creatures that no longer exist. Trilobites, urchins, ammonites, and other fossils are abundant in the local stone, and huge slabs are quarried, dissected, polished, and shaped here to create all manner of objects from tabletops to pendants. Most of the workshops give demonstrations as well as exhibit the finished articles.

Fossiles d'Erfoud

CRAFTS | This fossil showroom, workshop, and factory has English-speaking owners who are happy to show individuals and groups around the facilities. The showroom has just about every object you might imagine could be made from fossils, and there are plenty of un-"improved" fossils to go around as well. Credit cards are accepted and international shipping can be arranged. ✉ *107, av. Moulay Ismail, Erfoud* ☎ *0535/57-60-20* 🌐 *www.fossilesderfoud.com.*

Merzouga

53 km (33 miles) southeast of Erfoud, 134 km (83 miles) southeast of Errachidia.

Merzouga has an ever-expanding strip of hotels and guesthouses, with options ranging from simple to sublime. The village's main draw, though, is the easy access it offers to Erg Chebbi and its magnificent dunes. A dawn or dusk trip to the dunes has become a classic Moroccan adventure, and is worth the effort. A series of café-restaurant-hotels overlooks Erg Chebbi, and most run camel excursions to the top as well as to oases where you can spend the night in permanent bivouacs. Many tour operators now offer exclusive and luxurious camps tucked in dunes away from the crowds—picture tents kitted out with woven carpets, antiques, lanterns, four-poster beds strewn with rose petals, and en suite washing facilities. You can also expect chilled champagne and fine dining by candlelight, but be prepared—paradise doesn't come cheap!

■ TIP→ **If you have some extra time it is worth taking a day trip to the colorful local market at Rissani and the ruins of the once-great city of Sijilmassa—now just a few remaining walls but with a great sense of history.**

GETTING HERE AND AROUND

The N13 from Erfoud goes straight to Merzouga. Minibuses and grands taxis bring tourists from Rissani and Erfoud.

GUIDES AND TOURS

Once in Merzouga you get around either by foot, dune buggy, camel, or 4x4. If you haven't come on an organized tour,

It's a bit of a trek to reach the dunes at Erg Chebbi, in the Sahara Desert, but well worth it.

the hotel or guesthouse you choose will be able to make arrangements for you, using their own local guides and bivouac camps.

Berber Adventure Tours

ADVENTURE TOURS | For those who want a hiking adventure in the Sahara, look no further than this company that specializes in desert hikes. With 5-day, 8-day, or 10-day options, you're sure to go well off the beaten path and have a once-in-a-lifetime experience. ✉ *Merzouga* ☎ *0659/22–84–62* ⊕ *berberadventure-tours.com.*

Berber Space Morocco

ADVENTURE TOURS | Berber Space Morocco is an all-round activity-based tour company that can offer you everything from camel treks, 4x4 adventures, and dune buggy races to more sedate cycling tours and visits to the dunes and oases. It was set up by the young and entrepreneurial Hassan, who prides himself on his Amazigh heritage and on knowing everything—they call him Hassan

Google. ☎ *0670/13–76–63, 0662/47–57–17* ⊕ *www.berberspacemorocco.com.*

Camel Trekking

ADVENTURE TOURS | Omar grew up in the desert south of Merzouga and now lives near the dunes in the village of Hassi Labied. He has many different tours and offers available from one-day experiences to multiday tours. If trekking isn't your style it's also possible to do 4x4 or quad tours into the desert. ✉ *Hassi Labied* ☎ *0668/65–22–85* ⊕ *www.cameltrekking. com.*

Your Morocco Tour

ADVENTURE TOURS | This U.S.-Moroccan agency can organize tours from Marrakesh or Fez that include a night spent at its luxury bivouac in the dunes of Merzouga. The price is built into the cost of a longer tour package. ✉ *Merzouga* ☎ *0662/34–48–16* ⊕ *www.your-moroc-co-tour.com.*

TIMING AND PRECAUTIONS

In summer, prepare for the extreme daytime heat by bringing sunglasses, sunblock, and plenty of bottled water. In winter, the nights can be viciously cold, so pack extra layers if camping out.

■ TIP→ **The fine sand of the Sahara will find its way into everything. Carry zip-top plastic bags for keeping items sand-free, especially electronic equipment, and cosmetics.**

 Sights

Dayet Srji

Near the dunes, this seasonal salt lake is a surprising sight—sometimes you see pink flamingos in early spring. ⊠ *Dyet Srji, Merzouga.*

★ Erg Chebbi

VIEWPOINT | In most cases your hotel is your best bet for an organized tour of Erg Chebbi. Every auberge near the dunes is there because it's a prime jumping-off point for a sunrise or sunset journey, either on foot or by camel. Most auberges have their own permanent bivouac in the dunes, often not far from others but generally fairly well concealed—which lets you pretend no one else is around even if they are. Most bivouac areas are organized into series of small tents for couples and larger groups, so you don't have to share with everyone. If you want to be utterly private, make sure your auberge doesn't share a tented site with any other, or ask to camp in the dunes on your own. ⊠ *Erg Chebbi, Merzouga.*

 Hotels

There are nearly 100 guesthouses and hotels to choose from in the area, but the best are north of Merzouga in the desert village Hassi Labied; these also benefit from being closest to the towering sands. All will be able to arrange a night's stay in a bivouac camp, and you can usually return to the hotel for a shower the morning after.

Kasbah Mohayut

$$ | **B&B/INN** | A mud-built auberge in the Saharan tradition, Kasbah Mohayut has comfortable, air-conditioned rooms that are decorated in the local style (think tiled floors, date-palm ceiling, wrought-iron beds, and colorful rugs); there are also spacious family suites with huge king-size beds, a salon, and a private terrace looking out to the dunes. **Pros:** pretty pool; right beside the dunes; on-site swimming pool. **Cons:** can feel impersonal; food service can be a little slow and so-so quality; this part of dunes is often busy with other tourists. $ *Rooms from: DH600* ⊠ *Hassilabied, 1½ km (1 mile) south of the village proper, Hassi Labied* ☎ *0666/03–91–85* ⊕ *www.hotelmohayut. com* ⇌ *26 rooms* ⭐ *Free Breakfast.*

Kasbah Tombuctou

$$$$ | **HOTEL** | **FAMILY** | Another of the Xaluca luxury hotels, this rather ostentatious faux kasbah rises from the sand like a mirage; crenulated turrets and inner corridors lead to attractive, air-conditioned rooms with huge en suite bathrooms finished in colored tadlak. **Pros:** Wi-Fi throughout; magnificent view of the dunes; luxurious lodgings. **Cons:** it is a chain hotel; food is buffet style and mediocre; lights in rooms are very dim. $ *Rooms from: DH1200* ⊠ *Rte. Erfoud, 1½ km (1 mile) south of Hassi Labied, Hassi Labied* ☎ *0535/57–70–91* ⊕ *www.xaluca.com* ⇌ *77 rooms* ⭐ *Free Breakfast.*

Ksar Sania Eco-Lodge

$$ | **B&B/INN** | At the edge of the Sahara, this unique French-owned eco-lodge lets guests bed down in handsome, hexagonal bungalows that are built from straw-covered mud; the rooms are very spacious and stylish, with tasteful furnishings, rich colors, and traditional ceilings. **Pros:** environmentally friendly; highly original concept; nice swimming area. **Cons:** cash only; outside of Merzouga, so plan accordingly; service can be slack and limited English. $ *Rooms from:*

Did You Know?

There are many ways to experience the dunes at Erg Chebbi: take in the sunset or sunrise, overnight at a desert camp, and/or go sand boarding, off-roading, or camel-trekking.

DH640 ✉ *Ksar Sania, 2 km (1 mile) south of Merzouga, Merzouga* ☎ *0661/35–99–10* ⊕ *auberge-ksarsania-merzouga. com* ▭ *No credit cards* ⊘ *Closed during Ramadan when it falls in summer* ⇆ *15 rooms, 5 huts* ❖ *Free Breakfast.*

Riad Cafe Du Sud
$$$$ | HOTEL | An exclusive retreat of just four individually designed rooms set in a fabulous location on the dunes, the Riad Cafe Du Sud provides traditional, simple, and calm desert living with all the luxuries of the modern world such as plentiful hot water and a strong shower. **Pros:** exclusivity; individually designed rooms; rooms and tents are available. **Cons:** pricey; communication can be slow when booking; few rooms so reservations should be made in advance. Ⓢ *Rooms from: DH1500* ✉ *BP 120 Ksar Merzouga, Merzouga* ☎ *0661/21–61–66* ⊕ *riadcafedusud.com* ⇆ *4 rooms* ❖ *Free Breakfast.*

Riad Madu
$$$ | B&B/INN | Opened in 2013 by the Annam brothers from Merzouga, Riad Madu is a cut above the other Saharan inns dotting the edge of the Erg Chebbi dunes, showcasing the brothers' experience in the European tourism and hospitality sectors—good English is spoken, guests are greeted warmly, and attention to detail is evident throughout. **Pros:** attention to detail; enthusiastic staff; half-board meal plan available. **Cons:** a/c can have issues; cash only; not much to do nearby or at the hotel. Ⓢ *Rooms from: DH900* ✉ *Ksar Hassilabied, 5 km (3 miles) north of Merzouga, Hassi Labied* ☎ *0535/57–87–40* ⊕ *riadmadu.com* ▭ *No credit cards* ⇆ *12 rooms* ❖ *Free Breakfast.*

★ Sahara Stars Camp
$$$$ | ALL-INCLUSIVE | True to its name, this new camp in the dunes offers a stunning, unimpeded view of the stars, enjoyed from luxurious tents with hot power showers, plush beds, elegant decor, and lovely touches like flowers scattered on the bed and pom-pommed hats to guard against the sun. **Pros:** a secluded location; luxury tents; they can organize several activities. **Cons:** customer service can be hit or miss; quite pricey; only accessible by camel or quad. Ⓢ *Rooms from: DH2000* ✉ *Ras El Erg Chebbi* ☎ *0662/47–57–17, 0661/87–47–53* ✉ *saharastarscamp@gmail.com* ⊕ *www. saharastarscamp.com* ⇆ *6 rooms* ❖ *Free Breakfast.*

 ## Activities

Mouhou (Quad) Tours
FOUR-WHEELING | Mouhou Tours offer quad biking across the dunes or around the town of Merzouga. Phone ahead to organize a pick up from your hotel. ✉ *Merzouga* ☎ *0637/39–06–58* ✉ *mouhoutoursadventures@gmail.com* ⊕ *www. mouhoutours.com.*

Djebel Sarhro and Nekob

95 km (59 miles) east of Agdz, 165 km (103 miles) southwest of Rissani.

If you pick the southern oasis route, don't miss the chance to stay in Nekob, Morocco's most kasbah-filled village. Locals have come up with all sorts of reasons for why there are 45 of them. The amusing and believable theory is that members of a rich extended family settled here in the 18th and 19th centuries and quickly set to work trying to outbuild and out-impress each other. There's little in the way of showing off in the village today. The children are wild and the place a little untouched for the moment.

Visitors can pick up handcrafted carpets and headscarves made by local women at the weekly Sunday souk, or simply sit back, stare over the palmery, and savor the experience. If you're looking for a more active alternative, the trekking potential north of town stretches as far as Boumalne du Dadès, 150 km (93 miles) away and on the northern oasis route. It's a five-day hike to Tagdift or Iknioun.

GETTING HERE AND AROUND
Nekob lies on the southern oasis route between Agdz and Rissani, skirting the southern slopes of the Djebel Sarhro. Minibuses and grands taxis travel here from Rissani, Zagora, and Ouarzazate.

Exploring the mountain ranges and peaks of Djebel Sarhro requires a four-wheel-drive vehicle.

■ TIP→ **Walking in the Sarhro is a wonderful experience but to get the most out of it book with a specialist company before you arrive. Epic Morocco offers migration walks with the nomads in season.**

Sights

Djebel Sarhro Massif
SCENIC DRIVE | The wonderfully panoramic oasis Route 6956/R108 (which becomes 3454/N12 after Tazzarine) is one of the safest, fastest, least crowded roads in Morocco, and it offers unparalleled views up into the Djebel Sarhro Massif and all the way over to the Tafilalt date palmery. Count on four hours for the 233-km (140-mile) trip from Route P31/N9 (the Ouarzazate–Zagora road) to Rissani, in the date palmery. ⊠ *Rte. 6956/R108, Nekob.*

 Restaurants

Auberge Kasbah Meteorites
$ | AFRICAN | Morocco is a magnet for fossil fans, and much of the activity centers on the town of Alnif, on Route 3454/N12 between Rissani and Tazzarine. About 13 km (8 miles) west of Alnif is Auberge Kasbah Meteorites where you can enjoy a simple lunch, a dip in the immaculate pool, and a two- to three-hour excursion with a guide who'll show you the best places to hunt for fossils and ancient stone carvings. **Known for:** cash only; good local food; alcohol available for

purchase. $ *Average main: DH60* ⊠ *Ksar Tiguima, 13 km (8 miles) west of Alnif, Nekob* 🕾 *0661/70–26–30* ⊕ *www.kasbah-meteorites.com/* ▤ *No credit cards.*

Hotels

Kasbah Hotel Aït Omar
$$$ | B&B/INN | FAMILY | The premier address in the village of N'kob, this old family kasbah has been lovingly restored to high specifications. **Pros:** environmentally friendly ethic; very comfortable; great service. **Cons:** Wi-Fi can be patchy; minimal lighting in some areas; awkward, steep stairways. $ *Rooms from: DH900* ⊠ *Tansrite SARL Center N'Kob BP 95, Nekob* 🕾 *0524/83–99–81* ≤ *hotel.aitomar@gmail.com* ⊕ *www.hotel-aitomar.de* ▤ *No credit cards* ⊙ *Closed July and Aug.* ➪ *4 rooms, 10 apartments* Ɱ *Free Breakfast.*

Kasbah Imdoukal
$$$ | B&B/INN | This gorgeous Moroccan-owned kasbah sits in the heart of the village. **Pros:** plenty of atmosphere; in the center of Nekob; all rooms with a/c and heating. **Cons:** food is just ok; bed linens basic; prices are a bit high. $ *Rooms from: DH790* ⊠ *Douar N'Kob, Nekob* 🕾 *0524/83–97–98* ⊕ *kasbah-imdoukal.com* ▤ *No credit cards* ➪ *18 rooms, 2 suites* Ɱ *Free Breakfast.*

Riad Auberge Ouadjou
$$ | HOTEL | This pleasant, friendly hotel is a no-frills option with a manager who can speak English (with a British or American accent as required) and rooms that are simple, cool, and clean. **Pros:** Amazigh tent (added fee); clean, simple rooms; swimming pool. **Cons:** tent areas are rustic; shared bathrooms; basic. $ *Rooms from: DH500* ⊠ *N'kob* ⊹ *On left as you leave town on road to Agdz* 🕾 *0524/83–93–14* ≤ *ouadjou.aubergenkoub@gmail.com* ⊕ *www.ouadjou.com* ▤ *No credit cards* ➪ *6 rooms, 4 tents* Ɱ *Free Breakfast.*

Agdz

69 km (43 miles) southeast of Ouarzazate.

Agdz, at the junction of the Drâa and Tamsift rivers, marks the beginning of the Drâa palmery. A sleepy market town and administrative center, Agdz (pronounced *ah*-ga-dez) has little to offer at first glance other than the 5,022-foot peak Djebel Kissane and the Kasbah Dar el-Glaoui. But in the palm groves at the edge of town you'll discover some gorgeous boutique hotels and mini-kasbahs; these make an ideal base for a day or two of hiking and exploring. This is an ideal place to wander through the palmery and get to understand a little about how agriculture works in an oasis. There is also a center specializing in building from natural materials such as clay. From Agdz south to M'hamid, the P31/N9 road follows the river closely except for a 30-km (19-mile) section between the Tinfou Dunes and Tagounite.

GETTING HERE AND AROUND

Agdz is served by buses and grands taxis traveling between Ouarzazate and Zagora. The trip takes approximately two hours from either town.

TIMING AND PRECAUTIONS

A great time to visit is in October when the date harvest is in full swing, but it is wonderful at any time of the year. The market is stacked with boxes of the most delicious and succulent varieties.

Sights

Cascades du Drâa

NATURE SIGHT | Look for the turnoff to the Cascades du Drâa (also known as the Cascades de Tizgui) on the left, 30 km (19 miles) south of Ouarzazate and 10 km (6 miles) before Agdz. Over thousands of years, the water has carved out natural pools that are ideal for a refreshing dip. The waterfalls are not huge—not on the scale of Ouzoud—but if you want to see palm trees, figs, and oleander flowers springing from the rocks, and dip your toes (or all of you) in cold water, they are still worth a detour. ⊠ *Agdz* ✛ *10 km (6 miles) north of Agdz.*

Ksar Igdâoun

NOTABLE BUILDING | The truncated pyramidal towers and bastions of the Ksar Igdâoun are visible 15 km (9 miles) past the turnoff onto Route 6956/R108 to Tazzarine. There used to be three gates to the ksar: one for Jews; one for other people who lived nearby; and one for the local governor. ⊠ *Abranos, Agdz* ✛ *15 km (9 miles) past the turnoff onto Rte. 6956/R108 to Tazzarine* 🖭 *10 DH.*

Mt. Kissane

MOUNTAIN | This outcropping is one of the most prominent natural features in Agdz. The name itself means "glasses" in Arabic, referring to the shape of Moroccan tea glasses. There are paths that can be walked to the summit. The real show comes at sunset when the face of the mountain changes with shades of yellow, orange, purple, and pink. ⊠ *Agdz, Agdz.*

Tamnougalt

TOWN | Lining virtually the entire Drâa Valley from Agdz to Zagora are some two dozen ksour and kasbahs on both sides of the river. Perhaps the most amazing ksour in this region are at Tamnougalt, 6 km (4 miles) south of Agdz—the second group of red-pisé fortifications on the left. The resident Amazigh tribe, the Mezguita, governed its own independent republic from here until the late 18th century; the crenellated battlements and bastions were a necessary defense against desert nomads. For a deeper understanding of the tribe's traditional way of life, peruse the displays of farming and household implements in Tamnougalt's Kasbah des Caids du Mezguita museum. Occupying a restored 16th-century edifice, it is run by Hassan Aït el Caid (a descendant of the original caids who controlled the trade caravans passing through the region). Hassan can also take you on a walking tour through the village and the oasis, and explain the local Amazigh tribes and their origins en route. Donkey treks and picnics can be arranged as well. ✉ *Tamnougalt* ☎ *0667/34–56–02* 🌐 *www.facebook.com/KasbahDesCaidsTamnougalt/* 🎟 *Museum 20 DH.*

🍴 Restaurants

If you're passing though at lunchtime, the town has a slim selection of cafés; alternately you can continue on to Chez Yacob, located south toward Zagora in the village of Tamnougalt.

Agdz Café Restaurant

$ | **MOROCCAN** | **FAMILY** | Located at the edge of town as you arrive from the direction of Ouarzazate, this terrace café with easy parking outside is a good place to stop for lunch or a drink. It serves hearty tagines, brochettes, salads, and other snacks; the clean restrooms are an added bonus. **Known for:** clean restrooms (bring your own paper); hearty tagines; coffee and snacks available. [$] *Average main: DH60* ✉ *Centre, Agdz* 💳 *No credit cards.*

🛏 Hotels

Bab el Oued

$$$ | **B&B/INN** | **FAMILY** | Seven freestanding rooms await guests at this handsome eco-lodge, which is constructed in the typical mud-built style, tastefully mixing African and Moroccan decorative elements and equipped with modern showers and reversible air-conditioning—all of which are solar powered (though somewhat dark); other environmentally friendly details include natural soaps in the bathrooms and toilets with a water-saving flush option (this is the desert after all). **Pros:** environmentally sensitive; beautiful location; all rooms are separate from each other. **Cons:** cash only; no Wi-Fi by design (digital detox ethos); food quality inconsistent. [$] *Rooms from: DH950* ✉ *Palmeraie de Tamnougalt, Tamnougalt* ☎ *0660/18–84–84, 0619/40–28–32* 🌐 *ecolodgemaroc.com* 💳 *No credit cards* 🔑 *2 rooms, 5 suites* 🍽 *Free Breakfast.*

Chez Yacob

$$ | **B&B/INN** | This kasbah has been renovated to retain all its traditional charm including thick pisé walls pierced with tiny windows screened with *moucharabia* (carved wood latticework), and a central courtyard. **Pros:** en suite bathrooms and a/c; rooms face onto courtyard; great views over palmery (though windows are small). **Cons:** cash only; can be crowded at lunch time; very little parking. [$] *Rooms from: DH600* ✉ *6 km (4 miles) from Agdz on route to Zagora, Agdz* ☎ *0524/84–33–94* 🌐 *chez-yacob-tamnougalt.maroc-hebergement.fr/* 💳 *No credit cards* 🔑 *9 rooms* 🍽 *Free Breakfast.*

Dar Amazir

$$ | **B&B/INN** | Enter this warm and intimate guesthouse on the outskirts of Agdz through two Amazigh doors that lead into a courtyard with a swimming pool and the sound of birdsong. **Pros:** good Wi-Fi; good food and alcohol available; lovely pool. **Cons:** some ventilation issues; cash only; a bit difficult to book as a standalone reservation. [$] *Rooms from: DH620* ✉ *Aslim, Agdz* ✥ *After taxi rank in town in main square, take first left and follow that road down* ☎ *0665/46–63–39* 💳 *No credit cards* 🔑 *8 rooms* 🍽 *Free Breakfast.*

★ **Kasbah Azul**

$$$$ | **B&B/INN** | **FAMILY** | The aptly named "House of Peace" is tucked away in the palm groves outside Agdz. **Pros:** great for kids; arty vibe; eco-friendly; use of solar power and organic produce. **Cons:** low season can be quiet; a little isolated so will need transport; books up quickly. [$] *Rooms from: DH1155* ✉ *Douar Asslim, 2½ km (1½ miles) north of Agdz, Agdz* ☎ *0524/84–39–31* 🌐 *www.kasbahazul.com* ⏲ *Closed during Ramadan (call ahead)* 🔑 *7 rooms* 🍽 *Free Breakfast.*

Tinzouline

59 km (37 miles) southeast of Agdz, 130 km (81 miles) southeast of Ouarzazate.

Tinzouline holds an important weekly souk. If you're here on a Monday, take this opportunity to shop and make contact with the many peoples of this southern Moroccan region where Amazigh, Arab, Jewish, and Haratin communities have coexisted for centuries. The Tinzouline ksour are clustered around a majestic kasbah in the middle of an oasis that includes several villages. Tinzouline is also one of the most important prehistoric sites in pre-Saharan North Africa: from the ksour a 7-km (4½-mile) gravel path leads west of town to cave engravings depicting mounted hunters. These drawings are attributed to Iron Age Libyo-Imazighen, lending further substance to the theory that Morocco's first inhabitants may have originally come from Central Asia via central and eastern Africa.

Zagora

95 km (59 miles) southeast of Agdz, 170 km (106 miles) southeast of Ouarzazate.

Zagora is—and does feel like—the boundary between the Sahara and what some writers and travelers have referred to as "reality." After Zagora, time and distance are measured in camel days: a famous painted sign at the end of town (near the impressive new Zagora Province offices) features a camel and reads, "Tombouctu 52 Days"—that is, "52 days by camel." M'hamid, 97 km (60 miles) farther south, marks the actual end of the paved road and the beginning of the open desert, but Zagora is where the sensation of being in the desert kicks in.

On your way out of town, heading across the bridge signposted toward M'hamid,

you'll find the town of Amezrou, and in it, the fascinating **Kasbah des Juifs** (Kasbah of the Jews).

GETTING HERE AND AROUND

Zagora is easily reached by the main road from M'hamid and Ouarzazate. Buses and grands taxis navigate this route. The town's CTM bus station is on the main street. Zagora itself is easy to explore on foot or by inexpensive petit taxi. Numerous local tour agencies offer camel trips, oasis treks, and desert camping.

CONTACTS CTM Zagora. ⊠ *37, bd. Mohammed V, Zagora* ☎ *0524/84–73–27* ⊕ *www.ctm.ma.*

GUIDES AND TOURS

ATTA Desert Camp

ADVENTURE TOURS | A reliable local operator that offers desert excursions overnight or multiday options. Desert camp options include luxury and comfort with fantastic food and service. ⊠ *Zagora, Zagora* ☎ *0661/35–40–93* ⊕ *www. morocco-desert-camp.com.*

★ Caravane du Sud

ADVENTURE TOURS | This family-run agency specializes in the desert regions and villages around Zagora. Local guides with an eco-tourism ethos lead 4x4 and camel tours. You can get the best out of a tour by discussing it beforehand in some detail and letting them know what you really want to do. Service is excellent. ⊠ *BP 13, Zagora* ☎ *0524/84–75–69, 0661/87–68–74* ⊕ *www.caravanesud. com.*

Tombouctour

ADVENTURE TOURS | Long-established Tombouctour organizes tours throughout Morocco; the local office in Zagora will set up overnight excursions or desert safaris for travelers turning up at its door. ⊠ *79, av. Mohammed V, Zagora* ☎ *0524/84–82–07* ⊕ *tombouctour.com.*

Sights

Amezrou

MARKET | Three km (2 miles) south of Zagora, Amezrou is famous for its Jewish silversmiths, who made decorative jewelry in this small village until the creation of the Israeli State in 1948, when all but 30,000 of Morocco's 300,000 Jews left for Israel. Craftsmen continue the tradition in the Mellah here. It's a worthwhile stop if you don't mind the clamor of children eager to be hired as your guide. You may also be able to find some interesting Jewish antiques if you ask. ✉ *Zagora.*

Djebel Zagora

VIEWPOINT | The town's promontory, capped by an 11th-century Almoravid fortress, is an excellent sunset vantage point—it overlooks the Drâa palmery with the distant Djebel Sarhro Massif to the north and the Tinfou Dunes to the south. Djebel Zagora is reached via the first left turn south of the Kasbah Asmaa hotel; there's also a twisting footpath up the 3,195-foot mountain from the hotel itself. Most hotels in town will arrange for you to do the trip by camel, and it makes a nice sunset trek. ✉ *Zagora.*

Ksar Tissergate Museum

MUSEUM VILLAGE | Deep within the evocative alleys of the Ksar Tissergate—a 17th-century fortified village—this fascinating museum displays local costumes, agricultural implements, domestic utensils, jewelry, and other artifacts. Unlike most museums in southern Morocco, exhibits here have explanations in English. You access it through the Kasbah Ziwana and they can supply you with a guide for a small tip. ✉ *Next to Kasbah Ziwana, 8 km (5 miles) from Zagora on road to Ouarzazate* ☎ *0667/69–06–02* 🌐 *visitdraatafilalet.com/en/destinations/ksar-tissergate/* 🎫 *20 DH.*

Restaurants

Le Dromadaire Gourmand

$$ | **MOROCCAN** | Having hung up his *sheshe* (turban) after years of guiding tourists through the desert, Mustapha el Mekki has established one of the most popular eateries in Zagora. It serves regional specialties such as tagine *de mariage* (a slow-cooked casserole of beef with apricots, prunes, and almonds) and a Drâa Valley vegetable soup. **Known for:** lovely sidewalk terrace; classic tagines and other Moroccan dishes; BYOB and cash only. [$] *Average main: DH70* ✉ *Av. Mohammed V, near TOTAL gas station, Zagora* ☎ *0661/34–83–94* 🌐 *www.dromadaire-gourmand.com* 💳 *No credit cards.*

Hotels

★ Azalai Desert Lodge

$$$$ | **B&B/INN** | Hidden within the Drâa Valley oasis, the Azalai Desert Lodge is a luxurious retreat with secluded gardens, creative cuisine, and an interior that has been featured in several prestigious design magazines. **Pros:** beautiful decor; luxury at the edge of the desert; high-quality food served. **Cons:** pool is not heated; pricey option and cash only; remote location. [$] *Rooms from: DH1700* ✉ *Douar Tissergate, Zagora* ✣ *7 km (4 miles) north of Zagora* 🌐 *www.azalaidesertlodge.com* 💳 *No credit cards* ⏲ *Closed July and Aug.* 🛏 *8 rooms* 🍴 *Free Breakfast.*

Casa Juan

$$$ | **HOTEL** | A delightful and original hotel set in the small village of Aït Isoul, Casa Juan offers the best of both worlds here: the palmery and the desert, splendid in their green and gold, but there's not much nearby. **Pros:** original rooms full of interesting things; between the desert and the palmery; good food served. **Cons:** cash only; narrow rooms; off the beaten track. [$] *Rooms from: DH900* ✉ *Aït Isfoul, Tagounite* ✣ *70 km (43 miles)*

Ksour and Kasbahs

Ksour (plural for *ksar*) are fortified villages with houses, granaries, cemeteries (both Jewish and Muslim), hammams, and shops. Kasbahs are fortified castles belonging to a single family and often contain their own granaries, wells, and places for prayer. Moroccan ksour and kasbahs are all built of *pisé*, a sun-dried mixture of mud and clay. The Erfoud–Ouarzazate road through the Dadès Valley is billed as the "Route of the Thousand Kasbahs," with village after village of fortified pisé structures, many decorated with carved and painted geometrical patterns (the more intricate the motif, the wealthier the owner). The kasbahs served the caravan trains that passed along this trans-Saharan trade route. Camel trains loaded with salt or gold were targets for bandits so staying in a fortified village made sense. The merchants preempted what is now the tourist trade. The Drâa Valley is also rimmed with kasbahs and ksour for the length of the Agdz–Zagora road. Highlights of the Dadès route are the Kasbah Amerhidil, at the Skoura oasis, and the Aït Ben Haddou kasbahs, near Ouarzazate; showstoppers in the Drâa Valley include the 16th-century ksour at Tamnougalt, just south of Agdz, and the 17th-century Ksar Tissergate, just north of Zagora—both now feature interesting museums. Increasingly, these historic structures are being restored and converted into guesthouses. Staying in one that achieves the perfect balance is an unforgettable experience.

from Zagora on N9 ☎ 0661/74-37-10 ✉ casajuansahara@gmail.com ⊕ www.casajuansahara.com ▤ No credit cards ↬ 6 rooms, tents available ⦿ Free Breakfast.

Kasbah Sirocco

$$ | B&B/INN | FAMILY | A popular pit stop on the way to the desert, Kasbah Sirocco has clean, functional rooms; all have air-conditioning, and most have views of the relaxed pool terrace. **Pros:** full range of services; great pool; a/c standard in rooms. **Cons:** customer service can be brusque; lacks personalization; can be noisy. $ *Rooms from: DH660* ⊠ *Amezrou, Zagora* ✛ *2 km (1 mile) southeast of Zagora on road to M'hamid* ☎ *0524/84-61-25* ⊕ *www.kasbah-sirocco.com* ↬ *20 rooms* ⦿ *Free Breakfast.*

Riad Dar Sofian

$$$ | B&B/INN | FAMILY | Originally built as a family home, this rambling three-story riad is full of over-the-top Moroccan decor, with stucco plasterwork, colorful mosaic tiling, ornate ceilings, and antique furnishings competing for attention. **Pros:** lovely pool; lots of creature comforts; Wi-Fi available. **Cons:** no elevator; some rooms are small; some water flow issues. $ *Rooms from: DH900* ⊠ *Rte. de Nakhla BP 78, Zagora* ☎ *0524/84-73-19* ⊕ *www.riaddarsofian.com* ↬ *10 rooms* ⦿ *Free Breakfast.*

M'hamid

68 km (42 miles) south of Tinfou, 97 km (60 miles) south of Zagora, 260 km (161 miles) southeast of Ouarzazate, 395 km (245 miles) southwest of Rissani.

Properly known as M'hamid el-Ghizlane, or Plain of the Gazelles, M'hamid neatly marks the end of Morocco's Great Oasis Valleys and the end of the asphalt road. It was once an outpost for the camel corps of the French Foreign Legion, and a large military barracks reminds visitors that the Algerian border is not far away. Looking at modern M'hamid—a one-street village with overeager tour companies hustling for business—you may wonder what's worth defending, but consider the obvious upside. The Sahara awaits at the end of the main street, making this a vital departure point for desert forays, most notably to Morocco's highest dunes at Erg Chigaga, 50 km (31 miles) west.

In the palm groves just before M'hamid, the outlying villages of Ouled Driss and Bounou have interesting kasbahs that can be visited. A short hop across the dried riverbed of the Drâa, next to M'hamid's mosque, takes you toward the site of the original village, some 2 km (1 mile) away, where a 17th-century Jewish-built kasbah is still inhabited by the local Haratin population.

The sand drifting like snow across the road (despite the placement of palm-frond sand breaks and fences), the immensity of the horizon, plus the patient gait of camels combine to produce a palpable change in the sense of time and space at this final Drâa oasis. The ocean of dunes 7 km (4½ miles) beyond M'hamid will satisfy any craving for some real Saharan scenery.

GETTING HERE AND AROUND
Buses arrive here twice daily from Marrakesh via Zagora and Ouarzazate. Grands taxis and minibuses also make the journey to and from Zagora.

GUIDES AND TOURS
Arriving in M'hamid without having already reserved accommodation or excursions can be intimidating due to fiercely competing touts. That said, there are several local agencies to choose from if you want to trek or take a 4x4 expedition deeper into the dunes and surrounding desert.

Caravan of Dreams
ADVENTURE TOURS | Run by Ali Laghfiri, who grew up in the village of M'hamid,
this German-Moroccan outfit offers camel treks and 4x4 excursions to a picturesque camp in the Erg Lehoudi dunes. Cooking and drumming lessons at the camp can also be arranged. ⌂ Village center, M'hamid ☎ 0670/02–00–33 ⊕ www.caravane-de-reve.com.

Sahara Services
ADVENTURE TOURS | FAMILY | This full-service travel agency offers camel treks to the nearby dunes of Erg Lehoudi and 4x4 trips to a luxury bivouac in Erg Chigaga from its office in M'hamid. The agency also specializes in family-friendly trips. ⌂ Village Center, M'hamid ☎ 0661/77–67–66 ⊕ www.saharaservices.info.

Zbar Travel
ADVENTURE TOURS | The local office of Zbar Travel serves as a launchpad for sand-boarding adventures, camel treks, and 4x4 outings. The agency also has a very comfortable bivouac camp in the dunes of Erg Chigaga. ⌂ Main St., next to Hotel El Ghizlane, on right as you enter village, M'hamid ☎ 0668/51–72–80 ⊕ www.zbartravel.com.

TIMING AND PRECAUTIONS
M'hamid has a Monday souk that's famous for the occasional appearance of nomadic, trans-Saharan traders of the Reguibat tribe. Much chronicled by writer Paul Bowles, these traders habitually wear the indigo *sheish*, a linen cloth wrapped around the head and face for protection from the elements. The dye from the fabric runs, tingeing the men's faces blue and leading to their nickname, the "Blue Men." Don't expect too much in the way of merchandise, though; the souk has lost much of its appeal in recent years. Noteworthy annual events include the International Nomads Festival, staged in mid-March to promote understanding of the nomadic traditions of the Moroccan Sahara; and a world music festival called Taragalte, which takes place in the nearby dunes in November. ■ TIP→ **Many hotels and desert camps close during July and August due to the unbearable heat.**

Sights

★ Erg Chigaga

VIEWPOINT | The splendid Erg Chigaga dunes are the principal reason why visitors make the trek south to M'hamid. Wild, remote, and largely unspoiled, they're only accessible by heading west out of the village on 50 km (31 miles) of dusty and stony pistes. The journey takes three hours in a 4x4 vehicle or three days on a camel, though hurried jet-setters bound for Erg Chigaga's luxury bivouac camps sometimes come by helicopter direct from Marrakesh. Morocco's highest dunes, rising almost 1,000 feet, are approached by crossing smaller dunes, *hammada* (rocky Martian-like terrain), and flat expanses, which are sometimes flooded in winter. A few nomadic families still live in the region, herding their camels and goats through the pasture, which can be surprisingly lush. ✉ *50 km (31 miles) west of M'hamid, M'hamid.*

Ksebt el-Allouj

TOWN | The ruins of the ksar Ksebt el-Allouj, dating from the Saadian dynasty, lie across the Drâa riverbed on the other side from the village from M'hamid, about 2 km (1 mile) from the town center. The ksar is uninhabited and is interesting to explore. ✉ *M'hamid.*

Hotels

Chez le Pacha

$$$ | **HOTEL** | **FAMILY** | One of a string of kasbah-style hotels in palm groves as you approach M'hamid, Chez le Pacha is a well-run establishment that offers a lot at a reasonable price. **Pros:** helpful staff; stylish accommodations; large pool area. **Cons:** cash only; some rooms a bit tired; the half-board plan is compulsory. [$] *Rooms from: DH800* ✉ *Bounou, Ouled Driss, 5 km (3 miles) north of M'hamid, M'hamid* ☎ *0524/84-86-96* 🌐 *www.chezlepacha.com* 💳 *No credit cards* 🛏 *16 rooms, 10 huts* 🍴 *Free Breakfast.*

Le Drom' Blanc

$$ | **B&B/INN** | Hidden in the palm groves of Bounou, this guesthouse has simple en suite rooms set around a central patio, plus nomad-style tents and self-contained pisé bungalows in the garden. **Pros:** one wheelchair-accessible room; secluded location in palm groves; great views of the night sky. **Cons:** not much English spoken; not much nearby (but half-board included); rooms are very dark. [$] *Rooms from: DH580* ✉ *Bounou, 5 km (3 miles) north of M'hamid, Ouled Driss, M'hamid* ☎ *0524/84-68-52* 🌐 *www.ledromblanc.com* 🛏 *4 rooms, 6 tents, 3 bungalows* 🍴 *Free Breakfast.*

Kasbah Azalay

$$$$ | **HOTEL** | The only luxurious lodging actually in the village of M'hamid is this Spanish-owned kasbah hotel at the edge of the palmery. **Pros:** magnificent pool and spa; plenty of creature comforts; alcohol is available. **Cons:** often empty; dining area is basic; lack of communal terraces or salons for socializing. [$] *Rooms from: DH1300* ✉ *M'hamid el Ghizlane, M'hamid* ☎ *0524/84-80-96* 🌐 *azalay.com* 🛏 *43 rooms* 🍴 *Free Breakfast.*

Chapter 9

AGADIR AND THE SOUTHERN ATLANTIC COAST

Updated by
Erin Wilson

⊙ Sights	🍴 Restaurants	🛏 Hotels	🛍 Shopping	🍸 Nightlife
★★★★★	★★★★☆	★★★★☆	★★★☆☆	★☆☆☆☆

WELCOME TO AGADIR AND THE SOUTHERN ATLANTIC COAST

TOP REASONS TO GO

★ **Water sports:** The magnificent Atlantic coastline draws hundreds of surfers and other watersports fanatics every year to ride its huge breaks and test their wits against the winds.

★ **Satisfying seafood:** Whether you are haggling down by Essaouira port for your own fish or enjoying the day's catch at an upscale restaurant in Agadir's marina, both cities are a seafood-lover's paradise.

★ **Family fun:** Donkey and camel rides, swimming pools, and ice-cream stalls make Agadir heaven for children, while stylish resort hotels provide every luxury parents could possibly want.

★ **Walks in the Anti-Atlas:** Hikers can enjoy the spectacular scenery around Tafraoute and the pretty villages of the Ammeln Valley, without another tourist in sight.

★ **Taroudant:** This authentically Moroccan walled city has a strong crafts tradition, fascinating souks, and some lovely boutique hotels.

Morocco's southern coastal towns are just a few hours from bustling Marrakesh, but their laid-back vibe makes you feel you're a world away. Moroccans and Europeans flock to this region in summer for the sea breeze, the sandy beaches, the luxurious resorts, and the numerous music festivals. This is also argan country: otherwise known as "Morocco gold," this tree's oil is changing the economic prospects of local women and the beauty regimens of women across the world. The inland region around the Anti-Atlas Mountains, comprising Taroudant, Tafraoute, and Tiznit, is relatively undiscovered by visitors but attracts some nature lovers, walkers, and climbers.

1 Agadir. Essentially a large, regional trading city, Agadir is fronted by Morocco's premier beach resort, long popular with European sun worshippers and tourists. Visitors spend most of their time at the hotels near the sweeping sandy beach at the south end. Less crowded local beaches are to the north and south, and the Souss Massa National Park is nearby.

2 Essaouira. Quieter and more emblematically Moroccan than Agadir, Essaouira is becoming more popular with travelers. The beach stretches for miles in a curving bay with a breeze great for water sports, but most visitors are attracted by the medina and the busy port with its fish restaurants.

3 Taroudant. This market town in the Souss Valley is worth a visit for the stunning mountains nearby and the rich local Amazigh culture.

4 Tafraoute. Excellent outdoor adventures and striking natural beauty are plentiful near this town, from the Ammeln Valley to the palm groves of Aït Mansour.

5 Tiznit. The silver center of Morocco, Tiznit has strong appeal for lovers of jewelry and artisanal crafts.

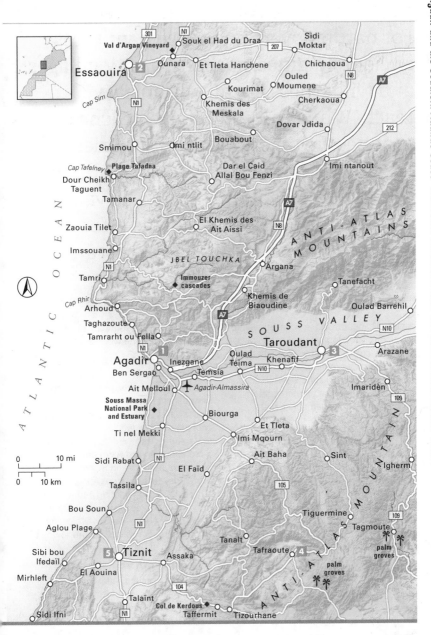

Whether your interests involve holing up in luxury or diving into the surf, this coastal area offers a great deal. For nature lovers and culture vultures, ancient medinas, kasbahs, pretty villages, and wilderness are all within easy reach. While they both have beaches that people rave about, tourist-oriented Agadir and bohemian Essaouira couldn't be more different. Inland, fertile valleys and the Anti-Atlas Mountains offer abundant opportunities to explore nature.

A hippie hangout whose secret travelers refused to reveal for years, Essaouira is only now coming into the limelight as a mainstream destination, but it nevertheless retains its distinctive ambience. Windy beaches attract water-sports enthusiasts rather than sunseekers, and riad-hotels cater to independent travelers.

Agadir, on the other hand, was made for mass tourism. It's a modern resort city with every kind of singing, dancing, and casino-betting distraction on hand along with long stretches of hot, sandy beaches, and calm seas perfect for sunbathing families. Both Agadir and Essaouira, however, have lively ports worth seeing in action and superb fresh fish and seafood. Between the two are less frequented spots good for surfing, windsurfing, kitesurfing, kayaking, and bodyboarding, or, for the less active, sunbathing and just hiding out from the world a little.

Head inland southeast of Agadir, and you'll find fruit orchards, argan trees, saffron crocus fields, pretty painted villages, and kasbahs. The plains of the Souss Valley and the jagged Anti-Atlas Mountains provide stunning vistas with plenty of scope for adventure. The picturesque walled town of Taroudant has historic sights and markets that attract day-trippers from Agadir, and it's a great base for exploring and trekking into the Anti-Atlas or western High Atlas mountains. A very worthwhile circuit from Taroudant will include the towns of Tafraoute and Tiznit.

MAJOR REGIONS
Souss Valley and Anti-Atlas Mountains.
Fewer visitors venture far south in Morocco to the Souss Valley and

Anti-Atlas Mountains, but those who do are rewarded with striking landscapes as well as insight into life and culture at the edge of the great Sahara. The region's character is strongly flavored by its Tashelhit-speaking Imazighen, who inhabited these mountains and plains before Arabs set foot in Morocco, giving the region a distinctive rural atmosphere. East and south of Agadir, scenic drives take you past hills covered with barley and almond trees, palm groves, and the Anti-Atlas Mountains themselves. In the towns, poke around the monuments and souks of Taroudant, take in the backdrop of towering granite boulders and nearby rock carvings in Tafraoute, or shop for Morocco's finest silver in Tiznit. Still, the towns are not the main attraction; people come here to commune with nature and get away from it all.

Planning

When to Go

Inland destinations can get too hot in summer, but high season for the coast is July and August, with other peaks in June and at Christmas and New Year's Day. The best months for visiting may be September and October, when it's off-season but still warm. Summer tends to be busy with vacationing Moroccan families; spring in Agadir is the main season for vacationers and families from abroad. Surfers and water-sports fans come year-round, although winter and early spring are by far the best times for surf.

In the Souss Valley, spring is the most spectacular time to visit, when almond trees and wildflowers are in bloom, the harvest is near, and the weather is sunny but not too hot. Fall temperatures are moderate, but landscapes are a bit drabber after the summer harvest.

As long as rains don't wash out the roads, winter is pleasant as well—it is particularly popular for climbers in the mountains. Coastal areas are mild, although inland temperatures can be cold and heated rooms hard to find.

If you must come in summer, stick to the coast: even an hour inland, in Taroudant, the July and August heat is unbearable in all but the nighttime hours.

Planning Your Time

Most visitors to the region fly into Agadir or reach Essaouira from Marrakesh, but there are now a few direct flights to Essaouira from Europe. Both cities easily warrant more than just a day trip, so it's worth booking at least a couple of nights in a local riad. You can decide to stick to just one city, but many people decide to explore both while in the area. From Agadir, the Anti-Atlas region is easily accessible in day excursions or with an overnight stay in Tafraoute or Taroudant. These trips can be arranged with a rental car or through one of the many local travel agencies. The area farther south of Agadir, where the desert meets the ocean, is beautiful and has a fascinating and turbulent history of occupation and independence, but it requires a longer trip as distances are great and public transportation is very limited. If you are fortunate to be traveling to any of the region's towns during a festival, book accommodations well in advance.

Festivals

Agadir and Essaouira are music hot spots and host popular music festivals. Held in July, Agadir's Festival Timitar celebrates native Amazigh music; Essaouira's world-famous Gnaoua and World Music Festival, held each June, hosts international musicians as well as native ones. Various towns around the Anti-Atlas have developed festivals to celebrate aspects of local culture, including events in Taroudant (focusing on traditional music every June); Tafraoute (celebrating the almond blossom in February and local music and culture in August); and Tiznit (honoring the traditional silversmiths in August).

Getting Here and Around

AIR

The key international air hub in the region is Agadir, although visitors based in Essaouira may fly in to Marrakesh or Essaouira itself. Agadir's Al Massira Airport (AGA) is 35 km (21 miles) east of town. *Grands taxis* (large shared taxis for up to six passengers) to downtown Agadir are a fixed price of 200 DH, but many drivers expect you to haggle. There is also a shuttle bus (4 DH) every 30 minutes from the airport to nearby Inezgane (13 km [8 miles] southeast of Agadir), where several bus services and grands taxis provide connections to other southern destinations as well as to the main bus station in Agadir. Otherwise, your hotel will usually be happy to arrange your airport transfer.

Essaouira's Mogador Airport (ESU) has several flights a week direct from the United Kingdom and some European cities. The airport is 16 km (10 miles) south of the town. There are no regular buses or shuttles from the airport, but grands taxis to Essaouira cost 150 DH, and your hotel can usually arrange transfers.

BUS

There is frequent bus service offered by both CTM and Supratours connecting to Essaouira, Marrakesh, and Casablanca, as well as grands taxis that travel between cities.

CAR

A freeway connects Marrakesh and Agadir; the journey takes approximately three hours. You can also rent a car in either Agadir or Essaouira if you want

to explore the region at your own pace. Explorations of the area around Taroudant and Tafraoute can be done as side trips from Agadir. If you don't want to drive yourself, one of the most enjoyable ways to cover this broad area is to organize a tour through one of several agencies based in Agadir.

Safety

Essaouira and Agadir are quite safe, with almost no violent crime. Lone female travelers will feel more comfortable in these towns than in some other parts of Morocco. Travelers should keep an eye on their personal belongings, however, as pickpockets are common, especially during festival time when the streets are jam-packed.

Restaurants

All along the coast and at any time of day, you can get great grilled or battered fresh fish and seafood that's inexpensive and tasty. For a better fish experience, go to a restaurant and try fish tagine or skewered and marinated fish brochettes. International cuisine is also readily available in both Agadir and Essaouira, including burger joints and pizza restaurants. Plenty of cafés around the area serve traditional Moroccan cuisine such as tagines, meat brochettes, and couscous.

Dining reviews have been shortened. For full information, visit Fodors.com.

Hotels

You'll find a full range of options, from small budget hotels to Agadir's five-star behemoths. In Essaouira, many old traditional family homes, or *riads,* have been restored and converted to beautiful guesthouses. In summer it's best to reserve rooms in advance, and for the more upscale boutique hotels, you may have to book several months in advance whatever the time of year. An increasing number of rental apartments in Essaouira and "apartment hotels" in Agadir offer self-catering options.

The Souss has some choice small hotels ranging from simple auberges (inns) and restored riads to former palaces and country retreats.

Hotel reviews have been shortened. For full information, visit Fodors.com

WHAT IT COSTS in Dirhams			
$	$$	$$$	$$$$
RESTAURANTS			
under 70 DH	70 DH–90 DH	91 DH–110 DH	over 110 DH
HOTELS			
under 450 DH	450 DH–700 DH	701 DH–1,000 DH	over 1,000 DH

Agadir

270 km (168 miles) southwest of Marrakesh, 460 km (285 miles) south of Casablanca.

Agadir is, above all else, a holiday resort, so don't hope for a medina, a souk, or a kasbah (although it does have all three, after a fashion). Think sun, sea, and sand. These are what it does best, as hundreds of thousands of visitors each year can testify.

There's no reason to begrudge the city its tourist aspirations. Razed by an earthquake in 1960 that killed 15,000 people in 13 seconds, Agadir had to be entirely rebuilt. Today it's a thoroughly modern city where travelers don't think twice about showing considerable skin, and Moroccans benefit from the growing number of jobs.

There's a reason why this popular European package vacation destination is overrun with enormous, characterless beachfront hotels. The beach, all 10 km (6 miles) of it, is dreamy. A 450-yard-wide strip, it bends in an elegant crescent along the bay, and is covered with fine-grain sand. The beach is sheltered and safe for swimming, making it perfect for families. Farther north, where small villages stand behind some of the best waves in the world, is a surfers' paradise.

Even if you have no interest in surfing, jet-skiing, golf, tennis, or horseback riding down the beach, you can treat Agadir as a modern bubble in which to kick back. It's equipped with familiar pleasurable pursuits—eating, drinking, and relaxing next to the ocean—and modern amenities such as car-rental agencies and ATMs. It isn't quite Europe, but neither is it quite Morocco.

GETTING HERE AND AROUND
Most travelers fly directly into Agadir's Al Massira airport. Although there are no direct flights from North America, connections from Casablanca and European airports are easy. Inexpensive buses are easy ways to get here from Essaouira, Marrakesh, and beyond. If all else fails, grands taxis can take you just about anywhere for the right price.

Once in Agadir, you'll find that downtown is easily navigable on foot, although you may prefer to taxi in from your hotel. The city's orange petits taxis are easy to flag down. Agadir also has many car-rental agencies, including Hertz and Avis.

BUS CONTACTS CTM. ⊠ *Gare Routiere Municipale, Bd. Al Akkad, Agadir* ☎ *0528/82–53–41* ⊕ *www.ctm.ma.* **Supratours.** ⊠ *Gare Routiere Municipale, Bd. Al Akkad, Agadir* ☎ *0528/22–40–10* ⊕ *www.supratours.ma.*

RENTAL CAR CONTACTS Avis. ⊠ *Bungalow Hotel Marhaba, Av. Mohammed V, Agadir* ☎ *0528/82–14–14 downtown, 0528/83–92–44 airport* ⊕ *www.avis.*

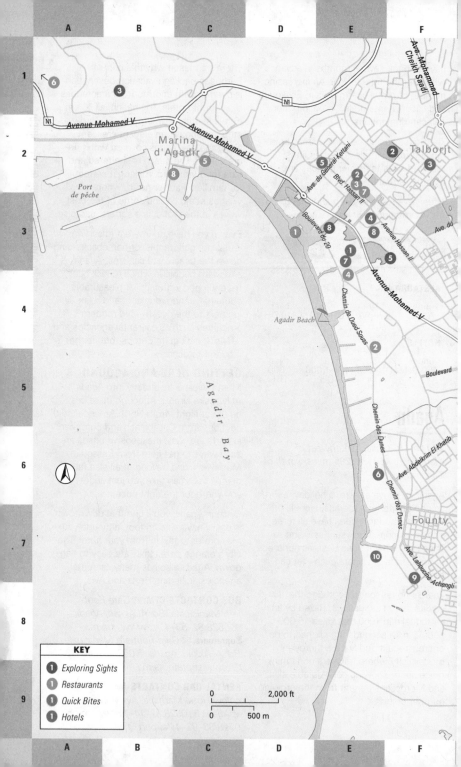

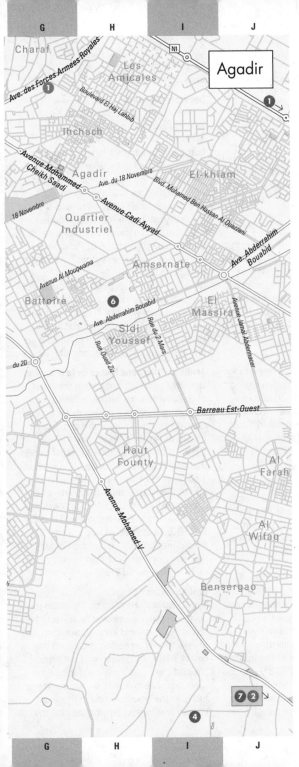

Agadir

Sights ▼

1 Imouzzer Cascades..................J1
2 Jardin de Olhão and
  Musée de la Mémoire.............. F2
3 Kasbah............................. B1
4 La Medina d'Agadir I9
5 Musée Municipale du
  Patrimonie Amazighe F3
6 Souk Al Had H4
7 Souss Massa National Park.......J9
8 Vallée des Oiseaux E3

Restaurants ▼

1 Camel's............................ D3
2 La Scala............................ E4
3 La Siciliana E2
4 Le 20............................... E4
5 Les Blancs......................... C2
6 Let's Be Healing Food A1
7 Little Italy E3
8 Pure Passion B2

Quick Bites ▼

1 Boulangerie Pâtisserie
  Tafarnout G1
2 Le 116 .... E2

Hotels ▼

1 Anezi Tower Hotel E3
2 Dar Maktoub J9
3 Hotel El Bahia F2
4 Hotel Kamal E3
5 Hôtel Petite Suède.................E2
6 Hotel Riu Tikida Dunas E6
7 Mogador Al Madina................E3
8 Résidence Yasmina................E3
9 Riad Villa Blanche F7
10 Sofitel Agadir Thalassa
   Sea & Spa E7

com. **Dan Car.** ⊠ *Av. Mohammed V, Agadir* ☎ *0528/84–46–00.* **Europcar.** ⊠ *Av. Mohammed V, Agadir* ☎ *0528/84–02–03 downtown, 0528/83–90–66 airport* ⊕ *www.europcar.com.* **Exotik Cars.** ⊠ *5, av. Général Kettani, Agadir* ✚ *Next to Hotel Aferni* ☎ *0528/84–11–42* ⊕ *www. exotikcars.net.* **Hertz.** ⊠ *Bungalow Marha-ba, Av. Mohammed V, Agadir* ☎ *0528/84– 09–39 downtown, 0528/83–90–71 airport* ⊕ *www.hertz.com.*

GUIDES AND TOURS

Complete Tours

OTHER TOURS | This English-run operation, based in Agadir with offices in Marrakesh and Casablanca, can put together your whole trip, including hotels, excursions, and meals—everything, in fact, but the flight. ⊠ *Immeuble Oumlil, 26, bd. Has-san II, Agadir* ☎ *0528/82–34–01* ⊕ *www. complete-tours.com.*

Massira Travel

PRIVATE GUIDES | The agency offers a range of private trips with an English-speaking guide all over Morocco, including excursions to Essaouira, Marrakesh, Imouzzer, Tafraoute, Tiznit, and farther afield. ⊠ *25, bd. du 20 Août, Agadir* ☎ *0528/84–77–13* 🖃 *From 300 DH for a full-day trip.*

VISITOR INFORMATION

You can pick up a copy of the bilingual French–English *Agadir Tour Guide* magazine or the French-only *Agadir Premiere Le Mag* in many shops and restaurants. Both offer a better idea of what's on than a trip to the local tourism office.

◉ Sights

For those looking for a more comprehensive tour of town, a touristy yet amusing way to see the town is with the Petit Train, a small white tram with three carriages pulled by a motorcar at the front. It leaves every 40 minutes (9:15 am until 6 pm) from the kiosk at the base of Vallée des Oiseaux on Boulevard 20 Août. Kids love it and it's a great way to get off your

feet. Tickets cost 18 DH, and the ride lasts 35 minutes.

Imouzzer Cascades

WATERFALL | If you're looking for a more isolated and less developed excursion away from the beach, the waterfalls in the Ida Outanane Mountains, near Immouzer des Ida Outananeup, make an ideal day trip from Agadir, with many opportunities for walking and hiking. Check with locals—the waterfalls are often dry when the region is experiencing drought. On your way you'll pass through the palm gorge of Paradise Valley, where the rocky riverbank welcomes picnicking Moroccan families and foreigners alike. The Amazigh souk in Immouzer is on Thursday and is a great place to buy local honey. To get here by car from Aourir (12 km [7 miles] north of Agadir), take the paved road 50 km (31 miles) up into the mountains. ⊠ *Agadir* 🖃 *Free.*

Jardin de Olhão and Musée de la Mémoire

CITY PARK | **FAMILY** | Located in the heart of the city, this garden (also called Jardin du Portugal) offers a pleasant, cool green retreat from the heat of the sun. Built in tribute to Agadir's "twin" city in Portugal, Olhão, it features architecture that recalls that of the Moors of southern Spain. Two pavilions attached to the garden house the Musée de la Mémoire, a moving exhibition of photos and writings documenting the earthquake of February 29,1960, which devastated the city. ⊠ *Av. President Kennedy, at Av. des Forces Armées Royales, Agadir* 🖃 *Museum 10 DH, playground 5 DH.*

Kasbah (*Agadir Oufella*)

RUINS | **FAMILY** | High up on the hill to the northwest that looks over Agadir are the few ruins of the old kasbah, the main site of Agadir until an earthquake razed the city in 1960. The devastating earthquake created the opportunity for the development of modern Agadir, which stands today to the south. Although there is little to see here of the former city, the panoramas are breathtaking, especially at sunset. The only way to get here is to take a bus with ALSA, the public transportation company, from the parking lot at the foot of the mountain. The bus leaves every 20 minutes from 8 am to 9:30 pm (8:30 pm on Saturdays) and costs 4 DH each way.

Emblazoned on the side of the hill below the kasbah are three Arabic words that keep guard over Agadir at all times. Their meaning? God, country, and the king. By day they're a patchwork of huge white stones against the green grass. At night they're lighted up powerfully against the dark. The huge hill is really a burial mound, covering the old medina and the impromptu graves of those who died in the earthquake. ⊠ *Agadir.*

La Medina d'Agadir

MUSEUM VILLAGE | FAMILY | This combination ethnological museum and bazaar is the dream of Moroccan-born Italian decorator-architect Coco Polizzi, who wanted to replace the medina Agadir lost to the 1960 earthquake with a new one on his own land. Located in Ben Sergao, a few miles south of Agadir, on the Inezgane road, the remarkable 13-acre project was completed in 2007 by hundreds of Moroccan craftspeople who used centuries-old techniques. Each stone was laid by hand, and the buildings are made of earth, rock from the Souss, slate from the High Atlas, and local woods such as thuya and eucalyptus. Decorations follow both Amazigh and Saharan motifs. You can find a few mosaic craftspeople, painters, jewelers, metalworkers, and carpenters in workshop nooks throughout the medina. The medina also houses a restaurant, shops, and even an amphitheater. Grands taxis to the medina from Agadir cost around 100 DH round-trip. ☎ *0528/28–02–53* ⊠ *40 DH* ⊗ *Closed during Eid el Adha.*

★ Musée Municipale du Patrimoine Amazighe (*Museum of Amazigh Culture*)

OTHER MUSEUM | Agadir's municipal museum celebrates the Amazigh heritage of the region with collections of photography, jewelry, artifacts, and local handicrafts, as well as temporary exhibits. It's worth a visit to learn about the symbolism seen in Amazigh carpets and jewelry; there's also information about the *Igouder* (plural of *agadir*, a communal granary) of the local villages. If you're lucky, an English-speaking intern may be on hand to guide you around. ⊠ *Passage Aït Souss, Av. Hassan II, Agadir* ☎ *0528/82–16–32* ⊠ *10 DH* ⊗ *Closed Sun.*

Souk Al Had

MARKET | FAMILY | In the northeastern corner of the city, this daily bazaar sells souvenirs, household goods, and the produce of the fertile Souss plains. It's one of the biggest in Morocco, and you'll need to bargain hard. The souk is a great place to witness and participate in real Moroccan life. ⊠ *Av. Abderrahim Bouabid, Agadir* ⊗ *Closed Mon.*

Souss Massa National Park

NATIONAL PARK | This sprawling, 338-square-km (131-square-mile) national park on the coast south of Agadir is a breeding ground for a number of indigenous and migratory bird species, including the bald ibis. There are also captive-breeding programs for four threatened North African antelope and gazelle species, as well as for ostriches, which were previously extinct in Morocco since 1945. Tours are available within the park, which also contains a number of guesthouses and other accommodation options. Many of these support sustainable tourism and offer bird- and animal-watching excursions. One entry point for the park is 15 km (9 miles) south of Agadir at Rokein information center; the other is 60 km (37 miles) south of Agadir at the Sidi Binzarne eco-guide kiosk. ⊠ *Parc National de Souss Massa, Sidi Binzarne* ☎ *0528/33–38–80* ⊠ *Free.*

The area around the Imouzzer Cascades is good for hiking but the waterfalls may be dry if there's a drought.

Vallée des Oiseaux (*Valley of the Birds*)
GARDEN | FAMILY | It's not so much a valley as a pleasure garden connecting Avenue Hassan II to the beach. The garden has not only birds but also monkeys, fountains, and lovely green surroundings. Very popular with Moroccan families and young couples as well as tourists, it makes for a pleasant stroll between downtown and the beachfront. ⊠ *Bd. du 20 Août, Agadir.*

 Beaches

Agadir Beach
BEACH | FAMILY | The beach here swings around a crescent from southeast to northwest; you're more likely to find a quiet spot if you wander south, although be careful to avoid the private beaches of the resorts. The most crowded areas, frequented year-round by families and locals, are to the north. Along the flanking thoroughfare, known as the Corniche (promenade), are cafés, bars, and restaurants. At the very northern end is the swanky marina development where

private yachts are moored. The promenade comes alive at dusk, when families and youngsters take their evening walks, but as night falls, it can become a little sketchy. Nonetheless, from the shelter of a café terrace, it's still a good spot to stop and watch the world go by. The northern tip is also the place to rent a Jet Ski, catamaran, or surf equipment. **Amenities:** food and drink; water sports. **Best for:** sunset. ⊠ *Agadir.*

Taghazout
BEACH | This is the area to visit if you want to tackle some of Morocco's best surfing, though you probably won't be alone. In summer the beaches on the Essaouira road—especially those in the rapidly expanding Taghazout area 20 km (12 miles) north of Agadir—are crammed with Moroccan families (who often camp there). Catering to their needs is a range of cafés, hostels, and rental apartments. While Taghazout village still feels like a rough-and-ready surfers' frontier town, the area just south, called Taghazout Bay, is being developed with luxury and

family resorts in the hopes of attracting a more upmarket clientele. **Amenities:** food and drink; water sports. **Best for:** sunset, surfing; swimming. ⊠ *Tagazout*.

Tamraght
BEACH | Smaller, less developed, and with much more of a local vibe, Tamraght is the laid-back little sibling of Taghazout. It spills down the side of a mountain toward the national coastal road and has a beautiful, spacious beach. New hotel and upscale vacation villa developments have begun to spring up, but there's still a natural feel to the coastline, where a new foot and bike path of about 5 km (3 miles) leads directly into Taghazout. You can stay in surf houses, private apartments, and small boutique hotels, enjoying the quiet nights and the sound of the rushing ocean. The area is 15 km (9 miles) north of Agadir. **Amenities:** food and drink; parking (fee); showers; toilets. *Best for:* sunset; surfing; swimming. ⊠ *Tamraght*.

🍴 Restaurants

Agadir is famous for its fish and seafood, as well as its lively deep-sea fishing port (Morocco's busiest), where you can eat lunch at the stalls. Each stall offers nearly identical food, including squid, prawns, sole, lobster, and whiting, and for nearly identical prices. So walk around and pick what you'd like; the better-organized stalls have chalkboards listing the catch of the day and the price. Frequented by locals and travelers alike, the port is a great bet for cheap and fun eats, and it shares space with Morocco's swankiest marina, which is becoming a sophisticated culinary hot spot.

Although neon signs throughout Agadir lure you in to sample not so much the delights of Moroccan cuisine as the woes of fast food and international menus, many of these restaurants do have convenient locations along the beachfront or in the town center. Downtown has a good selection of Italian, French, Thai, and even Japanese and Indian restaurants.

All major hotels have both Moroccan and international restaurants, a reality that has led to the sad demise of many well-established local restaurants.

Les Blancs
$$$$ | **SPANISH** | At the edge of Agadir's trendy Marina district, Les Blancs is a shiny, white, modernist retreat serving colorful Spanish paellas, including black squid ink rice, green rice with veggies, and red king prawns. In addition to the contemporary indoor dining room, an informal bar-cum-restaurant with board-walk-style flooring and huge windows overlooks the bay, as does the outdoor terrace with woven seagrass umbrellas. **Known for:** reservations advised in high season; Spanish-style tapas; good wine selection. $ *Average main: DH180* ⊠ *Rte. Marina, Agadir* ☎ *0528/82–83–68.*

Camel's
$$ | **INTERNATIONAL** | Fantastic camel tagines remain the highlight of the largely international menu at this beachside restaurant, as the name suggests. Like its neighbors, it caters to all audiences with candlelit tables, flat-screen TVs, live music, and a wine list. **Known for:** beach area with food delivery; worthy paella; jambalaya chicken. $ *Average main: DH90* ⊠ *Bd. Tawada (Rue de la Plage), Agadir* ☎ *0528/82–85–60.*

Let's Be Healing Food
$$$ | **ECLECTIC** | Located in Tamraght, a small surf village 15 km (9 miles) north of Agadir, this oasis of mostly plant-based and wellness-oriented foods is an unconventional experience for Morocco. **Known for:** superfood smoothies; raw chocolate desserts; house-made kombucha. $ *Average main: DH100* ⊠ *Tamraght* ☎ *0639/27–43–91.*

Little Italy

$$ | **ITALIAN** | One of the better choices among the many Moroccan-style Italian restaurants in the area, Little Italy is a little more subdued in decor and laid-back in style than others on the strip. You'll eat pasta and pizza surrounded by black-and-white photos and dark wooden banisters. **Known for:** extensive wine list; large portions; high-quality food. $ *Average main: DH80* ✉ *Av. Hassan II, Agadir* ☎ *0528/82–00–39* ⓦ *Closed Mon.*

★ Pure Passion

$$$$ | **MEDITERRANEAN** | The passion in the name of this sophisticated restaurant is for Mediterranean-style food made from fresh, local produce. This means lots of seafood and pasta dishes, but also steak and stunning desserts. **Known for:** attentive staff; terrace seating option with marina views; long wine list. $ *Average main: DH190* ✉ *Marina, Agadir* ☎ *0528/84–01–20* ⊕ *www.purepassion. ma.*

La Scala

$$$$ | **SEAFOOD** | At one of Agadir's finest fish restaurants, you can enjoy excellent quality seafood including lobster and John Dory; there's also a tasty duck breast for those who prefer meat. It's ideally located across from the beach-front strip of resort hotels. **Known for:** good service; better atmosphere inside than on the terrace; prix-fixe options. $ *Average main: DH200* ✉ *Rue de l'Oued Souss, Complexe Tamelt, Agadir* ☎ *0528/84–67–73.*

La Siciliana

$$ | **PIZZA** | With a broad menu of pizzas, homemade pasta, and Italian desserts, this Moroccan-run Italian eatery is a favorite among locals amid the string of Italian restaurants that line Avenue Hassan II. They can also deliver, should you crave a quiet night in, but they don't serve alcohol. **Known for:** credit cards have a minimum; best pizza in town; friendly service. $ *Average main: DH70*

✉ *65–67, av. Hassan II, near Vallée des Oiseaux, Agadir* ☎ *0528/82–09–73* ⓦ *Closed during Ramadan.*

★ Le 20

$$$ | **MOROCCAN** | This chic eatery, formerly Le P'tit Dôme (and still sometimes referred to as such), offers an impressive menu of Moroccan specialties and local seafood, with a large Moroccan and French wine list—champagne included—to boot. Sit on the terrace or in the black-and-white dining room. **Known for:** fine-dining atmosphere; good-value fixed menus; house-baked bread. $ *Average main: DH100* ✉ *20, bd. Août, Agadir* ☎ *0528/84–08–05* ⊕ *le20.ma.*

☕ Coffee and Quick Bites

Boulangerie Pâtisserie Tafarnout

$ | **CAFÉ** | A good stop in the center of town, this popular bakery serves a wide range of breads, cakes, and traditional Moroccan pastries for breakfast, lunch, or a light snack. Highlights include buttery croissants, indulgent cakes, savory panini, and sandwiches. **Known for:** excellent coffee; delicious French pastries; good, fast service. $ *Average main: DH40* ✉ *Av. Hassan II, Agadir* ☎ *0528/84–44–50* ⓦ *No dinner.*

★ Le 116

$ | **FAST FOOD** | Small but buzzy, this cash-only salad-and-crepe bar offers great-value healthy snacks and small meals, including DIY salads, quiches, and panini. It attracts local office workers, foreign residents, and tourists for its healthy food, excellent Italian espresso, and fresh juices and smoothies. **Known for:** lots of vegetarian options; salads in three sizes; fast service. $ *Average main: DH40* ✉ *116, av. des Forces Armées Royales, Agadir* ☎ *0528/82–03–12* ▤ *No credit cards* ⓦ *Closed Sun. and during Ramadan.*

The city of Agadir, rebuilt after an earthquake in 1960, is known for its wide beach and modern resorts.

Hotels

Besides a couple of boutique guesthouses, you can forget riad-style intimacy in Agadir; your choices are mainly executive-style functionality or giant beachfront complexes that cater primarily to European package tours. As a general rule the luxury (and price) increases as you move southward down the beach, where five-star resort complexes are still being built.

The hotels along Boulevard du 20 Août leading onto Chemin des Dunes have so many amenities and restaurants that you'll feel no need to leave their beachside complexes. Indeed, more and more hotels are becoming all-inclusive. Be wary of these, however, as they don't guarantee fine dining, and many local experts think they will lead to a slip in standards. If you just need a bed while passing through Agadir, less expensive, basic hotels can be found in the center of town, north of the beach. There's also a lively trade in "*résidences,*" self-catering apartments that you can rent by the night.

Anezi Tower Hotel

$$ | **HOTEL** | Although the Anezi has a crisp and somewhat sterile, business-oriented vibe, the guest rooms are spacious and comfortable, with balconies that have lovely views of the sea or the inner courtyard, pool, and garden areas. **Pros:** three beautiful swimming pools; easy beach access; wheelchair-accessible option. **Cons:** slow service; limited breakfast foods; Wi-Fi intermittent or nonexistent. [$] *Rooms from: DH700* ✉ *Bd. Mohammed V, Agadir* ☎ *0528/84–09–40* 🌐 *www.hotelaneziagadir.com* 🛏 *237 rooms* 🍴 *Free Breakfast.*

★ **Dar Maktoub**

$$$$ | **B&B/INN** | Set on the edge of the Souss-Massa National Park, within easy reach of Agadir, Dar Maktoub is a gorgeous, modern boutique hotel with a beautiful garden. **Pros:** large gardens and pool; stellar service in an intimate location; close to golf courses. **Cons:** no other restaurants nearby; not wheelchair accessible; a taxi or rented car required to reach Agadir. $ *Rooms from: DH1045* ✉ *Av. Moulay Ali Cherif, Inezgane, Agadir* ☎ *0661/37–63–44* ⊕ *www.darmaktoub. com* ⇨ *10 rooms* ⦿| *Free Breakfast.*

Hotel El Bahia

$ | HOTEL | If you're not desperate for beach views and don't mind a 20-minute walk to get there, then El Bahia is a central and good-value option. **Pros:** close to local markets and restaurants; some rooms have terraces; patio for relaxing. **Cons:** some rooms have shared bathroom; cash required for payment; few amenities. $ *Rooms from: DH250* ✉ *Rue el Mehdi Ibn Toumert, Agadir* ☎ *0528/82–39–54* ▭ *No credit cards* ⇨ *27 rooms* ⦿| *Free Breakfast.*

Hotel Kamal

$$ | HOTEL | If you don't need to be near the beach, this affordable option in downtown Agadir is pleasant and airy and offers consistently decent value. **Pros:** parking on-site; clean and neat; nice pool. **Cons:** can be busy with groups; roadside rooms noisy; no restaurant, but there are plenty nearby. $ *Rooms from: DH465* ✉ *Bd. Hassan II, Agadir* ☎ *0528/84–28–17* ⊕ *www.facebook.com/hotelkamalagadir/* ⇨ *128 rooms* ⦿| *Free Breakfast.*

Hôtel Petite Suède

$ | HOTEL | While the name is a little baffling (it means "small Sweden"), this is an inexpensive hotel run by a Moroccan family. **Pros:** close to beach; basic but very affordable option; friendly staff. **Cons:** Wi-Fi can be intermittent; cash only for payment; drab and old-fashioned design. $ *Rooms from: DH350* ✉ *Corner of Av. Hassan II and Av. General Kettani, Agadir* ☎ *0528/84–07–79* ⊕ *www.petitesuede. com* ▭ *No credit cards* ⇨ *24 rooms* ⦿| *Free Breakfast.*

Hotel Riu Tikida Dunas

$$$$ | RESORT | FAMILY | One of three Riu resorts on the beachfront, this one gives

you value for your money as all-inclusive options go (drinks are also included), and although rooms are nothing special, the huge complex as a whole is well designed. **Pros:** miniclub for kids; pretty pools; large gardens. **Cons:** 40-minute walk from city center; minimum five-night stay; very busy with package tour groups. $ *Rooms from: DH2500* ✉ *Chemin des Dunes, Agadir* ☎ *0528/84–90–90* ⊕ *www.riu.com* ⇨ *406 rooms* ⦿| *All-Inclusive.*

Mogador Al Madina

$$$ | HOTEL | Part of the Moroccan Mogador Hotels & Resorts chain, this complex, near but set back from the beach, lacks the wide-open vistas of other resorts but is slightly quieter. **Pros:** generous breakfast; friendly and helpful staff; nice pool. **Cons:** no Wi-Fi in rooms; no real views; overpriced for what you get. $ *Rooms from: DH980* ✉ *Bd. du 20 Août, Agadir* ☎ *0528/29–80–00* ⊕ *www. mogadorhotels.com* ⇨ *232 rooms* ⦿| *Free Breakfast.*

Résidence Yasmina

$$$ | HOTEL | FAMILY | Common areas at this self-catering complex have impressive hand-painted tiles and trickling fountains, but pass up the older, outdated apartments for one of the 30 newer suites and apartments on the upper floors. **Pros:** central location; two pools (one for kids); balconies with great views. **Cons:** can be noisy from road at night; elevator only goes to fifth floor (of six); not on the beachfront. $ *Rooms from: DH800* ✉ *Rue de la Jeunesse, off Av. Hassan II, Agadir* ☎ *0528/84–26–60* ⇨ *114 apartments* ⦿| *No Meals.*

★ Riad Villa Blanche

$$$$ | B&B/INN | An elegant boutique hotel—it was the first of its kind in Agadir—Riad Villa Blanche feels as though it has been plucked from the chicest Marrakesh address and dropped at the edge of the ocean. **Pros:** excellent service; sophisticated decor in mix of styles; spa and massage center on-site. **Cons:** the

bar can be noisy at night; far from main tourist beach or downtown; surrounded by large hotel resorts. [$] *Rooms from: DH1900* ⊠ *50 Baie des Palmiers, Cité Founty, Agadir* ☎ *0528/21–13–13* ⊕ *www.riadvillablanche.com* ⤳ *28 rooms* ⦿ *No Meals.*

⭐ **Sofitel Agadir Thalassa Sea & Spa**

$$$$ | **RESORT** | If luxury is important to you, or total relaxation and detox, this Sofitel in Agadir is for you. **Pros:** direct beach access; heated pool; great health and fitness facilities. **Cons:** far from town center and main tourist beach; rooms are open plan to the bathroom; corridors are rather dark. [$] *Rooms from: DH2300* ⊠ *Baie des Palmiers, Secteur Touristique, Cité Founty P5, Agadir* ☎ *0528/38–80–00* ⊕ *www.sofitel.com* ⤳ *173 rooms* ⦿ *Free Breakfast.*

Nightlife

For many in Agadir, nightlife constitutes a stroll along the waterfront and a coffee with friends. But with its relaxed mores, Agadir can be a clubbing hot spot, particularly for young people looking to cut loose. Many places don't get going until after midnight, but the beachfront is always busy earlier on, with diners and drinkers making the most of the beach environment. Although Agadir lacks the class of Marrakesh, a number of places, mostly based in the resort hotels, are putting up some decent competition.

Be warned: nighttime also attracts many prostitutes, some underage, who throng the cheap bars. The authorities aren't afraid to imprison foreigners who patronize them. Hotel clubs tend to have a more exclusive patronage; in general, the more expensive the drinks, the fancier the clientele. Many bars and clubs close during the Muslim holy month of Ramadan.

BARS
Maxwell

BARS | Live music and a cool, local atmosphere are the draws of this bar and restaurant near the beach. The crowd is mostly local thirty- and fortysomething local professionals. The live music is a house band that does English-language covers and some local English-language and contemporary Amazigh music as well. The vibe is that of a feel-good community. ⊠ *Rue Oued Souss, complexe Touristique Tamlelt, Agadir* ☎ *0528/84–05–80.*

Zanzibar

BARS | Those looking for postdinner, preclub drinks with a touch of East African colonial elegance should stop by Zanzibar at the Riu Tikida Beach Resort. ⊠ *Hotel Riu Tikida Beach, Rte. de L'Oued Sous (Chemin des Dunes), Agadir* ☎ *0528/84–54–00.*

CLUBS
Actor's

DANCE CLUBS | Part of the Royal Atlas Hotel, Actor's attracts a young crowd with its playlist of Western dance, house, and R&B music, often with well-known Moroccan and Arab hits toward the end of the night. *Shisha* (a hookah water pipe) is also available. ⊠ *Royal Atlas Hotel, Bd. 20 Août, Agadir* ☎ *0528/29–40–40.*

Papagayo

DANCE CLUBS | A long-standing favorite is Papagayo, attached to the Riu Tikida Beach resort, which attracts international DJs pumping out fairly mainstream tunes. ⊠ *Hotel Riu Tikida Beach, Rte. de L'Oued Sous (Chemin des Dunes), Agadir* ☎ *0528/84–54–00.*

Shopping

CRAFTS
Baz'Art Salam

CRAFTS | Offering a wide range of quality Moroccan-made items at fixed prices near the Lebanese mosque, the store features modern twists on classic

Western Sahara

In 1975 more than 350,000 unarmed Moroccans walked south in the Green March, taking possession from the Spanish of what are now officially known as Morocco's Southern Provinces (though internationally known as the Western Sahara). Since 1975, conflict between the Polisario (Saharan separatists) and the Moroccan military has been sporadic, and a referendum to determine the province's political future has been postponed numerous times. There is currently a ceasefire, and the U.N. has a large presence in the region's big cities. Foreign visitors to the area are likely to be surfers or here on business, as Morocco is encouraging significant investments in the area. The main attraction for the traveler, aside from the journey to the middle of nowhere, is a chance to set foot in the Sahara, as the cities are new and charmless, food and wine scarce, and the military presence pervasive. However, there are several towns worth visiting before crossing the disputed border.

At the time of writing, tourists with Moroccan entry stamps were free to travel to the Southern Provinces. However, the situation is politically charged, so check before you head this far south and be prepared for numerous police checkpoints. These are usually amicable, but it could be worth it to prepare a form with your vital information printed in French, especially if you don't speak the language (which has replaced the Spanish of the colonial era).

The Towns

Guelmim is known as the Gateway to the Sahara, and the ensuing drive south to Tan-Tan—along which the landscape turns ever more arid and desertlike—illustrates why. It's an easy trip (107 km [66 miles] south of Tiznit), shooting through empty stretches of flat *hamada* (stony desert) broken only by the occasional village or café and one gas station. Although you're likely to catch your first glimpse of large camel herds here, the town doesn't have much to entertain a tourist, and even the exotic-sounding camel market is little more than an average weekly souk.

As you approach **Tan-Tan** (125 km [78 miles] south of Guelmim), you may think you're seeing a giant mirage. Fear not, for your eyes do not deceive you: there really are two enormous kissing camels forming an archway over the road into town. Carved out of stone in the 1970s, these affectionate creatures are one of Tan-Tan's chief claims to fame and the subjects of many a Western Sahara postcard. Tan-Tan's main significance (beyond the kissing camels) is that it was the official starting point for the Green March of 1975. The southern end of Boulevard Mohammed V is Tan-Tan's main square, Place de la Marche Verte (Green March Square). This is the main transportation hub for taxis and cars headed back to Guelmim and on to Laayoune. The town makes a logical stop on a trip farther south and is a passable choice for an overnight stay, although some tourists report unfriendly locals. The beach here, Tan-Tan Plage, is popular with surfers.

At 150 km (93 miles) south of Tan-Tan, the modest fishing village of **Akhfenir** has the first gas station, cafés, and stores on the coastal route after Tan-Tan. Footpaths down to a gorgeous beach make Akhfenir a good place for an en-route swimming stop. At 85 km (53 miles) south of Akhfenir, you'll find the largest of the few coastal towns on this route and the last before the disputed border. **Tarfaya** offers panoramic ocean views, excellent seafood, and a nice place to explore before the road turns inland.

Laayoune, the former capital of the Spanish Sahara, has thrived under Moroccan rule. A calm and easy place to navigate, Laayoune (115 km [71 miles] south of Tarfaya) makes the best base for trips around the Western Sahara. It's quite impressive to look around at surrounding dunes and landscape and contemplate the very existence of a town this size in the middle of the Sahara Desert. Moroccan investment is pouring into the town to capitalize on the benefits of deep-sea fishing, and any Moroccans one encounters are as likely to be from elsewhere, drawn here by construction work, fishing, and government subsidies.

Smara's central site has long been an important Saharan caravan stop, but most of the fun, it must be said, is in getting here. Once you *are* in Smara, however, the remains of the Palace Ma el-Ainin make a great stopping point. There is a guardian who will be happy to show you around, if you can find him. Smara is 219 km (135 miles) east of Laayoune via N5 and N14.

Dakhla, 536 km (331 miles) south of Laayoune, is the last frontier for most travelers to the Western Sahara, as there is little else south of here until you reach the Mauritanian border. Dakhla's main attractions are its superb beaches and the surrounding cliff, and it's become a magnet for kitesurfers. As a result, many guesthouses and surf companies are setting up in Dakhla to meet the growing demand from this market. At least one well-established outfit also has a base in Essaouira: Ocean Vagabond (⊕www.oceanvagabond.com). In recent years, the Moroccan government has invested heavily in infrastructure development in the town, and since 2006 Dakhla has celebrated the meeting of ocean and desert with the annual Dakhla Festival, held in February.

Getting Here and Around

Unless you're arriving by plane, be prepared for a long journey to reach this region. The CTM (⊕www.ctm.ma) and Supratours (⊕www.supratours.ma) bus lines operate services most days from major cities to Laayoune (13 hours from Casablanca, 10 hours from Marrakesh, 8 hours from Agadir) and to Dakhla (20 hours from Casablanca, 17 hours from Marrakesh, 14 hours from Agadir). The national airline, Royal Air Maroc, operates flights from Casablanca to both Laayoune and Dakhla. Flying is probably the most convenient and hassle-free way to approach this less-developed area.

crafts such as Fez leather bags, glazed ceramics, oversize candles, and Sens de Marrakech cosmetics. It's owned by two brothers who speak excellent English and are happy to advise on purchases without being pushy. ✉ *124–126, av. des Forces Armées Royales, Agadir* ☎ *0528/82–45–53.*

★ Kasbat Souss
CRAFTS | Established by an association of local artisans, this complex of more than 60 shops a short distance outside town sells leather products, woodwork, jewelry, pottery, candles, sculpture, embroidery, and argan oil. It's a relaxed place to wander and browse without any of the usual souk hassle, and prices are reasonable. There's also a small café at the center. You can take a taxi from downtown Agadir for around 50 DH. ✉ *Rte. d' Inzegane, Km 5, Agadir ✛ Just after Palais Royale* ☎ *0528/28–19–43* ⊕ *kasbatsouss.com.*

Palais du Sud
CRAFTS | For an emporium of carpets, ceramics, leather, lanterns, and ornate boxes, visit Palais du Sud. Behind the golden doors, all goods have price tags, which makes buying hassle-free. It's closed Sunday. ✉ *Rue de la Foire, north of Av. Hassan II, Agadir* ☎ *0528/84–35–00.*

JEWELRY
Madd
JEWELRY & WATCHES | This boutique jewelry store selling some more modern designs entices you with 18-carat gold from behind a warm wooden exterior. Custom creations are a specialty. There's another branch in the Marina development at the north end of Agadir beach. ✉ *38–40, av. Hassan II, Agadir* ☎ *0528/84–05–92.*

MARKET
Uniprix
MARKET | A large indoor bazaar with fixed prices, the store offers Moroccan artisanal goods, souvenirs, a small grocery area with some Western foods

like peanut butter (not too common here), and a full selection of international wines, beers, and spirits. ✉ *Av. Hassan II, opposite Pl. de l'Espérance, Agadir* ☎ *0528/84–18–41* ⊕ *uniprix.ma.*

WOMEN'S CLOTHING
Nomad Boutique Concept Store
WOMEN'S CLOTHING | Owned and operated by Morgane and Majid, this boho-chic women's fashion boutique serves the women of Agadir and visitors from all over the world. The carefully curated mix of clothing from Europe and handmade Moroccan creations helps give your wardrobe a multicultural, eco-friendly makeover. The store is closed Sunday. ✉ *23, av. du Prince Moulay Abdallah, Agadir* ☎ *0682/15–84–96.*

Activities

GOLF
Golf de L'Océan
GOLF | Opened in 2009 along Agadir's coast, the Golf de L'Océan was designed by Belt Collins and is part of the Atlantic Palace Hotel resort (note: hotel is closed for renovations at time of writing). It's open to both resort guests and the public. ✉ *Agadir* ☎ *0528/27–35–42* ⊕ *www.golfdelocean.com* ⛳ *From 400 DH for 9 holes; from 700 DH for 18 holes* ⛳ *Desert course: 9 holes, 3128 yards, par 36; Garden course: 9 holes, 3126 yards, par 36; Dunes course: 9 holes, 2949 yards, par 35.*

Golf du Soleil
GOLF | This American-style, championship course was designed in a classic style amid a eucalyptus forest and has several challenging obstacles. Guests of any of the three Tikida resorts in Agadir receive a discount and shuttle bus service to and from the hotels. ✉ *Chemin des Dunes, Agadir* ☎ *0528/33–73–30* ⊕ *www.tikidagolfpalace.com* ⛳ *From 420 DH for 9 holes; from 700 DH for 18 holes* ⛳ *Championship course: 18 holes, 6057*

yards, par 72; Tikida course 18 holes, 6535 yards, par 72.

Golf Les Dunes

GOLF | At this American-style golf course 10 km (6 miles) south of central Agadir, the 27-hole course (three 9-hole courses) runs over hilly, thickly wooded country-side. Free shuttles operate from various hotels in town. ⊠ *Chemin Oued Souss, Agadir* ☎ *0528/83–46–90* ⊕ *www.golf-lesdunesagadir.com* 🖃 *From 500 DH for 9 holes; from 700 DH for 18 holes* 🏌. *Eucalyptus course: 9 holes, 3416 yards, par 36; Oued course: 9 holes, 3358 yards, par 36; Tamaris course: 9 holes, 3472 yards, par 36.*

Royal Golf Club

GOLF | Established in 1952 by a Scots-man, the Royal Golf Club is Agadir's oldest. One of the smaller courses in Agadir, covering more than 30 acres with English-style Bermuda 419 and Cucuyo grass, it is 12 km (7 miles) south of Aga-dir on the road to Aït Melloul. ⊠ *Km 12, Rte. Aït Melloul, Agadir* ☎ *0528/24–85–51* 🖃 *From 200 DH for 9 holes; from 280 DH for 18 holes* 🏌. *9 holes, 2932 yards, par 36.*

JET-SKIING

Club Royal de Jet Ski

JET SKIING | At the north end of Agadir beach, near the marina entrance, you'll find Jet Skis for rent. The honorary president of the Club Royal de Jet Ski is actually Moroccan king Mohammed VI, although it's unlikely you'll find him here. ⊠ *Agadir* 🖃 *From 350 DH for ½ hr.*

SPAS

Le Spa Villa Blanche

SPAS | Seven kinds of massages using Western and Eastern techniques and essential oils are offered in the sumptu-ous, candlelit spa of Riad Villa Blanche. It also has a heated swimming pool and a hamman. You can choose from a Sahara hot-sand massage, an "après-souk" massage, or an energizing massage with argan oil and lemon. A steam bath and

a scrub includes a full-body exfoliation, and steam bath packages including a massage and a blow-dry hair styling are available. ⊠ *Riad Villa Blanche, 50 Baie des Palmiers, Cité Founty, Agadir* ☎ *0528/21–13–13* ⊕ *riadvillablanche. com* 🖃 *From 200 DH for steam bath and scrub; from 600 DH for steam bath package with massage.*

SURFING

Surfers the world over rate Morocco's southern Atlantic coast one of the world's best places to catch waves. The recent surfer boom in the region has helped create countless surf schools, many run by foreigners who came to surf and then simply couldn't tear themselves away. Many surf shops and schools are based in Tamraght, 15 km (9 miles) north of Agadir, and Taghazout, 20 km (12 miles) north of Agadir. From there, instructors will take clients to local bays and points according to wind and tides.

Original Surf Morocco

SURFING | A professional, Moroc-can-owned outfit, Original Surf Morocco is based in Tamraght, a village famous for its bananas and beaches, about 15 km (9 miles) north of Agadir. It offers surfing lessons and accommodations in a surf hostel. ⊠ *Tamraght* ☎ *0707/73–77–98 WhatsApp, 0808/50–64–05* ⊕ *www. originalsurfmorocco.com.*

Surf Town Morocco

SURFING | At this surf school and guest-house 15 km (9 miles) north of Agadir in Tamraght, English-speaking instructors can take you to local surfing points like Boiler, Killer Point, and Devil's Rock. The type of instruction depends on the experience of the surfer and the length of time chosen. Inexpensive accommo-dations are also available with half-board. ⊠ *Tamraght* ☎ *0664/47–81–76* ⊕ *www. surftownmorocco.com* 🖃 *From 350 DH for ½-day surfing lesson; board rental 100 DH per day.*

Essaouira

171 km (106 miles) north of Agadir.

Once Morocco's main trading port and a stronghold of Jewish culture, Essaouira became famed as a hippie hangout for surfers and expat artists in the 20th century, though these days the city offers its cool breezes and relaxed atmosphere to a broader range of visitors. The windy city remains a favorite destination for its picturesque fishing harbor, medina walls, blue shutters, twisting *derbs* (alleyways), and sea, sand, and surf. The scenic waterfront has appeared on film and TV, too, including as Astapor in the third season of *Game of Thrones*.

Essaouira pretty much has a nine-month high season, from mid-March until early November, with extra peaks around Christmas, New Year's, and the hugely popular Gnaoua and World Music Festival in June. More hotels and guesthouses have opened in recent years, including a five-star resort and golf course south of the town in Diabat, but the town remains peaceful in its laid-back bustle—an enticing blend of fishing port, historical medina, and seaside haven.

GETTING HERE AND AROUND

Essaouira's airport is served by only a handful of European budget airlines, so the easiest and most common way to get here is by bus. There is no train service and little parking space for private cars, but road connections are good; and buses can get you efficiently and easily to and from Agadir, Casablanca, and Marrakesh. The drive from Marrakesh or Agadir to Essaouira takes about three hours, with bus companies Supratours and CTM operating several daily services. Grands taxis are also an option.

The coastal trip from Agadir on the P8/N1 road to Essaouira is one of the most stunning drives in Morocco. If you're driving, you can stop and relax at several turnoffs from the main road.

The medina of Essaouira is compact, pedestrian-friendly, and easily walkable. Outside the walls, the local petits taxis are blue and have a fixed price of 7 DH during the day and 8 DH after 8 pm. A journey to Diabat costs 30 DH to 50 DH. You can hail the taxis on the street or pick them up at taxi stands outside the main medina gates.

Several local travel agents can arrange day trips and longer tours in a minibus or 4x4.

BUS CONTACTS CTM Essaouira. ⊠ *Pl. 11 Janvier, Quartier Borj, Ville Nouvelle, Essaouira* ☎ *0524/78–47–64* ⊕ *www.ctm.ma.* **Supratours.** ⊠ *South Bastion, Essaouira* ⊹ *Across from Borj Bab Marrakech* ☎ *0524/47–53–17* ⊕ *www.supratours.ma.*

RENTAL CARS Chaaba Cars. ⊠ *7.01, rue Mae El Aaynine, Lotissement 4, Essaouira* ☎ *0600/05–15–30* ⊕ *www.chaabacar.com.* **El Ghazwa Car.** ⊠ *501, av. Al Aqaba, Lot 4, Essaouira* ☎ *0524/78–48–41, 0661/66–18–41.*

PLANNING YOUR TIME

Weekend visitors to Essaouira often leave wishing they had more time. If you can, plan to spend several days in this relaxing seaside town. The most popular time to visit is summer, but the best time is September when both tourist numbers and winds drop. Although the temperature is tolerable year-round, this is Africa's windy city, so don't expect to swim before May or after September.

FESTIVALS

Essaouira hosts three major festivals each year: Le Printemps Musical des Alizés, a classical and chamber music festival held in April; Gnaoua and World Music Festival, a mix of jazz, rock, pop, and world music held in June; and Le Festival des Andalousies Atlantiques, which showcases Arabo-Andalusian music and flamenco at the end of October.

★ Gnaoua and World Music Festival

MUSIC FESTIVALS | Essaouira is always packed over the third weekend of June, as tens of thousands of people from all over the world come to enjoy the annual four-day Gnaoua and World Music Festival. It's one of the best times to listen to traditional Gnaoua musicians. These descendants of enslaved Africans established associations across Morocco and are healers and mystics as well as musicians. Among their troupes of metal castanet (*krakab*) players, bass lute (*gimbri*) players, and drummers, they have mediums and clairvoyants who perform wild, spellbinding acts. ■TIP→ **If you plan to visit the festival, make sure you reserve accommodations at least three months in advance as hotels and guesthouses will be full.** ✉ *Essaouira* ⊕ *www.festival-gnaoua. net* 🎫 *Free; may have fees for special events.*

TOURS

Be in Nature Tours

GUIDED TOURS | This reliable outfitter puts together half or full day hiking excursions around Essaouira, into the dunes or oases. Guides trained in geology or bird-watching enhance the experience. ✉ *Essaouira* ⊕ *be-in-naturetours.com/en/ trekking-essaouira/.*

 Sights

Bayt Dakira (*House of Memory*)

HISTORY MUSEUM | A new historical, cultural, and spiritual landmark in Essaouira, this museum in the Mellah dedicated to Jewish heritage and culture celebrates the Moroccan Jewish culture that once dominated Essaouira, as well as the continuing mutual respect between Muslim and Jewish communities in Morocco. Within the space are the Simon Attias synagogue, the museum Bayt Dakira, and the Haim and Célia Zafrani International Research Center for the study of the history of relations between Judaism and Islam. The exhibits are based around rare objects and photographs illustrating the history of Jewish life and culture in the area. ✉ *Rue Ziry Ibn Atiyah, Essaouira* ☎ *0524/66-35-87* 🎫 *Free.*

Dar Souiri

ARTS CENTER | Home to the active Essaouira-Mogador Association, Dar Souiri is the hub of cultural life in Essaouira, with a notice board outside the door with information on upcoming festivals, concerts, film screenings, and other cultural events. Inside, the building is an excellent example of 18th-century Mogador (a former name of the city) architecture and houses an art gallery and a library. Free Wi-Fi is available. ✉ *2, rue de Caire, Medina* ☎ *0524/47-52-68* ⊕ *www.essaouiramogador.org* ⊘ *Closed Sun.*

Medina

HISTORIC DISTRICT | The medina isn't so much a sight as the essence of Essaouira, where you are likely to stay, eat, shop, and wander. It was designed by French architect Théodore Cornut in the late 18th century, on the instructions of Sidi Mohammed Ben Abdellah, who wanted to create a new town and port to rival Agadir and demonstrate Morocco's outward focus. Cornut built the kasbah, and the sultan invited prominent Jewish traders to settle here. Mogador (as it was then known) soon thrived.

The medina is a UNESCO World Heritage site, and restoration efforts are underway for some key buildings from Mogador's heyday, namely Simon Attias synagogue (already restored) and the Danish consulate. The former Portuguese consulate and church are earmarked for restoration. All feature the colonnaded ground floor and rooms off internal walkways on the higher levels that are typical of the era. From the kasbah, heading northwest, pass through the Mellah Kdim (old Mellah) before reaching the Mellah proper. It was in this latter area that less affluent Jews settled. Following the end of the French protectorate and the creation of the state of Israel, most of Mogador's

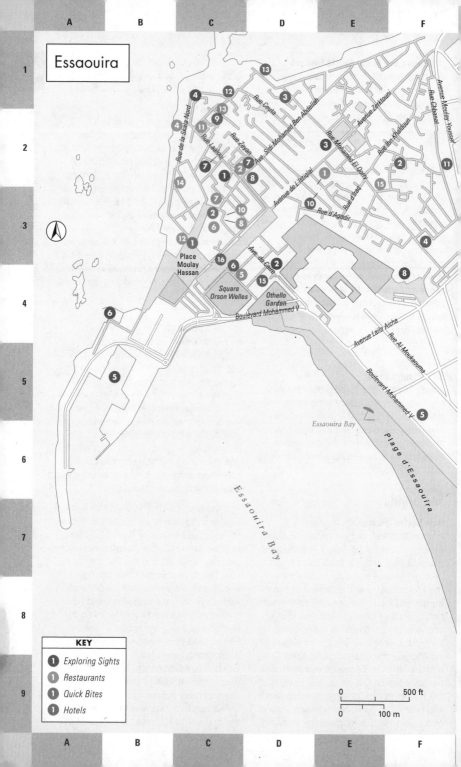

Sights ▼

1 Bayt Dakira **C2**
2 Dar Souiri **D4**
3 Medina **E2**
4 North Bastion and Medina Skala **C1**
5 Port of Essaouira **B5**
6 Port Skala **B4**
7 Sidi Mohammed Ben Abdellah Ethnological Museum **C2**
8 South Bastion **F4**
9 Val d'Argan Vineyard **I4**

Restaurants ▼

1 Caravane Café **D2**
2 Dar Mounia **C2**
3 La Fromagerie **I4**
4 La Licorne **C2**
5 La Table by Madada **C4**
6 Le Mogadorien **C3**
7 Le Patio **C3**
8 The Loft **C3**
9 Platinium **I7**
10 Restaurant Laayoune ... **C3**
11 Silvestro **C2**
12 Taros **C3**
13 Triskala **C1**
14 Umia **C2**
15 Vague Bleue **E2**

Quick Bites ▼

1 Gelateria Dolce Freddo **C3**
2 Pâtisserie Driss **C3**

Hotels ▼

1 Atlas Essaouira and Spa **H9**
2 Dar Liouba **F2**
3 Dar Maya **D1**
4 Heure Bleue Palais **F3**
5 Hotel Le Medina Essaouira Thalassa Sea & Spa MGallery **F5**
6 Madada Mogador **C4**
7 Maison du Sud **D2**
8 Riad Al Madina **D2**
9 Riad Baladin **C2**
10 Riad Chakir Mogador ... **D3**
11 Riad Chbanate **F2**
12 Riad Kafila **C1**
13 Riad Mimouna **D1**
14 Sofitel Essaouira Mogador Golf & Spa **I9**
15 Villa de L'Ô **D4**
16 Villa Maroc **C3**

Jews left and the area became home to poorer urban families and squatters. Today the area is under redevelopment. Two original synagogues can be visited: Synagogue Slat Lkahal and Haïm Pinto Synagogue. The area is best avoided after dark. ■TIP→ **As you approach the Mellah, look for the Star of David carved in stone above doorways.** ✉ *Medina*.

North Bastion and Medina Skala

HISTORIC SIGHT | The distinctive outlines of the medina *skala* (a fortified bastion) and its citadel, known as the North Bastion, frame the waves dramatically at sunset. The bastion once held emergency supplies of fresh water, and the large circle of stones in the center marks what was known as a call-point, or alarm system, to warn of approaching invaders. Guards would warn of danger by stomping on the resonant circle. ■TIP→ **If you stand in the middle of the circle and stomp your foot or yell, you'll hear the echo ring far.** ✉ *Essaouira*.

★ Port of Essaouira

MARINA/PIER | Built in 1769 in the reign of Sidi Mohammed Ben Abdellah by an Englishman who had converted to Islam, Essaouira's port is still going strong in the southwest corner of town, and it's the one must-see sight for any traveler coming here. Trawlers and other boats bob along the quay, and middlemen and independent sailors sell the daily catch of sardines, calamari, and skate from small dockside tables. You'll be selling yourself short if you don't have a meal of the freshest fish imaginable at one of the shoreside grill restaurants. As Moroccan ports go, it's also one of the most beautiful, not to mention accessible and tourist-friendly. ✉ *Essaouira*.

Port Skala

HISTORIC SIGHT | Essaouira has two principal skala, fortified bastions with fabulous cannons: the medina skala and the port skala. Each was a strategic maritime defense point. Unlike the straight-edged Moorish constructions in other Moroccan cities, the ramparts in Essaouira are triangular, so the insider looking out has a broader field of vision than the enemy peering in. Orson Welles filmed scenes of his 1951 film *Othello* from the tower of the port skala, picking up a magnificent panorama of town, port, and bay all in one that can still be seen today. ■TIP→ **The entrance fee is worth it to get the picture-postcard view of the medina through a round opening in the wall.** ✉ *Tangier* 🏛 *10 DH; free for Muslims on Fri.*

Sidi Mohammed Ben Abdellah Ethnological Museum

OTHER MUSEUM | The stunning former French colonial town hall holds this smartly arranged collection of items from everyday and ritual life in and around the Essaouira area. Exhibits include items related to the China tea trade, as part of its tea museum. The permanent collection includes musical instruments of both Gnaoua and Sufi sects; displays of regional carpet styles and wood-carving techniques and motifs; and examples of Muslim, Jewish, and rural Ishelhin Amazigh rites and dress. ✉ *7, rue Laalouj, Medina* ☎ *0524/47–23–00* 🏛 *10 DH* 🕐 *Closed Tues.*

South Bastion

NOTABLE BUILDING | Also known as the Bastion Bab Marrakech, the South Bastion is a carefully restored element of the original fortified medina walls. Managed by the local Delegation of the Culture Ministry, it is open to the public when exhibitions and events take place, like the annual Gnaoua and World Music Festival. The flat roof offers a view over the rooftops to the beach and is often the backdrop to concerts and other performances. The area in front of the bastion (now a parking lot) was the site of the town's original Muslim cemetery. ✉ *Bab Marrakech, Medina*.

Essaouira's medina is a wonderful place to wander, with art galleries, cafés, and traditional-style riads.

Val d'Argan Vineyard

WINERY | Just outside Ounagha, about 35½ km (22 miles) east of Essaouira, is Morocco's first organic vineyard. Established by Charles Melia, an experienced winemaker of the Rhône valley in France, it covers 128 acres, 100 of which are under cultivation. The vineyard produces a selection of ranges and labels featuring red, white, rosé, and—typical in Morocco—*vin gris* (a pale pink variation of rosé made from red grapes) wines. Many of the wines here are commonly featured on wine lists in Essaouira and Marrakesh restaurants. Tours and tastings can be arranged in French, English, or Arabic, and the restaurant on-site has a panoramic view of the vineyard and olive trees. ⊠ *Domaine du Val d'Argan, Ounagha, Essaouira* ☎ *0524/78–34–67* ⊕ *www.valdargan.com* ✉ *Tours free; tastings from 50 DH* ☺ *Closed Sun.*

Beaches

Diabat Beach

BEACH | Essaouira's beach is fine for an early-morning jog or a late-afternoon game of soccer, but serious sunbathers typically head south to quiet Diabat. Walking along the beach, cross over the mouth of the river and continue past the Borj el Baroud, a former Portuguese fortification. To your left, a few miles south of town nestled in eucalyptus fields, you'll see the ruins of the so-called Sultan's Palace. This building is said to have inspired Jimi Hendrix to write "Castles in the Sand," although he actually released the track a couple of years before his visit to this village, which has been trading on his name ever since. On a windy day the only escape is behind the Borj at low tide. **Amenities:** none. **Best for:** solitude; sunset. ⊠ *Diabat* ✛ *A petit taxi can take you to rotary at edge of town (from which point you can walk to beach via unpaved road) or into village of Diabat (via new Sofitel Golf complex).*

Essaouira Bay

BEACH | FAMILY | Essaouira's main beach is a sweep of sand along the bay that has provided shelter to seafarers from Atlantic storms since antiquity. Although temperatures are moderate all year and the sun is nearly always shining, the wind is consistently strong, making sunbathing or swimming less attractive than farther south in Agadir. Nonetheless, sunbed rentals are relatively inexpensive or even free if you eat at one of the cafés at the southern end of the beach.

The wind comes from the north and creates three main areas. The most northerly part, tucked up into the armpit of the port, has wind that comes in gusts. Just south of this the wind strengthens, with fewer gusts. Farther south are the steady, strong trade winds the town is known for, and that make it a mecca for wind and kitesurfers. The range of areas makes the bay perfect for every level of water-sports enthusiast.

The surrounding islets, the Iles de Mogador, are home to nine bird species, including the endangered Eleanora's falcon. They are closed to visitors during breeding season (April to October), but otherwise you can get a boat trip from the port, with boats leaving morning and afternoon depending on weather conditions. **Amenities:** food and drink; lifeguards (summer only); toilets; parking (fee); water sports. **Best for:** sunset; swimming; walking; windsurfing. ⊠ *Essaouira.*

Sidi Kaouki Beach

BEACH | The tranquil beach village of Sidi Kaouki is often touted as an alternative to Essaouira's beach and is a destination of choice for younger backpackers, surfers, and windsurfers, which should give you an idea of the typical wind velocity and wave size. It doesn't have the amenities of its larger neighbor, but the "town" consists of a number of guesthouses, a couple of shops, and some small restaurants all serving the same standard tourist menus. It's easy to rent mountain bikes, quad bikes, or ponies for a jaunt along the beach toward Ouassane (the village to the north) or Sidi M'barek (with a waterfall and wide sandy beach) to the south. ■**TIP→ It's possible to walk along the beach and over a cliff from Essaouira to Sidi Kaouki—about 21 km (13 miles) one-way. Walking in the opposite direction (against the wind) is not recommended. Amenities:** food and drink; parking (fee in summer); toilets; water sports. **Best for:** surfing; sunset; walking. ⊠ *Sidi Kaouki* ✛ *Sidi Kaouki is 27 km (17 miles) south of Diabat. Turnoff is 15 km (9 miles) south of Diabat on Agadir road. No. 2 Lima bus goes to Sidi Kaouki.*

🍴 Restaurants

In Essaouira, you can dine in some great restaurants, from port catches grilled in front of you to inventive and expensive fish dishes in the swankiest restaurants. Seafood tends to headline menus when the surf permits. A must-do experience is lunch or dinner in one of the seafood grills near the port: feast on charcoal-grilled sardines, calamari, red snapper, sea bass, whiting, and shrimp (crab is usually too dry) from among the array of stalls, and experience the color and bustle of the port. You choose your fish, then establish a price based on weight. The later in the day, the lower you'll be able to negotiate the price, but because Essaouira can be very windy, enjoying lunch alfresco in the sun makes more sense than a breezy dinner. This is a great place to go if you are tiring of tagine. You could also take a stroll along Avenue L'Istiqlal (known by locals as "Haddada"), or better still Avenue Mohammed el-Quori (known by locals as "Souk Waka"). Here you'll be able to pack a delicious, locally flavored picnic of salty battered fish, potato patties, stuffed sardines in fresh Moroccan bread, almonds and peanuts, fruit, and sticky Maghrebian sweets.

In addition, there are also lots of traditional Moroccan options and excellent examples of French, Italian, and even Asian food.

Caravane Café

$$$$ | ECLECTIC | This popular, renovated riad filled with the artwork and collections of its host, artist Didier Spindler, offers an imaginative menu that is a fusion of Moroccan, European, and Asian flavors. The decor is an eclectic mix, with Buddha statues, pop art, and palm trees. **Known for:** nightly entertainment; trio of desserts for sharing; hip clientele and atmosphere. $ *Average main: DH160* ⊠ *2 bis, rue Cadi Ayad, Essaouira* ☎ *0524/78–31–11* ☽ *Closed Mon.*

Dar Mounia

$$ | MOROCCAN | Located in the heart of the medina, this unpretentious Moroccan restaurant is spacious and cool. Hidden among the extensive menu of couscous, tagine, and pastilla variations are a few refreshing surprises like a grilled zucchini short-crust tart or a marinated fish kebab. **Known for:** credit cards not accepted; simple, tasty food at a reasonable price; lemon juice with ginger. $ *Average main: DH70* ⊠ *2, rue Laalouj, Medina* ☎ *0524/47–29–88* ⊟ *No credit cards.*

★ La Fromagerie

$$$$ | MEDITERRANEAN | A few miles outside town on the edge of thuya and olive groves, owner Abderrazak welcomes you warmly to his artisanal cheesery and open-air restaurant. Enjoy a fixed-menu lunch of salads topped with local goat- and sheep-milk cheeses, followed by (for nonvegetarians) a *mechoui* (lamb spit roast), and wine to complement. **Known for:** cash required for payment; large portions; wine served with meals. $ *Average main: DH225* ⊠ *Rte. de Safi, Douar Larabe, Essaouira* ✛ *1 km (½ mile) after rotary on Essaouira-Marrakesh road* ☎ *0666/23–35–34* ⊟ *No credit cards.*

La Licorne

$$$ | MOROCCAN | Come to this Moroccan restaurant for a selection of tagines with flavor combinations you don't often find, such as tagine of beef with honey and dried fruits or saffron chicken with almonds. It has an excellent selection of seafood dishes and desserts, along with a selection of Morocco's finest wines. **Known for:** cash required for payment; beautiful, romantic atmosphere; extensive selection of Moroccan and foreign wines. $ *Average main: DH95* ⊠ *26, rue de la Scala, Essaouira* ☎ *0524/47–36–26* ⊕ *www.restaurant-lalicorne-essaouira. com* ⊟ *No credit cards* ☽ *Closed Mon. No lunch.*

The Loft

$$ | MEDITERRANEAN | Cozy and chic, this café and restaurant offers a small seasonal, changing menu of fresh local produce and seafood, and a few surprises such as a mille-feuille of eggplant and goat cheese. After your meal, try a spiced coffee or Amazigh tea. **Known for:** cash required for payment; arty, bohemian decor; vegetarian options and spiced coffee. $ *Average main: DH70* ⊠ *5, rue Hajjali, Essaouira* ✛ *In alley behind clocktower square* ☎ *0524/78–44–62* ⊟ *No credit cards* ☽ *Closed Tues.*

Le Mogadorien

$$$ | MOROCCAN | Often overlooked in favor of the smaller, lounge-style restaurants farther along the street, Le Mogadorien has a similar menu but a lot more style, with decor that reflects Essaouira's Amazigh, Arab, Jewish, and Christian heritage and gives you a choice of low-slung Moroccan salon seats or regular chairs and tables. Chef Najiba prepares a range of Moroccan classics and local seafood. **Known for:** vegetarian options; hearty portions; excellent service. $ *Average main: DH110* ⊠ *7, pl. Chefchaouni, Essaouira* ✛ *In clocktower square* ☎ *0524/47–49–50.*

Le Patio

$$$ | **MOROCCAN** | Moroccan cooking comes with a twist at this French-run restaurant; for example, fish tagines are made with pears, apples, or prunes. The small tables are set around a large, starry lantern, and the deep-red walls, white muslin, and candles create a romantic atmosphere, although it's a little too dark for gazing into each other's eyes. **Known for:** large menu; local wines; fresh fish dishes. [$] *Average main: DH95* ✉ *28 bis, rue Moulay Rachid, Essaouira* ☎ *0524/47–41–66* ⏲ *No lunch.*

Platinium

$ | **EUROPEAN** | A few blocks east of the beach is one of the city's best cafés, where excellent salads, pasta, pizza, and meat and fish dishes are served all day. Breakfasts come in European or Moroccan style. **Known for:** modern, airy space with shaded outdoor terrace; cash required for payment; large selection of pizzas. [$] *Average main: DH50* ✉ *Av. Lalla Amina, Quartier des Dunes* ☎ *0524/78–50–91* 🌐 *platiniumrestaurant.com* 💳 *No credit cards.*

Restaurant Laayoune

$$ | **MOROCCAN** | The food here is simple, traditional, and tasty, but the atmosphere is particularly lovely, especially in the evening, when lights and candles bring the small space to life. This is the most popular of several salon-style Moroccan restaurants in the area, which means you may have to wait for a table. **Known for:** credit cards not accepted; organic ingredients; offers some fixed menus with large portions. [$] *Average main: DH70* ✉ *4 bis, rue El Hajjali, Essaouira* ☎ *0524/47–46–43* 💳 *No credit cards* ⏲ *No lunch Fri.*

★ **Silvestro**

$$ | **ITALIAN** | A long-standing favorite among locals, expats, and tourists, this authentic Italian restaurant serves the best crispy pizzas in the medina, straight from a wood-fired oven. The menu also features home-cooked pasta dishes. **Known for:** enclosed terrace for dining; large portions; alcoholic drinks. [$] *Average main: DH80* ✉ *70, rue Laalouj, Medina* ☎ *0524/47–35–55* ⏲ *Closed during Ramadan.*

La Table by Madada

$$$$ | **SEAFOOD** | Occupying a former warehouse of the sultan's Jewish traders, this is one of three Madada brand businesses in Essaouira. The restaurant and bar offers fresh seafood prepared imaginatively and according to the seasons, such as a monkfish tagine with caramelized apples. **Known for:** live music entertainment on weekends; lobster pastilla; books up, so reserve ahead. [$] *Average main: DH165* ✉ *7, rue Youssef el Fassi, Essaouira* ☎ *0524/47–21–06* 🌐 *madada.com* ⏲ *No lunch.*

★ **Taros**

$$$$ | **MEDITERRANEAN** | This restaurant and bar with a Mediterranean menu is the place to be in the evenings. It's named after the wind that blows off the sea, which you can feel firsthand if you're having cocktails on the terrific rooftop terrace with views of the port. **Known for:** Oualidia oysters in season; delicious food; nightly music. [$] *Average main: DH160* ✉ *Pl. Moulay Hassan, at Rue de la Skala, Essaouira* ☎ *0524/47–64–07.*

Triskala

$ | **VEGETARIAN** | Near the ramparts, this vegetarian restaurant creates a cozy atmosphere, with quirky design and simple, tasty, seasonal food such as the falafel platter, sardine ball tagine, and stuffed eggplant. The chocolate gâteau is pretty amazing, too. **Known for:** intimate corners and secret mezzanine areas for dining; cash required for payment; chocolate gâteau. [$] *Average main: DH65* ✉ *58 bis, rue Touahen, Essaouira* ☎ *0524/47–63–71* 💳 *No credit cards.*

★ **Umia**

$$$$ | **EUROPEAN** | Tucked away along the skala, this chic restaurant is a real treat, offering a daily changing menu—prepared

in an open kitchen—that blends seasonal and local ingredients with French *savoir faire.* The airy restaurant draws in a clientele of expats and tourists with its muted dove grays, glossy white furniture, and quirky art touches, such as a gorgeous Gnaoua mural. Be sure to try the goat cheese from a women's co-op in nearby Meskala; you also can't miss the chocolate fondant with salted caramel ice cream. **Known for:** sleek minimalist decor; chocolate fondant; good service. [$] *Average main: DH120* ✉ *22 bis, rue de la Skala, Essaouira* ☎ *0524/78–33–95.*

Vague Bleue
$ | ITALIAN | One of Essaouira's best-kept secrets, this little hole-in-the-wall restaurant never fails to impress. Manager Brahim offers freshly prepared Italian mains (fish, chicken, and pasta), all served with a trio of salads and two juices to start. **Known for:** cash required for payment; simple, good-value food; small and hard to find (but worth it). [$] *Average main: DH50* ✉ *2, rue Sidi Ali Ben Abdullah, Essaouira* ☎ *0611/28–37–91* 💳 *No credit cards* ⏲ *Closed Fri.*

Coffee and Quick Bites

Gelateria Dolce Freddo
$ | CAFÉ | Come here for the best coffee and the best ice cream in town; its location on the main square is also great for people-watching. ■ **TIP→ Pick a shady seat on the inside of the terrace under a parasol to avoid the passing street hawkers.** **Known for:** cash required for payment; homemade gelato; varieties of coffee drinks. [$] *Average main: DH12* ✉ *Pl. Moulay Hassan, Essaouira* ☎ *0663/57–19–28* 💳 *No credit cards.*

Pâtisserie Driss
$ | CAFÉ | This local institution off the main square dates back to 1929. Prices are very reasonable, so you can start your day with great coffee and breakfasts; you can also take your pick from the French and Moroccan pastries baked fresh every day. ■ **TIP→ Take away some cakes and coffee in the late afternoon and eat them at one of the cafés on the square—it's what the locals do.** **Known for:** cheap eats with local flavor; generously sized pastries; cash required for payment. [$] *Average main: DH10* ✉ *9, rue el Hajjali, Essaouira* ☎ *0524/47–27–93* 💳 *No credit cards.*

Hotels

The riad trend spread to Essaouira and is still going strong, although many of the first foreign riad renovators have now built villas in the countryside, where the winds and humidity are lower. Rooms are generally less opulent and less expensive than those in Marrakesh, but you'll find plenty of charm and elegance. There are also many even less expensive hotels, but fewer of the budget hippie hangouts of yesteryear.

For hotels with swimming pools you'll have only one expensive option within the medina: the Heure Bleue Palais. Other beachfront hotels with pools are fine if you have a large family, and may offer shelter on windier days, but the beach is never very far away on foot. Another option is to rent an apartment, by the night or by the week. Rooms book up quickly, especially in summer, so reserve (sometimes months) ahead. ■ **TIP→ You can only take a car as far as a medina gate, so you'll have to heave your luggage to your lodging by yourself. The best option? Pick up a carossa (a small cart on wheels) from the parking lot outside one of the gates and pay the owner and cart wheeler 20 DH for his trouble.**

Atlas Essaouira and Spa
$$$$ | HOTEL | The Atlas provides beachfront five-star service with all the facilities you would expect from the Moroccan brand. **Pros:** some rooms with beach views; private beach; delicious restaurant. **Cons:** popular with big groups; lacks local charm; corporate feel. [$] *Rooms from: DH1400* ✉ *Bd. Mohammed V,*

Did You Know?

Essaouira (originally called Mogador) is one of Morocco's best port towns to visit. A walk along the ramparts and a seafood dinner at one of the many local restaurants are two must-dos of any visit.

Essaouira ☎ *0524/47–99–99* 🌐 *atlashotelscollection.com* 🛏 *156 rooms* 🍴 *Free Breakfast.*

Dar Liouba

$$ | B&B/INN | Actually two properties combined, this riad in the medina has been remodeled to ensure that the atrium and bedrooms are flooded with light. **Pros:** rooftop terrace with sea views; more light than most riads; warm welcome. **Cons:** rooms on lower floors can be noisy from the street below; lots of stairs; can be difficult to find. [$] *Rooms from: DH650* ✉ *28, Impasse Moulay Ismail, Essaouira* ☎ *0677/54–32–84* 🌐 *www.darliouba.eu* 🛏 *9 rooms* 🍴 *Free Breakfast.*

Dar Maya

$$$$ | B&B/INN | With only five rooms but plenty of communal spaces, every inch of Dar Maya is designed to perfection, creating an elegant boutique experience in Essaouira. **Pros:** ocean views; intimate and chic; attentive English-speaking staff. **Cons:** owners have dogs that roam the house; may be too small for some people; rooms are often booked up. [$] *Rooms from: DH1595* ✉ *33, rue Oujda, Essaouira* ☎ *0524/78–56–87* 🌐 *www.riaddarmaya.com* 🛏 *5 rooms* 🍴 *Free Breakfast.*

★ **Heure Bleue Palais**

$$$$ | HOTEL | Enjoy ample space and amenities like nowhere else in the medina at Essaouira's most prestigious lodging, a meticulously designed, luxurious property that evokes a colonial ambience in decor that includes cream tones, granite, and dark wood. **Pros:** beautiful architecture; entertainment choices including a cinema; the only pool in a luxury property inside the medina walls. **Cons:** noise from the billiards room and bar can reverberate up to the rooms; by far the most expensive rates in the medina; not the typical Moroccan decor some might expect. [$] *Rooms from: DH1980* ✉ *2, rue Ibn Batouta, Essaouira* ☎ *0524/78–34–34* 🌐 *www.heure-bleue.com* 🛏 *33 rooms* 🍴 *Free Breakfast.*

Hotel Le Medina Essaouira Thalassa Sea & Spa MGallery

$$$$ | HOTEL | FAMILY | The closer to the medina of the city's two beachfront five-star hotels, this Accor property has a location and facilities that are second to none. **Pros:** large heated pool; private beach; fabulous spa. **Cons:** lacks Moroccan charm beyond the lobby; popular with large groups; service can be lacking despite its five-star status. [$] *Rooms from: DH1300* ✉ *Bd. Mohammed V, Essaouira* ☎ *0525/07–25–26* 🌐 *all.accor.com* 🛏 *117 rooms* 🍴 *Free Breakfast.*

Madada Mogador

$$$$ | B&B/INN | Stylized, elegant, and designed to perfection, Madada Mogador is perfectly poised just within the medina walls to ensure easy access and ocean views from most rooms. **Pros:** modern take on Moroccan style; attentive, English-speaking staff; cool lounge spaces. **Cons:** small common areas; two-night minimum stay; confusing shared entrance with hotel next door. [$] *Rooms from: DH1485* ✉ *5, rue Youssef el Fassi, Medina* ☎ *0524/47–55–12* 🌐 *www.madada.com* 🛏 *7 rooms* 🍴 *Free Breakfast.*

Maison du Sud

$$ | B&B/INN | FAMILY | A traditional, heavy, stone arch off a busy medina street marks the entrance to the cool interior of this long-established, Moroccan-run inn, made of two large town houses. **Pros:** substantial breakfast; great central location in the medina; triple and quadruple rooms available. **Cons:** can be dark; can fill up with groups; some rooms feel cramped. [$] *Rooms from: DH540* ✉ *29, av. Sidi Mohammed Ben Abdellah, Medina* ☎ *0524/47–41–41* 🌐 *www.riad-maisondusud.com* 🛏 *24 rooms* 🍴 *Free Breakfast.*

Riad Al Madina

$$$ | **HOTEL** | This beautiful 18th-century riad is wrapped around a stone courtyard with a trickling fountain. **Pros:** central location; sun-filled rooms and patio; in-house hammam. **Cons:** gets busy with groups; rooms can be cramped; can feel very crowded. [$] *Rooms from: DH880* ✉ *9, rue Attarine, Medina* ☎ *0524/47–59–07* 🌐 *www.riadalmadina.com* 🛏 *54 rooms* 🍴 *Free Breakfast.*

Riad Baladin

$$$ | **B&B/INN** | The personal attention from the manager is a highlight here and starts with a welcome briefing and introduction to the best-kept secrets of the medina. **Pros:** quiet cul-de-sac location; larger and lighter rooms than in most riads; Jacuzzi on the patio. **Cons:** confusing stairways can make it difficult to find your room; no meals other than breakfast; cash required for payment. [$] *Rooms from: DH810* ✉ *9, rue Sidi Magdoul, Medina* ☎ *0524/47–30–94* 🌐 *www.riadbaladin.com* 💳 *No credit cards* 🛏 *10 rooms* 🍴 *Free Breakfast.*

Riad Chakir Mogador

$ | **B&B/INN** | A good budget option, this colorful and friendly riad is actually made up of three neighboring houses. **Pros:** lovely roof terrace; great value for the location; friendly, English-speaking staff. **Cons:** used by a travel company, so often full; more homey comfort than boutique chic; some rooms cramped. [$] *Rooms from: DH385* ✉ *13, rue Malek Ben Morhal, off Av. Istiqlal, Medina* ☎ *0524/47–33–09* 🌐 *www.riadchakir.com* 🛏 *20 rooms* 🍴 *Free Breakfast.*

Riad Chbanate

$$$$ | **B&B/INN** | The former residence of an 18th-century *caid* (local official) has been transformed into a small boutique hotel flooded with light. **Pros:** modern architecture with some traditional elements; rooftop suite with 360-degree views of the city; beautifully decorated rooms. **Cons:** the street to the hotel can be dark at night; not suitable for people with limited mobility; some rooms have open-plan bathrooms, which are not to everyone's taste. [$] *Rooms from: DH1430* ✉ *179, rue Chbanate, Medina* ☎ *0524/78–33–34* 🌐 *www.riad-chbanate.com* 🛏 *8 rooms* 🍴 *Free Breakfast.*

Riad Kafila

$$ | **B&B/INN** | Located right on the medina walls, Riad Kafila has some of the best direct ocean views in the city. **Pros:** impressive hospitality; bright salon with stunning ocean views; homey ambience. **Cons:** property may be too small for some tastes; no air-conditioning; the windows of the sea-view rooms are too high for an actual view. [$] *Rooms from: DH650* ✉ *4 bis, rue Yamen, Medina* ☎ *0524/78–32–75* 🌐 *www.riadkafila.com* 🛏 *7 rooms* 🍴 *Free Breakfast.*

Riad Mimouna

$$$ | **HOTEL** | Tight against the northern side of the medina walls, this opulent riad sits over the water's edge, letting you have the raging sea all to yourself. **Pros:** traditional architectural features; newer rooms have floor-to-ceiling windows; central heating in winter. **Cons:** patchy Wi-Fi; atmosphere more like a hotel than an intimate riad; some rooms too weather-beaten. [$] *Rooms from: DH850* ✉ *62, rue d'Oujda, Medina* ☎ *0524/78–57–53* 🌐 *www.hotelriad-mimouna.com* 🛏 *33 rooms* 🍴 *Free Breakfast.*

Sofitel Essaouira Mogador Golf & Spa

$$$$ | **RESORT** | **FAMILY** | If you're done with the cutesy but crowded scene of the medina and yearn for space and views as far as the eye can see, this Sofitel near Diabat is for you. **Pros:** sea views; heaps of facilities including three pools, four restaurants, a hammam, and kids' club; extensive gardens. **Cons:** some parts of the hotel look run-down; beach is a 20-minute walk away; far from the medina, and the free shuttle stops at 6 pm. [$] *Rooms from: DH1500* ✉ *Domaine de Mogador, Diabat* ☎ *0524/47–94–00* 🌐 *sofitel.accor.com* 🛏 *175 rooms* 🍴 *Free Breakfast.*

Villa de l'Ô

$$$$ | B&B/INN | The Essaouira location of this small regional chain exudes sophistication, with its wood-paneled library, colonial-style decor, sleek roof terrace, and sweeping views of the whole beach. **Pros:** pool access at the sister hotel outside the medina; conveniently located and easily accessible; on-site hammam. **Cons:** some rooms can be cold in winter; parts of the hotel are looking a little tired; this kind of service gets pricey. [$] *Rooms from: DH1200* ✉ *3, rue Mohamed Ben Messaoud, Medina* ☎ *0524/47–63–75* 🌐 *www.villadelo.com* 🛏 *12 rooms* 🍴 *Free Breakfast.*

Villa Maroc

$$$$ | HOTEL | Embodying much of what international travelers seek in a Moroccan hotel, the intimate Villa Maroc is delightfully decorated to epitomize a "traditional" Moroccan style that never really was. **Pros:** on-site hammam; great service; sizable rooms. **Cons:** not suitable for people with limited mobility; half-board bookings preferred; when busy, a minimum stay may be required. [$] *Rooms from: DH1400* ✉ *10, rue Abdellah Ben Yassine, Medina* ☎ *0524/47–31–47* 🌐 *www.villa-maroc.com* 🛏 *21 rooms* 🍴 *Free Breakfast.*

Nightlife

Most Essaouira residents consider nightlife to involve simply hanging out at a café on the main square, but should you fancy partying into the night after dinner, there are a few options.

Le Chrysalis

DANCE CLUBS | At what is by far the most appealing of Essaouira's nightclubs, every night has a band playing an eclectic set of covers of popular Western tunes, as well as Moroccan and West African favorites. The drinks aren't cheap, but the atmosphere and dancing are lively and the place pulls in a range of tourists, locals, and expats of varying ages. ✉ *Complexe Bin Laswar, next to Bab Sbaa, Essaouira* ☎ *0524/47–26–63, 0666/45–00–93.*

The Roof Top

BARS | Known for spectacular sunset views and for being one of the coolest party spots among expats, this bar and restaurant offers creative cocktails, tasty tapas, and live music. ✉ *60, av. Mohammed V, Essaouira* ☎ *0524/78–48–28* 🌐 *theroofessaouira.business.site.*

So Lounge

DANCE CLUBS | Modeled after its successful older sibling in Agadir, the So Lounge at the Sofitel in Diabat is the height of sophistication. A cocktail bar and restaurant overlooks the main bar, stage, and dance area; live music is played every night except Monday. Admission is free, but it's recommended that diners book a table. ✉ *Sofitel Essaouira Mogador Golf & Spa, Domaine de Mogador, Diabat* ☎ *0524/47–94–00* 🌐 *sofitel.accor.com.*

Shopping

Essaouira is a great shopping destination. Although the range of goods may be more limited than in Marrakesh or Fez, the vendors are a lot more relaxed and starting prices are often reasonable.

Essaouira is famed as an artisan center expert in marquetry and inlay. Boxes, platters, and picture frames made of local thuya wood make excellent gifts, and the wood-carvers' souk below the skala is a popular place to purchase them. A hard, local wood that shines up to almost plastic perfection, thuya is sculpted for artistic and practical use. Almost-life-size statues and sculptures sit alongside boxes, bowls, and chess sets. Scan stores to see whether you prefer the even-toned thuya branch inlaid with mother-of-pearl or walnut or one with swirling root designs. To get a bulk price, buy a bunch of items from a craftsperson who specializes in them.

Did You Know?

Essaouira is a great shopping destination: it's known for its local artisans and the shops and stalls tend to be more low-key than in Fez and Marrakesh, making bargaining a more relaxed experience.

The main areas for purchasing local crafts and souvenirs are Rue Sidi Mohammed Ben Abdullah, Derb Laalouj, and along the skala. Colorful, woven baskets hang from herbalists' stores in the spice souk and Place Marché aux Grains across the road. While the bazaars, tended by turbaned men of the South, will sell antique (and faux-antique) silver jewelry, locals tend to buy new items from the jewelry souk off Avenue L'Istiqlal. Dive into the small, shady alleyways off the main areas to find more treasures such as carpets, cushion covers, jewelry and punched metal, and goatskin lamps. Argan oil products for culinary and cosmetic use are available around Essaouira, too.

Essaouira is home to a number of expat artists and craftspeople. Many restaurants and boutique stores sell their work in glass cabinets at fixed prices.

ANTIQUES

Galérie Aida

ANTIQUES & COLLECTIBLES | For tasteful used pewter platters, goblets, and ceramic teapots, as well as new and used English and French books, check this store underneath the ramparts. It also has a large selection of antique daggers. The gallery's owner, Joseph Sebag, one of Essaouira's last remaining Jewish residents, is knowledgeable about the city's Jewish history. ✉ 2, rue de la Skala, Medina ☎ 0524/47–62–90.

Galerie Boutique Elizir

ANTIQUES & COLLECTIBLES | Three floors of retro and vintage furnishings and decor at this gallery showcase the collections of Abdelatif, who ran a restaurant of the same name in this space. Explore this treasure trove to discover furniture, artwork, clothing, and decorative objects, both Moroccan and European, from bygone decades. ✉ Av. de l'Istiqlal, Medina ☎ 0524/47–21–03.

Galerie Jama

ANTIQUES & COLLECTIBLES | Tucked away at the end of the street, Galerie Jama seems more museum than shop. You can browse among wooden doors, mosaic vases, vintage Amazigh rugs, and all sorts of wonderful odds and ends. Get ready to negotiate if you see something you like. ✉ 22, rue Ibn Rochd, Medina ☎ 0670/01–64–29 ⊕ www.galeriejama.com.

ARGAN OIL AND SPICES

Au Petit Bonhomme de la Chance

OTHER HEALTH & BEAUTY | Habiba Ajaoui was the first female shopkeeper in the Essaouira medina, and she's always happy to pass the time chatting with clients (in Arabic, French, or English) over a cup of steaming tea. She sells spices and argan and cactus-seed oils at reasonable prices and can get you everything you need for the hammam. She also has a large repertoire of henna tattoo designs, which are priced according to their complexity. ✉ 30, rue Laalouj, Medina ☎ 0666/01–45–02.

Chez Makki

OTHER SPECIALTY STORE | The five Makki brothers have taken over their father's herbalist business and turned it into an empire, running several of the shops on Place Marché aux Grains and in the spice souk across the road. They know their stuff and are happy to explain, over a pot of royal tea, which spices are used in which recipes and the difference between real and fake saffron. They also sell a range of solid perfumes, argan-oil products, and ceramics. ✉ 221, Souk Laghzal, Spice Market, Medina ☎ 0524/47–30–90.

ART GALLERIES

Many galleries in the medina display contemporary Moroccan and expatriate mixed-media productions. These are also often exhibited at Dar Souiri or in the South Bastion at Bab Marrakech.

Espace Othello Gallerie d'Art

ART GALLERIES | Named after Orson Welles's film *Othello*, which was shot in town, this gallery exhibits the work

Berber Gold: Argan Oil

The Moroccan argan forest, which stretches from Essaouira down past Agadir and along the Souss Valley to the Anti-Atlas, is unique, as there is nowhere else in the world where the tree grows so well. As you travel across the region, you will see the short, spiny trees in fields and on hillsides.

Since the start of the 21st century, as the aesthetic properties of argan oil have been widely publicized, the Moroccan government has developed a strategy to support the creation of women's co-ops to extract and market the oil, as well as to preserve the unique biosphere and protect against overuse. As prices have risen, argan oil has become known as "Berber gold," with leading beauty brands including it in their products and famous television chefs developing recipes to include it.

The difference between cosmetic and culinary oils is that the latter is the result of grinding the almonds found inside the argan nut after toasting, while cosmetic oil is ground directly.

Without a doubt, the argan boom has brought much-needed employment opportunities to rural areas, particularly for women. However, many establishments that claim to operate on cooperative principles (especially those on main tourist thoroughfares) often do not. Also, many co-ops that tout "bio" or "organic" branding may use nuts that have not been sprayed with pesticides, but few have actually been able to secure organic certification.

When buying argan oil, try to buy from a genuine cooperative to ensure you get the real deal and that your money helps rural women. The UCFA is a union created with aid from foreign development agencies to help professionalize and support women's argan co-ops. They have a list of members online at ⊕ www.cooperative-argane.com.

If your concern is the oil being 100% organic, it may be that the production is less hands-on and more mechanized than in rural co-ops. The oils produced at Sidi Yassine outside Essaouira are widely exported and therefore rigorously certified. You can buy them at Histoire de Filles.

A great souvenir is *amlou*, a paste made from toasted almonds or peanuts, argan oil, and local honey. Often called "Berber Nutella," it tastes more like a kind of nut butter.

of local and international artists as well as antiques. Look out for Scottish artist Caroline Fulton's work, which features indigenous Moroccan animals in rural and medina settings. It's closed Monday. ⊠ *9, rue Mohammed Layachi, Medina* ☎ *0524/47–50–95.*

Galerie d'Art Damgaard

ART GALLERIES | Danish collector Frederic Damgaard is credited with bringing the naïve art (works by artists without formal art training) of Essaouira to an international audience. His Galerie d'Art Damgaard, across from the clock tower, has well-curated displays of work by Essaouira painters and sculptors, and it's also a great place to pick up souvenir books on local art and culture. ⊠ *Av. Oqba Ibn Nafiaa, Medina* ☎ *0524/78–44–46.*

Essaouira's Local Markets

If you don't mind getting up early to catch the action, your hotel or a local tour operator will be happy to arrange a visit to a local market (although all are also accessible by local bus or grand taxi). The highlight is Had Draa on a Sunday, where the earliest risers are rewarded with a view of camel trading. Cattle, donkeys, horses, sheep, and goats are also traded, the latter often taking a direct route to the on-site abattoir. This is a farmers' market in the true sense; it's unlikely you'll find many souvenirs to buy between the animal feed, fresh vegetables, cobblers, and vendors of plastic sheeting, but it is a fascinating insight into rural Moroccan life.

Other smaller markets are on Wednesday (Ida Ougourd), Thursday (Meskala), Saturday (Akermoud), and Sunday (Smimou). Rural Moroccans are often conservative, so please dress accordingly and cover thighs and shoulders to avoid unwanted attention. The markets are picturesque, but local people may be offended if you photograph them without asking and may say no if you do. All these markets are between 28 km (17 miles) and 50 km (31 miles) from Essaouira.

Yellow Workshop

ART GALLERIES | Danish artist Sanne Busk, who has made Essaouira her home, specializes in collage art made with hand-painted paper. Her husband, Hassan, is a master *guembri* (traditional Gnaoua stringed instrument) maker and crafts unusually decorated wood instruments. Their work is showcased in this gallery, along with workshops and demonstrations. ⊠ *Rue Mohamed Diouri, Medina* ☎ *0697/40–25–43 Sanne, 0660/31–36–05 Hassan* ⊕ *www.yellow-workshop.com.*

CRAFTS AND JEWELRY

Basma

CRAFTS | Hafida welcomes all her customers with a smile and offers a keenly curated selection of Morocco-made jewelry, leather bags, shoes, small paintings, and other decorative items. ⊠ *20 bis, rue Skala, Essaouira* ☎ *0524/78–34–66.*

La Fibule Berbère

CRAFTS | Amid dozens of other Ali Baba–cave-style shops in the Essaouira medina, La Fibule Berbère is one of the oldest and one of the few that accepts credit cards. The shop displays stunning jewelry, such as huge silver pendants, *fibules* (clasps for attaching pendants and closing shawls), and bulky necklaces made in the Amazigh and Toureg styles. ⊠ *51–53, rue Attarine, Essaouira* ☎ *0524/47–62–55, 0661/06–97–74* ⊕ *www.fibuleberbere-essaouira.com.*

Histoire de Filles

CRAFTS | Essaouira's only concept store is located near Bab Sbaa and offers a range of clothing, jewelry, accessories, organic argan oil, and small decorative items. Products are designed locally by Moroccan and international designers. This is the closest you'll get in Essaouira to the modern design stores of Marrakesh. ⊠ *1, rue Mohamed Ben Messaoud, Medina* ☎ *0524/78–51–93.*

Mashi Mushki

CRAFTS | Shopping at this store in the medina gives you the chance to pick up craft items with a conscience and support locals, as a percentage of the profits goes to Project 91, a charity that helps young Souiris (natives of Essaouira) improve their lives through job training and other activities. Some items, including paintings, prints, handwoven textiles, bags, gifts, and accessories, are made in the neighborhood or by co-ops, which benefits locals. Project 91 also runs Dar 91 (⊕ dar91.com), three serviced apartments for visitors. ⊠ *91, rue Chbanat, Medina.*

Trésor Kafila Shop
CRAFTS | This shop in the medina offers a range of handmade items from all over Morocco and the Sahara, including mirrors, jewelry, leather bags, and small pieces of furniture. The kettle is always on, and you'll eventually be invited to join in for a cup of sweet mint tea to seal your deal. ⊠ *86, rue Laalouj, Medina* ☎ *0662/82–55–46.*

WOODWORK
Thuya furniture is as unavoidable on the streets of Essaouira as in-line skaters in Malibu Beach. Try to buy from the artisans, as this is the only way they can make a decent return on their ancient craft. The cheap boxes you see in the tourist shops have passed through so many middlemen that the craftspeople end up with nearly nothing.

★ Coopérative Artisanale des Marqueteurs
CRAFTS | Walk through a nondescript passageway into a classic 19th-century riad and you'll find the Coopérative Artisanale des Marqueteurs, whose members have been turning out finely decorated boxes, ornaments, tables, and other furniture since 1948. Everything has a tag with the artisan's code number and reasonable fixed prices. At the end of the month, the craftspeople collect their income, and a small proportion goes to the upkeep of the building and the running of the co-op. You won't find tour groups here as guides get no commission, making it a tranquil place to stop and admire decades of craftsmanship. ⊠ *6, rue Khalid Ibn el Walid, off Pl. Moulay Hassan, Essaouira* ☎ *0524/47–56–76.*

🏃 Activities

BIKING
Mogador2Roues
BIKING | Bikes can be rented here for personal use, and guided tours along local trails are available; rates are cheaper for larger groups. Motor scooters are available for exploration farther afield. ⊠ *22, rue Al Attarine, Medina ⊹ Opposite Hotel Souiri* ☎ *0671/01–82–52, 0668/19–53–68* 🌐 *120 DH per day for bike rental; 350 DH per person for guided ½-day tours.*

COOKING CLASSES
Many riads offer cookery classes or demonstrations, but the two best places in Essaouira to learn about Moroccan cuisine are L'Atelier de Madada, a modern cooking school; and Khadija's Kuzina, where you cook in a local home.

★ L'Atelier by Madada
COOKING CLASSES | At the best cooking school in town, you'll get an authentic, step-by-step introduction to Moroccan cuisine from chef Mouna, who shares the secrets of generations of Moroccan home cooks with simultaneous English translation. The first person to reserve each day gets to choose from a range of menus, including tagines, pastilla, couscous, and traditional cooked salads. Classes in the modern space last around four hours and include a tour of the spice souk where some of the meal's ingredients come from. A glass of wine costs extra. ⊠ *Rue Mohamed Ben Massoud, Essaouira* ☎ *0700/18–90–17* 🌐 *www. lateliermadada.com* 🌐 *550 DH for 4½-hr cooking class.*

★ Khadija's Kuzina
COOKING CLASSES | For an authentic home-cooking experience in Moroccan cuisine, stop into Khadija and Hussein's home, where you will learn how to prepare several typical dishes, including salads, tagines, couscous, and pastilla. Afterward, sit together with the family to enjoy the fruits of your labors. You may often join other travelers, and the

first to reserve picks the menu. It's also possible to arrange a special class on Moroccan pastries. ⊠ *Av. Allal al Fassi, Quartier Bouhaira, Essaouira* ✛ *Opposite Pharmacie Bouhaira* ☎ *0613/98–58–90, 0670/07–12–32* 🍴 *350 DH for cooking class*.

FOUR-WHEELING
Diana Quad Essaouira
FOUR-WHEELING | The company offers a range of quad biking excursions from one-hour joy rides to longer experiences and trekking adventures, with meals included on trips all the way out to the beach village of Sidi Kaouki. ⊠ *60 Quartier Diabat, Diabat, Essaouira* ☎ *0600/02–20–77 WhatsApp* ⊕ *dianaquad-essaouira. com* 🍴 *From 450 DH for 1-hr quad ride for 2 people*.

GOLF
Golf de Mogador
GOLF | The 18-hole golf course at Diabat, designed by Gary Player, is an integral part of the same resort that includes the Sofitel hotel. Surrounded by sand dunes, the course rolls down toward the sea and sits among forests of eucalyptus and thuya. Lessons are available, and there are discounts for Sofitel guests. ⊠ *Sofitel Essaouira Mogador Golf & Spa, Domaine de Mogador, Diabat, Diabat* ☎ *0525/08–10–10* ⊕ *golf-mogador-essaouira.com* 🍴 *From 475 DH for 9 holes; from 750 DH for 18 holes* ⛳ *18 holes, 7227 yards, par 72*.

HAMMAMS AND SPAS
If you want an authentic hammam experience, collect the necessary soap, scrub mitt, and other products from a spice shop such as Au Petit Bonhomme de la Chance and prepare to get down and dirty with the locals. If you prefer something a little more refined, head to a spa; there are plenty in hotels and around the medina. The following hammams and spas are open to all (even nonguests, if the place is in a hotel).

PUBLIC HAMMAMS
Hammam Pabst
SPAS | Located in the Mellah, this is one of the oldest hammams in Essaouira. Now brightly painted, it has a plaque indicating that Orson Welles once used it as a location during the filming of *Othello*. Because of this, it's popular with tourists, and the ladies who are on hand to scrub and massage clients can get a little greedy. Check on the door for the most up-to-date male/female opening hours. ⊠ *Rue Annasr, Medina* ☎ *No phone* 🍴 *10 DH (massage or scrub extra)*.

Hammam Sidi Abdelsmih
SPAS | On the street of the same name in the medina, this women-only hammam is open all day until midnight, and you can get a great scrub-down by one of the local ladies. If your male partner wants the same, he should head over the Hammam Bolisi in Rue Dar Dheb, near Maison du Sud. Don't forget to bring a towel and a spare pair of underwear (because you wear one pair inside). ⊠ *Rue Sidi Abdelsmih, Medina* ☎ *No phone* 🍴 *50 DH*.

HOTEL HAMMAMS
Riad Al Madina Hammam
SPAS | This popular riad in the medina has a rather good hammam that nonguests can use. One option is a 30-minute scrub with argan oil, roses, sugar, and salt (200 DH). ⊠ *9, rue Attarine, Medina* ☎ *0524/47–59–07* ⊕ *www.riadalmadina. com* 🍴 *Treatments from 70 DH*.

Villa Maroc Hammam
SPAS | FAMILY | The Oriental Spa hammam in this riad guesthouse is open to nonguests and offers a range of treatment packages, including massages for children. One option is a traditional scrub with black soap and a scrub mitt plus a *ghassoul* (therapeutic mud) wrap and a 10-minute massage. ⊠ *10, rue Abdellah Ben Yassine, Medina* ☎ *0524/47–31–47* ⊕ *www.villa-maroc.com* 🍴 *45-minute massage with argan oil 320 DH; 600 DH for scrub, mud wrap, and massage*.

The beaches south of Essaouira are among Morocco's top surfing spots.

SPAS
Azur Spa
SPAS | A wide range of treatments are available at this spa in the medina—including aromatic massage, reflexology, seaweed baths, and exfoliation—but it's the beautiful, black-marble hammam that remains the star attraction. Fluffy robes, slippers, and black soap are provided, as is herbal tea after your treatments. Men, women, and couples can use the hammam together. ✉ *15, rue Khalid ben Walid, Medina* ☎ *0524/78–57–94* ⊕ *www.azur-spa-essaouira.com* 🖼 *Traditional hammam with scrub 200 DH; 1-hr massage 350 DH.*

Bio Spa Esthétique
SPAS | This spa and hammam offers great value in a clean and welcoming setting in the heart of the medina. The package deals frequently include an argan-oil scrub or massage. Treatment choices range from a simple hammam scrub to a 1½-hour package with an argan scrub, face scrub and mask, and back massage.

✉ *9, rue Irak, Medina* ☎ *0524/78–46–88* 🖼 *Treatments from 130 DH.*

Le P'tit Spa at Heure Bleue Palais
SPAS | Located at Bab Marrakech in the medina, this palatial riad hotel has a hammam plus treatment and massage rooms open to nonguests who book in advance (book either one or two days ahead). The full list of packages and treatments ranges from hand, foot, and face care to scrubs and massages and treatments with fragrances such as verbena. ✉ *2, rue Ibn Batouta, Bab Marrakech, Essaouira* ☎ *0524/78–34–34* ⊕ *www.heure-bleue.com* 🖼 *Treatments from 470 DH.*

HORSEBACK AND CAMEL RIDING
★ Ranch de Diabat
HORSEBACK RIDING | This long-standing family-run business can organize horse-riding and camel trips from a ranch in Diabat. Shorter camel and horseback rides are an option, as is a half-day camel trip with lunch. Horseback riding lessons and trail rides of several days can be organized for groups. They also have an

activity center with dune buggies and quad bikes for rent. ✉ *Ranch Diabat, Diabat, Diabat* ☎ *0524/47–63–82* ⊕ *www.ranchdediabat.com* ✉ *From 150 DH per hr for a camel or horseback ride; from 450 DH for a ½-day camel trip.*

Zouina Cheval

HORSEBACK RIDING | The company organizes horseback riding excursions on Diabat Beach and in the countryside around Essaouira, with treks from one hour to a full day for beginners and experienced riders alike. Longer multiday treks with camping for groups and camel trips are also possible. ✉ *Diabat, Diabat* ☎ *0669/80–71–01* ⊕ *www.zouina-cheval.com* ✉ *From 160 DH per hr; from 600 DH for a full day with picnic lunch.*

WATER SPORTS

If you are a water-sports enthusiast, it is important to understand where the wind and wave conditions are best for each sport. In Essaouira Bay and farther south to Sidi Kaouki, you will most often find kitesurfing. When the wind gets going, windsurfers come out in Essaouira and to the north at Moulay Bouzerktoun. Only beginner surfers attempt anything around Essaouira; the best breaks for experienced surfers are much farther south, between Imsouane and Agadir.

★ Explora

WATER SPORTS | **FAMILY** | A professional Moroccan-English company, Explora offers a range of water sports, including kitesurfing, surfing, and paddleboarding, with qualified instruction at prices considerably cheaper than the nearest competition. The company can also arrange your accommodation and other outdoor activities such as horseback riding, quad biking, camel treks, and mountain biking. The company has its activity base on the southern end of the beach (at Avenue Mohammed V near junction with Route d'Agadir) and also a supplies shop in the medina. ✉ *12, av. Istiqlal, Essaouira* ☎ *0611/47–51–88* ⊕ *explorawatersports.com* ✉ *From 300 DH for ½-hr group*

surfing class; from 660 DH for 2-hr kite-surfing lesson.

Ion Club - Ocean Vagabond

WATER SPORTS | This joint venture with Ocean Vagabond is the biggest outfit in town and prides itself on the quality of its equipment and its multidisciplinary and multilingual instruction in water sports such as surfing, kitesurfing, and windsurfing. Factor this into the cost of courses, which are pricier than elsewhere along the bay, and private lessons may be double the cost of group classes. The more experienced can rent everything they need to explore the coast: boards, windsurfers, and even roof racks. ✉ *Quartier des Dunes* ✥ *At southern end of beach* ☎ *0524/78–39–34* ⊕ *www.oceanvagabond.com* ✉ *From 825 DH for 2-hr kitesurfing class with a group.*

Kite Paradise

WATER SPORTS | **FAMILY** | Run by Marie, from France, and her husband, Taher, from Essaouira, Kite Paradise opened in 2018, offering water sports services including equipment rental, group and private classes, classes for kids, and surfing excursions to Sidi Kaouki and Imsouane. The surf school and all instructors are IKO (International Kitesurfing Organization) certified. Kite Paradise uses the highest-quality equipment and claims to have "the most beautiful location on the spot." ✉ *Rue Lalla Hasna, Essaouira* ☎ *0610/16–83–18* ⊕ *essaouira-kiteparadise.com* ✉ *From 250 DH for a 2-hr group surfing class.*

Taroudant

85 km (51 miles) east of Agadir, 277 km (172 miles) southwest of Marrakesh, 303 km (188 miles) south of Essaouira.

Known as the "Grandmother of Marrakesh," Taroudant is often promoted as an alternative destination to that other former Saadian capital, but these labels don't really acknowledge the essence of

Taroudant as a town serving a rural area. The Taroudant medina walls were built in the 16th century to defend the capital and are almost entirely complete. Today, they encircle a spacious, fully functional Moroccan market town serving a large hinterland where tourism plays only a limited role in the local economy. People in Taroudant are less jaded than in more tourist-focused areas and are happy to chat with visitors as they go about their daily business. You're more likely to see an artisan at one of the markets upcycling something for use on a farm than creating a trinket for a tourist. The town is known for its leather products and its olive and argan oils.

People, customs, and the Arabic and Tashelhit Amazigh languages mix in this Souss Valley town of around 80,000 inhabitants. The town's relaxed feel, the easy interaction with locals, inexpensive dining, and a couple of guesthouse gems make Taroudant an ideal base for exploring the Souss Valley and the western High Atlas.

GETTING HERE AND AROUND
The principal road routes to Taroudant are easily navigable and well signposted. The N10 runs east from Agadir and leads eventually to Taliouine, Tazenakht, and Ouarzazate. There are also scheduled buses from Agadir (1½ hours), Ouarzazate (5 hours), Casablanca (10 hours), Rabat (13 hours), and Marrakesh (6½ hours). Efficient and comfortable CTM buses leave from the gare routière outside Bab Zorgane on the southern side of the medina.

Once you arrive in the city, everything is within walking distance.

BUS CONTACT CTM. ⊠ *Gare Routière, Bab Zorgane, Taroudant* ✛ *Just inside city walls* ☎ *0528/85–38–58* ⊕ *www.ctm.ma.*

RENTAL CARS Malja Cars. ⊠ *Bab Targhount, Mbarek Oussalem, Taroudant* ☎ *0528/55–17–42.*

GUIDES AND TOURS
For a guided tour of the city, Moulay Brahim Bouchra has encyclopedic knowledge of Taroudant and speaks English very well. Tours cost from 150 DH for a half day.

TIMING AND PRECAUTIONS
Taroudant attracts visitors year-round thanks to its favorable climate, although it can get very hot in summer. Most visitors stay a night or two to explore the local region while en route to another destination such as Tafraoute or Ouarzazate.

Sights

Whatever you do in the late afternoon, don't miss the sight of colorfully dressed Roudani (Taroudant native) women lined up against the ramparts near the hospital like birds on a ledge, socializing in the cool hours before sunset. Sunset tours of the ramparts aboard a *calèche* (horse-drawn carriage) are available; the driver may expect you to haggle for your fare—around 70 DH per hour is about right.

City Walls
HISTORIC SIGHT | The city walls of Taroudant date from the 16th century and are unique in their completeness and for the fact that the new city has not yet encroached upon them, making the 7½ km (4½ miles) of walls easily visible and approachable. There are five main entry points into the city (from the northwest, going clockwise): Bab el Kasbah, Bab Zorgan, Bab Targhount, Bab Ouled Bounouna, and Bab el Khemis. The one place to climb upstairs onto the ramparts for a view across the town is at Bab el Kasbah. ■ **TIP→ The best way to see the ramparts is at sunset in a calèche (horse and trap) as the setting sun casts a golden glow over the walls.** ⊠ *Taroudant.*

Dar Baroud
NOTABLE BUILDING | Diagonally across from Bab Sedra, across Avenue Moulay Rachid and with the hospital on your right, is

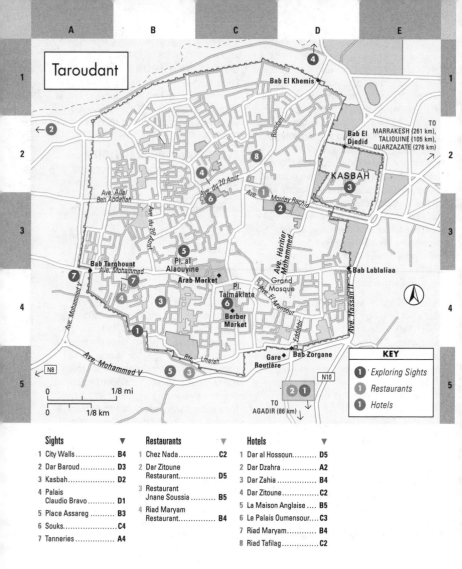

Taroudant

TO
MARRAKESH (261 km),
TALIOUINE (105 km),
OUARZAZATE (276 km)

KASBAH

Bab El Khemis
Bab El Djedid
Bab Lablaliaa
Bab Targhount
Ave. Mohammed
Pl. al Alaouyine
Arab Market
Pl. Talmaklate
Berber Market
Grand Mosque
Gare Routière
Bab Zorgane
Ave. du 20 Aout
Ave. Allal Ben Abdallah
Ave. Moulay Rachid
Ave. Héritier Mohammed
Ave. El Mensour
Ave. Hassan II
Ave. Mohammed V
Roudani
Eddahbi
Rte. Lmelah

N8
N10

0   1/8 mi
0   1/8 km

TO
AGADIR (86 km)

KEY

1 *Exploring Sights*

1 *Restaurants*

1 *Hotels*

Sights ▼	Restaurants ▼	Hotels ▼
1 City Walls **B4**	1 Chez Nada **C2**	1 Dar al Hossoun **D5**
2 Dar Baroud **D3**	2 Dar Zitoune Restaurant **D5**	2 Dar Dzahra **A2**
3 Kasbah **D2**		3 Dar Zahia **B4**
4 Palais Claudio Bravo **D1**	3 Restaurant Jnane Soussia **B5**	4 Dar Zitoune **C2**
5 Place Assareg **B3**	4 Riad Maryam Restaurant **B4**	5 La Maison Anglaise **B5**
6 Souks **C4**		6 Le Palais Oumensour **C3**
7 Tanneries **A4**		7 Riad Maryam **B4**
		8 Riad Tafilag **C2**

the Dar Baroud, once a French ammu-nition-storage facility. This high-walled building is closed to the public—and is locally rumored to be haunted—but stand back on the sidewalk opposite and you can admire its delicate carved stone walls from the exterior. ⊠ *Taroudant.*

Kasbah
HISTORIC SIGHT | In the northeast side of the city, you'll find the kasbah, or the former king's quarter. It was built by Alouite leader Moulay Ismail in the 17th century—some of the pasha's palace remains intact and has been converted into a hotel (Palais Salam, which you can visit for a drink or meal). On Avenue Mou-lay Rachid, with the main gate (Bab el Kasbah) behind you, you'll see a smaller gate (Bab Sedra) on the right, which is the old entrance into the kasbah quarter. Inside the walls is a typical medina resi-dential area with little left of any original structures apart from the gates. The area in front of the hotel is now a public park and a great place for watching the evening promenade. ⊠ *Taroudant.*

★ Palais Claudio Bravo
ART MUSEUM | **FAMILY** | Chilean artist Clau-dio Bravo came to Morocco in 1972 and built this palatial home-turned-museum with stunning gardens and stables 10 km (6 miles) outside Taroudant. Following his death in 2011, the estate became a museum showcasing his art and col-lections, including works by friends like Picasso. The palace is divided into several pavilions connected by inner courtyards and covered walkways, while inside the guest rooms, salons, and Bravo's private rooms and studios are paintings, sculp-tures, and artifacts, including Roman and North African ceramics. Wander through the gardens full of exotic plants to the large water basin, and rest in the shade of a pavilion with a cup of tea and views of the Atlas Mountains. A full guided tour takes two to three hours, but it's possible to do an unguided visit of the gardens. The hefty entry fee includes transportation by horse carriage from the entrance to the main building. You must reserve in advance to visit. You can also reserve for lunch or dinner (expect to pay 400 DH–500 DH per person). ⊠ *Rte. de Tamaloukt, Agwidir, Taroudant* ☎ *0691/24–21–61, 0661/96–81–21* ⊕ *www.palaisclaudiobravo.com/fr/hotel* 🏛 *Guided tour 200 DH, gardens only 100 DH* ⊘ *Closed Mon.*

Place Assareg
PLAZA/SQUARE | This plaza sits between the two main souks (the so-called Arab and Amazigh markets) and serves as the center of life in Taroudant. Although not as lively as Marrakesh's Place Djemâa el Fna, you still may be able to see perform-ers on the square in the late afternoon. Be sure to join the locals in taking a mint tea on a café terrace and watching the scene unfold. ⊠ *Taroudant.*

Souks
MARKET | In the city itself, the municipal market (also referred to as the Amazigh souk) sells spices, dried fruits, and other household essentials. In an open-air area to the east, you'll find men upcycling plastics and tires into saddles, water troughs, and panniers for donkeys. The older, so-called Arab market is the better one for souvenirs, and here you can pick up local terra-cotta, brass, and copper items, along with leather sandals, rugs, and jewelry. You can access the souks from Place Assareg. ⊠ *Taroudant.*

Tanneries
FACTORY | Just outside Bab Targhount, gifted artisans work at Taroudant's tanneries, and you can see them working the leather firsthand (not always a pleas-ant olfactory experience). Many places around town sell the locally made leather goods, such as bags, poufs, sandals, and decorations, for which Taroudant is famous. ⊠ *Taroudant.*

Some of Taroudant's well-preserved fortified walls date from the 16th century.

🍴 Restaurants

Chez Nada

$$ | **MOROCCAN** | If you want to stick within the city walls for some no-hassle Moroccan food, you can't go wrong at this father-and-son joint established in 1950. The menu features standards such as couscous, harira, and pigeon pastilla (order in advance). **Known for:** hearty portions of couscous; cash required for payment; nice views over public gardens. [$] *Average main: DH90* ✉ *15, rue Moulay el Rachid, Taroudant* ☎ *0528/85–17–26* 💳 *No credit cards.*

★ Dar Zitoune Restaurant

$$$ | **MEDITERRANEAN** | Set among gorgeous gardens and featuring a menu of local produce, Dar Zitoune is worth the visit from Taroudant. Serving a refined Mediterranean-style menu, it's a favorite with locals as well as with passing tour groups. **Known for:** good service; reservations essential, particularly for orders of pastilla and other special dishes; accommodating to vegetarians and special diets. [$] *Average main: DH100* ✉ *Boutarialt el Barrania, Taroudant* ✣ *2 km (1 mile) south of Taroudant, by N10* ☎ *0528/55–11–41* 🌐 *www.darzitoune.com.*

Restaurant Jnane Soussia

$$ | **MOROCCAN** | **FAMILY** | This outdoor restaurant is a long-standing favorite for Moroccan families, offering great food and lots of space. Traditional cuisine is served under a *caidal* (white canvas) tent around two small swimming pools, in a garden full of orange, fig, and papaya trees and flowers. **Known for:** swimming pool for children; mechoui (traditional roasted lamb; order in advance); local vibe. [$] *Average main: DH80* ✉ *Bab Zorgan, just outside gate, on right side of road as you head west, Taroudant* ☎ *0528/85–49–80.*

★ Riad Maryam Restaurant

$$$$ | **MOROCCAN** | Taroudant's oldest family-run riad prides itself on its restaurant for good reason. While Habib greets the guests, his wife, Latifa, works wonders in the kitchen to produce a spread of salads, pastilla, tagines, or couscous fit for a

king, not to mention the best *pastilla du lait* (a dessert of fine, crispy phyllo pastry layered with pastry crème) in town. **Known for:** homemade pastilla du lait for dessert; reservations essential; no credit cards; vegetarian-friendly options. [$] *Average main: DH200* ✉ *140, Derb Maalem Mohamed, Bab Targhount, Taroudant* ☎ *0666/12–72–85* 🌐 *www.riadmaryam.com* 💳 *No credit cards.*

Hotels

Dar al Hossoun
$$$$ | **RESORT** | This luxury boutique hotel is a true eco-lodge, located in the countryside 8 km (5 miles) from Taroudant; it was built using local materials and traditional techniques but offers all the modern conveniences. **Pros:** attentive service from staff; amenities including spa, two pools, and sundeck; individually decorated rooms. **Cons:** no other restaurants nearby; can be difficult to find; located a good distance from town. [$] *Rooms from: DH1300* ✉ *Qartier Hossoun, Sidi Mbark, Taroudant* ✣ *Off Amskroud–Agadir Rd.* ☎ *0528/85–34–76* 🌐 *www.alhossoun.com* 🛏 *16 rooms* 🍴 *Free Breakfast.*

Dar Dzahra
$$ | **B&B/INN** | Tucked away south of the main square, Dar Dzahra is full of surprises, starting with the unassuming entrance that leads into a house that is in fact two separate buildings: one over 300 years old and the other just a few years old. **Pros:** credit cards not accepted; friendly and knowledgeable owner; great pool. **Cons:** no air-conditioning; only basic amenities in rooms; easy to get lost on the way there. [$] *Rooms from: DH550* ✉ *73, Derb Akka, Taroudant* ☎ *0528/85–10–85* 🌐 *www.dzahra.com* 💳 *No credit cards* 🛏 *10 rooms* 🍴 *Free Breakfast.*

Dar Zahia
$$$ | **B&B/INN** | **FAMILY** | Hidden behind an unassuming door at the end of an alley, this unique guesthouse is an oasis in the bustling city. **Pros:** roof terrace; local Amazigh flavor in design and decor; beautifully designed. **Cons:** staff doesn't speak much English; bathrooms are shared; credit cards not accepted. [$] *Rooms from: DH935* ✉ *175, Derb Chrif, Taroudant* ☎ *0528/85–08–01* 🌐 *www.darzahia.com* 💳 *No credit cards* 🛏 *4 rooms* 🍴 *Free Breakfast.*

★ **Dar Zitoune**
$$$$ | **HOTEL** | Located just outside Taroudant, Dar Zitoune is a wonderful retreat from the bustling town. **Pros:** luxury tents are one room option; large gardens full of fruit trees and flowering plants; three swimming pools. **Cons:** often fully booked; can be busy with groups coming for lunch; a mile from old city. [$] *Rooms from: DH1200* ✉ *Boutarial El Berrania, Taroudant* ✣ *On road to Agadir Airport, 2 km (1 mile) from town* ☎ *0528/55–11–41* 🌐 *www.darzitoune.com* 🛏 *32 rooms* 🍴 *Free Breakfast.*

La Maison Anglaise
$$ | **B&B/INN** | **FAMILY** | This English-speaking, family-friendly guesthouse, which doubles as a cultural center, has been certified by Green Key for its sustainable operations and environmental responsibility. **Pros:** credit cards not accepted; extensive activity program; staff are very welcoming. **Cons:** a little difficult to find; often booked up in advance; not all rooms have air-conditioning or an en suite bathroom. [$] *Rooms from: DH600* ✉ *422, Derb Aferdou, Taroudant* ☎ *0661/23–66–27 in Morocco* 🌐 *cecu.co.uk* 💳 *No credit cards* 🛏 *9 rooms* 🍴 *Free Breakfast.*

★ **Le Palais Oumensour**
$$$ | **B&B/INN** | In the heart of Taroudant's medina, this luxurious boutique hotel has been beautifully renovated from an old riad. **Pros:** beautiful architecture; hotel can arrange many activities; good value. **Cons:** front rooms over the alley can be noisy; no credit cards accepted; often fully booked. [$] *Rooms from: DH990* ✉ *Borj Oumensour, Taroudant* ☎ *0528/55–02–15* 🌐 *www.palaisoumensour.com* 💳 *No*

credit cards ⤴ 11 rooms ⊙| Free Breakfast.

★ Riad Maryam

$$ | B&B/INN | FAMILY | Taroudant's oldest family-run riad is inside an authentic Moroccan town house dating from the early 19th century and has many period features. **Pros:** you are made to feel at home; quiet and calm; one of the best dining options in town. **Cons:** no parking nearby; credit cards not accepted; some kitschy room decor. $ *Rooms from: DH500 ⊠ 140, Derb Maalem Mohamed, Bab Targhount, Taroudant* ☎ *0666/12–72–85* ⊕ *www.riadmaryam.com* ⊟ *No credit cards* ⤴ *6 rooms* ⊙| *Free Breakfast.*

Riad Tafilag

$$$ | B&B/INN | FAMILY | In a typical Moroccan neighborhood, this riad is the kind of place you could stay for a week and unwind, whether on one of several terraces, in the shade of the lounge, or by either of the two pools. **Pros:** attentive staff; hammam and spa; good value. **Cons:** communal areas cluttered with craft and gift items for sale; lots of stairs; a little difficult to find. $ *Rooms from: DH715 ⊠ 31, Derb Taffellagt, Taroudant* ☎ *0528/85–06–07* ⊕ *www.riad-tafilag. com* ⤴ *9 rooms* ⊙| *Free Breakfast.*

Shopping

Taroudant is famous for leather: 200 shops here are dedicated to sandals alone. A walk down even the quietest of streets will feature the incessant tap-tapping of shoemakers at work. Other local products include saffron and lavender, sold by the ounce in herbal stores. The locally pressed olive and argan oils are nationally renowned; ask the herbalists if they can get you a liter. You can also pick up antique jewelry in Taroudant from local Muslim and Jewish Amazigh tribes.

Antiquaire Haut Atlas

CRAFTS | For serious collectors, this shop has one of the best collections of Amazigh jewelry in southern Morocco,

some of it dating from the 17th and 18th centuries. Even if you're not in the market for a trinket, wandering around the dusty rooms of carpets, candlesticks, and charms makes for a diverting half hour. And if you *are* in the market, Mr. Houssaine accepts all major credit cards and is open every day. ⊠ *61, Souk el Kabir, Taroudant* ☎ *0528/85–21–45.*

Sculpteur de Pierre

ART GALLERIES | Here's the best place to go for sculpture, both for quality and range of workmanship. Craftsman Larbi El Hare uses marble, limestone, and alabaster to create pieces of different sizes, some quite affordable. He also makes some of the best mint tea in town. The shop has been here awhile, so ask in the Grande Marché if you can't find it. ⊠ *Fondouk el Hare, 29, Rahba Kedima, near soap souk, Taroudant* ☎ *0668/80–78–35.*

Tafraoute

*148 km (92 miles) south of Taroudant,
152 km (94 miles) southeast of Agadir.*

Tafraoute is a pretty and quiet regional market and administrative center, nestled at the bottom of a valley. Usually overlooked by group travelers, it's a great base for exploring an area rich in natural beauty and overflowing with walks, many of which can be undertaken without bumping into another tourist. It is also a base for those wishing to experience some of Morocco's best rock climbing. Although the dizzying mountains around Tafraoute may prove forbidding to cyclists or light hikers, half-day excursions can take you to prehistoric rock carvings, the Ammeln Valley, or the villages off the main road to Tiznit. It's also worth planning a day's excursion to the Aït Mansour gorges to the south of town, where you'll find lush, verdant palm groves. The region around Tafraoute is a great place to visit some spectacular *agadirs*—hilltop granaries perched at the top of sheer

Tafraoute, in a quiet valley, offers beautiful walks in the surrounding countryside.

cliffs. They include those at Amtoudi, Tasguint, and Ikouka.

GETTING HERE AND AROUND

The R105 is a spectacular road running over mountains from Agadir to Tafraoute via Aït Baha. You can pick up this road coming from Taroudant to Tafraoute or travel via the alternative Igherm road. There are buses to Tafraoute from Aït Baha (2 hours), Agadir via Tiznit (5 hours), Marrakesh (10 hours), and Casablanca (14 hours). There are also grands taxis from Tiznit.

Once in Tafraoute, if you don't have a rental car, your best bet is to travel on foot or by bicycle.

TIMING AND PRECAUTIONS

This region can get extremely hot in summer. Climbers prefer to come in winter and spring, when almond blossoms cover the hillsides. Walkers and trekkers following less obvious routes should hire a local guide; if you want to include Tafraoute as part of a longer Souss Valley tour, then it's worth going through one of the many agencies based in Agadir.

Sights

Ammeln Valley

NATURE SIGHT | The Ammeln Valley is becoming a magnet not only for climbers but also for nature lovers and hikers. A walk in the valley might start at the village of Oumesnat, where the Maison Traditionelle is well worth a visit. ■ TIP→ **Wear sturdy shoes for the short walk from the car park.** At this museum in a traditional Amazigh house, the caretakers will happily explain the old ways of the Anti-Atlas, introducing you to domestic implements, the tea ceremony, and the local women's embroidered black wrap, the *tamelheft*. Express your appreciation for the tour by tipping generously. From Oumesnat you can follow paths to the neighboring villages. Taghdicte makes a good base for ambitious Anti-Atlas climbers. ⊠ *Tafraoute* ✛ *Oumesnat is 7 km (4½ miles) north of Tafraoute via R105.*

Gazelle Rock Carving

HISTORIC SIGHT | The prehistoric gazelle rock carving just 2 km (1 mile) south of Tafraoute is an easy walk or bike ride from town, and although the sparse etching has been retouched, it still gives you an idea about how long these desolate mountains have sustained human cultures. To get here, follow signs to "Tazka" from behind Hôtel Les Amandiers; go through the village to the palm and argan fields beyond. You may have offers to guide you from local children: if you accept, then be sure to thank them with a small gift, such as a pen or toy, but avoid giving money. Although everyone calls it a gazelle, locals in the know will tell you that the celebrated rock carving is in fact of a *mouflon* (wild sheep). Those energetic enough can visit more cave paintings at Ukas, south of the town of Souk Had Issi, 50 km (31 miles) southeast of Tafraoute. ✉ *Tafraoute.*

Painted Rocks

PUBLIC ART | A slightly bizarre tourist attraction, the Painted Rocks outside Tafraoute (follow signs) is most dramatically experienced in late afternoon, when the hillsides stacked with massive round boulders turn a rich mustard hue before sunset. Belgian artist Jean Veran painted a cluster of these natural curiosities in varying shades of blue in 1984, and they have been retouched ever since. Checking out amateur copies is as much fun as looking at the originals. On quieter days, it's also a great place to spot local geckos, lizards, and squirrels. The route to the rocks is now paved, making access easier than ever. ✉ *Tafraoute* 🎟 *Free.*

Palm Groves of Aït Mansour

NATURE SIGHT | The palm groves of the Aït Mansour Gorge southeast of Tafraoute deserve a day's excursion, although you could just take the road as a scenic (and longer) route to Tiznit. About 2 km (1 mile) south out of town, you'll see the so-called Napoleon's Hat of massive boulders on your right. Occasionally, you'll see climbers here. Continue past the pretty village of Aguerd Oudad. When the road forks, go left; the right branch goes to the Painted Rocks. A winding, paved road takes you higher into the Anti-Atlas Mountains. The views are spectacular as the road rises and then descends, crossing a riverbed, which—even when dry—betrays the presence of underground water by the cactus and oleander growing there. Twenty kilometers (12 miles) out of Tafraoute, turn right toward Aït Mansour.

After another 14 km (9 miles) of descent, you reach the palm groves. Water, shade, and greenery are abundant, and you may find a shop serving sweet mint tea or soda. The goatherds of the peaks are replaced here by shrouded women, either transporting palm-frond baskets of dates or walking to Timguilcht to visit its saint's shrine. Continue on the piste to Souk Had Issi, whose market is held on Sunday. From there, the piste loops back to Tafraoute, or you can take a lower road to connect to Tiznit over the dramatic Col de Kerdous. ✉ *Tafraoute.*

🍴 Restaurants

La Kasbah

$$ | **MOROCCAN** | The menu here is classic tourist fare (omelets, tagines, soups, and salads), but the quality is excellent. Try the vegetarian tagines with prunes, nuts, and plenty of veggies, or sample the house specialty, *Kalia*, a Saharan dish of thinly sliced beef and vegetables. **Known for:** credit cards not accepted; authentic local cuisine at local prices; friendly, hospitable owner. [$] *Average main: DH70* ✉ *Rte. Imiane (R107), Tafraoute* ✢ *On right as you leave town* ☎ *0672/30–39–09* 💳 *No credit cards.*

Restaurant L'Etoile du Sud

$$ | **MOROCCAN** | Since 1968 the "Star of the South" has been dishing up ample servings of couscous and tagines in a red-velvet dining room or under a huge red-and-green velvet caidal tent. The harira is hearty and satisfying after a long day's drive, and there is plenty of parking. **Known for:** credit cards not accepted; central location; popular with groups. [$] *Average main: DH90* ✉ *Av. Hassan II, next to post office, Tafraoute* ☎ *0528/80–00–38* 💳 *No credit cards.*

Restaurant Marrakech

$ | **MOROCCAN** | Haute cuisine it isn't, but the tagines here are fresh and cheap and appreciated by many locals. The cool, fresh-squeezed juices make this a nice spot to catch your breath and get out of the sun. **Known for:** credit cards not accepted; cleanliness and simplicity; popular with locals as well as tourists. [$] *Average main: DH50* ✉ *Av. Hassan II, in center of town, Tafraoute* ☎ *0663/22–92–50* 💳 *No credit cards.*

Hotels

★ **Auberge Kasbah Chez Amaliya**

$$ | **B&B/INN** | **FAMILY** | Nestled among the mountains and occasional almond blossoms of the Ammeln Valley 2 km (1 mile) from downtown, Chez Amaliya is a great base for hikers, climbers, and the less active. **Pros:** large pool and terrace with lounge chairs; vivacious host makes you feel right at home; great views and good restaurant. **Cons:** Wi-Fi can be limited in rooms; can be full of tour groups; outside the city center. [$] *Rooms from: DH500* ✉ *Valley d'Ammeln, signposted off R105 as you approach from Aït Baha, Tafraoute* ☎ *0528/80–00–65* 🌐 *www.chezamaliya.com* 🛏 *18 rooms* 🍴 *Free Breakfast.*

El Malara

$$$ | **B&B/INN** | Outside Tafraoute, this modern, kasbah-style guesthouse offers comfortable accommodation in a quiet rural setting. **Pros:** large, clean swimming pool; very welcoming hosts and staff; restaurant fuses Moroccan and Mediterranean flavors. **Cons:** credit cards not accepted; Wi-Fi is intermittent; 6 km (4 miles) outside town. [$] *Rooms from: DH720* ✉ *Afela Ouaday, Tafraoute* ✥ *6 km (4 miles) out of Tafraoute on Tiznit–Tahala road (R104)* ☎ *0658/18–18–36* 🌐 *www.elmalara.com* 💳 *No credit cards* 🕒 *Closed July* 🛏 *7 rooms.*

Hôtel Les Amandiers

$$$ | **HOTEL** | This former officers' mess of the French protectorate is a piece of Moroccan postcolonial history as well as a hotel that dominates the town, providing panoramic views of the mountains that surround it. **Pros:** good-size pool with nice views; large bathrooms; has a bar. **Cons:** Wi-Fi can be spotty; service can be slow; parts of the hotel still have a slightly institutional feel. [$] *Rooms from: DH815* ✉ *Town center, Tafraoute* ☎ *0528/80–00–88* 🌐 *www.lesamandiers-hotel.com/* 🛏 *60 rooms.*

Hotel Salama

$ | **HOTEL** | A favorite with groups and right in the center of town, the Salama overlooks the busy area around the market, where old men sell dates and local women bring their homemade argan oil. **Pros:** on-site parking; close to the market; nice views from rooftop lounge. **Cons:** credit cards not accepted; rooms quite basic; rooms overlooking the market can be noisy. [$] *Rooms from: DH372* ✉ *Town center, Tafraoute* ☎ *0528/80–00–26* 🌐 *www.hotelsalama.com* 💳 *No credit cards* 🛏 *37 rooms* 🍴 *Free Breakfast.*

Shopping

Tafraoute's market is held on Tuesday and Wednesday and often has a good selection of woven palm-frond baskets, argan oil, and *amalou* (almond and argan paste). Tafraoute is the place to come for mountain babouches (slippers). These are different from the slip-on varieties found in the souks of Marrakesh and Fez, as they are specially made with a heel covering to aid mountain walking. Take note of Amazigh babouche color-coding: yellow for men, red for women, pompoms for unmarried girls, and spangled designs only for special occasions. The traditional local women's dress is a large black piece of fabric with braiding or embroidery at the edges.

Maison du Troc

CRAFTS | With a great range of carpets and other artisanal goods, this place is worth a visit if you feel the need for souvenirs. Although the area isn't well-known for carpet making, Mohammed and his team are happy to explain the different types of rugs from various regions. ✉ *Rte. Imiane, Tafraoute* ☎ *0528/80–00–35.*

Maison Touareg

CRAFTS | Not to be confused with the excellent Maison Traditionelle museum in Oumesnat, the Maison Touareg is a bazaar, carrying a nice selection of regional Amazigh carpets. ✉ *Rte. de l'Hotel Les Amandiers, Av. Mohammed V, Tafraoute* ☎ *0528/80–02–10* ⊕ *www. maisontouareg.com.*

Tiznit

100 km (62 miles) west of Tafraoute, 98 km (61 miles) south of Agadir.

Typically a lunch stop en route to somewhere else, Tiznit is not a popular destination for tourists, despite being surrounded by breathtaking North African nature. It does make a good base for people exploring the surrounding area and for those who dislike the high-rise, beach-resort feel of Agadir. The restaurant scene isn't great, but a couple of smaller guesthouses serve excellent homemade cuisine. One big draw of Tiznit is its reputation as Morocco's silver center. It's worthwhile to go to this source of silver jewelry and see some of the more creative and unique designs available. Otherwise, the town itself has few sights.

GETTING HERE AND AROUND
Tiznit is well signposted if traveling by road, with the N1 bringing you from Agadir, and the R104 from Tafraoute. Several daily buses arrive from Sidi Ifni (1½ hours), Agadir (2 hours), and Tafraoute (2 hours). The bus station is a 15-minute walk along Boulevard Mohamed Hafidi from the medina entrance at Bab Jdid. The CTM office is located at the bus station. There are also grands taxis from Agadir.

Tiznit is a compact city and everything within the medina walls is within walking distance. Bikes can be hired on Méchouar Square or from certain riads.

TIMING AND PRECAUTIONS
Tiznit makes for an easy day trip from Agadir or for a break in an exploration of the Anti-Atlas and southern Morocco region. In summer it gets extremely hot, and it may be more pleasant to stay on the coast at nearby Aglou Plage or in Agadir.

 Sights

Grande Mosquée (*Great Mosque*)

MOSQUE | The minaret of the Grande Mosquée is the oldest example in Morocco of a Saharan–style minaret, an architectural feature more commonly seen in Niger and Mali. Perches poke out from all sides, making it look like someone forgot to take out the scaffolding after it was completed. These perches are said to assist the dead in their ascent to paradise. Non-Muslims cannot enter the mosque. ✉ *Rue de la Grande Mosquée, old town, Tiznit.*

Lalla Zninia Spring

POOL | Near the Grand Mosquée, the Lalla Zninia Spring (also known as the Source Bleue) is touted as Tiznit's main sight. In the evenings, the pool is lit up, while locals take in the night air in the adjacent square. The spring honors the saint after whom Tiznit is named. Of the several legends relating to this woman, one has it that she was a shepherd girl who brought her flocks to this spot and smelled the then-undiscovered spring below; her sheep dug (if you can imagine sheep digging) until they found the water, and the town was born. Another story talks of a repentant prostitute who later became a saint. In any case, to catch a glimpse of her tomb on afternoons when devotees visit, follow the prison wall and turn left on the first narrow neighborhood street; the tomb is behind a green-painted door on your left. ✉ *Tiznit.*

Méchouar

BUSINESS DISTRICT | The main square, the Méchouar, is the heart of town and was once a military parade ground, though nowadays it has become a car park with a clutch of cheap hotels and cafés around it. Down a side street off the main square (heading in the direction of the ramparts), in a smaller square lined with orange trees, locals buy from the mint, date, and dried-thyme vendors whose carts park between the rows of clothing and housewares. Off the Méchouar are the town's main souks. ✉ *Pl. el Méchouar, Tiznit.*

🍴 Restaurants

À l'Ombre du Figuier

$$ | **MOROCCAN** | Behind a small blue door in an unusually buttressed wall, this quaint restaurant welcomes diners with a fig tree–shaded courtyard (hence the name) and Moroccan dishes, including a fish tagine, spiced chicken, beef brochettes, couscous, and pastilla. The menu changes regularly, as everything is freshly made. **Known for:** credit cards not accepted; fresh local produce; large portions at reasonable prices. [$] *Average main: DH75* ✉ *22, passage Akchouch, dit "Métro" Idzakri, Tiznit* ✥ *From Pl. Mechouar, take passage marked "entrée 4" to Gallery Riad Akchouch and look for signs* ☎ *0528/86–12–04* 🌐 *facebook.com/ombredufiguier* 💳 *No credit cards.*

Riad Le Lieu Restaurant

$ | **MOROCCAN** | Popular among the guests of local riads and hotels, Riad Le Lieu is a beacon in the dining scene of Tiznit. In a part of the former palace next door, chef Jihad prepares a range of Moroccan specialties, which are served on the patio and terraces; the rabbit and camel tagines are always great choices. **Known for:** pretty, vine-covered patio; credit cards not accepted; kind, attentive staff. [$] *Average main: DH65* ✉ *273, Impasse Issaoui, Rue Imzilen, Pl. Méchouar, Tiznit* ☎ *0528/60–00–19* 🌐 *www.riadlelieu.com* 💳 *No credit cards.*

🛏 Hotels

Hotel Idou Tiznit

$$$$ | **HOTEL** | This large four-star hotel caters primarily to the business market but is the only option in town for accommodation other than a small guesthouse. **Pros:** located at the entrance of the old town; full range of facilities, including a pool; helpful staff. **Cons:** the bar can get noisy at night; feels a bit sterile; can get busy with large groups. [$] *Rooms from: DH1100* ✉ *Av. Hassan II, Tiznit* ☎ *0528/60–03–33* 🛏 *93 rooms* 🍽 *Free Breakfast.*

★ **Riad Janoub**

$$$ | **B&B/INN** | The design of this luxury riad, hidden behind nondescript walls in the medina, was inspired by the Andalusian and Moorish architecture of grand old residences. **Pros:** easily accessed by car; stunning Moorish architecture with arched colonnades; a little bit of luxury at a great price. **Cons:** can be noisy when pool is busy; swimming pool is unheated; the dining room is cramped. [$] *Rooms from: DH825* ✉ *193, rue de la Grande Mosquée, Quartier Tafrgant, Tiznit* ☎ *0528/60–27–26* 🌐 *www.riadjanoub.com* 🛏 *7 rooms* 🍽 *Free Breakfast.*

Tigmi Kenza

$$ | **B&B/INN** | Chic and sophisticated, this riad near Place Méchouar infuses a modern flavor to traditional Moroccan architectural techniques. **Pros:** lovely roof terrace; excellent on-site restaurant; good-size rooms. **Cons:** Wi-Fi only in reception; no air-conditioning; credit cards not accepted. [$] *Rooms from: DH500* ✉ *30, rue al Mourabitine, Hay Idzekri, Tiznit* ☎ *0528/60–03–62* 🌐 *www.tigmi-kenza.com* 💳 *No credit cards* 🛏 *7 rooms* 🍴 *Free Breakfast.*

Shopping

Tiznit has earned a reputation as *the* place to buy silver jewelry in Morocco, and the local market has responded accordingly. The silver markets of Tiznit sell more—and better—silver per square foot than any other market in Morocco. Some vendors also sell handwoven cream-color blankets, traded by local women for a few pieces of new silver. Merchants cater increasingly to Western tastes and wallets. Many shops around the main square are really wholesalers, trading their silver all over Morocco and abroad, so don't expect any encounters with the artisans. **■ TIP→ Most items are produced in the home, so tourists are unlikely to see any actual production, and the shops advertising it are unlikely to be manufacturing real silver jewelry.**

Bijouterie Aziz

CRAFTS | This low-pressure jewelry store sells Saharan and Amazigh silver jewelry. ✉ *5, Souk Joutia, Tiznit* ☎ *0615/57–12–79.*

Coin des Berberes

CRAFTS | Located next to the Lalla Zninia Spring, this large jewelry shop showcases new and old Amazigh jewelry, as well as artisans at work. Also for sale are carpets, pottery, and other Moroccan crafts. ✉ *4, rue de la Source Bleue, Tiznit* ☎ *0528/60–16–17.*

Trésor du Sud

CRAFTS | Located away from the souk, Trésor du Sud has an enormous showroom of high-quality handcrafted Amazigh jewelry. In addition, the workshops allow you to see the silversmiths in action. Carpets and other Moroccan crafts are also for sale. This is not the cheapest jewelry showroom in town, but you can pay with a credit card. ✉ *Bab al-Khemis, Tiznit* ☎ *0528/86–47–89.*

Index

Photo Credits

Notes

Notes

Notes

Fodor's ESSENTIAL MOROCCO

Publisher: Stephen Horowitz, *General Manager*

Editorial: Douglas Stallings, *Editorial Director*; Jill Fergus, Amanda Sadlowski, Caroline Trefler, *Senior Editors*; Kayla Becker, Alexis Kelly, *Editors*; Angelique Kennedy-Chavannes, *Assistant Editor*

Design: Tina Malaney, *Director of Design and Production*; Jessica Gonzalez, *Graphic Designer*

Production: Jennifer DePrima, *Editorial Production Manager*; Elyse Rozelle, *Senior Production Editor*; Monica White, *Production Editor*

Maps: Rebecca Baer, *Senior Map Editor*; David Lindroth, Mark Stroud (Moon Street Cartography), *Cartographers*

Photography: Viviane Teles, *Senior Photo Editor*; Namrata Aggarwal, Payal Gupta, Ashok Kumar, *Photo Editors*; Rebecca Rimmer, *Photo Production Associate*; Eddie Aldrete, *Photo Production Intern*

Business and Operations: Chuck Hoover, *Chief Marketing Officer*; Robert Ames, *Group General Manager*; Devin Duckworth, *Director of Print Publishing*

Public Relations and Marketing: Joe Ewaskiw, *Senior Director of Communications and Public Relations*

Fodors.com: Jeremy Tarr, *Editorial Director*; Rachael Levitt, *Managing Editor*

Technology: Jon Atkinson, *Director of Technology*; Rudresh Teotia, *Lead Developer*; Jacob Ashpis, *Content Operations Manager*

Writers: Rachel Blech, Sarah Gilbert, Amanda Mouttaki, Helen Ranger, Erin Wilson

Editor: Caroline Trefler

Production Editor: Jennifer DePrima

2nd Edition

ISBN 978-1-64097-350-3

ISSN 2574-0652

All details in this book are based on information supplied to us at press time. Always confirm information when it matters, especially if you're making a detour to visit a specific place. Fodor's expressly disclaims any liability, loss, or risk, personal or otherwise, that is incurred as a consequence of the use of any of the contents of this book.

SPECIAL SALES
This book is available at special discounts for bulk purchases for sales promotions or premiums. For more information, e-mail SpecialMarkets@fodors.com.

PRINTED IN CANADA

10 9 8 7 6 5 4 3 2 1

About Our Writers

 Rachel Blech is a travel writer and former broadcaster for Ireland's RTÉ Radio. While making a radio documentary about Essaouira's Gnawa Music Festival in 2006, she met Saharoui nomads from southern Morocco who invited her to visit their local festival and experience their way of life. She juggled her music and travel projects between Ireland and Morocco until 2013, but now lives full-time in Morocco, organizing cultural tours to the southern oases and desert regions. Her company, SheherazadVentures, is run in partnership with the nomads she met on that first visit. Rachel has also written for Footprint and Time Out guides and has recently written and illustrated her own short stories. She updated the Morocco Experience chapter of this edition of Fodor's Morocco.

Sarah Gilbert is a freelance writer and photographer who calls London home when she's not traveling for numerous magazines, newspapers, and websites such as Condé Nast Traveller (U.K.), Wanderlust, The Guardian, and The Independent. She fell in love with Morocco in 2002 and has returned many times. A former resident of Fez and honorary Fassi, Sarah finds its history, culture, and people endlessly fascinating. She updated the Fez and the Middle Atlas chapter, the Tangier and the Mediterranean chapter, and the Travel Smart section of this edition.

 Amanda Mouttaki is a freelance writer and blogger who has lived in Marrakesh for the last 10 years with her Moroccan husband and children. She first visited Morocco in 2004 and has since immersed herself in all things Moroccan—especially the food! You can follow her @marocmama on Instagram or on her website marocmama.com.

 Helen Ranger—who updated the Rabat and Casablanca chapter for this edition—has lived in her 400-year-old house in the medieval medina of Fez in Morocco for 18 years. Traveling and writing are passions. She concentrates on African destinations including Morocco, Madagascar, South Africa, Gabon, and Equatorial Guinea. When not writing guidebooks, Helen runs a bespoke travel consultancy in Morocco and translates art books from French into English. Find her on Instagram and Twitter @helenranger.

 Erin Wilson is a creative writer, life coach, and Reiki Master living in the small surf village of Tamraght, Morocco. Her worldview has been largely shaped by the 22 years she has spent living and traveling in Morocco and learning about the country as well as about other parts of the Islamic world. You can follow Erin on her instagram account @thepermissionist.